Classic Readings in American Politics

Third Edition

Classic Readings in American Politics

THIRD EDITION

EDITED BY

Pietro S. Nivola

The Brookings Institution

David H. Rosenbloom

American University

With Forewords by
John W. Kingdon
Nelson W. Polsby
and
Theodore J. Lowi

St. Martin's / WORTH

Classic Readings in American Politics
Third Edition

Executive Editor: James R. Headley
Project Director: Scott E. Hitchcock
Editorial Assistant: Brian Nobile
Design Director: Jennie R. Nichols
Production Editor: Douglas Bell
Production Manager: Barbara Anne Seixas
Project Coordination: Publisher's Studio,
    a division of Stratford Publishing Services
Text Design: Levavi & Levavi
Cover Design: Paul Lacy
Cover Photos: Signatures on the Declaration of Independence: Baldwin H. Ward/
    Corbis-Bettmann; Typewriter keys: Todd Gipstein/Corbis
Cover Printer: Phoenix Color Corporation
Composition: Stratford Publishing Services
Printing and Binding: R. R. Donnelley & Sons Company

Worth Publishers
33 Irving Place
New York, NY 10003

www.worthpublishers.com

Acknowledgments

Acknowledgment and copyrights are continued at the back of the book on page 582, which constitutes an extension of the copyright page.

Peter Bachrach and Morton S. Baratz. "Two Faces of Power." *American Political Science Review*, Vol. 56, December 1962, pp. 947–952. Reprinted by permission of the American Political Science Association.
Edward C. Banfield. "Influence and the Public Interest." Excerpt from Chapter 12, pp. 324–341, in *Political Influence* by Edward C. Banfield. Copyright ©1961 by The Free Press; renewed 1989 by Edward C. Banfield. Reprinted with the permission of The Free Press, a Division of Simon and Schuster.
Charles A. Beard. "The Constitution as an Economic Document." From *An Economic Interpretation of the Constitution of the United States*, pp. 152–188, by Charles Beard. Copyright ©1935 by Macmillan Publishing Company; renewed 1963 by William Beard and Mrs. Miriam Beard Vagts. Reprinted with the permission of Simon and Schuster.
Samuel H. Beer. "The National Idea in American Politics." Lecture delivered to the faculty and officers of Boston College, Chestnut Hill, MA, 02167, on April 21, 1982.
Edward S. Corwin. "The 'Higher Law' Background of American Constitutional Law." *Harvard Law Review*, Vol. XLII, 1928–1929: 149–185, 369–409. Copyright ©1928, 1929 by the Harvard Law Review Association. Reprinted by permission.
Robert A. Dahl. Excerpt from "On the Species *Homo Politicus*" in *Who Governs?* by Robert A. Dahl. Copyright ©1961 by Robert A. Dahl. Reprinted by permission of Yale University Press.
Martha Derthick. "The Enduring Features of American Federalism." *The Brookings Review*, Summer 1989: 34–38. Copyright ©1989 by Brookings Publications. Reprinted by permission of The Brookings Institution.

About the Editors

Pietro S. Nivola is a Senior Fellow in the Governmental Studies Program at The Brookings Institution in Washington, D.C. Dr. Nivola has published a large number of books and articles on subjects ranging from trade and industrial policy to energy taxation, social regulation, and urban studies. He is the author of *Regulating Unfair Trade* (Brookings, 1993) and, with Robert W. Crandall, *The Extra Mile: Rethinking Energy Policy for Automotive Transportation*, a Twentieth Century Fund book published by Brookings in 1995. Two of his earlier works were *The Politics of Energy Conservation* (Brookings, 1986) and *The Urban Service Problem* (Heath, 1979). In 1997, Nivola produced the major conference volume *Comparative Disadvantages? Social Regulations and the Global Economy* (Brookings, 1997). His latest study is titled *Laws of Unintended Consequence: How Policies Shape the Cityscapes of Europe and America* (Brookings, forthcoming). Formerly an associate professor of political science at the University of Vermont and a lecturer in government at Harvard University, Pietro Nivola received his A.B. and Ph.D. from Harvard.

David H. Rosenbloom is Distinguished Professor of Public Administration at American University in Washington, D.C. He previously held faculty appointments at Syracuse University's Maxwell School of Citizenship and Public Affairs, the University of Vermont, Tel Aviv University, and the University of Kansas. He specializes in constitutional law, public administration, and bureaucratic politics. Widely published, his most recent titles include *Public Administration: Understanding Management; Politics and Law in the Public Sector*, fourth ed. (McGraw Hill, 1998); and *Public Administration and Law*, second ed., with Rosemary O'Leary (Marcel Dekker, 1997). Among Rosenbloom's awards are the Policy Studies Organization's Thomas Dye Award for Outstanding Service (1996) and the American Society for Public Administration/National Association of Schools of Public Affairs and Administration's Charles H. Levine Award for Excellence in Public Administration (1993) and Distinguished Research Award (1992). Rosenbloom holds Ph.D. and M.A. degrees in political science from the University of Chicago, as well as a B.A. in political science and an honorary doctor of laws degree from Marietta College.

For our sons and daughters,
Adrian, Alessandro, Asia, Joshua, Leah, Lila, and Sarah

CONTENTS

III. POLITICAL POWER 95

IV. POLITICAL PARTIES AND ELECTIONS 123

V. INTEREST GROUPS AND LOBBYING 189

VI. THE CONGRESS 275

VII. THE PRESIDENCY 349

VIII. THE BUREAUCRACY 403

IX. THE JUDICIARY 431

X. THE POLICY PROCESS 529

PREFACE

In truth, we approached the task of preparing a third edition of this book with some hesitancy. The continuing success of the first two editions made us wonder whether a third one was necessary. More basically, a book that purports to assemble "classics" cannot supply a new table of contents every few years. Put another way, we thought we got it right the first time, and that subsequent revisions would be mostly cosmetic, not substantive.

Well, we were less than half right. The original edition did provide a core of what we still deem to be works of truly enduring importance. Indeed, in the present volume we restore some selections that were dropped from the second edition. On the sound advice of various reviewers, for example, we reintroduce an entire section on "Political Power," reinstating contributions on the subject by C. Wright Mills, Robert A. Dahl, and others. But we also add new material to most chapters.

Some of the additions correct earlier oversights. The section on the "Policy Process," for instance, is strengthened by including John W. Kingdon's work on agenda setting. The "Political Parties and Elections" section now has a better sample of the work of V. O. Key, and includes parts of Anthony Downs's *An Economic Theory of Democracy*—a glaring omission in earlier editions. Elsewhere, we believe we have greatly improved the contents by broadening most sections. "The Judiciary," for example, now has an excerpt from Walter F. Murphy's *Elements of Judicial Strategy*. Herbert Kaufman's splendid essay on red tape bolsters the section on "The Bureaucracy," while writings by Charles O. Jones and by Doris Kearns fortify "The Presidency." And Gordon S. Wood's analysis, especially when juxtaposed with Charles A. Beard's essay from the first edition, adds elegance to the opening section on "Political Culture and Traditions."

We have tried not to follow trendy topics, but at the same time, we did not want to be oblivious to revived interest in certain subject areas or in the insights of some great writers. The question of federalism is one example. Here, amid today's renewed attention to devolution, we consider it highly useful to draw more heavily from such scholars as Martha Derthick and Samuel H. Beer, as well as the essays of Alexander Hamilton. It is not too much to say that Hamilton has been rediscovered in recent years—and with good reason. We think students would do well to familiarize themselves with more of what he had to say not only on federalism, but on the presidency and the courts as well.

Likewise, in an age of divided party control of the federal government, reading at least parts of David R. Mayhew's *Divided We Govern* is essential. As lobbies acquire distinctive characteristics and methods in modern American politics, it is appropriate to call on scholars such as Hugh Heclo, or Richard L. Hall and Frank W. Wayman, whose studies have helped shed unusual light on contemporary political realities. Finally, with institutions such as the Supreme Court seemingly delivering surprises, it may be important to recall some blockbusters of the past— *Roe v. Wade* (1973), for example, or *Korematsu v. United States* (1944). Accordingly, we reproduce them in this edition.

Once again, the book has benefitted immensely from the comments and suggestions of a large number of individuals who gave generously of their time and reflections: Roger Davidson, University of Maryland, University Park; Henry Hogue, American University; Richard Johnson, University of Illinois, Chicago; Douglas Rose, Tulane University; Michael Stathis, Southern Utah University; and Edward Uliassi, Northeastern Illinois University. Our special thanks go to Thomas E. Mann, Charles O. Jones, Martha Derthick, and above all to John W. Kingdon, who advised us on all parts of the book and wrote a foreword that any student of American government ought to read carefully.

Pietro S. Nivola
Senior Fellow
Governmental Studies Program
The Brookings Institution
Washington, D.C.

David H. Rosenbloom
Distinguished Professor
    of Public Administration
American University
Washington, D.C.

FOREWORD

TO THE THIRD EDITION

BY

JOHN W. KINGDON

Many observers and commentators on American government and politics have a massive stake in change. Journalists, for instance, report what they regard as the "news." But practically by definition, what is newsworthy excludes things that stay the same; after all, news is new. Many scholars also concentrate on change, because that is a sure way to say something that other scholars have not said before, and incidentally, to argue that previous scholarship is out of date. Politicians and other practitioners, eager to show constituents and each other that they are on the cutting edge, are also preoccupied with the latest news, the latest proposal, the latest wrinkle.

This concentration on change, of course, is often entirely appropriate. Some things do change substantially and rapidly. Public policy agendas, for instance, often change abruptly in response to such events as shifts in the partisan or ideological makeup of Congress, the election of a new president, an international crisis, or an unanticipated and dramatic focusing event like an airplane crash or bridge collapse. Indeed, large patterns of public policies can shift suddenly, as in the New Deal period of the 1930s, the Great Society initiatives of the 1960s, and the Reagan revolution in 1981. The emergence of a new social movement or a different set of interest groups can produce dramatic changes in short periods of time. Public opinion sometimes shifts substantially.

Still, change takes place within the context of enduring features of the American political system. Such fundamental features of the constitutional system as separation of powers, bicameralism, checks and balances, and federalism change only slowly. Basic themes in American political thought, including a pervasive individualism and a commitment to equality of opportunity, persist from one era to another. The configuration of partisan forces—party loyalties in the electorate, the two-party system reinforced by single-member district elections, the coalitions that support the major parties, and the parties' ideologies—is rather stable most of the time and is disrupted only rarely. A pattern of relatively limited government has distinguished the United States from most other advanced industrialized countries for most of its history. In other words, there's a lot of stability.

Given that stability, students of American government and politics are well-served by pondering the classics—writings that help them understand the enduring fundamentals. This book assembles many of those classics, some quite old and others more modern, into one volume. As professors of political science design American government courses, they often ask themselves what major themes should form central parts of a well-crafted course, what is essential reading, and to which authors should every well-educated student be exposed. Different professors, of course, would arrive at different answers, and their choices of writings to excerpt might differ around the edges from those included here. But most of them would recognize the selections in this book as writings that have profoundly shaped the field of political science. In other words, this is not a book of current events or trendy commentary, but is instead a selection of classics with lasting value. Not all of the authors in this volume are right; indeed, partly because there often is no single correct position, their ideas often conflict. But these writers are all important figures whose ideas have had major impacts on our understanding of the American political system.

That system is unusual, as compared to the governmental and political systems of other industrial representative democracies. American governmental institutions, for one thing, are far more fragmented; the combination of separation of powers (division among branches) and federalism (division between national and regional governments) does not exist elsewhere. American political parties are weaker than other countries' parties. The public sector makes up a smaller proportion of the economy, taxes are lower, and with a few exceptions, government is smaller and public policies are less ambitious than in most comparable countries. Although Americans often complain about big government, in other words, American government is actually more limited than in most other countries.

A substantial literature yields some clues about why the United States is different. We learn from that literature about distinctive themes in American political thought, for instance, and about the origins of the constitutional regime. The American pattern started very early, with the suspicion of governmental authority that followed from the values of early immigrants and the tremendous diversity and localism in the original colonies. Those considerations prompted the founders to design limited governmental institutions, using devices both to directly limit government (e.g., the Bill of Rights and independent courts) and to fragment government (e.g., by separation of powers) so that no one faction could control everything. The limits were reinforced down through the years by the deliberate weakening of political parties and the failure of democratic socialism to emerge, among other things. It's a complicated story, of course, but a careful reading of the classics can help us understand why America has come to be unusual.

That reading can also help us understand other central features of the American political system. Students of American government, for one thing, should reflect on the relationship between the public and government. A system like this one, after all, is founded on the principles that the bulk of the people select governmental decision makers in elections, that important decisions are made by those elected representatives, and that people can turn them out of office if they are not satisfied with their performance. But what level of competence and information is required of citizens in such a system, and how well do citizens measure up? Do elections actually provide for the accountability that theory prescribes, or are officeholders quite free from their constituents' views to decide as they see fit? Do elected officials actually make decisions, or are they manipulated by hidden nonelected elites? There may not be foolproof answers to such questions, but the large amount of political science literature on voting, elections, interest groups, and political parties does help the motivated student to grapple with them. There is a substantial body of writing on representation, for instance, some of which is included in this book, that tries to answer questions about how responsive elected officials are to their constituents, how well-equipped constituents are to hold them to account, and what limits constituencies set on representatives' discretion. Writings on political power, interest groups, and governmental institutions, furthermore, help us understand how, and by whom, important decisions are made.

A good part of this book is devoted to the workings of the various governmental institutions — the Congress, the presidency, the bureaucracy, and the courts — and how public policy is made within those institutions. The interplay among institutions, interests, and ideas in the American context is actually quite intriguing. Many scholars have argued, for instance, that American public policy is more limited and less ambitious than in European countries because American ideas are distinctive. That is, Americans think that government should be more limited than citizens of other countries do, and this sort of philosophy affects public policy outcomes. Other scholars disagree, and point instead to the workings of the institutions. They point out that American governmental institutions are limited by fragmentation and even by direct constitutional prohibition on many activities, which makes it impossible to enact social policies of the reach and scope that most European countries enact, even if American people preferred them.

It seems likely, actually, that both institutions and ideas affect policy outcomes, and in fact, that each affects the other. Institutions are limited because the founders deliberately designed them that way; that is, American ideas affected institutional design. But limited institutions then affect ideas, as Americans come to believe that government rarely gets things right and that it's better to trust private actions and markets. Interests also build up around, and reinforce, this powerful interaction of institutions and ideas, as some groups are advantaged and others are neglected. So institutions, ideas, and interests combine to produce distinctive American patterns.

At any rate, it is well for students of American government and politics to direct their attention to the fundamentals, rather than the ephemera that so often occupy us. A book like this one helps us understand many of those fundamentals.

Foreword

TO THE SECOND EDITION

BY

NELSON W. POLSBY

Education—higher education not excepted—is all about the transfer of information between generations. The purpose of a book of readings of this kind is to provide members of a student generation with information about some of the signposts their elders have been using to guide themselves through the world of politics. "Classic" readings aspire not merely to give facts and figures, although many of them do that. Many of these essays and excerpts also embody ideas that have been influential in guiding thought, in sorting out categories of causes and relating them to categories of effects. The expression of key ideas that readers—sometimes a great many readers—have found so useful gives articles like those reprinted here their capacity to "stick to the ribs" and entitles them to be considered "classics."

It is not required, however, that the articles be right. Some of the ideas in these writings have been superseded by time, some have been ably rebutted, and some were never strongly supported by evidence. Some are, thus, to put it mildly, regarded as scientifically controversial. It is characteristic of the social sciences that even with controversy, many such contributions remain very much a part of the literature if the proposals they make about how social and political life are organized are sufficiently interesting. So it is important for readers to read this book critically, attentively, and skeptically—as they should any work of political science.

That a collection of important works about the American political system should show great diversity is no surprise. Although it is unfashionable even to entertain such a thought, it seems to me plain enough that the American experiment in self-government, now a remarkable 200 years old, has properties that make it unique. Seen in a comparative perspective, the United States is one of the world's few federal systems, one of the world's few separation-of-powers systems, and one of the world's few systems embodying a written, legally enforced Bill of Rights. All three of these features, when taken together, have produced over time a political system that is unusual in the extreme—indeed singular.

The American political system is singular in its capacity to absorb change, and, hence, has proven to have unusual adaptability and, therefore, longevity, as constitutional orders go. No doubt it has helped enormously that the United States has grown extremely rich, has been geographically isolated from rival powers during its development as a nation, and has been militarily strong. But the very diversity of its inhabitants has provided much material for internal combustion, as the Civil War illustrated. And so it is not entirely inappropriate that we look inward for sources of adaptation.

Two such sources are embodied in the party system and in the judicial system. A Western European parliamentarian from a nation a little less than one-quarter the size of the United States once asked me how a nation as large and diverse as the United States made do with only two major political parties when other democratic nations had three, four, or more parties regularly represented in their Parliaments. Surely, he conjectured, we must be suppressing major strands of opinion by having so narrow a set of realistic alternatives.

It seems to me a fascinating question. One possible response is to agree that our two-party democracy does indeed suppress broader expressions of opinion. If we were to seek independent confirmation of the factual premise of this explanation, however, especially as compared with other, smaller, multiparty democracies, we would, I think, come up short. A second possibility, equally implausible, is that a smaller variety of opinions actually exist in America — that Americans are more homogeneous than Spaniards or Italians or Swedes. That a continental multiethnic nation of a quarter of a billion souls should be less varied than 7 million or so Swedes seems a dubious proposition indeed.

A third possible explanation suggests itself. Perhaps we do not really have a two-party system at all, but rather two party labels, under which many parties group themselves. Parties in America have a devolved, state-by-state, legal, and ideological basis. State parties are not franchises of a central, national party, like so many fast-food restaurants serving the same menu everywhere. Rather, they are fried clams in New England and catfish in the south, intimately expressive of sectional ideas and histories, of local populations and cultures. This is possible because we are a federal system, and hence have not a two-party but a hundred-party system (more or less).

A claim like this one deserves a longer exposition, and a more careful defense, than can be supplied here. If it turns out to have merit, however, it might explain how the federal structure of the union supplies some of the extraordinary flexibility and adaptiveness that our political system undeniably seems to have.

A second possible source of adaptiveness is a feature of the American political system that is frequently criticized: its litigiousness. The existence of a Bill of a Rights, guaranteeing citizens protection against the government, to a large extent also guarantees a strong form of judicial review. These rights provide incentives to litigate, and rather soon in our constitutional history produced a political system deeply influenced by lawyers and legalities. Many commentators have observed that other democratic political systems make do with fewer lawyers and with less-influential judges. And so they do. But they are also systems far more capable of solving problems concerning the assignment of prerogatives and responsibilities through the strength of their status systems. The American legal system, in part, is a response to the weakness of social status as a means of giving Americans their place in the world. It provides, in effect, for the renegotiation of status, and a capacity to renegotiate is a form of adaptiveness.

If the American political system is unusually long-lasting and unusually adaptive, as I believe, it seems to be so because it is unusually complex, providing numerous alternative points of entry, access, and innovation for those fortunate enough to be able to take advantage of them. The observant reader of the pages that follow will find numerous examples of the exercise of power, exercised by a wide range of actors who are diversely situated in the system. These actors can sometimes act alone, but more frequently they must persuade, lobby, build coalitions, and engage in cooperative behavior. These are signs of a complex political system, one which requires the mastery of process in order to understand it, or influence it. Actors in the American political drama, no matter how compelling, are, in the end, the creatures of process. And there are a great many of them. The sheer size of the cast of players in the American political system makes it unusual in a comparative perspective. Each and every one of the fifty state capitals has a full complement of political actors who make policy pertaining to health, welfare, education, transportation, the maintenance of public order, local economic growth, and other issues of intimate day-to-day public concern. And then there are the thousands of policymakers—large and small—executive, legislative, and judicial, who influence the outcomes of national government.

The sheer size of American government, over and above its great complexity, has no real analogue anywhere in the world. Nations larger than our own—and there are only three—are governed by relatively tiny oligarchies. Nations smaller than ours are mostly governed by oligarchies as well, but those nations that are democracies are nevertheless served by rather small and close-knit political classes. It is common to find in the annals of these democratic nation-states that political rivals of the same generation were schoolmates—the relationships among key actors in the political class having been cemented long before any of them came to power. The analyst of American politics who expects to find a similar close-knit framework in the United States will be disappointed.

One consequence of the extraordinary properties of the American political system is that it requires a great deal of attention from analysts. Analogies with the rest of the systems of the world will usually not do. And as a literature on American politics has developed, some contributions have proven to be especially helpful in getting a grasp on how this sizeable, long-lasting, complex, and adaptive system works—and how its parts fit into a whole. Some of those contributions are among the articles reprinted here.

Foreword

TO THE FIRST EDITION

BY

THEODORE J. LOWI

In music, the term *classic* refers to the age of Haydn and Mozart because that was the period when musical forms, instruments, and ensembles became standardized, providing the framework for most subsequent Western musical composition and performance. *Classic* was not intended to refer to superior results; nor was it intended to distinguish between serious music and popular music. As one music historian put it, "To group all music which does not come under the head of popular music as classical is a mark of lack of cultivation."

This musical usage is consistent with the *Oxford English Dictionary*, where, although the primary definition identifies *classic* as referring to things of the highest quality, the brief history of its usage affirms that the meaning of *classic* arises out of references to "classes of colleges or schools." It is probable that this notion influenced the extension of the word to the ancient authors themselves, as studied in school or college. It is also probable that "the transference of the epithet from the first-class or standard writers in Greek and Latin to these languages themselves has been partly owing to the notion that the latter are intrinsically excellent or of the first order, in comparison to the modern tongues." Thus, a musical composition or an essay is referred to as "classic" if it is thought to perform as the model or standard for other works in a school of thought or a discipline.

But here's the rub. If a work qualifies as "classic" only when it is loyally imitated by all successors, then not even the masterpieces of the great Haydn or Mozart would fit the definition because significant departures from their model occurred even before they were cold in the grave. The classical era of music was rather quickly replaced by the romantic era. What we can say, however, is that the works of Haydn and Mozart were classic because, as the models, they set the terms of discourse, even for the dissenters and the innovators.

How are the essays in this volume classics? Each is considered something of a classic because it has helped shape the terms of discourse in political science. Each has served as a kind of jumping-off point for other scholars. Actually, I should say jumping-*on* point, since many scholars have found it useful to criticize one or more of these works as a way of distinguishing their own. In other words, a work can become a classic regardless of its weaknesses. The hundreds of citations of these works in the footnotes of others indicate how influential they have been. To cite another author's work does not mean it is being used as the authority to clinch the argument. More often, a work is cited because it has been integrated into the thought on that subject. Even a cursory reading of the essays in this volume shows that the authors were seeking to be part of a discourse outside the confines of their own research by saying something lasting about the conditions of political life—especially about the conditions of that most delicate of all political specimens, institutionalized democracy.

In the introduction to his own classic work, *American Capitalism*, John Kenneth Galbraith characterized the U.S. economy by observing that "such are the aerodynamics and wing-loading of the bumblebee that, in principle, it cannot fly. It does, and the knowledge that it defies the august authority of Issac Newton and Orville Wright must keep the bee in constant fear of a crack-up."[1] Such a comparison is more appropriate for the American polity, because it has been relatively stable for over two hundred years despite the fact that American society and the American economy have been unstable. To add to the mystery, American democracy itself was built on contradictions: How is it possible to balance free thought and free choice with the requirements of public order? In a representative legislature? But is it possible to set up a legislature that gives equality of access to policy making and still makes important decisions in time to meet the collective needs of an immensely complex society? And how can we have intelligent policymakers if a very substantial fraction of the American electorate is ignorant of the issues? Or an accountable bureaucracy without giving its leader, the president, powers far in excess of what a legislature can oversee or the people or the courts will accept?

Political scientists address themselves to these difficult issues with one hand tied behind their backs; that is, they are trying to study with scientific precision matters as complex and ever-changing as the institutions of government. Science requires analysis, it has its own language—that of variables and hypotheses—and it holds to its own standards of truth, which presume strict canons of evidence and demonstration, and an attitude of utmost objectivity. Few political scientists want to reject the scientific method, but they use it at a heavy cost. While being scientific, political scientists sacrifice at least some concern for the questions of history, context, and value, which attend all political issues. Does this mean that we yield to others the joy of confrontation with big questions, even when our findings may bear on them?

The authors in this collection have indicated an unwillingness to yield. But this does not mean they have abandoned their discipline. An outstanding characteristic of these selections, especially those drawn from the professional political science of the twentieth century, is that each started on a fairly solid evidentiary base and each *lifted the discourse* from that base to an entirely different language—from a language of variables to a language of argument, from a language of causes to a language of consequences. That, to me, is the secret of a classic, whether it succeeds or whether it fails; and that is the only way to make political science interesting.

Lifting the discourse toward the larger consequences that are of concern to the whole political community also makes authors more vulnerable than if they stayed within the confines of what has been carefully studied. As Woodrow Wilson said in 1911 in his address as president of the American Political Science

Association, "There is no such thing as an expert in human relationships."[2] Inevitably, those who seek to engage in the larger, continuing discourse concerning human—and political—relationships must go a considerable distance beyond their professional competence.

Not everyone wants to take such a risk, but those who do have something in common: They are both teachers and scholars. Although four of the six pre-twentieth century authors represented here—Madison, Hamilton, Chief Justice Marshall, and de Tocqueville—were not academicians, they were, in their own way teachers of politics. For example, Madison and Hamilton addressed their arguments in *Federalist 10* and 78 to the New York voters and the members of the New York State Assembly who were polarized over whether to ratify the new Constitution, Alexis de Tocqueville wrote about democracy in the America of the 1830s but aimed his argument at the French public. All the others, including the late nineteenth-century authors Woodrow Wilson and Lord Bryce, were card-carrying academic political scientists (with the exception of a half dozen who took Ph.D.s in some related academic field but addressed a large number of their writings to political scientists); and all but one had a career in college teaching.

Is this dominance by teacher-scholars merely a reflection of editorial bias? I doubt it, because the primary interest of the editors is to provide selections, regardless of the source or author, most likely to be considered essential reading by the largest segment of the relevant market, namely, the professors who select books and students who are assigned to purchase and read them. I think the explanation is to be found in the creative contradiction faced by college teachers who embrace their discipline by carrying on a parallel career in research and writing. Writing for the discipline of political science subjects the author to the anonymous, professional peer review process of scholarly journals and book publishing. The college classroom subjects the teacher to the contrary pressure of trying to transcend the methods and results of research in the discipline by explaining its value to students. College students require of their teachers at least some concern for consequential argument as well as causal analysis. They want to know "So what?" In the classroom, professors rarely can talk down to their students; generally they have to talk *up* to their students because they have the difficult task of bringing specialized research and unspecialized students to a community of common concern: how we govern ourselves.

A teacher's attempt to be memorable by being consequential is the important bridge between the down-to-earth science of our research and the more elevated argument of our teaching. The contradiction between the stringencies of science and the goal of a higher, more consequence-oriented level of discourse is not only creative, it is also invaluable. If in the process we reveal our incompetence, that is in itself good teaching, because it encourages students to join the process as bona fide participants.

In the preface to his intellectual history of political science (*The Tragedy of Political Science*, 1984) David Ricci observes that with the rise of academic political science, "The line of first-rate thinkers in the Western tradition came to an end." Those whose writings form the basis for the history of political science—from Plato and Aristotle to Marx and Mill—were not the product of an academic environment, though some of them did teach for a living. As Ricci put it, "The longer I thought about the declining number of great thinkers and the growing prominence of universities, the more I was convinced that these two trends must be significantly related."[3] It is difficult to disagree with Ricci's contention that the twentieth century has yet to produce a single political thinker of the stature of a Marx or Mill, the last of the great thinkers before political writing and teaching became organized into the discipline of political science. But it would be equally difficult for him to disagree with the contention that in the 2,000-plus years between Plato and Mill, *no* country or century—not even the Greece of classical antiquity—could lay claim to many great thinkers. Great thinkers just don't come along very often. And it's even possible that their appearance may drop still further because of the tendency of both democracy and science to reduce issues to manageable proportions, while thinkers tend to magnify issues. America's greatest thinkers all appeared at the time of our founding, with the possible exception of Abraham Lincoln and a half dozen members of the U.S. Supreme Court—and all for the same reason: They confronted issues too big to trivialize, and they crafted their responses accordingly.

Modern academic political scientists from Woodrow Wilson to the present, including all the contemporary authors in this volume, have overcome many of the constraints of science and democracy, and although there are still no Aristotles or Rousseaus, we can consider ourselves keepers of the flame. If enough political scientists can transcend the discipline without unsciencing it, we can maintain a discourse worthy of the great thinkers to come—who may be in our classrooms at this very moment. We cannot yet know who they are, and we cannot create them. But we can encourage them by exposing them to the best thinking our field of study can offer.

NOTES

1. John Kenneth Galbraith, *American Capitalism*, 2d ed., revised (Boston: Houghton Mifflin, 1956), p. 1.

2. Raymond Seidelman, with the assistance of Edward J. Harpham, *Disenchanted Realists: Political Science and the American Crisis* (Albany: State University of New York Press, 1985).

3. David Ricci, *The Tragedy of Political Science: Politics, Scholarship, and Democracy* (New Haven, Conn.: Yale University Press, 1984).

PART ONE

POLITICAL CULTURE AND TRADITIONS

American and foreign observers have long considered government and politics in the United States to be unique. This uniqueness is suggested by structural features such as a written constitution, a two-party system, an elaborate separation of powers, a bicameral legislature, federalism, and judicial review—features that are not found together in other political systems. But the unique qualities of the American polity reach well beyond structures and institutions; they go to the very core of the United States' political culture.

Political culture involves the ways in which the members of a political community think about and evaluate their government and politics. This is a broad concern upon which almost all general theories of the American political experience dwell. Although different scholars have stressed various keys to understanding the United States' political culture, the classic interpretations tend to stress two related elements—equality and constitutionalism.

The first selection on political culture is drawn from the seminal work of Alexis de Tocqueville, whom many consider still the keenest observer of the American political community. In *Democracy in America* (Vol. I, 1835; Vol. II, 1840), this visitor from France identified equality as the fundamental aspect of the developing American political culture, but he also addressed the very breaches of equality that still confound the political system today. Thus, in perhaps his best-known words, Tocqueville wrote, "The great advantage of the Americans is that they have arrived at a state of democracy without having to endure a democratic revolution; and that they are born equal, instead of becoming so." But in a lesser-known passage, he commented that "in no country has such constant care been taken as in America to trace two clearly distinct lines of action for the two sexes, and to make them keep pace one with the other, but in two pathways which are always different." Moreover, he referred to the existence of three distinct races within the United States polity as one of the "dangers which menace that confederation," as these groups might almost be termed "hostile to each other" and "do not amalgamate," but rather "each race fulfils its destiny apart." Consequently, although we have titled the selections from Tocqueville "Equality," his understanding of the fundamental social cleavages facing the nation is also stressed.

Although Tocqueville presents a sound beginning for the student of American political culture, Louis Hartz is correct in pointing out that "no school of American historians has ever come out of the well-known work of the greatest foreign critic

1

America ever had—Tocqueville." Hence, while often rooted in Tocqueville's work, intellectual traditions concerning American political culture have frequently moved beyond his formulations in addressing additional dimensions.

In his *Liberal Tradition in America* (1955), Hartz argues that what sets America apart from other countries is its liberal consensus. Although "liberalism" eludes a precise definition, Hartz uses it to refer to a democratic ethos stressing individual rights, political equality, and limited government. In his view, this liberalism developed naturally from the absence of a feudal past in America. Essentially, a nonfeudal society lacks both a genuine revolutionary tradition and a tradition of reaction; this makes it possible for what would be revolutionary elsewhere (liberalism) to be a matter of consensus in a political community such as the United States.

Were the Founders of the American republic motivated in large part by material concerns or chiefly by a common public philosophy? Charles Beard's *Economic Interpretation of the Constitution of the United States* (1913) places emphasis on the first of these sources of inspiration. Analyzing the commercial activities and holdings of those who attended the Constitutional Convention in 1787, Beard inferred that the Founders sought to advance or defend their economic interests. Their instrument, Beard argued, was the Constitution, which conferred "great powers . . . on the new government: taxation, war, commercial control, and disposition of western lands." "Through them," he wrote, "public creditors may be paid in full, domestic peace maintained, advantages obtained in dealing with foreign nations, manufacturers protected, and the development of the territories go forward with full swing." In addition, Beard stressed, "None of the powers conferred by the Constitution on Congress permits a direct attack on property."

Gordon S. Wood provides a contrasting perspective. In the excerpt from his treatise, *The Creation of the American Republic, 1776–1787* (1969), Professor Wood shows how the American revolutionaries were not only animated by political ideas, nor mere economic pursuits, but came to embrace a truly revolutionary theory of governance. A sober assessment of human nature, with all its vices, underlaid the new conception of politics. The republic would be organized to pursue just ends by ultimately conferring sovereign power on the people, and also by harnessing for their common good their often divergent self-interests.

In the end, however, there is no better source for understanding the roots of American constitutional democracy than the writings of the Founders themselves. *The Federalist Papers* (1787–1788), authored by James Madison, Alexander Hamilton, and John Jay, provide if not a detailed blueprint for the Constitution, surely a clear outline of its theoretical framework—including its central public purpose, its conception of republicanism, and its rationale for the separation of powers. In these pages, we reproduce one of the most important and comprehensive essays, *Federalist 10*. Subsequent sections include several others that help shed light on how the Founders debated issues such as federalism and the scope of executive power.

1

ALEXIS DE TOCQUEVILLE

EQUALITY OF CONDITION

The French aristocrat Alexis de Tocqueville (1805–1859) visited the United States for nine months in 1831. His observations and deep insights were subsequently compiled in what may be the greatest treatise ever written about American society and politics, Democracy in America *(Vol. I, 1835; Vol. II, 1840). In the following selection, composed of excerpts from that book, Tocqueville marvels at the relative equality of the citizenry and notes the absence of an aristocracy in the European sense. He comments on how much easier it is for democracy to take root in a land with these attributes.*

Among the novel objects that attracted my attention during my stay in the United States, nothing struck me more forcibly than the general equality of conditions. I readily discovered the prodigious influence which this primary fact exercises on the whole course of society, by giving a certain direction to public opinion, and a certain tenor to the laws; by imparting new maxims to the governing powers, and peculiar habits to the governed.

I speedily perceived that the influence of this fact extends far beyond the political character and the laws of the country, and that it has no less empire over civil society than over the government; it creates opinions, engenders sentiments, suggests the ordinary practices of life, and modifies whatever it does not produce.

The more I advanced in the study of American society, the more I perceived that the equality of conditions is the fundamental fact from which all others seem to be derived, and the central point at which all my observations constantly terminated. . . .

The emigrants who fixed themselves on the shores of America in the beginning of the seventeenth century, severed the democratic principle from all the principles which repressed it in the old communities of Europe, and transplanted it unalloyed to the New World. It has there been allowed to spread in perfect freedom, and to put forth its consequences in the laws by influencing the manners of the country.

✳   ✳   ✳

THE STRIKING CHARACTERISTIC OF THE SOCIAL CONDITION OF THE ANGLO-AMERICANS IS ITS ESSENTIAL DEMOCRACY

Many important observations suggest themselves upon the social condition of the Anglo-Americans; but there is one which takes precedence of all the rest. The social condition of the Americans is eminently democratic; this was its character at the foundation of the colonies, and is still more strongly marked at the present day.

I have stated . . . that great equality existed among the emigrants who settled on the shores of New England. The germ of aristocracy was never planted in that part of the Union. The only influence which obtained there was that of intellect; the people were used to reverence certain names as the emblems of knowledge and virtue. Some of their fellow-citizens acquired a power over the rest which might truly have been called aristocratic, if it had been capable of invariable transmission from father to son.

This was the state of things to the east of the Hudson: to the southwest of that river, and in the direction of the Floridas, the case was different. In most of the states situated to the southwest of the Hudson some great English proprietors had settled, who had imported with them aristocratic principles and the English law of descent. I have explained the reasons why it was impossible ever to establish a powerful aristocracy in America; these reasons existed with less force to the southwest of the Hudson. In the south, one man, aided by slaves, could cultivate a great extent of country: it was therefore common to see rich landed proprietors. But their influence was not altogether aristocratic as that term is understood in Europe, since they possessed no privileges; and the cultivation of their estates being carried on by slaves, they had no tenants depending on them, and consequently no patronage. Still, the great proprietors south of the Hudson constituted a superior class, having ideas and tastes of its own, and forming the centre of political action. This kind of aristocracy sympathized with the body of the people, whose passions and interests it easily embraced; but it was too weak and too short-lived to excite either love or hatred for itself. This was the class which headed the insurrection in the south, and furnished the best leaders of the American revolution.

At the period of which we are now speaking, society was shaken to its centre: the people, in whose name the struggle had taken place, conceived the desire of exercising the authority which it had acquired; its democratic tendencies were awakened; and having thrown off the yoke of the mother-country, it aspired to independence of every kind. The influence of individuals gradually ceased to be felt, and custom and law united together to produce the same result.

But the law of descent was the last step to equality. I am surprised that ancient and modern jurists have not attributed to this law a greater influence on human affairs. It is true that these laws belong to civil affairs: but they ought nevertheless to be placed at the head of all political institutions; for, while political laws are only the symbol of a nation's condition, they exercise an incredible influence upon its social state. They have, moreover, a sure and uniform manner of operating upon society, affecting, as it were, generations yet unborn.

Through their means man acquires a kind of preternatural power over the future lot of his fellow-creatures. When the legislator has once regulated the law of inheritance, he may rest from his labour. The machine once put in motion will go on for ages, and advance, as if self-guided, toward a given point. When framed in a particular manner, this law unites, draws together, and vests property and power in a few hands: its tendency is clearly aristocratic. On opposite principles its action is still more rapid; it divides, distributes, and disperses both property and power.

*   *   *

In the United States [the law of inheritance] has nearly completed its work of destruction, and there we can best study its results. The English laws concerning the transmission of property were abolished in almost all the states at the time of the revolution. The law of entail was so modified as not to interrupt the free circulation of property. The first having passed away, estates began to be parcelled out; and the change became more and more rapid with the progress of time. At this moment, after a lapse of little more than sixty years, the aspect of society is totally altered; the families of the great landed proprietors are almost all commingled with the general mass. In the state of New York, which formerly contained many of these, there are but two who still keep their heads above the stream; and they must shortly disappear. The sons of these opulent citizens have become merchants, lawyers, or physicians. Most of them have lapsed into obscurity. The last trace of hereditary ranks and distinctions is destroyed—the law of partition has reduced all to one level.

I do not mean that there is any deficiency of wealthy individuals in the United States; I know of no country, indeed, where the love of money has taken stronger hold on the affections of men, and where a profounder contempt is expressed for the theory of the permanent equality of property. But wealth circulates with inconceivable rapidity, and experience shows that it is rare to find two succeeding generations in the full enjoyment of it. . . .

It is not only the fortunes of men which are equal in America; even their acquirements partake in some degree of the same uniformity. I do not believe there is a country in the world where, in proportion to the population, there are so few uninstructed, and at the same time so few learned individuals. Primary instruction is within the reach of everybody; superior instruction is scarcely to be obtained by any. This is not surprising; it is in fact the necessary consequence of what we have advanced above. Almost all the Americans are in easy circumstances, and can therefore obtain the first elements of human knowledge.

In America there are comparatively few who are rich enough to live without a profession. Every profession requires an apprenticeship, which limits the time of instruction to the early years of life. At fifteen they enter upon their calling, and thus their education ends at the age when ours begins. Whatever is done afterward, is with a view to some special and lucrative object; a science is taken up as a matter of business, and the only branch of it which is attended to is such as admits of an immediate practical application.

In America most of the rich men were formerly poor: most of those who now enjoy leisure were absorbed in business during their youth; the consequence of which is, that when they might have had a taste for study they had no time for it, and when the time is at their disposal they have no longer the inclination.

There is no class, then, in America in which the taste for intellectual pleasures is transmitted with hereditary fortune and leisure, and by which the labours of the intellect are held in honour. Accordingly there is an equal want of the desire and the power of application to these objects.

A middling standard is fixed in America for human knowledge. All approach as near to it as they can; some as they rise, others as they descend. Of course, an immense multitude of persons are to be found who entertain the same number of

ideas on religion, history, science, political economy, legislation, and government. The gifts of intellect proceed directly from God, and man cannot prevent
their unequal distribution. But in consequence of the state of things which we
have here represented, it happens, that although the capacities of men are widely
different, as the Creator has doubtless intended they should be, they are submitted to the same method of treatment.

In America the aristocratic element has always been feeble from its birth; and
if at the present day it is not actually destroyed, it is at any rate so completely disabled that we can scarcely assign to it any degree of influence in the course of
affairs.

The democratic principle, on the contrary, has gained so much strength by
time, by events, and by legislation, as to have become not only predominant but
all-powerful. There is no family or corporate authority, and it is rare to find even
the influence of individual character enjoy any durability.

America, then, exhibits in her social state a most extraordinary phenomenon.
Men are there seen on a greater equality in point of fortune and intellect, or in
other words, more equal in their strength, than in any other country of the world,
or, in any age of which history has preserved the remembrance.

POLITICAL CONSEQUENCES OF THE SOCIAL CONDITION
OF THE ANGLO-AMERICANS

The political consequences of such a social condition as this are easily
deducible.

It is impossible to believe that equality will not eventually find its way into the
political world as it does everywhere else. To conceive of men remaining for ever
unequal upon one single point, yet equal on all others, is impossible; they must
come in the end to be equal upon all.

Now I know of only two methods of establishing equality in the political world:
every citizen must be put in possession of his rights, or rights must be granted to
no one. For nations which have arrived at the same stage of social existence as the
Anglo-Americans, it is therefore very difficult to discover a medium between the
sovereignty of all and the absolute power of one man: and it would be vain to
deny that the social condition which I have been describing is equally liable to
each of these consequences.

There is, in fact, a manly and lawful passion for equality, which excites men to
wish all to be powerful and honoured. This passion tends to elevate the humble
to the rank of the great; but there exists also in the human heart a depraved taste
for equality, which impels the weak to attempt to lower the powerful to their own
level, and reduces men to prefer equality in slavery to inequality with freedom.
Not that those nations whose social condition is democratic naturally despise liberty; on the contrary, they have an instinctive love of it. But liberty is not the chief
and constant object of their desires; equality is their idol: they make rapid and
sudden efforts to obtain liberty, and if they miss their aim, resign themselves to

their disappointment; but nothing can satisfy them except equality, and rather than lose it they resolve to perish.

On the other hand, in a state where the citizens are nearly on an equality, it becomes difficult for them to preserve their independence against the aggressions of power. No one among them being strong enough to engage singly in the struggle with advantage, nothing but a general combination can protect their liberty: and such a union is not always to be found.

From the same social position, then, nations may derive one or the other of two great political results; these results are extremely different from each other, but they may both proceed from the same cause.

The Anglo-Americans are the first who, having been exposed to this formidable alternative, have been happy enough to escape the dominion of absolute power. They have been allowed by their circumstances, their origin, their intelligence, and especially by their moral feeling, to establish and maintain the sovereignty of the people.

⚜   ✻   ⚜

INDIVIDUALISM STRONGER AT THE CLOSE OF A DEMOCRATIC REVOLUTION THAN AT OTHER PERIODS

. . . An aristocracy seldom yields without a protracted struggle, in the course of which implacable animosities are kindled between the different classes of society. These passions survive the victory, and traces of them may be observed in the midst of the democratic confusion which ensues.

Those members of the community who were at the top of the late gradations of rank cannot immediately forget their former greatness; they will long regard themselves as aliens in the midst of the newly composed society. They look upon all those whom this state of society has made their equals as oppressors, whose destiny can excite no sympathy; they have lost sight of their former equals, and feel no longer bound by a common interest to their fate: each of them, standing aloof, thinks that he is reduced to care for himself alone. Those, on the contrary, who were formerly at the foot of the social scale, and who have been brought up to the common level by a sudden revolution, cannot enjoy their newly acquired independence without secret uneasiness; and if they meet with some of their former superiors on the same footing as themselves, they stand aloof from them with an expression of triumph and of fear. . . .

The great advantage of the Americans is that they have arrived at a state of democracy without having to endure a democratic revolution; and that they are born equal, instead of becoming so.

✻   ✻   ✻

OF CERTAIN PECULIAR AND ACCIDENTAL CAUSES WHICH EITHER LEAD A PEOPLE TO COMPLETE CENTRALIZATION OF GOVERNMENT, OR WHICH DIVERT THEM FROM IT

. . . These observations explain why the supreme power is always stronger, and private individuals weaker, among a democratic people which has passed through a long and arduous struggle to reach a state of equality, than among a democratic community in which the citizens have been equal from the first. The example of the Americans completely demonstrates the fact. The inhabitants of the United States were never divided by any privileges; they have never known the mutual relation of master and inferior, and as they neither dread nor hate each other, they have never known the necessity of calling in the supreme power to manage their affairs. The lot of the Americans is singular: they have derived from the aristocracy of England the notion of private rights and the taste for local freedom; and they have been able to retain both the one and the other, because they have had no aristocracy to combat.

2

LOUIS HARTZ

THE CONCEPT OF A LIBERAL SOCIETY

In his famous book, The Liberal Tradition in America *(1955), Louis Hartz (1919–1986) built on Alexis de Tocqueville's reportage about the American polity. Among the unique features Tocqueville had observed in the United States was the absence of a feudal past. Hartz, a professor at Harvard University, explored the implications of this legacy. America's classical liberal consensus, he argued, became uniquely broad because the society had not passed through a historical sequence of ideologically charged class conflicts, beginning with those that broke feudal bonds.*

1. AMERICA AND EUROPE

The analysis which this book contains is based on what might be called the storybook truth about American history: that America was settled by men who fled from the feudal and clerical oppressions of the Old World. If there is anything in this view, as old as the national folklore itself, then the outstanding thing about the American community in Western history ought to be the nonexistence of those oppressions, or since the reaction against them was in the broadest sense liberal, that the American community is a liberal community. We are confronted, as it were, with a kind of inverted Trotskyite law of combined development, America skipping the feudal stage of history as Russia presumably skipped the liberal stage. I know that I am using broad terms broadly here. "Feudalism" refers technically to the institutions of the medieval era, and it is well known that aspects of the decadent feudalism of the later period, such as primogeniture, entail, and quitrents, were present in America even in the eighteenth century.[1] "Liberalism" is an even vaguer term, clouded as it is by all sorts of modern social reform connotations, and even when one insists on using it in the classic Lockian sense, as I shall insist here, there are aspects of our original life in the Puritan colonies and the South which hardly fit its meaning. But these are the liabilities of any large generalization, danger points but not insuperable barriers. What in the end is more interesting is the curious failure of American historians, after repeating endlessly that America was grounded in escape from the European past, to interpret our history in the light of that fact. There are a number of reasons for this which we shall encounter before we are through, but one is obvious at the outset: the separation of the study of American from European history and politics. Any attempt to uncover the nature of an American society without feudalism can only be accomplished by studying it in conjunction with a European society where the feudal structure and the feudal ethos did in fact survive. This is not to deny our national uniqueness, one of the reasons curiously given for studying America alone, but actually to affirm it. How can we know the uniqueness of anything except by contrasting it with what is not unique? The rationale for a separate American study, once you begin to think about it, explodes the study itself.

In the end, however, it is not logic but experience, to use a Holmesian phrase, which exposes the traditional approach. We could use our uniqueness as an excuse for evading its study so long as our world position did not really require us to know much about it. Now that a whole series of alien cultures have crashed in upon the American world, shattering the peaceful landscape of Bancroft and Beard, the old non sequitur simply will not do. When we need desperately to know the idiosyncrasies which interfere with our understanding of Europe, we can hardly break away from "European schemes" of analysis, as J. Franklin Jameson urged American historians to do in 1891 (not that they ever really used them in the first place) on the ground that we are idiosyncratic. But the issue is deeper than foreign policy, for the world involvement has also brought to the surface of American life great new domestic forces which must remain inexplicable without comparative study. It has redefined, as Communism shows, the issue of our internal freedom in terms of our external life. So in fact it is the entire crisis of our time which compels us to make that journey to Europe and back which ends in the discovery of the American liberal world.

2. "NATURAL LIBERALISM": THE FRAME OF MIND

One of the central characteristics of a nonfeudal society is that it lacks a genuine revolutionary tradition, the tradition which in Europe has been linked with the Puritan and French revolutions: that it is "born equal," as Tocqueville said. And this being the case, it lacks also a tradition of reaction: lacking Robespierre it lacks Maistre, lacking Sydney it lacks Charles II. Its liberalism is what Santayana called, referring to American democracy, a "natural" phenomenon. But the matter is curiously broader than this, for a society which begins with Locke, and thus transforms him, stays with Locke, by virtue of an absolute and irrational attachment it develops for him, and becomes as indifferent to the challenge of socialism in the later era as it was unfamiliar with the heritage of feudalism in the earlier one. It has within it, as it were, a kind of self-completing mechanism, which ensures the universality of the liberal idea. Here, we shall see, is one of the places where Marx went wrong in his historical analysis, attributing as he did the emergence of the socialist ideology to the objective movement of economic forces. Actually socialism is largely an ideological phenomenon, arising out of the principles of class and the revolutionary liberal revolt against them which the old European order inspired. It is not accidental that America which has uniquely lacked a feudal tradition has uniquely lacked also a socialist tradition. The hidden origin of socialist thought everywhere in the West is to be found in the feudal ethos. The *ancien régime* inspires Rousseau; both inspire Marx.

Which brings us to the substantive quality of the natural liberal mind. And this poses no easy problem. For when the words of Locke are used and a prior Filmer is absent, how are we to delineate the significance of the latter fact? In politics men who make speeches do not go out of their way to explain how differently they would speak if the enemies they had were larger in size or different in character. On the contrary whatever enemies they fight they paint in satanic terms, so that a problem sufficiently difficult to begin with in a liberal society becomes complicated further by the inevitable perspectives of political battle. Take the American Revolution. With John Adams identifying the Stamp Act with the worst of the historic European oppressions, how can we distinguish the man from Lilburne or the philosophers of the French Enlightenment? And yet if we study the American liberal language in terms of intensity and emphasis, if we look for silent omissions as well as explicit inclusions, we begin to see a pattern emerging that smacks distinctively of the New World. It has a quiet, matter of fact quality, it does not understand the meaning of sovereign power, the bourgeois class passion is scarcely present, the sense of the past is altered, and there is about it all, as compared with the European pattern, a vast and almost charming innocence of mind. Twain's "Innocents Abroad" is a pretty relevant concept, for the psyche that springs from social war and social revolution is given to far suspicions and sidelong glances that the American liberal cannot easily understand. Possibly this is what people mean when they say that European thought is "deeper" than American, though anyone who tries to grapple with America in Western terms will wonder whether the term "depth" is the proper one to use. There can be an appalling complexity to innocence, especially if your point of departure is guilt.

Now if the *ancien régime* is not present to begin with, one thing follows automatically: it does not return in a blaze of glory. It does not flower in the nineteenth century in a Disraeli or a Ballanche, however different from each other these men may be. I do not mean to imply that no trace of the feudal urge, no shadow whatsoever of Sir Walter Scott, has been found on the hills and plains of the New World. One can get into a lot of useless argument if he affirms the liberalness of a liberal society in absolute mathematical fashion. The top strata of the American community, from the time of Peggy Hutchinson to the time of Margaret Kennedy, have yearned for the aristocratic ethos. But instead of exemplifying the typical Western situation, these yearnings represent an inversion of it. America has presented the world with the peculiar phenomenon, not of a frustrated middle class, but of a "frustrated aristocracy"—of men, Aristotelian-like, trying to break out of the egalitarian confines of middle class life but suffering guilt and failure in the process. The South before the Civil War is the case par excellence of this, though New England of course exemplifies it also. Driven away from Jefferson by abolitionism, the Fitzhughs of the ante-bellum era actually dared to ape the doctrinal patterns of the Western reaction, of Disraeli and Bonald. But when Jefferson is traditional, European traditionalism is a curious thing indeed. The Southerners were thrown into fantastic contradictions by their iconoclastic conservatism, by what I have called the "Reactionary Enlightenment," and after the Civil War for good historical reasons they fell quickly into oblivion. The South, as John Crowe Ransom has said, has been the part of America closest to Old World Europe, but it has never really been Europe. It has been an alien child in a liberal family, tortured and confused, driven to a fantasy life which, instead of disproving the power of Locke in America, portrays more poignantly than anything else the tyranny he has had.

But is not the problem of Fitzhugh at once the problem of De Leon? Here we have one of the great and neglected relationships in American history: the

common fecklessness of the Southern "feudalists" and the modern socialists. It is
not accidental, but something rooted in the logic of all of Western history, that
they should fail alike to leave a dent in the American liberal intelligence. For if
the concept of class was meaningless in its Disraelian form, and if American liberalism had never acquired it in its bourgeois form, why should it be any more
meaningful in its Marxian form? This secret process of ideological transmission is
not, however, the only thing involved. Socialism arises not only to fight capitalism but remnants of feudalism itself, so that the failure of the Southern Filmeri-
ans, in addition to setting the pattern for the failure of the later Marxists, robbed
them in the process of a normal ground for growth. Could De Leon take over the
liberal goal of extended suffrage as Lasalle did in Germany or the crusade against
the House of Lords as the Labor Party did in England? Marx himself noted the
absence of an American feudalism, but since he misinterpreted the complex origins of European socialism in the European *ancien régime*, he did not grasp the
significance of it.

Surely, then, it is a remarkable force: this fixed, dogmatic liberalism of a liberal
way of life. It is the secret root from which have sprung many of the most puzzling of American cultural phenomena. Take the unusual power of the Supreme
Court and the cult of constitution worship on which it rests. Federal factors apart,
judicial review as it has worked in America would be inconceivable without the
national acceptance of the Lockian creed, ultimately enshrined in the Constitution, since the removal of high policy to the realm of adjudication implies a prior
recognition of the principles to be legally interpreted. At the very moment that
Senator Benton was hailing the rise of America's constitutional fetishism, in
France Royer Collard and the Doctrinaires were desperately trying to build precisely the same atmosphere around the Restoration Charter of 1814, but being a
patchwork of Maistre and Rousseau, that constitutional document exploded in
their faces in the July Revolution. *Inter arma leges silent.* If in England a mar-
velous organic cohesion has held together the feudal, liberal, and socialist ideas,
it would still be unthinkable there that the largest issues of public policy should
be put before nine Talmudic judges examining a single text. But this is merely
another way of saying that law has flourished on the corpse of philosophy in
America, for the settlement of the ultimate moral question is the end of speculation upon it. Pragmatism, interestingly enough America's great contribution to
the philosophic tradition, does not alter this, since it feeds itself on the Lockian
settlement. It is only when you take your ethics for granted that all problems
emerge as problems of technique. Not that this is a bar in America to institutional
innovations of highly non-Lockian kind. Indeed, as the New Deal shows, when
you simply "solve problems" on the basis of a submerged and absolute liberal
faith, you can depart from Locke with a kind of inventive freedom that European
Liberal reformers and even European socialists, dominated by ideological systems, cannot duplicate. But the main point remains: if Fitzhugh and De Leon
were crucified by the American general will, John Marshall and John Dewey
flourished in consequence of their crucifixion. The moral unanimity of a liberal
society reaches out in many directions.

At bottom it is riddled with paradox. Here is a Lockian doctrine which in the West as a whole is the symbol of rationalism, yet in America the devotion to it has been so irrational that it has not even been recognized for what it is: liberalism. There has never been a "liberal movement" or a real "liberal party" in America: we have only had the American Way of Life, a nationalist articulation of Locke which usually does not know that Locke himself is involved; and we did not even get that until after the Civil War when the Whigs of the nation, deserting the Hamiltonian tradition, saw the capital that could be made out of it. This is why even critics who have noticed America's moral unity have usually missed its substance. Ironically, "liberalism" is a stranger in the land of its greatest realization and fulfillment. But this is not all. Here is a doctrine which everywhere in the West has been a glorious symbol of individual liberty, yet in America its compulsive power has been so great that it has posed a threat to liberty itself. Actually Locke has a hidden conformitarian germ to begin with, since natural law tells equal people equal things, but when this germ is fed by the explosive power of modern nationalism, it mushrooms into something pretty remarkable. One can reasonably wonder about the liberty one finds in Burke.

I believe that this is the basic ethical problem of a liberal society: not the danger of the majority which has been its conscious fear, but the danger of unanimity, which has slumbered unconsciously behind it: the "tyranny of opinion" that Tocqueville saw unfolding as even the pathetic social distinctions of the Federalist era collapsed before his eyes. But in recent times this manifestation of irrational Lockianism, or of "Americanism," to use a favorite term of the American Legion, one of the best expounders of the national spirit that Whiggery discovered after the Civil War, has neither slumbered nor been unconscious. It has been very much awake in a red scare hysteria which no other nation in the West has really been able to understand. And this suggests a very significant principle: that when a liberal community faces military and ideological pressure from without it transforms eccentricity into sin, and the irritating figure of the bourgeois gossip flowers into the frightening figure of an A. Mitchell Palmer or a Senator McCarthy. Do we not find here, hidden away at the base of the American mind, one of the reasons why its legalism has been so imperfect a barrier against the violent moods of its mass Lockianism? If the latter is nourished by the former, how can we expect it to be strong? We say of the Supreme Court that it is courageous when it challenges Jefferson, but since in a liberal society the individualism of Hamilton is also a secret part of the Jeffersonian psyche, we make too much of this. The real test of the Court is when it faces the excitement both of Jefferson and Hamilton, when the Talmudic text is itself at stake, when the general will on which it feeds rises to the surface in anger. And here, brave as the Court has been at moments, its record has been no more heroic than the logic of the situation would suggest.

The decisive domestic issue of our time may well lie in the counter resources a liberal society can muster against this deep and unwritten tyrannical compulsion it contains. They exist. Given the individualist nature of the Lockian doctrine, there is always a logical impulse within it to transcend the very conformitarian spirit it breeds in a Lockian society: witness the spirit of Holmes and Hand. Given the fact, which we shall study at length later, that "Americanism" oddly disadvantages the Progressive despite the fact that he shares it to the full, there is always a strategic impulse within him to transcend it: witness the spirit of Brandeis, Roosevelt, and Stevenson. In some sense the tragedy of these movements has lain in the imperfect knowledge they have had of the enemy they face, above all in their failure to see their own unwitting contribution to his strength. The record of Brandeis was good on civil liberties, but anyone who studies his Progressive thought will see that he was, for good or bad, on that score a vital part of the compulsive "Americanism" which bred the hysteria he fought. The Progressive tradition, if it is to transcend the national general will, has got to realize, as it has not yet done, how deeply its own Jacksonian heroes have been rooted in it.

But the most powerful force working to shatter the American absolutism is, paradoxically enough, the very international involvement which intensifies it. This involvement is complex in its implications. If in the context of the Russian Revolution it elicits a domestic red scare, in the context of diplomacy it elicits an impulse to impose Locke everywhere. The way in which "Americanism" brings McCarthy together with Wilson is of great significance and it is, needless to say, another one of Progressivism's neglected roots in the Rousseauean tide it often seeks to stem. Thus to say that world politics shatters "Americanism" at the moment it intensifies it is to say a lot: it is to say that the basic horizons of the nation both at home and abroad are drastically widened by it. But has this not been the obvious experience of the recent past? Along with the fetish that has been made of Locke at peace conferences and at Congressional investigations has not Locke suffered a relativistic beating at the same time? You can turn the issue of Wilsonianism upside down: when has the nation appreciated more keenly the limits of its own cultural pattern as applied to the rest of the world? You can turn the issue of McCarthyism upside down: when has the meaning of civil liberties been more ardently understood than now? A dialectic process is at work, evil eliciting the challenge of a conscious good, so that in difficult moments progress is made. The outcome of the battle between intensified "Americanism" and new enlightenment is still an open question.

Historically the issue here is one for which we have little precedent. It raises the question of whether a nation can compensate for the uniformity of its domestic life by contact with alien cultures outside it. It asks whether American liberalism can acquire through external experience that sense of relativity, that spark of philosophy which European liberalism acquired through an internal experience of social diversity and social conflict. But if the final problem posed by the American liberal community is bizarre, this is merely a continuation of its historic record. That community has always been a place where the common issues of the West have taken strange and singular shape. . . .

NOTE

1. There is no precise term for feudal institutions and feudal ideas as they persisted into the modern period amid the national states and economic movements which progressively undermined them. The phrases "quasi-feudal" and "ancien régime" are nebulous enough. Some historians speak of "corporate society," but since a good deal more is involved than a congeries of associational units and since "corporate" is often used to describe current fascist states, the term has disadvantages. Under the circumstances it seems best to retain the simple word "feudal," realizing that its technical meaning is stretched when one applies it in the modern era.

3

CHARLES A. BEARD

THE CONSTITUTION
AS AN ECONOMIC DOCUMENT

The following is an excerpt from An Economic Interpretation of the Constitution of the United States, *the book Charles A. Beard (1874–1948) published in 1913 when he was a professor at Columbia University. Behind key provisions of the Constitution, Beard argued, were a variety of vested economic interests, including those of slave holders. Beard's closely argued thesis has long stimulated debate as to whether particular material interests or broader political values were the dominant inspirations for the constitutional framework that was drafted in 1787.*

It is difficult for the superficial student of the Constitution, who has read only the commentaries of the legists, to conceive of that instrument as an economic document. It places no property qualifications on voters or officers; it gives no outward recognition of any economic groups in society; it mentions no special privileges to be conferred upon any class. It betrays no feeling, such as vibrates through the French constitution of 1791; its language is cold, formal, and severe.

The true inwardness of the Constitution is not revealed by an examination of its provisions as simple propositions of law; but by a long and careful study of the voluminous correspondence of the period, contemporary newspapers and pamphlets, the records of the debates in the Convention at Philadelphia and in the several state conventions, and particularly, *The Federalist*, which was widely circulated during the struggle over ratification. The correspondence shows the exact character of the evils which the Constitution was intended to remedy; the records of the proceedings in the Philadelphia Convention reveal the successive steps in the building of the framework of the government under the pressure of economic interests; the pamphlets and newspapers disclose the ideas of the contestants over the ratification; and *The Federalist* presents the political science of the new system as conceived by three of the profoundest thinkers of the period, Hamilton, Madison, and Jay. . . .

THE POWERS CONFERRED
UPON THE FEDERAL GOVERNMENT

1. The powers for positive action conferred upon the new government were few, but they were adequate to the purposes of the framers. They included, first, the power to lay and collect taxes; but here the rural interests were conciliated by the provision that direct taxes must be apportioned among the states according to population, counting three-fifths of the slaves. This, in the opinion of contemporaries eminently qualified to speak, was designed to prevent the populations of

the manufacturing states from shifting the burdens of taxation to the sparsely settled agricultural regions.

In a letter to the governor of their state, three delegates from North Carolina,
Blount, Spaight, and Williamson, explained the advantage of this safeguard on
taxation to the southern planters and farmers: "We had many things to hope from
a National Government and the chief thing we had to fear from such a Government was the risque of unequal or heavy Taxation, but we hope you will believe
as we do that the Southern states in general and North Carolina in particular are
well secured on that head by the proposed system. It is provided in the 9th section
of article the first that no Capitation or direct Tax shall be laid except in proportion to the number of inhabitants, in which number five blacks are only counted
as three. If a land tax is laid, we are to pay the same rate; for example, fifty citizens
of North Carolina can be taxed no more for all their Lands than fifty Citizens in
one of the Eastern States. This must be greatly in our favour, for as most of their
farms are small and many of them live in Towns we certainly have, one with
another, land of twice the value that they possess. When it is also considered that
five Negroes are only to be charged the same Poll Tax as three whites, the advantage must be considerably increased under the proposed Form of Government.
The Southern states have also a better security for the return of slaves who might
endeavour to escape than they had under the original Confederation."

The taxing power was the basis of all other positive powers, and it afforded the
revenues that were to discharge the public debt in full. Provision was made for
this discharge in Article VI to the effect that "All debts contracted and engagements entered into before the adoption of this Constitution shall be valid against
the United States under this Constitution as under the Confederation."

But the cautious student of public economy, remembering the difficulties
which Congress encountered under the Articles of Confederation in its attempts
to raise the money to meet the interest on the debt, may ask how the framers of
the Constitution could expect to overcome the hostile economic forces which
had hitherto blocked the payment of the requisitions. The answer is short. Under
the Articles, Congress had no power to lay and collect taxes immediately; it could
only make requisitions on the state legislatures. Inasmuch as most of the states
relied largely on direct taxes for their revenues, the demands of Congress were
keenly felt and stoutly resisted. Under the new system, however, Congress is
authorized to lay taxes on its own account, but it is evident that the framers contemplated placing practically all of the national burden on the consumer. The
provision requiring the apportionment of direct taxes on a basis of population
obviously implied that such taxes were to be viewed as a last resort when indirect
taxes failed to provide the required revenue.

With his usual acumen, Hamilton conciliates the freeholders and property
owners in general by pointing out that they will not be called upon to support the
national government by payments proportioned to their wealth. Experience has
demonstrated that it is impracticable to raise any considerable sums by direct taxation. Even where the government is strong, as in Great Britain, resort must be
had chiefly to indirect taxation. The pockets of the farmers "will reluctantly yield

but scanty supplies, in the unwelcome shape of impositions on their houses and lands; and personal property is too precarious and invisible a fund to be laid hold of in any other way than by the imperceptible agency of taxes on consumption." Real and personal property are thus assured a generous immunity from such burdens as Congress had attempted to impose under the Articles; taxes under the new system will, therefore, be less troublesome than under the old.

2. Congress was given, in the second place, plenary power to raise and support military and naval forces, for the defence of the country against foreign and domestic foes. These forces were to be at the disposal of the President in the execution of national laws; and to guard the states against renewed attempts of "desperate debtors" like Shays, the United States guaranteed to every commonwealth a republican form of government and promised to aid in quelling internal disorder on call of the proper authorities.

The army and navy are considered by the authors of *The Federalist* as genuine economic instrumentalities. As will be pointed out below, they regarded trade and commerce as the fundamental cause of wars between nations; and the source of domestic insurrection they traced to class conflicts within society. "Nations in general," says Jay, "will make war whenever they have a prospect of getting anything by it"; and it is obvious that the United States dissevered and discordant will be the easy prey to the commercial ambitions of their neighbors and rivals.

The material gains to be made by other nations at the expense of the United States are so apparent that the former cannot restrain themselves from aggression. France and Great Britain feel the pressure of our rivalry in the fisheries; they and other European nations are our competitors in navigation and the carrying trade; our independent voyages to China interfere with the monopolies enjoyed by other countries there; Spain would like to shut the Mississippi against us on one side and Great Britain fain would close the St. Lawrence on the other. The cheapness and excellence of our productions will excite their jealousy, and the enterprise and address of our merchants will not be consistent with the wishes or policy of the sovereigns of Europe. But, adds the commentator, by way of clinching the argument, "if they see that our national government is efficient and well administered, our trade prudently regulated, our militia properly organized and disciplined, our resources and finances discreetly managed, our credit reestablished, our people free, contented, and united, they will be much more disposed to cultivate our friendship than provoke our resentment."

All the powers of Europe could not prevail against us. "Under a vigorous national government the natural strength and resources of the country, directed to a common interest, would baffle all the combinations of European jealousy to restrain our growth. . . . An active commerce, an extensive navigation, and a flourishing marine would then be the offspring of moral and physical necessity. We might defy the little arts of the little politicians to control or vary the irresistible and unchangeable course of nature." In the present state of disunion the profits of trade are snatched from us; our commerce languishes; and poverty threatens to overspread a country which might outrival the world in riches.

The army and navy are to be not only instruments of defence in protecting the United States against the commercial and territorial ambitions of other countries; but they may be used also in forcing open foreign markets. What discriminatory tariffs and navigation laws may not accomplish the sword may achieve. The authors of *The Federalist* do not contemplate that policy of mild and innocuous isolation which was later made famous by Washington's farewell address. On the contrary—they do not expect the United States to change human nature and make our commercial classes less ambitious than those of other countries to extend their spheres of trade. A strong navy will command the respect of European states. "There can be no doubt that the continuance of the Union under an efficient government would put it within our power, at a period not very distant, to create a navy which, if it could not vie with those of the great maritime powers, would at least be of respectable weight if thrown into the scale of either of two contending parties. . . . A few ships of the line sent opportunely to the reinforcement of either side, would often be sufficient to decide the fate of a campaign, on the event of which interests of the greatest magnitude were suspended. Our position is, in this respect, a most commanding one. And if to this consideration we add that of the usefulness of supplies from this country, in the prosecution of military operations in the West Indies, it will be readily perceived that a situation so favorable would enable us to bargain with great advantage for commercial privileges. A price would be set not only upon our friendship, but upon our neutrality. By a steady adherence to the Union, we may hope, ere long, to become the arbiter of Europe in America, and to be able to incline the balance of European competitions in this part of the world as our interest may dictate."

As to dangers from class wars within particular states, the authors of *The Federalist* did not deem it necessary to make extended remarks: the recent events in New England were only too vividly impressed upon the public mind. "The tempestuous situation from which Massachusetts has scarcely emerged," says Hamilton, "evinces that dangers of this kind are not merely speculative. Who can determine what might have been the issue of her late convulsions, if the malcontents had been headed by a Caesar or by a Cromwell." The strong arm of the Union must be available in such crises.

In considering the importance of defence against domestic insurrection, the authors of *The Federalist* do not overlook an appeal to the slave-holders' instinctive fear of a servile revolt. Naturally, it is Madison whose interest catches this point and drives it home, by appearing to discount it. In dealing with the dangers of insurrection, he says: "I take no notice of an unhappy species of population abounding in some of the states who, during the calm of regular government are sunk below the level of men; but who, in the tempestuous scenes of civil violence, may emerge into human character and give a superiority of strength to any party with which they may associate themselves."

3. In addition to the power to lay and collect taxes and raise and maintain armed forces on land and sea, the Constitution vests in Congress plenary control over foreign and interstate commerce, and thus authorizes it to institute protective and discriminatory laws in favor of American interests, and to create a wide

sweep for free trade throughout the whole American empire. A single clause thus reflects the strong impulse of economic forces in the towns and young manufacturing centres. In a few simple words the mercantile and manufacturing interests wrote their *Zweck im Recht*; and they paid for their victory by large concessions to the slave-owning planters of the south.

While dealing with commerce in *The Federalist* Hamilton does not neglect the subject of interstate traffic and intercourse. He shows how free trade over a wide range will be to reciprocal advantage, will give great diversity to commercial enterprise, and will render stagnation less liable by offering more distant markets when local demands fall off. "The speculative trader," he concludes, "will at once perceive the force of these observations and will acknowledge that the aggregate balance of the commerce of the United States would bid fair to be much more favorable than that of the thirteen states without union or with partial unions."

4. Another great economic antagonism found its expression in the clause conferring upon Congress the power to dispose of the territories and make rules and regulations for their government and admission to the Union. In this contest, the interests of the states which held territories came prominently to the front; and the ambiguity of the language used in the Constitution on this point may be attributed to the inability of the contestants to reach precise conclusions. The leaders were willing to risk the proper management of the land problem after the new government was safely launched; and they were correct in their estimate of their future political prowess. . . .

RESTRICTIONS LAID UPON STATE LEGISLATURES

Equally important to personalty as the positive powers conferred upon Congress to tax, support armies, and regulate commerce were the restrictions imposed on the states. Indeed, we have the high authority of Madison for the statement that of the forces which created the Constitution, those property interests seeking protection against omnipotent legislatures were the most active.

In a letter to Jefferson, written in October, 1787, Madison elaborates the principle of federal judicial control over state legislation, and explains the importance of this new institution in connection with the restrictions laid down in the Constitution on laws affecting private rights. "The mutability of the laws of the States," he says, "is found to be a serious evil. The injustice of them has been so frequent and so flagrant as to alarm the most steadfast friends of Republicanism. I am persuaded I do not err in saying that the evils issuing from these sources contributed more to that uneasiness which produced the Convention, and prepared the public mind for a general reform, than those which accrued to our national character and interest from the inadequacy of the Confederation to its immediate objects. A reform, therefore, which does not make provision for private rights must be materially defective."

Two small clauses embody the chief demands of personalty against agrarianism: the emission of paper money is prohibited and the states are forbidden to impair the obligation of contract. The first of these means a return to a specie basis—when coupled with the requirement that the gold and silver coin of the United States shall be the legal tender. The Shays and their paper money legions, who assaulted the vested rights of personalty by the process of legislative depreciation, are now subdued forever, and money lenders and security holders may be sure of their operations. Contracts are to be safe, and whoever engages in a financial operation, public or private, may know that state legislatures cannot destroy overnight the rules by which the game is played. . . .

4

GORDON S. WOOD

THE AMERICAN SCIENCE OF POLITICS

Gordon S. Wood's book The Creation of the American Republic *offers an excellent contrast to the preceding selection. Here, Wood, a professor of history at Brown University, stresses that the American experiment in 1787 did much more than reflect the claims of various stakeholders, including economic interests. It was also designed to prevent them "from incorporating themselves too firmly in the government." The idea, Wood insists, was truly revolutionary.*

The Americans had reversed in a revolutionary way the traditional conception of politics: the stability of government no longer relied, as it had for centuries, upon its embodiment of the basic social forces of the state. Indeed, it now depended upon the prevention of the various social interests from incorporating themselves too firmly in the government. Institutional or governmental politics was thus abstracted in a curious way from its former associations with the society. But at the same time a more modern and more realistic sense of political behavior in the society itself, among the people, could now be appreciated. This revolution marked an end of the classical conception of politics and the beginning of what might be called a romantic view of politics. The eighteenth century had sought to understand politics, as it had all of life, by capturing in an integrated, ordered, changeless ideal the totality and complexity of the world—an ideal that the concept of the mixed constitution and the proportioned social hierarchy on which it rested perfectly expressed. In such an ideal there could be only potential energy, no kinetic energy, only a static equilibrium among synthetic orders, and no motion among the particular, miscellaneous parts that made up the society. By destroying this ideal Americans placed a new emphasis on the piecemeal and the concrete in politics at the expense of order and completeness. The Constitution represented both the climax and the finale of the American Enlightenment, both the fulfillment and the end of the belief that the endless variety and perplexity of society could be reduced to a simple and harmonious system. By attempting to formulate a theory of politics that would represent reality as it was, the Americans of 1787 shattered the classical Whig world of 1776.

Americans had begun the Revolution assuming that the people were a homogeneous entity in society set against the rulers. But such an assumption belied American experience, and it took only a few years of independence to convince the best American minds that distinctions in the society were "various and unavoidable," so much so that they could not be embodied in the government.[1] Once the people were thought to be composed of various interests in opposition to one another, all sense of a graduated organic chain in the social hierarchy became irrelevant, symbolized by the increasing emphasis on the image of a

[Notes have been renumbered.—Eds.]

social contract. The people were not an order organically tied together by their unity of interest but rather an agglomeration of hostile individuals coming together for their mutual benefit to construct a society. The Americans transformed the people in the same way that Englishmen a century earlier had transformed the rulers: they broke the connectedness of interest among them and put them at war with one another, just as seventeenth-century Englishmen had separated the interests of rulers and people and put them in opposition to each other.

As Joel Barlow noted in 1792, the word "people" in America had taken on a different meaning from what it had in Europe. In America it meant the whole community and comprehended every human creature in the society; in Europe, however, it meant "something else more difficult to define." "Society," said Enos Hitchcock in 1788, "is composed of individuals—they are parts of the whole." And such individuals in America were the entire society: there could be nothing else—no orders, no lords, no monarch, no magistrates in the traditional sense. "Without the distinctions of titles, families, or nobility," wrote Samuel Williams, "they acknowledged and reverenced only those distinctions which nature had made, in a diversity of talents, abilities, and virtues. There were no family interests, connexions, or estates, large enough to oppress them. There was no excessive wealth in the hands of a few, sufficient to corrupt them." The Americans were thus both equal and unequal at the same time.

> They all feel that nature has made them equal in respect to their rights; or rather that nature has given to them a common and an equal right to liberty, to property, and to safety; to justice, government, laws, religion, and freedom. They all see that nature has made them very unequal in respect to their original powers, capacities, and talents. They become united in claiming and in preserving the equality, which nature has assigned to them; and in availing themselves of the benefits, which are designed, and may be derived from the inequality, which nature has also established.[2]

Politics in such a society could no longer be simply described as a contest between rulers and people, between institutionalized orders of the society. The political struggles would in fact be among the people themselves, among all the various groups and individuals seeking to create inequality out of their equality by gaining control of a government divested of its former identity with the society. It was this disembodiment of government from society that ultimately made possible the conception of modern politics and the eventual justification of competing parties among the people. Those who criticized such divisive jealousy and opposition among the people, said William Hornby of South Carolina in 1784, did not understand "the great change in politics, which the revolution must have necessarily produced. . . . In *these* days we are equal citizens of a DEMOCRATIC REPUBLIC, in which *jealousy* and *opposition* must naturally exist, while there exists a difference in the minds, interests, and sentiments of mankind." While few were as yet willing to justify factionalism so blatantly, many now realized with Madison that "the regulation of these various and interfering interests forms the principal task of modern legislation, and involves the spirit of party and faction in the necessary and ordinary operations of the government." Legislation in such a society could not be the transcending of the different interests but the reconciling of them. Despite Madison's lingering hope, the public good could not be an entity distinct from its parts; it was rather "the general combined interest of all the state put together, as it were, upon an average."[3]

Under the pressure of this transformation of political thought old words and concepts shifted in emphasis and took on new meanings. Tyranny was now seen as the abuse of power by any branch of the government, even, and for some especially, by the traditional representatives of the people. "The accumulation of all powers," said Madison, "legislative, executive, and judiciary, in the same hands, whether of one, a few, or many, and whether hereditary, self-appointed. or elective, may justly be pronounced the very definition of tyranny." The separation of this governmental power, rather than simply the participation of the people in a part of the government, became the best defense of liberty. Therefore liberty, as the old Whigs had predominantly used the term—public or political liberty, the right of the people to share in the government—lost its significance for a system in which the people participated throughout.[4]

The liberty that was now emphasized was personal or private, the protection of individual rights against all governmental encroachments, particularly by the legislature, the body which the Whigs had traditionally cherished as the people's exclusive repository of their public liberty and the surest weapon to defend their private liberties. Such liberties, like that of freedom of the press, said both Madison and Paine, were now in less danger from "any direct attacks of Power" than they were from "the silent awe of a predominant party" or "from a fear of popular resentment." The assumptions behind such charges were radically new and different from those of the Whigs of 1776: men now began to consider "the interests of society and the rights of individuals as distinct," and to regard public and private liberty as antagonistic rather than complementary. In such circumstances the aim of government, in James Iredell's words, became necessarily twofold: to provide "for the security of every individual, as well as a fluctuating majority of the people." Government was no longer designed merely to promote the collective happiness of the people, but also, as the Tories had urged in the early seventies, "to protect citizens in their personal liberty and their property" even against the public will. Indeed, Madison could now say emphatically, "Justice is the end of government. It is the end of civil society." Unless individuals and minorities were protected against the power of majorities no government could be truly free.[5]

Because of this growing sense of discrepancy between the rights of the society and the rights of individuals and because the new federal government was designed to prevent the emergence of any "common passion" or sense of oneness among large numbers of persons "on any other principles than those of justice and the general good," comprehensible only by a natural elite, the older emphasis on public virtue existing throughout the society lost some of its thrust; and men could now argue that "virtue, patriotism, or love of country, never was nor never will be till men's natures are changed, a fixed, permanent principle and support of government." The problem was, as Charles Thompson lamented in 1786, that most Americans had no other "Object" than their own "individual happiness." While Thompson still hoped that the people would eventually become "sufficiently impressed with a sense of what they owe to their national character," others began recasting their thinking. As early as 1782 Jefferson told Monroe that it was ridiculous to suppose that a man should surrender himself to the state. "This would be slavery, and not that liberty which the bill of rights has made inviolable, and for the preservation of which our government has been changed." Freedom, said Jefferson, would be destroyed by "the establishment of the opinion that the state has a *perpetual* right to the services of all it's members." The aim of instilling a spartan creed in America thus began to seem more and more nonsensical. By 1785 Noah Webster was directly challenging Montesquieu's opinion that public virtue was a necessary foundation for democratic republics. Such virtue or patriotism, said Webster, could never predominate. Local attachments would always exist, self-interest was all there ever was. But under a democracy, argued Webster, a self-interested man must court the people, thus tending to make self-love coincide with the people's interest.[6]

William Vans Murray devoted an entire chapter of his *Political Sketches*, published in 1787, to a denial of the conventional view that republicanism was dependent upon virtue. The compulsion for such arguments was obvious. America, as Murray admitted, was "in a state of refinement and opulence," and was increasingly being permeated by "luxurious habits"—characteristics which time-honored writers on politics had declared incompatible with republican virtue and simplicity, and thus foreboding signs of an inevitable declension of the state. Yet the political scientists who spouted these maxims of republicanism had never known America. "The truth is," said Murray, "Montesquieu had never study'd a free Democracy." All the notions of these "refining speculists" had come from impressions of the ancient republics which possessed only "undefined constitutions, . . . constructed in days of ignorance." The republics of antiquity had failed because they had "attempted to force the human character into distorted shapes." The American republics, on the other hand, said Murray, were built upon the realities of human nature. They were free and responsive to the people, framed so as to give "fair play" to the actions of human nature, however unvirtuous. They had been created rationally and purposefully—for the first time in history—without attempting to pervert, suppress, or ignore the evil propensities of all men. Public virtue—the "enthusiasm," as Murray called it, of a rude and simple society, the public proscription of private pursuits for luxury—had at last "found a happy substitution in the energy of true freedom, and in a just sense of civil liberty." The American governments possessed "the freedom of Democracy, without its anarchy."[7]

Although they were "so extremely popular," wrote John Stevens, "yet the checks which have been invented (particularly in some of them) have rendered these governments capable of a degree of stability and consistency beyond what could have been expected, and which will be viewed with surprise by foreigners." Undoubtedly virtue in the people had been an essential substitute for the lack of good laws and the indispensable remedy for the traditional defects of most democratic governments. But in America where the inconveniences of the democratic form of government had been eliminated without destroying the substantial benefits of democracy—where there was introduced, said James Wilson, "into the very form of government, such particular checks and controls, as to make it advantageous even for bad men to act for the public good"—the need for a society of simple, equal, virtuous people no longer seemed so critical. America alone, wrote Murray, had united liberty with luxury and had proved "the consistency of the social nature with the political happiness of man."[8]

Such depreciations of public virtue were still sporadic and premature, yet they represented the beginnings of a fundamental shift in thought. In place of individual self-sacrifice for the good of the state as the bond holding the republican fabric together, the Americans began putting an increasing emphasis on what they called "public opinion" as the basis of all governments. Montesquieu in his *Spirit of the Laws*, wrote Madison in 1792, had only opened up the science of politics. Governments could not be divided simply into despotisms, monarchies, and republics sustained by their "operative principles" of fear, honor, and virtue. Governments, suggested Madison, were better divided into those which derived their energy from military force, those which operated by corrupt influence, and those which relied on the will and interest of the society. While nearly all governments, including the British monarchy, rested to some extent on public opinion, only in America had public consent as the basis of government attained its greatest perfection. No government, Americans told themselves over and over, had ever before so completely set its roots in the sentiments and aims of its citizens. All the power of America's governments, said Samuel Williams, was "derived from the public opinion." America would remain free not because of any quality in its citizens of spartan self-sacrifice to some nebulous public good, but in the last analysis because of the concern each individual would have in his own self-interest and personal freedom. The really great danger to liberty in the extended republic of America, warned Madison in 1791, was that each individual may become insignificant in his own eyes—hitherto the very foundation of republican government.[9]

Such a total grounding of government in self-interest and consent had made old-fashioned popular revolutions obsolete. Establishments whose foundations rest on the society itself, said Wilson, cannot be overturned by any alteration of the government which the society can make. The decay and eventual death of the republican body politic now seemed less inevitable. The prevailing opinion of political writers, noted Nathaniel Chipman, had been "that man is fatally incapable of forming any system which shall endure without degeneration," an opinion that appeared "to be countenanced by the experience of ages." Yet America had lighted the way to a reversal of this opinion, placing, as David Ramsay put it, "the science of politics on a footing with the other sciences, by opening it to improvements from experience, and the discoveries of future ages." Governments had never been able to adjust continually to the operations of human nature. It was "impossible," said Chipman, "to form any human institution, which should accommodate itself to every situation in progress." All previous peoples had been compelled to suffer with the same forms of government—probably unplanned and unsuitable in the first place—despite extensive changes in the nature of their societies. "The confining of a people, who have arrived at a highly improved state of society, to the forms and principles of a government, which originated in a simple, if not barbarous state of men and manners," was, said Chipman, like Chinese foot-binding, a "perversion of nature," causing an incongruity between the form of government and the character of the society that usually ended in a violent eruption, in a forceful effort to bring the government into accord with the new social temperament of the people.[10]

However, the American republics possessed what Thomas Pownall called "a healing principle" built into their constitutions. Each contained "within itself," said Samuel Williams, "the means of its own improvement." The American governments never pretended, said Chipman, to perfection or to the exclusion of future improvements. "The idea of incorporating, in the constitution itself, a plan of reformation," enabling the people periodically and peacefully to return to first principles, as Machiavelli had urged, the Americans realized, was a totally new contribution to politics. The early state constitutions, David Ramsay admitted, possessed many defects. "But in one thing they were all perfect. They left the people in the power of altering and amending them, whenever they pleased." And the Americans had demonstrated to the world how a people could fundamentally and yet peaceably alter their forms of government. "This revolution principle—that, the sovereign power residing in the people, they may change their constitution and government whenever they please—is," said James Wilson, "not a principle of discord, rancour, or war: it is a principle of melioration, contentment, and peace." Americans had in fact institutionalized and legitimized revolution. Thereafter, they believed, new knowledge about the nature of government could be converted into concrete form without resorting to violence. Let no one, concluded Chipman, now rashly predict "that this beautiful system is, with the crazy empires of antiquity, destined to a speedy dissolution; or that it must in time, thro' the degeneracy of the people, and a corruption of its principles, of necessity give place to a system of remediless tyranny and oppression." By actually implementing the old and trite conception of the sovereignty of the people, by infusing political and even legal life into the people, Americans had created, said Wilson, "the great panacea of human politics."[11] The illimitable progress of mankind promised by the Enlightenment could at last be made coincident with the history of a single nation. For the Americans at least, and for others if they followed, the endless cycles of history could finally be broken.

The Americans of the Revolutionary generation believed that they had made a momentous contribution to the history of politics. They had for the first time demonstrated to the world how a people could diagnose the ills of its society and work out a peaceable process of cure. They had, and what is more significant they knew they had, broken through the conceptions of political theory that had imprisoned men's minds for centuries and brilliantly reconstructed the framework for a new republican polity, a reconstruction that radically changed the future discussion of politics. The Federalists had discovered, they thought, a constitutional antidote "wholly popular" and "strictly republican" for the ancient diseases of a republican polity—an antidote that did not destroy the republican vices, but rather accepted, indeed endorsed and relied upon them. The Federalist image of a public good undefinable by factious majorities in small states but somehow capable of formulation by the best men of a large society may have been a chimera. So too perhaps was the Federalist hope for the filtration of the natural social leaders through a federal sieve into political leadership. These were partisan and aristocratic purposes that belied the Federalists' democratic language. Yet the Federalists' intellectual achievement really transcended their particular political and social intentions and became more important and more influential than they themselves anticipated. Because their ideas were so popularly based and embodied what Americans had been groping towards from the beginning of their history, the Federalists' creation could be, and eventually was, easily adopted and expanded by others with quite different interests and aims at stake, indeed, contributing in time to the destruction of the very social world they had sought to maintain. The invention of a government that was, in James Sullivan's words, "perhaps without example in the world" could not long remain a strictly Federalist achievement. "As this kind of government," wrote Samuel Williams, "is not the same as that, which has been called monarchy, aristocracy, or democracy; as it had a conspicuous origin in America, and has not been suffered to prevail in any other part of the globe, it would be no more than just and proper, to distinguish it by its proper name, and call it, *The American System of Government.*"[12]

So piecemeal was the Americans' formulation of this system, so diverse and scattered in authorship, and so much a simple response to the pressures of democratic politics was their creation, that the originality and the theoretical consistency and completeness of their constitutional thinking have been obscured. It was a political theory that was diffusive and open-ended; it was not delineated in a single book; it was peculiarly the product of a democratic society, without a precise beginning or an ending. It was not political theory in the grand manner, but it was political theory worthy of a prominent place in the history of Western thought.

NOTES

1. Madison to Jefferson, Oct. 24, 1787, Boyd, ed., *Jefferson Papers*, XII, 277.

2. Joel Barlow, *Advice to the Privileged Orders in the Several States of Europe Resulting from the Necessity and Propriety of a General Revolution in the Principles of Government* (Ithaca, N.Y., 1956, first published, London 1792), 17; Hitchcock, *Oration, Delivered July 4, 1788*, 18; Williams, *History of Vermont*, 344, 330.

3. Charleston *Gazette of the St. of S.-C.*, July 29, 1784; *The Federalist Papers*, No. 10; Charleston *Gazette Extra. of the St. of S.-C.*, July 17, 1784.

4. *The Federalist*, No. 47, No. 48.

5. Madison's "Observations on Jefferson's Draft of a Constitution for Virginia" (1788), Boyd, ed., *Jefferson Papers*, VI, 316; Paine, *Letter to Raynal*, in Foner, ed., *Writings of Paine*, II, 250; *Rudiments of Law and Government*, v; James Iredell, "To the Public" (1786), McRee, *Life of Iredell*, II, 146; *Providence Gazette*, Nov. 7, 1789; *The Federalist*, No. 51. For a new definition of liberty similar to that being formed by the Americans see De Lolme, *Constitution of England* (London, 1788), 244–46: Liberty was not, as men used to think, the establishing of a governmental order or the participating in legislation through voting for representatives; for "these are functions, are acts of Government, but not constituent parts of Liberty." "To concur by one's suffrage in enacting laws, is to enjoy a share,

whatever it may be, of Power," while liberty, "so far as it is possible for it to exist in a Society of Beings whose interests are almost perpetually opposed to each other, consists in this, that, *every Man, while he respects the persons of others, and allows them quietly to enjoy the produce of their industry, be certain himself likewise to enjoy the produce of his own industry, and that his person be also secure.*"

6. *The Federalist*, No. 50, No. 51; *Providence Gazette*, Dec. 29, 1787; Thompson to Jefferson, Apr. 6, 1786, Boyd, ed., *Jefferson Papers*, IX, 380; Jefferson to Monroe, May 20, 1782, ibid., VI, 185–86; Webster, *Sketches of American Policy*, 25. For Hamilton's disavowal of "the necessity of disinterestedness in republics" and his ridiculing of the seeking "for models in the simple ages of Greece and Rome" see "The Continentalist No. VI," July 4, 1782, Syrett and Cooke, eds., *Hamilton Papers*, III, 103.

7. [Murray], *Political Sketches*, Chap. II, "Virtue," 24, 25, 28–30, 47, 43, 38, 10. On Murray and the circumstances of the writing of his pamphlet see Alexander DeConde, "William Vans Murray's *Political Sketches:* A Defense of the American Experiment," *Miss. Valley Hist. Rev.*, 41 (1954–55), 623–40.

8. [Stevens], *Observations on Government*, 51; Wilson, "Lectures on Law," Wilson, ed., *Works of Wilson*, I, 393; [Murray], *Political Sketches*, 47–48. See also [Jackson], *Thoughts upon the Political Situation*, 22–24; Taylor, *Inquiry into the Principles*, 386, 390, 461–62.

9. [Madison], Phila. *National Gazette*, Feb. 20, Jan. 19, 30, 1792, Dec. 19, 1791, Hunt, ed., *Writings of Madison*, VI, 93–94, 85, 87, 70; Williams, *History of Vermont*, 206–07, 344–45; Wilson, "Lectures on Law," Wilson, ed., *Works of Wilson*, II, 125.

10. Wilson, "Lectures on Law," Wilson, ed., *Works of Wilson*, I, 384, Chipman, *Principles of Government*, 282, 286, 288–89; Ramsay, *American Revolution*, I, 357.

11. Pownall, *Memorial to America*, 53; Williams, *History of Vermont*, 345; Chipman, *Principles of Government*, 289–90, 291–92; Ramsay, *American Revolution*, I, 357; Wilson, "Lectures on Law," Wilson, ed., *Works of Wilson*, I, 21, 420; Jefferson to David Humphreys, Mar. 18, 1789, Boyd, ed., *Jefferson Papers*, XIV, 678; Wilson, in McMaster and Stone, eds., *Pennsylvania and the Federal Constitution*, 230.

12. Sullivan, *Observations upon the Government*, 38, Williams, *History of Vermont*, 346.

5

JAMES MADISON

FEDERALIST 10

In this renowned essay, Madison (1751–1836) outlines his remedy for what he called "the mischiefs of faction"—that is, the potential for tyranny, either by a ruling minority or a majority. He argues that a "republican" regime, delegating authority to elected representatives to govern a large polity, offers a better safeguard than does a small-scale, "pure democracy." The extended republic will introduce a diversity of interests, making it harder for any one group or party to oppress the rest.

Among the numerous advantages promised by a well-constructed Union, none deserves to be more accurately developed than its tendency to break and control the violence of faction. The friend of popular governments never finds himself so much alarmed for their character and fate as when he contemplates their propensity to this dangerous vice. He will not fail, therefore, to set a due value on any plan which, without violating the principles to which he is attached, provides a proper cure for it. The instability, injustice, and confusion introduced into the public councils have, in truth, been the mortal diseases under which popular governments have everywhere perished, as they continue to be the favorite and fruitful topics from which the adversaries to liberty derive their most specious declamations. The valuable improvements made by the American constitutions on the popular models, both ancient and modern, cannot certainly be too much admired; but it would be an unwarrantable partiality to contend that they have as effectually obviated the danger on this side, as was wished and expected. Complaints are everywhere heard from our most considerate and virtuous citizens, equally the friends of public and private faith and of public and personal liberty, that our governments are too unstable, that the public good is disregarded in the conflicts of rival parties, and that measures are too often decided, not according to the rules of justice and the rights of the minor party, but by the superior force of an interested and overbearing majority. However anxiously we may wish that these complaints had no foundation, the evidence of known facts will not permit us to deny that they are in some degree true. It will be found, indeed, on a candid review of our situation, that some of the distresses under which we labor have been erroneously charged on the operation of our governments; but it will be found, at the same time, that other causes will not alone account for many of our heaviest misfortunes; and, particularly, for that prevailing and increasing distrust of public engagements and alarm for private rights which are echoed from one end of the continent to the other. These must be chiefly, if not wholly, effects of the unsteadiness and injustice with which a factious spirit has tainted our public administration.

By a faction I understand a number of citizens, whether amounting to a majority or minority of the whole, who are united and actuated by some common impulse of passion, or of interest, adverse to the rights of other citizens, or to the permanent and aggregate interests of the community.

There are two methods of curing the mischiefs of faction: the one, by removing its causes; the other, by controlling its effects.

There are again two methods of removing the causes of faction: the one, by destroying the liberty which is essential to its existence; the other, by giving to every citizen the same opinions, the same passions, and the same interests.

It could never be more truly said than of the first remedy that it was worse than the disease. Liberty is to faction what air is to fire, an aliment without which it instantly expires. But it could not be a less folly to abolish liberty, which is essential to political life, because it nourishes faction than it would be to wish the annihilation of air, which is essential to animal life, because it imparts to fire its destructive agency.

The second expedient is as impracticable as the first would be unwise. As long as the reason of man continues fallible, and he is at liberty to exercise it, different opinions will be formed. As long as the connection subsists between his reason and his self-love, his opinions and his passions will have a reciprocal influence on each other; and the former will be objects to which the latter will attach themselves. The diversity in the faculties of men, from which the rights of property originate, is not less an insuperable obstacle to a uniformity of interests. The protection of these faculties is the first object of government. From the protection of different and unequal faculties of acquiring property, the possession of different degrees and kinds of property immediately results; and from the influence of these on the sentiments and views of the respective proprietors ensues a division of the society into different interests and parties.

The latent causes of faction are thus sown in the nature of man; and we see them everywhere brought into different degrees of activity, according to the different circumstances of civil society. A zeal for different opinions concerning religion, concerning government, and many other points, as well of speculation as of practice; an attachment to different leaders ambitiously contending for pre-eminence and power; or to persons of other descriptions whose fortunes have been interesting to the human passions, have, in turn, divided mankind into parties, inflamed them with mutual animosity, and rendered them much more disposed to vex and oppress each other than to co-operate for their common good. So strong is this propensity of mankind to fall into mutual animosities that where no substantial occasion presents itself the most frivolous and fanciful distinctions have been sufficient to kindle their unfriendly passions and excite their most violent conflicts. But the most common and durable source of factions has been the various and unequal distribution of property. Those who hold and those who are without property have ever formed distinct interests in society. Those who are creditors, and those who are debtors, fall under a like discrimination. A landed interest, a manufacturing interest, a mercantile interest, a moneyed interest, with many lesser interests, grow up of necessity in civilized nations, and divide them into different classes, actuated by different sentiments and views. The regulation of these various and interfering interests forms the principal task of modern legislation and involves the spirit of party and faction in the necessary and ordinary operations of government.

No man is allowed to be a judge in his own cause, because his interest would certainly bias his judgment, and, not improbably, corrupt his integrity. With equal, nay with greater reason, a body of men are unfit to be both judges and parties at the same time; yet what are many of the most important acts of legislation but so many judicial determinations, not indeed concerning the rights of single persons, but concerning the rights of large bodies of citizens? And what are the different classes of legislators but advocates and parties to the causes which they determine? Is a law proposed concerning private debts? It is a question to which the creditors are parties on one side and the debtors on the other. Justice ought to hold the balance between them. Yet the parties are, and must be, themselves the judges; and the most numerous party, or in other words, the most powerful faction must be expected to prevail. Shall domestic manufacturers be encouraged, and in what degree, by restrictions on foreign manufacturers? are questions which would be differently decided by the landed and the manufacturing classes, and probably by neither with a sole regard to justice and the public good. The apportionment of taxes on the various descriptions of property is an act which seems to require the most exact impartiality; yet there is, perhaps, no legislative act in which greater opportunity and temptation are given to a predominant party to trample on the rules of justice. Every shilling with which they overburden the inferior number is a shilling saved to their own pockets.

It is in vain to say that enlightened statesmen will be able to adjust these clashing interests and render them all subservient to the public good. Enlightened statesmen will not always be at the helm. Nor, in many cases, can such an adjustment be made at all without taking into view indirect and remote considerations, which will rarely prevail over the immediate interest which one party may find in disregarding the rights of another or the good of the whole.

The inference to which we are brought is that the *causes* of faction cannot be removed and that relief is only to be sought in the means of controlling its *effects*.

If a faction consists of less than a majority, relief is supplied by the republican principle, which enables the majority to defeat its sinister views by regular vote. It may clog the administration, it may convulse the society; but it will be unable to execute and mask its violence under the forms of the Constitution. When a majority is included in a faction, the form of popular government, on the other hand, enables it to sacrifice to its ruling passion or interest both the public good and the rights of other citizens. To secure the public good and private rights against the danger of such a faction, and at the same time to preserve the spirit and the form of popular government, is then the great object to which our inquiries are directed. Let me add that it is the great desideratum by which alone this form of government can be rescued from the opprobrium under which it has so long labored and be recommended to the esteem and adoption of mankind.

By what means is this object attainable? Evidently by one of two only. Either the existence of the same passion or interest in a majority at the same time must be prevented, or the majority, having such coexistent passion or interest, must be rendered, by their number and local situation, unable to concert and carry into effect schemes of oppression. If the impulse and the opportunity be suffered to coincide, we well know that neither moral nor religious motives can be relied on as an adequate control. They are not found to be such on the injustice and violence of individuals, and lose their efficacy in proportion to the number combined together, that is, in proportion as their efficacy becomes needful.

From this view of the subject it may be concluded that a pure democracy, by which I mean a society consisting of a small number of citizens, who assemble and administer the government in person, can admit of no cure for the mischiefs of faction. A common passion or interest will, in almost every case, be felt by a majority of the whole; a communication and concert results from the form of government itself; and there is nothing to check the inducements to sacrifice the weaker party or an obnoxious individual. Hence it is that such democracies have ever been spectacles of turbulence and contention; have ever been found incompatible with personal security or the rights of property; and have in general been as short in their lives as they have been violent in their deaths. Theoretic politicians, who have patronized this species of government, have erroneously supposed that by reducing mankind to a perfect equality in their political rights, they would at the same time be perfectly equalized and assimilated in their possessions, their opinions, and their passions.

A republic, by which I mean a government in which the scheme of representation takes place, opens a different prospect and promises the cure for which we are seeking. Let us examine the points in which it varies from pure democracy, and we shall comprehend both the nature of the cure and the efficacy which it must derive from the Union.

The two great points of difference between a democracy and a republic are: first, the delegation of the government, in the latter, to a small number of citizens elected by the rest; secondly, the greater number of citizens and greater sphere of country over which the latter may be extended.

The effect of the first difference is, on the one hand, to refine and enlarge the public views by passing them through the medium of a chosen body of citizens, whose wisdom may best discern the true interest of their country and whose patriotism and love of justice will be least likely to sacrifice it to temporary or partial considerations. Under such a regulation it may well happen that the public voice, pronounced by the representatives of the people, will be more consonant to the public good than if pronounced by the people themselves, convened for the purpose. On the other hand, the effect may be inverted. Men of factious tempers, of local prejudices, or of sinister designs, may, by intrigue, by corruption, or by other means, first obtain the suffrages, and then betray the interests of the people. The question resulting is, whether small or extensive republics are most favorable to the election of proper guardians of the public weal; and it is clearly decided in favor of the latter by two obvious considerations.

In the first place it is to be remarked that however small the republic may be the representatives must be raised to a certain number in order to guard against the cabals of a few; and that however large it may be they must be limited to a certain number in order to guard against the confusion of a multitude. Hence, the number of representatives in the two cases not being in proportion to that of the constituents, and being proportionally greatest in the small republic, it follows that if the proportion of fit characters be not less in the large than in the small republic, the former will present a greater option, and consequently a greater probability of a fit choice.

In the next place, as each representative will be chosen by a greater number of citizens in the large than in the small republic, it will be more difficult for unworthy candidates to practise with success the vicious arts by which elections are too often carried; and the suffrages of the people being more free, will be more likely to center on men who possess the most attractive merit and the most diffusive and established characters.

It must be confessed that in this, as in most other cases, there is a mean, on both sides of which inconveniencies will be found to lie. By enlarging too much the number of electors, you render the representative too little acquainted with all their local circumstances and lesser interests; as by reducing it too much, you render him unduly attached to these, and too little fit to comprehend and pursue great and national objects. The federal Constitution forms a happy combination in this respect; the great and aggregate interests being referred to the national, the local and particular to the State legislatures.

The other point of difference is the greater number of citizens and extent of territory which may be brought within the compass of republican than of democratic government; and it is this circumstance principally which renders factious combinations less to be dreaded in the former than in the latter. The smaller the society, the fewer probably will be the distinct parties and interests composing it; the fewer the distinct parties and interests, the more frequently will a majority be found of the same party; and the smaller the number of individuals composing a majority, and the smaller the compass within which they are placed, the more easily will they concert and execute their plans of oppression. Extend the sphere and you take in a greater variety of parties and interests; you make it less probable that a majority of the whole will have a common motive to invade the rights of other citizens; or if such a common motive exists, it will be more difficult for all who feel it to discover their own strength and to act in unison with each other. Besides other impediments, it may be remarked that, where there is a consciousness of unjust or dishonorable purposes, communication is always checked by distrust in proportion to the number whose concurrence is necessary.

Hence, it clearly appears that the same advantage which a republic has over a democracy in controlling the effects of faction is enjoyed by a large over a small republic—is enjoyed by the Union over the States composing it. Does this advantage consist in the substitution of representatives whose enlightened views and virtuous sentiments render them superior to local prejudices and to schemes of injustice? It will not be denied that the representation of the Union will be most likely to possess these requisite endowments. Does it consist in the greater security afforded by a greater variety of parties, against the event of any one party being able to outnumber and oppress the rest? In an equal degree does the increased variety of parties comprised within the Union increase this security. Does it, in fine, consist in the greater obstacles opposed to the concert and accomplishment of the secret wishes of an unjust and interested majority? Here again the extent of the Union gives it the most palpable advantage.

The influence of factious leaders may kindle a flame within their particular States but will be unable to spread a general conflagration through the other States. A religious sect may degenerate into a political faction in a part of the Confederacy; but the variety of sects dispersed over the entire face of it must secure the national councils against any danger from that source. A rage for paper money, for an abolition of debts, for an equal division of property, or for any other improper or wicked project, will be less apt to pervade the whole body of the Union than a particular member of it, in the same proportion as such a malady is more likely to taint a particular county or district than an entire State.

In the extent and proper structure of the Union, therefore, we behold a republican remedy for the diseases most incident to republican government. And according to the degree of pleasure and pride we feel in being republicans ought to be our zeal in cherishing the spirit and supporting the character of federalists.

PART TWO

FEDERALISM

Relations between the national and state governments have been perhaps the single most persistent source of conflict in American politics. The protracted struggles over such issues as slavery and civil rights, government regulation of business, and the provision of social welfare programs all reflect in one manner or another the underlying tension of the federal system: the conflict between national interests and states' rights. While other nations such as Great Britain have debated how to extend basic rights (such as the right to vote) to certain groups, to provide forms of social insurance, or to nationalize the railroads, the United States has debated a different question—whether the central government has the right to do such things.[1] Even now, after many of these disputes have been resolved—usually with the national government successfully asserting its right to intervene—the states have retained leverage over the final administration of federal programs, ensuring that the distribution of power between levels of government remains in flux.

Complicating American intergovernmental relations is the fact that the Constitution does not always state clearly where federal authority begins and state sovereignty ends. In part, the Framers, faced with the difficult task of winning ratification of the document, often found it inexpedient to be precise. But in part, also, it was hard to be precise when creating a novel form of government that, unlike the known models of the past, was to be neither a confederation of loosely allied provinces nor a strictly unitary regime, but rather an unfamiliar admixture of both.

The ambiguities of the Constitution also reflect the tension between two competing theories of the American federation. The states' rights concept was advanced first by Thomas Jefferson and later enunciated more radically by southern secessionists. South Carolina's John C. Calhoun, for example, regarded the national union as a mere compact among its member states, one that the signatories could maintain or disband at will. The opposing view, held by the federalist framers of the Constitution, and most forcefully by Alexander Hamilton, deemed the republic greater than the sum of its parts. Rejecting the contractual theory of the union, "nationalists" such as Hamilton saw a legitimate role for an active

1. James Q. Wilson, *American Government: Institutions and Policies* (Lexington, Mass.: D.C. Heath and Company, 1980), pp. 42–44.

central government. According to them, the scope of federal authority would have to expand frequently to attend to the nation's common good, as distinct from local interests, and to "consolidate" the union. In an elegant essay, Samuel H. Beer traces the evolution of this national ideal, from the early ruminations of Hamilton and the magnificent orations of Daniel Webster to the missions of Abraham Lincoln, Theodore Roosevelt, and Franklin D. Roosevelt.

In the nineteenth century, "dual federalism" was the prevailing judicial interpretation of the Constitution. It held that the federal government was restricted to some functions, the states to others, and that each was sovereign in its own legal domain. However, by the 1950s, this concept of federalism appeared increasingly antiquated. In 1960, Morton Grodzins advanced the view that American federalism is a system characterized by *mutual* influence among levels of government. Grodzins provided a now-famous analogy: contrary to what the old doctrine of dual federalism suggested, the federal system is not a "layer cake," in which clear functional distinctions can be drawn between the national and subordinate governments, but a "marble cake." "As colors are mixed in the marble cake," Grodzins wrote, "so functions are mixed in the American federal system." Moreover, in the article reprinted here, Grodzins affirmed that the marble cake model was not a recent development, but a suitable description of federal-state relations from the start: ". . . relative to what governments did, intergovernmental cooperation during the last century was comparable with that existing today."

Martha Derthick offers a somewhat different perspective. In her brilliant essay, "The Enduring Features of American Federalism," she argues that states have been subordinated in practice—increasingly so amid the voluminous unfunded mandates imposed on them by Congress and federal courts. Constitutionally, of course, the states are governments in their own right. Without them the overload of tasks wrought by an ever-expanding federal agenda would be far greater than it already is. But as indispensable as their administrative functions are, the state governments also need to reassert a role as policy-making partners, not mere supplicants, in their relations with the federal establishment. Professor Derthick urges the states to "talk back." They can impart their pragmatism to policymakers in Washington, perhaps helping to match the ends of policy more practically with the means available. Although Derthick's essay was written a decade ago, it detected signs that such a renaissance of state leadership already might be underway.

6

SAMUEL H. BEER

THE NATIONAL IDEA IN AMERICAN POLITICS

How America forged a strong union out of a loose confederation of disparate states is a question that has fascinated generations of historians and political scientists. One scholar who has written most thoughtfully on the subject is Samuel H. Beer, a professor emeritus of Harvard University. In the following lecture given at Boston College in 1982, Beer examines the origins and development of the idea that a central government has a legitimate role to play in consolidating the nation and advancing its public interest.

THE NATIONAL IDEA

My subject is The National Idea in American Politics. I can most quickly explain what I mean by introducing a difference of opinion that I entertain with President Reagan. You have all heard of the President's New Federalism and his proposal to cut back on the activities of the Federal government by reducing or eliminating certain programs and transferring others to the states. He wishes to do this because he finds these activities to be inefficient and wasteful. He also claims that they are improper under the U.S. Constitution. Not in the sense that the courts have found them to violate our fundamental law, but in the larger philosophical and historical sense that the present distribution of power between levels of government offends against the true meaning and intent of that document.

In justification of this conclusion, he has relied upon a certain view of the founding of the Republic. In his Inaugural he summarized its essentials when he said: "The Federal government did not create the states; the states created the Federal government." This allegation of historical fact did not pass without comment. Richard B. Morris of Columbia took issue with the President, called his view of the historical facts "a hoary myth about the origin of the Union" and went on to summarize the evidence showing that "the United States was created by the people in collectivity, not by the individual states." No less bluntly Henry Steele Commager of Amherst said the President did not understand the Constitution, which in its own words asserts that it was ordained by "We, the people of the United States," not by the states severally.

We may smile at this exchange between the President and the professors. They are talking about something that happened a long time ago. To be sure, the conflict of ideas between them did inform the most serious crisis of our first century—the grim struggle that culminated in the Civil War. In that conflict, President Reagan's view—the compact theory of the Constitution—was championed by Jefferson Davis, the President of the seceding South. The first Republican President, on the other hand, espoused the national theory of the Constitution. "The Union," said Abraham Lincoln, "is older than any of the states and, in fact, it created them as States. . . . The Union and not the states separately produced their independence and their liberty. . . . The Union gave each of them whatever of independence and liberty it has."

As stated by President Lincoln, the national idea is a theory of where ultimate authority lies in the United States. It identifies the whole people of the nation as the source of the legitimate power of both the federal government and the state governments. But admirable as we may find this conception of popular sovereignty in principle, we must doubt its relevance to our problems today. The republic is untroubled by threats of secession, except occasionally in a rhetorical flourish by candidates for public office. Nullification and interposition, those other offspring of the compact theory, were asserted in the 1960s against the enforcement of civil rights, only to flicker out with the collapse of what had been called "massive resistance."

The national idea, however, is not only a theory of authority, but also a theory of purpose, a perspective on public policy, a guide to the ends for which power should be used. It invites us to ask ourselves what sort of a people we are and whether we are a people and what we wish to make of ourselves as a people. In this sense the national idea is as alive and contentious today as it was when Alexander Hamilton set the course of the first Administration of George Washington.

THE PROMISE OF NATIONHOOD

Like the other Founders, Hamilton sought to establish a regime of republican liberty, that is, a system of government which would protect the individual rights of person and property and which would be founded upon the consent of the governed. He was by no means satisfied with the legal framework produced by the Philadelphia convention. Fearing the states, he would have preferred a much stronger central authority and, distrusting the common people, he would have set a greater distance between them and the exercise of power. He was less concerned, however, with the legal framework than with the use that would be made of it. He saw in the Constitution not only a regime of liberty, but also and especially the promise of nationhood.

He understood, moreover, that this promise of nationhood would have to be fulfilled if the regime of liberty itself was to endure. The scale of the country almost daunted him. At Philadelphia, as its chief diarist reported, Hamilton "confessed that he was much discouraged by the amazing extent of the Country in expecting the desired blessings from any general sovereignty that could be substituted." This fear echoed the conventional wisdom of the time. The great Montesquieu had warned that popular government was not suitable for a large and diverse country. If attempted, he predicted that its counsels would be distracted by "a thousand private views" and its extent would provide cover for ambitious men seeking despotic power.

One reply to Montesquieu turned this argument on its head by declaring that such pluralism would be a source of stability. In his famous *Federalist 10* James Madison argued that the more extensive republic, precisely because of its diversity, would protect popular government by making oppressive combinations less likely. Hamilton did not deny Madison's reasoning, but perceived that something more than a balance of groups would be necessary if the more extensive republic was to escape the disorder that would destroy its liberty.

Hamilton summarized his views in the Farewell Address that he drafted for Washington in 1796. Its theme is the importance of union. But this union does not consist merely in a balance of groups or a consensus on values, and certainly not merely in a strong central government or a common framework of constitutional law. It is rather a condition of the people, uniting them by both sympathy and interest, but above all in "an indissoluble community of interest as *one nation.*"

Hamilton's nationalism did not consist solely in his belief that the Americans were "one people" rather than thirteen separate peoples. The father of the compact theory himself, Thomas Jefferson, at times shared that opinion, to which he gave expression in the Declaration of Independence. The contrast with Jefferson lay in Hamilton's activism, his belief that this American people must make vigorous use of its central government for the tasks of nationbuilding. This difference between the two members of Washington's cabinet, the great individualist and the great nationalist, achieved classic expression in their conflict over the proposed Bank of the United States. Jefferson feared that the bank would corrupt his cherished agrarian order and discovered no authority for it in the Constitution. Hamilton, believing that a central bank was necessary to sustain public credit, promote economic development and—in his graphic phrase—"cement the union," found in a broad construction of the necessary and proper clause ample Constitutional authorization. Looking back today and recognizing that the words of the Constitution can be fitted into either line of reasoning, we must sigh with relief that President Washington and in later years the Supreme Court preferred the Hamiltonian doctrine.

Hamilton was not only a nationalist and centralizer, he was also an elitist. Along with the bank, his first steps to revive and sustain the public credit were the full funding of the federal debt and the federal assumption of the debts incurred by the states during the war of independence. These measures had their fiscal and economic purposes. Their social impact, moreover, favored the fortunes of those members of the propertied classes who had come to hold the federal and state obligations. This result, while fully understood, was incidental to Hamilton's ultimate purpose, which was political. As with the bank, that purpose was to strengthen the newly empowered central government by attaching to it the interests of these influential members of society. Hamilton promoted capitalism. Not because he was a lackey of the capitalist class—indeed as he once wrote to a close friend, "I hate moneying men"—but just the opposite. His elitism was subservient to his nationalism.

In the same cause he was not only an elitist, but also an integrationist. I use that term expressly because of its current overtones, wishing to suggest Hamilton's perception of how diversity need not always be divisive, but may lead to mutual dependence and union. Here again he broke from Jefferson who valued homogeneity. Hamilton, on the other hand, planned for active federal intervention to diversify the economy by the development of commerce and industry. His great report on manufactures is at once visionary and far-seeing—"the embryo of modern America," a recent writer terms it. The economy he foresaw would be free, individualist, and competitive—no other scheme was conceivable to Americans at that time or any other time. The federal government, however, would take action to ensure that entrepreneurs invested their money in ways most advantageous to the national welfare. In addition to a moderately protective tariff, bounties, premiums, and other aids would be employed to develop industry, along with a federal commission to allocate funds. There would be federal inspection of manufactured goods to protect the consumer and to enhance the reputation of American goods in foreign markets. The purpose was to make the country rich and powerful. At the same time, the interdependence of agriculture and industry and especially of South and North would enhance the union. The outcome, writes a biographer, would be to make the United States "one nation indivisible, bound together by common wants, common interests, and a common prosperity."

Hamilton is renowned for his statecraft: for his methods of using the powers of government for economic, political, and social ends. But that emphasis obscures his originality, which consisted in his conceptualization of those ends. His methods were derivative, being taken from the theory and practice of state-builders of the seventeenth and eighteenth centuries from Colbert to Pitt. Hamilton used this familiar technology, however, to forward the unprecedented attempt to establish republican government on a continental scale. In his scheme the unities of nationhood would sustain the authority of such a regime. By contrast those earlier craftsmen of the modern state in Bourbon France or Hohenzollern Prussia or Whig Britain could take for granted the established authority of a monarchic and aristocratic regime. They too had their techniques for enhancing the attachment of the people to the prince. But in America the people were the prince. To enhance their attachment to the ultimate governing power, therefore, meant fortifying the bonds that united them as a people. If the authority of this first nation-state was to suffice for its governance, the purpose of the state would have to become the development of the nation. This was the distinctive Hamiltonian end: to make the nation more of a nation.

THE CRISIS OF SECTIONALISM

The national idea, so engendered, confronted three great crises: the crisis of sectionalism, culminating in the civil war; the crisis of industrialism, culminating in the great depression and the New Deal; and the crisis of racism, which continues to rack our country today.

In the course of the struggle with sectionalism, John C. Calhoun defined the issue and threw down the challenge to nationalism when he said: ". . . the very idea of an *American People*, as constituting a single community, is a mere chimera. Such a community never for a single moment existed—neither before nor since the Declaration of Independence." This was a logical deduction from the compact theory, which in Calhoun's system made of each state a "separate sovereign community."

His leading opponent, Daniel Webster, has been called the first great champion of the national theory of the union. If we are thinking of speech rather than action, that is true, since Hamilton's contribution, while earlier, was in the realm of deeds rather than words. Webster never won the high executive power that he sought and the cause of union for which he spent himself suffered continual defeat during his lifetime. But the impact on history of words such as his is not to be underestimated. "When finally, after his death, civil war did eventuate," concludes his biographer, "it was Webster's doctrine, from the lips of Abraham Lincoln, which animated the North and made its victory inevitable." Webster gave us not only doctrine, but also imagery and myth. He was not the narrow legalist and materialistic Whig of some critical portraits. His oratory is too florid for our taste today. Its effect on his audiences, however, was overpowering. "I was never so excited by public speaking before in my life," exclaimed George Ticknor, an otherwise cool Bostonian, after one address. "Three or four times I thought my temples would burst with the gush of blood." Those who heard him, it has been said, "experienced the same delight which they might have received from a performance of *Hamlet* or Beethoven's Fifth Symphony." Poets have been called "the unacknowledged legislators of the world." This legislator, I submit, was the unacknowledged poet of the young Republic.

To say this is to emphasize his style. What was the substance of his achievement? Historians of political thought usually and correctly look first to his memorable debate with Senator Robert Hayne of South Carolina in January of 1830. Echoing Calhoun's deductions from the compact theory, Hayne had stated the doctrine of nullification. This doctrine would deny to the federal judiciary the right to draw the line between federal and state authority, leaving such questions of constitutionality to be decided—subject to various qualifications—by each state itself.

In reply Webster set forth with new boldness the national theory of authority. Asking what was the origin of "this general government," he concluded that the Constitution is not a compact between the states. It was not established by the governments of the several states, or by the people of the several states, but by "the people of the United States in the aggregate." In Lincolnian phrases he called it "the people's Constitution, the people's government, made for the people, made by the people, and answerable to the people," and clinched his argument for the dependence of popular government on nationhood with that memorable and sonorous coda, "Liberty and union, one and inseparable, now and forever."

These later passages of his argument have almost monopolized the attention of historians of political thought. Yet it is in an earlier and longer part that he developed the Hamiltonian thrust, looking not to the origins, but to the purpose of government. These initial passages of the debate had not yet focused on the problem of authority and nullification. The question was rather what to do with a great national resource—the public domain, already consisting of hundreds of millions of acres located in the states and territories and owned by the federal government. Large tracts had been used to finance internal improvements—such as roads, canals, and schools—as envisioned by Hamilton and ardently espoused by the previous President, John Quincy Adams.

When Webster defended such uses, citing the long-standing agreement that the public domain was for "the common benefit of all the States," Hayne made a revealing reply. If that was the rule, said he, how could one justify "voting away immense bodies of these lands—for canals in Indiana and Illinois, to the Louisville and Portland Canal, to Kenyon College in Ohio, to Schools for the Deaf and Dumb." "If grants of this character," he continued, "can fairly be considered as made for the common benefit of all the states, it can only be because all the states are interested in the welfare of each—a principle, which, carried to the full extent, destroys all distinction between local and national subjects."

Webster seized the objection and set out to answer it. His task was to show when a resource belonging to the whole country could legitimately be used to support works on "particular roads, particular canals, particular rivers, and particular institutions of education in the West." Calling this question "the real and wide difference in political opinion between the honorable gentleman and myself," he asserted that there was a "common good" distinguishable from "local goods," yet embracing such particular projects. Senator Hayne, he said, "may well ask what interest has South Carolina in a canal in Ohio. On his system, it is true, she has no interest. On that system, Ohio and Carolina are different governments and different countries. . . . On that system, Carolina has no more interest in a canal in Ohio than in Mexico." For Webster, on the contrary, "Carolina and Ohio are parts of the same country, states, united under the same general government, having interests, common, associated, intermingled."

In these passages the rhetoric is suggestive, but one would like a more specific answer: What is the difference between a local and a general good? Suddenly Webster's discourse becomes quite concrete. His approach is to show what the federal government must do by demonstrating what the states cannot do. Using the development of transportation after the peace of 1815 for illustration, he shows why a particular project within a state, which also has substantial benefits for other states, will for that very reason probably not be undertaken by the state within which it is located.

"Take the instance of the Delaware breakwater," he said. (This was a large artificial harbor then under federal construction near the mouth of Delaware Bay.) "It will cost several millions of money. Would Pennsylvania ever have constructed it? Certainly never, . . . because it is not for her sole benefit. Would Pennsylvania, New Jersey, and Delaware have united to accomplish it at their joint expense? Certainly not, for the same reason. It could not be done, therefore, but by the general government."

The example illustrates a standard argument of political economy for centralization. Where the effects of government activity within one jurisdiction spill over into other jurisdictions, there is a case for central intervention to promote this activity, if it is beneficial, or to restrain it, if it is harmful. This spillover argument is one criterion of the "common good" and, as Webster pointed out, its logic calls for action in such cases by the government representing the whole country.

Hayne was right to shrink from the logic of this argument. For its logic does mean that in a rapidly developing economy such as that of America in the nineteenth century, increasing interdependence would bring more and more matters legitimately within the province of the federal government. But logic was not the only aspect of Webster's argument that Hayne was resisting. In the spirit of Hamilton, Webster did perceive the prospect of increasing interdependence and recognized that it could fully realize its promise of wealth and power only with the assistance of the federal government. Moreover, he looked beyond the merely material benefits that such intervention would bring to individuals, classes, and regions toward his grand objective, "the consolidation of the union." This further criterion of the common good could under no circumstances be reconciled with Hayne's "system."

Like Hamilton, Webster sought to make the nation more of a nation. As he conceived this objective, however, he broke from the bleak eighteenth-century realism of Hamilton and turned his imagination toward the vistas of social possibility being opened by the rising romantic movement of his day. By "consolidation" Webster did not mean merely attachment to the union arising from economic benefits. Indeed, he blamed Hayne for regarding the union "as a mere question of present and temporary expedience; nothing more than a mere matter of profit and loss . . . to be preserved, while it suits local and temporary purposes to preserve it; and to be sundered whenever it shall be found to thwart such purposes."

The language brings to mind the imagery of another romantic nationalist, Edmund Burke, when in his famous assault upon the French Revolution and social contract theory, he proclaimed that "the state ought not to be considered as nothing better than a partnership agreement in a trade of pepper and coffee, calico or tobacco, or some other such low concern, to be taken up for a little temporary interest, and to be dissolved at the fancy of the parties," but rather as "a partnership in all science; a partnership in all art; a partnership in every virtue, and in all perfection."

A later formulation echoes Burke's words and phrasing even more exactly, as Webster sets forth the organic conception of the nation: "The Union," he said, "is not a temporary partnership of states. It is an association of people, under a constitution of government, uniting their power, joining together their highest interests, cementing their present enjoyments, and blending into one indivisible mass, all their hopes for the future."

Webster articulated this conception most vividly not in Congress or before the Supreme Court, but at public gatherings on patriotic occasions. There the constraints of a professional and adversarial audience upon his imagination were relaxed and his powers as myth-maker released. Consider what some call the finest of his occasional addresses, his speech at the laying of the cornerstone of the Bunker Hill Monument on June 17th, 1825. As in his advocacy and in his debates, his theme was the union. What he did, however, was not to make an argument for the union, but to tell a story about it—a story about its past with a lesson for its future.

The plot was simple: how American union foiled the British oppressors in 1775. They had thought to divide and conquer, anticipating that the other colonies would be cowed by the severity of the punishment visited on Massachusetts and that the other seaports would be seduced by the prospect of gain from trade diverted from Boston. "How miserably such reasoners deceived themselves!" exclaimed the orator. "Everywhere the unworthy boon was rejected with scorn. The fortunate occasion was seized, everywhere, to show to the whole world that the Colonies were swayed by no local interest, no partial interest, no selfish interest." In the imagery of Webster, the battle of Bunker Hill was a metaphor of that united people. As Warren, Prescott, Putnam, and Stark had fought side by side; as the four colonies of New England had on that day stood together with "one cause, one country, one heart"; so also "the feeling of resistance . . . possessed the whole American people." So much for Calhoun and his "system."

From this myth of war Webster drew a lesson for peace. "In a day of peace, let us advance the arts of peace and the works of peace. . . . Let us develop the resources of our land, call forth its powers, build up its institutions, and see whether we also, in our day and generation, may not perform something worthy to be remembered." Then he concluded with abrupt and brutal rhetoric: "Let our object be: OUR COUNTRY, OUR WHOLE COUNTRY, AND NOTHING BUT OUR COUNTRY."

THE CRISIS OF INDUSTRIALISM

With his own matchless sensibility, Abraham Lincoln deployed the doctrine and imagery of Webster to animate the North during the civil war. Lincoln's nationalism, like Webster's, also had a positive message for peacetime and it was this message that set the course of the country's development for the next several generations. Much that he did derived from the original Hamiltonian program, which, long frustrated by the dominance of the compact theory, now burst forth in legislative and executive action. During the very war years, not only was slavery given the death blow, but also an integrated program of positive federal involvement was put through in the fields of banking and currency, transportation, the tariff, land grants to homesteaders, and aid to higher education. In the following decades, an enormous expansion of the economy propelled America into the age of industrialism, which in due course engendered its typical problems of deprivation, inequality, and class conflict.

A Republican, Teddy Roosevelt, first attempted to cope with these problems in terms of the national idea. Throughout his public career, an associate has written, Roosevelt "kept one steady purpose, the solidarity, the essential unity of our country. . . . All the details of his action, the specific policies he stated, arise from his underlying purpose for the Union." Like other Progressives, Roosevelt was disturbed by the rising conflicts between groups and classes and sought to offset them by timely reform. In this sense integration was T.R.'s guiding aim and he rightly christened his cause "The New Nationalism." Effective advocacy of this cause, however, fell to another Roosevelt a generation later, when the failings of industrialism were raising far greater dangers to the union.

None of the main points in Franklin Roosevelt's famous Inaugural of March 4, 1933, can be summarized without reference to the nation. The emergency is national because of "the interdependence of the various elements in, and parts of, the United States." Our purpose must be, first, "the establishment of a sound national economy" and beyond that "the assurance of a rounded and permanent national life." The mode of action must be national, conducted by the federal government and carried out "on a national scale," helped "by national planning." No other thematic term faintly rivals the term "nation" as noun or adjective, in emphasis. Democracy is mentioned only once; liberty, equality, or the individual not at all.

Franklin Roosevelt's nationalism was threefold. First it was a doctrine of federal centralization and in his administration, in peace as well as war, the balance of power in the federal system swung sharply toward Washington. Roosevelt called not only for a centralization of government, but also a nationalization of politics. In these years a new kind of mass politics arose. The old rustic and sectional politics gave way to a new urban and class politics dividing electoral forces on a nation-wide basis.

The third aspect of Roosevelt's nationalism was expressed in his policies. Those policies do not make a neat package and include many false starts and failures and ad hoc expedients. Yet in their overall impact one can detect the old purpose of "consolidation of the union."

During the very first phase of the New Deal, based on the National Industrial Recovery Act, this goal was explicit. In its declaration of policy, the act, having declared a "national emergency," called for "cooperative action among trade groups" and "united action of labor and management" under "adequate government sanctions and supervision." Engulfed in red, white, and blue propaganda, the NRA, after a first brief success, failed to achieve that coordinated effort and had virtually collapsed by the time it was declared unconstitutional in 1935. The second New Deal which followed, however, brought about fundamental and lasting changes in the structure of the American government and economy.

The paradox of the second New Deal is that although at the time it was intensely divisive, in the end it enhanced national solidarity.

The divisiveness will be readily granted by anyone who remembers the campaign of 1936. The tone was set by Roosevelt's speech accepting the Democratic nomination. In swollen and abrasive hyperbole he promised that, just as 1776 had wiped out "political tyranny" so 1936 would bring "economic tyranny" to an end. The "economic royalist" metaphor that was launched into the political battle by this speech expressed the emerging purpose of the New Deal to create a new balance of power in the economy by means of a series of basic structural reforms. I have always thought that the Wagner Act was the most important and characteristic. Utilizing its protections of the right to organize and to bargain collectively, trade unions swept through industry in a massive organizing effort. Despite bitter and sometimes bloody resistance in what can only be called class war, over the years not only practices but also attitudes were altered. The life of the working stiff was never again the same. For illustration of the extremes we may contrast the recent pact between the UAW and the Ford Motor Company with the battle of the Underpass outside the company's River Rouge Plant in 1937.

The Rooseveltian reforms had two aspects. In their material aspect they brought about a redistribution of power in favor of certain groups. No less important was their symbolic significance as recognition of the full membership of these groups in the national community. (I like De Gaulle's expression, "citizens with a full share.") Industrial labor and recent immigrants won a degree of acceptance in the national consciousness and in everyday social intercourse that they had not previously enjoyed. In Roosevelt's appointments to the judiciary, Catholics and Jews were recognized as never before. He named the first Italo-American and the first Negroes ever appointed to the federal bench. As Joseph Alsop has recently observed, "the essence of his achievement" was that he "included the excluded." And with such high spirits; I can never forget the impact when he opened an address to the Daughters of the American Revolution with the greetings: "Fellow Immigrants!"

The other day I had a letter from a friend who asked: Did not "the new social democracy, which arose with the New Deal, make popular sacrifice, not least for foreign policy, more difficult to obtain?" Just the opposite, I replied. And I went on to recall how during the war it often occurred to me that we were lucky that those sudden, vast demands being put upon the people in the name of national defense had been preceded by a period of radical national reform. An anecdote will illustrate my point. One hot day in the late summer of 1944 while crossing France we stopped to vote by absentee ballot in the Presidential election. "Well, Guthrie," I said to one of the non-coms, "let's line up these men and vote them for Roosevelt." That light-hearted remark was entirely in keeping with the situation. Most of the GIs were from fairly poor families in the Bronx and New Jersey. Politics didn't greatly concern them, but nothing was more natural to them than to vote for the man who had brought WPA, Social Security, and other benefits to their families. Even among the battalion officers I can think of only two who did not vote for Roosevelt—the colonel and a staff officer from New York City named something or other the Fourth.

THE CRISIS OF RACISM

None of these conflicts in nation-building is ever wholly terminated. Sectionalism still flares up from time to time, as between frostbelt and sunbelt. So also does class struggle. Similarly today, the cleavages between ethnic groups that boiled up with a new bitterness in the 1960s are far from being resolved. In this nation of immigrants, "ethnicity" has been an old and fundamental feature of our politics. In the sixties the new word came into use to signify new facts as ethnic identity gained as a ground of claims and denials. "From the mid-sixties," one writer has reported, ". . . the ethnic identity began to gain on the general American identity. Indeed the very term 'American' became depreciated in the late 1960s." Once again the question whether we were one nation and one people was put in doubt.

The issue is not just ethnicity, but race. To be sure, ethnic pluralism is a fact— there are said to be ninety-two ethnic groups in the New York area alone—but this broad focus obscures the burning issue which is the coexistence of blacks and whites in large numbers on both sides. That question of numbers is crucial. In other times and places one can find instances of a small number of one race living in relative peace in a society composed overwhelmingly of the other race. "Tokenism" is viable. But the facts rule out that solution for the United States.

Another option is the model of "separate but equal." In some circumstances this option could be carried out on a decent and democratic basis. It is, for instance, the way the French-speaking citizens of Quebec would like to live, in relation to Canada as a whole. And, commonly, Canadians contrast favorably what they call their "mosaic society" with the American "melting pot." But in the present crisis Americans have rejected this option in the law and in opinion as segregation. American nationalism demands that diversity be dealt with not by separation, but by integration.

For John F. Kennedy and Lyndon Johnson, the question was, first of all, civil rights. This meant securing for blacks the legal and political rights that had been won for whites in other generations. But the problem of civil rights, which was mainly a problem of the South, merged with the problem of black deprivation, which was especially a problem of northern cities. Johnson's "poverty program" characterized the main thrust of the Great Society measures which he built on the initiatives of Kennedy. To think of these measures as concerned simply with "the poor" is to miss the point. The actual incidence of poverty meant that their main concern would be with the living conditions and opportunities of blacks, and especially those who populated the decaying areas of the great urban centers swollen by migration from the South to the North during and after World War II.

These programs were based on the recognition that membership in one ethic group rather than another can make a great difference to your life chances. In trying to make the opportunities somewhat less unequal, they sought to bring the individuals belonging to disadvantaged groups—as was often said—"into the mainstream of American life." The rhetoric of one of Johnson's most impassioned speeches echoes this purpose. Only a few days after a civil rights march led by Martin Luther King had been broken up by state troopers in full view of national television, he introduced the Voting Rights Act of 1965 into Congress. Calling upon the myths of former wars, like other nationalist orators before him, he harked back to Lexington and Concord and to Appomattox Court House in his summons to national effort.

"What happened in Selma," he continued, "is part of a larger movement which reaches into every section and state of America. It is the effort of American Negroes to secure for themselves the full blessings of American life. . . ." Then, declaring that "their cause must be our cause too," he closed with solemn echo of the song of the marchers: "And . . . we . . . shall . . . overcome."

That effort to consolidate the union has proved no less difficult than the others. Theodore White has characterized the contrast in mood and behavior. In the early sixties, he has said, "the dominant theme was invincibility. America was going to the moon. America was going to end poverty. America was going to end discrimination." Then he asked, "What's the mood of the seventies?" and replied:

"It's a life-style mood. It's a period when each group and sect is trying to find its own virtue and trying to tyrannize over the other groups."

Considering where we started from some thirty years ago, our progress has been substantial. One incredible event stands out in my recollection as a symbol of that success. This was the ceremony in 1976 in Mississippi when after a long and bitter struggle for black participation in the Democratic party, Governor Finch, formerly an arch-segregationist, and Aaron Henry, an original member of the Mississippi Freedom Democratic Party, on the same platform integrated the state party organization.

Still, few will assert that our statecraft—from poverty programs to affirmative action to busing—has been adequate to the objective. This problem still awaits its Alexander Hamilton. We may take some slight comfort from the fact that it is continuous with his great work. The Fathers confronted the task of founding a nationstate. Our present exercise in nation-building is no less challenging. What we are attempting has never before been attempted by any country at any time. It is to create within a liberal, democratic framework a society in which vast numbers of both black and white people live in free and equal intercourse, political, economic, and social. It is a unique, a stupendous demand, but the national idea will let us be satisfied with nothing less.

THE NEW FEDERALISM

The federal system that confronts Ronald Reagan is the outcome of these three great waves of centralization: the Lincolnian, the Rooseveltian, and the Johnsonian. By means of his new federalism President Reagan seeks radically to decentralize that system. Does this brief review of the history of the national idea in American politics suggest any criticism or guidance?

I hope it has done something to undermine the appeal of compact theory rhetoric. Rhetoric is important, although not all-important. Words are means by which politicians reach the motivations of voters and by which leaders may shape those motivations. Both the compact theory and the national theory touch nerves of the body politic. Each conveys a very different sense of nationhood—or the lack thereof. I have spoken for the national theory, which envisions one people, at once sovereign and subject, source of authority and substance of history, asserting, through conflict and in diversity, our unity of origin and of destiny.

Such an image does not yield a decision rule for allocating functions between levels of government. That is for practical men, assisted no doubt by the policy sciences. But the imagery of the national idea can prepare the minds of practical men to recognize in the facts of our time the call for renewed effort to consolidate the union. The vice of the compact theory is that it obscures this issue, diverts attention from the facts and muffles the call for action.

Today this issue is real. A destructive pluralism, sectional, economic and ethnic, disrupts our common life. It is foolish so to use the rhetoric of political discourse as to divert attention from that fact. I ask the new federalists not only to give up their diversionary rhetoric, but positively to advocate the national idea.

This does not mean they must give up federal reform. A nationalist need not always be a centralizer. For philosophical and for pragmatic reasons he may prefer a less active federal government. The important thing is to keep alive in our speech and our intentions the thrust toward the consolidation of the union. People will differ on what and how much needs to be done. The common goal should not be denied. We may need a new federalism. We surely need a new nationalism. I plead with the new federalists: Come out from behind that Jeffersonian verbiage and take up the good old Hamiltonian cause.

7

MORTON GRODZINS

THE FEDERAL SYSTEM

A political scientist at the University of Chicago during the 1950s and early 1960s, Morton Grodzins (1917–1964) devoted the greater part of his career to studying American federalism. Writing in rebuttal to major reform efforts of the period that sought to separate the functions and revenue sources of the levels of government, Grodzins argued that the American system had been designed to promote a sharing of functions and power. The overlapping governmental authority built into the system, he argues, promotes decentralization and local autonomy.

Federalism is a device for dividing decisions and functions of government. As the constitutional fathers well understood, the federal structure is a means, not an end. The pages that follow are therefore not concerned with an exposition of American federalism as a formal, legal set of relationships. The focus, rather, is on the purpose of federalism, that is to say, on the distribution of power between central and peripheral units of government.

THE SHARING OF FUNCTIONS

The American form of government is often, but erroneously, symbolized by a three-layer cake. A far more accurate image is the rainbow or marble cake, characterized by an inseparable mingling of differently colored ingredients, the colors appearing in vertical and diagonal strands and unexpected whirls. As colors are mixed in the marble cake, so functions are mixed in the American federal system. Consider the health officer, styled "sanitarian," of a rural county in a border state. He embodies the whole idea of the marble cake of government.

The sanitarian is appointed by the state under merit standards established by the federal government. His base salary comes jointly from state and federal funds, the county provides him with an office and office amenities and pays a portion of his expenses, and the largest city in the county also contributes to his salary and office by virtue of his appointment as a city plumbing inspector. It is impossible from moment to moment to tell under which governmental hat the sanitarian operates. His work of inspecting the purity of food is carried out under federal standards; but he is enforcing state laws when inspecting commodities that have not been in interstate commerce; and somewhat perversely he also acts under state authority when inspecting milk coming into the county from producing areas across the state border. He is a federal officer when impounding impure drugs shipped from a neighboring state; a federal-state officer when distributing typhoid immunization serum; a state officer when enforcing standards of industrial hygiene; a state-local officer when inspecting the city's water supply; and (to complete the circle) a local officer when insisting that the city butchers adopt more hygienic methods of handling their garbage. But he cannot and does not think of himself as acting in these separate capacities. All business in the county that concerns public health and sanitation he considers his business. Paid largely from federal funds, he does not find it strange to attend meetings of the city council to give expert advice on matters ranging from rotten apples to rabies control. He is even deputized as a member of both the city and county police forces.

The sanitarian is an extreme case, but he accurately represents an important aspect of the whole range of governmental activities in the United States. Functions are not neatly parceled out among the many governments. They are shared functions. It is difficult to find any governmental activity which does not involve all three of the so-called "levels" of the federal system. In the most local of local functions—law enforcement or education, for example—the federal and state governments play important roles. In what, a priori, may be considered the purest central government activities—the conduct of foreign affairs, for example—the state and local governments have considerable responsibilities, directly and indirectly.

The federal grant programs are only the most obvious example of shared functions. They also most clearly exhibit how sharing serves to disperse governmental powers. The grants utilize the greater wealth-gathering abilities of the central government and establish nationwide standards, yet they are "in aid" of functions carried out under state law, with considerable state and local discretion. The national supervision of such programs is largely a process of mutual accommodation. Leading state and local officials, acting through their professional organizations, are in considerable part responsible for the very standards that national officers try to persuade all state and local officers to accept.

Even in the absence of joint financing, federal-state-local collaboration is the characteristic mode of action. Federal expertise is available to aid in the building of a local jail (which may later be used to house federal prisoners), to improve a local water purification system, to step up building inspections, to provide standards for state and local personnel in protecting housewives against dishonest butchers' scales, to prevent gas explosions, or to produce a land use plan. States and localities, on the other hand, take important formal responsibilities in the development of national programs for atomic energy, civil defense, the regulation of commerce, and the protection of purity in foods and drugs; local political weight is always a factor in the operation of even a post office or a military establishment. From abattoirs and accounting through zoning and zoo administration, any governmental activity is almost certain to involve the influence, if not the formal administration, of all three planes of the federal system.

ATTEMPTS TO UNWIND THE FEDERAL SYSTEM

Within the past dozen years there have been four major attempts to reform or reorganize the federal system: the first (1947–1949) and second (1953–1955) Hoover Commissions on Executive Organization; the Kestnbaum Commission on Intergovernmental Relations (1953–1955); and the Joint Federal-State Action

Committee (1957–1959). All four of these groups have aimed to minimize federal activities. None of them has recognized the sharing of functions as the characteristic way American governments do things. Even when making recommendations for joint action, these official commissions take the view (as expressed in the Kestnbaum report) that "the main tradition of American federalism [is] the tradition of separateness." All four have, in varying degrees, worked to separate functions and tax sources.

The history of the Joint Federal-State Action Committee is especially instructive. The committee was established at the suggestion of President Eisenhower, who charged it, first of all, "to designate functions which the States are ready and willing to assume and finance that are now performed or financed wholly or in part by the Federal Government." He also gave the committee the task of recommending "Federal and State revenue adjustments required to enable the States to assume such functions."[1]

The committee subsequently established seemed most favorably situated to accomplish the task of functional separation. It was composed of distinguished and able men, including among its personnel three leading members of the President's Cabinet, the director of the Bureau of the Budget, and ten state governors. It had the full support of the President at every point, and it worked hard and conscientiously. Excellent staff studies were supplied by the Bureau of the Budget, the White House, the Treasury Department, and, from the state side, the Council of State Governments. It had available to it a large mass of research data, including the sixteen recently completed volumes of the Kestnbaum Commission. There existed no disagreements on party lines within the committee and, of course, no constitutional impediments to its mission. The President, his Cabinet members, and all the governors (with one possible exception) on the committee completely agreed on the desirability of decentralization-via-separation-of-functions-and-taxes. They were unanimous in wanting to justify the committee's name and to produce action, not just another report.

The committee worked for more than two years. It found exactly two programs to recommend for transfer from federal to state hands. One was the federal grant program for vocational education (including practical-nurse training and aid to fishery trades); the other was federal grants for municipal waste treatments plants. The programs together cost the federal government less than $80 million in 1957, slightly more than two percent of the total federal grants for that year. To allow the states to pay for these programs, the committee recommended that they be allowed a credit against the federal tax on local telephone calls. Calculations showed that this offset device, plus an equalizing factor, would give every state at least 40 percent more from the tax than it received from the federal government in vocational education and sewage disposal grants. Some states were "equalized" to receive twice as much.

The recommendations were modest enough, and the generous financing feature seemed calculated to gain state support. The President recommended to Congress that all points of the program be legislated. None of them was, none has been since, and none is likely to be.

A POINT OF HISTORY

The American federal system has never been a system of separated governmental activities. There has never been a time when it was possible to put neat labels on discrete "federal," "state," and "local" functions. Even before the Constitution, a statute of 1785, reinforced by the Northwest Ordinance of 1787, gave grants-in-land to the states for public schools. Thus the national government was a prime force in making possible what is now taken to be the most local function of all, primary and secondary education. More important, the nation, before it was fully organized, established by this action a first principle of American federalism: the national government would use its superior resources to initiate and support national programs, principally administered by the states and localities.

The essential unity of state and federal financial systems was again recognized in the earliest constitutional days with the assumption by the federal government of the Revolutionary War debts of the states. Other points of federal-state collaboration during the Federalist period concerned the militia, law enforcement, court practices, the administration of elections, public health measures, pilot laws, and many other matters.

The nineteenth century is widely believed to have been the preeminent period of duality in the American system. Lord Bryce, at the end of the century described (in *The American Commonwealth*) the federal and state government as "distinct and separate in their action." The system, he said, was "like a great factory wherein two sets of machinery are at work, their revolving wheels apparently intermixed, their bands crossing one another, yet each set doing its own work without touching or hampering the other." Great works may contain gross errors. Bryce was wrong. The nineteenth century, like the early days of the republic, was a period principally characterized by intergovernmental collaboration.

Decisions of the Supreme Court are often cited as evidence of nineteenth-century duality. In the early part of the century the Court, heavily weighted with Federalists, was intent upon enlarging the sphere of national authority; in the later years (and to the 1930s) its actions were in the direction of paring down national powers and indeed all governmental authority. Decisions refered to "areas of exclusive competence" exercised by the federal government and the states; to their powers being "separated and distinct"; and to neither being able "to intrude within the jurisdiction of the other."

Judicial rhetoric is not always consistent with judicial action, and the Court did not always adhere to separatist doctrine. Indeed, its rhetoric sometimes indicated a positive view of cooperation. In any case, the Court was rarely, if ever, directly confronted with the issue of cooperation versus separation as such. Rather it was concerned with defining permissible areas of action for the central government and the states; or with saying with respect to a point at issue whether any government could take action. The Marshall Court contributed to intergovernmental cooperation by the very act of permitting federal operations where they had not existed before. Furthermore, even Marshall was willing to allow interstate commerce to be affected by the states in their use of the police power. Later courts also upheld state laws that had an impact on interstate commerce, just as they approved the expansion of the national commerce power, as in statutes providing for the control of telegraphic communication or prohibiting the interstate transportation of lotteries, impure foods and drugs, and prostitutes. Similar room for cooperation was found outside the commerce field, notably in the Court's refusal to interfere with federal grants-in-land or cash to the states. Although research to clinch the point has not been completed, it is probably true that the Supreme Court from 1800 to 1936 allowed far more federal-state collaboration than it blocked.

Political behavior and administrative action of the nineteenth century provide positive evidence that, throughout the entire era of so-called dual federalism, the many governments in the American federal system continued the close administrative and fiscal collaboration of the earlier period. Governmental activities were not extensive. But relative to what governments did, intergovernmental cooperation during the last century was comparable with that existing today.

Occasional presidential vetoes (from Madison to Buchanan) of cash and land grants are evidence of constitutional and ideological apprehensions about the extensive expansion of federal activities which produced widespread intergovernmental collaboration. In perspective, however, the vetoes are a more important evidence of the continuous search, not least by state officials, for ways and means to involve the central government in a wide variety of joint programs. The search was successful.

Grants-in-land and grants-in-services from the national government were of first importance in virtually all the principal functions undertaken by the states and their local subsidiaries. Land grants were made to the states for, among other purposes, elementary schools, colleges, and special educational institutions; roads, canals, rivers, harbors, and railroads; reclamation of desert and swamp lands; and veterans' welfare. In fact whatever was at the focus of state attention became the recipient of national grants. (Then, as today, national grants established state emphasis as well as followed it.) If Connecticut wished to establish a program for the care and education of the deaf and dumb, federal money in the form of a land grant was found to aid that program. If higher education relating to agriculture became a pressing need, Congress could dip into the public domain and make appropriate grants to states. If the need for swamp drainage and flood control appeared, the federal government could supply both grants-in-land and, from the Army's Corps of Engineers, the services of the only trained engineers then available.

Aid also went in the other direction. The federal government, theoretically in exclusive control of the Indian population, relied continuously (and not always wisely) on the experience and resources of state and local governments. State militias were an all-important ingredient in the nation's armed forces. State governments became unofficial but real partners in federal programs for homesteading, reclamation, tree culture, law enforcement, inland waterways, the nation's internal communications system (including highway and railroad routes), and veterans' aid of various sorts. Administrative contacts were voluminous, and the whole process of interaction was lubricated, then as today, by constituent-conscious members of Congress.

The essential continuity of the collaborative system is best demonstrated by the history of the grants. The land grant tended to become a cash grant based on the calculated disposable value of the land, and the cash grant tended to become an annual grant based upon the national government's superior tax powers. In 1887, only three years before the frontier was officially closed, thus signalizing the end of the disposable public domain, Congress enacted the first continuing cash grants.

A long, extensive, and continuous experience is therefore the foundation of the present system of shared functions characteristic of the American federal system, what we have called the marble cake of government. It is a misjudgment of our history and our present situation to believe that a neat separation of governmental functions could take place without drastic alterations in our society and system of government.

DYNAMICS OF SHARING: THE POLITICS
OF THE FEDERAL SYSTEM

Many causes contribute to dispersed power in the federal system. One is the simple historical fact that the states existed before the nation. A second is in the form of creed, the traditional opinion of Americans that expresses distrust of centralized power and places great value in the strength and vitality of local units of government. Another is pride in locality and state, nurtured by the nation's size and by variations of regional and state history. Still a fourth cause of decentralization is the sheer wealth of the nation. It allows all groups, including state and local governments, to partake of the central government's largesse, supplies room for experimentation and even waste, and makes unnecessary the tight organization of political power that must follow when the support of one program necessarily means the deprivation of another.

In one important respect, the Constitution no longer operates to impede centralized government. The Supreme Court since 1937 has given Congress a relatively free hand. The federal government can build substantive programs in many areas on the taxation and commerce powers. Limitations of such central programs based on the argument, "it's unconstitutional," are no longer possible as long as Congress (in the Court's view) acts reasonably in the interest of the whole nation. The Court is unlikely to reverse this permissive view in the foreseeable future.

Nevertheless, some constitutional restraints on centralization continue to operate. The strong constitutional position of the states—for example, the assignment of two Senators to each state, the role given the states in administering even national elections, and the relatively few limitations on their lawmaking powers—establish the geographical units as natural centers of administrative and political strength. Many clauses of the Constitution are not subject to the same latitude of interpretation as the commerce and tax clauses. The simple, clearly stated, unambiguous phrases—for example, the President "shall hold his office during the term of four years"—are subject to change only through the formal amendment process. Similar provisions exist with respect to the terms of Senators and Congressmen and the amendment process. All of them have the effect of retarding or restraining centralizing action of the federal government. The fixed terms of the President and members of Congress, for example, greatly impede the development of nationwide, disciplined political parties that almost certainly would have to precede continuous large-scale expansion of federal functions.

The constitutional restraints on the expansion of national authority are less important and less direct today than they were in 1879 or in 1936. But to say that they are less important is not to say that they are unimportant.

The nation's politics reflect these decentralizing causes and add some of their own. The political parties of the United States are unique. They seldom perform the function that parties traditionally perform in other countries, the function of gathering together diverse strands of power and welding them into one. Except during the period of nominating and electing a President and for the essential but nonsubstantive business of organizing the houses of Congress, the American parties rarely coalesce power at all. Characteristically they do the reverse, serving as a canopy under which special and local interests are represented with little regard for anything that can be called a party program. National leaders are elected on a party ticket, but in Congress they must seek cross-party support if their leadership is to be effective. It is a rare President during rare periods who can produce legislation without facing the defection of substantial numbers of his own party. (Wilson could do this in the first session of the Sixty-Third Congress; but Franklin D. Roosevelt could not, even during the famous hundred days of 1933.) Presidents whose parties form the majority of the Congressional houses must still count heavily on support from the other party.

The parties provide the pivot on which the entire governmental system swings. Party operations, first of all, produce in legislation the basic division of functions between the federal government, on the one hand, and state and local governments, on the other. The Supreme Court's permissiveness with respect to the expansion of national powers has not in fact produced any considerable extension of exclusive federal functions. The body of federal law in all fields has remained, in the words of Henry M. Hart, Jr., and Herbert Wechsler, "interstitial in its nature," limited in objective and resting upon the principal body of legal relationships defined by state law. It is difficult to find any area of federal legislation that is not significantly affected by state law.

In areas of new or enlarged federal activity, legislation characteristically provides important roles for state and local governments. This is as true of Democratic as of Republican administrations and true even of functions for which arguments of efficiency would produce exclusive federal responsibility. Thus the unemployment compensation program of the New Deal and the airport program of President Truman's administration both provided important responsibilities for state governments. In both cases attempts to eliminate state participation were defeated by a cross-party coalition of pro-state votes and influence. A large fraction of the Senate is usually made up of ex-governors, and the membership of both houses is composed of men who know that their reelection depends less upon national leaders or national party organization than upon support from their home constituencies. State and local officials are key members of these constituencies, often central figures in selecting candidates and in turning out the vote. Under such circumstances, national legislation taking state and local views heavily into account is inevitable.

Second, the undisciplined parties affect the character of the federal system as a result of Senatorial and Congressional interference in federal administrative programs on behalf of local interests. Many aspects of the legislative involvement in administrative affairs are formalized. The Legislative Reorganization Act of 1946, to take only one example, provided that each of the standing committees "shall exercise continuous watchfulness" over administration of laws within its jurisdiction. But the formal system of controls, extensive as it is, does not compare in importance with the informal and extralegal network of relationships in producing continuous legislative involvement in administrative affairs.

Senators and Congressmen spend a major fraction of their time representing problems of their constituents before administrative agencies. An even larger fraction of Congressional staff time is devoted to the same task. The total magnitude of such "case work" operations is great. In one five-month period of 1943 the Office of Price Administration received a weekly average of 842 letters from members of Congress. If phone calls and personal contacts are added, each member of Congress on the average presented the OPA with a problem involving one of his constituents twice a day in each five-day work week. Data for less vulnerable agencies during less intensive periods are also impressive. In 1958, to take only one example, the Department of Agriculture estimated (and underestimated) that it received an average of 159 Congressional letters per working day. Special Congressional liaison staffs have been created to service this mass of business, though all higher officials meet it in one form or another. The Air Force in 1958 had, under the command of a major general, 137 people (55 officers and 82 civilians) working in its liaison office.

The widespread, consistent, and in many ways unpredictable character of legislative interference in administrative affairs has many consequences for the tone and character of American administrative behavior. From the perspective of this paper, the important consequence is the comprehensive, day-to-day, even hour-by-hour, impact of local views on national programs. No point of substance or procedure is immune from Congressional scrutiny. A substantial portion of the entire weight of this impact is on behalf of the state and local governments. It is a weight that can alter procedures for screening immigration applications, divert the course of a national highway, change the tone of an international negotiation, and amend a social security law to accommodate local practices or fulfill local desires.

The party system compels administrators to take a political role. This is a third way in which the parties function to decentralize the American system. The administrator must play politics for the same reason that the politician is able to play in administration: the parties are without program and without discipline.

In response to the unprotected position in which the party situation places him, the administrator is forced to seek support where he can find it. One ever-present task is to nurse the Congress of the United States, that crucial constituency which ultimately controls his agency's budget and program. From the administrator's view, a sympathetic consideration of Congressional requests (if not downright submission to them) is the surest way to build the political support without which the administrative job could not continue. Even the completely task-oriented administrator must be sensitive to the need for Congressional support and to the relationship between case work requests, on one side, and budgetary and legislative support, on the other. "You do a good job handling the personal problems and requests of a Congressman," a White House officer said, "and you have an easier time convincing him to back your program." Thus there is an important link between the nursing of Congressional requests, requests that largely concern local matters, and the most comprehensive national programs. The administrator must accommodate to the former as a price of gaining support for the latter.

One result of administrative politics is that the administrative agency may become the captive of the nationwide interest group it serves or presumably regulates. In such cases no government may come out with effective authority: the winners are the interest groups themselves. But in a very large number of cases, states and localities also win influence. The politics of administration is a process of making peace with legislators who for the most part consider themselves the guardians of local interests. The political role of administrators therefore contributes to the power of states and localities in national programs.

Finally, the way the party system operates gives American politics their overall distinctive tone. The lack of party discipline produces an openness in the system that allows individuals, groups, and institutions (including state and local governments) to attempt to influence national policy at every step of the legislative-administrative process. This is the "multiple-crack" attribute of the American government. "Crack" has two meanings. It means not only many fissures or access points; it also means, less statically, opportunities for wallops or smacks at government.

If the parties were more disciplined, the result would not be a cessation of the process by which individuals and groups impinge themselves upon the central government. But the present state of the parties clearly allows for a far greater operation of the multiple crack than would be possible under the conditions of centralized party control. American interest groups exploit literally uncountable access points in the legislative-administrative process. If legislative lobbying, from committee stages to the conference committee, does not produce results, a Cabinet secretary is called. His immediate associates are petitioned. Bureau chiefs and their aides are hit. Field officers are put under pressure. Campaigns are instituted by which friends of the agency apply a secondary influence on behalf of the interested party. A conference with the President may be urged.

To these multiple points for bringing influence must be added the multiple voices of the influencers. Consider, for example, those in a small town who wish to have a federal action taken. The easy merging of public and private interest at the local level means that the influence attempt is made in the name of the whole community, thus removing it from political partisanship. The Rotary Club as well as the City Council, the Chamber of Commerce and the mayor, eminent citizens and political bosses—all are readily enlisted. If a conference in a Senator's office will expedite matters, someone on the local scene can be found to make such a conference possible and effective. If technical information is needed, technicians will supply it. State or national professional organizations of local officials, individual Congressmen and Senators, and not infrequently whole state delegations will make the local cause their own. Federal field officers, who service localities, often assume local views. So may elected and appointed state officers. Friendships are exploited, and political mortgages called due. Under these circumstances, national policies are molded by local action.

In summary, then, the party system functions to devolve power. The American parties, unlike any other, are highly responsive when directives move from the bottom to the top, highly unresponsive from top to bottom. Congressmen and Senators can rarely ignore concerted demands from their home constituencies; but no party leader can expect the same kind of response from those below, whether he be a President asking for Congressional support or a Congressman seeking aid from local or state leaders.

Any tightening of the party apparatus would have the effect of strengthening the central government. The four characteristics of the system, discussed above, would become less important. If control from the top were strictly applied, these hallmarks of American decentralization might entirely disappear. To be specific, if disciplined and program-oriented parties were achieved: (1) It would make far less likely legislation that takes heavily into account the desires and prejudices of the highly centralized power groups and institutions of the country, including the state and local governments. (2) It would to a large extent prevent legislators, individually and collectively, from intruding themselves on behalf of non-national interests in national administrative programs. (3) It would put an end to the administrator's search for his own political support, a search that often results in fostering state, local, and other non-national powers. (4) It would dampen the process by which individuals and groups, including state and local political leaders, take advantage of multiple cracks to steer national legislation and administration in ways congenial to them and the institutions they represent.

Alterations of this sort could only accompany basic changes in the organization and style of politics which, in turn, presuppose fundamental changes at the parties' social base. The sharing of functions is, in fact, the sharing of power. To end this sharing process would mean the destruction of whatever measure of decentralization exists in the United States today.

GOALS FOR THE SYSTEM OF SHARING

The Goal of Understanding

Our structure of government is complex, and the politics operating that structure are mildly chaotic. Circumstances are ever-changing. Old institutions mask intricate procedures. The nation's history can be read with alternative glosses, and what is nearest at hand may be furthest from comprehension. Simply to understand the federal system is therefore a difficult task. Yet without understanding there is little possibility of producing desired changes in the system. Social structures and processes are relatively impervious to purposeful change. They also exhibit intricate interrelationships so that change induced at point "A" often produces unanticipated results at point "Z." Changes introduced into an imperfectly understood system are as likely to produce reverse consequences as the desired ones.

This is counsel of neither futility nor conservation for those who seek to make our government a better servant of the people. It is only to say that the first goal for those setting goals with respect to the federal system is that of understanding it.

Two Kinds of Decentralization

The recent major efforts to reform the federal system have in large part been aimed at separating functions and tax sources, at dividing them between the federal government and the states. All of these attempts have failed. We can now add that their success would be undesirable.

It is easy to specify the conditions under which an ordered separation of functions could take place. What is principally needed is a majority political party, under firm leadership, in control of both Presidency and Congress, and, ideally but not necessarily, also in control of a number of states. The political discontinuities, or the absence of party links, (1) between the governors and their state legislatures, (2) between the President and the governors, and (3) between the President and Congress clearly account for both the picayune recommendations of the Federal-State Action Committee and for the failure of even those recommendations in Congress. If the President had been in control of Congress (that is, consistently able to direct a majority of House and Senate votes), this alone would have made possible some genuine separation and devolution of functions. The failure to decentralize by order is a measure of the decentralization of power in the political parties.

Stated positively, party centralization must precede governmental decentralization by order. But this is a slender reed on which to hang decentralization. It implies the power to centralize. A majority party powerful enough to bring about ordered decentralization is far more likely to choose in favor of ordered centralization. And a society that produced centralized national parties would, by that very fact, be a society prepared to accept centralized government.

Decentralization by order must be contrasted with the different kind of decentralization that exists today in the United States. It may be called the decentralization of mild chaos. It exists because of the existence of dispersed power centers. This form of decentralization is less visible and less neat. It rests on no discretion of central authorities. It produces at times specific acts that many citizens may consider undesirable or evil. But power sometimes wielded even for evil ends may be desirable power. To those who find value in the dispersion of power, decentralization by mild chaos is infinitely more desirable than decentralization by order. The preservation of mild chaos is an important goal for the American federal system.

Oiling the Squeak Points

In a governmental system of genuinely shared responsibilities, disagreements inevitably occur. Opinions clash over proximate ends, particular ways of doing things become the subject of public debate, innovations are contested. These are not basic defects in the system. Rather, they are the system's energy-reflecting life blood. There can be no permanent "solutions" short of changing the system itself by elevating one partner to absolute supremacy. What can be done is to attempt to produce conditions in which conflict will not fester but be turned to constructive solutions of particular problems.

A long list of specific points of difficulty in the federal system can be easily identified. No adequate congressional or administrative mechanism exists to review the patchwork of grants in terms of national needs. There is no procedure by which to judge, for example, whether the national government is justified in spending so much more for highways than for education. The working force in some states is inadequate for the effective performance of some nationwide programs, while honest and not-so-honest graft frustrates efficiency in others. Some federal aid programs distort state budgets, and some are so closely supervised as to impede state action in meeting local needs. Grants are given for programs too narrowly defined, and overall programs at the state level consequently suffer. Administrative, accounting, and auditing difficulties are the consequence of the multiplicity of grant programs. City officials complain that the states are intrusive fifth wheels in housing, urban redevelopment, and airport building programs.

Some differences are so basic that only a demonstration of strength on one side or another can solve them. School desegregation illustrates such an issue. It also illustrates the correct solution (although not the most desirable method of reaching it): in policy conflicts of fundamental importance, touching the nature of democracy itself, the view of the whole nation must prevail. Such basic ends, however, are rarely at issue, and sides are rarely taken with such passion that loggerheads are reached. Modes of settlement can usually be found to lubricate the squeak points of the system.

A pressing and permanent state problem, general in its impact, is the difficulty of raising sufficient revenue without putting local industries at a competitive disadvantage or without an expansion of sales taxes that press hardest on the least wealthy. A possible way of meeting this problem is to establish a state-levied income tax that could be used as an offset for federal taxes. The maximum level of the tax which could be offset would be fixed by federal law. When levied by a state, the state collection would be deducted from federal taxes. But if a state did not levy the tax, the federal government would. An additional fraction of the total tax imposed by the states would be collected directly by the federal government and used as an equalization fund, that is, distributed among the less wealthy states. Such a tax would almost certainly be imposed by all states since not to levy it would give neither political advantage to its public leaders nor financial advantage to its citizens. The net effect would be an increase in the total personal and corporate income tax.

The offset has great promise for strengthening state governments. It would help produce a more economic distribution of industry. It would have obvious financial advantages for the vast majority of states. Since a large fraction of all state income is used to aid political subdivisions, the local governments would also profit, though not equally as long as cities are underrepresented in state legislatures. On the other hand, such a scheme will appear disadvantageous to some low-tax states which profit from the in-migration of industry (though it would by no means end all state-by-state tax differentials). It will probably excite the opposition of those concerned over governmental centralization, and they will not be assuaged by methods that suggest themselves for making both state and central governments bear the psychological impact of the tax. Although the offset would probably produce an across-the-board tax increase, wealthier persons, who are affected more by an income tax than by other levies, can be expected to join forces with those whose fear is centralization. (This is a common alliance and, in the nature of things, the philosophical issue rather than financial advantage is kept foremost.)

Those opposing such a tax would gain additional ammunition from the certain knowledge that federal participation in the scheme would lead to some federal standards governing the use of the funds. Yet the political strength of the states would keep these from becoming onerous. Indeed, inauguration of the tax offset as a means of providing funds to the states might be an occasion for dropping some of the specifications for existing federal grants. One federal standard, however, might be possible because of the greater representation of urban areas in the constituency of Congress and the President than in the constituency of state legislatures: Congress might make a state's participation in the offset scheme dependent upon a periodic reapportionment of state legislatures.

The income tax offset is only one of many ideas that can be generated to meet serious problems of closely meshed governments. The fate of all such schemes ultimately rests, as it should, with the politics of a free people. But much can be done if the primary technical effort of those concerned with improving the federal system were directed not at separating its interrelated parts but at making them work together more effectively. Temporary commissions are relatively inefficient in this effort, though they may be useful for making general assessments and for generating new ideas. The professional organizations of government workers do part of the job of continuously scrutinizing programs and ways and means of improving them. A permanent staff, established in the President's office and working closely with state and local officials, could also perform a useful and perhaps important role.

The Strength of the Parts

Whatever governmental "strength" or "vitality" may be, it does not consist of independent decision-making in legislation and administration. Federal-state interpenetration here is extensive. Indeed, a judgment of the relative domestic strength of the two planes must take heavily into account the influence of one on the other's decisions. In such an analysis the strength of the states (and localities) does not weigh lightly. The nature of the nation's politics makes federal functions more vulnerable to state influence than state offices are to federal influence. Many states, as the Kestnbaum Commission noted, live with "self-imposed constitutional limitations" that make it difficult for them to "perform all of the services that their citizens require." If this has the result of adding to federal responsibilities, the states' importance in shaping and administering federal programs eliminates much of the sting.

The geography of state boundaries, as well as many aspects of state internal organization, are the products of history and cannot be justified on any grounds of rational efficiency. Who, today, would create major governmental subdivisions the size of Maryland, Delaware, New Jersey, or Rhode Island? Who would write into Oklahoma's fundamental law an absolute state debt limit of $500,000? Who would design (to cite only the most extreme cases) Georgia's and Florida's gross underrepresentation of urban areas in both houses of the legislature?

A complete catalogue of state political and administrative horrors would fill a sizeable volume. Yet exhortations to erase them have roughly the same effect as similar exhortations to erase sin. Some of the worst inanities—for example, the boundaries of the states, themselves—are fixed in the national constitution and defy alteration for all foreseeable time. Others, such as urban underrepresentation in state legislatures, serve the overrepresented groups, including some urban ones, and the effective political organization of the deprived groups must precede reform.

Despite deficiencies of politics and organizations that are unchangeable or slowly changing, it is an error to look at the states as static anachronisms. Some of them—New York, Minnesota, and California, to take three examples spanning the country—have administrative organizations that compare favorably in many ways with the national establishment. Many more in recent years have moved rapidly towards integrated administrative departments, statewide budgeting, and central leadership. The others have models-in-existence to follow, and active professional organizations (led by the Council of State Governments) promoting their development. Slow as this change may be, the states move in the direction of greater internal effectiveness.

The pace toward more effective performance at the state level is likely to increase. Urban leaders, who generally feel themselves disadvantaged in state affairs, and suburban and rural spokesmen, who are most concerned about national centralization, have a common interest in this task. The urban dwellers want greater equality in state affairs, including a more equitable share of state financial aid; nonurban dwellers are concerned that city dissatisfactions should not be met by exclusive federal, or federal-local, programs. Antagonistic, rather than amiable, cooperation may be the consequence. But it is a cooperation that can be turned to politically effective measures for a desirable upgrading of state institutions.

If one looks closely, there is scant evidence for the fear of the federal octopus, the fear that expansion of central programs and influence threatens to reduce the states and localities to compliant administrative arms of the central government. In fact, state and local governments are touching a larger proportion of the people in more ways than ever before; and they are spending a higher fraction of the total national product than ever before. Federal programs have increased, rather than diminished, the importance of the governors; stimulated professionalism in state agencies; increased citizen interest and participation in government; and, generally, enlarged and made more effective the scope of state action.[2] It may no longer be true in any significant sense that the states and localities are "closer" than the federal government to the people. It is true that the smaller governments remain active and powerful members of the federal system.

Central Leadership: The Need for Balance

The chaos of party processes makes difficult the task of presidential leadership. It deprives the President of ready-made congressional majorities. It may produce, as in the chairmen of legislative committees, power-holders relatively hidden from public scrutiny and relatively protected from presidential direction. It allows the growth of administrative agencies which sometimes escape control by central officials. These are prices paid for a wide dispersion of political power. The cost is tolerable because the total results of dispersed power are themselves desirable and because, where clear national supremacy is essential, in foreign policy and military affairs, it is easiest to secure.

Moreover, in the balance of strength between the central and peripheral governments, the central government has on its side the whole secular drift towards the concentration of power. It has on its side technical developments that make central decisions easy and sometimes mandatory. It has on its side potent purse powers, the result of superior tax-gathering resources. It has potentially on its side national leadership capacities of the presidential office. The last factor is the controlling one, and national strength in the federal system has shifted with the leadership desires and capacities of the Chief Executive. As these have varied, so there has been an almost rhythmic pattern: periods of central strength put to use alternating with periods of central strength dormant.

Following a high point of federal influence during the early and middle years of the New Deal, the postwar years have been, in the weighing of central-peripheral strength, a period of light federal activity. Excepting the Supreme Court's action in favor of school desegregation, national influence by design or default has not been strong in domestic affairs. The danger now is that the central government is doing too little rather than too much. National deficiencies in education and health require the renewed attention of the national government. Steepening population and urbanization trend lines have produced metropolitan area problems that can be effectively attacked only with the aid of federal resources. New definitions of old programs in housing and urban redevelopment, and new programs to deal with air pollution, water supply, and mass transportation are necessary. The federal government's essential role in the federal system is that of organizing, and helping to finance, such nationwide programs.

The American federal system exhibits many evidences of the dispersion of power not only because of formal federalism but more importantly because our politics reflect and reinforce the nation's diversities-within-unity. Those who value the virtues of decentralization, which writ large are virtues of freedom, need not scruple at recognizing the defects of those virtues. The defects are principally the danger that parochial and private interests may not coincide with, or give way to, the nation's interest. The necessary cure for these defects is effective national leadership.

The centrifugal force of domestic politics needs to be balanced by the centripetal force of strong presidential leadership. Simultaneous strength at center and periphery exhibits the American system at its best, if also at its noisiest. The interests of both find effective spokesmen. States and localities (and private interest groups) do not lose their influence opportunities, but national policy becomes more than the simple consequence of successful, momentary concentrations of non-national pressures: it is guided by national leaders.

NOTES

1. The President's third suggestion was that the committee "identify functions and responsibilities likely to require state or federal attention in the future and . . . recommend the level of state effort, or federal effort, or both, that will be needed to assure effective action." The committee initially devoted little attention to this problem. Upon discovering the difficulty of making separatist recommendations, i.e., for turning over federal functions and taxes to the states, it developed a series of proposals looking to greater effectiveness in intergovernmental collaboration. The committee was succeeded by a legislatively based, 26-member Advisory Commission on Intergovernmental Relations, established September 29, 1959.

2. See the valuable report, *The Impact of Federal Grants-in-Aid on the Structure and Functions of State and Local Governments*, submitted to the Commission on Intergovernmental Relations by the Governmental Affairs Institute (Washington, D.C., 1955).

8

MARTHA DERTHICK

THE ENDURING FEATURES
OF AMERICAN FEDERALISM

Under the Constitution, the states are governments in their own right. In practice, however, their policy-making role has been eclipsed by that of the federal government. Martha Derthick, a professor of government at the University of Virginia, sees a need for the states to lead, not just follow. Within these subnational entities is where the rubber meets the road, so to speak, in much domestic policy. As such, much can be learned from them about what works, and what doesn't. Derthick's essay anticipated the revival of interest in devolution during the 1990s.

It is a commonplace of scholarship that American federalism constantly changes. And it is a commonplace of contemporary comment that the states are enjoying a renaissance. Their historic role as laboratories of experiment is acknowledged with praise. Their executives and legislatures are increasingly active, seizing issues, such as economic development, that the federal government has failed to come to grips with. State courts are staking out positions on individual rights in advance of those defined by the U.S. Supreme Court, while state attorneys general pursue consumer protection and antitrust cases that federal agencies have ignored. The states' share of government revenue has gained slightly on that of the federal government in the 1980s, and considerably surpasses that of local governments, contrary to a pattern that prevailed until the 1960s. The states' standing with the public and with prospective employees has improved. The governors are getting their share of good press and, what may be almost as important, of presidential nominations. As a result, state governments are perceived to have improved their position in the federal system.

Yet it is worth recalling how different the impression was but a short time ago, and how little has changed in some respects. Early in 1984 the Advisory Commission on Intergovernmental Relations published a much-noticed report, *Regulatory Federalism*, detailing a wide range of new or expanded federal controls over state government. In 1985, in the case of *Garcia v. San Antonio Metropolitan Transit Authority*, the Supreme Court declined to protect the state governments from congressional regulation under the Constitution's commerce clause and then washed its hands of this crucial federalism question. In the spring of 1988 the court removed the constitutional prohibition on federal taxation of income from interest on state and local government bonds (*South Carolina v. Baker*).

Certain regulatory excesses of the federal government vis-à-vis the states have been modified in the past several years; rules regarding transportation of the disabled and bilingual education are two examples. Yet not even under Ronald Reagan did the federal government step back from the new constitutional frontiers mapped out in the last decade or two—frontiers such as the Clean Air Act of 1970, which addresses the states with the language of outright command ("Each state shall . . ."). The president's executive order of October 1987 on federalism may be interpreted as an attempt to draw back, with its rhetorical statement of federalism principles and its instructions to executive agencies to refrain from using their discretion to preempt state action. But to read it is to be reminded of how little unilateral power the president has. The drawing back can succeed only to the extent the national legislature and courts concur. Nor did the Reagan administration consistently adhere to its professed principles. Substantive policy goals often were in tension with devolution of power to the states; the Reagan administration could be counted on to opt for devolution only when that tactic was consistent with its pursuit of a freer market and lower federal spending.

American federalism is a very large elephant indeed, and it is hard for a lone observer to grasp the properties of the whole beast. One needs to be abreast of constitutional doctrines; of legislative, judicial, and administrative practices over the whole range of government activities, from taxation to protection of civil liberties to pollution control; of the development or disintegration of political parties (are they decaying at the grass roots? at the center? both? neither?); of the volume and locus of interest group activity; of trends in public opinion and public employment, and more. To understand the condition of federalism, one needs to comprehend the functioning of the whole polity.

Granting that the federal system is always in flux, it is harder than one might suppose even to detect the dominant tendencies. While most academic analysts probably would assert that centralization is the secular trend, such distinguished scholars as Princeton political scientist Richard P. Nathan and Brandeis historian Morton Keller have argued that centralization is not inexorable and that the evolution of American federalism follows a cyclical pattern, with the federal government and the states alternately dominating.

MAPPING THE TERRAIN

Fighting the customary temptation to concentrate on change, I want to try to identify some elemental and enduring truths of American federalism. I want to map the features of the terrain, a metaphor that may be in fact apt. Our federalism is much like a piece of earth that is subject to constant redevelopment. It can be bulldozed and built up, flattened and regraded, virtually beyond recognition. Yet certain elemental properties of it, the bedrock and the composition of the soil, endure. I will start with propositions that I take to be purely factual and then proceed to others that are more analytical and normative, hence debatable.

The states are governments in their own right. They have constitutions that derive from the people and guarantee specific rights. They have elected legislatures that make laws, elected executives that enforce laws, and courts that interpret them — and not incidentally interpret the laws of the United States as well. State governments levy taxes. Their territorial integrity is protected by the U.S. Constitution, which also guarantees them equal representation in the Senate and a republican form of government. These creatures that walk like ducks and squawk like ducks must be ducks.

Nevertheless, the states are inferior governments. In our pond, they are the weaker ducks. The stubbornly persistent mythology that governments in the American federal system are coordinate should not obscure that fact. The two levels of government are *not* coordinate and equal, nor did the winning side in 1787 intend them to be. One cannot deny the existence of the Constitution's supremacy clause and the prescription that state officers take an oath to uphold the Constitution of the United States, or the fact that the framers of the Constitution fully expected an instrumentality of the federal government, the Supreme Court, to settle jurisdictional issues in the "compound republic," as James Madison called it. See *Federalist* No. 39, in which Madison makes a feeble, unsuccessful attempt to deny that the court's having this function gives the federal government a crucial advantage.

Whether the federal government has always been superior in fact can certainly be debated. At various times and places its writ did not run very strong. Ours was a different system in the nineteenth century, and it is significant that the full impact on federalism of the post–Civil War Amendments on civil rights was long delayed. Only recently has the South ceased to have a deviant social system. But on the whole, the federal government has won the crucial conflicts. Surely its ascendancy is not currently in dispute. Not only are the states treated as its administrative agents; they accept such treatment as a fact of life. Not since *Brown v. Board of Education* (1954) and *Baker v. Carr* (1962) have truly strenuous protests been heard from the states against their palpably inferior status.

The states' status as governments, even though inferior ones, gives Congress a range of choice in dealing with them. It may choose deference, displacement, or interdependence. In domestic affairs Congress always has the option of doing nothing, knowing that the states can act whether or not it does. Sometimes Congress consciously defers to the states, judging that the subject properly "belongs" to them. Perhaps just as often, Congress today is not deliberately deferential but fails to act for lack of time or the ability to reach agreement. It defaults. The area of congressional inaction, be it through deference or default, is reliably quite large. It normally includes new issues, such as AIDS or comparable worth. States remain on the front lines of domestic policy, the first to deal with newly perceived problems. Congress tends to defer or default on particularly difficult issues, such as the amount of support to be given to needy single mothers with children.

Congress rarely employs its second option, complete displacement, although explicit invocations of it, using the term "preemption," are more frequent now than they used to be. The third option, interdependence, is very common, I would think predominant. Through some combination of inducements, sanctions, or contractual agreements, Congress enters into collaborative arrangements with the states in the pursuit of national ends. The most common techniques are conditional grants-in-aid, which are characteristic of programs for income support and infrastructure development, and qualified preemptions, which are typical of the "new" regulation, including environmental protection and occupational health and safety. Congress sets standards but tells states that if they meet or exceed the national standards, they may retain the function, including administration.

The vigor and competence with which state governments perform functions left to them does not protect them against congressional incursions. Here I mean to challenge one of the leading canards of American federalism. Whenever Congress takes domestic action, that action is rationalized as a response to the failures of the states. Congress has had to step in, it is said, because states were not doing the job. The only thing one can safely say about the origins of nationalizing acts is that they are responses to the power of nationalizing coalitions. When Congress acts, in other words, it is not necessarily because states have failed; it is because advocates of national action have succeeded in mustering enough political force to get their way. State inaction may constitute part of their case, but state actions that are offensive to their interests may do so as well. Pathbreaking states have often demonstrated what can be done.

Congress's usual choice, moreover, is to cooperate with the states, not to displace them, and in the relationships of mutual dependence that result, it is a nice question just whose deficiencies are being compensated for. The federal government typically contributes uniform standards and maybe money. The states typically do the work of carrying out the function. The more they do and the better they do it, the more they are likely to be asked or ordered by Congress to do.

In cooperating with the states, Congress again has a choice. It can emphasize their status as governments, or it can emphasize their inferiority as such. Our ambiguous constitutional system enables Congress to view the states as equals or as agents. Congress gradually has abandoned the former view in favor of the latter. It has done so with the acquiescence of the Supreme Court, which once tried to defend "dual federalism" that is, the notion that the states were sovereign, separate, and equal—but which has long since abandoned that doctrine. And Congress does not indulge its agents. Ask any federal bureau chief. Congress is very poor at balancing the ends and means of action. All major federal executive agencies—the Environmental Protection Agency, the Social Security Administration, the Immigration and Naturalization Service, to cite just a few—are laboring under a burden of excessive obligation

Because states are governments, they may bargain with Congress. Bargaining is the usual mode of intergovernmental relations. State governments, even when treated by Congress as administrative agents, are agents with a difference. Unlike federal executive agencies, they are not Congress's creatures. Therefore they can talk back to it. They can influence the terms of cooperation.

This bargaining between levels of governments is good, depending on how the states use it. Here again I mean to challenge what I take to be a conventional view. Fragmentation of authority in the federal system is ordinarily portrayed, at least in academic literature, as a severe handicap to the federal government's pursuit of its goals. The federal government would be more effective, it is commonly said, if it did not have to rely so heavily on other governments. I believe, to the contrary, that the federal government needs a great deal of help, of a kind that can best be supplied—perhaps can only be supplied—by governments. It needs help with all aspects of governing, that is, with all the functions that legislatures, courts, and executives perform. Beyond that, it needs a great deal of help quite specifically in adjusting its goals to social and economic realities and to the capacities of administrative organizations.

Madison may be cited in support of this view—not the famous passage in *Federalist* No. 51 that one might anticipate, in which he argues that "the different governments will control each other, at the same time that each will be controlled by itself," but a passage less remarked, yet perhaps more prescient, in No. 62. In this essay on the Senate, Madison wrote: "A good government implies two things: first, fidelity to the object of government, which is the happiness of the people; secondly, a knowledge of the means by which that object can be best attained. Some governments are deficient in both these qualities; most governments are deficient in the first. I scruple not to assert, that in American governments too little attention has been paid to the last."

The deficiency in our attention to the means of government has never been more glaring. All institutions of the federal government—Congress, presidency, courts—have far more to do than they can do, but the executive agencies as the instruments of government action are arguably the most overburdened of all. Perhaps even more glaring today than the federal government's shortfall of institutional capacity is its shortfall of fiscal capacity. It has obligations far in excess of its willingness or ability to meet them. Whether that is a product of party politics or has other causes need not concern us here. The fact of the deficit is plain enough.

State governments help fill the federal government's performance gaps. They do much of the work of governing, as Madison anticipated. Even as an ardent nationalist, at the time of the Constitutional Convention, he held to the view that the national government would not be suited to the entire task of governing "so great an extent of country and over so great a variety of objects." Just how right he was has never been clearer. But if the states help fill the federal government's implementation gaps, they also are very much at risk of being victimized by them. Congress will try to close the distance between what it wants and what the federal government is able to do independently by ordering the states to do it.

AN APPEAL TO TALK BACK

The states are entitled to talk back. As governments in their own right, they have an independent responsibility to set priorities and balance means against ends. Because they are closer to the practical realities of domestic problems and because they lack the power to respond to deficits by printing money, state governments are in a superior position to do that balancing.

This appeal to the states to talk back is not a call to defiance, but a call to engage federal officials in a policy dialogue—and, having done so, to address those officials with language suitable to governments. If states habitually present themselves as supplicants for assistance—supplicants like any other interest group—they will inevitably contribute to the erosion of their own status.

I believe that the states *are* increasingly using the language of governments, rather than supplicants, in their dialogue with the federal government. The enactment in 1988 of welfare reform legislation, which a working group of the National Governors Association helped to shape, is an example. The governors drew on the state governments' experience with welfare programs to fashion changes that would be both politically and administratively feasible, besides containing improved assurances of federal funding for welfare.

There are numerous explanations for the new, more authoritative voice of the states. One is that individually the states have heightened competence and self-confidence as governments, whatever the range among them (and the range between, say, Virginia and Louisiana is very great). Another is that the decline of federal aid under Presidents Carter and Reagan has compelled greater independence. A third is that self-consciousness and cohesion of the states as a class of governments have increased, as indicated by the development of organized, well-staffed mechanisms of cooperation. Their shared status as agents of Congress and objects of its influence has caused the states to cooperate with one another today to a degree unprecedented in history, even if they remain intensely competitive in some respects, such as the pursuit of economic development.

I have concentrated on relations between the states and Congress to keep the subject focused and relatively simple. But the federal judiciary rivals the legislature as a framer of federal-state relations. Federal courts, like Congress, can choose to emphasize the states' standing as governments or their inferiority as such. Like Congress, over time the courts have come to favor the latter choice, so that states today are routinely commanded to implement the detailed policy decisions of national courts as well as the national legislature.

For the states, it is one thing to talk back to Congress, quite another and much harder thing to talk back to the federal courts. Yet here as well, they have been trying to find ways to talk back more effectively. The National Association of Attorneys General and the State and Local Legal Center, both with offices in Washington, now offer advice and assistance to state and local governments involved in litigation before the Supreme Court. Such governments in the past have often suffered from a lack of expert counsel.

It is no use to portray these developments in federal-state relations as a transgression of the framers' intentions, at least if we take the *Federalist* as our authoritative guide to those intentions. Alexander Hamilton foresaw with evident satisfaction the federal-state relation that obtains today. In *Federalist* No. 27, he wrote that "the plan reported by the convention, by extending the authority of the federal head to the individual citizens of the several States, will enable the government to employ the ordinary magistracy of each, in the execution of its laws. . . . Thus the legislatures, courts, and magistrates, of the respective [states], will be, incorporated into the operations of the national government . . . and will be rendered auxiliary to the enforcement of its laws." This is exactly what has happened.

What Hamilton would certainly not be satisfied with, however, is the federal government's management of its own administrative and fiscal affairs. One therefore feels entitled to invoke Madison on the states' behalf. It is not enough today that the states help the national government with governing, the function that both Hamilton and Madison foresaw. It is important as well that they perform a modern version of the balancing function that Madison in particular foresaw. This requires that in their policy dialogue with the federal government they assert, as governments in their own right, the importance of balancing ends and means.

9

ALEXANDER HAMILTON

FEDERALIST 27 AND 28

In the first of these two key essays, Hamilton (1755–1804) spelled out the basis of federal authority: namely, that (within limits) it would reach citizens directly, not merely through the intermediary of the states. In the second paper, he explained how federal sovereignty coexisting alongside that of the states protects the people from "tyranny." "If their rights are invaded by either, they can makes use of the other as the instrument of redress." Notice that Hamilton's case for federation is not identical to Madison's in Federalist 10. *The emphasis here is on the ability of the "general government" to "check" the possible "disposition" of state governments to usurp power for themselves, and likewise on the ability of the states to defend citizens from "usurpations" by the national government.*

FEDERALIST 27

To the People of the State of New York:

It has been urged, in different shapes, that a Constitution of the kind proposed by the convention cannot operate without the aid of a military force to execute its laws. This, however, like most other things that have been alleged on that side, rests on mere general assertion, unsupported by any precise or intelligible designation of the reasons upon which it is founded. As far as I have been able to divine the latent meaning of the objectors, it seems to originate in a presupposition that the people will be disinclined to the exercise of federal authority in any matter of an internal nature. Waiving any exception that might be taken to the inaccuracy or inexplicitness of the distinction between internal and external, let us inquire what ground there is to presuppose that disinclination in the people. Unless we presume at the same time that the powers of the general government will be worse administered than those of the State government, there seems to be no room for the presumption of ill-will, disaffection, or opposition in the people. I believe it may be laid down as a general rule that their confidence in and obedience to a government will commonly be proportioned to the goodness or badness of its administration. It must be admitted that there are exceptions to this rule; but these exceptions depend so entirely on accidental causes, that they cannot be considered as having any relation to the intrinsic merits or demerits of a constitution. These can only be judged of by general principles and maxims.

Various reasons have been suggested, in the course of these papers, to induce a probability that the general government will be better administered than the particular governments: the principal of which reasons are that the extension of the spheres of election will present a greater option, or latitude of choice, to the people; that through the medium of the State legislatures—which are select bodies of men, and which are to appoint the members of the national Senate—there is reason to expect that this branch will generally be composed with peculiar care and judgment; that these circumstances promise greater knowledge and more extensive information in the national councils, and that they will be less apt to be tainted by the spirit of faction, and more out of the reach of those occasional ill-humors, or temporary prejudices and propensities, which, in smaller societies, frequently contaminate the public councils, beget injustice and oppression of a part of the community, and engender schemes which, though they gratify a momentary inclination or desire, terminate in general distress, dissatisfaction, and disgust. Several additional reasons of considerable force, to fortify that probability, will occur when we come to survey, with a more critical eye, the interior structure of the edifice which we are invited to erect. It will be sufficient here to remark, that until satisfactory reasons can be assigned to justify an opinion, that the federal government is likely to be administered in such a manner as to render it odious or contemptible to the people, there can be no reasonable foundation for the supposition that the laws of the Union will meet with any greater obstruction from them, or will stand in need of any other methods to enforce their execution, than the laws of the particular members.

The hope of impunity is a strong incitement to sedition; the dread of punishment, a proportionably strong discouragement to it. Will not the government of the Union, which, if possessed of a due degree of power, can call to its aid the collective resources of the whole Confederacy, be more likely to repress the *former* sentiment and to inspire the *latter,* than that of a single State, which can only command the resources within itself? A turbulent faction in a State may easily suppose itself able to contend with the friends to the government in that State; but it can hardly be so infatuated as to imagine itself a match for the combined efforts of the Union. If this reflection be just, there is less danger of resistance from irregular combinations of individuals to the authority of the Confederacy than to that of a single member.

I will, in this place, hazard an observation, which will not be the less just because to some it may appear new; which is, that the more the operations of the national authority are intermingled in the ordinary exercise of government, the more the citizens are accustomed to meet with it in the common occurrences of their political life, the more it is familiarized to their sight and to their feelings, the further it enters into those objects which touch the most sensible chords and put in motion the most active springs of the human heart, the greater will be the probability that it will conciliate the respect and attachment of the community. Man is very much a creature of habit. A thing that rarely strikes his senses will generally have but little influence upon his mind. A government continually at a distance and out of sight can hardly be expected to interest the sensations of the people. The inference is, that the authority of the Union, and the affections of the citizens towards it, will be strengthened, rather than weakened, by its extension to what are called matters of internal concern; and will have less occasion to recur to force, in proportion to the familiarity and comprehensiveness of its agency. The more it circulates through those channels and currents in which the passions of mankind naturally flow, the less will it require the aid of the violent and perilous expedients of compulsion.

One thing, at all events, must be evident, that a government like the one proposed would bid much fairer to avoid the necessity of using force, than that species of league contended for by most of its opponents; the authority of which should only operate upon the States in their political or collective capacities. It has been shown that in such a Confederacy there can be no sanction for the laws but force; that frequent delinquencies in the members are the natural offspring of the very frame of the government; and that as often as these happen, they can only be redressed, if at all, by war and violence.

The plan reported by the convention, by extending the authority of the federal head to the individual citizens of the several States, will enable the government to employ the ordinary magistracy of each, in the execution of its laws. It is easy to perceive that this will tend to destroy, in the common apprehension, all distinction between the sources from which they might proceed; and will give the federal government the same advantage for securing a due obedience to its authority which is enjoyed by the government of each State, in addition to the influence on public opinion which will result from the important consideration of its having power to call to its assistance and support the resources of the whole Union. It merits particular attention in this place, that the laws of the Confederacy, as to the *enumerated* and *legitimate* objects of its jurisdiction, will become the SUPREME LAW of the land; to the observance of which all officers, legislative, executive, and judicial, in each State, will be bound by the sanctity of an oath. Thus the legislatures, courts, and magistrates, of the respective members, will be incorporated into the operations of the national government *as far as its just and constitutional authority extends*; and will be rendered auxiliary to the enforcement of its laws.* Any man who will pursue, by his own reflections, the consequences of this situation, will perceive that there is good ground to calculate upon a regular and peaceable execution of the laws of the Union, if its powers are administered with a common share of prudence. If we will arbitrarily suppose the contrary, we may deduce any inferences we please from the supposition; for it is certainly possible, by an injudicious exercise of the authorities of the best government that ever was, or ever can be instituted, to provoke and precipitate the people into the wildest excesses. But though the adversaries of the proposed Constitution should presume that the national rulers would be insensible to the motives of public good, or to the obligations of duty, I would still ask them how the interests of ambition, or the views of encroachment, can be promoted by such a conduct?

FEDERALIST 28

To the People of the State of New York:

That there may happen cases in which the national government may be necessitated to resort to force, cannot be denied. Our own experience has corroborated the lessons taught by the examples of other nations; that emergencies of this sort will sometimes arise in all societies, however constituted; that seditions and insurrections are, unhappily, maladies as inseparable from the body politic as tumors

---

* The sophistry which has been employed to show that this will tend to the destruction of the State governments, will, in its proper place, be fully detected.

and eruptions from the natural body; that the idea of governing at all times by the simple force of law (which we have been told is the only admissible principle of republican government), has no place but in the reveries of those political doctors whose sagacity disdains the admonitions of experimental instruction.

Should such emergencies at any time happen under the national government, there could be no remedy but force. The means to be employed must be proportioned to the extent of the mischief. If it should be a slight commotion in a small part of a State, the militia of the residue would be adequate to its suppression; and the natural presumption is that they would be ready to do their duty. An insurrection, whatever may be its immediate cause, eventually endangers all government. Regard to the public peace, if not to the rights of the Union, would engage the citizens to whom the contagion had not communicated itself to oppose the insurgents; and if the general government should be found in practice conducive to the prosperity and felicity of the people, it were irrational to believe that they would be disinclined to its support.

If, on the contrary, the insurrection should pervade a whole State, or a principal part of it, the employment of a different kind of force might become unavoidable. It appears that Massachusetts found it necessary to raise troops for repressing the disorders within that State; that Pennsylvania, from the mere apprehension of commotions among a part of her citizens, has thought proper to have recourse to the same measure. Suppose the State of New York had been inclined to reestablish her lost jurisdiction over the inhabitants of Vermont, could she have hoped for success in such an enterprise from the efforts of the militia alone? Would she not have been compelled to raise and to maintain a more regular force for the execution of her design? If it must then be admitted that the necessity of recurring to a force different from the militia, in cases of this extraordinary nature, is applicable to the State governments themselves, why should the possibility, that the national government might be under a like necessity, in similar extremities, be made an objection to its existence? Is it not surprising that men who declare an attachment to the Union in the abstract, should urge as an objection to the proposed Constitution what applies with tenfold weight to the plan for which they contend; and what, as far as it has any foundation in truth, is an inevitable consequence of civil society upon an enlarged scale? Who would not prefer that possibility to the unceasing agitations and frequent revolutions which are the continual scourges of petty republics.

Let us presume this examination in another light. Suppose, in lieu of one general system, two, or three, or even four Confederacies were to be formed, would not the same difficulty oppose itself to the operations of either of these Confederacies? Would not each of them be exposed to the same casualties; and when these happened, be obliged to have recourse to the same expedients for upholding its authority which are objected to in a government for all the States? Would the militia, in this supposition, be more ready or more able to support the federal authority than in the case of a general union? All candid and intelligent men must, upon due consideration, acknowledge that the principle of the objection is equally applicable to either of the two cases; and that whether we have one government for all the States, or different governments for different parcels of them,

or even if there should be an entire separation of the States,* there might sometimes be a necessity to make use of a force constituted differently from the militia,
to preserve the peace of the community and to maintain the just authority of the
laws against those violent invasions of them which amount to insurrections and
rebellions.

Independent of all other reasonings upon the subject, it is a full answer to
those who require a more peremptory provision against military establishments
in time of peace, to say that the whole powers of the proposed government is to be
in the hands of the representatives of the people. This is the essential, and, after
all, only efficacious security for the rights and privileges of the people, which is
attainable in civil society.†

If the representatives of the people betray their constituents, there is then no
resource left but in the exertion of that original right of self-defence which is
paramount to all positive forms of government, and which against the usurpations of the national rulers, may be exerted with infinitely better prospect of success than against those of the rulers of an individual state. In a single state, if the
persons intrusted with supreme power become usurpers, the different parcels,
subdivisions, or districts of which it consists, having no distinct government in
each, can take no regular measures for defence. The citizens must rush tumul-
tuously to arms, without concert, without system, without resource; except in
their courage and despair. The usurpers, clothed with the forms of legal authority, can too often crush the opposition in embryo. The smaller the extent of
the territory, the more difficult will it be for the people to form a regular or systematic plan of opposition, and the more easy will it be to defeat their early
efforts. Intelligence can be more speedily obtained of their preparations and
movements, and the military force in the possession of the usurpers can be more
rapidly directed against the part where the opposition has begun. In this situation
there must be a peculiar coincidence of circumstances to insure success to the
popular resistance.

The obstacles to usurpation and the facilities of resistance increase with the
increased extent of the state, provided the citizens understand their rights and are
disposed to defend them. The natural strength of the people in a large community, in proportion to the artificial strength of the government, is greater than in a
small, and of course more competent to a struggle with the attempts of the government to establish a tyranny. But in a confederacy the people, without exaggeration, may be said to be entirely the masters of their own fate. Power being almost
always the rival of power, the general government will at all times stand ready to
check the usurpations of the state governments, and these will have the same disposition towards the general government. The people, by throwing themselves
into either scale, will infallibly make it preponderate. If their rights are invaded
by either, they can make use of the other as the instrument of redress. How wise
will it be in them by cherishing the union to preserve to themselves an advantage
which can never be too highly prized!

---

* In the revised text, "or if there should be as many unconnected governments as there are States."
† Its full efficacy will be examined hereafter.

It may safely be received as an axiom in our political system, that the State governments will, in all possible contingencies, afford complete security against invasions of the public liberty by the national authority. Projects of usurpation cannot be masked under pretences so likely to escape the penetration of select bodies of men, as of the people at large. The legislatures will have better means of information. They can discover the danger at a distance; and possessing all the organs of civil power, and the confidence of the people, they can at once adopt a regular plan of opposition, in which they can combine all the resources of the community. They can readily communicate with each other in the different States, and unite their common forces for the protection of their common liberty.

The great extent of the country is a further security. We have already experienced its utility against the attacks of a foreign power. And it would have precisely the same effect against the enterprises of ambitious rulers in the national councils. If the federal army should be able to quell the resistance of one State, the distant States would have it in their power to make head with fresh forces. The advantages obtained in one place must be abandoned to subdue the opposition in others; and the moment the part which had been reduced to submission was left to itself, its efforts would be renewed, and its resistance revive.

We should recollect that the extent of the military force must, at all events, be regulated by the resources of the country. For a long time to come, it will not be possible to maintain a large army; and as the means of doing this increase, the population and natural strength of the community will proportionably increase. When will the time arrive that the federal government can raise and maintain an army capable of erecting a despotism over the great body of the people of an immense empire, who are in a situation, through the medium of their State governments, to take measures for their own defence, with all the celerity, regularity, and system of independent nations? The apprehension may be considered as a disease, for which there can be found no cure in the resources of argument and reasoning.

10

JAMES MADISON

FEDERALIST 39

In this essay, Madison reviews, feature by feature, the extent to which the proposed Constitution establishes a "national" government as opposed to a confederation of states. He concludes that the system of government will be a hybrid, "a composition of both." Interestingly, however, Madison tucks into his discussion an institutional issue that would acquire greater significance several years later: the position of the Supreme Court as the final arbiter of disputes between federal and state jurisdictions. In his words, "the tribunal which is ultimately to decide is to be established under the general government."

The last paper having concluded the observations which were meant to introduce a candid survey of the plan of government reported by the convention, we now proceed to the execution of that part of our undertaking.

The first question that offers itself is whether the general form and aspect of the government be strictly republican. It is evident that no other form would be reconcilable with the genius of the people of America; with the fundamental principles of the Revolution; or with that honorable determination which animates every votary of freedom to rest all our political experiments on the capacity of mankind for self-government. If the plan of the convention, therefore, be found to depart from the republican character, its advocates must abandon it as no longer defensible.

What, then, are the distinctive characters of the republican form? Were an answer to this question to be sought, not by recurring to principles but in the application of the term by political writers to the constitutions of different States, no satisfactory one would ever be found. Holland, in which no particle of the supreme authority is derived from the people, has passed almost universally under the denomination of a republic. The same title has been bestowed on Venice, where absolute power over the great body of the people is exercised in the most absolute manner by a small body of hereditary nobles. Poland, which is a mixture of aristocracy and of monarchy in their worst forms, has been dignified with the same appellation. The government of England, which has one republican branch only, combined with an hereditary aristocracy and monarchy, has with equal impropriety been frequently placed on the list of republics. These examples, which are nearly as dissimilar to each other as to a genuine republic, show the extreme inaccuracy with which the term has been used in political disquisitions.

If we resort for a criterion to the different principles on which different forms of government are established, we may define a republic to be, or at least may bestow that name on, a government which derives all its powers directly or indirectly from the great body of the people, and is administered by persons holding their offices during pleasure for a limited period, or during good behavior. It is *essential* to such a government that it be derived from the great body of the society, not from an inconsiderable proportion or a favored class of it; otherwise a handful of tyrannical nobles, exercising their oppressions by a delegation of their powers, might aspire to the rank of republicans and claim for their government the honorable title of republic. It is *sufficient* for such a government that the persons administering it be appointed, either directly or indirectly, by the people; and that they hold their appointments by either of the tenures just specified; otherwise every government in the United States, as well as every other popular government that has been or can be well organized or well executed, would be degraded from the republican character. According to the constitution of every State in the Union, some or other of the officers of government are appointed indirectly only by the people. According to most of them, the chief magistrate himself is so appointed. And according to one, this mode of appointment is extended to one of the co-ordinate branches of the legislature. According to all the constitutions, also, the tenure of the highest offices is extended to a definite period, and in many instances, both within the legislative and executive departments, to a period of years. According to the provisions of most of the constitutions, again, as well as according to the most respectable and received opinions on the subject, the members of the judiciary department are to retain their offices by the firm tenure of good behavior.

On comparing the Constitution planned by the convention with the standard here fixed, we perceived at once that it is, in the most rigid sense, conformable to it. The House of Representatives, like that of one branch at least of all the State legislatures, is elected immediately by the great body of the people. The Senate, like the present Congress and the Senate of Maryland, derives its appointment indirectly from the people. The President is indirectly derived from the choice of the people, according to the example in most of the States. Even the judges, with all other officers of the Union, will, as in the several States, be the choice, though a remote choice, of the people themselves. The duration of the appointments is equally conformable to the republican standard and to the model of State constitutions. The House of Representatives is periodically elective, as in all the States; and for the period of two years, as in the State of South Carolina. The Senate is elective for the period of six years, which is but one year more than the period of the Senate of Maryland, and but two more than that of the Senates of New York and Virginia. The President is to continue in office for the period of four years; as in New York and Delaware the chief magistrate is elected for three years, and in South Carolina for two years. In the other States the election is annual. In several of the States, however, no explicit provision is made for the impeachment of the chief magistrate. And in Delaware and Virginia he is not impeachable till out of office. The President of the United States is impeachable at any time during his continuance in office. The tenure by which the judges are to hold their places is, as it unquestionably ought to be, that of good behavior. The tenure of the ministerial offices generally will be a subject of legal regulation, conformably to the reason of the case and the example of the State constitutions.

Could any further proof be required of the republican complexion of this system, the most decisive one might be found in its absolute prohibition of titles of nobility, both under the federal and the State governments; and in its express guaranty of the republican form to each of the latter.

"But it was not sufficient," say the adversaries of the proposed Constitution, "for the convention to adhere to the republican form. They ought with equal care to have preserved the *federal* form, which regards the Union as a *Confederacy* of sovereign states; instead of which they have framed a *national* government, which regards the Union as a *consolidation* of the States." And it is asked by what authority this bold and radical innovation was undertaken? The handle which has been made of this objection requires that it should be examined with some precision.

Without inquiring into the accuracy of the distinction on which the objection is founded, it will be necessary to a just estimate of its force, first, to ascertain the real character of the government in question; secondly, to inquire how far the convention were authorized to propose such a government; and thirdly, how far the duty they owed to their country could supply any defect of regular authority.

First.—In order to ascertain the real character of the government, it may be considered in relation to the foundation on which it is to be established; to the sources from which its ordinary powers are to be drawn; to the operation of those powers; to the extent of them; and to the authority by which future changes in the government are to be introduced.

On examining the first relation, it appears, on one hand, that the Constitution is to be founded on the assent and ratification of the people of America, given by deputies elected for the special purpose; but, on the other, that this assent and rat- ification is to be given by the people, not as individuals composing one entire nation, but as composing the distinct and independent States to which they respectively belong. It is to be the assent and ratification of the several States, derived from the supreme authority in each State—the authority of the people themselves. The act, therefore, establishing the Constitution will not be a *national* but a *federal* act.

That it will be a federal and not a national act, as these terms are understood by the objectors—the act of the people, as forming so many independent States, not as forming one aggregate nation—is obvious from the single consideration: that it is to result neither from the decision of a *majority* of the people of the Union, nor from that of a *majority* of the States. It must result from the *unanimous* assent of the several States that are parties to it, differing no otherwise from their ordinary assent than in its being expressed, not by the legislative authority, but by that of the people themselves. Were the people regarded in this transaction as forming one nation, the will of the majority of the whole people of the United States would bind the minority, in the same manner as the majority in each State must bind the minority; and the will of the majority must be determined either by a comparison of the individual votes, or by considering the will of the majority of the States as evidence of the will of a majority of the people of the United States. Neither of these rules has been adopted. Each State, in ratifying the Constitu- tion, is considered as a sovereign body independent of all others, and only to be bound by its own voluntary act. In this relation, then, the new Constitution will, if established, be a *federal* and not a *national* constitution.

The next relation is to the sources from which the ordinary powers of govern- ment are to be derived. The House of Representatives will derive its powers from the people of America; and the people will be represented in the same proportion and on the same principle as they are in the legislature of a particular State. So far the government is *national*, not *federal*. The Senate, on the other hand, will derive its powers from the States as political and coequal societies; and these will be represented on the principle of equality in the Senate, as they now are in the existing Congress. So far the government is *federal*, not *national*. The executive power will be derived from a very compound source. The immediate election of the President is to be made by the States in their political characters. The votes allotted to them are in a compound ratio, which considers them partly as distinct and coequal societies, partly as unequal members of the same society. The eventual election, again, is to be made by that branch of the legislature which consists of the national representatives; but in this particular act they are to be thrown into the form of individual delegations from so many distinct and coequal bodies politic. From this aspect of the government it appears to be of a mixed character, presenting at least as many *federal* as *national* features.

The difference between a federal and national government, as it relates to the *operation of the government*, is by the adversaries of the plan of the convention supposed to consist in this, that in the former the powers operate on the political bodies composing the Confederacy in their political capacities; in the latter, on the individual citizens composing the nation in their individual capacities. On trying the Constitution by this criterion, it falls under the *national* not the *federal* character; though perhaps not so completely as has been understood. In several cases, and particularly in the trial of controversies to which States may be parties, they must be viewed and proceeded against in their collective and political capacities only. But the operation of the government on the people in their individual capacities, in its ordinary and most essential proceedings, will, in the sense of its opponents, on the whole, designate it, in this relation, a *national* government.

But if the government be national with regard to the *operation of its powers*, it changes its aspect again when we contemplate it in relation to the extent of its powers. The idea of a national government involves in it not only an authority over the individual citizens, but an indefinite supremacy over all persons and things, so far as they are objects of lawful government. Among a people consolidated into one nation, this supremacy is completely vested in the national legislature. Among communities united for particular purposes, it is vested partly in the general and partly in the municipal legislatures. In the former case, all local authorities are subordinate to the supreme; and may be controlled, directed, or abolished by it at pleasure. In the latter, the local or municipal authorities form distinct and independent portions of the supremacy, no more subject, within their respective spheres, to the general authority than the general authority is subject to them, within its own sphere. In this relation, then, the proposed government cannot be deemed a *national* one; since its jurisdiction extends to certain enumerated objects only, and leaves to the several States a residuary and inviolable sovereignty over all other objects. It is true that in controversies relating to the boundary between the two jurisdictions, the tribunal which is ultimately to decide is to be established under the general government. But this does not change the principle of the case. The decision is to be impartially made, according to the rules of the

Constitution; and all the usual and most effectual precautions are taken to secure this impartiality. Some such tribunal is clearly essential to prevent an appeal to the sword and a dissolution of the compact; and that it ought to be established under the general rather than under the local governments, or, to speak more properly, that it could be safely established under the first alone, is a position not likely to be combated.

If we try the Constitution by its last relation to the authority by which amendments are to be made, we find it neither wholly *national* nor wholly *federal*. Were it wholly national, the supreme and ultimate authority would reside in the *majority* of the people of the Union; and this authority would be competent at all times, like that of a majority of every national society to alter or abolish its established government. Were it wholly federal, on the other hand, the concurrence of each State in the Union would be essential to every alteration that would be binding on all. The mode provided by the plan of the convention is not founded on either of these principles. In requiring more than a majority, and particularly in computing the proportion by *States*, not by *citizens*, it departs from the national and advances towards the *federal* character; in rendering the concurrence of less than the whole number of States sufficient, it loses again the *federal* and partakes of the *national* character.

The proposed Constitution, therefore, even when tested by the rules laid down by its antagonists, is, in strictness, neither a national nor a federal Constitution, but a composition of both. In its foundation it is federal, not national; in the sources from which the ordinary powers of the government are drawn, it is partly federal and partly national; in the operation of these powers, it is national, not federal; in the extent of them, again, it is federal, not national; and, finally in the authoritative mode of introducing amendments, it is neither wholly federal nor wholly national.

11

McCULLOCH v. MARYLAND (1819)

Though it was understood that the Supreme Court would preside over "controversies"
pertaining to the jurisdictional "boundary" between the central government and the
states (as Madison wrote in Federalist 39), *it was hardly clear how elastic that bound-*
ary could become and that assertions of federal authority would prevail. The case of
McCulloch v. Maryland *that came before the court in 1819 set a broad precedent.*
The decision delivered by Chief Justice John Marshall affirmed an expansive inter-
pretation of the enumerated powers of Congress, and invoked the Constitution's
"supremacy clause" to defend a "necessary and proper" act of Congress from state
measures that could challenge or weaken it.

Mr. Chief Justice Marshall delivered the opinion of the Court:

The first question . . . is: Has Congress power to incorporate a bank?

It has been truly said, that this can scarcely be considered as an open question,
entirely unprejudiced by the former proceedings of the nation respecting it. The
principle now contested was introduced at a very early period of our history, has
been recognized by many successive legislatures, and has been acted upon by
the judicial department, in cases of peculiar delicacy, as a law of undoubted
obligation. . . .

The power now contested was exercised by the first Congress elected under the
present Constitution. The bill for incorporating the Bank of the United States did
not steal upon an unsuspecting legislature, and pass unobserved. Its principle was
completely understood, and was opposed with equal zeal and ability. After being
resisted, first in the fair and open field of debate, and afterwards in the executive
cabinet, with as much persevering talent as any measure has ever experienced,
and being supported by arguments which convinced minds as pure and as intelligent as this country can boast, it became a law. The original act was permitted to
expire; but a short experience of the embarrassments to which the refusal to
revive it exposed the government, convinced those who were most prejudiced
against the measure of its necessity, and induced the passage of the present law. It
would require no ordinary share of intrepidity to assert, that a measure adopted
under these circumstances, was a bold and plain usurpation, to which the Constitution gave no countenance. . . .

In discussing this question, the counsel for the state of Maryland have deemed
it of some importance, in the construction of the Constitution, to consider that
instrument not as emanating from the people, but as the act of sovereign and

The question whether in the absence of specific constitutional authorization the federal government
could establish a national bank had been an issue since the 1790s. In 1818, Maryland directly confronted the Bank of the United States, established by Congress in 1816, by requiring that all banks not
chartered in that state pay a fee or tax for the issuance of bank notes. The cashier of the Baltimore
branch of the Bank of the United States, James McCulloch, refused to pay the required tax and was
convicted of violating the law by the Maryland courts. His case was appealed to the U.S. Supreme
Court, where Chief Justice Marshall delivered a wide-ranging discourse on the nature of Congress's
constitutional powers and the states' limited sovereignty. —Eds.

independent states. The powers of the general government, it has been said, are delegated by the states, who alone are truly sovereign; and must be exercised in subordination to the states, who alone possess supreme dominion.

. . . It would be difficult to sustain this proposition. The convention which framed the Constitution was, indeed, elected by the state legislatures. But the instrument, when it came from their hands, was a mere proposal, without obligation, or pretensions to it. It was reported to the then existing Congress of the United States, with a request that it might "be submitted to a convention of delegates, chosen in each state by the people thereof, under the recommendation of its legislature, for their assent and ratification." This mode of proceeding was adopted; and by the convention, by Congress, and by the state legislatures, the instrument was submitted to the *people*. They acted upon it, in the only manner in which they can act safely, effectively, and wisely, on such a subject by assembling in convention. It is true, they assembled in their several states; and where else should they have assembled? No political dreamer was ever wild enough to think of breaking down the lines which separate the states, and of compounding the American people into one common mass. Of consequence, when they act, they act in their states. But the measures they adopt do not, on that account, cease to be the measures of the people themselves, or become the measures of the state governments. . . .

It has been said that the people had already surrendered all their powers to the state sovereignties, and had nothing more to give. But, surely, the question whether they may resume and modify the powers granted to government, does not remain to be settled in this country. Much more might the legitimacy of the general government be doubted, had it been created by the states. The powers delegated to the state sovereignties were to be exercised by themselves, not by a distinct and independent sovereignty, created by themselves. To the formation of a league, such as was the confederation, the state sovereignties were certainly competent. But when, "in order to form a more perfect union," it was deemed necessary to change this alliance into an effective government, possessing great and sovereign powers, and acting directly on the people, the necessity of referring it to the people, and of deriving its powers directly from them, was felt and acknowledged by all.

The government of the Union, then (whatever may be the influence of this fact on the case), is emphatically and truly a government of the people. In form and in substance it emanates from them, its powers are granted by them, and are to be exercised directly on them, and for their benefit.

This government is acknowledged by all to be one of the enumerated powers. . . . But the question respecting the extent of the powers actually granted, is perpetually arising, and will probably continue to rise, as long as our system shall exist. In discussing these questions, the conflicting powers of the general and state governments must be brought into view, and the supremacy of their respective laws, when they are in opposition, must be settled.

If any one proposition could command the universal assent of mankind, we might expect that it would be this—that the government of the Union, though limited in its powers, is supreme within its sphere of action. This would seem to result, necessarily, from its nature. It is the government of all; its powers are delegated by all; it represents all, and acts for all. Though any one state may be willing to control its operations, no state is willing to allow others to control them. The nation, on those subjects on which it can act, must necessarily bind its component parts. But this question is not left to mere reason: the people have, in express terms, decided it, by saying, "this Constitution, and the laws of the United States, which shall be made in pursuance thereof," "shall be the supreme law of the land," and by requiring that the members of the state legislatures, and the officers of the executive and judicial departments of the states, shall take the oath of fidelity to it.

The government of the United States, then, though limited in its powers, is supreme; and its laws, when made in pursuance of the Constitution, form the supreme law of the land, "anything in the constitution or laws of any state, to the contrary notwithstanding."

Among the enumerated powers, we do not find that of establishing a bank or creating a corporation. But there is no phrase in the instrument which, like the Articles of Confederation, excludes incidental or implied powers; and which requires that everything granted shall be expressly and minutely described. Even the Tenth Amendment, which was framed for the purpose of quieting the excessive jealousies which had been excited, omits the word "expressly," and declares only that the powers "not delegated to the United States, nor prohibited to the states, are reserved to the states or to the people"; thus leaving the question, whether the particular power which may become the subject of contest, has been delegated to the one government, or prohibited to the other, to depend on a fair construction of the whole instrument. The men who drew and adopted this amendment had experienced the embarrassments resulting from the insertion of this word in the Articles of Confederation, and probably omitted it, to avoid those embarrassments. A constitution, to contain an accurate detail of all the subdivisions of which its great powers will admit, and of all the means by which they may be carried into execution, would partake of the prolixity of a legal code, and could scarcely be embraced by the human mind. It would, probably, never be understood by the public. Its nature, therefore, requires, that only its great outlines should be marked, its important objects designated, and the minor ingredients which compose those objects, be deduced from the nature of the objects themselves. That this idea was entertained by the framers of the American Constitution, is not only to be inferred from the nature of the instrument, but from the language. Why else were some of the limitations, found in the ninth section of Article I, introduced? It is also, in some degree, warranted, by their having omitted to use any restrictive term which might prevent its receiving a fair and just interpretation. In considering this question, then, we must never forget, that it is a *constitution* we are expounding.

Although, among the enumerated powers of government, we do not find the work "bank," or "incorporation," we find the great powers, to lay and collect taxes; to borrow money; to regulate commerce; to declare and conduct war; and to raise and support armies and navies. The sword and the purse, all the external relations, and no inconsiderable portion of the industry of the nation, are intrusted to its government. It can never be pretended, that these vast powers draw after them others of inferior importance, merely because they are inferior. Such an idea can never be advanced. But it may with great reason be contended, that a government, intrusted with such ample powers, on the due execution of which the happiness and prosperity of the nation so vitally depends, must also be intrusted with ample means for their execution. The power being given, it is the interest of the nation to facilitate its execution. It can never be their interest, and cannot be presumed to have been their intention, to clog and embarrass its execution, by withholding the most appropriate means. Throughout this vast republic . . . , from the Atlantic to the Pacific, revenue is to be collected and expended, armies are to be marched and supported. The exigencies of the nation may require, that the treasure raised in the north should be transported to the south, that raised in the east, conveyed to the west, or that this order should be reversed. Is that construction of the Constitution to be preferred, which would render these operations difficult, hazardous, and expensive? Can we adopt that construction (unless the words imperiously require it), which would impute to the framers of that instrument, when granting these powers for the public good, the intention of impeding their exercise by withholding a choice of means? If, indeed, such be the mandate of the Constitution, we have only to obey; but that instrument does not profess to enumerate the means by which the powers it confers may be executed; nor does it prohibit the creation of a corporation, if the existence of such a being be essential to the beneficial exercise of those powers. It is, then, the subject of fair inquiry, how far such means may be employed. . . .

The creation of a corporation, it is said, appertains to sovereignty. This is admitted. But to what portion of sovereignty does it appertain? Does it belong to one more than to another? . . . The power of creating a corporation, though appertaining to sovereignty, is not, like the power of making war, or levying taxes, or of regulating commerce, a great substantive and independent power, which cannot be implied as incidental to other powers, or used as a means of executing them. It is never the end for which other powers are exercised, but a means by which other objects are accomplished. No contributions are made to charity for the sake of an incorporation, but a corporation is created to administer the charity; no seminary of learning is instituted in order to be incorporated, but the corporate character is conferred to subserve the purposes of education. . . . The power of creating a corporation is never used for its own sake, but for the purpose of effecting something else. No sufficient reason is, therefore, perceived, why it may not pass as incidental to those powers which are expressly given, if it be a direct mode of executing them.

But the Constitution of the United States has not left the right of Congress to employ the necessary means for the execution of the powers conferred on the government to general reasoning. To its enumeration of powers is added that of making "all laws which shall be necessary and proper, for carrying into execution the foregoing powers, and all other powers vested by this Constitution, in the government of the United States, or in any department thereof."

The counsel for the state of Maryland have urged . . . that this clause, though in terms a grant of power, is not so in effect; but is really restrictive of the general right, which might otherwise be implied, of selecting means for executing the enumerated powers. . . .

. . . [T]he argument on which most reliance is placed, is drawn from the peculiar language of this clause. Congress is not empowered by it to make all laws, which may have relation to the powers conferred on the government, but such only as may be "necessary and proper" for carrying them into execution. The word "necessary" is considered as controlling the whole sentence, and as limiting the right to pass laws for the execution of the granted powers, to such as are indispensable, and without which the power would be nugatory. That it excludes the choice of means, and leaves to Congress, in each case, that only which is most direct and simple.

Is it true, that this is the sense in which the world "necessary" is always used? Does it always import an absolute physical necessity, so strong, that one thing, to which another may be termed necessary, cannot exist without that other? We think it does not. If reference be had to its use, in the common affairs of the world, or in approved authors, we find that it frequently imports no more than that one thing is convenient, or useful, or essential to another. To employ the means necessary to an end, is generally understood as employing any means calculated to produce the end, and not as being confined to those single means, without which the end would be entirely unattainable. . . . A thing may be necessary, very necessary, absolutely or indispensably necessary. To no mind would the same idea be conveyed by these several phrases. This comment on the word is well illustrated by the passage cited at the bar, from the tenth section of Article I of the Constitution. It is, we think, impossible to compare the sentence which prohibits a state from laying "imposts, or duties on imports or exports, except what may be *absolutely* necessary for executing its inspection laws," with that which authorizes Congress "to make all laws which shall be necessary and proper for carrying into execution" the powers of the general government, without feeling a conviction, that the convention understood itself to change materially the meaning of the word "necessary" by prefixing the word "absolutely." This word, then, like others, is used in various senses; and, in its construction, the subject, the context, the intention of the person using them, are all to be taken into view.

Let this be done in the case under consideration. The subject is the execution of those great powers on which the welfare of a nation essentially depends. It must have been the intention of those who gave these powers, to insure, as far as human prudence could insure, their beneficial execution. This could not be done, by confining the choice of means to such narrow limits as not to leave it in the power of Congress to adopt any which might be appropriate, and which were conducive to the end. This provision is made in a constitution, intended to endure for ages to come, and consequently, to be adapted to the various *crises* of human affairs. To have prescribed the means by which government should, in all future time, execute its powers, would have been to change, entirely, the character of the instrument, and give it the properties of a legal code. It would have been an unwise attempt to provide, by immutable rules, for exigencies which, if foreseen at all, must have been seen dimly, and which can be best provided for as they occur. To have declared that the best means shall not be used, but those alone without which the power given would be nugatory, have been to deprive the legislature of the capacity to avail itself of experience, to exercise its reason, and to accommodate its legislation to circumstances. . . .

Take, for example, the power "to establish post offices and post roads." This power is executed by the single act of making the establishment. But, from this has been inferred the power and duty of carrying the mail along the post road, from one post office to another. And, from this implied power, has again been inferred the right to punish those who steal letters from the post office, or rob the mail. It may be said, with some plausibility, that the right to carry the mail, and to punish those who rob it, is not indispensably necessary to the establishment of a post office and post road. This right is indeed essential to the beneficial exercise of the power, but not indispensably necessary to its existence. So, of the punishment of the crimes of stealing or falsifying a record or process of a court of the United States, or of perjury in such court. To punish these offences is certainly conducive to the due administration of justice. But courts may exist, and may decide the causes brought before them, though such crimes escape punishment. . . .

If this limited construction of the word "necessary" must be abandoned, in order to punish, whence is derived the rule which would reinstate it, when the government would carry its powers into execution, by means not vindictive in their nature? If the word "necessary" means "needful," "requisite," "essential," "conducive to," in order to let in the power of punishment for the infraction of law; why is it not equally comprehensive, when required to authorize the use of means which facilitate the execution of the powers of government, without the infliction of punishment?

In ascertaining the sense in which the word "necessary" is used in this clause of the Constitution, we may derive some aid from that with which it is associated. Congress shall have power "to make all laws which shall be necessary and proper to carry into execution" the powers of the government. If the word "necessary" was used in that strict and rigorous sense for which the counsel for the state of Maryland contend, it would be an extraordinary departure from the usual course of the human mind, as exhibited in composition, to add a word, the only possible effect of which is, to qualify that strict and rigorous meaning; to present to the mind the idea of some choice of means of legislation, not strained and compressed within the narrow limits for which gentlemen contend.

But the argument which most conclusively demonstrates the error of the construction contended for by the counsel for the state of Maryland, is founded on the intention of the convention, as manifested in the whole clause. . . .

We think so for the following reasons:

1st. The clause is placed among the powers of Congress, not among the limitations on those powers.

2d. Its terms purport to enlarge, not to diminish the powers vested in the government. It purports to be an additional power, not a restriction on those already granted. . . . The framers of the Constitution wished its adoption, and well knew that it would be endangered by its strength, not by its weakness. Had they been capable of using language which would convey to the eye one idea, and, after deep reflection, impress on the mind, another, they would rather have disguised the grant of power, than its limitation. If then, their intention had been, by this clause, to restrain the free use of means which might otherwise have been implied, that intention would have been inserted in another place, and would have been expressed in terms resembling these. "In carrying into execution the foregoing powers and all others," &c., "no laws shall be passed but such as are necessary and proper." Had the intention been to make this clause restrictive, it would unquestionably have been so in form as well as in effect.

The result of the most careful and attentive consideration bestowed upon this clause is, that if it does not enlarge, it cannot be construed to restrain the powers of Congress, or to impair the right of the legislature to exercise its best judgment in the selection of measures, to carry into execution the constitutional powers of the government. If no other motive for its insertion can be suggested, a sufficient one is found in the desire to remove all doubts respecting the right to legislate on that vast mass of incidental powers which must be involved in the Constitution, if that instrument be not a splendid bauble.

We admit, as all must admit, that the powers of the government are limited, and that its limits are not to be transcended. But we think the sound construction of the Constitution must allow to the national legislature that discretion, with respect to the means by which the powers it confers are to be carried into execution, which will enable that body to perform the high duties assigned to it, in the manner most beneficial to the people. Let the end be legitimate, let it be within the scope of the Constitution, and all means which are appropriate, which are plainly adapted to that end, which are not prohibited, but consistent with the letter and spirit of the Constitution, are constitutional. . . .

It being the opinion of the Court, that the act incorporating the bank is constitutional; and that the power of establishing a branch in the state of Maryland might be properly exercised by the bank itself, we proceed to inquire—

Whether the state of Maryland may, without violating the Constitution, tax that branch? . . .

The power of Congress to create, and of course, to continue, the bank, was the subject of the preceding part of this opinion; and is no longer to be considered as questionable.

That the power of taxing it by the states may be exercised so as to destroy it, is too obvious to be denied. But taxation is said to be an absolute power, which acknowledges no other limits than those expressly prescribed in the Constitution, and like sovereign power of every other description, is trusted to the discretion of those who use it. But the very terms of this argument admit, that the sovereignty of the state, in the article of taxation itself, is subordinate to, and may be controlled by, the Constitution of the United States. How far it has been controlled by that instrument must be a question of construction. In making this construction, no principle not declared, can be admissible, which would defeat the legitimate operations of a supreme government. It is of the very essence of supremacy, to remove all obstacles to its action within its own sphere, and so to modify every power vested in subordinate governments, as to exempt its own operations from their own influence. This effect need not be stated in terms. It is so involved in the declaration of supremacy, so necessarily implied in it, that the expression of it could not make it more certain. We must, therefore, keep it in view, while construing the Constitution. . . .

The sovereignty of a state extends to everything which exists by its own authority, or is introduced by its permission; but does it extend to those means which are employed by Congress to carry into execution—powers conferred on that body by the people of the United States? We think it demonstrable that it does not. Those powers are not given by the people of a single state. They are given by the people of the United States, to a government whose laws, made in pursuance of the Constitution, are declared to be supreme. Consequently, the people of a single state cannot confer a sovereignty which will extend over them.

If we measure the power of taxation residing in a state, by the extent of sovereignty which the people of a single state possess, and can confer on its government, we have an intelligible standard, applicable to every case to which the power may be applied. We have a principle which leaves the power of taxing the people and property of a state unimpaired; which leaves to a state the command of all its resources, and which places beyond its reach, all those powers which are conferred by the people of the United States on the government of the Union, and all those means which are given for the purpose of carrying those powers into execution. We have a principle which is safe for the states, and safe for the Union. We are relieved, as we ought to be, from clashing sovereignty; from interfering powers; from a repugnancy between a right in one government to pull down, what there is an acknowledged right in another to build up; from the incompatibility of a right in one government to destroy, what there is a right in another to preserve. We are not driven to the perplexing inquiry, so unfit for the judicial department, what degree of taxation is the legitimate use, and what degree may amount to the abuse of the power. . . .

. . . That the power to tax involves the power to destroy; that the power to destroy may defeat and render useless the power to create; that there is a plain repugnancy in conferring on one government a power to control the constitutional measures of another, which other, with respect to those very measures, is declared to be supreme over that which exerts the control, are propositions not to be denied. But all inconsistencies are to be reconciled by the magic of the word *confidence*. Taxation, it is said, does not necessarily and unavoidably destroy. To carry it to the excess of destruction, would be an abuse, to presume which, would banish that confidence which is essential to all government.

But is this a case of confidence? Would the people of any state trust those of another with a power to control the most significant operations of their state government? We know they would not. Why, then, should we suppose, that the people of any one state should be willing to trust those of another with a power to control the operations of a government to which they have confided their most important and valuable interests? In the legislature of the Union alone, are all represented. The legislature of the Union alone, therefore, can be trusted by the people with the power of controlling measures which concern all, in the confidence that it will not be abused. . . .

If we apply the principle for which the state of Maryland contends, to the Constitution generally, we shall find it capable of changing totally the character of that instrument. We shall find it capable of arresting all the measures of the government, and of prostrating it at the foot of the states. The American people have declared their Constitution and the laws made in pursuance thereof, to be supreme; but this principle would transfer the supremacy, in fact, to the states.

If the states may tax one instrument, employed by the government in the execution of its powers, they may tax any and every other instrument. They may tax the mail; they may tax the mint; they may tax patent rights; they may tax the papers of the custom-house; they may tax judicial process; they may tax all the means employed by the government, to an excess which would defeat all the ends of government. This was not intended by the American people. . . .

It has also been insisted, that, as the power of taxation in the general and state governments is acknowledged to be concurrent, every argument which would sustain the right of the general government to tax banks chartered by the states, will equally sustain the rights of the states to tax banks chartered by the general government.

But the two cases are not on the same reason. The people of all the states have created the general government, and have conferred upon it the general power of taxation. The people of all the states, and the states themselves, are represented in Congress, and, by their representatives, exercise this power. When they tax the chartered institutions of the states, they tax their constituents; and these taxes must be uniform. But when a state taxes the operations of the government of the United States, it acts upon institutions created, not by their own constituents, but by people over whom they claim no control. It acts upon the measures of a government created by others as well as themselves, for the benefit of others in common with themselves. The difference is that which always exists, and always must exist, between the action of the whole on a part, and the action of a part on the whole—between the laws of a government declared which, when in opposition to those laws, is not supreme.

But if the full application of this argument could be admitted, it might bring into question the right of Congress to tax the state banks, and could not prove the right of the states to tax the Bank of the United States.

The Court has bestowed on this subject its most deliberate consideration. The result is a conviction that the states have no power, by taxation or otherwise, to retard, impede, burden, or in any manner control, the operations of the constitutional laws enacted by Congress to carry into execution the powers vested in the general government. This is, we think, the unavoidable consequence of that supremacy which the Constitution had declared.

We are unanimously of opinion, that the law passed by the legislature of Maryland, imposing a tax on the Bank of the United States, is unconstitutional and void.

This opinion does not deprive the states of any resources which they originally possessed. It does not extend to a tax paid by the real property of the bank, in common with the other real property within the state, nor to a tax imposed on the interest which the citizens of Maryland may hold in this institution, in common with other property of the same description throughout the state. But this is a tax on the operations of the bank, and is, consequently, a tax on the operation of an instrument employed by the government of the Union to carry its powers into execution. Such a tax must be unconstitutional.

Reversed.

PART THREE

POLITICAL POWER

What is the actual distribution of power in the American polity? No issue has pre-occupied political scientists more or provoked greater debate among them. It is easy to see why. Democracy is predicated on the dispersion of political power. An excessive concentration of power in the hands of few individuals or groups implies, not democracy, but autocracy or oligarchy. Thus, to answer the question "How democratic is the American regime?" one must first ask (as Robert Dahl docs in the title of his celebrated book), "Who governs?"

Over the years, those who have pondered this issue have divided themselves roughly into two schools of thought. One sees American government as characterized by elitism, the other by pluralism. The first theory was most forcefully expressed by C. Wright Mills in his book *The Power Elite*. (The article we have chosen to reprint here is essentially an abridged version of that work.) According to Mills, American society is dominated by a "triangle of power" composed of corporate leaders, top military officers, and a handful of key political leaders. Some elite theorists believe "The Establishment" is limited to fewer participants (chiefly corporate interests, for instance), while others would widen Mills's triangle to include, say, the major communications media and even the big labor leaders. But the gist of the argument is the same: government is manipulated, largely from without, by a few top leaders who possess great advantages in wealth, status, and organizational position. Other actors and institutions, such as the mass political parties and the Congress, that once provided autonomous bases of power, are now increasingly inert or subservient to the "power elite" that operates mostly in and around the national executive. Although Mills is careful not to assert that the power elite is engaged in some sort of conscious conspiracy to subvert the democratic system, he perceives subtle forces enabling its members to concert their actions. Among the conditions facilitating coordination are a coincidence of interest (as between defense contractors and the military); the interconnected patterns of recruitment between public and private institutions; and the social milieus at the highest reaches of government and business (i.e., the intermingling of men with similar social origins, educations, professional backgrounds, and lifestyles).

Although the alternative, pluralist theory, has no single intellectual parent, Robert Dahl's work is probably the best known exposition of it. At the heart of the pluralist perspective is the notion that *political resources* are not limited to wealth and social standing, but encompass a broad range of factors that can be translated into political power. In fact, as Dahl contends in the brief excerpt that follows, political resources now tend to be so diverse and widely scattered in American politics that no single elite can have anything like a monopoly on them. Rather, the effectiveness of any given set of resources depends in large measure on the nature of the particular issue in question; the forms of influence that may prove efficient in decision making on, say, foreign policy may be quite distinct from those required to shape some domestic program. Accordingly, different groups are influential in different issue areas. Note that Dahl does not claim that political resources are distributed equally in society, only that the distribution was more uneven in the past than it is now; control has moved, in his terms, from a system of "cumulative inequalities" to one of "dispersed inequalities." Put another way, elites continue to govern, even in the pluralist model, but there is a difference: here we have a multiplicity of elites. They are seldom in collusion with one another (though ad hoc coalitions or alliances often arise); instead, the elites tend to be independent and competitive. Indeed, so numerous are the conflicting groups that all, or almost all, relevant interests in society have a chance to affect government policy.

At the same time, the pluralists sometimes overstate the diffusion of power in American life. (Dahl may be right in saying that "certainly no group of more than a few individuals is entirely lacking in some influence resources." Yet, at least before the civil rights legislation of the 1960s, the influence resources of, for example, many blacks were, for all intents and purposes, trivial.) And the pluralists sometimes underemphasize the extent to which national policy is determined, not by discrete organizations, but by complex networks of public and private interests.

At bottom, the dispute between exponents of the two schools may never be resolved conclusively. To resolve it, political scientists would have to ascertain the manifestations of power and the wielders of such power in all contexts. A methodology capable of doing this perspicuously does not exist. As Peter Bachrach and Morton S. Baratz demonstrate in their brilliant article "Two Faces of Power" (1962), it is misleading to assume that persons reputed to be powerful necessarily *exercise* power. By the same token, it is not enough to observe overt instances of decision making in selected issue areas to discern exactly who the influential actors are. Power is sometimes exerted covertly, where no external investigator can see it. At times, also, policies will be made, not in response to political pressures, but in *anticipation* of them. In such cases, no act of power can be identified; there is only an unstated quid pro quo. Finally, power is often exercised by confining the scope of decision making to "safe" issues—that is, by delimiting the political agenda. A given set of decision makers may appear, to the outside observer, as highly active in certain visible spheres. But behind the scenes may lie an entirely different group, one that defines the rules of the game (so to speak) and that is able to decide *what sorts* of issues can be freely ventilated. In the last analysis, with so many possible forms that political power can take, a rigorous, definitive response to the question "Who really rules?" is likely to remain elusive.

12

C. WRIGHT MILLS

THE STRUCTURE OF POWER
IN AMERICAN SOCIETY

Have national polities in the United States been dominated by a few elites with inter-locking interests and membership? C. Wright Mills (1916–1962) has hardly been the only social scientist who subscribed to this proposition, but he was perhaps its best known exponent. Mills, a sociologist at Columbia University, fully developed the notion of an essentially oligarchic pattern of governance in his famous book, The Power Elite *(1956). The following piece is basically an abridged version of that work.*

I

Power has to do with whatever decisions men make about the arrangements under which they live, and about the events which make up the history of their times. Events that are beyond human decision do happen; social arrangements do change without benefit of explicit decision. But in so far as such decisions are made, the problem of who is involved in making them is the basic problem of power. In so far as they could be made but are not, the problem becomes who fails to make them?

We cannot today merely assume that in the last resort men must always be governed by their own consent. For among the means of power which now prevail is the power to manage and to manipulate the consent of men. That we do not know the limits of such power, and that we hope it does have limits, does not remove the fact that much power today is successfully employed without the sanction of the reason or the conscience of the obedient.

Surely nowadays we need not argue that, in the last resort, coercion is the 'final' form of power. But then, we are by no means constantly at the last resort. Authority (power that is justified by the beliefs of the voluntarily obedient) and manipulation (power that is wielded unbeknown to the powerless)—must also be considered, along with coercion. In fact, the three types must be sorted out whenever we think about power.

In the modern world, we must bear in mind, power is often not so authoritative as it seemed to be in the medieval epoch: ideas which justify rulers no longer seem so necessary to their exercise of power. At least for many of the great decisions of our time—especially those of an international sort—mass 'persuasion' has not been 'necessary'; the fact is simply accomplished. Furthermore, such ideas as are available to the powerful are often neither taken up nor used by them.

A draft of this lecture was presented at a residential weekend at the Beatrice Webb House, Surrey, on March 2, 1957, and at the University of Frankfurt on May 3, 1957. A more detailed exposition of the general argument, as well as documentation, will be found in *The Power Elite* (New York: Oxford University Press), 1956.

Such ideologies usually arise as a response to an effective debunking of power; in the United States such opposition has not been effective enough recently to create the felt need for new ideologies of rule.

There has, in fact, come about a situation in which many who have lost faith in prevailing loyalties have not acquired new ones, and so pay no attention to politics of any kind. They are not radical, not liberal, not conservative, not reactionary. They are inactionary. They are out of it. If we accept the Greek's definition of the idiot as an altogether private man, then we must conclude that many American citizens are now idiots. And I should not be surprised, although I do not know, if there were not some such idiots even in Germany. This—and I use the word with care—this spiritual condition seems to me the key to many modern troubles of political intellectuals, as well as the key to much political bewilderment in modern society. Intellectual 'conviction' and moral 'belief' are not necessary, in either the rulers or the ruled, for a ruling power to persist and even to flourish. So far as the role of ideologies is concerned, their frequent absences and the prevalence of mass indifference are surely two of the major political facts about the western societies today.

How large a role any explicit decisions do play in the making of history is itself an historical problem. For how large that role may be depends very much upon the means of power that are available at any given time in any given society. In some societies, the innumerable actions of innumerable men modify their milieux, and so gradually modify the structure itself. These modifications—the course of history—go on behind the backs of men. History is drift, although in total 'men make it.' Thus, innumerable entrepreneurs and innumerable consumers by ten thousand decisions per minute may shape and re-shape the free-market economy. Perhaps this was the chief kind of limitation Marx had in mind when he wrote, in *The 18th Brumaire*: that 'Men make their own history, but they do not make it just as they please; they do not make it under circumstances chosen by themselves. . . .'

But in other societies—certainly in the United States and in the Soviet Union today—a few men may be so placed within the structure that by their decisions they modify the milieux of many other men, and in fact nowadays the structural conditions under which most men live. Such elites of power also make history under circumstances not chosen altogether by themselves, yet compared with other men, and compared with other periods of world history, these circumstances do indeed seem less limiting.

I should contend that 'men are free to make history', but that some men are indeed much freer than others. For such freedom requires access to the means of decision and of power by which history can now be made. It has not always been so made; but in the later phases of the modern epoch it is. It is with reference to this epoch that I am contending that if men do not make history, they tend increasingly to become the utensils of history-makers as well as the mere objects of indeed seem less limiting [sic].

The history of modern society may readily be understood as the story of the enlargement and the centralization of the means of power—in economic, in political, and in military institutions. The rise of industrial society has involved these developments in the means of economic production. The rise of the nation-state has involved similar developments in the means of violence and in those of political administration.

In the western societies, such transformations have generally occurred gradually, and many cultural traditions have restrained and shaped them. In most of the Soviet societies, they are happening very rapidly indeed and without the great discourse of western civilization, without the Renaissance and without the Reformation, which so greatly strengthened and gave political focus to the idea of freedom. In those societies, the enlargement and the coordination of all the means of power has occurred more brutally, and from the beginning under tightly centralized authority. But in both types, the means of power have now become international in scope and similar in form. To be sure, each of them has its own ups and downs; neither is as yet absolute; how they are run differs quite sharply.

Yet so great is the reach of the means of violence, and so great the economy required to produce and support them, that we have in the immediate past witnessed the consolidation of these two world centres, either of which dwarfs the power of Ancient Rome. As we pay attention to the awesome means of power now available to quite small groups of men we come to realize that Caesar could do less with Rome than Napoleon with France; Napoleon less with France than Lenin with Russia. But what was Caesar's power at its height compared with the power of the changing inner circles of Soviet Russia and the temporary administrations of the United States? We come to real realize — indeed they continually remind us — how a few men have access to the means by which in a few days continents can be turned into thermonuclear wastelands. That the facilities of power are so enormously enlarged and so decisively centralized surely means that the powers of quite small groups of men, which we may call elites, are now of literally inhuman consequence.

My concern here is not with the international scene but with the United States in the middle of the twentieth century. I must emphasize 'in the middle of the twentieth century' because in our attempt to understand any society we come upon images which have been drawn from its past and which often confuse our attempt to confront its present reality. That is one minor reason why history is the shank of any social science: we must study it if only to rid ourselves of it. In the United States, there are indeed many such images and usually they have to do with the first half of the nineteenth century. At that time the economic facilities of the United States were very widely dispersed and subject to little or to no central authority.

The state watched in the night but was without decisive voice in the day.

One man meant one rifle and the militia were without centralized orders.

Any American as old-fashioned as I can only agree with R. H. Tawney that 'Whatever the future may contain, the past has shown no more excellent social order than that in which the mass of the people were the masters of the holdings which they ploughed and the tools with which they worked, and could boast . . . It is a quietness to a man's mind to live upon his own and to know his heir certain.'

But then we must immediately add: all that is of the past and of little relevance to our understanding of the United States today. Within this society three broad levels of power may now be distinguished. I shall begin at the top and move downward.

II

The power to make decisions of national and international consequence is now so clearly seated in political, military, and economic institutions that other areas of society seem off to the side and, on occasion, readily subordinated to these. The scattered institutions of religion, education and family are increasingly shaped by the big three, in which history-making decisions now regularly occur. Behind this fact there is all the push and drive of a fabulous technology; for these three institutional orders have incorporated this technology and now guide it, even as it shapes and paces their development.

As each has assumed its modern shape, its effects upon the other two have become greater, and the traffic between the three has increased. There is no longer, on the one hand, an economy, and, on the other, a political order, containing a military establishment unimportant to politics and to moneymaking. There is a political economy numerously linked with military order and decision. This triangle of power is now a structural fact, and it is the key to any understanding of the higher circles in America today. For as each of these domains has coincided with the others, as decisions in each have become broader, the leading men of each—the high military, the corporation executives, the political directorate—have tended to come together to form the power elite of America.

The political order, once composed of several dozen states with a weak federal-centre, has become an executive apparatus which has taken up into itself many powers previously scattered, legislative as well as administrative, and which now reaches into all parts of the social structure. The long-time tendency of business and government to become more closely connected has since World War II reached a new point of explicitness. Neither can now be seen clearly as a distinct world. The growth of executive government does not mean merely the 'enlargement of government' as some kind of autonomous bureaucracy: under American conditions, it has meant the ascendency of the corporation man into political eminence. Already during the New Deal, such men had joined the political directorate; as of World War II they came to dominate it. Long involved with government, now they have moved into quite full direction of the economy of the war effort and of the post-war era.

The economy, once a great scatter of small productive units in somewhat automatic balance, has become internally dominated by a few hundred corporations, administratively and politically interrelated, which together hold the keys to economic decision. This economy is at once a permanent-war economy and a private-corporation economy. The most important relations of the corporation to the state now rest on the coincidence between military and corporate interests, as defined by the military and the corporate rich, and accepted by politicians and public. Within the elite as a whole, this coincidence of military domain and corporate realm strengthens both of them and further subordinates the merely political man. Not the party politician, but the corporation executive, is now more likely to sit with the military to answer the question: what is to be done?

The military order, once a slim establishment in a context of civilian distrust, has become the largest and most expensive feature of government; behind smiling public relations, it has all the grim and clumsy efficiency of a great and sprawling bureaucracy. The high military have gained decisive political and economic relevance. The seemingly permanent military threat places a premium upon them and virtually all political and economic actions are now judged in terms of military definitions of reality: the higher military have ascended to a firm position within the power elite of our time.

In part at least this is a result of an historical fact, pivotal for the years since 1939; the attention of the elite has shifted from domestic problems—centered in the thirties around slump—to international problems—centered in the forties and fifties around war. By long historical usage, the government of the United States has been shaped by domestic clash and balance; it does not have suitable agencies and traditions for the democratic handling of international affairs. In considerable part, it is in this vacuum that the power elite has grown.

(i) To understand the unity of this power elite, we must pay attention to the psychology of its several members in their respective milieux. In so far as the power elite is composed of men of similar origin and education, of similar career and style of life, their unity may be said to rest upon the fact that they are of similar social type, and to lead to the fact of their easy intermingling. This kind of unity reaches its frothier apex in the sharing of that prestige which is to be had in the world of the celebrity. It achieves a more solid culmination in the fact of the interchangeability of positions between the three dominant institutional orders. It is revealed by considerable traffic of personnel within and between these three, as well as by the rise of specialized go-betweens as in the new style high-level lobbying.

(ii) Behind such psychological and social unity are the structure and the mechanics of those institutional hierarchies over which the political directorate, the corporate rich, and the high military now preside. How each of these hierarchies is shaped and what relations it has with the others determine in large part the relations of their rulers. Were these hierarchies scattered and disjointed, then their respective elites might tend to be scattered and disjointed; but if they have many interconnections and points of coinciding interest, then their elites tend to form a coherent kind of grouping. The unity of the elite is not a simple reflection of the unity of institutions, but men and institutions are always related; that is why we must understand the elite today in connection with such institutional trends as the development of a permanent-war establishment, alongside a privately incorporated economy, inside a virtual political vacuum. For the men at the top have been selected and formed by such institutional trends.

(iii) Their unity, however, does not rest solely upon psychological similarity and social intermingling, nor entirely upon the structural blending of commanding positions and common interests. At times it is the unity of a more explicit co-ordination.

To say that these higher circles are increasingly coordinated, that this is *one* basis of their unity, and that at times—as during open war—such coordination is quite wilful, is not to say that the co-ordination is total or continuous, or even that it is very surefooted. Much less is it to say that the power elite has emerged as the realization of a plot. Its rise cannot be adequately explained in any psychological terms.

Yet we must remember that institutional trends may be defined as opportunities by those who occupy the command posts. Once such opportunities are recognized, men may avail themselves of them. Certain types of men from each of these three areas, more far-sighted than others, have actively promoted the liaison even before it took its truly modern shape. Now more have come to see that their several interests can more easily be realized if they work together, in informal as well as in formal ways, and accordingly they have done so.

The idea of the power elite is of course an interpretation. It rests upon and it enables us to make sense of major institutional trends, the social similarities and psychological affinities of the men at the top. But the idea is also based upon what has been happening on the middle and lower levels of power, to which I now turn.

III

There are of course other interpretations of the American system of power. The most usual is that it is a moving balance of many competing interests. The image of balance, at least in America, is derived from the idea of the economic market: in the nineteenth century, the balance was thought to occur between a great scatter of individuals and enterprises; in the twentieth century, it is thought to occur between great interest blocs. In both views, the politician is the key man of power because he is the broker of many conflicting powers.

I believe that the balance and the compromise in American society—the 'countervailing powers' and the 'veto groups', of parties and associations, of strata and unions—must now be seen as having mainly to do with the middle levels of power. It is these middle levels that the political journalist and the scholar of politics are most likely to understand and to write about—if only because, being mainly middle class themselves, they are closer to them. Moreover these levels provide the noisy content of most 'political' news and gossip; the images of these levels are more or less in accord with the folklore of how democracy works; and, if the master-image of balance is accepted, many intellectuals, especially in their current patrioteering, are readily able to satisfy such political optimism as they wish to feel. Accordingly, liberal interpretations of what is happening in the United States are now virtually the only interpretations that are widely distributed.

But to believe that the power system reflects a balancing society is, I think, to confuse the present era with earlier times, and to confuse its top and bottom with its middle levels.

By the top levels, as distinguished from the middle, I intend to refer, first of all, to the scope of the decisions that are made. At the top today, these decisions have to do with all the issues of war and peace. They have also to do with slump and poverty which are now so very much problems of international scope. I intend also to refer to whether or not the groups that struggle politically have a chance to gain the positions from which such top decisions are made, and indeed whether their members do usually hope for such top national command. Most of the competing interests which make up the clang and clash of American politics are strictly concerned with their slice of the existing pie. Labour unions, for example, certainly have no policies of an international sort other than those which given unions adopt for the strict economic protection of their members. Neither do farm organizations. The actions of such middle-level powers may indeed have consequence for top-level policy; certainly at times they hamper these policies. But they are not truly concerned with them, which means of course that their influence tends to be quite irresponsible.

The facts of the middle levels may in part be understood in terms of the rise of the power elite. The expanded and centralized and interlocked hierarchies over which the power elite preside have encroached upon the old balance and relegated it to the middle level. But there are also independent developments of the middle levels. These, it seems to me, are better understood as an affair of intrenched and provincial demands than as a centre of national decision. As such, the middle level often seems much more of a stalemate than a moving balance.

(i) The middle level of politics is not a forum in which there are debated the big decisions of national and international life. Such debate is not carried on by nationally responsible parties representing and clarifying alternative policies. There are no such parties in the United States. More and more, fundamental issues never come to any point or decision before the Congress, much less before the electorate in party campaigns. In the case of Formosa, in the spring of 1955, the Congress abdicated all debate concerning events and decisions which surely bordered on war. The same is largely true of the 1957 crisis in the Middle East. Such decisions now regularly by-pass the Congress, and are never clearly focused issues for public decision.

The American political campaign distracts attention from national and international issues, but that is not to say that there are no issues in these campaigns. In each district and state, issues are set up and watched by organized interests of sovereign local importance. The professional politician is of course a party politician, and the two parties are semi-feudal organizations: they trade patronage and other favours for votes and for protection. The differences between them, so far as national issues are concerned, are very narrow and very mixed up. Often each seems to be forty-eight parties, one to each state; and accordingly, the politician as campaigner and as Congressman is not concerned with national party lines, if any are discernible. Often he is not subject to any effective national party discipline. He speaks for the interests of his own constituency, and he is concerned with national issues only in so far as they affect the interests effectively organized there, and hence his chances of re-election. That is why, when he does speak of national matters, the result is so often such an empty rhetoric. Seated in his sovereign locality, the politician is not at the national summit. He is on and of the middle levels of power.

(ii) Politics is not an arena in which free and independent organizations truly connect the lower and middle levels of society with the top levels of decision. Such organizations are not an effective and major part of American life today. As more people are drawn into the political arena, their associations become mass in scale, and the power of the individual becomes dependent upon them; to the extent that they are effective, they have become larger, and to that extent they have become less accessible to the influence of the individual. This is a central fact about associations in any mass society: it is of most consequence for political parties and for trade unions.

In the thirties, it often seemed that labour would become all insurgent power independent of corporation and state. Organized labour was then emerging for the first time on an American scale, and the only political sense of direction it needed was the slogan, 'organize the unorganized': Now without the mandate of the slump, labour remains without political direction. Instead of economic and political struggles it has become deeply entangled in administrative routines with both corporation and state. One of its major functions, as a vested interest of the new society, is the regulation of such irregular tendencies as may occur among the rank and file.

There is nothing, it seems to me, in the make-up of the current labour leadership to allow us to expect that it can or that it will lead, rather than merely react. In so far as it fights at all it fights over a share of the goods of a single way of life and not over that way of life itself. The typical labour leader in the U.S.A. today is better understood as an adaptive creature of the main business drift than as an independent actor in a truly national context.

(iii) The idea that this society is a balance of powers requires us to assume that the units in balance are of more or less equal power and that they are truly independent of one another. These assumptions have rested, it seems clear, upon the historical importance of a large and independent middle class. In the latter nineteenth century and during the Progressive Era, such a class of farmers and small businessmen fought politically—and lost—their last struggle for a paramount role in national decision. Even then, their aspirations seemed bound to their own imagined past.

This old, independent middle class has of course declined. On the most generous count, it is now 40 percent of the total middle class (at most 20 percent of the total labour force). Moreover, it has become politically as well as economically dependent upon the state, most notably in the case of the subsidized farmer.

The *new* middle class of white-collar employees is certainly not the political pivot of any balancing society. It is in no way politically unified. Its unions, such as they are, often serve merely to incorporate it as hanger-on of the labour interest. For a considerable period, the old middle class *was* an independent base of power; the new middle class cannot be. Political freedom and economic security *were* anchored in small and independent properties; they are not anchored in the worlds of the white-collar job. Scattered property holders were economically united by more or less free markets; the jobs of the new middle class are integrated by corporate authority. Economically, the white-collar classes are in the same condition as wage workers; politically, they are in a worse condition, for they are not organized. They are no vanguard of historic change; they are at best a rear guard of the welfare state.

The agrarian revolt of the nineties, the small-business revolt that has been more or less continuous since the eighties, the labour revolt of the thirties—each of these has failed as an independent movement which could countervail against the powers that be; they have failed as politically autonomous third parties. But they have succeeded, in varying degree, as interests vested in the expanded corporation and state; they have succeeded as parochial interests seated in particular districts, in local divisions of the two parties, and in the Congress. What they would become, in short, are well-established features of the *middle* levels of balancing power, on which we may now observe all those strata and interests which in the course of American history have been defeated in their bids for top power or which have never made such bids.

Fifty years ago many observers thought of the American state as a mask behind which an invisible government operated. But nowadays, much of what was called the old lobby, visible or invisible, is part of the quite visible government. The 'governmentalization of the lobby' has proceeded in both the legislative and the executive domain, as well as between them. The executive bureaucracy becomes not only the centre of decision but also the arena within which major conflicts of power are resolved or denied resolution. 'Administration' replaces electoral politics; the manoeuvring of cliques (which include leading Senators as well as civil servants) replaces the open clash of parties.

The shift of corporation men into the political directorate has accelerated the decline of the politicians in the Congress to the middle levels of power; the formation of the power elite rests in part upon this relegation. It rests also upon the semi-organized stalemate of the interests of sovereign localities, into which the legislative function has so largely fallen; upon the virtually complete absence of a civil service that is a politically neutral but politically relevant, depository of brainpower and executive skill; and it rests upon the increased official secrecy behind which great decisions are made without benefit of public or even of Congressional debate.

IV

There is one last belief upon which liberal observers everywhere base their interpretations and rest their hopes. That is the idea of the public and the associated idea of public opinion. Conservative thinkers, since the French Revolution, have of course Viewed With Alarm the rise of the public, which they have usually called the masses, or something to that effect. 'The populace is sovereign,' wrote Gustave Le Bon, 'and the tide of barbarism mounts.' But surely those who have supposed the masses to be well on their way to triumph are mistaken. In our time, the influence of publics or of masses within political life is in fact decreasing, and such influence as on occasion they do have tends, to an unknown but increasing degree, to be guided by the means of mass communication.

In a society of publics, discussion is the ascendant means of communication, and the mass media, if they exist, simply enlarge and animate this discussion, linking one face-to-face public with the discussions of another. In a mass society, the dominant type of communication is the formal media, and publics become mere markets for these media: the 'public' of a radio programme consists of all those exposed to it. When we try to look upon the United States today as a society of publics, we realize that it has moved a considerable distance along the road to the mass society.

In official circles, the very term, 'the public', has come to have a phantom meaning, which dramatically reveals its eclipse. The deciding elite can identify some of those who clamour publicly as 'Labour', others as 'Business', still others as 'Farmer'. But these are not the public. 'The public' consists of the unidentified and the non-partisan in a world of defined and partisan interests. In this faint echo of the classic notion, the public is composed of these remnants of the old and new middle classes whose interests are not explicitly defined, organized, or clamorous. In a curious adaptation, 'the public' often becomes, in administrative fact, 'the disengaged expert', who, although ever so well informed, has never taken a clear-cut and public stand on controversial issues. He is the 'public' member of the board, the commission, the committee. What 'the public' stands for, accordingly, is often a vagueness of policy (called 'open-mindedness'), a lack of involvement in public affairs (known as 'reasonableness'), and a professional disinterest (known as 'tolerance').

All this is indeed far removed from the eighteenth-century idea of the public of public opinion. That idea parallels the economic idea of the magical market. Here is the market composed of freely competing entrepreneurs; there is the public composed of circles of people in discussion. As price is the result of anonymous, equally weighted, bargaining individuals, so public opinion is the result of each man's having thought things out for himself and then contributing his voice to the great chorus. To be sure, some may have more influence on the state of opinion than others, but no one group monopolizes the discussion, or by itself determines the opinions that prevail.

In this classic image, the people are presented with problems. They discuss them. They formulate viewpoints. These viewpoints are organized, and they compete. One viewpoint 'wins out'. Then the people act on this view, or their representatives are instructed to act it out, and this they promptly do.

Such are the images of democracy which are still used as working justifications of power in America. We must now recognize this description as more a fairy tale than a useful approximation. The issues that now shape man's fate are neither raised nor decided by any public at large. The idea of a society that is at bottom composed of publics is not a matter of fact; it is the proclamation of an ideal, and as well the assertion of a legitimation masquerading as fact.

I cannot here describe the several great forces within American society as well as elsewhere which have been at work in the debilitation of the public. I want only to remind you that publics, like free associations, can be deliberately and suddenly smashed, or they can more slowly wither away. But whether smashed in a week or withered in a generation, the demise of the public must be seen in connection with the rise of centralized organizations, with all their new means of power, including those of the mass media of distraction. These, we now know, often seem to expropriate the rationality and the will of the terrorized or—as the case may be—the voluntarily indifferent society of masses. In the more democratic process of indifference the remnants of such publics as remain may only occasionally be intimidated by fanatics in search of 'disloyalty.' But regardless of that, they lose their will for decision because they do not possess the instruments for decision; they lose their sense of political belonging because they do not belong; they lose their political will because they see no way to realize it.

The political structure of a modern democratic state requires that such a public as is projected by democratic theorists not only exist but that it be the very forum within which a politics of real issues is enacted.

It requires a civil service that is firmly linked with the world of knowledge and sensibility, and which is composed of skilled men who, in their careers and in their aspirations, are truly independent of any private, which is to say, corporation, interests.

It requires nationally responsible parties which debate openly and clearly the issues which the nation, and indeed the world, now so rigidly confronts.

It requires an intelligentsia, inside as well as outside the universities, who carry on the big discourse of the western world, and whose work is relevant to and influential among parties and movements and publics.

And it certainly requires, as a fact of power, that there be free associations standing between families and smaller communities and publics, on the one hand, and the state, the military, the corporation, on the other. For unless these do exist, there are no vehicles for reasoned opinion, no instruments for the rational exertion of public will.

Such democratic formations are not now ascendant in the power structure of the United States, and accordingly the men of decision are not men selected and formed by careers within such associations and by their performance before such publics. The top of modern American society is increasingly unified, and often seems wilfully coordinated: at the top there has emerged an elite whose power probably exceeds that of any small group of men in world history. The middle levels are often a drifting set of stalemated forces: the middle does not link the bottom with the top. The bottom of this society is politically fragmented, and even as a passive fact, increasingly powerless: at the bottom there is emerging a mass society.

These developments, I believe, can be correctly understood neither in terms of the liberal nor the marxian interpretation of politics and history. Both these ways of thought arose as guidelines to reflection about a type of society which does not now exist in the United States. We confront there a new kind of social structure, which embodies elements and tendencies of all modern society, but in which they have assumed a more naked and flamboyant prominence.

That does not mean that we must give up the ideals of these classic political expectations. I believe that both have been concerned with the problem of rationality and of freedom: liberalism, with freedom and rationality as supreme facts about the individual; marxism, as supreme facts about man's role in the political making of history. What I have said here, I suppose, may be taken as an attempt to make evident why the ideas of freedom and of rationality now so often seem so ambiguous in the new society of the United States of America.

13

ROBERT A. DAHL

ON *THE SPECIES* HOMO POLITICUS

This excerpt from Robert A. Dahl's great book Who Governs? *captures the essence of so-called pluralist theory. Dahl, a professor emeritus at Yale University, argued that groups who possess wealth and social status have but two of the political assets that can help exert influence on government in this country. Many other types of resources can provide political actors with a basis for power. No single elite, or small collection of elites, has a monopoly on power. Multiple groups, resourceful in varying ways, share it.*

. . . Let us start with man himself: with his opportunities and resources for gaining influence and the way he exploits—or more often neglects to exploit—his political potentialities.

HOMO CIVICUS

Civic man is, at heart, simply man; man is the child grown up; the child is the human species after millions of years of evolution. In spite of ideas and ideals, the human organism still relentlessly insists on its primordial quest for gratifications and release from pain. The child and the youth learn various forms of gratifying experience; they learn of love, and food, of play, work, and rest, of the pursuit of curiosity, the perception of order and pattern, sex, friendship, self-esteem, social esteem. Throughout man's life, experiences like these channel his efforts, his energies, his attention. They represent his hungers, his needs, his wants.

The child, the budding civic man, learns all too soon that he cannot indulge himself without stint. Constraints are imposed on his liberty to gratify himself, both by nature herself in the form of physiological, mechanical, and psychological limitations and also by other individuals—his family, to begin with, then playmates, teachers, and later a host of others. The child struggles, resists, and is caught, more or less firmly, in a net woven by himself and his society.

He learns how to delay his gratifying experiences; because of the various barriers imposed on him, the routes he now chooses to his goals are frequently complex and time-consuming, sometimes boring, occasionally painful, at times dangerous.

He discovers that just as others constrain him in his efforts to achieve his primary goals, he too has resources that he can use to influence others to gain his own ends. At first these resources are closely attached to his own person and consist of simple,

[This study is part of a larger study of the distribution of political power in New Haven, Connecticut.—Eds.]

direct actions and reactions like affection, friendliness, anger, hostility, crying, destructiveness. But the world, as he gradually learns, contains many resources that can be used more indirectly. In our own culture, for example, he soon finds that money has a magical power to induce the compliance of many different people for many different purposes.

Thus *homo civicus* begins to develop strategies, ways of using his resources to achieve his goals. Even in choosing strategies, he discovers, he does not enjoy complete freedom. Some strategies are banned, some are permissible, others are encouraged, many are all but unavoidable. Schooling and a job are presented to him as compulsory strategies; it is made clear that any attempt to depart from these paths will be visited not only by a great loss in his capacity to attain his goals but possibly even by outright punishment. Schooling is considered instrumental in gaining knowledge, and knowledge is a resource of widespread applicability; a job is instrumental in acquiring income and social standing, resources that are important for a variety of ends.

Young *homo civicus* learns that his choices are constrained by laws enforced by the police, by courts, and by many other officials. He learns of clusters of institutions and men called governments, toward some of which he develops sentiments of loyalty or cynicism. He may accept the constraints on his choices flowing from the actions of these governments, or he may try to evade them, but in either case he gradually learns that the range of permissible strategies in dealing with governments is a good deal wider and includes many subtler alternatives than he had first assumed. Among his resources for influencing officials, *homo civicus* discovers the ballot. Although the prevailing public doctrine of American society places a high value on this resource, and *homo civicus* may himself give lip service to that doctrine, in fact he may doubt its value and rarely if ever employ it, or he may vote merely out of habit and sense of duty. Or he may see the ballot as a useful device for influencing politicians.

Homo civicus has other resources, too. For example, he can forego a movie or two in order to make a contribution to a political campaign; he can forego all evening of television in order to distribute propaganda for a candidate. But the chances are very great that political activity will always seem rather remote from the main focus of his life. Typically, as a source of direct gratifications political activity will appear to *homo civicus* as less attractive than a host of other activities; and, as a strategy to achieve his gratifications indirectly, political action will seem considerably less efficient than working at his job, earning more money, taking out insurance, joining a club, planning a vacation, moving to another neighborhood or city, or coping with all uncertain future in manifold other ways.

Sometimes, however, the actions or inactions of governments may threaten the primary goals of *homo civicus*. . . . Then *homo civicus* may set out deliberately to use the resources at his disposal in order to influence the actions of governments. But when the danger passes, *homo civicus* may usually be counted on to revert to his normal preoccupation with nonpolitical strategies for attaining his primary goals.

Homo civicus is not, by nature, a political animal.

HOMO POLITICUS

Despite several thousand years of richly insightful speculation, not much can be said with confidence about the factors that shape *homo politicus* out of the apolitical clay of *homo civicus*. Presumably, in the course of development some individuals find that political action is a powerful source of gratifications, both direct and indirect. If and when the primary goals that animate *homo civicus* become durably attached to political action, a new member of the genus *homo politicus* is born. Political man, unlike civic man, deliberately allocates a very sizable share of his resources to the process of gaining and maintaining control over the policies of government. Control over policies usually requires control over officials. And where, as in the United States, key officials are elected by voters, political man usually allocates an important share of his resources to the process of gaining and maintaining influence over voters. Because the acquiescence of *homo civicus* is always a necessary condition for rulership, and to gain his consent is often economical, in all political systems *homo politicus* deliberately employs some resources to influence the choices of *homo civicus*. Political man invariably seeks to influence civic man directly, but even in democratic systems civic man only occasionally seeks to influence political man directly.

Like civic man, political man develops strategies that govern the ways in which he uses the resources at his disposal. Like civic man, political man chooses his strategies from a narrowly limited set. In some political systems, the limits imposed on *homo politicus* are broad; in others the limits are relatively narrow. In pluralistic, democratic political systems with wide political consensus the range of acceptable strategies is narrowed by beliefs and habits rooted in traditions of legality, constitutionality, and legitimacy that are constantly reinforced by a great variety of social processes for generating agreement on and adherence to political norms. Whoever departs from these acceptable strategies incurs a high risk of defeat, for the resources that will be mounted against the political deviant are almost certain to be vastly greater than the resources the political deviant can himself muster. Even *homo civicus* (under the prodding of rival political leaders) can be counted on to rise briefly out of his preoccupation with apolitical goals and employ some of his resources to smite down the political man who begins to deviate noticeably in his choice of strategies from the norms prescribed in the political culture.

RESOURCES

The resources available to political man for influencing others are limited, though not permanently fixed. For our purposes in this book, a resource is anything that can be used to sway the specific choices or the strategies of another individual. Or, to use different language, whatever may be used as an inducement is a resource.

How one classifies resources is to some extent arbitrary. It would be possible to list resources in great detail, distinguishing one from the other with the utmost subtlety or to deal in very broad categories. One could search for a comprehensive and logically exhaustive classification or simply list resources according to the dictates of common sense. One could employ elaborate psychological categories derived from theories of modern psychology, or one could use more commonplace terms to classify resources. . . . it will do, I think, to use categorics dictated by common sense; to do more at this stage of our knowledge would be pseudoscientific window dressing.

Some resources can be used more or less directly as inducements. Or, put another way, the kinds of effective and cognitive experiences mentioned a moment ago as peculiarly fundamental and universal depend rather directly on some kinds of resources and more indirectly on others.

A list of resources in the American political system might include an individual's own time; access to money, credit, and wealth; control over jobs; control over information; esteem or social standing; the possession of charisma, popularity, legitimacy, legality; and the rights pertaining to public office. The list might also include solidarity: the capacity of a member of one segment of society to evoke support from others who identify him as like themselves because of similarities in occupation, social standing, religion, ethnic origin, or racial stock. The list would include the right to vote, intelligence, education, and perhaps even one's energy level.

One could easily think of refinements and additions to this list; it is not intended as an exhaustive list so much as an illustration of the richness and variety of political resources. All too often, attempts to explain the distribution and patterns of influence in political systems begin with an *a priori* assumption that everything can be explained by reference to only one kind of resource. On the contrary, . . . various manifestations of influence . . . can be explained, as we shall see, only by taking into account a number of different political resources.

Although the kinds and amounts of resources available to political man are always limited and at any given moment fixed, they are not, as was pointed out a moment ago, permanently fixed as to either kind or amount. Political man can use his resources to gain influence, and he can then use his influence to gain more resources. Political resources can be pyramided in much the same way that a man who starts out in business sometimes pyramids a small investment into a large corporate empire. To the political entrepreneur who has skill and drive, the political system offers unusual opportunities for pyramiding a small amount of initial resources into a sizable political holding. . . .

HYPOTHESES

In [an earlier part of this study] we saw how the monopoly over public life enjoyed by the Congregational patrician families of New Haven was destroyed, how the entrepreneurs without inherited social position and education acquired the prerogatives of office, and how these men were in their turn displaced by explebes who lacked the most salient resources of influence possessed by their predecessors: hereditary social status, wealth, business prominence, professional attainments, and frequently even formal education beyond high school. The change in the New Haven political system from the election of Elizur Goodrich in 1803 to John W. Murphy in 1931—the first a descendant of a sixteenth-century Anglican Bishop, a Yale graduate, a Congregationalist, a lawyer, a judge, congressman, Federalist; the second a descendant of Irish immigrants, a Catholic, a Democrat, and a union official in Samuel Gompers' old Cigar Makers International Union—represented nothing less than an extended and peaceful revolution that transformed the social, economic, and political institutions of New Haven.

This change in New Haven is fully consistent with three of the key hypotheses in this study. First, a number of old American cities, of which New Haven is one, have passed through a roughly similar transformation from a system in which resources of influence were highly concentrated to a system in which they are highly dispersed. Second, the present dispersion is a consequence of certain fundamental aspects of the social, economic, and political structures of New Haven. Third, the present dispersion does not represent equality of resources but fragmentation. The revolution in New Haven might be said to constitute a change from a system of *cumulative inequalities* in political resources to a system of noncumulative or *dispersed inequalities* in political resources.

This system of dispersed inequalities is, I believe, marked by the following six characteristics.

1. Many different kinds of resources for influencing officials are available to different citizens.
2. With few exceptions, these resources are unequally distributed.
3. Individuals best off in their access to one kind of resource are often badly off with respect to many other resources.
4. No one influence resource dominates all the others in all or even in most key decisions.
5. With some exceptions, an influence resource is effective in some issue-areas or in some specific decisions but not in all.
6. Virtually no one, and certainly no group of more than a few individuals, is entirely lacking in some influence resources. . . .

14

PETER BACHRACH AND MORTON S. BARATZ

TWO FACES OF POWER

In 1962, Peter Bachrach, a professor at Temple University, and Morton S. Baratz, who was teaching at Bryn Mawr, published an important critique of both the "ruling elite" model and the "pluralist" model of the political process. The chief insight of these scholars was that the question "Who really governs?" cannot be answered satisfactorily without examining what they called "the mobilization of bias"—that is, the ability of some political actors to influence not only the making of decisions but also of nondecisions. Control of the political agenda—which issues get on and which issues remain off limits—is an exercise of power at least as consequential as the affirmative formulation of policies.

The concept of power remains elusive despite the recent and prolific outpourings of case studies on community power. Its elusiveness is dramatically demonstrated by the regularity of disagreement as to the locus of community power between the sociologists and the political scientists. Sociologically oriented researchers have consistently found that power is highly centralized, while scholars trained in political science have just as regularly concluded that in "their" communities power is widely diffused.[1] Presumably, this explains why the latter group styles itself "pluralist," its counterpart "elitist."

There seems no room for doubt that the sharply divergent findings of the two groups are the product, not of sheer coincidence, but of fundamental differences in both their underlying assumptions and research methodology. The political scientists have contended that these differences in findings can be explained by the faulty approach and presuppositions of the sociologists. We contend in this paper that the pluralists themselves have not grasped the whole truth of the matter; that while their criticisms of the elitists are sound, they, like the elitists, utilize an approach and assumptions which predetermine their conclusions. Our argument is cast within the frame of our central thesis: that there are two faces of power, neither of which the sociologists see and only one of which the political scientists see.

I

Against the elitist approach to power several criticisms may be, and have been levelled.[2] One has to do with its basic premise that in every human institution there is an ordered system of power, a "power structure" which is an integral part

This paper is an outgrowth of a seminar in Problems of Power in Contemporary Society, conducted jointly by the authors for graduate students and undergraduate majors in political science and economics.

and the mirror image of the organization's stratification. This postulate the pluralists emphatically—and, to our mind, correctly—reject, on the ground that

> nothing categorical can be assumed about power in any community. . . . If anything, there seems to be an unspoken notion among pluralist researchers that at bottom *nobody* dominates in a town, so that their first question is not likely to be, "Who runs this community?," but rather, "Does anyone at all run this community?" The first query is somewhat like, "Have you stopped beating your wife?," in that virtually any response short of total unwillingness to answer will supply the researchers with a "power elite" along the lines presupposed by the stratification theory.[3]

Equally objectionable to the pluralists—and to us—is the sociologists' hypothesis that the power structure tends to be stable over time.

> Pluralists hold that power may be tied to issues, and issues can be fleeting or persistent, provoking coalitions among interested groups and citizens, ranging in their duration from momentary to semi-permanent. . . . To presume that the set of coalitions which exists in the community at any given time is a timelessly stable aspect of social structure is to introduce systematic inaccuracies into one's description of social reality.[4]

A third criticism of the elitist model is that it wrongly equates reputed with actual power:

> If a man's major life work is banking, the pluralist presumes he will spend his time at the bank, and not in manipulating community decisions. This presumption holds until the banker's activities and participations indicate otherwise. . . . If we presume that the banker is "really" engaged in running the community, there is practically no way of disconfirming this notion, even if it is totally erroneous. On the other hand, it is easy to spot the banker who really *does* run community affairs when we presume he does not, because his activities will make this fact apparent.[5]

This is not an exhaustive bill of particulars; there are flaws other than these in the sociological model and methodology[6]—including some which the pluralists themselves have not noticed. But to go into this would not materially serve our current purposes. Suffice it simply to observe that whatever the merits of their own approach to power, the pluralists have effectively exposed the main weaknesses of the elitist model.

As the foregoing quotations make clear, the pluralists concentrate their attention, not upon the sources of power, but its exercise. Power to them means "participation in decision making"[7] and can be analyzed only after "careful examination of a series of concrete decisions."[8] As a result, the pluralist researcher is uninterested in the reputedly powerful. His concerns instead are to (a) select for study a number of "key" as opposed to "routine" political decisions, (b) identify the people who took an active part in the decision-making process, (c) obtain a full account of their actual behavior while the policy conflict was being resolved, and (d) determine and analyze the specific outcome of the conflict.

The advantages of this approach, relative to the elitist alternative, need no further exposition. The same may not be said, however, about its defects—two of which seem to us to be of fundamental importance. One is that the model takes no account of the fact that power may be, and often is, exercised by confining the scope of decision making to relatively "safe" issues. The other is that the model provides no *objective* criteria for distinguishing between "important" and "unimportant" issues arising in the political arena.

II

There is no gainsaying that an analysis grounded entirely upon what is specific and visible to the outside observer is more "scientific" than one based upon pure speculation. To put it another way,

> If we can get our social life stated in terms of activity, and of nothing else, we have not indeed succeeded in measuring it, but we have at least reached a foundation upon which a coherent system of measurements can be built up. . . . We shall cease to be blocked by the intervention of unmeasurable elements, which claim to be themselves the real causes of all that is happening, and which by their spook-like arbitrariness make impossible any progress toward dependable knowledge.[9]

The question is, however, how can one be certain in any given situation that the "unmeasurable elements" are inconsequential, are not of decisive importance? Cast in slightly different terms, can a sound concept of power be predicated on the assumption that power is totally embodied and fully reflected in "concrete decisions" or in activity bearing directly upon their making?

We think not. Of course power is exercised when A participates in the making of decisions that affect B. But power is also exercised when A devotes his energies to creating or reinforcing social and political values and institutional practices that limit the scope of the political process to public consideration of only those issues which are comparatively innocuous to A. To the extent that A succeeds in doing this, B is prevented, for all practical purposes, from bringing to the fore any issues that might in their resolution be seriously detrimental to A's set of preferences.[10]

Situations of this kind are common. Consider, for example, the case—surely not unfamiliar to this audience—of the discontented faculty member in an academic institution headed by a tradition-bound executive. Aggrieved about a long-standing policy around which a strong vested interest has developed, the professor resolves in the privacy of his office to launch an attack upon the policy at the next faculty meeting. But, when the moment of truth is at hand, he sits frozen in silence. Why? Among the many possible reasons, one or more of these could have been of crucial importance: (a) the professor was fearful that his intended action would be interpreted as an expression of his disloyalty to the institution; or (b) he decided that, given the beliefs and attitudes of his colleagues on the faculty, he would almost certainly constitute on this issue a minority of one; or (c) he concluded that, given the nature of the law-making process in the institution, his proposed remedies would be pigeonholed permanently. But whatever the case, the central point to be made is the same: to the extent that a person or group—consciously or unconsciously—creates or reinforces barriers to the public airing of policy conflicts, that person or group has power. Or, as Professor Schattschneider has so admirably put it:

> All forms of political organization have a bias in favor of the exploitation of some kinds of conflict and the suppression of others because *organization is the mobilization of bias.* Some issues are organized into politics while others are organized out.[11]

Is such bias not relevant to the study of power? Should not the student be continuously alert to its possible existence in the human institution that he studies, and be ever prepared to examine the forces which brought it into being and sustain it? Can he safely ignore the possibility, for instance, that an individual or group in a community participates more vigorously in supporting the *nondecision-making* process than in participating in actual decisions within the process? Stated differently, can the researcher overlook the chance that some person or association could limit decision making to relatively non-controversial matters, by influencing community values and political procedures and rituals, notwithstanding that there are in the community serious but latent power conflicts?[12] To do so is, in our judgment, to overlook the less apparent, but nonetheless extremely important, face of power.

III

In his critique of the "ruling-elite model," Professor Dahl argues that "the hypothesis of the existence of a ruling elite can be strictly tested only if . . . [t]here is a fair sample of cases involving key political decisions in which the preferences of the hypothetical ruling elite run counter to those of any other likely group that might be suggested."[13] With this assertion we have two complaints. One we have already discussed, viz., in erroneously assuming that power is solely reflected in concrete decisions, Dahl thereby excludes the possibility that in the community in question there is a group capable of preventing contests from arising on issues of importance to it. Beyond that, however, by ignoring the less apparent face of power Dahl and those who accept his pluralist approach are unable adequately to differentiate between a "key" and a "routine" political decision.

Nelson Polsby, for example, proposes that "by pre-selecting as issues for study those which are generally agreed to be significant, pluralist researchers can test stratification theory."[14] He is silent, however, on how the researcher is to determine *what* issues are "generally agreed to be significant," and on how the researcher is to appraise the reliability of the agreement. In fact, Polsby is guilty here of the same fault he himself has found with elitist methodology: by presupposing that in any community there are significant issues in the political arena, he takes for granted the very question which is in doubt. He accepts as issues what are reputed to be issues. As a result, his findings are fore-ordained. For even if there is no "truly" significant issue in the community under study, there is every likelihood that Polsby (or any like-minded researcher) will find one or some and, after careful study, reach the appropriate pluralistic conclusions.[15]

Dahl's definition of "key political issues" in his essay on the ruling-elite model is open to the same criticism. He states that it is "a necessary although possibly not a sufficient condition that the [key] issue should involve actual disagreement in preferences among two or more groups."[16] In our view, this is an inadequate characterization of a "key political issue," simply because groups can have disagreements in preferences on unimportant as well as on important issues. Elite preferences which border on the indifferent are certainly not significant in determining whether a monolithic or polylithic distribution of power prevails in a given community. Using Dahl's definition of "key political issues," the researcher would have little difficulty in finding such in practically any community; and it would not be surprising then if he ultimately concluded that power in the community was widely diffused.

The distinction between important and unimportant issues, we believe, cannot be made intelligently in the absence of an analysis of the "mobilization of bias" in the community; of the dominant values and the political myths, rituals, and institutions which tend to favor the vested interests of one or more groups, relative to others. Armed with this knowledge, one could conclude that any challenge to the predominant values or to the established "rules of the game" would constitute an "important" issue; all else, unimportant. To be sure, judgments of this kind cannot be entirely objective. But to avoid making them in a study of power is both to neglect a highly significant aspect of power and thereby to undermine the only sound basis for discriminating between "key" and "routine" decisions. In effect, we contend, the pluralists have made each of these mistakes; that is to say, they have done just that for which Kaufman and Jones so severely taxed Floyd Hunter: they have begun "their structure at the mezzanine without showing us a lobby or foundation,"[17] *i.e.*, they have begun by studying the issues rather than the values and biases that are built into the political system and that, for the student of power, give real meaning to those issues which do enter the political arena.

IV

There is no better fulcrum for our critique of the pluralist model than Dahl's recent study of power in New Haven.[18]

At the outset it may be observed that Dahl does not attempt in this work to define his concept, "key political decision." In asking whether the "Notables" of New Haven are "influential overtly or covertly in the making of government decisions," he simply states that he will examine "three different 'issue areas' in which important public decisions are made: nominations by the two political parties, urban redevelopment, and public education." These choices are justified on the grounds that "nominations determine which persons will hold public office. The

New Haven redevelopment program measured by its cost—present and potential—is the largest in the country. Public education, aside from its intrinsic
importance, is the costliest item in the city's budget." Therefore, Dahl concludes,
"It is reasonable to expect . . . that the relative influence over public officials
wielded by the . . . Notables would be revealed by an examination of their participation in these three areas of activity."[19]

The difficulty with this latter statement is that it is evident from Dahl's own
account that the Notables are in fact uninterested in two of the three "key" decisions he has chosen. In regard to the public school issue, for example, Dahl
points out that many of the Notables live in the suburbs and that those who do
live in New Haven choose in the main to send their children to private schools.
"As a consequence," he writes, "their interest in the public schools is ordinarily
rather slight."[20] Nominations by the two political parties as an important "issue
area," is somewhat analogous to the public schools, in that the apparent lack of
interest among the Notables in this issue is partially accounted for by their suburban residence—because of which they are disqualified from holding public
office in New Haven. Indeed, Dahl himself concedes that with respect to both
these issues the Notables are largely indifferent: "Business leaders might ignore
the public schools or the political parties without any sharp awareness that their
indifference would hurt their pocketbooks . . ." He goes on, however, to say that

> the prospect of profound changes [as a result of the urban-redevelopment program] in
> ownership, physical layout, and usage of property in the downtown area and the effects
> of these changes on the commercial and industrial prosperity of New Haven were all
> related in an obvious way to the daily concerns of businessmen.[21]

Thus, if one believes—as Professor Dahl did when he wrote his critique of the
ruling-elite model—that an issue, to be considered as important, "should involve
actual disagreement in preferences among two or more groups,"[22] then clearly he
has now for all practical purposes written off public education and party nominations as key "issue areas." But this point aside, it appears somewhat dubious at
best that "the relative influence over public officials wielded by the Social Notables" can be revealed by an examination of their nonparticipation in areas in
which they were not interested.

Furthermore, we would not rule out the possibility that even on those issues to
which they appear indifferent, the Notables may have a significant degree of *indirect* influence. We would suggest, for example, that although they send their children to private schools, the Notables do recognize that public school expenditures
have a direct bearing upon their own tax liabilities. This being so, and given their
strong representation on the New Haven Board of Finance,[23] the expectation must
be that it is in their direct interest to play an active role in fiscal policy making, in
the establishment of the educational budget in particular. But as to this, Dahl is
silent: he inquires not at all into either the decisions made by the Board of Finance
with respect to education nor into their impact upon the public schools.[24] Let it
be understood clearly that in making these points we are not attempting to
refute Dahl's contention that the Notables lack power in New Haven. What we

are saying, however, is that this conclusion is not adequately supported by his analysis of the "issue areas" of public education and party nominations.

The same may not be said of redevelopment. This issue is by any reasonable standard important for purposes of determining whether New Haven is ruled by "the hidden hand of an economic elite."[25] For the Economic Notables have taken an active interest in the program and, beyond that, the socio-economic implications of it are not necessarily in harmony with the basic interests and values of businesses and businessmen.

In an effort to assure that the redevelopment program would be acceptable to what he dubbed "the biggest muscles" in New Haven, Mayor Lee created the Citizens Action Commission (CAC) and appointed to it primarily representatives of the economic elite. It was given the function of overseeing the work of the mayor and other officials involved in redevelopment, and, as well, the responsibility for organizing and encouraging citizens' participation in the program through an extensive committee system.

In order to weigh the relative influence of the mayor, other key officials, and the members of the CAC, Dahl reconstructs "all the *important* decisions on redevelopment and renewal between 1950–58 . . . [to] determine which individuals most often initiated the proposals that were finally adopted or most often successfully vetoed the proposals of the others."[26] The results of this test indicate that the mayor and his development administrator were by far the most influential, and that the "muscles" on the Commission, excepting in a few trivial instances, "never directly initiated, opposed, vetoed, or altered any proposal brought before them. . . ."[27]

This finding is, in our view, unreliable, not so much because Dahl was compelled to make a subjective selection of what constituted *important* decisions within what he felt to be an *important* "issue area," as because the finding was based upon an excessively narrow test of influence. To measure relative influence solely in terms of the ability to initiate and veto proposals is to ignore the possible exercise of influence or power in limiting the scope of initiation. How, that is to say, can a judgment be made as to the relative influence of Mayor Lee and the CAC without knowing (through prior study of the political and social views of all concerned) the proposals that Lee did *not* make because he anticipated that they would provoke strenuous opposition and, perhaps, sanctions on the part of the CAC?[28]

In sum, since he does not recognize *both* faces of power, Dahl is in no position to evaluate the relative influence or power of the initiator and decisionmaker, on the one hand, and of those persons, on the other, who may have been indirectly instrumental in preventing potentially dangerous issues from being raised.[29] As a result, he unduly emphasizes the importance of initiating, deciding, and vetoing, and in the process casts the pluralist conclusions of his study into serious doubt.

V

We have contended in this paper that a fresh approach to the study of power is called for, an approach based upon a recognition of the two faces of power. Under this approach the researcher would begin—not, as does the sociologist who asks, "Who rules?" nor as does the pluralist who asks, "Does anyone have power?"—but by investigating the particular "mobilization of bias" in the institution under scrutiny. Then, having analyzed the dominant values, the myths and the established political procedures and rules of the game, he would make a careful inquiry into which persons or groups, if any, gain from the existing bias and which, if any, are handicapped by it. Next, he would investigate the dynamics of *nondecision-making;* that is, he would examine the extent to which and the manner in which the *status quo* oriented persons and groups influence those community values and those political institutions (as, e.g., the unanimity "rule" of New York City's Board of Estimate[30]) which tend to limit the scope of actual decision-making to "safe" issues. Finally, using his knowledge of the restrictive face of power as a foundation for analysis and as a standard for distinguishing between "key" and "routine" political decisions, the researcher would, after the manner of the pluralists, analyze participation in decision making of concrete issues.

We reject in advance as unimpressive the possible criticism that this approach to the study of power is likely to prove fruitless because it goes beyond an investigation of what is objectively measurable. In reacting against the subjective aspects of the sociological model of power, the pluralists have, we believe, made the mistake of discarding "unmeasurable elements" as unreal. It is ironical that, by so doing, they have exposed themselves to the same fundamental criticism they have so forcefully levelled against the elitists: their approach to and assumptions about power predetermine their findings and conclusions.

NOTES

1. Compare, for example, the sociological studies of Floyd Hunter, *Community Power Structure* (Chapel Hill, 1953); Roland Pellegrini and Charles H. Coates, "Absentee-Owned Corporations and Community Power Structure," *American Journal of Sociology* 61 (March 1956): pp. 413–419; and Robert O. Schulze, "Economic Dominants and Community Power Structure," *American Sociological Review* 23 (February 1958): pp. 3–9; with political science studies of Wallace S. Sayre and Herbert Kaufman, *Governing New York City* (New York, 1960); Robert A. Dahl, *Who Governs?* (New Haven, 1961); and Norton E. Long and George Belknap, "A Research Program on Leadership and Decision-Making in Metropolitan Areas" (New York: Governmental Affairs Institute, 1956). See also Nelson W. Polsby, "How to Study Community Power: The Pluralist Alternative," *Journal of Politics* 22 (August, 1960): pp. 474–484.

2. See especially N. W. Polsby, *op. cit.,* p. 475f.

3. *Ibid.,* pp. 476.

4. *Ibid.,* pp. 478–479.

5. *Ibid.,* pp. 480–491.

6. See especially Robert A. Dahl, "A Critique of the Ruling-Elite Model," *American Political Science Review,* Vol. 52 (June 1958), pp. 463–469; and Lawrence J. R. Herson, "In the Footsteps of Community Power," *American Political Science Review* 55 (December 1961): pp. 817–831.

7. This definition originated with Harold D. Lasswell and Abraham Kaplan, *Power and Society* (New Haven, 1950), p. 75.

8. Robert A. Dahl, "A Critique of the Ruling-Elite Model," *loc. cit.,* p. 466.

9. Arthur Bentley, *The Process of Government* (Chicago, 1908), p. 202, quoted in Polsby, *op. cit.*, p. 418n.

10. As is perhaps self-evident, there are similarities in both faces of power. In each, A participates in decisions and thereby adversely affects B. But there is an important difference between the two: in the one case, A openly participates; in the other, he participates only in the sense that he works to sustain those values and rules of procedure that help him keep certain issues out of the public domain. True enough, participation of the second kind may at times be overt; that is the case, for instance, in cloture fights in the Congress. But the point is that it need not be. In fact, when the maneuver is most success-fully executed, it neither involves nor can be identified with decisions arrived at on specific issues.

11. E. E. Schattschneider, *The Semi-Sovereign People* (New York, 1960), p. 71.

12. Dahl *partially* concedes this point when he observes ("A Critique of the Ruling-Elite Model," pp. 468–469) that "one could argue that even in a society like ours a ruling elite might be so influen-tial over ideas, attitudes, and opinions that a kind of false consensus will exist—not the phony consen-sus of a terroristic totalitarian dictatorship but the manipulated and superficially self-imposed adherence to the norms and goals of the elite by broad sections of a community. . . . This objection points to the need to be circumspect in interpreting the evidence." But that he largely misses our point is clear from the succeeding sentence: "Yet here, too, it seems to me that the hypothesis cannot be satisfactorily confirmed without something equivalent to the test I have proposed," and that is "by an examination of a series of concrete cases where key decisions are made. . . ."

13. *Op. cit.*, p. 466.

14. *Op. cit.*, p. 478.

15. As he points out, the expectations of the pluralist researchers "have seldom been disappointed" (*Ibid.*, p. 477).

16. *Op. cit.*, p. 467.

17. Herbert Kaufman and Victor Jones, "The Mystery of Power," *Public Administration Review* 14 (Summer 1954): p. 207.

18. Robert A. Dahl, *Who Governs?* (New Haven, 1961).

19. *Ibid.*, p. 64.

20. *Ibid.*, p. 70.

21. *Ibid.*, p. 71.

22. *Op. cit.*, p. 467.

23. *Who Governs?*, p. 82. Dahl points out that "the main policy thrust of the Economic Notables is to oppose tax increases; this leads them to oppose expenditures for anything more than minimal tradi-tional city services. In this effort their two most effective weapons ordinarily are the mayor and the Board of Finance. The policies of the Notables are most easily achieved under a strong mayor if his policies coincide with theirs or under a weak mayor if they have the support of the Board of Finance. . . . New Haven mayors have continued to find it expedient to create confidence in their financial policies among businessmen by appointing them to the Board." (pp. 81–82).

24. Dahl does discuss in general terms (pp. 79–84) changes in the level of tax rates and assessments in past years, but not actual decisions of the Board of Finance or their effects on the public school system.

25. *Ibid.*, p. 124.

26. *Ibid.* "A rough test of a person's overt or covert influence," Dahl states in the first section of the book, "is the frequency with which he successfully initiates an important policy over the opposition of others, or vetoes policies initiated by others, or initiates a policy where no opposition appears." (*Ibid.*, p. 66).

27. *Ibid.*, p. 131.

28. Dahl is, of course, aware of the "law of anticipated reactions." In the case of the mayor's rela-tionship with the CAC, Dahl notes that Lee was "particularly skillful in estimating what the CAC could be expected to support or reject" (p. 137). However, Dahl was not interested in analyzing or appraising to what extent the CAC limited Lee's freedom of action. Because of his restricted concept of power, Dahl did not consider that the CAC might in this respect have exercised power. That the CAC did not initiate or veto actual proposals by the mayor was to Dahl evidence enough that the CAC was virtually powerless; it might as plausibly be evidence that the CAC was (in itself or in what it represented) so powerful that Lee ventured nothing it would find worth quarreling with.

29. The fact that the initiator of decisions also refrains—because he anticipates adverse reactions—from initiating other proposals does not obviously lessen the power of the agent who limited his initiative powers. Dahl missed this point: "It is," he writes, "all the more improbable, then, that a secret cabal of Notables dominates the public life of New Haven through means so clandestine that not one of the fifty prominent citizens interviewed in the course of this study—citizens who had participated extensively in various decisions—hinted at the existence of such a cabal . . ." (p. 185).

In conceiving of elite domination exclusively in the form of a conscious cabal exercising the power of decision making and vetoing, he overlooks a more subtle form of domination; one in which those who actually dominate are not conscious of it themselves, simply because their position of dominance has never seriously been challenged.

30. Sayre and Kaufman, *op. cit.*, p. 640. For perceptive study of the "mobilization of bias" in a rural American community, see Arthur Vidich and Joseph Bensman, *Small Town in Mass Society* (Princeton, 1958).

PART FOUR

POLITICAL PARTIES AND ELECTIONS

Elections lie at the heart of the democratic process, and because in any large democracy political parties organize electoral competition, a vital party system is essential to democratic politics. On this general proposition, few political scientists would disagree. Opinions differ, however, as to exactly what a vital party system is, whether the United States still has one, and hence, how "democratic" American national elections will be with the passage of time.

In 1950, the American Political Science Association issued a famous report that called for thorough reform of the political parties to promote a "more responsible two-party system." By "more responsible," the authors meant an arrangement analogous to the British model, that is, a system with the following attributes. The parties would offer the electorate a clear choice between alternative platforms; the party garnering a popular majority in a general election could then claim the consent of the people when adopting its announced course of action; and representatives elected to office would deliver on their campaign promises. If the voters grew disenchanted with the governing party's program, they could withdraw their mandate by voting in the opposition at the next election. Until that time, however, the minority party would mostly be in a position to criticize government policies and to articulate alternatives, but not to frustrate continually, or compromise, the policies. Finally, to make the party system dependable and acountable in this fashion, the stature of party leaders would have to improve, the national party organizations would have to be strengthened, and greater party loyalty would have to be encouraged, principally by sharpening the programmatic differences between the contenders.

It is hard to think of a time in American history when the political parties closely approximated this ideal. To be sure, there have been periods—the election of 1896, for instance—when the ideological breach between Democrats and Republicans was particularly wide. But seldom has party discipline in Congress, for example, resembled that in most European parliaments. Nor is it likely to. The separation of powers provides Congress and the presidency with different constituencies and functions that inevitably hinder party cohesion in ways parliamentary structures do not.

In a two-party system, moreover, there is a tendency for both parties to gravitate ideologically toward the center of the political spectrum. "In fact," as Anthony Downs observes in his well-known book, *An Economic Theory of Democracy*, "in two-party systems there is a large area of overlapping policies near the middle of the scale, so that parties closely resemble each other." The similarity often requires "deliberate equivocation" about issues. Indeed, Downs argues, the policies of the respective parties "may become so vague, and parties so alike, that voters find it difficult to make rational decisions."

The late Donald E. Stokes came to view Downs's model of two-party politics, excerpted here, as empirically deficient. In his essay "Spatial Models of Party Competition," Stokes noted that American political parties have not always aligned themselves along a linear left-to-right axis, nor converged at the center of it. In reality, party orientations involve a mix of *"position-issues,"* wherein politicians pose specific policy alternatives based on a perceived distribution of voter preferences, and *"valence-issues,"* wherein the electorate attaches to the parties credit or blame for particular social or economic conditions ("crime," "unemployment," etc.). The role of these "valence" questions, so important in many U.S. presidential elections, renders the ideal of "responsible," platform-committed parties even more remote— especially since political leaders are often credited or inculpated for conditions that policymakers may not be able to control or influence.

Nonetheless, parties in American politics once played a more central role than they do today. Not only did the party organizations nominate candidates, simplify the choices before the public, and actively mobilize voters, but party identification also ran deep in the electorate. The large-scale voting study conducted by Angus Campbell and his associates at the University of Michigan's Survey Research Center during the 1950s discovered that no variable better predicted voting decisions than did party affiliation. According to the Michigan researchers' findings, party attachments are formed early in life and internalized; once established, they tend to be remarkably stable.[1] Only the most wrenching personal experiences (such as migrations, occupational shifts, or fundamental changes in one's social milieu) or cataclysmic historical events (e.g., the Civil War, the Great Depression) could be expected to alter partisan orientations.

In "The Decline of Collective Responsibility in American Politics," Morris P. Fiorina laments the degeneration of political parties during the twentieth century and its impact on the accountability of elected officials. He notes that each of the following has been declining: the strength of party organization, voter identification with the parties, and unified party control of the executive and legislative branches. Among the consequences of the decline of parties (the only instruments that can promote collective responsibility) are immobilism, the increased importance of single-issue politics, and popular alienation from government. Fiorina concludes that "through a complex mixture of accident and intention we have constructed for ourselves a system that articulates interests superbly but aggregates them poorly. We hold our politicians individually accountable for the proposals they advocate, but less so for the adoption of those proposals, and not at all for overseeing the implementation of those proposals and the evaluation of their results."

1. Angus Campbell, Philip Converse, Warren Miller, and Donald Stokes, "The Development of Party Identification," *The American Voter: An Abridgement* (New York: John Wiley & Sons, 1964).

The last part of Fiorina's conclusion may be overstating matters. For if there is one lasting generalization that can be made about electoral behavior, it is that the electorate tends to judge candidates "retrospectively," even if it has trouble assessing them prospectively. V. O. Key, the original source of this insight, made the point plainly: "The public can express itself with greatest clarity when it speaks in disapprobation of the past policy or performance of an administration, though the collective decision may not specify with minuteness the elements of policy or performance of which it disapproves." Hence, what elections do least clearly is "indicate with precision the lines of policy that should be pursued."

15

ANTHONY DOWNS

AN ECONOMIC THEORY OF DEMOCRACY

Critics of America's political parties sometimes bemoan the tendency to blur, or not adhere to, distinct policy platforms. "There's not a dime's worth of difference between them," is the common impression. In this excerpt from his classic book An Economic Theory of Democracy, *Anthony Downs, a senior fellow at the Brookings Institution, shows how and why parties in a two-party system tend to converge toward the midpoint of the ideological spectrum. Inevitably, competing parties often find themselves equivocating about key issues and espousing policies that overlap.*

INTRODUCTION

If political ideologies are truly means to the end of obtaining votes, and if we know something about the distribution of voters' preferences, we can make specific predictions about how ideologies change in content as parties maneuver to gain power. Or, conversely, we can state the conditions under which ideologies come to resemble each other, diverge from each other, or remain in some fixed relationship.

OBJECTIVES

In this chapter we attempt to prove the following propositions:

1. A two-party democracy cannot provide stable and effective government unless there is a large measure of ideological consensus among its citizens.
2. Parties in a two-party system deliberately change their platforms so that they resemble one another; whereas parties in a multiparty system try to remain as ideologically distinct from each other as possible.
3. If the distribution of ideologies in a society's citizenry remains constant, its political system will move toward a position of equilibrium in which the number of parties and their ideological positions are stable over time.
4. New parties can be most successfully launched immediately after some significant change in the distribution of ideological views among eligible voters.
5. In a two-party system, it is rational for each party to encourage voters to be irrational by making its platform vague and ambiguous.

I. THE SPATIAL ANALOGY AND ITS EARLY USE

To carry out this analysis, we borrow and elaborate upon an apparatus invented by Harold Hotelling. It first appeared in a famous article on spatial competition published in 1929, and was later refined by Arthur Smithies.[1] Our version of

Hotelling's spatial market consists of a linear scale running from zero to 100 in the usual left-to-right fashion. To make this politically meaningful, we assume that political preferences can be ordered from left to right in a manner agreed upon by all voters. They need not agree on which point they personally prefer, only on the ordering of parties from one extreme to the other.

In addition, we assume that every voter's preferences are single-peaked and slope downward monotonically on either side of the peak (unless his peak lies at one extreme on the scale). For example, if a voter likes position 35 best, we can immediately deduce that he prefers 30 to 25 and 40 to 45. He always prefers some point X to another point Y if X is closer to 35 than Y and both are on the same side of 35. The slope downward from the apex need not be identical on both sides, but we do presume no sharp asymmetry exists.

These assumptions can perhaps be made more plausible if we reduce all political questions to their bearing upon one crucial issue: how much government intervention in the economy should there be? If we assume that the left end of the scale represents full government control, and the right end means a completely free market, we can rank parties by their views on this issue in a way that might be nearly universally recognized as accurate. In order to coordinate this left-right orientation with our numerical scale, we will arbitrarily assume that the number denoting any party's position indicates the percentage of the economy it wants left in private hands (excluding those minimal state operations which even the most Hayekian economists favor). Thus the extreme left position is zero, and the extreme right is 100. Admittedly, this apparatus is unrealistic for the following two reasons: (1) actually each party is leftish on some issues and rightish on others, and (2) the parties designated as right wing extremists in the real world are for fascist control of the economy rather than free markets. However, we will ignore these limitations temporarily and see what conclusions of interest we can draw from this spatial analogy.

Both Hotelling and Smithies have already applied their versions of this model to politics. Hotelling assumed that people were evenly spaced along the straight-line scale, and reasoned that competition in a two-party system would cause each party to move towards its opponent ideologically. Such convergence would occur because each party knows that extremists at its end of the scale prefer it to the opposition, since it is necessarily closer to them than the opposition party is. Therefore the best way for it to gain more support is to move toward the other extreme, so as to get more voters outside of it—i.e., to come between them and its opponent. As the two parties move closer together, they become more moderate and less extreme in policy in an effort to win the crucial middle-of-the-road voters, i.e., those whose views place them between the two parties. This center area becomes smaller and smaller as both parties strive to capture moderate votes; finally the two parties become nearly identical in platforms and actions. For example, if there is one voter at every point on the scale, and parties A and B start at points 25 and 75 respectively, they will move towards each other and meet at 50, assuming they move at the same speed (Figure 1). Like the two grocery stores in Hotelling's famous example, they will converge on the same location until practically all voters are indifferent between them.

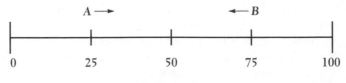

FIGURE 1

Note for Figures 1–9: Horizontal scale represents political orientation. Vertical scale represents number of citizens.

Smithies improved this model by introducing elastic demand at each point on the scale. Thus as the grocery stores moved away from the extremes, they lost customers there because of the increased cost of transportation; this checked them from coming together at the center. In our model, this is analogous to political extremists becoming disgusted at the identity of the parties, and refusing to vote for either if they become too much alike. At exactly what point this leakage checks the convergence of A and B depends upon how many extremists each loses by moving towards the center compared with how many moderates it gains thereby.

II. THE EFFECTS OF VARIOUS DISTRIBUTIONS OF VOTERS

A. *In Two-Party Systems*

An important addition we can make to this model is a variable distribution of voters along the scale. Instead of assuming there is one voter at each point on the scale, let us assume there are 100,000 voters whose preferences cause them to be normally distributed with a mean of 50 (Figure 2). Again, if we place parties A and B initially at 25 and 75, they will converge rapidly upon the center. The possible loss of extremists will not deter their movement toward each other, because there are so few voters to be lost at the margins compared with the number to be gained in the middle. However, if we alter the distribution to that shown in Figure 3, the two parties will not move away from their initial positions at 25 and 75 at all; if they did, they would lose far more voters at the extremes than they could possibly gain in the center. Therefore a two-party system need not lead to the convergence on moderation that Hotelling and Smithies predicted. If voters' preferences are distributed so that voters are massed bimodally near the extremes, the parties will remain poles apart in ideology.

The possibility that parties will be kept from converging ideologically in a two-party system depends upon the refusal of extremist voters to support either party if both become alike—not identical, but merely similar. In a certain world—where information is complete and costless, there is no future-oriented voting, and the act of voting uses up no scarce resources—such abstention by extremists would be irrational. As long as there is even the most infinitesimal difference between A and B, extremist voters would be forced to vote for the one closest to them, no

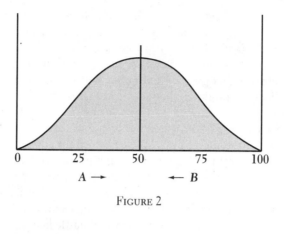

FIGURE 2

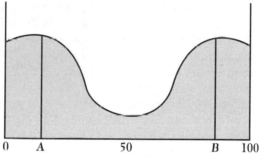

FIGURE 3

matter how distasteful its policies seemed in comparison with those of their ideal government. It is always rational *ex definitione* to select a greater good before a lesser, or a lesser evil before a greater; consequently abstention would be irrational because it increases the chances of the worse party for victory.

Even in a certain world, however, abstention is rational for the extremist voters who are future oriented. They are willing to let the worse party win today in order to keep the better party from moving towards the center, so that in future elections it will be closer to them. Then when it does win, its victory is more valuable in their eyes. Abstention thus becomes a threat to use against the party nearest one's own extreme position so as to keep it away from the center.[2]

Uncertainty increases the possibility that rational extremist voters will abstain if the party nearest them moves toward its opponent even if it does not become ideologically identical with the latter. When information is limited and costly, it is difficult to detect infinitesimal differences between parties. Perhaps even relatively significant differences will pass unnoticed by the radical whose own views are so immoderate that all moderates look alike. This means that the differential threshold of such extremists is likely to be very high—they will regard all small differences between moderate parties as irrelevant to their voting decision, i.e., as unreal distinctions.

Having established the rationality of abstention by extremist voters, let us again consider a bimodal distribution of voters with modes near each extreme (Figure 3). In a two-party system, whichever party wins will attempt to implement policies radically opposed to the other party's ideology, since the two are at opposite extremes. This means that government policy will be highly unstable, and that democracy is likely to produce chaos. Unfortunately, the growth of balancing center parties is unlikely. Any party which forms in the center will eventually move toward one extreme or the other to increase its votes, since there are so few moderate voters. Furthermore, any center party could govern only in coalition with one of the extremist parties, which would alienate the other, and thus not eliminate the basic problem. In such a situation, unless voters can somehow be moved to the center of the scale to eliminate their polar split, democratic government is not going to function at all well. In fact, no government can operate so as to please most of the people; hence this situation may lead to revolution.

The political cycle typical of revolutions can be viewed as a series of movements of men along the political scale.[3] Preliminary to the upheaval, the once centralized distribution begins to polarize into two extremes as the incumbents increasingly antagonize those who feel themselves oppressed. When the distribution has become so split that one extreme is imposing by force policies abhorred by the other extreme, open warfare breaks out, and a clique of underdogs seizes power. This radical switch from one extreme to the other is partly responsible for the reign of terror which marks most revolutions; the new governors want to eliminate their predecessors, who have bitterly opposed them. Finally violence exhausts itself, a new consensus is reached on the principles of the revolution, and the distribution becomes centralized again—often under a new dictatorship as rigid as the old, but not faced with a polarized distribution of opinions.[4]

Under more normal circumstances, in countries where there are two opposite social classes and no sizeable middle class, the numerical distribution is more likely to be skewed to the left, with a small mode at the right extreme (Figure 4). The large mode at the left represents the lower or working class; on the right is the upper class. Here democracy, if effective, will bring about the installation of a leftish government because of the numerical preponderance of the lower classes. Fear of this result is precisely what caused many European aristocrats to fight the introduction of universal suffrage. Of course, our schema oversimplifies the situation considerably. On our political scale, every voter has equal weight with every other, whereas in fact the unequal distribution of income allows a numerically small group to control political power quite disproportionate to its size. . . .

In spite of oversimplification, it is clear that the numerical distribution of voters along the political scale determines to a great extent what kind of democracy will develop. For example, a distribution like that of Figure 2 encourages a two-party system with both parties located near the center in relatively moderate positions. This type of government is likely to have stable policies, and whichever party is in power, its policies will not be far from the views of the vast majority of people. On the other hand, if a nation's voters are distributed as shown in Figure 5, a multiparty system will almost inevitably result.

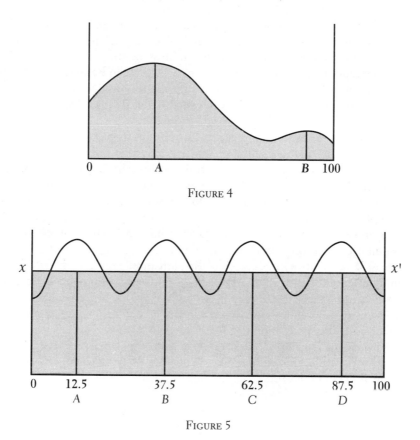

FIGURE 4

FIGURE 5

B. *The Number of Parties in Equilibrium*

Before examining the dynamics of multiparty systems, we should point out that our political version of Hotelling's model does not suffer from the outstanding limitation of the economic version he used. In Hotelling's spatial market, it was impossible to reach stable equilibrium with more than two grocery stores. The ones in the middle would always become the target of convergence from either side; consequently they would leap to the outside to keep from being squeezed. There was no device to restrict the perfect mobility that caused this disequilibrium.

But political parties cannot move ideologically past each other. . . . integrity and responsibility create relative immobility, which prevents a party from making ideological leaps over the heads of its neighbors. Thus ideological movement is restricted to horizontal progress at most up to—and never beyond—the nearest party on either side. Coupled with our device of variable distribution, this attribute of the model nearly always insures stable equilibrium.

It is true that new parties can be introduced between two formerly adjacent ones or outside one of them. Nevertheless, this possibility cannot upset stable equilibrium in the long run for two reasons. First, once a party has come into being, it cannot leap over the heads of its neighbors, as explained. Second, there is a limit to the number of parties which can be supported by any one distribution. When that limit is reached, no more new parties can be successfully introduced. The parties extant at that point arrange themselves through competition so that no party can gain more votes by moving to the right than it loses on the left by doing so, and vice versa. The political system thus reaches a state of long-run equilibrium in so far as the number and positions of its parties are concerned, assuming no change in the distribution of voters along the scale.

Whether the political system contains two or many parties in this state of equilibrium depends upon (1) the nature of the limit upon the introduction of new parties and (2) the shape of the distribution of voters. We will examine these factors in order.

In our model, every party is a team of men who seek to attain office—a party cannot survive in the long run if none of its members get elected.[5] But in order to get at least some of its members elected, the party must gain the support of a certain minimum number of voters. The size of this minimum depends upon the type of electoral system in operation.

To get any of its members in office at all, a party in our model must win more votes than any other party running. This arrangement encourages parties which repeatedly lose to merge with each other so as to capture a combined total of votes larger than the total received by the party which repeatedly wins. Such amalgamation continues until each of the survivors has a reasonable chance of winning a majority of the votes cast, which is the only way it can be sure of gaining office. Thus the winner-take-all outcome of a plurality electoral structure tends to narrow the field to two competing parties.[6]

Where proportional representation exists, a party which wins only a small percentage of the total vote may place some of its members in the government, since coalition governments often rule.[7] Thus the minimum amount of support necessary to keep a party going is much smaller than in a plurality system; so a multiparty system is encouraged. Nevertheless, each party must still obtain a certain minimum number of votes in order to elect members of the legislature who might possibly enter a coalition. For this reason, a given distribution of voters can support only a limited number of parties even under proportional representation.[8] Therefore the conditions for equilibrium exist in both two- and multiparty systems.

The type of electoral structure extant in a political system may be either a cause or a result of the original distribution of voters along the scale. Thus if the distribution has a single mode around which nearly all voters are clustered, the framers of the electoral structure may believe that plurality rule will not cause any large group to be ignored politically. Or if the distribution has many small modes, the lawmakers may choose proportional representation in order to allow sizeable extremist groups to have a voice in government.

Causality can also be reversed because the number of parties in existence molds the political views of rising generations, thereby influencing their positions on the scale. In a plurality structure, since a two-party system is encouraged and the two parties usually converge, voters' tastes may become relatively homogeneous in the long run; whereas the opposite effect may occur in a proportional representation structure.

From this analysis it is clear that both the electoral structure and the distribution of voters are important in determining how many parties a given democracy will contain when it reaches equilibrium. Each factor influences the other indirectly, but it also has some impact independent of the other. For example, if a proportional representation system is established in a society where the distribution of voters has a single mode and a small variance, it is possible that only two parties will exist in equilibrium because there is not enough political room on the scale for more than two significantly different positions to gain measurable support.[9]

Having explored the impact of the two major types of electoral structure upon the number of parties in a political system, we will concentrate our attention from now on upon the impact of the distribution of voters along the scale. In order to do so, we assume that this distribution is the only factor in determining how many parties there are.[10]

C. In Multiparty Systems

Multiparty systems—those with three or more major parties—are likely to occur whenever the distribution of voters is polymodal. The existence of two or more outstanding modes creates conditions favorable to one party at each mode, and perhaps balancing parties between them. Figure 5 represents an extreme example of this structure, since voters are equally distributed along the scale (on XX′); i.e., each point on the scale is a mode (or the distribution can be seen as having no modes). However, not every point can support a party if we assume that the electoral structure allows only a certain number of parties to compete for power with reasonable chances of success. Therefore a definite number of parties will spring up along the scale and maneuver until the distance between each party and its immediately adjacent neighbors is the same for all parties. In Figure 5 we have assumed that the total number of parties is limited to four; hence in equilibrium they will space themselves as shown (assuming extremists abstain if parties A and D move toward the center).[11]

An important difference between a distribution like that in Figure 5 and one like that in Figure 2 is that the former provides no incentive for parties to move toward each other ideologically. Party B in Figure 5, for example, cannot gain more votes by moving toward A or towards C. If it started toward C, it would win votes away from C, but it would lose just as many to A; the reverse happens if it moves toward A. Therefore it will stay at 37.5 and maintain its ideological purity—unlike party B in Figure 2.[12] The latter party is pulled toward the center because, by moving toward A, it wins more votes among the moderates than it loses among the extremists, as mentioned before.

Thus it is likely that in multiparty systems, parties will strive to distinguish themselves ideologically from each other and maintain the purity of their positions; whereas in two-party systems, each will try to resemble its opponent as closely as possible.[13]

This phenomenon helps to explain certain peculiarities of the two political systems. If our reasoning is correct, voters in multiparty systems are much more likely to be swayed by doctrinal considerations—matters of ideology and policy—than are voters in two-party systems. The latter voters are massed in the moderate range where both ideologies lie; hence they are likely to view personality, or technical competence, or some other nonideological factor as decisive. Because they are not really offered much choice between policies, they may need other factors to discriminate between parties.

Voters in multiparty systems, however, are given a wide range of ideological choice, with parties emphasizing rather than soft-pedalling their doctrinal differences. Hence regarding ideologies as a decisive factor in one's voting decision is usually more rational in a multiparty system than in a two-party system. In spite of this fact, the ideology of the government in a multiparty system (as opposed to the parties) is often less cohesive than its counterpart in a two-party system, as we shall see in the next chapter.

III.   THE ORIGIN OF NEW PARTIES

In analyzing the birth of new parties, we must distinguish between two types of new parties. The first is designed *to win elections*. Its originators feel that it can locate itself so as to represent a large number of voters whose views are not being expressed by any extant party. The second type is designed *to influence already existent parties* to change their policies, or not to change them; it is not primarily aimed at winning elections.

Of course, no party is ever begun by people who think it will never get any votes, or win any offices, especially if our hypothesis about party motivation is true. Nevertheless, some parties—founded by perfectly rational men—are meant to be threats to other parties and not means of gaining immediate power or prestige. An example is the States' Rights Party of 1948, intended to threaten the Democrats because of their policy on civil rights. Such blackmail parties are future oriented, since their purpose is to alter the choices offered to voters by the extant parties at some future date.

To distinguish between these two kinds of parties is often difficult, because many parties founded primarily to gain office actually perform the function of influencing the policies of previously existing parties. This impact has been typical of third parties in United States history, none of which ever won a national election, though many had great influence upon the platforms of parties that did win. Thus if we classify new parties by intention, nearly all of them are of the "real" type; whereas if we classify them by results, most of them, at least in American history, are of the "influence" type. However, we will assume that the new parties we discuss are designed to win elections, unless otherwise specified.

No party, new or old, can survive without gaining the support of a sizeable fraction of the electorate—a support active enough to be expressed by votes in elections. This does not mean that a party must locate right in the midst of a big lump of voters on our political scale; rather it must be nearer a large number of voters than any other parties are. Its location is as dependent upon where other parties are as it is upon where voters are.

New parties are most likely to appear and survive when there is an opportunity for them to cut off a large part of the support of an older party by sprouting up between it and its former voters. An outstanding case in point is the birth of the Labour Party in England, which can be illustrated very roughly by Figure 6. Before 1900, there were two major British parties, the Liberals (A) and the Tories (B). They were under the usual two-party pressure to converge. However, the enfranchisement of the working class in the late nineteenth century had shifted the center of voter distribution far to the left of its old position. And the Liberal Party, even after it moved to the left, was to the right of the new center of gravity, although it was the more left of the two parties. The founders of the Labour Party correctly guessed that they could out-flank the Liberals by forming a new party (C) to the left of the latter, which they did. This trapped the Liberals between the two modes of the electorate, and their support rapidly diminished to insignificant size.[14]

The crucial factor in this case was the shift of the electorate's distribution along the political scale as a result of the extension of suffrage to a vast number of new voters, many of whom were near the extreme left. Whenever such a radical change in the distribution of voters occurs, existent parties will probably be unable to adjust rapidly because they are ideologically immobile. New parties, however, are not weighed down by this impediment. Unencumbered by ideological commitments, they can select the most opportune point on the scale at which to locate, and structure their ideologies accordingly. Opportunities to do so will be especially tempting if the old parties have converged toward the previous center of gravity as a result of the normal two-party process, and the new distribution is heavily skewed to one or both extremes. This is roughly what happened in the case of the Labour Party.

Another situation which may be productive of new parties is a social stalemate caused by a voter distribution like that in Figure 3. Where voters are massed bimodally at opposite ends of the scale, peaceful democratic government is difficult, as mentioned previously. A faction desirous of compromise may grow up, thus altering the distribution so it resembles the one shown in Figure 7. Here an opportunity exists for a new party to be formed at C. If this party grows as a result of continuous shifts of voters to the center, eventually a new situation like that in Figure 8 may appear. The center has become preponderant, but has split into three parts because new parties have arisen to exploit the large moderate voting mass.

It is clear that a major prerequisite for the appearance of new parties is a change in the distribution of voters along the political scale. A shift in the universality of franchise, a weakening of traditional views by some cataclysmic event like World War II, a social revolution like that following upon industrialization— any such disturbing occurrence may move the modes on the political scale. A change in the number of voters *per se* is irrelevant; it is the distribution which counts. Hence women's suffrage does not create any new parties, although it raises the total vote enormously.

There is one situation in which a new party is likely to appear without any change in voter distribution, but this will be the influence type of party, not the

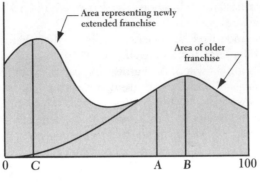

FIGURE 6

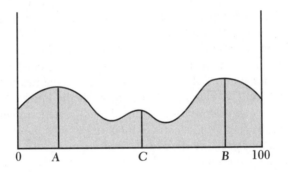

FIGURE 7

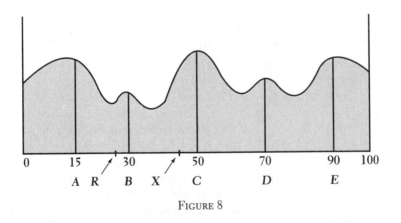

FIGURE 8

kind that aims at getting itself elected. When one of the parties in a two-party system has drifted away from the extreme nearest it toward the moderate center, its extremist supporters may form a new party to pull the policies of the old one back toward them. In Figure 9, party B has moved away to the left of its right-wing members because it wants to gain votes from the large mass of voters near

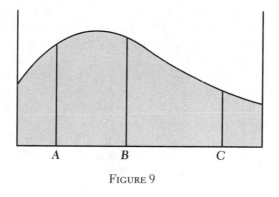

Figure 9

the leftish mode. In order to threaten party *B* with defeat unless it moves back toward the right, the right-wing extremists found party *C*. This party cannot possibly win itself, but it can throw the election to *A* by diverting extremist votes from *B*.

To get rid of this menace, party *B* must adopt some of *C*'s policies, thus moving back to the right and taking the wind out of *C*'s sails. This will cause party *C* to collapse, but it will have accomplished its purpose of improving the platform of one of the real contenders, *B*, in the eyes of its extremist supporters. As mentioned previously, the States' Rights Party formed in 1948 had just such an aim.

In situations like this, it is a movement of party ideology, not of voter distribution, which gives rise to a new party. Party ideologies are relatively immobile in multiparty systems; so this type of new party will appear almost exclusively in two-party systems. Fear of these blackmail parties may strongly counteract the centripetal pull normal to such systems.

IV. IDEOLOGICAL COHERENCE AND INTEGRATION

A. *Alteration of Our Model to Include Multipolicy Parties*

[Earlier] we showed that each party's ideology will be coherent but not integrated. That is, it will not contain internal contradictions, but neither will it be too closely tied to any one philosophic *Weltanschauung*. This outcome results from the conflicting desires each party feels when forming its ideology. On the one hand, it wishes to appeal to as many voters as possible; on the other hand, it wishes to have a strong appeal for each individual voter. The first desire implies a platform containing a wide range of policies representing many different ideological outlooks. The second desire implies a close integration of policies around the philosophic viewpoint of whichever voter is being wooed. Obviously, the more either desire is achieved, the less will the other be satisfied.

This dualism can be depicted on our graph of political space. First we must remove the assumption that each party's platform contains only its stand on the proper degree of government intervention in the economy. Let us assume instead that each party takes stands on many issues, and that each stand can be assigned a position on our left-right scale.[15] Then the party's net position on this scale is a weighted average of the positions of all the particular policies it upholds.

Furthermore, each citizen may apply different weights to the individual policies, since each policy affects some citizens more than others. Therefore the party has no unique, universally recognized net position. Some voters may feel it is more right-wing than others, and no one view can be proved correct. However, there will be some consensus as to the range in which the party's net position lies; so we can still distinguish right-wing parties from center and left-wing ones.

Under these conditions, the rational party strategy is to adopt a spread of policies which covers a whole range of the left-right scale. The wider this spread is, the more viewpoints the party's ideology and platform will appeal to. But a wider spread also weakens the strength of the appeal to any one viewpoint, because each citizen sees the party upholding policies he does not approve of.

Thus a voter's judgment of each party becomes two-dimensional: he must balance its net position (the mean of its policies) against its spread (their variance) in deciding whether he wants to support it. If some party has a mean identical with his own position (which we assume single-valued) but an enormous variance, he may reject it in favor of another party with a mean not as close to him but with a much smaller variance. In short, voters choose policy vectors rather than policy scalars, and each vector is really a weighted frequency distribution of policies on the left-right scale.

B. Integration Strategies in Two-Party and Multiparty Systems

If we assume that each point on the political scale represents a definite *Weltanschauung*, the width of the spread formed by a party's policies varies inversely with their integration around a single such *Weltanschauung*. Therefore, the degree of integration in a party's ideology depends upon what fraction of the scale it is trying to cover with its policy spread. We have already seen that this fraction will be smaller in a multiparty system than in a two-party system, simply because dividing a constant in half yields larger parts than dividing it into any greater number of equal pieces. If we rule out any overlapping of policy spreads, we may conclude that ideologies will be more integrated in multiparty systems than in two-party systems. Each party's platform will more clearly reflect some one philosophic viewpoint, around which its policies will be more closely grouped. This accords with our previous conclusion that each party in a multiparty system will try to differentiate its product sharply from the products of all other parties, whereas each party in a two-party system will try to resemble its rival.

To illustrate this conclusion, let us compare Figure 2 with Figure 5. In Figure 2, after parties A and B have approached each other near the center of the scale, each is drawing votes from half the scale. Its supporters range in viewpoint from those at one extreme to those at dead center; hence it must design a policy spread which includes all of them. But there are more voters in the middle than at the extremes. Therefore each party structures its policies so that its net position is moderate, even though it makes a few concessions to the extremists. In this way, it hopes to keep the extremists from abstaining and yet woo the middle-of-the-roaders massed around 50.

In contrast to the parties in Figure 2, those in Figure 5 do not have to appeal to a wide range of viewpoints. The policy span of each is much narrower, and any attempt to widen it soon causes a collision with another party. This restricts each party's spread even if we allow overlapping to occur.

For example, party B in Figure 5 cannot gain by trying to spread its policies so as to please voters at positions 10 and 60. If it wishes to retain its net position at 35, it can only cast a few policies out as far as 10 and 60. But parties A and C are massing most of their policies so as to please voters at 10 and 60 respectively; hence B cannot hope to compete with A and C in these locations. In fact, B is much better off concentrating its policies around 35, since this keeps it from spreading itself too thin and losing votes to A and C from its own bailiwick. Thus no party in a multiparty system has much incentive to spread out or to overlap another ideologically, and each will closely integrate its policies around some definite philosophic outlook.

C. Overlapping and Ambiguity in Two-Party Systems

If we allow overlapping in a two-party system, the results are radically different from those just described. Each party casts some policies into the other's territory in order to convince voters there that its net position is near them. In such maneuvering, there is much room for skill because different voters assign different weights to the same policies. For example, assume that there are two social groups, farmers and workers, whose positions are respectively right and left of 50. They have exactly opposite views on two laws, one on farm price supports and the other on labor practices. However, the farmers weigh the farm law heavily in their voting decisions and consider the labor law much less significant; whereas the workers' emphasis is just the reverse. Each group thus views any party's net position differently from the way the other views it. Realizing this, a clever party will take a stand favoring farmers on the farm law and workers on the labor law. By doing so, it can establish a net position simultaneously close to both groups, even though they are far apart from each other!

This possibility of having a net position in many different places at once makes overlapping policies a rational strategy in a two-party system. Therefore, in the middle of the scale where most voters are massed, each party scatters its policies on both sides of the midpoint. It attempts to make each voter in this area feel that it is centered right at his position. Naturally, this causes an enormous overlapping of moderate policies.

However, each party will sprinkle these moderate policies with a few extreme stands in order to please its far-out voters. Obviously, each party is trying to please an extreme opposite to that being pleased by the other party. Therefore it is possible to detect on which side of the midpoint each party is actually located by looking at the extremist policies it espouses. In fact, this may be the only way to tell the two parties apart ideologically, since most of their policies are conglomerated in an overlapping mass in the middle of the scale.

Clearly, both parties are trying to be as ambiguous as possible about their actual net position. Therefore why should they not accomplish the same end by being equally ambiguous about each policy? Then every policy stand can cover a spread of voters, too. Not only can voters differently weight individual policies, they can, also interpret the meaning of each policy differently—each seeing it in a light which brings it as close as possible to his own position. This vastly widens the band on the political scale into which various interpretations of a party's net position may fall.

Ambiguity thus increases the number of voters to whom a party may appeal. This fact encourages parties in a two-party system to be as equivocal as possible about their stands on each controversial issue. And since both parties find it rational to be ambiguous, neither is forced by the other's clarity to take a more precise stand.

Thus political rationality leads parties in a two-party system to becloud their policies in a fog of ambiguity. True, their tendency towards obscurity is limited by their desire to attract voters to the polls, since citizens abstain if all parties seem identical or no party makes testable promises. Nevertheless, competition forces both parties to be much less than perfectly clear about what they stand for. Naturally, this makes it more difficult for each citizen to vote rationally; he has a hard time finding out what his ballot supports when cast for either party. As a result, voters are encouraged to make decisions on some basis other than the issues, i.e., on the personalities of candidates, traditional family voting patterns, loyalty to past party heroes, etc. But only the parties' decisions on issues relevant to voters' utility incomes from government, so making decisions on any other basis is irrational. We are forced to conclude that rational behavior by political parties tends to discourage rational behavior by voters.

This conclusion may seem startling, since it implies that there is a conflict between party rationality and voter rationality in a two-party system. But in fact this conflict has also been observed by students of political behavior, as the following quotation shows:

> The tendency toward agreement between parties under a bipartisan system flows from the fact that party leaders must seek to build a majority of the electorate. In the nation as a whole a majority cannot be built upon the support of organized labor alone; the farmers cannot muster enough votes to form a majority; businessmen are decidedly in a minority. Given the traditional attachment to one party or another of large blocs of voters in all these classes, about the only way in which a party can form a majority is to draw further support from voters of all classes and interests. To succeed in this endeavor party leaders cannot afford to antagonize any major segment of the population. A convenient way to antagonize an element in the population is to take at an inopportune moment an unequivocal stand on an issue of importance. Similarities of composition, hence, contribute to two features of American parties: their similarity of view and their addiction to equivocation and ambiguity.[16]

Our model of "political space" has led us to exactly the same conclusion: parties will try to be similar and to equivocate. And the more they succeed, the more difficult it is for voters to behave rationally.

Does this mean that our assumption of rationality leads to a contradiction in a two-party system? Apparently the more rational political parties are, the less rational voters must be, and vice versa. How does this affect our model?

D. *A Fundamental Tension in Our Model*

To answer these questions, we must review briefly the basic structure of our mythical political system. In it are two sets of agents: voters and parties. Each set uses the other to achieve its own goal. Voters have as their goal the attainment of a government responsive to their wants; they make use of parties to run this government. Parties have as their goal the rewards of being in office; they make use of voters to get elected. Thus the interlocking of two different goal-pursuing processes forms the political system.

The only end common to both sets of agents is the continuance of the system. Otherwise, neither set cares whether the other's goals are achieved unless that achievement is beneficial to itself. Therefore if a member of one set can gain by impairing the ability of all the members of the other set to attain their goals, he will do so. This follows from our axiom that each man seeks his own good and to get it will sacrifice the good of others, if necessary.

To put it more concretely, if any party believes it can increase its chances of gaining office by discouraging voters from being rational, its own rational course is to do so. The only exception to this rule occurs when voter irrationality is likely to destroy the political system. Since parties have a stake in this system, they are irrational if they encourage anything which might wreck it.

However, it is not obvious that ambiguous policies and similar ideologies are likely to destroy democracy. What they might do is make voting less than perfectly rational as a mechanism for selecting governments. But rationality as we define it is not a dichotomous concept; i.e., the possible states of rationality are not limited to 100 percent and 0 percent. Therefore making voting less than perfectly rational does not render it absolutely useless but merely reduces its efficiency as a government-selection process. Knowing this, parties will not be deterred by fear of the end of democracy when they increase ambiguity and match each other's platforms.

Voters have two defenses against being forced into irrationality. The first is to limit the operations of parties by law. In the United States, parties have been forced to make financial reports, refrain from fraudulent statements, submit their primaries to public control, accept only limited contributions from any one source, and otherwise act in ways not likely to exploit the citizenry. Since it would be irrational for citizens to allow parties to exploit them, these laws indirectly protect voters from being forced into irrationality. But voters can hardly expect to induce government to pass laws against platform ambiguity and similarity, so this defense is not much help.

The second defense is to change the political system from a two-party one to a multiparty one. This will cause parties to narrow the spread of their policies, differentiate their platforms more sharply, and reduce ambiguity. However, such a conversion will also give rise to tremendous problems not present in two-party systems, as we shall see in the next chapter. Therefore it is doubtful whether the change would improve prospects for rational voting; they might get worse.

After weighing all these considerations, we may conclude that our model is not necessarily contradictory. However, it does contain two sets of agents in tension with each other. If either of these is allowed to dominate the other fully, the model may become contradictory; i.e., one of the two sets of agents may cease to behave rationally. Thus if parties succeed in obscuring their policy decisions in a mist of generalities, and voters are unable to discover what their votes really mean, a *rationality crisis* develops. Since such a crisis is even more likely to occur in a multiparty system, we will defer our analysis of it until the next chapter.

V. A BASIC DETERMINANT OF A NATION'S POLITICS

From everything we have said, it is clear that a basic determinant of how a nation's political life develops is the distribution of voters along the political scale, assuming our oversimplified model has some application in the real world. In the first place, the number of modes in the distribution helps determine whether the political system will be two-party or multiparty in character. This in turn determines whether party ideologies will be similar and ambiguous or different and definite; hence it influences the difficulties voters face in behaving rationally. Second, whether democracy can lead to stable government depends upon whether the mass of voters is centrally conglomerated, or lumped at the extremes with low density in the center; only in the former case will democracy really work. Third, the distribution's stability determines whether new parties will constantly be replacing the old, or the old will dominate and new ones merely influence their policy.

Of course, the distribution of voters is not the only factor basic to a nation's policies. For example, some theorists argue that the use of single-member districts instead of proportional representation is the main cause of a two-party political system.[17] Nevertheless, whether it is seen as a cause in itself or as a result of more fundamental factors, the distribution is a crucial political parameter.

What forces shape this important parameter? At the beginning of our study, we assumed that voters' tastes were fixed, which means that the voter distribution is given. Thus we dodged the question just posed, and have been evading it ever since. Even now we cannot answer, because the determinants are historic, cultural, and psychological, as well as economic; to attempt to analyze them would be to undertake a study vast beyond our scope.

All we can say is the following: (1) the distribution of voters is a crucial determinant molding a nation's political life, (2) major changes in it are among the most important political events possible, and (3) though parties will move ideologically to adjust to the distribution under some circumstances, they will also attempt to move voters toward their own locations, thus altering it.

VI. SUMMARY

We can turn Harold Hotelling's famous spatial market into a useful device for analyzing political ideologies by adding to it (1) variable distribution of population, (2) an unequivocal left-to-right ordering of parties, (3) relative ideological immobility, and (4) peaked political preferences for all voters.

This model confirms Hotelling's conclusion that the parties in a two-party system converge ideologically upon the center, and Smithies' addendum that fear of losing extremist voters keeps them from becoming identical. But we discover that such convergence depends upon a unimodal distribution of voters which has a low variance and most of its mass clustered around the mode.

If the distribution of voters along the scale remains constant in a society, its political system tends to move towards an equilibrium in which the number of parties and their ideological positions are fixed. Whether it will then have two or many parties depends upon (1) the shape of the distribution and (2) whether the electoral structure is based upon plurality or proportional representation.

No tendency toward imitation exists in a multiparty system; in fact, parties strive to accentuate ideological "product differentiation" by maintaining purity of doctrine. This difference between the two systems helps explain why certain practices are peculiar to each.

New parties are usually intended to win elections, but they are often more important as means of influencing the policies of previously existent parties. Since old parties are ideologically immobile, they cannot adjust rapidly to changes in voter distribution, but new parties can enter wherever it is most advantageous. Influence parties may crop up in two-party systems whenever convergence has pulled one of the major parties away from the extreme, and its extremist supporters want to move it back towards them.

If we assume a party's position on the scale is a weighted average of the positions occupied by each of its policy decisions, we can account for the tendency of parties to spread their policies: they wish to appeal to many different viewpoints at once. Parties in a two-party system have a much wider spread of policies—hence a looser integration of them—than those in a multiparty system. In fact, in two-party systems there is a large area of overlapping policies near the middle of the scale, so that parties closely resemble each other.

This tendency towards similarity is reinforced by deliberate equivocation about each particular issue. Party policies may become so vague, and parties so alike, that voters find it difficult to make rational decisions. Nevertheless, fostering ambiguity is the rational course for each party in a two-party system.

A basic determinant of a nation's political development is the distribution of its voters along the political scale. Upon this factor, to a great extent, depend whether the nation will have two or many major parties, whether democracy will lead to stable or unstable government, and whether new parties will continually replace old or play only a minor role.

NOTES

1. Harold Hotelling, "Stability in Competition," *Economic Journal* XXXIX (1929): 41–57, and Arthur Smithies, "Optimum Location in Spatial Competition," *Journal of Political Economy* XLIX (1941): 423–439. For other aspects of the spatial-competition problem, see F. Zeuthen, "Theoretical Remarks on Price Policy: Hotelling's Case with Variations," *Quarterly Journal of Economics* XLVII (1933): 231–253; Erich Schneider, "Bermerkungen zu Einer Theorie der Raumwirtschaft," *Econometrica* III (1935): 79–105; A. P. Lerner and H. W. Singer, "Some Notes on Duopoly and Spatial Competition," *Journal of Political Economy* XLV (1937): 145–186; and August Lösch, *The Economics of Location* (New Haven, Conn.: Yale University Press, 1954).

2. In reality, since so many ballots are cast, each individual voter has so little influence upon the election that his acts cannot be realistically appraised as a threat to any party, assuming the actions of all other citizens are given. Since we deal with this atomistic problem fully in [a later chapter], we evade it here by assuming each man behaves as though his vote has a high probability of being decisive.

3. The following description should not be construed as a causal explanation of revolutions; it is rather a translation of the events that occur in them into movements along the scale we have developed. Hence we make no attempt to discuss why revolutions follow the cycle portrayed. For an analysis of this problem, see Lyford P. Edwards, *The Natural History of Revolution* (Chicago: University of Chicago Press, 1927).

4. The application of this model to revolutions was suggested by Robert A. Dahl and Kenneth Arrow. Professor Dahl develops a similar model in A *Preface to Democratic Theory* (Chicago: University of Chicago Press, 1956), pp. 90–102.

5. This definition of party does not cover many actual parties that continue to exist even though their chances for election are practically zero; e.g., the Vegetarians and Socialists in the United States. These parties are politically irrational from the point of view of our hypothesis; i.e., the motives we posit as politically rational are not the ones impelling their members. Even future-oriented rationality does not cover them, since past experience demonstrates that their future chances of election are also nearly nonexistent unless some highly unlikely catastrophe occurs.

6. For a more extensive discussion of this assertion, see V. O. Key, Jr., *Politics, Parties, and Pressure Groups* (New York: Thomas Y. Crowell Company, 1953), pp. 224–231.

7. A detailed analysis of the problems raised by coalition governments is presented in the next chapter.

8. Another reason why new parties cannot form *ad infinitum* is that political parties are specialized agencies in the division of labor. Therefore not everyone can be in a political party; in fact, in a given society, there is probably a definite limit imposed by efficiency on the number of persons who can specialize in being party members. The size of this limit depends upon such factors as the importance of government action in that society, the need for differing representation (i.e., the scattering of voters on the scale), the social prestige and economic income attached to being in politics, and the general standard of living produced by the division of labor.

9. This example ignores the possibility of a tiny third party occupying a crucial balancing position between two other large parties. Actually such an outcome is also possible in a plurality system if the government is chosen by a series of district elections rather than a single national election. As in Great Britain, a small party may gain only a few seats in the legislature, but if the two large parties are equally powerful, its decisive role in the balance of power may keep it alive even though it never gains office in the government directly. Our plurality model precludes this outcome because we posit election on a strictly national basis. In the next chapter we present a proportional representation model in which such small but powerful parties can exist.

10. Of course there are many factors influencing the number of parties in a given system, but most of them can be subsumed under the electoral structure (which we just discussed) or the distribution of voters (which we are about to discuss).

11. As new voters appear on the scene, they may cluster around the four locations where parties exist and thus form a tetramodal distribution like that shown by the dotted line in Figure 5. In other

words, a perfectly even distribution is probably not stable over time but tends to become a distribution with definite modes and less populated areas between them. Such a development further restricts the manner in which new parties may enter the system, since it makes some locations much more desirable than others but also concentrates at the most favorable spots.

12. At this point we are ignoring the possibility of B's gaining power by forming a coalition with either A or C or both. . . .

13. A two-party system like that shown in Figure 3 will not exhibit ideological convergence. However, as we have pointed out, it is doubtful whether such a distribution can function as a democracy, since internal conflict will be intense no matter which party wins.

14. Interestingly enough, now that the Liberal Party has dwindled in support, the British electoral system has reverted to its former two-party pattern. Since the new center of gravity is far left of the old, the Conservative Party has moved farther leftward than the Labour Party has moved rightward. Nevertheless, a tendency toward convergence clearly exists.

15. We can state this assumption formally as follows: all citizens agree on a left-right ordering of the stands taken by the various parties on any given issue. Thus it is not necessary for every citizen to have the same cardinal ordering of stands on the left-right scale as every other; i.e., citizen A may feel that party X's stand on some issue is at point 35, while citizen B may believe the same stand is at point 30, but both must agree it is on the same side of party Y's stand on that issue and bears the same ordinal relation to the stands of parties W, Y and Z. Although in the text we implicitly assume agreement on the exact location of each party stand in order to simplify the argument, our conclusions also follow from purely ordinal premises.

16. V. O. Key, Jr., *op. cit.*, pp. 231–232.

17. We have already discussed this point in Section II of this chapter.

DONALD E. STOKES

SPATIAL MODELS OF PARTY COMPETITION

Donald E. Stokes (1927–1997), a professor at Princeton University, described party orientations in American elections as based on a combination of "position-issues" and what he called "valence-issues." The first delineate policy alternatives based on the perceived preferences of party constituencies. The second, "valence" effects, reflect the credit or blame that the electorate attaches to the parties for social and economic circumstances deemed salient at the time. Stokes's formulation modified, if not challenged, the Downsian model.

The use of spatial ideas to interpret party competition is a universal phenomenon of modern politics. Such ideas are the common coin of political journalists and have extraordinary influence in the thought of political activists. Especially widespread is the conception of a liberal-conservative dimension on which parties maneuver for the support of a public that is itself distributed from left to right. This conception goes back at least to French revolutionary times and has recently gained new interest for an academic audience through its ingenious formalization by Downs and others.[1] However, most spatial interpretations of party competition have a very poor fit with the evidence about how large-scale electorates and political leaders actually respond to politics. Indeed, the findings on this point are clear enough so that spatial ideas about party competition ought to be modified by empirical observation. I will review here evidence that the "space" in which American parties contend for electoral support is very unlike a single ideological dimension, and I will offer some suggestions toward revision of the prevailing spatial model.

I. THE HOTELLING-DOWNS MODEL

Because spatial ideas have been woven into popular and scholarly commentaries on politics with remarkable frequency, my observations reach well beyond recent efforts to formalize the spatial model of party competition. However, the work of Downs gives this conception admirable clarity without removing it too far from familiar usage, and I begin with a brief review of his system. The root idea of Downs's model is that the alternatives of government action on which political controversy is focused can be located in a one-dimensional space, along a left-right scale. At least for illustration, Downs interprets this dimension as the degree of government intervention in the economy. At the extreme left is complete government control, and at the extreme right no government intervention beyond the most limited state operations. Each voter can be located on the scale according to how much government control he wants and each party according to how much government control it advocates.[2]

As Downs is careful to make clear, this model extends a line of thought tracing back to the work of Harold Hotelling.[3] Thirty years ago Hotelling had sought to answer the question of why two competing firms are so often found in adjacent positions near the middle of a spatial market (Kresge's and Woolworth's are not at opposite ends of Main Street; they are right next door). Assuming (1) that the buying public is evenly distributed along a linear market (a transcontinental railroad, say), and (2) that demand is inelastic (that is, consumers at a given point of the market will buy a fixed amount of goods from whichever of two producers is closer and, hence, can offer the lower transportation costs to consumers located at that point), Hotelling was able to show that two competing firms would converge toward adjacent positions at the middle of the market. If one firm is farther from the middle than its competitor, it can increase its share of the market by moving toward the middle; and so on, until equilibrium is reached. Substituting voters for consumers, parties for firms, and the "costs" of ideological distance for transportation costs, Hotelling felt that his model could explain why the Democratic and Republican parties are so often found close to the center a liberal-conservative dimension.

Those who have extended Hotelling's ideas have done so by relaxing one or both of the assumptions given above. Arthur Smithies and several other economists dispensed with (2), the assumption of inelastic demand.[4] Smithies assumed instead that demand depends on price and that sales at any given point of the market will vary according to how much delivered prices are raised by transportation costs. For this reason two competing firms will be under pressure not only to move closer together to improve sales in their "competitive region"; they will also be under pressure to move farther apart to improve sales in their respective "hinterlands." When these two opposite forces are in equilibrium the competing firms could well be some distance apart. Continuing the side discussion of politics, Smithies argued that electoral "demand" also is elastic, since a voter who feels that both parties are too far from his ideological position can simply stay away from the polls. With this assumption added, Smithies felt that the model could explain why the Republicans and Democrats (by the time of the New Deal era) were some distance apart, ideologically speaking.

Downs has retained Smithies's assumption of elastic demand and has further modified the Hotelling model by dispensing with (1), the assumption that the public is evenly distributed over a one-dimensional space. Indeed, in Downs's system, the way the public is distributed along the liberal-conservative scale is a *variable* of great importance, one that he uses to explain some very notable attributes of (constructed) political systems.[5] Under Downs's revision, the model not only can explain the strategic choices of existing parties as they place themselves along the left- right scale. It can also explain the emergence of new parties and the disappearance of old ones. Downs's discussion can be read equally as a theory of voter choice, a theory of party positioning, and a theory of party number.

Like any good theorist, Downs should be read in the original. However, the inferences he makes to the number and positions of competing parties from different distributions of the public on the left-right scale may be summarized as follows. If the distribution has a single mode, the party system will be in equilibrium when two parties have converged to positions that are fairly close together. Just how close depends on how elastic the turnout is and on how sharp the peak of the distribution is, as well as other factors.[6] If the distribution has two modes, the system will be in equilibrium when two parties are present, each having assumed a position somewhere near one of the modes. If the distribution has more than two modes, the system will be in equilibrium when a party occupies each of the several modal positions. In this sense, the presence of more than two modes of opinion encourages the development of a multiparty system.

Reviewing these ideas, one must first admire the ingenuity with which Downs has transformed Hotelling's brilliant analogy into a model of party systems. However, the model includes some cognitive postulates that need to be drastically qualified in view of what is known about the parties and electorates of actual political systems. Of course, it is in the nature of models not to represent the real world exactly. The more general and powerful a model is, the more severely it will cut away unnecessary aspects of reality, and any first-class formalization should be forgiven a host of empirical peccadilloes. However, what is wrong with the hidden postulates of Downs's model is more than a petty fault. Those postulates are introduced when the argument shifts from economic competition in a spatial market to political competition in an ideological market. In Downs's (and Hotelling's) exposition, this transition is rather too easily accomplished. The consequences of placing competitors and consumers in a linear space are developed persuasively for the economic problem, where the meaning of the space is clear, and transferred too easily to the political problem, where the meaning of the space can be far from clear. The ground over which the parties contend is *not* a space in the sense that Main Street or a transcontinental railroad is. Treating it as if it were introduces assumptions about the unidimensionality of the space, the stability of its structure, the existence of ordered dimensions and the common frame of reference of parties and electorate that are only poorly supported by available evidence from real political systems.[7]

II. THE AXIOM OF UNIDIMENSIONALITY

The most evident—and perhaps least fundamental—criticism to be made of the spatial model is that the conception of a single dimension of political conflict can hardly be sustained. Such an assumption clearly is false to the realities of two-party systems, including the American, on which intensive studies have been made. And there is evidence that it falsifies the realities of many multiparty systems, in which the appearance or continued existence of parties depends less on the electorate's distribution along a single dimension than on the presence of several dimensions of political conflict.

The unreality of a one-dimensional account of political attitudes in America is attested by several kinds of evidence from the electoral studies of the Survey Research Center at the University of Michigan. The relative independence of various attitude dimensions is a repeated finding of these studies. For example, over a period of years this research has measured public attitudes toward social and economic welfare action by government and toward American involvement in foreign affairs. The lore of popular journalism would make these two domains one, with the liberal internationalist position going hand in hand with the liberal social welfare position. However, the empirical support for this conception is weak indeed. Across a national sample of the electorate, there is *no* relation between attitudes toward social welfare policies and American involvement abroad.[8] These dimensions of attitude are independent in a statistical sense; knowing how "liberal" a person is on one gives no clue whatever as to how "liberal" he will be on the other.

If the voters' own positions on social welfare and foreign involvement prevent our treating these two dimensions as one, their reactions to the domestic and foreign policies of the parties can also be strongly discrepant. For example, in the presidential election of 1952 the Democratic Party was approved for its domestic economic record but strongly disapproved for its record in foreign affairs, particularly the unfinished conflict in Korea. With even-handed justice the public rewarded the party for prosperity and punished it for war without reducing the Democrats' performance to a summary position on some over-arching dimension of political controversy.

An intensive search for such a dimension has met little success. In the presidential elections of 1952, 1956, and 1960 the Center's interviews opened with an extended series of questions designed to elicit the ideas that are actually associated with the parties and their presidential candidates. When the answers, amounting on the average to a quarter hour of conversation, are examined closely for ideological content, only about a tenth of the electorate by the loosest definition is found to be using the liberal-conservative distinction or any other ideological concept. By a more reasonable count, the proportion is something like three percent.[9] What is more, when our respondents are asked directly to describe the parties in terms of the liberal-conservative distinction, nearly half confess that the terms are unfamiliar. And the bizarre meanings given the terms by many of those who do attempt to use them suggest that we are eliciting artificial answers that have little to do with the public's everyday perceptions of the parties.

The axiom of unidimensionality is difficult to reconcile with the evidence from multiparty systems as well. The support for the parties of a multiparty system is often more easily explained by the presence of several dimensions of political conflict than it is by the distribution of the electorate along any single dimension. At least since Marx, the dimension we would choose to account for party support, if allowed only one, would be socio-economic or class-related. Yet the politics even of western nations exhibit many parties that owe their existence to religious or racial or ethnic identifications or to specialized social and economic interests (such as the agrarian) that do not fit readily into the stratification order. For example, the *Zentrum* of Weimar Germany and before, as the prototype confessional party, drew support from Catholics at all levels of German society. The party could scarcely have survived if its strength had depended entirely on public response to its socio-economic policies.[10] My colleague, Philip Converse, and Georges Dupeux have found that the party preferences of the mass French public are more highly associated with attitudes toward religious issues than with attitudes toward socio-economic issues, despite the immensely greater attention given the latter by government and elite circles. If the parties and electorate of contemporary France are to be located in spatial terms, the space must be one of at least two dimensions.

Even support for the occasional third party of American politics may be understood better if more than one dimension is considered. The Dixiecrat Party of 1948 is a good case in point. Downs himself describes the Dixiecrats as a "blackmail party" whose intent was to force the national Democratic party farther to the right on the general liberal-conservative dimension.[11] But it is at least as plausible to say that their rebellion was directed at Truman's civil rights program, as the southern walkout over adoption of a civil rights plank by the national Democratic convention of 1948 would suggest. Undoubtedly for some southerners civil rights were closely linked with issues of economic and social welfare policy. But for others these issue domains were quite distinct. American political beliefs are sufficiently multidimensional so that many Dixiecrat votes were cast by southern economic liberals.

Although the assumption of unidimensionality is a familiar part of prevailing spatial conceptions of party competition, it might well he dispensed with. Hotelling's original argument can easily be generalized to two dimensions, as Hotelling himself observed (in most of the towns we know about, Kresge's and Woolworth's are still right together, even though their customers live on a two-dimensional surface).[12] That the model has not been extended may be due in part to the fact that introducing more dimensions raises questions about its fit with the real world that are not likely to be asked about the simple one-dimensional model. In particular, accommodating a greater number of dimensions draws attention to the assumption that the space of party competition, whether unidimensional or multidimensional, has a stable structure.

III. THE AXIOM OF FIXED STRUCTURE

The mischief of too facile a shift from the economic to the political problem is plainly seen in connection with the assumption of stable structure. Since the space represented by a transcontinental railroad depends on physical distance, its structure is fixed, as the structure of Main Street is. The distribution of consumers within these spaces may vary; the space itself will not. Hotelling applied his economic model to some kinds of spaces whose structure was not derived from physical distance: for example, the degree of sweetness of cider. But these, too, were spaces of fixed structure.

By comparison, the space in which political parties compete can be of highly variable structure. Just as the parties may be perceived and evaluated on several dimensions, so the dimensions that are salient to the electorate may change widely over time. The fact of such change in American politics is one of the best-supported conclusions to be drawn from the Survey Research Center's studies of voting behavior over a decade and a half. For example, between the elections of 1948 and 1952 a far-reaching change took place in the terms in which the parties and candidates were judged by the electorate. Whereas the voter evaluations of 1948 were strongly rooted in the economic and social issues of the New Deal–Fair Deal era, the evaluations of 1952 were based substantially on foreign concerns.

A dimension that had touched the motives of the electorate scarcely at all in the Truman election was of great importance in turning the Democratic administration out of power four years later. If the difference between these two elections is to be interpreted in spatial terms, we would have to say that the intrusion of a new issue dimension had changed the structure of the space in which the parties competed for electoral support.

However, this way of putting it implies that a dimension either *is* part of the structure of the space or it is *not*, whereas the presence of a given evaluative dimension is often a matter of degree. What is needed is language that would express the fact that different weights should be given different dimensions at different times. At some moments of political history class or religious or foreign or regional dimensions are of greater cognitive and motivational significance to the electorate than they are at other times, quite apart from shifts in the positions of the competing parties and their consuming public. Drastic electoral changes can result from changes in the *coordinate system* of the space rather than changes in the distribution of parties and voters.

I think the evidence shows that party managers are very sensitive to changes in the grounds of electoral evaluation. Political fortunes are made and lost according to the ability of party leaders to sense what dimensions will be salient to the public as it appraises the candidates and party records. To be sure, this awareness is not universal, and some political leaders have imputed to the electorate a stereotyped cognitive map that is very close to the Downs model. The discrepancy between these imputed cognitions and the electorate's actual cognitions is a point to which I will return. But the skills of political leaders who must maneuver for public support in a democracy consist partly in knowing what issue dimensions are salient to the electorate or can be made salient by suitable propaganda. The deftness with which Republican leaders turned the changing concerns of the country to their advantage in 1952 provides an excellent modern example. Dewey and the other Eisenhower managers knew that victory lay in exploiting relatively new and transitory political attitudes, including the one they could inject into the campaign by nominating an immensely popular military figure who was seen in wholly non-ideological terms. The brilliant slogan of the "three K's"—Korea, Corruption, Communism—with which the Republicans pressed the 1952 campaign was hardly the work of men who perceived the cognitions and motives of the electorate as tied primarily to the left-right distinction. The dominant Republican leadership showed a highly pragmatic understanding of the changing dimensions of political evaluation.

The case of 1952 leads to a further point of great importance. I have called the new issues of that year "dimensions" to keep them within the terms of this discussion. But one does not have to take a very searching look at these issues to feel that some at least are not dimensions in any ordinary sense. The issue of corruption, for example, was hardly one on which the Democratic Party took a position *for* the "mess in Washington" and the Republicans a position *against* it in appealing to an electorate that was itself distributed on a dimension extending from full probity in government to full laxity and disarray. A consideration of this point raises a third difficulty in applying the Downs model to actual party systems.

IV. THE AXIOM OF ORDERED DIMENSIONS

For the spatial model to be applied, the parties and voters of a political system must be able to place themselves on one or more common dimensions. That is, there must be at least one ordered set of alternatives of government action that the parties may advocate and the voters prefer. Degrees of government intervention in the economy is such a set, as Downs observed; so is the extent of American involvement in foreign affairs or the extent of federal action to protect the rights of Negroes. Obviously a good deal depends on how many elements the set has. A spatial language tends to suggest that the number is indefinitely large, like the number of points in Euclidean one-space or the real line of mathematics. The number of alternatives in a political dimension is clearly more limited, though it cannot be too limited if such ideas as modal position and relative distance are to have more than trivial meaning. However, to make my point as strong as possible, let me include within the notion of an ordered set one in which there are only *two* alternatives of government action that the parties may endorse and the voters prefer.

The empirical point that needs to be made is that many of the issues that agitate our politics do not involve even a shriveled set of two alternatives of government action. The corruption issue of 1952 did not find the Democrats taking one position and the Republicans another. And neither were some voters in favor of corruption while others were against it. If we are to speak of a dimension at all, both parties and all voters were located at a single point—the position of virtue in government. To be sure, enough evidence of malfeasance had turned up in the Democratic administration so that many voters felt the party had strayed from full virtue. But throwing the rascals out is very different from choosing between two or more parties on the basis of their advocacy of alternatives of government action. The machinery of the spatial model will not work if the voters are simply reacting to the association of the parties with some goal or state or symbol that is positively or negatively valued.

To emphasize the difference involved here I will call "*position*-issues" those that involve advocacy of government actions from a set of alternatives over which a distribution of voter preferences is defined. And borrowing a term from Kurt Lewin I will call "*valence*-issues" those that merely involve the linking of the parties with some condition that is positively or negatively valued by the electorate.[13] If the condition is past or present ("You never had it so good," "800 million people have gone behind the Iron Curtain"), the argument turns on where the credit or blame ought to be assigned. But if the condition is a future or potential one, the argument turns on which party, given possession of the government, is the more likely to bring it about.

It will not do simply to exclude valence-issues from the discussion of party competition. The people's choice too often depends upon them. At least in American presidential elections of the past generation it is remarkable how many valence-issues have held the center of the stage. The great themes of depression and recovery, which dominated electoral choice during the Thirties and Forties, were a good deal of this kind. What happened to Hoover and the Republicans was that they got bracketed with hard times, much as the Democrats later, although less clearly, were to be bracketed with war. Twenty years after the Hoover disaster the Republicans were returned to power in an election that was saturated with the valence-issues of the Korean War and corruption in Washington. And the question of American prestige abroad, to which Kennedy and Nixon gave so much attention in the campaign of 1960, was a pure specimen of valence-issue. Both parties and all voters, presumably, were for high prestige. The only issue was whether or not America had it under the existing Republican Administration.

The failure to distinguish these types of issues, whatever they are called, is one reason why journalistic accounts of political trends so often go astray. Apparently the urge to give an ideological, position-issue interpretation of election results can be irresistible, despite the reams of copy that have been devoted to Madison Avenue technique and the art of image-building. One becomes aware of how often the impact of valence-issues is mistaken for ideological movements ("with the election of Kennedy America has again moved to the left") simply by reading what the newspapers have continued to say even after careful studies of American voting behavior began to report their findings.

It is of course true that position-issues lurk behind many valence-issues. The problem of Korea, which benefited the Republicans so handsomely in 1952, is a good case. The successful Republican treatment of this issue was to link the unfinished Korean conflict with the fact of Democratic presidents during two world wars to hang the "war party" label on the Democrats. However, it is not hard to find alternatives of government action that *might* have provided a focus to the debate. For example, the controversy might have centered on how aggressive a policy toward the Red Chinese forces America should adopt. Should the United States carry the war to Manchuria, using all weapons? prosecute the war more vigorously within Korea? negotiate a settlement on the basis of existing conditions, essentially the course the Eisenhower administration took? or pull back to Japan? The point is that neither this ordered set of alternatives nor any other provided the terms of the debate. Both in Republican propaganda and popular understanding the issue was simply a matter of the Democrats having gotten the country into a war from which Eisenhower would extract us—whether by bombing Manchuria or evacuating South Korea was not made clear.

The question whether a given problem poses a position- or valence-issue is a matter to be settled empirically and not on *a priori* logical grounds. This point is illustrated by the issue of the country's economic health. At least since the panic of 1837 did Van Buren in, prosperity has been one of the most influential valence-issues of American politics. All parties and the whole electorate have wanted it. The argument has had to do only with which party is more likely to achieve it, a question on which the public changed its mind between McKinley's full dinner pail and Franklin Roosevelt's New Deal. However, to make the point as sharp as possible, let us imagine that part of the electorate wants something less than full prosperity—even that it wants economic distress, for the bracing effect that economic difficulties have on individual conduct and the moral fiber of society as a whole. If this unlikely condition came to pass and the parties maneuvered for support by advocating different degrees of prosperity or distress, the issue would have been transformed from a valence-issue into a position-issue. That it is *not* such an issue in our politics is due solely to the fact that there is overwhelming consensus as to the goal of government action.

Since the preferences of parties and voters must be distributed over an ordered set of policy alternatives for the spatial model to work, valence-issues plainly do not fit the spatial scheme. Unless the interaction of voters and parties is focused on position-dimensions the model cannot serve as a theory either of the motivation of voters or of the positioning of parties.[14] This is not to say that the interaction of parties and voters on valence-issues is uninteresting or incapable of being represented by a different model. It is only to say that the model would be different. When the parties maneuver for support on a position-dimension, they choose policies from an ordered set of alternatives belonging to the same problem or issue. But when the parties maneuver in terms of valence-issues, they choose one or more issues from a set of distinct issue domains. As the Republicans looked over the prospective issues for 1952, their problem was not whether to come out *for* or *against* Communist subversion or prosperity or corruption in Washington. It was rather to put together a collection of issues of real or potential public concern whose positive and negative valences would aid the Republicans and embarrass the Democrats.

To be sure, Downs makes allowance for valence-issues by granting that some voting is "irrational," that is, non-ideological in his spatial sense. He asserts, in fact, that rational behavior by the parties of a two-party system tends to encourage irrational behavior by voters. As the parties converge to ideologically similar positions (assuming a unimodal distribution of voters) their relative position provides fewer grounds for choice and the voters are driven to deciding between them on some irrational basis. This is an admirable defense—indeed, Downs has come close to constructing a theory that cannot be disproved, since evidence of voter motivation and party propaganda outside the bounds of the theory can be cited as evidence that the model applies. For the defense to be convincing, however, we must be shown that the ideological dimension on which the parties are presumed to be close together has empirical validity.

But empirical validity for whom? The space of Downs's model is formed out of the perceptions held by the actors who play roles in the political system. However, the model includes at least two classes of actors—voters and party managers—and their perceptions of what the political fighting is all about can diverge markedly. Here again, the economic problem has left its imprint; Kresge's Main Street and the customer's Main Street are the same, and the question of divergent spaces does not arise. Yet it can easily arise in the political context. It is quite possible that the voters see political conflict in terms that differ widely from those in which the parties see it, and this possibility draws attention to a fourth unstated assumption of the Downs model.

V. THE AXIOM OF COMMON REFERENCE

The versatility of the spatial scheme as an interactional model is enhanced a good deal by assuming that the public and those who seek its support impose a common frame of reference on the alternatives of government action. In particular, it is the assumption of a commonly perceived space of party competition that allows the model to serve at once as a theory of voter motivation and of party positioning. But with the space formed out of perceptions, there is no logically necessary reason why the space of voters and of parties should be identical, and there is good empirical reason to suppose that it often is not. Indeed, in view of the emphasis on imperfect information elsewhere in his discussion, one might expect Downs to regard such an assumption with considerable skepticism. The postulate may be faithful to the realities of economic competition, and it serves the cause of theoretical parsimony, but its factual validity in the political context is doubtful, to say the least.

If the model's assumption of common reference is relaxed, its unified theory of voter behavior and party positioning breaks at least in two. The behavior of voters depends not on where or whether the parties are on an ideological dimension but only on the electorate's *perception* of these things. It would be possible, although highly improbable in view of what is known about large-scale publics, for the motivation of voters to be governed by a calculus of ideological distance, even though the parties were not competing for support in these terms at all. And it would be possible, and a good deal more probable, for the parties to seek electoral support by positioning themselves on an ideological dimension, even though the public evaluated their stands in wholly non-ideological terms. Admittedly, it is extreme to think of the pieces into which the spatial model divides (without the assumption of common reference) as two *completely intrapsychic* theories, since the voters' perceptions of parties depend to some degree on what the parties are actually doing and vice versa. But it is equally extreme to assume away the possibility of divergence between the space that is real to voters and the space that is real to party leaders.

Relaxing the assumption of common reference necessarily opens Pandora's box. If we are willing to assume that Kresge's and the customer's Main Street are not the same, there is no reason why Woolworth's Main Street cannot be different, too. We may, in fact, have as many perceived spaces as there are perceiving actors. Certainly the way public policy alternatives are perceived varies widely across the electorate. A few voters, as we have seen, impose a clear ideological structure on political conflict. But the vast majority rely on assorted non-ideological ways of structuring the political world. And an appreciable stratum of voters can scarcely be said to have any cognitive structure at all as it tries to make sense out of that distant and confusing world.

Likewise, different political leaders may impose different frames of reference on the alternatives of government policy. And they may attribute very different cognitive structures to the public. In the intraparty struggle preceding the 1952 Republican convention, the late Senator Taft and his lieutenants offered a diagnosis of the Republican situation that was remarkably faithful to the one-dimensional ideological model. According to Taft, the country had been moving strongly to the right on the liberal-conservative dimension since the heyday of the New Deal, but millions of potential Republican voters had been kept from the polls by the party's liberal, "me-too" candidates (because demand is elastic, Willkie and Dewey were said to have lost more votes in the party's hinterland than they gained in its competitive region). Hence, victory lay in nominating an unmistakably conservative candidate. The Taft diagnosis and prescription had an appealing simplicity, but the convention was dominated by men whose view of popular thought was very different and far more realistic. Their struggle to control the nomination was fought at least in part on the issue of how the public looks at party competition.

The truth is that we do not yet have very careful evidence about what frames of reference party leaders use in their perceptions of the alternatives of government policy and little enough evidence about the cognitive structures the voters use. Various scaling studies of legislatures suggest that at least the political space of legislators has a fairly definite structure, although it is typically multidimensional.[15] In a variety of multiparty systems the simple factor of seating legislators from left to right helps give political conflict a dimensional character—and has done so as far back as the National Convention of revolutionary France.[16] It is likely that political leaders impute more structure to the perceptions formed by the public than actually exists; in some cases party activists see the electorate in thoroughly Downsian terms, as Senator Taft did. But the question of what cognitive structures are meaningful to political leaders remains an immensely important matter for future inquiry.

VI. TOWARD REFORMULATION

The conclusion I would draw from all this is not that the spatial model should be rejected root-and-branch but rather that we should treat as explicit variables the cognitive phenomena that the prevailing model removes from the discussion by assumption. Bringing these variables into the model would lessen its elegance and parsimony in some respects but would vastly increase the scientific interest of the model as a theory of party systems. Without these variables the model is likely to remain a kind of instructive insight that seems plausible in some contexts, implausible in others, and only poorly suited to guide empirical observation of real political events.

One implication of treating these cognitive factors as variables is to acknowledge that they can assume a configuration of values in the real world that approximates the assumptions of the classical spatial model. Political conflict *can* be focused on a single, stable issue domain which presents an ordered-dimension that is perceived in common terms by leaders and followers. Let us call this the case of *strong ideological focus*. On the other hand, political controversy can be diffused over a number of changing issue concerns which rarely present position-dimensions and which are perceived in different ways by different political actors. Let us call this the case of *weak ideological focus*, a case that is well illustrated by the contemporary American scene.

Treating these cognitive phenomena as variables would lead naturally to a comparison of political systems in these terms. Certainly there are very significant differences in the values these variables assume in different party systems, just as there are very important differences in their values for the same system over time. Although the historical evidence is tantalizingly ambiguous, I think it reasonable to conclude that the strength of ideological focus in the United States was greater during the Roosevelt New Deal than it is today. Then, more than now, the intervention of government in the domestic economy and related social problems provided a position-dimension that could organize the competition of parties and the motivation of electors.

However, the moment of American political history when political conflict was most intensely focused on a single ordered-dimension was undoubtedly the period just prior to the Civil War. As the prewar crisis deepened, political discussion became more and more absorbed in the overriding issue of slavery and its attendant controversies. The fact that the struggle over slavery had overtones of economic interest and constitutional theory and regional loyalty does not undermine the point; it is exactly the gathering of several facets of conflict into a single dimension that characterized the politics of the day. The focusing of controversy on this dimension became at last so strong that it provided a basis for the dissolution of long-standing party loyalties in much of the electorate, something that has not happened again to an equal degree in a hundred years. This historical case is the more interesting since the all-consuming dimension of conflict had so little to do with the class-related dimensions that we usually associate with the spatial model.

If a single position-dimension was of transcendant importance in the convulsions leading to civil war, the spatial model ought to predict the appearance of the new party of the prewar era. The period of the Republican Party's early success exhibited the strong ideological focus that would make the model applicable. Then the period ought also to exhibit the conditions from which we would predict the birth of a new party. There is persuasive evidence that it did. As the dimension of slavery became more and more salient, almost certainly there was an anti-slavery shift of opinion in the older states of the North, just as there was a shift to a more aggressively pro-slavery opinion in the South. And what is equally important, the Northern electorate was rapidly extended in the fifteen years prior to 1860 by the granting of statehood to five new states—Wisconsin, Iowa, Minnesota, California, and Oregon—all anti-slavery. These changes in the North presented the Republican Party with the chance to exploit a new "mode" of anti-slavery opinion to which the Democrats and Whigs, in seeking to keep the allegiance of old friends, were much less able to respond. Yet if the slavery dimension had been only one of several influencing the electorate, the new party would hardly have succeeded. Only with the cognitive preconditions of the spatial model satisfied could the distribution of voters on the slavery question bring a revolutionary change in the structure of the party system.

Elaborating the model to take account of these cognitive variables is more than a matter of seeing that Downs's assumptions are met before plugging the model in. In particular, extending the model to the case of two or more stable, ordered dimensions will lead to results that do not have any analogues in the one-dimensional case. For example, the degree of orthogonality of several dimensions clearly has implications for electoral behavior, party positioning, and party number. And in the multidimensional case a good deal would rest on whether the electoral support of the parties is defined in terms of several dimensions at once;

that is, on whether the parties' support is based on joint distributions or marginal distributions. At the very least the formation of coalitions will differ according to whether the parties' electoral strength is differentiated on common or distinct dimensions. The politics of Israel, for instance, will be quite different according to whether the parties are referred to *all* major dimensions of conflict—Zionism, secularism, socialism, attitude toward the West, and so forth—or tend to attract their support on the basis of one or a very few dimensions only.

The reaction to political models is likely to depend partly on taste for some time to come. So few formalizations have added to our knowledge of politics that their potential value can be a matter for honest debate. The Hotelling-Downs model makes a good case for model-building in political research. Certainly no one who compares the inferences this apparatus permits with the inferences that can be drawn from loose popular ideas of spatial competition will fail to gain new respect for a model of this sort. However, the usefulness of models depends absolutely on the interchange between theory-building and empirical observation. This interchange is essential to show the limits of a model's application and guide its future development. No theory is unconditionally true. Learning what the conditions are is an indispensable step toward giving the theory a more significant domain of application.

If anything, the exchange between theory-building and empirical observation is more important in social than in natural science, since the social scientist so rarely has it in his power to make the conditions of his theory come true, as the natural or physical scientist often can. One reason the physicist is untroubled by the fact that his law of gravity does not describe the behavior of many falling bodies (snowflakes, for example) is that he is able to control the disturbing factors whenever the need arises. But the social or political theorist cannot manipulate the conditions of party systems whose dynamics he would predict or explain. No engineering is available to produce the conditions of strong ideological focus so that the prevailing model of spatial competition will apply. If it is to be empirically successful the theory itself must be extended to take account of the varying cognitive elements found in the competition of parties in the real world.

NOTES

1. For expositions of Downs's model, see Anthony Downs, *An Economic Theory of Democracy* (New York: Harper and Brothers, 1957), pp. 114–141, and "An Economic Theory of Political Action in a Democracy," *Journal of Political Economy*, 65 (1957), pp. 135–150. For a similar model, developed independently, see Duncan MacRae, Jr., *Dimensions of Congressional Voting: a Statistical Study of the House of Representatives in the Eighty-First Congress* (Berkeley and Los Angeles: University of California Press, 1958), pp. 354–382.

2. Downs's model is a little more complicated than this. Each voter has not only a most-preferred degree of government intervention (let us say his "point" on the scale); he has some amount of preference for every other degree of government intervention (the other points on the scale), the amount decreasing monotonically the farther the point is from his optimum. Hence, the preference of the

electorate as a whole for a given degree of government intervention is the sum of the preferences of individual voters for that degree or intervention. Moreover, a party's position on the scale may be thought of as the sum or average of the positions it takes on a variety of particular issues.

3. Harold Hotelling, "Stability in Competition," *Economic Journal*, 39 (1929), pp. 41–57.

4. Arthur Smithies, "Optimum Location in Spatial Competition," *Journal of Political Economy*, 49 (1941), pp. 423–429.

5. Downs makes several other modifications of Hotelling's and Smithies's models in addition to treating the distribution of the public on the scale as a variable. Especially important is the assumption that one party will not "jump over" the position of another on the liberal-conservative dimension.

6. The assumption that no party can move past another on the left-right scale makes the equilibrium positions of two competing parties less well defined than it is for the competing firms of the models of Hotelling and Smithies.

7. My remarks here are directed solely to Downs's spatial model of party competition. *An Economic Theory of Democracy* (*op. cit.*) sets forth a whole collection of models, elaborated from a few central variables. All are worth detailed study. Paradoxically, the spatial model described here is likely to have great intuitive appeal for a wide audience, yet its postulates are almost certainly as radical as those of any model in Downs's collection.

8. Angus Campbell, Philip E. Converse, Warren E. Miller, and Donald E. Stokes, *The American Voter* (New York: John Wiley and Sons, 1960), pp. 197–198.

9. *Ibid.*, Chapter 10, "The Formation of Issue Concepts and Partisan Change," pp. 227–234.

10. It is a curious and interesting fact that the agrarian party of modern Norway, like the Catholic party of pre-Hitler Germany, has chosen to call itself the "Center" party, that is, to call itself by a name that refers to a dimension other than the one on which the party's main support is based. By selecting a title that is neutral in terms of a primary dimension of political conflict, the party invites potential supporters to ignore that dimension and rally to the party's special cause.

11. Downs, *op. cit.*, 1957, p. 128.

12. A troublesome problem in applying a more general model to the real world is that of defining some kind of distance function over all pairs of points in the space. The need for such a function is less acute in the one-dimensional case, because an approximate ordering of distances between points can be derived from the strong ordering of points in the space. However, the points of a multidimensional space are no longer strongly ordered, and it may not be possible to compare the appeal of two or more parties for voters located at a given point by measuring how far from the point the parties are. Of course, if the space can be interpreted in physical terms, as Hotelling's could, this problem does not arise.

13. These terms may recall the distinction between "position issues" and "style issues" made by Bernard R. Berelson, Paul F. Lazarsfeld, and William N. McPhee, *Voting* (Chicago: University of Chicago Press, 1954), pp. 184–198. If I understand their point, the difference between issues of position and style rests on a material-ideal distinction and hence tends to oppose class-related issues to all others. Their account of style issues sounds at places like the conception of valence-issues here. But many of the style issues they cite (e.g., prohibition, civil liberties) would be position-issues under the definitions I have given.

14. Because the public's evaluation of political actors is so often and so deeply influenced by valence-issues the Survey Research Center has used a model of individual electoral choice (and, by extension, of the national vote decision) that measures only the valence and intensity of the affect associated with the parties and candidates. The model is described in Donald E. Stokes, Angus Campbell, and Warren E. Miller, "Components of Electoral Decision," this *Review*, 52 (June 1958), pp. 367–387, and Campbell, Converse, Miller, and Stokes, *op. cit.*, pp. 68–88 and 524–531.

15. See, among others, Duncan MacRae, Jr., "The Role of the State Legislator in Massachusetts," *American Sociological Review*, 19 (1954), pp. 185–194; Duncan MacRae, Jr., and Hugh D. Price, "Scale Positions and 'Power' in the Senate," *Behavioral Science*, 4 (1959), pp. 212–218; and George M. Belknap, "A Method for Analyzing Legislative Behavior," *Midwest Journal of Political Science*, 2 (November 1958), pp. 377–402.

16. In view of the ambiguity of party ideologies and the multidimensional grounds of party conflict, the necessity of agreeing upon a unidimensional seating order can itself lead to conflict in a legislative chamber that follows a left-right scheme. An interesting example of this is the attempt of the Finnish People's Party to move its seats to the left of the Agrarian Party in Finland's Eduskunta after the 1951 election.

17

MORRIS P. FIORINA

THE DECLINE OF COLLECTIVE
RESPONSIBILITY IN AMERICAN POLITICS

American national government suffers increasingly from single-issue politics, weak leadership in the face of important challenges, and a trend toward short-term approaches to long-term problems. In the past, the political parties helped clarify accountability for public policies. As the strength and coherence of political parties has declined in the United States, it has become more difficult to concert governmental action and assign responsibility clearly. Morris P. Fiorina, professor of government at Harvard, discusses these issues in the following piece.

Though the Founding Fathers believed in the necessity of establishing a genuinely national government, they took great pains to design one that could not lightly do things *to* its citizens; what government might do *for* its citizens was to be limited to the functions of what we know now as the "watchman state." Thus the Founders composed the constitutional litany familiar to every schoolchild: they created a federal system, they distributed and blended powers within and across the federal levels, and they encouraged the occupants of the various positions to check and balance each other by structuring incentives so that one officeholder's ambitions would be likely to conflict with others'. The resulting system of institutional arrangements predictably hampers efforts to undertake major initiatives and favors maintenance of the status quo.

Given the historical record faced by the Founders, their emphasis on constraining government is understandable. But we face a later historical record, one that shows two hundred years of increasing demands for government to act positively. Moreover, developments unforeseen by the Founders increasingly raise the likelihood that the uncoordinated actions of individuals and groups will inflict serious damage on the nation as a whole. The by-products of the industrial and technological revolutions impose physical risks not only on us, but on future generations as well. Resource shortages and international cartels raise the spectre of economic ruin. And the simple proliferation of special interests with their intense, particularistic demands threatens to render us politically incapable of taking actions that might either advance the state of society or prevent foreseeable deteriorations in that state. None of this is to suggest that we should forget about what government can do *to* us—the contemporary concern with the proper scope and methods of government intervention in the social and economic orders is long overdue. But the modern age demands as well that we worry about our ability to make government work *for* us. The problem is that we are gradually

[Tables and figures have been renumbered.—Eds.]

losing that ability, and a principal reason for this loss is the steady erosion of *responsibility* in American politics.

What do I mean by this important quality, responsibility? To say that some person or group is responsible for a state of affairs is to assert that he or they have the ability to take legitimate actions that have a major impact on that state of affairs. More colloquially, when someone is responsible, we know whom to blame. Human beings have asymmetric attitudes toward responsibility, as captured by the saying "Success has a thousand fathers, but failure is an orphan." This general observation applies very much to politicians, not surprisingly, and this creates a problem for democratic theory, because clear location or responsibility is vitally important to the operation of democratic governments. Without responsibility, citizens can only guess at who deserves their support; the act of voting loses much of its meaning. Moreover, the expectation of being held responsible provides representatives with a personal incentive to govern in their constituents' interest. As ordinary citizens we do not know the proper rate of growth of the money supply, the appropriate level of the federal deficit, the advantages of the MX over alternative missile systems, and so forth. We elect people to make those decisions. But only if those elected know they will be held accountable for the results of their decisions (or nondecisions, as the case may be), do they have a personal incentive to govern in our interest.[1]

Unfortunately, the importance of responsibility in a democracy is matched by the difficulty of attaining it. In an autocracy, individual responsibility suffices; the location of power in a single individual locates responsibility in that individual as well. But individual responsibility is insufficient whenever more than one person shares governmental authority. We can hold a particular congressman individually responsible for a personal transgression such as bribe-taking. We can even hold a president individually responsible for military moves where he presents Congress and the citizenry with a *fait accompli*. But on most national issues individual responsibility is difficult to assess. If one were to go to Washington, randomly accost a Democratic congressman, and berate him about a 20-percent rate of inflation, imagine the response. More than likely it would run, "Don't blame me. If 'they' had done what I've advocated for *x* years, things would be fine today." And if one were to walk over to the White House and similarly confront President Carter, he would respond as he already has, by blaming Arabs, free-spending congressmen, special interests, and, of course, us.

American institutional structure makes this kind of game-playing all too easy. In order to overcome it we must lay the credit or blame for national conditions on all those who had any hand in bringing them about: some form of *collective responsibility* is essential.

The only way collective responsibility has ever existed, and can exist given our institutions, is through the agency of the political party; in American politics, responsibility requires cohesive parties. This is an old claim to be sure, but its age does not detract from its present relevance.[2] In fact, the continuing decline in public esteem for the parties and continuing efforts to "reform" them out of the political process suggest that old arguments for party responsibility have not been made often enough or, at least, convincingly enough, so I will make these arguments once again in this essay.

A strong political party can generate collective responsibility by creating incentive for leaders, followers, and popular supporters to think and act in collective terms. First, by providing party leaders with the capability (e.g., control of institutional patronage, nominations, and so on) to discipline party members, genuine leadership becomes possible. Legislative output is less likely to be a least common denominator—a residue of myriad conflicting proposals—and more likely to consist of a program actually intended to solve a problem or move the nation in a particular direction. Second, the subordination of individual officeholders to the party lessens their ability to separate themselves from party actions. Like it or not, their performance becomes identified with the performance of the collectivity to which they belong. Third, with individual candidate variation greatly reduced, voters have less incentive to support individuals and more incentive to support or oppose the party as a whole. And fourth, the circle closes as party-line voting in the electorate provides party leaders with the incentive to propose policies that will earn the support of a national majority, and party back-benchers with the personal incentive to cooperate with leaders in the attempt to compile a good record for the party as a whole.

In the American context, strong parties have traditionally clarified politics in two ways. First, they allow citizens to assess responsibility easily, at least when the government is unified, which it more often was in earlier eras when party meant more than it does today.[3] Citizens need only evaluate the social, economic, and international conditions they observe and make a simple decision for or against change. They do not need to decide whether the energy, inflation, urban, and defense policies advocated by their congressman would be superior to those advocated by Carter—were any of them to be enacted!

The second way in which strong parties clarify American politics follows from the first. When citizens assess responsibility on the party as a whole, party members have personal incentives to see the party evaluated favorably. They have little to gain from gutting their president's program one day and attacking him for lack of leadership the next, since they share in the president's fate when voters do not differentiate within the party. Put simply, party responsibility provides party members with a personal stake in their collective performance.

Admittedly, party responsibility is a blunt instrument. The objection immediately arises that party responsibility condemns junior Democratic representatives to suffer electorally for an inflation they could do little to affect. An unhappy situation, true, but unless we accept it, Congress as a whole escapes electoral retribution for an inflation they *could* have done something to affect. Responsibility requires acceptance of both conditions. The choice is between a blunt instrument or none at all.

Of course, the United States is not Great Britain. We have neither the institutions nor the traditions to support a British brand of responsible party government, and I do not see either the possibility or the necessity for such a system in America. In the past the United States has enjoyed eras in which party was a much stronger force than today. And until recently—a generation, roughly—parties have provided an "adequate" degree of collective responsibility. They have done so by connecting the electoral fates of party members, via presidential coattails, for example, and by transforming elections into referenda on party performance, as with congressional off-year elections.

In earlier times, when citizens voted for the party, not the person, parties had incentives to nominate good candidates, because poor ones could have harmful fallout on the ticket as a whole.[4] In particular, the existence of presidential coattails (positive and negative) provided an inducement to avoid the nomination of narrowly based candidates, no matter how committed their supporters. And, once in office, the existence of party voting in the electorate provided party members with the incentive to compile a good *party* record. In particular, the tendency of national midterm elections to serve as referenda on the performance of the president provided a clear inducement for congressmen to do what they could to see that their president was perceived as a solid performer. By stimulating electoral phenomena such as coattail effects and midterm referenda, party transformed some degree of personal ambition into concern with collective performance.

In the contemporary period, however, even the preceding tendencies toward collective responsibility have largely dissipated. As background for a discussion of this contemporary weakening of collective responsibility and its deleterious consequences, let us briefly review the evidence for the decline of party in America.

THE CONTINUING DECLINE OF PARTY IN THE UNITED STATES

Party is a simple term that covers a multitude of complicated organizations and processes. It manifests itself most concretely as the set of party organizations that exist principally at the state and local levels. It manifests itself most elusively as a psychological presence in the mind of the citizen. Somewhere in between, and partly a function of the first two, is the manifestation of party as a force in government. The discussion in this section will hold to this traditional schema, though it is clear that the three aspects of party have important interconnections.

Party Organizations

In the United States, party organization has traditionally meant state and local party organization. The national party generally has been a loose confederacy of subnational units that swings into action for a brief period every four years. This characterization remains true today, despite the somewhat greater influence and augmented functions of the national organizations.[5] Though such things are difficult to measure precisely, there is general agreement that the formal party organizations have undergone a secular decline since their peak at the end of the nineteenth century. The prototype of the old-style organization was the urban machine, a form approximated today only in Chicago.

Several long-term trends have served to undercut old-style party organizations. The patronage system has been steadily chopped back since passage of the Civil

Service Act of 1883. The social welfare functions of the parties have passed to the government as the modern welfare state developed. And, less concretely, the entire ethos of the old-style party organization is increasingly at odds with modern ideas of government based on rational expertise. These long-term trends spawned specific attacks on the old party organizations. In the late nineteenth and early twentieth centuries the Populists, Progressives, and assorted other reformers fought electoral corruption with the Australian Ballot and personal registration systems. They attempted to break the hold of the party bosses over nominations by mandating the direct primary. They attacked the urban machines with drives for nonpartisan at-large elections and nonpartisan city managers. None of these reforms destroyed the parties; they managed to live with the reforms better than most reformers had hoped. But the reforms reflected changing popular attitudes toward the parties and accelerated the secular decline in the influence of the party organizations.

The New Deal period temporarily arrested the deterioration of the party organizations, at least on the Democratic side. Unified party control under a "political" president provided favorable conditions for the state and local organizations.[6] But following the heyday of the New Deal (and ironically, in part, because of government assumption of subnational parties' functions) the decline continued.

In the 1970s two series of reforms further weakened the influence of organized parties in American national politics. The first was a series of legal changes deliberately intended to lessen organized party influence in the presidential nominating process. In the Democratic party, "New Politics" activists captured the national party apparatus and imposed a series of rules changes designed to "open up" the politics of presidential nominations. The Republican party—long more amateur and open than the Democratic party—adopted weaker versions of the Democratic rules changes. In addition, modifications of state electoral laws to conform to the Democratic rules changes (enforced by the federal courts) stimulated Republican rules changes as well. Table 1 shows that the presidential nominating process has indeed been opened up. In little more than a decade after the disastrous 1968 Democratic conclave, the number of primary states has more than doubled, and the number of delegates chosen in primaries has increased from little more than a third to three-quarters. Moreover, the remaining delegates emerge from caucuses far more open to mass citizen participation, and the delegates themselves are more likely to be amateurs, than previously.[7] For example, in the four conventions from 1956 to 1968 more than 70 percent of the Democratic party's senators, 40 percent of their representatives, and 80 percent of their governors attended. In 1976 the figures were 18 percent, 15 percent, and 47 percent, respectively.[8] Today's youth can observe the back-room maneuvers of party bosses and favorite sons only by watching *The Best Man* on late night television.

A second series of 1970s reforms lessened the role of formal party organizations in the conduct of political campaigns. These are financing regulations growing out of the Federal Election Campaign Act [FECA] of 1971 as amended in 1974 and 1976. In this case the reforms were aimed at cleaning up corruption in the financing of campaigns; their effects on the parties were a by-product, though many individuals accurately predicted its nature. Serious presidential candidates

TABLE 1. RECENT CHANGES IN PRESIDENTIAL NOMINATION PROCESS

	Number of States Holding Primaries	PERCENTAGES OF DELEGATES SELECTED IN PRIMARIES	
		Democratic	Republican
1968	17	38	34
1972	23	61	53
1976	30	73	68
1980	36	76	76

Source: 1968–1976 figures from Austin Ranney, "The Political Parties: Reform and Decline," in *The New American Political System*, Anthony King (ed.) (Washington, D.C.: American Enterprise Institute, 1978), Table 6-1. Figures for 1980 are from *National Journal*, October 20, 1979: 1738–1739.

are now publicly financed. Though the law permits the national party to spend two cents per eligible voter on behalf of the nominee, it also obliges the candidate to set up a finance committee separate from the national party. Between this legally mandated separation and fear of violating spending limits or accounting regulations, for example, the law has the effect of encouraging the candidate to keep his party at arm's length.[9]

At present only presidential candidates enjoy public financing, but a series of new limits on contributions and expenditures affects other national races. Prior to the implementation of the new law, data on congressional campaign financing were highly unreliable, but consider some of the trends that have emerged in the short time the law has been in effect. Table 2 shows the diminished role of the parties in the financing of congressional races. In House races, the decline in the party proportion of funding has been made up by the generosity of political action committees (also stimulated by the new law). In the Senate, wealthy candidates appear to have picked up the slack left by the diminished party role. The party funding contribution in congressional races has declined not only as a proportion of the total, but also in absolute dollars, and considerably in inflation-adjusted dollars. The limits in the new law restrict a House candidate to no more than $15,000 in funding from each of the national and relevant state parties (the average campaign expenditure of an incumbent in 1978 was about $121,000; of a challenger, about $54,000). A candidate for the Senate is permitted to receive a maximum of $17,500 from his senatorial campaign committee, plus two cents per eligible voter from the national committee and a like amount from the relevant state committee (twenty-one senatorial candidates spent over $1 million in 1978).

There is no detailed work on the precise effects of the contribution limits, but it appears doubtful that they are binding. If the national party were to contribute $15,000 to each of its congressional candidates, and a flat $17,500 to each of its senatorial candidates, that would be more than $8 million. *All* levels of the parties contributed only $10.5 million of the $157 million spent in 1978 congressional races.

Probably more constraining than limits on what the parties can contribute to the candidates are limits on what citizens and groups can contribute to the parties. Under current law, individual contributors may give $1,000 per election to a candidate (primary, runoff, general election), $5,000 per year to a political action

TABLE 2. RECENT SOURCES OF CONGRESSIONAL CAMPAIGN CONTRIBUTIONS
(IN PERCENTAGES)

	HOUSE			
	Individual	*PACs*	*Parties*	*Personal*
1972	59	14	17	NA
1978	57	25	7	11
	SENATE			
1972	67	12	14	1
1978	70	13	6	11

Source: Michael Malbin, "Of Mountains and Molehills: PACs, Campaigns, and Public Policy," in Malbin (ed.), *Parties, Interest Groups, and Campaign Finance Laws* (Washington, D.C.: American Enterprise Institute, 1980), Table 1.

committee, and $20,000 per year to a party. From the standpoint of the law, each of the two great national parties is the equivalent of four PACs. The PACs themselves are limited to a $15,000 per year contribution to the national party. Thus financial angels are severely restricted. They must spread contributions around to individual candidates, each of whom is likely to regard the contribution as an expression of personal worthiness and, if anything, as less reason than ever to think in terms of the party.

The ultimate results of such reforms are easy to predict. A lesser party role in the nominating and financing of candidates encourages candidates to organize and conduct independent campaigns, which further weakens the role of parties. Of course, party is not the entire story in this regard. Other modern day changes contribute to the diminished party role in campaign politics. For one thing, party foot soldiers are no longer so important, given the existence of a large leisured middle class that participates out of duty or enjoyment, but that participates on behalf of particular candidates and issues rather than parties. Similarly, contemporary campaigns rely heavily on survey research, the mass media, and modern advertising methods—all provided by independent consultants outside the formal party apparatus. Although these developments are not directly related to the contemporary reforms, their effect is the same: the diminution of the role of parties in conducting political campaigns. And if parties do not grant nominations, fund their choices, and work for them, why should those choices feel any commitment to their party?

Party in the Electorate

In the citizenry at large, party takes the form of a psychological attachment. The typical American traditionally has been likely to identify with one or the other of the two major parties. Such identifications are transmitted across generations to some degree, and within the individual they tend to be fairly stable.[10] But there is mounting evidence that the basis of identification lies in the individual's experiences (direct and vicarious, through family and social groups) with the parties in the past.[11] Our current party system, of course, is based on the dislocations of the Depression period and the New Deal attempts to alleviate them. Though only a small proportion of those who experienced the Depression directly are active voters today, the general outlines of citizen party identifications much resemble those established at that time.

Again, there is reason to believe that the extent of citizen attachments to parties has undergone a long-term decline from a nineteenth century high.[12] And again, the New Deal appears to have been a period during which the decline was arrested, even temporarily reversed. But again, the decline of party has reasserted itself in the 1970s.

Since 1952 the Center for Political Studies at the University of Michigan has conducted regular national election surveys. The data elicited in such studies give us a graphic picture of the state of party in the electorate (Table 3). As the 1960s wore on, the heretofore stable distribution of citizen party identifications began to change in the general direction of weakened attachments to the parties. Between 1960 and 1976, independents, broadly defined, increased from less than a quarter to more than a third of the voting-age population. Strong identifiers declined from slightly more than a third to about a quarter of the population.

As the strength and extent of citizen attachments to the parties declined, the influence of party on the voting decisions of the citizenry similarly declined. The percentage of the voting-age population that reports consistent support of the same party's presidential candidate dropped from more than two-thirds in 1952 to less than half in 1976. As Table 4 shows, the percentage of voters who report a congressional vote consistent with their party identification has declined from over 80 percent in the late 1950s to under 70 percent today. And as Table 5 shows, ticket-splitting, both at the national and subnational levels, has probably doubled since the time of the first Eisenhower election.

Indisputably, party in the electorate has declined in recent years. Why? To some extent the electoral decline results from the organizational decline. Few party organizations any longer have the tangible incentives to turn out the faithful and assure their loyalty. Candidates run independent campaigns and deemphasize their partisan ties whenever they see any short-term electoral gain in doing so. If party is increasingly less important in the nomination and election of candidates, it is not surprising that such diminished importance is reflected in the attitudes and behavior of the voter.

Certain long-term sociological and technological trends also appear to work against party in the electorate. The population is younger, and younger citizens

TABLE 3. SUBJECTIVE PARTY IDENTIFICATION, 1960–1976 (IN PERCENTAGES)

Party ID	1960	1964	1968	1972	1976
Strong Democrat	21	27	20	15	15
Weak Democrat	25	25	25	26	25
Independent Democrat	8	8	9	10	12
Independent	8	8	11	13	14
Independent Republican	7	6	9	11	10
Weak Republican	13	13	14	13	14
Strong Republican	14	11	10	10	9

Source: National Election Studies made available by the InterUniversity Consortium for Political and Social Research, University of Michigan.

TABLE 4. PARTY-LINE VOTES IN HOUSE ELECTIONS

YEAR	1956	1958	1960	1962	1964	1966
PERCENTAGE	82	84	80	83	79	76

YEAR	1968	1970	1972	1974	1976	1978
PERCENTAGE	74	76	73	74	72	69

Source: National Election Studies made available by the InterUniversity Consortium for Political and Social Research, University of Michigan.

TABLE 5. TRENDS IN TICKET-SPLITTING, 1952–1976 (IN PERCENTAGES)

	President/House	State/Local
1952	12	34
1956	16	42
1960	14	46
1964	15	42
1968	18	48
1972	30	54
1976	25	—

Source: National Election Studies made available by the InterUniversity Consortium for Political and Social Research, University of Michigan.

traditionally are less attached to the parties than their elders. The population is more highly educated; fewer voters need some means of simplifying the choices they face in the political arena, and party, of course, has been the principal means of simplification. And the media revolution has vastly expanded the amount of information easily available to the citizenry. Candidates would have little incentive to operate campaigns independent of the parties if there were no means to apprise the citizenry of their independence. The media provide the means.

Finally, our present party system is an old one. For increasing numbers of citizens, party attachments based on the Great Depression seem lacking in relevance to the problems of the late twentieth century. Beginning with the racial issue in the 1960s, proceeding to the social issue of the 1970s, and to the energy, environment, and inflation issues of today, the parties have been rent by internal dissension. Sometimes they failed to take stands, at other times they took the wrong ones from the standpoint of the rank and file, and at most times they have failed to solve the new problems in any genuine sense. Since 1965 the parties have done little or nothing to earn the loyalties of modern Americans.

Party in Government

If the organizational capabilities of the parties have weakened, and their psychological ties to the voters have loosened, one would expect predictable consequences for the party in government. In particular, one would expect to see an increasing degree of split party control within and across the levels of American government. The evidence on this point is overwhelming.

At the state level, twenty-seven of the fifty governments were under divided party control after the 1978 election. In seventeen states a governor of one party opposed a legislature controlled by the other, and in ten others a bicameral legislature was split between the parties. By way of contrast, twenty years ago the number of states with divided party control was sixteen.

At the federal level the trend is similar. In 1953 only twelve states sent a senator of each party to Washington. The number increased to sixteen by 1961, to twenty-one by 1972, and stands at twenty-seven today. Of course, the senators in each state are elected at different times. But the same patterns emerge when we examine simultaneous elections. There is an increasing tendency for congressional districts to support a congressman of one party and the presidential candidate of the other (Table 6). At the turn of the century it was extremely rare for a congressional district to report a split result. But since that time the trend has been steadily upward. We may well be heading for a record in 1980 as a vulnerable Democratic president runs with 250-odd not-so-vulnerable Democratic congressmen.

Seemingly unsatisfied with the increasing tendencies of the voters to engage in ticket-splitting, we have added to the split of party in government by changing electoral rules in a manner that lessens the impact of national forces. For example, in 1920 thirty-five states elected their legislators, governors, and other state officials in presidential election years. In 1944 thirty-two states still did so. But in the past generation the trend has been toward isolation of state elections from national currents: as of 1970 only twenty states still held their elections concurrently with the national ones.[13] This legal separation of the state and national electoral arenas helps to separate the electoral fates of party officeholders at different levels of government, and thereby lessens their common interest in a good party record.

The increased fragmentation of the party in government makes it more difficult for government officeholders to work together than in times past (not that it has ever been terribly easy). Voters meanwhile have a more difficult time attributing responsibility for government performance, and this only further fragments party control. The result is lessened collective responsibility in the system.

In recent years it has become a commonplace to bemoan the decline of party in government. National commentators nostalgically contrast the Senate under Lyndon Johnson with that under Robert Byrd. They deplore the cowardice and paralysis of a House of Representatives, supposedly controlled by a two-thirds Democratic majority under the most activist, partisan speaker since Sam Rayburn. And, of course, there are the unfavorable comparisons of Jimmy Carter to previous presidents—not only FDR and LBJ, but even Kennedy. Such observations may be

TABLE 6. SPLIT RESULTS, CONGRESS AND PRESIDENT

YEAR	1900	1908	1916	1924	1932	1940
PERCENTAGE OF DISTRICTS	3	7	11	12	14	15

YEAR	1948	1956	1964	1972	1980	
PERCENTAGE OF DISTRICTS	23	30	33	42	?	

Source: The 1900–1964 figures are from Walter Dean Burham, *Critical Elections and the Mainspring of American Politics* (New York: Norton, 1970), p. 109. The 1972 figures are from *Congressional Quarterly's* compilation of official election returns.

descriptively accurate, but they are not very illuminating. It is not enough to call for more inspiring presidential leadership and to demand that the majority party in Congress show more readiness to bite the bullet. Our present national problems should be recognized as the outgrowths of the increasing separation of the presidential and congressional electoral arenas.

By now it is widely understood that senatorial races are in a class by themselves. The visibility of the office attracts the attention of the media as well as that of organized interest groups. Celebrities and plutocrats find the office attractive. Thus massive media campaigns and the politics of personality increasingly affect these races. Senate elections now are most notable for their idiosyncrasy, and consequentially for their growing volatility; correspondingly, such general forces as the president and the party are less influential in senatorial voting today than previously.

What is less often recognized is that House elections have grown increasingly idiosyncratic as well. I have already discussed the declining importance of party identification in House voting and the increasing number of split results at the district level. These trends are both cause and consequence of incumbent efforts to insulate themselves from the electoral effects of national conditions. Figure 1 shows the distribution of the vote garnered by the Democratic candidate in incumbent-contested districts in 1948 and 1972.[14] Evidently, a massive change took place in the past generation. In 1948 most congressional districts were clustered around the 50-percent mark (an even split between the parties); most districts now are clustered away from the point of equal division. Two obvious questions arise: Why has the change occurred, and does it matter?

Taking the second question first, Figure 1 suggests a bleak future for such electoral phenomena as presidential coattails and midterm referenda on presidential performance. Consider a swing of 5 percent in the congressional vote owing to a particularly attractive (or repulsive) presidential candidate or an especially poor performance by a president. In the world represented by the 1948 diagram, such a swing has major consequences: it shifts a large proportion of districts across the 50-percent mark. The shift provides a new president with a "mandate" in an on-year election and constitutes a strong "message" to the president in an off-year election. In the world represented by the 1972 diagram, however, the hypothesized 5-percent shift has little effect: few seats are close enough to the tipping point to shift parties under the hypothesized swing. The president's victory is termed a "personal" victory by the media, or the midterm result is interpreted as a reflection of personal and local concerns rather than national ones.

Why has the distribution of the congressional voting results changed over time? Elsewhere I have argued that much of the transformation results from a temporal change in the basis of congressional voting.[15] We have seen that party influence in House voting has lessened. And, judging by the number of Democrats successfully hanging onto traditional Republican districts, programmatic and ideological influences on House voting probably have declined as well. What has taken up the slack left by the weakening of the traditional determinants of congressional voting? It appears that a variety of personal and local influences now play a major role in citizen evaluations of their representatives.[16] Along with the expansion of the

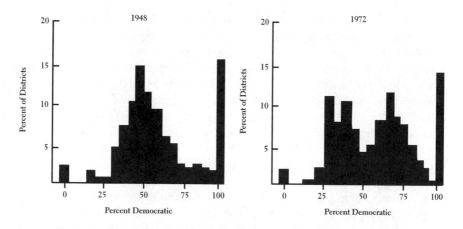

FIGURE 1. CONGRESSIONAL VOTE IN DISTRICTS WITH INCUMBENTS RUNNING

federal presence in American life, the traditional role of the congressman as an all-purpose ombudsman has greatly expanded. Tens of millions of citizens now are directly affected by federal decisions. Myriad programs provide opportunities to profit from government largesse, and myriad regulations impose costs and/or constraints on citizen activities. And, whether seeking to gain profit or avoid costs, citizens seek the aid of their congressmen. When a court imposes a desegregation plan on an urban school board, the congressional offices immediately are contacted for aid in safeguarding existing sources of funding and in determining eligibility for new ones. When a major employer announces plans to quit an area, the congressional offices immediately are contacted to explore possibilities for using federal programs to persuade the employer to reconsider. Contractors appreciate a good congressional word with DOD [Department of Defense] procurement officers. Local artistic groups cannot survive without NEA [National Endowment for the Arts] funding. And, of course, there are the major individual programs such as social security and veterans' benefits that create a steady demand for congressional information and aid services. Such activities are nonpartisan, nonideological, and, most important, noncontroversial. Moreover, the contribution of the congressman in the realm of district service appears considerably greater than the impact of his or her single vote on major national issues. Constituents respond rationally to this modern state of affairs by weighing nonprogrammatic constituency service heavily when casting their congressional votes. And this emphasis on the part of constituents provides the means for incumbents to solidify their hold on the office. Even if elected by a narrow margin, diligent service activities enable a congressman to neutralize or even convert a portion of those who would otherwise oppose him on policy or ideological grounds. Emphasis on local, nonpartisan factors in congressional voting enables the modern congressman to withstand national swings, whereas yesteryear's uninsulated congressmen were more dependent on preventing the occurrence of the swings.

Actually, the insulation of the modern congressman from national forces is even more complete than the preceding discussion suggests. Not only are few representatives so vulnerable that a reaction to a presidential candidate or his performance would turn them out of office, but such reactions themselves are less likely to find a reflection in the congressional voting. Several years ago Professor Edward Tufte formulated an elegant statistical model that predicts the magnitude of the in-party's losses in midterm elections as a function of two variables, the popularity of the incumbent president and the state of the national economy as measured by changes in real income.[17] For most of the post–World War II period the model predicts quite accurately. But in recent years the predictions have begun to go awry; specifically, in 1974 and 1978 the model significantly overpredicts the losses of the in-party.[18] The reason is quite apparent. As congressmen increasingly build personal organizations (largely with taxpayer-provided offices, staff, and communications resources) and base their campaigns on local issues and their personal record of service to the district, national conditions and the performance of the party leader have less and less of an impact on House races. In fact, analysis of the 1978 Center for Political Studies Congressional Election Study reveals that evaluations of President Carter's performance had no effect on the electoral fortunes of Democratic incumbents, and citizen evaluations of government's handling of the national economy had only the barest trace of an impact.[19]

The effects of the insulation of congressional incumbents have begun to show up in a systematic way in the governmental arena. Table 7 presents data on presidential success and presidential support in Congress for the first two years of the administrations of our last five elected presidents. As is evident, Carter (1977–1978) was less successful than earlier presidents who enjoyed a Congress controlled by their own party; he was only as successful as Nixon, who faced an opposition Congress. Moreover, in the House, Carter has done relatively poorly in gaining the support of his own party. It is noteworthy that John F. Kennedy (1961–1962) earned a significantly higher level of support from a congressional party that was nearly half Southern, whereas Carter enjoyed a majority in which the regional split was much less severe.[20]

Of course, it is possible to discount the preceding argument as an unjustified generalization of a unique situation—a particularly inept president, a Congress full of prima donnas still flexing their post-Watergate muscles, and so on. But I think not. The withering away of the party organizations and the weakening of party in the electorate have begun to show up as disarray in the party in government. As the electoral fates of congressmen and the president have diverged, their incentives to cooperate have diverged as well. Congressmen have little personal incentive to bear any risk in their president's behalf, since they no longer expect to gain much from his successes or suffer much from his failures. Only those who personally agree with the president's program and/or those who find that program well suited for their particular district support the president. And there are not enough of these to construct the coalitions necessary for action on the major issues now facing the country. By holding only the president responsible for national conditions, the electorate enables officialdom as a whole to escape

TABLE 7. RECENT TRENDS IN CONGRESSIONAL SUPPORT OF THE EXECUTIVE
(IN PERCENTAGES)

Congress	Year	Presidential Success	PRESIDENTIAL SUPPORT WITHIN HIS PARTY	
			House	Senate
83rd	1953–1954	83	72	72
87th	1961–1962	83	73	64
89th	1965–1966	87	69	61
91st	1969–1970	76	62	63
95th	1977–1978	77	61	67

Source: *Congressional Quarterly Almanacs.*

responsibility. This situation lies at the root of many of the problems that now plague American public life.

SOME CONSEQUENCES OF THE DECLINE OF COLLECTIVE RESPONSIBILITY

The weakening of party has contributed directly to the severity of several of the important problems the nation faces. For some of these, such as the government's inability to deal with inflation and energy, the connections are obvious. But for other problems, such as the growing importance of single-issue politics and the growing alienation of the American citizenry, the connections are more subtle.

Immobilism

As the electoral interdependence of the party in government declines, its ability to act also declines. If responsibility can be shifted to another level or to another officeholder, there is less incentive to stick one's neck out in an attempt to solve a given problem. Leadership becomes more difficult, the ever-present bias toward the short-term solution becomes more pronounced, and the possibility of solving any given problem lessens.

Consider the two critical problems facing the country today, energy and inflation. Major energy problems were forecast years ago, the 1973 embargo underlined the dangers, and yet what passes for our national energy policy is still only a weak set of jerry-built compromises achieved at the expense of years of political infighting. The related inflation problem has festered for more than a decade, and our current president is on his fourth anti-inflation plan, a set of proposals widely regarded as yet another instance of too little, too late. The failures of policy making in these areas are easy to identify and explain. A potential problem is identified, and actions that might head it off are proposed "for discussion." But the problem lies in the future, while the solutions impose costs in the present. So politicians dismiss the solutions as unfeasible and act as though the problem will go away. When it doesn't, popular concern increases. The president, in particular, feels compelled to act—he will be held responsible, both at election time and in the judgment of history. But congressmen expect to bear much less responsibility; moreover, the representatives face an election in less than two years, whereas the president can wait at least four (longer for the lame duck) for the results of his policy to become evident. Congressmen, logically enough, rebel. They denounce every proposed initiative as unfair, which simply means that it imposes costs on their constituents, whereas they prefer the costs to fall on everyone else's constituents. At first, no policy will be adopted; later, as pressure builds, Congress adopts a weak and ineffectual policy for symbolic purposes. Then, as the problem continues to worsen, congressmen join with the press and the public and attack the president for failures of leadership.

The preceding scenario is simplified, to be sure, but largely accurate, and in my opinion, rather disgusting. What makes it possible is the electoral fragmentation produced by the decline of party. Members of Congress are aware that national problems arising from inaction will have little political impact on them, and that the president's failures in dealing with those problems will have similarly little impact. Responsibility for inflation and energy problems? Don't look at congressmen.

In 1958 the Fourth Republic of France collapsed after years of immobilism. The features of congressional policy making just discussed were carried to their logical extremes in that Parliamentary regime. According to contemporary observers, the basic principle of the French Deputy was to avoid responsibility.[21] To achieve that goal the deputies followed subsidiary rules, the most important of which was delay. Action would take place only when crisis removed any possible alternative to action (and most of the alternative actions as well). A slogan of the time was "Those who crawl do not fall."

No one seriously believes that the American constitutional order is in danger of collapse (and certainly we have no de Gaulle waiting in the wings). But political inability to take actions that entail short-run costs ordinarily will result in much higher costs in the long run—we cannot continually depend on the technological fix. So the present American immobilism cannot be dismissed lightly. The sad thing is that the American people appear to understand the depth of our present problems and, at least in principle, appear prepared to sacrifice in furtherance of the long-run good. But they will not have an opportunity to choose between two or more such long-term plans. Although both parties promise tough, equitable policies, in the present state of our politics, neither can deliver.

Single-Issue Politics

In recent years both political analysts and politicians have decried the increased importance of single-issue groups in American politics. Some in fact would claim that the present immobilism in our politics owes more to the rise of single-issue groups than to the decline of party. A little thought, however, should reveal that the two trends are connected. Is single-issue politics a recent phenomenon? The contention is doubtful; such groups have always been active participants in American politics. The gun lobby already was a classic example at the time of President Kennedy's assassination. And however impressive the antiabortionists appear today, remember the temperance movement, which succeeded in getting its constitutional amendment. American history contains numerous forerunners of today's groups, from anti-Masons to abolitionists to the Klan—singularity of purpose is by no means a modern phenomenon. Why, then, do we hear all the contemporary hoopla about single-issue groups? Probably because politicians fear them now more than before and thus allow them to play a larger role in our politics. Why should this be so? Simply because the parties are too weak to protect their members and thus to contain single-issue politics.

In earlier times single-issue groups were under greater pressures to reach accommodations with the parties. After all, the parties nominated candidates, financed candidates, worked for candidates, and, perhaps most important, party voting protected candidates. When a contemporary single-issue group threatens to "get" an officeholder, the threat must be taken seriously. The group can go into his district, recruit a primary or general election challenger, or both, and bankroll that candidate. Even if the sentiment espoused by the group is not the majority sentiment of the district, few officeholders relish the thought of a strong, well-financed opponent. Things were different when strong parties existed. Party leaders controlled the nomination process and would fight to maintain that control. An outside challenge would merely serve to galvanize the party into action to protect its prerogatives. Only if a single-issue group represented the dominant sentiment in a given area could it count on controlling the party organization itself, and thereby electoral politics in that area.

Not only did the party organization have greater ability to resist single-issue pressures at the electoral level, but the party in government had greater ability to control the agenda, and thereby contain single-issue pressures at the policy-making level. Today we seem condemned to go through an annual agony over federal abortion funding. There is little doubt that politicians on both sides would prefer to reach some reasonable compromise at the committee level and settle the issue. But in today's decentralized Congress there is no way to put the lid on. In contrast, historians tell us that in the late nineteenth century a large portion of the Republican constituency was far less interested in the tariff and other questions of national economic development than in whether German immigrants should be permitted to teach their native language in their local schools, and whether Catholics and "liturgical Protestants" should be permitted to consume alcohol.[22] Interestingly, however, the national agenda of the period is devoid of such issues. And when they do show up on the state level, the exceptions prove the rule; they produce party splits and striking defeats for the party that allowed them to surface.[23]

One can cite more recent examples as well. Prior to 1970 popular commentators frequently criticized the autocratic antimajoritarian behavior of congressional committee chairmen in general, and of the entire Rules Committee in particular. It is certainly true that the seniority leadership killed many bills the rank and file might have passed if left to their own devices. But congressional scholars were always aware as well that the seniority leadership buried many bills that the rank and file wanted buried but lacked the political courage to bury themselves. In 1961, for example, the House Rules Committee was roundly condemned for killing a major federal aid to education bill over the question of extension of that aid to parochial schools. Contemporary accounts, however, suggest that congressmen regarded the action of the Rules Committee as a public service.[24] Of course, control of the agenda is a double-edged sword (a point we return to below), but today commentators on single-issue groups clearly are concerned with too little control rather than too much.

In sum, a strong party that is held accountable for the government of a nation-state has both the ability and the incentive to contain particularistic pressures. It controls nominations, elections, and the agenda, and it collectively realizes that small minorities are small minorities no matter how intense they are. But as the parties decline they lose control over nominations and campaigns, they lose the loyalty of the voters, and they lose control of the agenda. Party officeholders cease to be held collectively accountable for party performance, but they become individually exposed to the political pressure of myriad interest groups. The decline of party permits interest groups to wield greater influence, their success encourages the formation of still more interest groups, politics becomes increasingly fragmented, and collective responsibility becomes still more elusive.

Popular Alienation from Government

For at least a decade political analysts have pondered the significance of survey data indicative of a steady increase in the alienation of the American public from the political process. Table 8 presents some representative data: two-thirds of the American public feel the government is run for the benefit of big interests rather than for the people as a whole, three-quarters believe that government officials waste a lot of tax money and half flatly agree with the statement that government officials are basically incompetent. The American public is in a nasty mood, a cynical, distrusting, and resentful mood. The question is, Why?

Specific events and personalities clearly have some effect: we see pronounced "Watergate effects" between 1972 and 1976. But the trends clearly began much earlier. Indeed, the first political science studies analyzing the trends were based on data no later than 1972.[25] At the other extreme it also appears that the American data are only the strongest manifestation of a pattern evident in many democracies, perhaps for reasons common to all countries in the present era, perhaps not. I do think it probable, however, that the trends thus far discussed bear some relation to the popular mood in the United States.

If the same national problems not only persist but worsen while ever-greater amounts of revenue are directed at them, why shouldn't the typical citizen conclude that most of the money must be wasted by incompetent officials? If narrowly based interest groups increasingly affect our politics, why shouldn't citizens increasingly conclude that the interests run the government? For fifteen years the citizenry has listened to a steady stream of promises but has seen very little in the way of follow-through. An increasing proportion of the electorate does not

TABLE 8. RECENT TRENDS IN POLITICAL ALIENATION AND DISTRUST (IN PERCENTAGES)

	Government Run for Few Big Interests	Government Officials Waste "A Lot"	Government Officials Don't Know What They're Doing
1964	29	46	27
1968	39	57	36
1972	45	56	34
1976	66	74	49
1978	68	77	50

Source: National Election Studies made available by the InterUniversity Consortium for Political and Social Research, University of Michigan.

believe that elections make a difference, a fact that largely explains the much-discussed post-1960 decline in voting turnout.[26]

Continued public disillusionment with the political process poses several real dangers. For one thing, disillusionment begets further disillusionment. Leadership becomes more difficult if citizens do not trust their leaders and will not give them the benefit of a doubt. Policy failure becomes more likely if citizens expect the policy to fail. Waste increases and government competence decreases as citizen disrespect for politics encourages a lesser breed of person to make careers in government. And "government by a few big interests" becomes more than a cliché if citizens increasingly decide the cliché is true and cease participating for that reason.

Finally, there is the real danger that continued disappointment with particular government officials ultimately metamorphoses into disillusionment with government per se. Increasing numbers of citizens believe that government is not simply overextended but perhaps incapable of any further bettering of the world. Yes, government is overextended, inefficiency is pervasive, and ineffectiveness is all too common. But government is one of the few instruments of collective action we have, and even those committed to selective pruning of government programs cannot blithely allow the concept of an activist government to fall into disrepute.

The concept of democracy does not submit to precise definition, a claim supported by the existence of numerous nonidentical definitions. To most people democracy embodies a number of valued qualities. Unfortunately, there is no reason to believe that all such valued qualities are mutually compatible. At the least, maximizing the attainment of one quality may require accepting middling levels of another.

Recent American political thought has emphasized government *of* the people and *by* the people. Attempts have been made to [ensure] that all preferences receive a hearing, especially through direct expression of those preferences, but if not, at least through faithful representation. Citizen *participation* is the reigning value, and arrangements that foster widespread participation are much in favor.

Of late, however, some political commentators have begun to wonder whether contemporary thought places sufficient emphasis on government *for* the people.

In stressing participation have we lost sight of *accountability?* Surely, we should be as concerned with what government produces as with how many participate. What good is participation if the citizenry is unable to determine who merits their support?[27]

Participation and responsibility are not logically incompatible, but there is a degree of tension between the two, and the quest for either may be carried to extremes. Participation maximizers find themselves involved with quotas and virtual representation schemes, while responsibility maximizers can find themselves with a closed shop under boss rule.[28] Moreover, both qualities can weaken the democracy they supposedly underpin. Unfettered participation produces Hyde Amendments and immobilism. Responsible parties can use agenda power to thwart democratic decision—for more than a century the Democratic party used what control it had to suppress the racial issue. Neither participation nor responsibility should be pursued at the expense of all other values, but that is what has happened with participation over the course of the past two decades, and we now reap the consequences in our politics.

In 1970 journalist David Broder wrote:

> What we have is a society in which discontent, disbelief, cynicism, and political inertia characterize the public mood; a country whose economy suffers from severe dislocations, whose currency is endangered, where unemployment and inflation coexist, where increasing numbers of people and even giant enterprises live on the public dole; a country whose two races continue to withdraw from each other in growing physical and social isolation; a country whose major public institutions command steadily less allegiance from its citizens; whose education, transportation, law enforcement, health and sanitation systems fall far short of filling their functions; a country whose largest city is close to being ungovernable and uninhabitable; and a country still far from reconciling its international responsibilities with its unmet domestic needs.
>
> We are in trouble.[29]

Broder is not a Cassandra, and he was writing before FECA before the OPEC [Organization of Petroleum Exporting Countries] embargo, before Watergate, and before Jimmy Carter. If he was correct that we were in trouble then, what about now?

The depressing thing is that no rays of light shine through the dark clouds. The trends that underlie the decline of parties continue unabated, and the kinds of structural reforms that might override those trends are too sweeping and/or outlandish to stand any chance of adoption.[30] Through a complex mixture of accident and intention we have constructed for ourselves a system that articulates interests superbly but aggregates them poorly. We hold our politicians individually accountable for the proposals they advocate, but less so for the adoption of those proposals, and not at all for overseeing the implementation of those proposals and the evaluation of their results. In contemporary America officials do not govern, they merely posture.

NOTES

My thinking on the matters discussed in this essay has benefitted from the critical commentary of Lawrence Joseph and Robert Salisbury.

1. This may sound cynical, but it is a standard assumption in American democratic theory. Certainly the Founders believed that the government should not depend on the nobility of heart of officialdom in order to operate properly.

2. This argument was expounded at the turn of the century by writers such as Woodrow Wilson and A. Lawrence Lowell. It enjoyed a resurgence at mid-century in the thinking of scholars such as E. E. Schattschneider. For a thorough exegesis of the party responsibility argument, see Austin Ranney, *The Doctrine of Responsible Party Government* (Urbana: University of Illinois Press, 1962).

3. During the postwar period the national government has experienced divided party control about half the time. In the preceding half century there were only six years of divided control.

4. At this point skeptics invariably ask, "What about Warren G. Harding?" The statement in the text is meant to express a tendency. Certainly, in the first sixty years of this century we did not see a string of candidates comparable to the products of the amateur politics of the past fourteen years (Goldwater, McGovern, Carter, Reagan).

5. See Gerald Pomper, "The Decline of the Party in American Elections," *Political Science Quarterly* 92 (1977): 21–41; John Kessel, *Presidential Campaign Politics: Coalition Strategies and Citizen Responses* (Homewood, Ill.: Dorsey, 1980), ch. 10; Austin Ranney, "The Political Parties: Reform and Decline," in Anthony King (ed.), *The New American Political System* (Washington, D.C.: American Enterprise Institute, 1978), pp. 213–247. Both Kessel and Pomper have discussed the increased importance of the national party organizations in terms of maintenance of continuing operations, imposition of national rules and standards on the local parties, and so on. I believe with Ranney, however, that, considering all levels of the party together, there has been a decline in organizational strength even as the national party apparatuses have grown more influential.

6. Though federal employment increased considerably during the New Deal era, the proportion covered by civil service declined. Thus the erosion of the patronage system was temporarily halted. In addition, scholars have documented the political basis of New Deal spending and program decisions. See Gavin Wright, "The Political Economy of New Deal Spending: An Econometric Analysis," *Review of Economics and Statistics* 56 (1974): 30–38.

7. Jeanne Kirkpatrick, *The New Presidential Elite* (New York: Russell Sage Foundation and Twentieth Century Fund, 1976).

8. Ranney, "The Political Parties," p. 233.

9. Michael Malbin (ed.), *Parties, Interest Groups, and Campaign Finance Laws* (Washington, D.C.: American Enterprise Institute, 1980), pt. 3.

10. Angus Campbell, et al., *The American Voter* (New York: John Wiley & Sons, 1960), chs. 6, 7.

11. See Morris Fiorina, *Retrospective Voting in American National Elections* (New Haven, Conn.: Yale University Press, forthcoming), ch. 5.

12. For a discussion, see Walter Dean Burnham, *Critical Elections and the Mainsprings of American Politics* (New York: Norton, 1970).

13. Ibid., p. 95.

14. These diagrams are representative of the pre-1950 and post-1970 periods. To see how the earlier world gradually changed to the later, examine the series of diagrams in David Mayhew, "Congressional Elections: The Case of the Vanishing Marginals," *Polity* 6 (1974): 295–317.

15. See Morris Fiorina, *Congress—Keystone of the Washington Establishment* (New Haven, Conn.: Yale University Press, 1977).

16. Thomas Mann, *Unsafe at Any Margin* (Washington, D.C.: American Enterprise Institute, 1978).

17. Edward Tufte, "Determinants of the Outcomes of Midterm Congressional Elections," *American Political Science Review* 69 (1975): 812–826.

18. Gary Jacobson and Samuel Kernell, *The Structure of Choice*, forthcoming, ch. 5.

19. Fiorina, *Retrospective Voting*, ch. 10.

20. This compositional change in the Democratic party has a lot to do with the recent increase in party cohesion in Congress, which some might regard as evidence inconsistent with the argument in the text. Kennedy faced a congressional party that was almost half Southern; Carter faces one only about a quarter Southern. *Ceteris paribus,* this fact should have produced significantly higher levels of party cohesion and presidential support. But party cohesion has only marginally increased, and, as shown in the text, party support for its nominal leader has declined. I suspect that the increase in party cohesion also stems partly from the explosion in roll-call votes. Under the electronic voting system it is now common to record votes on relatively minor legislation. If the Republicans perfunctorily object on a proportion of these, party votes would result, and the overall party cohesion figures would be inflated by such relatively unimportant votes.

21. Nathan Leites, *On the Game of Politics in France* (Stanford, Calif.: Stanford University Press, 1959).

22. Paul Kleppner, *The Cross of Culture: A Social Analysis of Midwestern Politics, 1850–1900* (New York: Free Press, 1970), ch. 2.

23. Ibid., chs. 3, 4.

24. James Sundquist, *Politics and Policy* (Washington, D.C.: Brookings Institution, 1968).

25. Arthur Miller, "Political Issues and Trust in Government: 1964–1970," *American Political Science Review* 68 (1974): 951–972; Jack Citrin, "The Political Relevance of Trust in Government," *American Political Science Review* 68 (1974): 973–988.

26. John Ferejohn and Morris Fiorina, "The Decline in Turnout in Presidential Elections," paper presented at the Conference on Voter Turnout, San Diego, 1979.

27. There is, of course, a school of thought, dating back at least to John Stuart Mill, that holds that participation is a good in itself. While I am prepared to concede that self-expression is nice, I strongly object to making it the raison d'être of democratic politics.

28. S. E. Finer, *The Changing British Party System, 1945–1979* (Washington, D.C.: American Enterprise Institute, 1980).

29. *The Party's Over* (New York: Harper & Row, 1972), p. xxv.

30. For example, party cohesion would no doubt be strengthened by revising existing statutes to prevent split-ticket voting and to permit campaign contributions only to parties. At the constitutional level, giving the president the power of dissolution and replacing the single-member district system with proportional representation would probably unify the party in government much more than at present. Obviously, changes such as these are not only highly improbable but also exceedingly risky, since we cannot accurately predict the unintended consequences that surely would accompany them.

18

V. O. KEY, JR.

ELECTIONS AS COLLECTIVE DECISIONS

*This excerpt is from one of several seminal works by V. O. Key, Jr. (1908–1963), Pub-
lic Opinion and American Democracy (1961). Into this broad-ranging book, the
great Harvard political scientist had slipped perhaps the most fundamental insight
ever advanced about electoral behavior: Voters are more likely to cast their ballots "retrospectively"—passing judgment on the prior policies or performances of officeholders—than they are able to affirm precise policy preferences for the future.*

If elections express a public opinion, it should be possible to assign meaning to
them as they are examined in the context of the circumstances of the moment at
which they occur. Scholars habitually shy away from the task of translating the
indistinct mutterings of the people's voice as it projects itself through the ballot
boxes and the voting machines, but politicians must as a matter of course attribute
a decisional content to elections. While their readings of the verdict of the people
may on occasion be erroneous, they have a quality of authority. Scholars, too,
should by the findings of electoral research be able to make appraisals of the
meaning of the grand decisions by the electorate. In a minor referendum—as, for
example, a vote on a proposal for the issuance of building bonds by a school district—the expression of public opinion is direct and unmistakable in its meaning,
but interpretation of the meaning of great national electoral contests presents a
problem of far greater complexity. Granted that these grand electoral decisions
have a meaning whose clarity differs from election to election, the problem
remains of appraising particular elections or types of elections in their total context to divine the nature of the collective purpose expressed in the balloting. Such
an attempt assumes that, despite the variety of motives and preferences that guide
individual voters, their individual actions can be summed into a broad decision of
one or more major components of some clarity, at least in some elections.

Disapprobation

Perhaps the public can express itself with greatest clarity when it speaks in disapprobation of the past policy or performance of an administration, though the
collective decision may not specify with minuteness the elements of policy or performance of which it disapproves and cannot indicate with precision the lines of
policy that should be pursued, save that changes should be made. The presidential election of 1932 could be regarded as one in which the collective decision
was one of disapproval of past performance. Although from the vantage point of
hindsight, many elements of the New Deal may be read into Roosevelt's campaign speeches and into his earlier record as Governor of New York, the dominant element of the collective decision consisted in a rejection of the broad

[Tables and notes have been renumbered.—Eds.]

policies of the Hoover Administration rather than a mandate for future action. About the only clear prospective instruction contained in the electoral verdict was a mandate for the repeal of the Prohibition Amendment, and that action itself constituted to a degree a judgment of past experience.

Another election in which a major component of the decision consisted in the disapproval of past performance was that of 1952. From data presented earlier, the conclusion is inescapable that the election marked no majority rejection of the major trends of domestic policy under the New Deal and the Fair Deal, although Eisenhower had the support of those bitterly opposed to intervention in the economy. The major content of the decision related rather to the performance of the Truman Administration in the field of foreign policy. That interpretation is supported by the relationships between party identification and vote that appear in Table 1. The question of whether "it was our government's fault that China went Communist" or whether there was "nothing that we could do to stop it" separated out with some clarity those who deserted the Democratic party to vote for Eisenhower. Of those strong Democrats who thought that it was our government's fault that China went communist, only 69 percent voted Democratic. Of those who thought that there was nothing "we could do to stop it," 89 percent voted Democratic. Similar contrasts appear at other levels of party identification. This is not to say that the election turned on the China issue alone. Rather, the probabilities are that this question tapped a broad dimension of dissatisfaction with the conduct of foreign affairs that found expression in the vote. And that dissatisfaction was compounded by an unhappiness about the conduct of domestic affairs as well.[1]

Confirmation and Ratification

If public opinion expresses itself with relative clarity in retrospective disapproval of performance or policy, it may also express itself in the same manner in confirmation or ratification of past policy or performance. Only infrequently is a new program or a new course of action advocated with such force and the attention it receives so widespread that the polling may be regarded as advance

TABLE 1. PRESIDENTIAL VOTE IN RELATION TO PARTY IDENTIFICATION AND TO OPINION ON UNITED STATES RESPONSIBILITY FOR COMMUNIST CAPTURE OF CONTROL OF CHINA[a]

PARTY IDENTIFICATION	OPINION ON CHINA POLICY		
	Our Fault	Don't Know	Nothing U.S. Could Do
Strong D	69%	84%	89%
Weak D	40	66	67
Independent	28	20	45
Weak R	3	6	8
Strong R	1	0	1

[a] Entries are Democratic percentages of reported presidential vote for the groups in each cell in 1952. The question was: "Some people feel that it was our government's fault that China went Communist, others say there was nothing that we could do to stop it. How do you feel about this?"
Data source: Survey Research Center, University of Michigan, 1951.

approval of a proposed course of action. Those governments that regard elections as clear mandates for new policy actions probably often mirror the beliefs of the political elite rather than reflect an understanding of the vote widely shared in the population.

The congressional election of 1934 and the presidential election of 1936 are probably the elections in recent American history that could most certainly be regarded as mass approvals of newly instituted public policies. The actions taken from 1933 to the election of 1936 constituted a program of unusual range and novelty in American domestic policy. Subjected to frontal challenge by the minority, that program undoubtedly won broad popular ratification in the increased Democratic congressional majorities of 1934 and in the overwhelming vote by which Roosevelt was re-elected in 1936.

At a different level the election of 1956 could be regarded as a mass confirmation or approval of the performance of the Eisenhower Administration perhaps principally in the field of foreign affairs. The motivation of the vote contained a generous component of a political admiration for Eisenhower as a person; it contained practically no motivation of approbation for his innovations in domestic policy which were, of course, negligible. Probably the approval of past performance in the foreign field, as well as expectations about the future, were captured by the responses to the question: "Now looking ahead, do you think the problem of keeping out of war would be handled better in the next four years by the Republicans, or by the Democrats, or about the same by both?" Comments in the replies to this inquiry were heavily loaded with professions of confidence in Eisenhower based on his military and diplomatic experience and with expressions of approbation for his success in "keeping us out of war." And the position on this question, as may be seen from Table 2, was closely associated with the vote. Those Democrats who thought the problem of "keeping out of war" would be better handled by the Republicans deserted their candidate with far greater frequency than did those Democrats who had confidence with the peace-maintaining capacity of their own party.[2] The consideration was not an issue of policy; the Democrats had

TABLE 2. PRESIDENTIAL VOTE IN RELATION TO PARTY IDENTIFICATION AND TO OPINION ABOUT PARTY CAPABILITIES IN HANDLING "PROBLEM OF KEEPING OUT OF WAR"[a]

Party Identification	Better by Democrats	Same by Both	Better by Republicans
Strong D	87%	90%	47%
Weak D	96[b]	71	24
Independent	[c]	42	11
Weak R	[c]	14	2
Strong R	[d]	0	[e]

[a] Entries are percentages of those in each cell reporting a Democratic presidential vote. The question was: "Now looking ahead, do you think the problem of keeping out of war would be handled better in the next four years by the Republicans, or by the Democrats, or about the same by both?"
[b] This percentage rests on only 24 cases.
[c] Too few cases to percentage.
[d] No case fell in this cell.
[e] Less than one-half of 1 percent.
Data source: Survey Research Center, University of Michigan, 1956.

not advocated war. Although expressed as an expectation about the future, it reflected fundamentally a broad approval of past performance.

Rejection

As has been said, one source of difficulty in discerning the import of the popular decision in an election has been the supposition that elections do, or ought to, involve a choice between new and alternative policies for the future. American public policy rarely develops in this manner. Its evolution is more commonly by gradual stages. Policy breaks with the past, when they occur, more generally come about without precise prospective mandate; popular action takes place mainly in retrospect rather than in prospect.

Something can be said, however, for the existence of a type of election in which the electorate rejects a proposed panacea. By so doing, it may or may not give positive approval to the alternative. A clear-cut instance of an election of this type is that of 1896. William Jennings Bryan took control of the Democratic party from the conservative Cleveland forces and crusaded in advocacy of the free coinage of silver as a cure for the ills that beset the country. Here was a positive proposal, certainly widely known if not always understood in its details, to depart from the prevailing monetary policy. If we had for 1896 data of the kind that have been available for recent elections, we could speak with more confidence about what was in the minds of people as they rejected Bryan for McKinley. But the electors clearly rejected the radical alternative offered by Bryan, and it is not implausible to suppose that doubt and anxiety about free silver had more to do with their actions than did a powerful attraction to the gold standard.

Frustration of Policy-Motivated Decision

The structure of the American electoral system is such that certain types of policy-motivated decisions are frustrated or cannot be made by election. Or the more correct interpretation may be that certain types of combinations of opinions encounter obstruction as they percolate through almost any electoral system. When two or more issues divide an electorate along different planes, if a majority on one of the issues prevails, the majority on the other may be defeated. These problems were touched upon in the earlier discussion of the interrelationship of opinions. In recent decades those who cherished both isolationist and liberal views have suffered some inconvenience in adapting themselves to the alternatives offered by the American party system. Similarly, those who embraced both internationalist and conservative opinions had some uncertainty about how their opinions might best be translated into electoral preference. On lesser issues such conflict is commonplace.

In the American system several routes are open for the avoidance of the political dead-ends created by the existence of noncongruent majorities on a series of issues. Some of these ways around the problem are individual; others are institutional. The individual often places a higher value on his position on this issue than on another; or one issue may be more salient than the other. This permits him as he votes to bring his candidate preference into line with his dominant policy preference. Berelson, Lazarsfeld, and McPhee suggest that the unity of the supporters of a candidate may consist, not in their agreement on a series of issues, but in their opposition to one or another of the policy positions of the candidate they reject. "One Republican," they conclude from their Elmira study, "may be most concerned with foreign policy, and on that subject he is against the Democrats. Another Republican may be most concerned with domestic economics, and on that subject he is against the Democrats."[3] Unity may thus exist along a common denominator of disagreement with the opposition on a series of issues, but this is unity for election day only. Someone is bound to find himself in the majority on election day and in a minority on policies of interest to him the next day. Nevertheless, individuals may accommodate themselves to the situation to some extent by emphasizing in their actions those considerations most important to them.

Institutional structures also enable, or even require, governments to take into account the circumstance of the simultaneous existence of noncongruent majorities. The looseness of the party system, especially in its nominating practices, permits the election of Senators and Representatives with unorthodox combinations of policy outlook. Thus, the isolationist-liberal combination of opinion can find its spokesmen through the representative system. Witness the career of the late Senator William Langer, of North Dakota. A New Dealer with most pronounced convictions on domestic matters and a man markedly lacking in zeal for one-worldism, he probably reflected relatively well the mixed policy pattern of his constituency. Such adjustments through the representative system are commonplace.

In a more notable fashion, the system of separated powers on occasion, perhaps accidentally, permits governmental adaptation to the requirements of noncongruent majorities. The most striking case, or at least the one on which the data are most complete, is that of the election of 1952 and its consequences. A foreign policy majority supported Eisenhower in his promise to do something other than that which Truman had been doing. That majority, though, was not also, as some dedicated Republicans believed, committed to a rollback in domestic-welfare policy. The two noncongruent majorities, as a result of the congressional elections of 1954, found their voice through different organs of government. The President spoke for one majority; Congress, with its Democratic complexion, was beholden to the other majority.

When noncongruent majorities exist, the meaning of the outcome of an election may be obscure; the election may, in fact, settle only one of the great issues. There are also other types of questions that are not apt to be settled in any clear fashion by elections. Those are questions on which the popular opinion distribution is of the type we earlier denominated as "concentrated"—that is, questions about which comparatively few persons have an opinion one way or another. In the excitement of the presidential campaign these matters are overshadowed by more important questions, and few persons would regard their vote as an expression of opinion on them. Such questions are not likely to be settled by elections unless they are definitely related to some major ideological position of the winner or governed by the group interests associated with the winner.

Acceptability of Election Results

It is plain that elections involve broad decisions on policy questions, although estimation of precisely what those determinations are requires a degree of artistry. A more important feature of elections, whatever else they decide, is their production of acceptable decisions on the succession to power in the state. At the leadership levels that quality of elections manifests itself when the losers surrender the seals of authority to the winners of the popular majority. The development of norms, expectations, and restraints that enable those with authority to surrender it in response to popular decision is a rare phenomenon among the rulers of men; they usually fear that they may suffer personal discomfort if they transfer the apparatus of state power to their enemies. Nevertheless, in a few regimes those who occupy office have learned how to accomplish the peaceable transfer of authority. Or perhaps they have learned how to conduct themselves in office so that they will not be shot by the outs who win an election.

Within the mass of the people, too, some sort of reconciliation to the defeat of one's candidate evidently occurs. Though the opposition winner may not be embraced with enthusiasm, many people accomplish a psychological adjustment to the loss of an election. That adjustment may take the form of concluding that the stakes of the election were not after all so important as they were thought to be in the heat of the campaign. That process is illustrated by the data of Table 3. Before the election in 1952 a national sample was asked whether it thought that it would "make a good deal of difference to the country whether the Democrats or the Republicans win the election." About three fourths of the strong Democrats and strong Republicans opined that important differences, big differences, or at least some difference was at stake. After the election a substantial proportion of the strong Democrats made their peace with the situation by adopting the view

TABLE 3. APPRAISALS OF IMPORTANCE OF OUTCOME OF 1952 ELECTION BEFORE AND AFTER THE ELECTION BY STRONG PARTY IDENTIFIERS[a]

OPINIONS ON ELECTION IMPORTANCE	STRONG DEMOCRATS		STRONG REPUBLICANS	
	Pre-	Post-	Pre-	Post-
Very important differences; big difference; important differences; some difference	72%	46%	78%	80%
Minor differences; no difference; about the same; depends	24	45	20	18
Don't know	4	8	1	2
NA	—	1	1	—
	100%	100%	100%	100%
N	392	402	241	217

[a] The pre-election question was: "Do you think it will make a good deal of difference to the country whether the Democrats or the Republicans win the elections this November or that it won't make much difference which side wins?" The post-election question was: "Do you think it will make a good deal of difference to the country that Eisenhower won instead of Stevenson, or don't you think it will make much difference?"
Data source: Survey Research Center, University of Michigan, 1952.

that the Eisenhower victory would make no difference, only minor differences, or perhaps no difference at all.

This phenomenon of reconciliation to defeat has been noted in many surveys.[4] It also manifests itself in other ways. In postelection surveys that inquire about the vote, an overreport of the vote for the winner ordinarily occurs. Some people do not wish to admit that they were on the losing side and, ex post facto, change their vote, so to speak. The odds are that some of the acceptance of election outcomes may be attributable to a sportsmanship whose efficacy may be most marked among people with the least knowledge and awareness of the stakes of the political game. Then, too, after an election other persons may come around to the view that, though their man lost, the result was the "best thing" for the country.[5]

NOTES

1. Expression of electoral disapprobation, it is relevant to note, depends on the existence of political parties with some continuity and some sense of corporate accountability. When a President seeks re-election, he cannot avoid that accountability; his record is approved or it is not approved. When the President's party puts forward a nominee as a successor to the incumbent, the candidate must, if the electorate is to be effective, be accountable for the record of his party. When such a presidential candidate seeks to work out of such responsibility, he attempts to subvert a basic tenet of the constitutional customs.

2. It should not be presumed that these Democrats voted Republican necessarily because they had greater confidence in Eisenhower on the peace question. In some instances they may have had this confidence because they had decided to vote for Eisenhower. However it came about, the parallelism of expectation and vote had an importance.

3. Berelson, et al., *Voting* (Chicago: University of Chicago Press; 1954), p. 206.

4. See, for example, Arthur Kornhauser et al., *When Labor Votes* (New York: University Books; 1956), pp. 135, 161.

5. *Fortune*, February, 1941, has a relevant post-mortem on the 1940 presidential election; a goodly number of Willkie voters concluded that it was the "best thing" for the country that Roosevelt had won.

PART FIVE

INTEREST GROUPS AND LOBBYING

Private groups such as trade associations, labor unions, and farmers' organizations have long been recognized as an important feature of the American political community. Americans have a reputation for forming interest groups to promote their economic, political, or social objectives, and American government is thought to be responsive to, if not actually dependent upon, these associations. The classic literature on interest groups falls into three main categories. First, some authors have sought to explain why groups are formed and to delineate the different characteristics of associations according to such attributes as their size and purpose. It could be argued that this approach dates back to the 1830s when Alexis de Tocqueville observed that "Americans of all ages, all conditions, and all dispositions constantly form associations. They have not only commercial and manufacturing companies . . . but associations of a thousand other kinds, religious, moral, serious, futile, general or restricted, enormous or diminutive. . . . Wherever at the head of some new undertaking you see the government in France or a man of rank in England, in the United States you will be sure to find an association." Second, many have concentrated on the process by which groups advance their political interests. And, third, some have examined the impact of interest groups and their activities on the political system as a whole.

Mancur Olson's chapter on the logic of collective action from *The Rise and Decline of Nations* (1982) is a preeminent example of the first approach, dealing with the dynamics of forming and maintaining private associations. Olson seeks to explain why individuals join and work for groups by addressing a fundamental paradox: "The individual in any large group with a common interest will reap only a minute share of the gains from whatever sacrifices the individual makes to achieve this common interest. Since any gain goes to everyone in the group, those who contribute nothing to the effort will get just as much as those who made a contribution. It pays to 'let George do it,' but George has little or no incentive to do anything in the group interest either. . . . The paradox, then, is that . . . large groups, at least if they are composed of rational individuals, will *not* act in their group interest." However, as Olson argues, this paradox can be resolved in practice through the use of selective incentives, both positive and negative, to prompt individuals to contribute to group activities. Olson also notes that since small organizations may not be able to function without contributions from each of their few members, the logic of individual participation indicates that "smaller groups will have a greater likelihood of engaging in collective action than larger ones."

An excellent article which duly recognizes the powerful role of money from interest groups in congressional deliberations, is a paper by Richard L. Hall and Frank W. Wayman published in the *American Political Science Review* in 1990. "Buying Time: Moneyed Interests and the Mobilization of Bias in Congressional Committees" provides some rare balance to the more conventional view of interest groups as often divided, ineffectual, or mere "auxiliary" suppliers of information for legislators.[1]

The insights of Hugh Heclo in his penetrating essay on what he calls "issue networks" introduce some additional contemporary realism. Heclo shows how the traditional notion of interest group dynamics within the federal policy establishment has become outmoded. The "groups" that matter are no longer only, or even primarily, formal associations with a membership base and stable ties to the executive bureaus and congressional committees that attend to their interests. Instead of these old "iron triangles," Heclo sees a fluid, "loose-jointed" interplay of influence among professional policy activists and technocrats, political executives, and an assortment of "issue-watchers" insinuating themselves in policy debates and decisions. Many of the players are not organized groups in any true sense of the term, but rather participants "inside the Beltway's policy community," such as law firms that share none of the problems of incentives and collective action that concerned Olson. Some of the public agenda is still set by the initiatives of the customary lobbies, such as organized labor or the National Association of Manufacturers, but increasingly, the expanding scope of government itself creates new vested interests, mobilizing new clients and policy aficionados. This environment has profound implications, both positive and negative. Heclo suggests it can impart flexibility to governance, but also cause gridlock or indecision. And it raises questions of political control, accountability, and representativeness.

The latter concern—how "democratic" or "in touch" are Washington's policy deliberations?—is actually a new take on an old issue. Early on, E. E. Schattschneider, writing about "The Scope and Bias of the Pressure System," turned his attention to the consequences of interest group activism for the political system as a whole. Schattschneider's conception of "pressure groups," of course, was not as complex and nuanced as Heclo's "networks," but both were preoccupied with systemic imbalances. In his seminal work excerpted here, Schattschneider concluded that "the notion that the pressure system is automatically representative of the whole community is a myth fostered by the universalizing tendency of modern group theories. Pressure politics is skewed, loaded, and unbalanced in favor of a fraction of a minority." Institutional intermediaries, such as effective political parties, are needed to offset this bias and to advance the public interest, the whole of which is greater than the sum of compromises among special interests.

1.   Raymond A. Bauer, Ithiel de Sola Pool, and Lewis Anthony Dexter, *American Business and Public Policy* (Chicago: Aldine-Atherton, 1972), p. 357.

19

MANCUR OLSON, JR.

COLLECTIVE ACTION: THE LOGIC

In his book, The Logic of Collective Action: Public Goods and the Theory of Groups *(1965), the late Mancur Olson, Jr. (1932–1998) challenged conventional assumptions about political behavior and the formation of interest groups. The thrust of his reasoning is summarized in the following excerpt, taken from another of his important works,* The Rise and Decline of Nations *(1982). Olson, an economist at the University of Maryland, examined the calculations of gains and losses that rational individuals make when deciding whether to act collectively in groups. The maintenance of large voluntary associations is complicated by the free rider problem that often results when individuals make those calculations.*

I

. . . It has often been taken for granted that if everyone in a group of individuals or firms had some interest in common, then there would be a tendency for the group to seek to further this interest. Thus many students of politics in the United States for a long time supposed that citizens with a common political interest would organize and lobby to serve that interest. Each individual in the population would be in one or more groups and the vector of pressures of these competing groups explained the outcomes of the political process. Similarly, it was often supposed that if workers, farmers, or consumers faced monopolies harmful to their interests, they would eventually attain countervailing power through organizations such as labor unions or farm organizations that obtained market power and protective government action. On a larger scale, huge social classes are often expected to act in the interest of their members; the unalloyed form of this belief is, of course, the Marxian contention that in capitalist societies the bourgeois class runs the government to serve its own interests, and that once the exploitation of the proletariat goes far enough and "false consciousness" has disappeared, the working class will in its own interest revolt and establish a dictatorship of the proletariat. In general, if the individuals in some category or class had a sufficient degree of self-interest and if they all agreed on some common interest, then the group would to some extent also act in a self-interested or group-interested manner.

If we ponder the logic of the familiar assumption described in the preceding paragraph, we can see that it is fundamentally and indisputably faulty. Consider those consumers who agree that they pay higher prices for a product because of some objectionable monopoly or tariff, or those workers who agree that their skill deserves a higher wage. Let us now ask what would be the expedient course of action for an individual consumer who would like to see a boycott to combat a monopoly or a lobby to repeal the tariff, or for an individual worker who would like a strike threat or a minimum wage law that could bring higher wages. If the consumer or worker contributes a few days and a few dollars to organize a boycott or a union or to lobby for favorable legislation, he or she will have sacrificed time and money. What will this sacrifice obtain? The individual will at best succeed in advancing the cause to a small (often imperceptible) degree. In any case he will get only a minute share of the gain from his action. The very fact that the object or interest is common to or shared by the group entails that the gain from any sacrifice an individual makes to serve this common purpose is shared with everyone in the group. The successful boycott or strike or lobbying action will bring the better price or wage for everyone in the relevant category, so the individual in any large group with a common interest will reap only a minute share of the gains from whatever sacrifices the individual makes to achieve this common interest. Since any gain goes to everyone in the group, those who contribute nothing to the effort will get just as much as those who made a contribution. It pays to "let George do it," but George has little or no incentive to do anything in the group interest either, so (in the absence of factors that are completely left out of the conceptions mentioned in the first paragraph) there will be little, if any, group action. The paradox, then, is that (in the absence of special arrangements or circumstances to which we shall turn later) large groups, at least if they are composed of rational individuals, will *not* act in their group interest.

This paradox is elaborated and set out in a way that lets the reader check every step of the logic in a book I wrote entitled *The Logic of Collective Action.* . . .[1]

II

One finding in *The Logic* is that the services of associations like labor unions, professional associations, farm organizations, cartels, lobbies (and even collusive groups without formal organization) resemble the basic services of the state in one utterly fundamental respect. The services of such associations, like the elemental services or "public goods" provided by governments, if provided to anyone, go to everyone in some category or group. Just as the law and order, defense, or pollution abatement brought about by government accrue to everyone in some country or geographic area, so the tariff obtained by a farm organization's lobbying effort raises the price to all producers of the relevant commodity. Similarly, as I argued earlier, the higher wage won by a union applies to all employees in the pertinent category. More generally, every lobby obtaining a general change in legislation or regulation thereby obtains a public or collective good for everyone who benefits from that change, and every combination—that is, every "cartel"—using market or industrial action to get a higher price or wage must, when it restricts the quantity supplied, raise the price for every seller, thereby creating a collective good for all sellers.

If governments, on the one hand, and combinations exploiting their political or market power, on the other, produce public or collective goods that inevitably go to everyone in some group or category, then both are subject to the paradoxical logic set out above: that is, the individuals and firms they serve have in general no incentive voluntarily to contribute to their support.[2] It follows that if there is only voluntary and rational individual behavior,[3] then for the most part neither governments nor lobbies and cartels will exist, unless individuals support them for some reason *other* than the collective goods they provide. Of course, governments exist virtually everywhere and often there arc lobbies and cartelistic organizations as well. If the argument so far is right, it follows that something *other* than the collective goods that governments and other organizations provide accounts for their existence.[4]

In the case of governments, the answer was explained before *The Logic of Collective Action* was written; governments are obviously supported by compulsory taxation. Sometimes there is little objection to this compulsion, presumably because many people intuitively understand that public goods cannot be sold in the marketplace or financed by any voluntary mechanism; as I have already argued, each individual would get only a minute share of any governmental services he or she paid for and would get whatever level of services was provided by others in any event.

In the case of organizations that provide collective goods to their client groups through political or market action, the answer has not been obvious, but it is no less clear-cut. Organizations of this kind, at least when they represent large groups, are again not supported because of the collective goods they provide, but rather because they have been fortunate enough to find what I have called *selective incentives*. A selective incentive is one that applies selectively to the individuals depending on whether they do or do not contribute to the provision of the collective good.

A selective incentive can be either negative or positive; it can, for example, be a loss or punishment imposed only on those who do *not* help provide the collective good. Tax payments are, of course, obtained with the help of negative selective incentives, since those who are found not to have paid their taxes must then suffer both taxes and penalties. The best-known type of organized interest group in modern democratic societies, the labor union, is also usually supported, in part, through negative selective incentives. Most of the dues in strong unions are obtained through union shop, closed shop, or agency shop arrangements which make dues paying more or less compulsory and automatic. There are often also informal arrangements with the same effect; David McDonald, former president of the United Steel Workers of America, describes one of these arrangements used in the early history of that union. It was, he writes, a technique

> which we called . . . visual education, which was a high-sounding label for a practice much more accurately described as dues picketing. It worked very simply. A group of dues-paying members, selected by the district director (usually more for their size than their tact) would stand at the plant gate with pick handles or baseball bats in hand and confront each worker as he arrived for his shift.[5]

As McDonald's "dues picketing" analogy suggests, picketing during strikes is another negative selective incentive that unions sometimes need; although picketing in industries with established and stable unions is usually peaceful, this is because the union's capacity to close down an enterprise against which it has called a strike is clear to all; the early phase of unionization often involves a great deal of violence on the part of both unions and anti-union employers and scabs.[6]

Some opponents of labor unions argue that, since many of the members of labor unions join only through the processes McDonald described or through legally enforced union-shop arrangements, most of the relevant workers do not want to be unionized. The Taft-Hartley Act provided that impartial governmentally administered elections should be held to determine whether workers did in fact want to belong to unions. As the collective-good logic set out here suggests, the same workers who had to be coerced to pay union dues voted for the unions with compulsory dues (and normally by overwhelming margins), so that this feature of the Taft-Hartley Act was soon abandoned as pointless.[7] The workers who as individuals tried to avoid paying union dues at the same time that they voted to force themselves all to pay dues are no different from taxpayers who vote, in effect, for high levels of taxation, yet try to arrange their private affairs in ways that avoid taxes. Because of the same logic, many professional associations also get members through covert or overt coercion (for example, lawyers in those states with a "closed bar"). So do lobbies and cartels of several other types; some of the contributions by corporate officials, for instance, to politicians useful to the corporation are also the result of subtle forms of coercion.[8]

Positive selective incentives, although easily overlooked, are also commonplace, as diverse examples in *The Logic* demonstrate.[9] American farm organizations offer prototypical examples. Many of the members of the stronger American farm organizations are members because their dues are automatically deducted from the "patronage dividends" of farm cooperatives or are included in the insurance premiums paid to mutual insurance companies associated with the farm organizations. Any number of organizations with urban clients also provide similar positive selective incentives in the form of insurance policies, publications, group air fares, and other private goods made available only to members. The grievance procedures of labor unions usually also offer selective incentives, since the grievances of active members often get most of the attention. The symbiosis between the political power of a lobbying organization and the business institutions associated with it often yields tax or other advantages for the business institution, and the publicity and other information flowing out of the political arm of a movement often generates patterns of preference or trust that make the business activities of the movement more remunerative. The surpluses obtained in such ways in turn provide positive selective incentives that recruit participants for the lobbying efforts.

III

Small groups, or occasionally large "federal" groups that are made up of many small groups of socially interactive members, have an additional source of both negative and positive selective incentives. Clearly most people value the companionship and respect of those with whom they interact. In modern societies solitary confinement is, apart from the rare death penalty, the harshest legal punishment. The censure or even ostracism of those who fail to bear a share of the burdens of collective action can sometimes be an important selective incentive. An extreme example of this occurs when British unionists refuse to speak to uncooperative colleagues, that is, "send them to Coventry." Similarly, those in a socially interactive group seeking a collective good can give special respect or honor to those who distinguish themselves by their sacrifices in the interest of the group and thereby offer them a positive selective incentive. Since most people apparently prefer relatively like-minded or agreeable and respectable company, and often prefer to associate with those whom they especially admire, they may find it costless to shun those who shirk the collective action and to favor those who oversubscribe.

Social selective incentives can be powerful and inexpensive, but they are available only in certain situations. As I have already indicated, they have little applicability to large groups, except in those cases in which the large groups can be federations of small groups that are capable of social interaction. It also is not possible to organize most large groups in need of a collective good into small, socially interactive subgroups, since most individuals do not have the time needed to maintain a huge number of friends and acquaintances.

The availability of social selective incentives is also limited by the social heterogeneity of some of the groups or categories that would benefit from a collective good. Everyday observation reveals that most socially interactive groups are fairly homogeneous and that many people resist extensive social interaction with those they deem to have lower status or greatly different tastes. Even Bohemian or other nonconformist groups often are made up of individuals who are similar to one another, however much they differ from the rest of society. Since some of the categories of individuals who would benefit from a collective good are socially heterogeneous, the social interaction needed for selective incentives sometimes cannot be arranged even when the number of individuals involved is small.

Another problem in organizing and maintaining socially heterogeneous groups is that they are less likely to agree on the exact nature of whatever collective good is at issue or on how much of it is worth buying. All the arguments showing the difficulty of collective action mentioned so far in this chapter hold even when there is perfect consensus about the collective good that is desired, the amount that is wanted, and the best way to obtain the good. But if anything, such as social heterogeneity, reduces consensus, collective action can become still less likely. And if there is nonetheless collective action, it incurs the extra cost (especially for the leaders of whatever organization or collusion is at issue) of accommodating and compromising the different views. The situation is slightly different in the very small groups to which we shall turn shortly. In such groups differences of opinion can sometimes provide a bit of an incentive to join an organization seeking a collective good, since joining might give the individual a significant influence over the organization's policy and the nature of any collective good it would obtain. But this consideration is not relevant to any group that is large enough so that a single individual cannot expect to affect the outcome.

Consensus is especially difficult where collective goods are concerned because the defining characteristic of collective goods—that they go to everyone in some group or category if they are provided at all—also entails that everyone in the relevant group gets more or less of the collective good together, and that they all have to accept whatever level and type of public good is provided. A country can have only one foreign and defense policy, however diverse the preferences and incomes of its citizenry, and (except in the rarely attainable case of a "Lindahl equilibrium")[10] there will not be agreement within a country on how much should be spent to carry out the foreign and defense policy. This is a clear implication of the arguments for "fiscal equivalence"[11] and of the rigorous models of "optimal segregation"[12] and "fiscal federalism."[13] Heterogeneous clients with diverse demands for collective goods can pose an even greater problem for private associations, which not only must deal with the disagreements but also must find selective incentives strong enough to hold dissatisfied clients.

In short, the political entrepreneurs who attempt to organize collective action will accordingly be more likely to succeed if they strive to organize relatively homogeneous groups. The political managers whose task it is to maintain organized or collusive action similarly will be motivated to use indoctrination and selective recruitment to increase the homogeneity of their client groups. This is true in part because social selective incentives are more likely to be available to the more nearly homogeneous groups, and in part because homogeneity will help achieve consensus.

IV

Information and calculation about a collective good is often itself a collective good. Consider a typical member of a large organization who is deciding how much time to devote to studying the policies or leadership of the organization. The more time the member devotes to this matter, the greater the likelihood that his or her voting or advocacy will favor effective policies and leadership for the organization. This typical member will, however, get only a small share of the gain from the more effective policies and leadership: in the aggregate, the other members will get almost all the gains, so that the individual member does not have an incentive to devote nearly as much time to fact-finding and thinking about the organization as would be in the group interest. Each of the members of the group would be better off if they all could be coerced into spending more time finding out how to vote to make the organization best further their interests. This is dramatically evident in the case of the typical voter in a national election in a large country. The gain to such a voter from studying issues and candidates until it is clear what vote is truly in his or her interest is given by the difference in the value to the individual of the "right" election outcome as compared with the "wrong" outcome, *multiplied by the probability a change in the individual's vote will alter the outcome of the election.* Since the probability that a typical voter will change the outcome of the election is vanishingly small, the typical citizen is usually "rationally ignorant" about political affairs.[14] Often, information about public affairs is so interesting or entertaining that it pays to acquire it for these reasons alone—this appears to be the single most important source of exceptions to the generalization that *typical* citizens are rationally ignorant about public affairs.

Individuals in a few special vocations can receive considerable rewards in private goods if they acquire exceptional knowledge of public goods. Politicians, lobbyists, journalists, and social scientists, for example, may earn more money, power, or prestige from knowledge of this or that public business. Occasionally, exceptional knowledge of public policy can generate exceptional profits in stock exchanges or other markets. Withal, the typical citizen will find that his or her income and life chances will not be improved by zealous study of public affairs, or even of any single collective good.

The limited knowledge of public affairs is in turn necessary to explain the effectiveness of lobbying. If all citizens had obtained and digested all pertinent information, they could not then be swayed by advertising or other persuasion. With perfectly informed citizens, elected officials would not be subject to the blandishment of lobbyists, since the constituents would then know if their interests were betrayed and defeat the unfaithful representative at the next election. Just as lobbies provide collective goods to special-interest groups, so their effectiveness is explained by the imperfect knowledge of citizens, and this in turn is due mainly to the fact that information and calculation about collective goods is also a collective good.

This fact—that the benefits of individual enlightenment about public goods are usually dispersed through a group or nation, rather than concentrated upon the individual who bears the costs of becoming enlightened—explains many other phenomena as well. It explains, for example, the "man bites dog" criterion of what is newsworthy. If the television newscasts were watched or newspapers were read solely to obtain the most important information about public affairs, aberrant events of little public importance would be ignored and typical patterns of quantitative significance would be emphasized; when the news is, by contrast, for most people largely an alternative to other forms of diversion or entertainment, intriguing oddities and human-interest items are in demand. Similarly, events that unfold in a suspenseful way or sex scandals among public figures are fully covered by the media, whereas the complexities of economic policy or quantitative analyses of public problems receive only minimal attention. Public officials, often able to thrive without giving the citizens good value for their tax monies, may fall over an exceptional mistake striking enough to be newsworthy. Extravagant statements, picturesque protests, and unruly demonstrations that offend much of the public they are designed to influence are also explicable in this way: they make diverting news and thus call attention to interests and arguments that might otherwise be ignored. Even some isolated acts of terrorism that are described as "senseless" can, from this perspective, be explained as effective means of obtaining the riveted attention of a public that otherwise would remain rationally ignorant.

This argument also helps us to understand certain apparent inconsistencies in the behavior of modern democracies. The arrangement of the income-tax brackets in all the major developed democracies is distinctly progressive, whereas the loopholes are more often tilted toward a minority of more prosperous taxpayers.

Since both are the results of the same democratic institution, why do they not have the same incidence? As I see it, the progression of the income tax is a matter of such salience and political controversy that much of the electorate knows about it, so populist and majoritarian considerations dictate a considerable degree of progression. The details of tax laws are far less widely known, and they often reflect the interests of small numbers of organized and usually more prosperous taxpayers. Several of the developed democracies similarly have adopted programs such as Medicare and Medicaid that are obviously inspired by the concerns about the cost of medical care to those with low or middle incomes, yet implemented or administered these programs in ways that resulted in large increases in income for prosperous physicians and other providers of medical care. Again, these diverse consequences seem to be explained by the fact that conspicuous and controversial choices of overall policies become known to the majorities who consume health care, whereas the many smaller choices needed to implement these programs are influenced primarily by a minority of organized providers of health care.

The fact that the typical individual does not have an incentive to spend much time studying many of his choices concerning collective goods also helps to explain some otherwise inexplicable individual contributions toward the provision of collective goods. The logic of collective action that has been described in this chapter is not immediately apparent to those who have never studied it; if it were, there would be nothing paradoxical in the argument with which this chapter opened, and students to whom the argument is explained would not react with initial skepticism.[15] No doubt the practical implications of this logic for the individual's own choices were often discerned before the logic was ever set out in print, but this does not mean that they were always understood even at the intuitive and practical level. In particular, when the costs of individual contributions to collective action are very small, the individual has little incentive to investigate whether or not to make a contribution or even to exercise intuition. If the individual knows the costs of a contribution to collective action in the interest of a group of which he is a part are trivially small, he may rationally not take the trouble to consider whether the gains are smaller still. This is particularly the case since the size of these gains and the policies that would maximize them are matters about which it is usually not rational for him to investigate.

This consideration of the costs and benefits of calculation about public goods leads to the testable prediction that voluntary contributions toward the provision of collective goods for large groups without selective incentives will often occur when the costs of individual contributions are negligible, but that they will *not* often occur when the costs of the individual contributions are considerable. In other words, when the costs of individual action to help to obtain a desired collective good are small enough, the result is indeterminate and sometimes goes one way and sometimes the other, but when the costs get larger this indeterminacy disappears. We should accordingly find that more than a few people are willing to take the moment of time needed to sign petitions for causes they support, or to express their opinions in the course of discussion, or to vote for the candidate or party they prefer. Similarly, if the argument here is correct, we should not find many instances where individuals voluntarily contribute substantial sums of resources year after year for the purpose of obtaining some collective good for some large group of which they are a part. Before parting with a large amount of money or time, and particularly before doing so repeatedly, the rational individual will reflect on what this considerable sacrifice will accomplish. If the individual is a typical individual in a large group that would benefit from a collective good, his contribution will not make a perceptible difference in the amount that is provided. The theory here predicts that such contributions become less likely the larger the contribution at issue.[16]

V

Even when contributions are costly enough to elicit rational calculation, there is still only one set of circumstances in which collective action can occur without selective incentives. This set of circumstances becomes evident the moment we think of situations in which there are only a few individuals or firms that would benefit from collective action. Suppose there are two firms of equal size in an industry and no other firms can enter the industry. It still will be the case that a higher price for the industry's product will benefit both firms and that legislation favorable to the industry will help both firms. The higher price and the favorable legislation are then collective goods to this "oligopolistic" industry, even though there are only two in the group that benefit from the collective goods. Obviously, each of the oligopolists is in a situation in which if it restricts output to raise the industry price, or lobbies for favorable legislation for the industry, it will tend to get half of the benefit. And the cost-benefit ratio of action in the common interest easily could be so favorable that, even though a firm bears the whole cost of its action and gets only half the benefit of this action, it could still profit from acting in the common interest. Thus if the group that would benefit from collective action is sufficiently small and the cost-benefit ratio of collective action for the group sufficiently favorable, there may well be calculated action in the collective interest even without selective incentives.

When there are only a few members in the group, there is also the possibility that they will bargain with one another and agree on collective action—then the action of each can have a perceptible effect on the interests and the expedient courses of actions of others, so that each has an incentive to act strategically, that is, in ways that take into account the effect of the individual's choices on the choices of others. This interdependence of individual firms or persons in the group can give them an incentive to bargain with one another for their mutual advantage. Indeed, if bargaining costs were negligible, they would have an incentive to continue bargaining with one another until group gains were maximized, that is, until what we shall term a *group-optimal outcome* (or what economists sometimes call a "Pareto-optimal" outcome for the group) is achieved. One way the two firms mentioned in the previous paragraph could obtain such an outcome is by agreeing that each will bear half the costs of any collective action; each firm would then bear half the cost of its action in the common interest and receive half the benefits. It therefore would have an incentive to continue action in the collective interest until the aggregate gains of collective action were maximized. In any bargaining, however, each party has an incentive to seek the largest possible share of the group gain for itself, and usually also an incentive to threaten to block or undermine the collective action—that is, to be a "holdout"—if it does not get its preferred share of the group gains. Thus the bargaining may very well not succeed in achieving a group-optimal outcome and may also fail to achieve agreement on any collective action at all. The upshot of all this, as I explain elsewhere,[17] is that "small" groups can often engage in collective action without selective incentives. In certain small groups ("privileged groups") there is actually a presumption that some of the collective good will be provided. Nonetheless, even in the best of circumstances collective action is problematic and the outcomes in particular cases are indeterminate.

Although some aspects of the matter are complex and indeterminate, the essence of the relationship between the size of the group that would benefit from collective action and the extent of collective action is beautifully simple—yet somehow not widely understood. Consider again our two firms and suppose that they have *not* worked out any agreement to maximize their aggregate gains or to coordinate their actions in any way. Each firm will still get half the gains of any action it takes in the interest of the group, and thus it may have a substantial incentive to act in the group interest even when it is acting unilaterally. There is, of course, also a *group external economy*, or gain to the group for which the firm acting unilaterally is not compensated, of 50 percent, so unilateral behavior does not achieve a group-optimal outcome.[18] Now suppose there were a third firm of the same size—the group external economy would then be two thirds, and the individual firm would get only a third of the gain from any independent action it took in the group interest. Of course, if there were a hundred such firms, the group external economy would be 99 percent, and the individual firm would get only 1 percent of the gain from any action in the group interest. Obviously, when we get to large groups measured in millions or even thousands, the incentive for group-oriented behavior in the absence of selective incentives becomes insignificant and even imperceptible.

Untypical as my example of equal-sized firms may be, it makes the general point intuitively obvious: other things being equal, *the larger the number of individuals or firms that would benefit from a collective good, the smaller the share of the gains from action in the group interest that will accrue to the individual or firm that undertakes the action. Thus, in the absence of selective incentives, the incentive for group action diminishes as group size increases, so that large groups are less able to act in their common interest than small ones.* If an additional individual or firm that would value the collective good enters the scene, then the share of the gains from group-oriented action that anyone already in the group might take must diminish. This holds true whatever the relative sizes or valuations of the collective good in the group. . . .

The number of people who must bargain if a group-optimal amount of a collective good is to be obtained, and thus the costs of bargaining, must rise with the size of the group. This consideration reinforces the point just made. Indeed, both everyday observation and the logic of the matter suggest that for genuinely large groups, bargaining among all members to obtain agreement on the provision of a collective good is out of the question. The consideration mentioned earlier in this chapter, that social selective incentives are available only to small groups and (tenuously) to those larger groups that are federations of small groups, also suggests that small groups are more likely to organize than large ones.

The significance of the logic that has just been set out can best be seen by comparing groups that would have the same net gain from collective action, if they could engage in it, but that vary in size. Suppose there are a million individuals who would gain a thousand dollars each, or a billion in the aggregate, if they were to organize effectively and engage in collective action that had a total cost of a hundred million. If the logic set out above is right, they could not organize or engage in effective collective action without selective incentives. Now suppose that, although the total gain of a billion dollars from collective action and the aggregate cost of a hundred million remain the same, the group is composed instead of five big corporations or five organized municipalities, each of which would gain two hundred million. Collective action is not an absolute certainty even in this case, since each of the five could conceivably expect others to put up the hundred million and hope to gain the collective good worth two hundred million at no cost at all. Yet collective action, perhaps after some delays due to bargaining, seems very likely indeed. In this case any one of the five would gain a hundred million from providing the collective good even if it had to pay the whole cost itself; and the costs of bargaining among five would not be great, so they would sooner or later probably work out an agreement providing for the collective action. The numbers in this example are arbitrary, but roughly similar situations occur often in reality, and the contrast between "small" and "large" groups could be illustrated with an infinite number of diverse examples.

The significance of this argument shows up in a second way if one compares the operations of lobbies or cartels within jurisdictions of vastly different scale, such as a modest municipality on the one hand and a big country on the other. Within the town, the mayor or city council may be influenced by, say, a score of petitioners or a lobbying budget of a thousand dollars. A particular line of business may be in the hands of only a few firms, and if the town is distant enough from other markets only these few would need to agree to create a cartel. In a big country, the resources needed to influence the national government are likely to be much more substantial, and unless the firms are (as they sometimes are) gigantic, many of them would have to cooperate to create an effective cartel. Now suppose that the million individuals in our large group in the previous paragraph were spread out over a hundred thousand towns or jurisdictions, so that each jurisdiction had ten of them, along with the same proportion of citizens in other categories as before. Suppose also that the cost-benefit ratios remained the same, so that there was still a billion dollars to gain across all jurisdictions or ten thousand in each, and that it would still cost a hundred million dollars across all jurisdictions or a thousand in each. It no longer seems out of the question that in many jurisdictions the groups of ten, or subsets of them, would put up the thousand-dollar total needed to get the thousand for each individual. Thus we see that, if all else were equal, small jurisdictions would have more collective action per capita than large ones.

Differences in intensities of preference generate a third type of illustration of the logic at issue. A small number of zealots anxious for a particular collective good are more likely to act collectively to obtain that good than a larger number with the same aggregate willingness to pay. Suppose there are twenty-five individuals, each of whom finds a given collective good worth a thousand dollars in one case, whereas in another there are five thousand, each of whom finds the collective good worth five dollars. Obviously, the argument indicates that there would be a greater likelihood of collective action in the former case than in the latter, even though the aggregate demand for the collective good is the same in both. The great historical significance of small groups of fanatics no doubt owes something to this consideration.

VI

The argument in this chapter predicts that those groups that have access to selective incentives will be more likely to act collectively to obtain collective goods than those that do not, and that smaller groups will have a greater likelihood of engaging in collective action than larger ones. The empirical portions of *The Logic* show that this prediction has been correct for the United States. More study will be needed before we can be utterly certain that the argument also holds for other countries, but the more prominent features of the organizational landscape of other countries certainly do fit the theory. In no major country are large groups without access to selective incentives generally organized—the masses of consumers are not in consumers' organizations, the millions of taxpayers are not in taxpayers' organizations, the vast number of those with relatively low incomes are not in organizations for the poor, and the sometimes substantial numbers of unemployed have no organized voice. These groups are so dispersed that it is not feasible for any nongovernmental organization to coerce them; in this they differ dramatically from those, like workers in large factories or mines, who are susceptible to coercion through picketing. Neither does there appear to be any source of the positive selective incentives that might give individuals in these categories an incentive to cooperate with the many others with whom they share common interests.[19] By contrast, almost everywhere the social prestige of the learned professions and the limited numbers of practitioners of each profession in each community has helped them to organize. The professions have also been helped to organize by the distinctive susceptibility of the public to the assertion that a professional organization, with the backing of government, ought to be able to determine who is "qualified" to practice the profession, and thereby to control a decisive selective incentive. The small groups of (often large) firms in industry after industry, in country after country, are similarly often organized in trade associations or organizations or collusions of one kind or another. So, frequently, are the small groups of (usually smaller) businesses in particular towns or communities.

Even though the groups that the theory says cannot be organized do not appear to be organized anywhere, there are still substantial differences across societies and historical periods in the extent to which the groups that our logic says *could* be organized *are* organized. . . .

NOTES

1. Cambridge: Harvard University Press, 1965, 1971. The 1971 version differs from the first 1965 printing only in the addition of an appendix. Some readers may have access to the first paperback edition published by Schocken Books (New York: 1968), which is identical to the 1965 Harvard version. Readers whose first language is not English may prefer *Die Logik des Kollektiven Handelns* (Tübingen: J. C. B. Mohr [Paul Siebeck], 1968), or *Logique de l'Action Collective* (Paris: Presses Universitaires de France, 1978). Translations in Japanese (from Minerva Shobo) and in Italian (from Feltrinelli) are forthcoming.

2. There is a logically possible exception to this association, although not of wide practical importance, that is explained in footnote 68 of Chapter 1 of *The Logic*, pp. 48–49.

3. *Rational* need not imply *self-interested*. The argument in the text can hold even when there is altruistic behavior, although if particular types of altruistic behavior are strong enough it will not hold. Consider first altruistic attitudes about observable outcomes or results—suppose an individual would be willing to sacrifice some leisure or other personal consumption to obtain some amount of a collective good because of an altruistic concern that others should have this collective good. In other words, the individual's preference ordering takes account of the collective good obtained by others as well as personal consumption. This assumption of altruism does not imply irrationality, or a tendency to make choices that are inconsistent with the maximal satisfaction of the values or preferences the individual has. Altruism also does not call into question the normal diminishing marginal rates of substitution between any pair of goods or objectives; as more of any good or objective (selfish or altruistic) is attained, other things being equal, the extent to which other goods or objectives (selfish or altruistic) will be given up to attain more of that good or objective will diminish.

A typical altruistic and rational individual of the sort described will not make any substantial voluntary contributions to obtain a collective good for a large group. The reason is that in a sufficiently large group the individual's contribution will make only a small and perhaps imperceptible difference to the amount of collective good the group obtains, whereas at the same time every contribution reduces dollar-for-dollar the amount of personal consumption and private-good charity, and the diminishing marginal rates of substitution entail that these sacrifices become progressively more onerous. In equilibrium in large groups there is accordingly little or no voluntary contribution by the rational altruist to the provision of a collective good.

Jarring as it is to the common-sense notion of rationality, let us now make the special assumption that the altruist gets satisfaction not from observably better outcomes for others, but rather from his or her own sacrifices for them. On this assumption we can secure voluntary provision of collective goods even in the largest groups. Here each dollar of personal consumption that is sacrificed can bring a significant return in moral satisfaction, and the problem that substantial personal sacrifices bring little or no perceptible change in the level of public good provided is no longer relevant. Even though this latter participatory or "Kantian" altruism is presumably not the usual form of altruism, I think it does exist and helps to account for some observations of voluntary contributions to large groups. (Yet another possibility is that the altruist is result-oriented but neglects the observable levels of the public good, simply assuming that his or her sacrifices of personal consumption increase the utility of others enough to justify the personal sacrifice.) My own thinking on this issue has been clarified by reading Howard Margolis, *Selfishness, Altruism, and Rationality* (Cambridge: University Press, 1982).

4. This argument need not apply to small groups, which are discussed later in the chapter.

5. David J. McDonald, *Union Man* (New York: Dutton, 1969), p. 121, quoted in William A. Gamson, *The Strategy of Social Protest* (Homewood, Ill.: Dorsey Press, 1975), p. 68.

6. The references to the often violent interaction between employers and employees in the early stages of unionization should not obscure the consensual and informal "unionization" that also sometimes occurs because of employers' initiatives. This sort of labor organization or collusion arises because some types of production require that workers collaborate effectively. When this is the case, the employer may find it profitable to encourage team spirit and social interaction among employees. Staff conferences and work-group meetings, newsletters for employees, firm-sponsored employee athletic teams, employer-financed office parties, and the like are partly explained by this consideration. In firms that have the same employment pattern for some time, the networks for employee interaction that the employer created to encourage effective cooperation at work may evolve into informal collusions, or occasionally even unions, of workers, and tacitly or openly force the employer to deal with his employees as a cartelized group. This evolution is unlikely when employees are, for example, day laborers or consultants, but when stable patterns of active cooperation are important to production, the employer may gain more from the extra production that this cooperation brings about than he loses from the informal or formal cartelization that he helps to create. The evolution of this type of informal unionization implies that there is more organization of labor than the statistics imply, and that the differences between some ostensibly unorganized firms and unionized firms are not as great as might appear on the surface.

7. *The Logic*, p. 85.

8. This means in turn that sometimes individual corporations of substantial size can be political combinations with significant lobbying power. On less than voluntary corporate contributions, see J. Patrick Wright, *On a Clear Day You Can See General Motors* (Grosse Pointe, Mich.: Wright Enterprises, 1979), pp. 69–70.

9. *The Logic*, pp. 132–167.

10. Erik Lindahl, "Just Taxation—A Positive Solution," in Richard Musgrave and Alan T. Peacock, eds., *Classics in the Theory of Public Finance* (London: Macmillan, 1958), pp. 168–177 and 214–233. In a Lindahl equilibrium, the parties at issue are each charged a tax-price for marginal units of the public good that is equal to the value each places on a marginal unit of the good. When this condition holds, even parties that have vastly different evaluations of the collective good will want the same amount. It would take us far afield to discuss the huge literature on this matter now, but it may be helpful to nonspecialists to point out that in most circumstances in which the parties at issue expect Lindahl-type taxation, they would have an incentive to understate their true valuations of the collective good, since they would get whatever amount was provided however low their tax-price. There is an interesting literature on relatively subtle schemes that could give individuals an incentive to reveal their true valuations for public goods, thereby making Lindahl-equilibria attainable, but most of these schemes are a very long way indeed from practical application.

11. See my primitive, early article, "The Principle of 'Fiscal Equivalence,' " *American Economic Review, Papers and Proceedings* 59 (May 1969):479–487.

12. See, for a leading example, Martin C. McGuire, "Group Segregation and Optimal Jurisdictions," *Journal of Political Economy* 82 (1974):112–132.

13. See most notably Wallace Oates, *Fiscal Federalism* (New York: Harcourt Brace Jovanovich, Inc., 1972).

14. For very early work on the limited information voters may be expected to have, see Anthony Downs's classic *Economic Theory of Democracy* (New York: Harper, 1957).

15. I am indebted to Russell Hardin for calling this point to my attention. For a superb and rigorous analysis of the whole issue of collective action, see Hardin's *Collective Action* (Baltimore: The Johns Hopkins University Press, 1982).

16. There is another consideration that works in the same direction. Consider individuals who get pleasure from participating in efforts to obtain a collective good just as they would from ordinary consumption, and so are participation altruists (described in note 3). If the costs of collective action to the individual are slight, the costs of consuming the participation pleasure or satisfying the moral impulse to be a participant are unlikely to prevent collective action. With the diminishing marginal rates of substitution that are described in note 3, however, the extent of collective action out of these motives will decrease as its price rises.

17. *The Logic*, pp. 5–65.

18. The assumption that there are two firms that place an equal value on the collective good is expositionally useful but will not often be descriptively realistic. In the much more common case, where the parties place different valuations on the public good, the party that places the larger absolute valuation on the public good is at an immense disadvantage. When it provides the amount of the collective good that would be optimal for it alone, then the others have an incentive to enjoy this amount and provide none at all. But the reverse is not true. So the larger party bears the whole burden of the collective good. (The party that places the larger value on the collective good has the option of trying to force the others to share the cost by withholding provision, but it is also at a disadvantage in the bargaining because it will lose more from this action than those with whom it is bargaining.) Thus a complete analysis of the likelihood of collective action must consider the relative sizes or valuations of the collective good of the parties involved as well as the size of the group; see the references in the next note [not printed here] on "the exploitation of the great by the small" and other consequences of intragroup variations in valuations of collective goods.

If the corner solution with the larger party bearing all the burden does not occur, and both firms provide some amount of the collective good under Cournot assumptions, then the two firms will tend to be of exactly the same size, as in the example chosen for expositional convenience in the text. Assume that each firm has to pay the same price for each unit of the collective good and that they have identical production functions for whatever private good they produce. Since they must, by the definition of a pure collective good, both receive the same amount of it, they can both be in equilibrium under Cournot assumptions only if their isoquants have the same slope at the relevant point. That is, the isoquants describing the output that results from each combination of the private good and public good inputs for each of the firms must have the same slope if the two firms enjoying the same amount of the collective good are each purchasing some of it at the same time. Under my identical production function and factor price assumptions, the two firms must then have exactly the same output or size.

Similarly remarkable results hold for consumers who share a collective good. Either the consumer that places the higher absolute valuation on the public good will bear the entire cost or else they will end up with equal incomes! When both consumers get the same amount of a collective good, they both can be continuing to purchase some under Cournot behavior only if they both have the same marginal rate of substitution between the public good and the private good, and thus (with identical utility functions and prices) identical incomes. Unless the two consumers have identical incomes *in the beginning*, there is inevitably exploitation of the great by the small. One possibility is that the richer consumer will bear the whole cost of the collective good. The only other possibility with independent adjustment is that the public good is so valuable that the richer consumer's initial purchases of it have such a large income effect on the poorer consumer that this poorer consumer ends up just as well off as the initially richer consumer, so both buy some amount of the collective good in equilibrium. I have profited from discussion of this point with my colleague Martin C. McGuire. For a stimulating and valuable, if partially incorrect, argument along related lines, see Ronald Jeremias and Asghar Zardkoohi, "Distributional Implications of Independent Adjustment in an Economy with Public Goods," *Economic Inquiry* 14 (June 1976):305–308.

19. Even groups or causes that are so large or popular that they encompass almost everyone in the society cannot generate very substantial organizations. Consider those concerned about the quality of the environment. Although environmental extremists are a small minority, almost everyone is interested in a wholesome environment, and poll results suggest that in the United States, for example, there are tens of millions of citizens who think more ought to be done to protect the environment. In the late 1960s and early 1970s, certainly, environmentalism was faddish as well. Despite this, and despite subsidized postal rates for nonprofit organizations and reductions in the cost of direct mail solicitation due to computers, relatively few people pay dues each year to environmental organizations. The major environmental organizations in the United States have memberships measured in the tens or hundreds of thousands, with at least the larger (such as the Audubon Society, with its products for bird-watchers) plainly owing much of their membership to selective incentives. There are surely more than 50 million Americans who value a wholesome environment, but in a typical year probably fewer than one in a hundred pays dues to any organization whose main activity is lobbying for a better environment. The proportion of physicians in the American Medical Association, or automobile workers in the United Automobile Workers union, or farmers in the Farm Bureau, or manufacturers in trade associations is incomparably greater.

20

RICHARD L. HALL AND FRANK W. WAYMAN

BUYING TIME: MONEYED INTERESTS
AND THE MOBILIZATION OF BIAS

To what extent, if at all, do moneyed interests dominate congressional decisions? Richard L. Hall and Frank W. Wayman, professors at the University of Michigan, tackle the question in an innovative way. Instead of testing for the effects of campaign contributions on the floor votes of congressmen, Hall and Wayman probe the influence of donors at the agenda-setting stage: in committee deliberations. By examining the committee stage of the legislative process, rather than the often less revealing roll-call stage, these authors discern significant links between contributions and policy outcomes.

At least since Madison railed about the mischiefs of faction, critics of U.S. political institutions have worried about the influence of organized interests in national policy making. In this century, one of the most eloquent critics of the interest group system was E. E. Schattschneider, who warned of the inequalities between private, organized, and upper-class groups on the one hand and public, unorganized, and lower-class groups on the other. The pressure system, he argued in *The Semisovereign People* (1960), "mobilized bias" in national policy making in favor of the former, against the interests of the latter, and hence against the interests of U.S. democracy. Such concerns have hardly abated thirty years since the publication of Schattschneider's essay. In particular, the precipitous growth in the number and financial strength of political action committees has refueled the charge that moneyed interests dominate the policy making process. The current Congress is *The Best Congress Money Can Buy* according to one critic (Stern 1988), one where *Honest Graft* is an institutional imperative (Jackson 1988; see also Drew 1982; Etzioni 1984). "The rising tide of special-interest money," one close observer concludes, "is changing the balance of power between voters and donors, between lawmakers' constitutional constituents and their cash constituents" (Jackson 1988, 107).

Despite the claims of the institutional critics and the growing public concern over PACs during the last decade, the scientific evidence that political money matters in legislative decision making is surprisingly weak. Considerable research on members' voting decisions offers little support for the popular view that PAC money permits interests to buy or rent votes on matters that affect them. Based on an examination of 120 PACs in 10 issue areas over four congresses, one recent study concludes flatly that PAC contributions do not affect members' voting patterns (Grenzke 1989a). Another study, designed to explore the "upper bounds" of PAC influence on House roll calls, emphasizes "the relative inability of PACs to determine congressional voting" (Wright 1985, 412). Other studies have come to similar conclusions (see e.g., Chappell 1982; Wayman 1985; Welch 1982), though there are also dissenting voices (e.g., Kau and Rubin 1982; Silberman and Durden 1976). On the whole, then, this literature certainly leads one to a more sanguine view of moneyed interests and congressional politics than one gets from the popular commentaries. Does money matter?

Our approach to this question is two-pronged. In the first two sections, we revisit the question by developing a theoretical account of the constrained exchange between legislator and donor quite different from the one evident in the substantial literature cited above. In particular, we adopt the premise that PACs are rational actors, seeking to maximize their influence on the legislative outcomes that affect their affiliates; but we take issue with the standard account of PAC rationality. Our approach does not lead us to predict a strong causal relationship between PAC money and floor votes. House members and interest group representatives are viewed as parties to an implicit cooperative agreement, but the constraints on member behavior and the rational calculations of group representatives limit the extent to which votes become the currency of exchange. Instead, we advance two hypotheses about the effect of money on congressional decision making.

First, we suggest that in looking for the effects of money in Congress, one must look more to the politics of committee decision making than those of the floor. This view, of course, is neither original nor remarkable. Students of Congress have long contended that interest group influence flourishes at the committee level, and recent students of PAC influence invariably advocate that work move in this direction (e.g., Grenzke 1989a, 18; Schlozman and Tierney 1986, 256). To date, however, systematic studies of PACs and committee decision making have been altogether rare (for an important exception, see Wright 1989). We focus here at the committee level and emphasize the theoretical reasons for doing so.

Second, and more importantly, our account of the member-donor exchange leads us to focus on the *participation* of particular members, not on their votes. This variable, we believe, is a crucial but largely neglected element of congressional decision making. It is especially important in any analysis of interest group influence in a decentralized Congress. In their famous study of lobbying on foreign trade policy, for instance, Bauer, Pool, and Dexter concluded that a member's principal problem is "not how to vote but what to do with his time, how to allocate his resources, and where to put his energy" (1963, 405). More recently, Denzau and Munger (1986) have modeled the interest group-member relationship as an exchange of contributions and electoral support for legislative services or effort. If money does not necessarily buy votes or change minds, in other words, it can buy members' time. The intended effect is to mobilize bias in congressional committee decision making.

We then develop and estimate a model of committee participation that permits a direct test of whether moneyed interests do mobilize bias in committee decision making. Analyzing data from three House committees on three distinct issues, we find that they do. In the final section we briefly discuss the implications of the findings for our understanding of money, interest groups, and representation in Congress.

THE RATIONAL PAC REVISITED

The interdependencies of legislators and moneyed interests have been widely discussed by political scientists and widely lamented by critics of pluralism (see esp. Hayes 1981). The basis for political exchange is clear. Each depends at least partially on the other to promote its goals. Interest groups seek, among other things, favorable action on legislation that will affect them; members of Congress seek financial and political support from particular groups. Like the relationship between legislators and bureaucrats, however, the relationship between legislators and interest groups is one of *implicit* exchange: the actors "trade speculatively and on credit" (Arnold 1979, 36; see also Denzau and Munger 1986; Hayes 1981). Contributions are marked somewhere in the invisible ledger, and a group's political strategists presumably can use them to their momentary legislative ends.

This account of the legislator-interest group relationship underpins the now-considerable literature on contributions and roll call voting. The working hypothesis is that contributions influence legislative outcomes by "purchasing" the votes of particular members or, less directly, by serving as "investments" that will pay dividends in legislative support at some later date (e.g., Chappell 1982; Jacobson 1980, 77, 82). The scientific evidence that such effects appear only infrequently may be cause for relief among critics of the system, but it is puzzling to theorists of institutional behavior. Why should PACs flourish, both in number and financial strength, when their legislative efficacy is so low? The payoffs would appear inadequate to sustain the cooperative relationship.

One possible explanation is that PACs raise and disburse money with local congressional elections, not specific legislative ends, in mind. Wright (1985) argues, in fact, that the decentralized nature of most PAC organizations inclines them to do just that. But this account simply moves the issue of PAC rationality to a second, institutional level. Why would PACs organize in this way? Wright suggests that the typical national PAC office permits local officials substantial discretion because it wants to encourage them to continue raising funds. But the organization's fund-raising and disbursement, presumably, are intended for some more ultimate purpose, namely, to increase the net political benefits associated with governmental action (or inaction) on issues that affect it. On the whole, using money solely to affect election outcomes is not likely to be a rational means to this end. The probability that any single group's contribution will affect the outcome of a congressional election—in which a wide range of more powerful forces are at work—is almost certainly slight. In the aggregate it might affect the organization's political support within Congress by only a member or two (Wayman 1985). While organizational arrangements may create some inefficiency in the way PACs employ funds to promote their political ends, one should still expect to find systematic patterns of allocation that are driven by legislative considerations, even among PACs that are highly decentralized (and especially among those that are not). Indeed, there is growing evidence that this is the case (Grenzke 1989b).

If the principal value of contributions lies in their potential to affect floor roll calls, however, a second puzzle appears. One would expect to find contribution strategies that favor the swing legislators in anticipated floor battles, since these are the cases where the marginal utility in votes purchased per dollar spent is likely to be greatest (Denzau and Munger 1986). Money allocated to almost certain supporters (or almost certain opponents) should be counted as irrational behavior, evidence of scarce resources wasted. In fact, however, the evidence suggests that such "misallocations" systematically occur. The Business-Industry Political Action Committee (BIPAC) and the National Chamber of Commerce give overwhelmingly to conservative Republicans (Kau and Rubin 1982, 88; Maitland 1985). Labor PACs such as the AFL-CIO's Committee on Political Education give overwhelmingly to incumbent Democrats loyal to labor's agenda (Chappell 1982; Grier and Munger 1986; Jacobson 1980). Oil PACs give to conservative incumbents regardless of party and to friends regardless of ideology (Evans 1988). In general, PACs are prone to reward their friends—even when their friends are not in danger of defeat. In a specific test of the swing hypothesis, in fact, Welch found that if anything, dairy PACs were *less* likely to contribute to swing legislators on dairy issues, all other things being equal (1982).[1] On the whole, it would seem that if, as Schattschneider (1960) said, moneyed interests sing with an upper-class accent, they also spend a good deal of effort singing to the choir.

One oft-mentioned solution to these puzzles is that contributions buy not votes but "access" to members and their staffs (e.g., Berry 1984; Gopoian 1984; Schlozman and Tierney, 1986). But this solution only provokes a second query: If money buys access, what does access buy? (see esp. Herndon, 1982, 1017). Presumably, it gives the representatives of contributing groups important opportunities to directly lobby and potentially persuade legislators to the group's point of view. In this scenario the language of *access* may serve symbolically to launder the money going from group to roll call vote, but the effect of the group on the vote should still appear in systematic analysis (Grenzke 1989a). As we note above, it does not.

THE RATIONAL PAC REVISED

The literature on PAC contribution strategies and members' roll call voting behavior thus suggests two puzzles. First, if group strategists are reasonably rational, why would they continue to allocate scarce resources to efforts where the expected political benefits are so low? Second, if PAC allocation strategies are designed to influence members' votes, why do they contribute so heavily to their strongest supporters and occasionally to their strongest opponents? Is it the case that PACs are systematically irrational (e.g., Welch 1982, 492) and, by extension, that claims about the influence of money on legislative process almost certainly exaggerated? We believe that the premise of rationality need not be rejected but that theoretical work in this area requires a more complete account of rational

PAC behavior. We extend here an account developed formally in Denzau and Munger's model of a supply price for public policy (1986). Simply put, interest group resources are intended to accomplish something different from, and more than, influencing elections or buying votes. Specifically, we argue that PAC money should be allocated in order to *mobilize* legislative support and *demobilize* opposition, particularly at the most important points in the legislative process.

This argument turns directly on what we already know about the nature of legislators' voting decisions from a very rich literature. The simple but important point is that a number of powerful factors exist that predispose a member to vote a certain way, among them party leaders, ideology, constituency, and the position of the administration (Fiorina 1974; Jackson 1974; Kingdon 1981).[2] Kingdon notes, moreover, that members' votes on particular issues are also constrained by their past voting histories (1981, 274–278). Members attach some value to consistency, independent of the other factors that influence their voting behavior. A third and related point is that the public, recorded nature of the vote may itself limit the member's discretion: a risk-averse member may fear the appearance of impropriety in supporting major campaign contributors in the absence of some other, legitimate force pushing her in the same direction. Finally, the dichotomous nature of the vote acts as a constraint. Money must not only affect members' attitudes at the margin but do so enough to push them over the threshold between *nay* and *yea*. In short, the limits on member responsiveness to messages wrapped in money are substantial, perhaps overwhelming, at least insofar as floor voting is concerned.

Of course, almost all studies of PAC contributions and roll calls acknowledge the importance of such factors and build them into their statistical models of the voting decision. But it is also important to consider the implications of these findings for the vote-buying hypothesis itself. Interest group strategists tend to be astute-enough observers of the legislative process to appreciate the powerful constraints that shape members' voting behavior. To the extent that this is true the rational PAC should expect little in the way of marginal benefits in votes bought for dollars spent, especially when individual PAC contributions are limited by the Federal Election Campaign Act to ten thousand dollars—a slight fraction of the cost of the average House race. Individual votes, that is, simply aren't easy to change; and even if some are changed, the utility of the votes purchased depends on their net cumulative effect in turning a potentially losing coalition into a winning one. For the rational PAC manager, the expected marginal utility approximates zero in most every case. All other things being equal, scarce resources should be allocated heavily elsewhere and to other purposes.

How, then, should the strategic PAC distribute its resources? The first principle derives from the larger literature on interest group influence in Congress. Well aware of the decentralized nature of congressional decision making, interest groups recognize that resources allocated at the committee stage are more efficiently spent (e.g., Berry 1984; Grier and Munger 1986; Kingdon 1981, 170–171). Interest group preferences incorporated there have a strong chance of surviving as the bill moves through subsequent stages in the sequence, while provisions not in the committee vehicle are difficult to attach later. Second, the nature of the committee assignment process increases the probability that organized interests will find a sympathetic audience at the committee or subcommittee stage. Members seek and often receive positions that will permit them to promote the interests that, in turn, help them to get reelected (Shepsle 1978). Finally, the less public, often informal nature of committee decision making suggests that members' responsiveness to campaign donors will receive less scrutiny. Indeed, a long tradition of research on subgovernments emphasizes that such clientelism flourishes at the committee stage (e.g., Ripley and Franklin 1980; Shepsle 1978, chap. 10; but see Gais, Peterson, and Walker 1984). In short, groups will strategically allocate their resources with the knowledge that investments in the politics of the appropriate committee or subcommittee are likely to pay higher dividends than investments made elsewhere. Indeed, this principle is especially important in the House, where the sheer size of the chamber's membership, the greater importance of the committee stage, and the frequent restrictions on floor participation recommend a more targeted strategy (see, esp., Grenzke 1989b and Grier and Munger 1989).

If PACs concentrate at the committee level, what, specifically, do they hope to gain there? Purchasing votes is one possibility; and, in fact, the rationale for allocating campaign money to buy votes in committee is somewhat stronger than for vote-buying on the floor. But even within committee, PACs still tend to give to their strongest supporters. In addition, committee votes, like floor votes, are dichotomous decisions. And despite the lower visibility of committee decision making, the factors of constituency, ideology, party, and administration are almost certainly at work. In fact, while research on PACs and committee voting is just now beginning to emerge, there is little evidence that contributions influence voting in committee any more than they do voting on the floor (Wright 1989).

The alternative hypothesis that we test here is that political money alters members' patterns of legislative involvement, a point that emerges from an older literature on interest group influence in Congress (e.g., Bauer, Pool, and Dexter 1963; Matthews [1960] 1973, esp. 192–193) but is given its fullest theoretical expression in the recent work of Denzau and Munger (1986). Denzau and Munger suggest that interest groups provide political resources in an implicit effort to purchase policy-relevant "services" from members or their staffs. Stated somewhat differently, the object of a rational PAC allocation strategy is not simply the *direction* of legislators' preferences but the *vigor* with which those preferences are promoted in the decision making process. Such strategies should take the form of inducing sympathetic members to get actively involved in a variety of activities that directly affect the shape of committee legislation: authoring or blocking a legislative vehicle; negotiating compromises behind the scenes, especially at the staff level; offering friendly amendments or actively opposing unfriendly ones; lobbying colleagues; planning strategy; and last and sometimes least, showing up to vote in favor of the interest group's position. The purposes of PACs in allocating selective benefits, then, are analogous to the purposes that Arnold attributes to legislatively strategic bureaucrats: the goal is not simply to purchase support but to provide incentives for supporters to act as agents—at the extreme, to serve as "coalition leaders" on the principal's behalf (see Arnold 1979, 40–42 and esp. 98–100).

Several arguments support this view. First, participation is crucial to determining legislative outcomes; and voting is perhaps the least important of the various ways in which committee members participate (Hall 1989; Mayhew 1974, 95). Second, while members' voting choices are highly constrained, how they allocate their time, staff, and political capital is much more discretionary (Bauer, Pool, and Dexter 1963, 406–407). At any given moment, each member confronts a wide range of opportunities and demands, the response to any subset of which will serve one or more professional goals. To be sure, the member must choose among them. Legislative resources are scarce, and their allocation to one activity results in other beneficial opportunities foregone (Bauer, Pool, and Dexter 1963; Hall 1987, Matthews [1960] 1973, 182–193). But for the most part, the purposive legislator is free to choose among the abundant alternatives with only modest constraints imposed by constituents, colleagues, or other actors. Hence, the member's level of involvement is something that a strategic PAC can reasonably expect to affect. The contribution need not weigh so heavily in a member's mind that it changes his or her position in any material way; it need only weigh heavily enough to command some increment of legislative resources. The minimum threshold that must be passed is thus a fairly modest one, and the potential effect of contributions on behavior is one of degree. Specifically, the member will allocate scarce legislative resources on the group's behalf so long as the marginal utility of the contribution to the member exceeds the expected marginal utility of the most valuable remaining use of the member's resources (see also Denzau and Munger 1986).

A third advantage of this view is that it explains the ostensibly anomalous tendency of PACs to contribute so heavily to members who are almost certain to win reelection and almost certain to support the group's point of view. Such behavior now appears quite rational. It is precisely one's supporters that one wants to mobilize: the more likely certain members are to support the group, the more active it should want them to be. Furthermore, this view of purposive PACs makes sense of the evidence that PACs sometimes contribute to members who will almost certainly oppose them and whose involvement in an issue stands to do the group harm. The PAC may have no hope of changing the opponent's mind, but it may, at the margin at least, diminish the intensity with which the member pursues policies that the organization does not like. The intent of the money, then, is not persuasion but demobilization: "We know you can't support us, but please don't actively oppose us." However, we should not expect the demobilizing effect of money to be nearly so strong as the mobilizing effect. The message provided through contributions to one's supporters is widely perceived as a legitimate one: in asking for help, the group is encouraging members to do precisely what they would do were resources plentiful. In contrast, contributions to opponents are meant to encourage them to go against their predispositions: the implicit message is to "take a walk" on an issue that they may care about. In short, the expected effects are not symmetric; the mobilization hypothesis is on stronger theoretical ground.

A final advantage of the view of rational action employed here is that it renders the matter of access more comprehensible. We have already noted that according to the standard account of PAC behavior, the importance that both legislators and lobbyists attach to the money-access connection makes little sense, given the evidence that money has little ultimate effect on votes. In light of the theory sketched here, however, access becomes an important, proximate goal of the interest group pursuing a legislative agenda. Access is central to stimulating agency. It gives the group the opportunity to let otherwise sympathetic members (and their staffs) know that some issue or upcoming activity is important to them. The ideal response they seek is not simply "I'll support you on this" but "What can I do to help?" Perhaps more importantly, access refers to the reciprocal efforts of the group. It is the pipeline through which the group effectively subsidizes the considerable time and information costs associated with their supporters' participation in the matters the group cares about. As various accounts reveal, group representatives often serve as "service bureaus" or adjuncts to congressional staff (e.g., Bauer, Pool, and Dexter 1963, chap. 24; Kingdon 1981, 154–155). They provide technical information and policy analysis; they provide political intelligence; they draft legislation and craft amendments; they even write speeches or talking points that their supporters can employ in efforts on their behalf. Such subsidies to the "congressman-as-enterprise" (Salisbury and Shepsle 1981) do not necessarily persuade, but they should affect the patterns of activity and abdication that have a direct bearing on legislative deliberations and outcomes (Hall 1987, 1989).

THE DATA: MONEY AND MOBILIZATION
ON THREE COMMITTEES

The data for this investigation are drawn from staff interviews and markup records of three House committees on three issues: (1) the Dairy Stabilization Act, considered by the Agriculture Committee in 1982; (2) the Job Training Partnership Act (JTPA), considered by Education and Labor in 1982; and (3) the Natural Gas Market Policy Act, considered by Energy and Commerce during 1983–1984.

Several features of these cases make them particularly appropriate for exploring the effects of money on the participation of committee members. First, all were highly significant pieces of legislation, the stakes of each measuring in the billions of dollars. At issue in the Natural Gas Market Policy Act was the deregulation of natural gas prices, a proposal that would transfer billions of dollars from one region to another, from consumer to industry, and within the industry from interstate pipelines and distributors to the major natural gas producers (Uslaner 1989, chap. 5; Maraniss 1983). Annual spending on the Job Training Partnership Act was expected at the time of its passage to be in the four-to-five-billion-dollar range (Donnelly 1982, 1035), and it replaced one of the most important domestic programs of the 1970s (Franklin and Ripley 1984). While more narrow than these in scope, the Dairy Stabilization Act also entailed significant economic effects. The principal purpose of the act was to adjust the scheduled support price for milk downward by as much as a dollar per hundredweight over two years, creating budget savings of 4.2 billion dollars for fiscal years 1983–1985 and decreasing the profitability of milk production by as much as 30% for the typical dairy farmer. In each case, then, evidence of the influence of PAC money on congressional decision making can hardly be counted narrow or trivial. The deliberations in each case bore in significant ways on major interests, both public and private.

A second feature relevant to this investigation follows from the economic importance attached to these issues. All three were salient among actors other than the private groups immediately affected, a feature that the considerable research on roll call voting suggests should depress the effect of PAC contributions on congressional decision making (see, esp., Evans 1986). This was especially true for the natural gas and job training bills. While the Natural Gas Market Policy Act never received action on the House floor in the 98th Congress, it was a highly visible issue while still in committee. Consumer interest in the issue of natural gas pricing was unusually high. Gas heating costs had been climbing quickly in much of the country despite a substantial surplus of domestic natural gas (Davis 1984; Murray 1983; Uslaner 1989, chap. 5); and this fact was widely publicized through the efforts of the Citizen/Labor Energy Coalition (Pressman 1983). The *Washington Post*, in turn, gave Commerce Committee deliberations front-page coverage, and the issue was a high priority for the Reagan administration. The job training bill, likewise, was one of the most important domestic initiatives of Reagan's first term and received considerable media attention. The principal purpose of the bill was to replace the much maligned but widely used public jobs program, the Comprehensive Employment and Training Act (CETA), at a time when the national unemployment rate threatened to exceed 10% for the first time in four decades. To a lesser degree, finally, the 1982 dairy bill was also salient among actors off the committee and outside the industry. While the interest of the general public in dairy policy was slight, the burgeoning budget deficit loomed large on Capitol Hill, and it clearly motivated the decision to change dairy policy only one year after passage of an omnibus farm bill (Wehr 1982a, 1982b). Indeed, relative to other domestic nonentitlements, dairy subsidies were widely perceived as a major budget offender. The administration thus counted the price adjustments a high priority, one that commanded considerable attention from Budget Director David Stockman, and the House Budget Committee was involved at every stage of the process.

Finally, each of the policy areas we examine here has received the attention of previous scholars studying PAC contributions and floor roll calls; and in each case the effects of PAC money were found to be slight. In a study of dairy legislation considered in the House in 1975, for instance, Welch (1982) concluded that dairy PAC contributions were the least important determinant of voting on milk price supports and that their effect on the legislation was negligible (see also Chappell 1982). Grenzke (1989a) estimated a dynamic model of members' voting behavior over four congresses and found that labor union contributions had either a negligible or a *negative* effect on members' propensity to take pro-labor positions on the House floor (but see Wilhite and Theilmann 1987). And Wayman and Kutler (1985) found no effect of natural gas industry campaign contributions on members' votes during House consideration of natural gas deregulation in 1975.

At two levels, then, past research indicates that our selection of cases is biased against our argument. It suggests that high salience issues should exhibit little PAC influence on legislative behavior, yet each of the cases here commanded the attention of a wide range of political actors. Second, past research suggests that we will find little PAC influence in precisely these three policy areas. Should we find support for the hypothesis that money mobilizes support (or demobilizes opposition) at the committee level, we should be on reasonably solid ground to conclude that (1) the results of this exploration are apt to generalize to other committees and other issues and (2) the null results of past research are more likely to be artifacts of the legislative behavior and the legislative stage studied than evidence that moneyed interests do not matter in congressional decision making.

THE MODEL

The model of participation we use to test for the hypothesized effects is adapted from Hall 1987.[3] The model begins from the same motivational premise that we employed in our discussion of PAC contribution behavior. Members of Congress are purposive actors who allocate their time, staff, and other legislative resources in such a way as to advance certain personal goals or interests. There are several goals that commonly figure in these calculations. The one most prominently cited in the literature on legislative behavior is reelection or, more generally, service to the district (see, esp., Mayhew 1974); but we report elsewhere that the relevance of any particular goal to a member's participation depends directly on the nature of the issue and the legislative context (Hall 1987). To use language borrowed from Kingdon (1981), goals are "evoked." Any particular issue may evoke several goals simultaneously or may evoke none at all. In the latter case, a member is simply uninterested, the expected benefits of participation slight; in the former, the level of interest is intense, the expected benefits of participation high.

In the three cases under study here, in fact, several goals were probably at work in the resource allocation decisions of most committee members. For instance, the natural gas bill raised issues of government intervention in the economy and the country's long-term dependence on foreign energy sources. The budgetary implications of the dairy bill undoubtedly evoked some committee members' concerns about good fiscal policy and its macroeconomic consequences. The Job Training Partnership Act concerned the government's obligation to redress inequalities of economic opportunity resulting from inadequate or outdated job skills. But the goal most consistently evident in staff interviews, markup debates, and secondary accounts of the three bills was promoting or protecting district interests. For the purposes of this analysis, then, we adopt the simpler and more tractable motivational assumption common to most models of legislative behavior.[4] In deciding whether and to what extent to participate on a particular issue, the member estimates both the expected benefits and expected costs, where benefits are a direct function of the issue's economic relevance to the district.[5]

If the interests of one's constituents motivate a member to become involved, the costs of participation are also important and highly variable: resources are scarce, and the allocation to one activity results in other profitable opportunities foregone. Several factors affect the resources available to particular members on particular issues. First, assignment to the subcommittee of jurisdiction provides members both with greater formal opportunities to participate and access to an earlier stage of the sequential process. It also gives the member greater access to staff and to lines of communication with other interested actors both on and off the committee. For similar reasons, a committee or subcommittee leadership position subsidizes participation even more. The greater staff allocations that these positions bestow, the procedural control over the agenda, and the central place in the committee communication network diminish the time and information costs associated with meaningful involvement in the issue at hand. Finally, freshman status tends to increase the information costs and diminish the opportunities or resources a member enjoys for any particular bill.

The variable of greatest interest in this investigation, however, is the level of contributions each member receives from PACs interested in the issue at hand. To what degree, that is, does money affect members' decisions regarding whether and to what extent they will participate in the committee deliberations? Two points require emphasis here. First, the foregoing discussion suggests that the effects of money on participation should not be simply linear. The positive effect of contributions on participation should be contingent on probable support; this is the mobilization hypothesis. To the extent that contributions are given to probable opponents, on the other hand, they should diminish participation; this is the demobilization hypothesis.

Second, contributions may well be related to other activities that moneyed interests employ to further their legislative aims, making it difficult to isolate the effects of any particular part of their effort (Rothenberg 1989; Wright 1989). For instance, it may be the case that those groups that organize PACs for the purpose of channeling money to candidates are also the most active in developing grass roots campaigns or direct lobbying efforts. While there is evidence to suggest that the correlation among these activities is modest for the cases under study here,[6] our data on interest group activity are limited to political action committee campaign contributions. Hence, while our model tests for the effect that money has on committee behavior, one might more accurately characterize our results as capturing the effect of the several resources that moneyed interests employ.[7]

The dependent variable is the participation of member i on bill j, where participation refers to a member's activity both during formal committee markups and committee action behind the scenes. Our data on activity are drawn from two sources: semistructured interviews with both the majority and minority staffers assigned to cover each bill and the largely unpublished but meticulously kept committee and subcommittee markup records. The summary measure of participation that we use for the purposes of this exploration is a simple scale score derived from a factor analysis of six activities: attendance; voting participation; speaking; offering amendments during committee markups; role in authoring the legislative vehicle or an amendment in the nature of a substitute; and negotiating behind the scenes at either the member or the staff level.[8] The measurement of the independent variables, in turn, follows directly from the preceding discussion. Members' institutional positions and status are measured with dichotomous variables that are set at zero except as the following conditions hold: subcommittee membership takes a value of one if a member sat on the subcommittee with jurisdiction over the bill; leadership position takes a value of one if a member was chair or ranking minority member of either the full or subcommittee; and freshman status takes a value of one for members in their first term in the House.

In measuring the relevance of each issue to committee members' districts, we assume that relevance is primarily economic in nature. In the natural gas case, this takes two quite different forms: total district-level natural gas production[9] and the economic effect of gas price increases on residential consumers in the member's district, which we measure using industry data on natural gas price increases and census data regarding congressional district natural gas use.[10] If high production and high inflation capture dimensions of intradistrict salience, however, the presence of both at once should produce intradistrict conflict. The member is torn between two significant economic interests, and activity on behalf of one may alienate the other. Indeed, Fiorina (1974) suggests that unrequited constituents are likely to punish more than the requited are to reward. As intradistrict conflict increases, in any case, the expected benefits of activity on the issue should diminish, ceteris paribus. In the natural gas case, then, intradistrict conflict occurs as the production and inflation variables both approach their upper limits. We measure this condition as the product of two terms: "high production" is the extent to which natural gas production in the district exceeds the mean district production for all members of the committee; similarly, "high inflation" is the extent to which the district inflationary effect exceeds the mean for all committee members. When either district gas production or inflationary effect is below the committee mean, then, intradistrict conflict is zero.

In the other two cases the measurement of district interest is uncomplicated by potential conflicts within members' geographic constituencies. In the dairy stabilization case district relevance is directly related to the importance of dairy farming, measured simply by the total number of dairy cows in the member's district as reported by the United States Department of Agriculture biennial census. Given that milk prices were not a salient consumer issue per se and that the Dairy Stabilization Act was not likely to affect retail prices in any significant way, we do not assume a more general public concern with this issue. For the Job Training Partnership Act, likewise, district relevance is directly related to the importance of federal jobs programs in addressing structural unemployment, which we measure as the current level of CETA expenditures in the member's district.[11] This variable not only taps the district-specific economic benefits of clients of the expiring job training program but (given that CETA allocations were directly tied to local unemployment rates) also captures the severity of structural unemployment in the district.

Consistent with the preceding theoretical discussion, we estimate the effect of group expenditures on participation by including pairs of interactions between group contributions (measured as the amount contributed during the two-year election cycle prior to committee action) and indicators of probable support or opposition. For each case, the exact specification of the interactions is straightforward. In the dairy stabilization case, we measure probable support or opposition using the ratings of the National Farmers' Union (NFU),[12] an organization that strongly supports federal intervention in the agricultural economy to control supply and support the commodity prices paid to farmers. Given that we expect very different effects for contributions on the behavior of likely supporters and opponents, however, the model requires two separate interactions: *Money to supporters* is the product of contributions[13] and the member's distance from the mean NFU score where the members' rating is greater than the mean; the money-support term is zero otherwise. *Money to opponents* is the product of contributions and the member's distance from the mean NFU score, where the member's rating is less than the mean; the money-opposition term is zero otherwise. Following the theoretical reasoning of the last section, then, the expected effect on participation is positive for money to supporters. The expected effect is negative for money to opponents in each case.

Any attempt to model the effect of contribution activity on legislative behavior cannot assume that a particular industry is necessarily unified, however: one segment of an industry may have different interests and work in ways that offset some other segment. In the case of the federal dairy legislation, no such split within the industry was apparent among the principal actors, thus permitting the fairly simple specification described above. But in general—and in the natural gas case in particular—an industry may not be so easily simplified. While the gas producers were by far the most visible and most vigorous among the corporate actors and gave by far the most money in campaign contributions among energy PACs, the natural gas industry was seriously divided (Pressman 1983; Uslaner 1989, chap. 5), a feature that we attempt to capture. The alignments were by no means perfect, but the principal issues at stake in the legislation before House Energy and Commerce pitted the major gas producers and intrastate pipelines against the interstate pipelines and distributors. As a result, different segments of the industry were likely to target different members to serve as legislative agents and identify different members as their likely opponents. Our first task therefore was to distinguish the various energy PACs according to the principal business activities of their affiliates. Using the detailed descriptions of individual companies provided by Moody's Investor Service (1983a and 1983b), we classified each affiliate according to its principal interests in the natural gas area.[14] We then divided the contributions a member received according to whether they came from producers or intrastate pipelines on the one hand and interstates or distributors on the other. The measure of contributions that we employ, then, is the producer-intrastate contributions minus the interstate-distributor contributions, the value of which was positive in almost every case.

The operationalization of the interactions tapping the net producer-intrastate effects, in turn, was handled in a fashion analogous to the dairy stabilization case. In the natural gas case, however, members' Americans for Democratic Action (ADA) scores were more appropriate as an indicator of likely support or opposition. For the producer-intrastate segment of the gas industry at least, the issue of greatest concern was the extent to which the government continued its intervention in the natural gas market by controlling the price of old gas. The ADA score should tap members' historical tendency to support such federal interventions quite well. *Money to supporters*, then, is the product of net producer-intrastate contributions and the member's distance from the mean ADA score where the member's rating is less than the mean; the money-support term is zero otherwise; and *money to opponents* is the product of contributions and the member's distance from the mean ADA score where the member's rating is greater than the mean; the money-opposition term is zero otherwise.

Unlike the dairy and natural gas cases, finally, the job training bill did not involve issues specific to a particular industry. The organized interests most concerned with CETA and its prospective replacement were the national labor unions: public service employment and training programs were at the top of labor's agenda, especially in 1982, when unemployment was approaching postwar records. Moreover, labor unions were one of the single largest categories of contributors to congressional campaigns and gave to five-sixths of the members of House Education and Labor. It is the effect of these contributions on committee behavior with which we are primarily concerned. This is not to say, however, that labor unions were the only groups interested in mobilizing support on this bill.[15] On the business side, national business associations generally opposed any public service employment provisions and favored an expanded role for private industry councils so that federally subsidized training would be tailored to meet the changing needs of the private sector (Baumer and Van Horn 1985, 173). As in the natural gas case, we thus employ a net contributions variable, which takes the value of the member's total labor contributions less the total contributions received from national business organizations.[16] As in the other two cases, likewise, the indicator of probable support or opposition was constructed using the appropriate group rating, in this case, the AFL-CIO's Committee on Political Education (COPE) score. *Money to supporters*, then, is the product of net labor contributions and the member's distance from the mean COPE score, where the member's rating is greater than the mean; and *money to opponents* is the product of contributions and the member's distance from the mean COPE score where the member's rating is less than the mean.

RESULTS AND INTERPRETATIONS

In estimating the model of participation, we explicitly account for the possibility that contributions are effectively endogenous, that is, that in allocating contributions to committee members during the previous election cycle, a group may attempt to anticipate who the principal players will be on issues it cares about.[17] To the extent this is true, at least, the error term will be correlated with contributions and the ordinary least squares coefficient on the latter will be upwardly biased. We thus estimate the participation model using two-stage least squares, with the second stage results reported in the tables.[18] In each of the three cases, the model performs quite well, explaining over 55% of the variance in participation. More importantly, the analysis provides solid support for the principal hypothesis of this study, that moneyed interests mobilize bias in committee decision making.

This finding is clear for all three cases.[19] The campaign contributions that dairy industry PACs gave to their likely supporters significantly increased their participation, even when we controlled for the importance of the issue to individual members' districts, whether they sat on the subcommittee of jurisdiction, and whether they held a leadership position (Table 1). Such factors are reported elsewhere to be strong determinants of committee participation (Hall 1987), and each is also likely to affect contributions since interest groups tend to concentrate their resources on members who hold positions of institutional power (e.g., Grenzke 1989b; Grier and Munger 1986, 1989), as well as on members who have a district stake in their industry. That the mobilization coefficient remains positive and significant in the face of the multivariate controls reinforces the interpretation that the connection between group resources and mobilization is causal. When dairy PACs did give to their probable opponents, moreover, there is some evidence that the contributions diminished participation. While the coefficient on the money-opposition variable is statistically insignificant, its size is substantively non-trivial, and the negative sign is consistent with the demobilization hypothesis. In short, the more money a supporter received from the dairy PACs and the stronger the member's support, the more likely he or she was to allocate time and effort on the industry's behalf (e.g., work behind the scenes, speak on the group's behalf, attach amendments to the committee vehicle, as well as show up and vote at committee markups). Alternatively, money may have diminished the intensity of the opposition. The effect of money on decision making in the House Agriculture Committee, then, was to encourage industry supporters to be active and, if anything, to encourage industry opponents to abdicate.

The results of the job training case are also clear, and the specific estimates are striking in their similarity to the dairy stabilization case. As Table 2 shows, the contributions that labor groups made to their supporters had a substantial, statistically significant effect on participation during Education and Labor deliberations. Remarkably, the unstandardized coefficient for the money support variable is almost identical in size to the analogous coefficient in the dairy stabilization model despite the fact that the two cases are drawn from different committees

TABLE 1. PAC MONEY AND COMMITTEE PARTICIPATION: 1982 DAIRY STABILIZATION ACT

Independent Variables	Unstandardized 2SLS Coefficient	t-statistic
Intercept	.01	.05
Number of dairy cows in district	.27**	2.21
Dairy PAC contributions to supporters	.26**	2.42
Dairy PAC contributions to opponents	−.11	−.61
Membership on reporting subcommittee	.17**	3.54
Committee or subcommittee leadership position	.35**	4.50
Freshman status	−.02	−.31

Note: Adjusted R-squared = .60; number of observations = 41. All variables are measured on a 0–1 scale. The contributions term is the predicted value from the first-stage equation.
** Statistically significant at .05 level, one-tailed test.

TABLE 2. PAC MONEY AND COMMITTEE PARTICIPATION:
1982 JOB TRAINING PARTNERSHIP ACT

Independent Variables	Unstandardized 2SLS Coefficient	t-statistic
Intercept	.13	.77
CETA expenditures in district	.03	.23
Labor union net contributions to supporters	.25*	1.62
Labor union net contributions to opponents	−.18	−.80
Membership on reporting subcommittee	.19**	2.61
Committee or subcommittee leadership position	.47**	4.55
Freshman status	−.05	−.51

Note: Adjusted R-squared = .56; number of observations = 32. All variables are measured on a 0–1 scale. The net contributions term is the predicted value from the first-stage equation.
 * Statistically significant at .10 level, one-tailed test.
** Statistically significant at .05 level, one-tailed test.

with qualitatively different jurisdictions and policy environments (Smith and Deering 1984). In each case, a change in the money support variable from its minimum to its maximum value moves a member approximately one-fourth of the way along the participation scale, almost exactly one standard deviation. In both cases, likewise, this coefficient is greater than that for subcommittee membership, a variable generally considered central to understanding participation in the postreform House. As in the dairy stabilization case, finally, the Education and Labor bill provides some support for the demobilization hypothesis. While it fails to meet conventional levels of statistical significance, the size of the money-opposition term proves negative and substantively significant, nearly matching the size of subcommittee membership.

The results regarding moneyed interests and mobilization are only slightly less compelling in the natural gas case, a case complicated both by divisions within the industry and the apparent importance of both organized and unorganized interests. As we note above, such conditions are likely to mitigate the efficacy of interest group efforts, and they complicate the measurement of anticipated support and opposition. Still, the mobilization hypothesis finds strong support in the behavior of Energy and Commerce members. While the size of the unstandardized coefficient for the money support variable is somewhat smaller than for the other two cases, it is still substantial and statistically significant at the .05 level. A change in the money support variable from its minimum to its maximum moves a Commerce Committee member approximately one-sixth of the way along the participation scale. By way of illustration, this amounts to the difference between Minnesota Representative Gerry Sikorski, who did little more than faithfully attend and vote during formal markups, and Alabama Representative Richard Shelby, whose staff participated in behind-the-scenes negotiations and who offered two substantive amendments during subcommittee markup, both of which passed.

As Table 3 shows, finally, the demobilization hypothesis is not supported in the natural gas case. While the coefficient on the money opponents interaction is slight, its positive sign is inconsistent with our prediction. The foundation for the

TABLE 3. PAC MONEY AND COMMITTEE PARTICIPATION:
1984 NATURAL GAS MARKET POLICY ACT

Independent Variables	Unstandardized 2SLS Coefficient	t-statistic
Intercept	.08	.40
Natural gas production in district	.32*	1.65
Natural gas price increase effect on district	.17*	1.35
High production/high inflation interaction	−.18	−1.28
Producer-intrastate net contributions to supporters	.17**	1.69
Producer-intrastate net contributions to opponents	.01	.06
Membership on reporting subcommittee	.23**	3.17
Committee or subcommittee leadership position	.54**	4.77
Freshman status	.13*	1.31

Note: Adjusted R-squared = .57; number of observations = 42. All variables are measured on a 0–1 scale. The net contributions term is the predicted value from the first stage equation.

 * Statistically significant at .10 level, one-tailed test.
** Statistically significant at .05 level, one-tailed test.

demobilization hypothesis being theoretically weaker, however, the null result here, as well as the weak results in the dairy and job training cases, are not altogether surprising. The theoretically stronger hypothesis, that money mobilizes a pro-PAC bias at the committee level, is confirmed in all three.

For the most part, the other variables in the model also perform as predicted and suggest interesting implications for the politics of representation in a decentralized Congress. The relevance of an issue to the member's district enhances member participation in two cases, providing evidence that Agriculture and Commerce members purposively allocate their legislative time and resources to promote the interests of their constituencies. On House Agriculture, the more important dairy farming was to the member's district, the more likely he or she was to participate in committee deliberations. Likewise, the greater the presence of natural gas production in the district, the more likely the Energy and Commerce member was to participate in deliberations on the Natural Gas Market Policy Act. Indeed, a change in gas production from its minimum to its maximum corresponds to a 32% change along the participation scale, the difference between simply showing up and being a major player on the bill. By comparison, however, the effect of natural gas price increases on district consumers appears smaller by half. And the importance of structural unemployment and program spending in the districts of Education and Labor members had at best a slight effect on their involvement in the Job Training Partnership Act.

Pending better measurement of unorganized constituents' interest at the district level, of course, we cannot draw unqualified conclusions regarding their importance in shaping committee behavior. Should such patterns hold up under subsequent analysis, however, the implications for member responsiveness to industry interests and industry money relative to more general constituency concerns would be several and important. If members allocate their scarce legislative time and resources with district interests in mind, they perceive their districts in terms of different constituencies; and these perceptions affect their behavior as representatives (Fenno 1978). In part, the results presented here suggest that organized economic interests within districts figure more prominently in the psychology of representation than the diffuse and unorganized interests of rank-and-file voters. Such was the charge that Schattschneider made thirty years ago, one which critics of pluralism have echoed repeatedly since.

At the same time, however, the findings in the natural gas case also suggest that the preferences of unorganized interests sometimes constrain the responsiveness of members to organized groups, thus confronting the thesis of Denzau and Munger (1986) regarding how unorganized interests get represented. Beyond the positive coefficient for the inflationary effect variable, this is evident in the size and significance of the coefficient on the high production-high inflation interaction. Even if members are inclined to respond to producer interests, in short, this tendency is mitigated when consumer interests are also high. However, we should point out two things. First, the simultaneous occurrence of both strong producer interests and high consumer-voter salience is rare. Indeed, this distinguishes the natural gas issue from most of the issues with which members of Congress typically deal, and even in this case only 1 of the 42 members of Energy and Commerce were seriously cross-pressured. Second, we found no such constraint on the behavioral effect of producer contributions. One might expect, for instance, that the mobilizing effect of producer contributions would be diminished for a member who also represents a high inflation district. In one variant of the model tested here we included an interaction between the money support and high inflation variables, with the result that the coefficient was correct in sign (negative) but very near zero and the money-support coefficient was unchanged.

Finally, most of the variables that tap members' institutional positions prove to be strong determinants of committee participation. While the coefficients on freshman status differ in sign, both subcommittee membership and leadership position are positive, statistically significant, and substantively large in all three cases. Even on issues that are widely perceived among the committee membership to be important, issues where the organized interests in the policy environment are themselves active, the opportunities and resources provided by formal institutional position are major factors in determining who makes the laws at the committee stage. Such findings are generally consistent with findings from other committees and larger samples of issues (Evans n.d.; Hall 1987, 1989; Hall and Evans 1990) and reinforce the assumption that the model of participation employed here is specified correctly.

CONCLUSION

We have elaborated a theory of the member-group exchange relationship that comprehends the general patterns of PAC contributions reported in the literature. House members and interest group representatives are parties to an implicit cooperative agreement, but the constraints on member behavior and the rational calculations of group strategists limit the extent to which votes become the basis for exchange. This view suggests expectations about the effects of money on congressional decision making quite different from the ones that motivate the substantial research on the subject. We should find little causal connection between contributions and votes, especially on the floor—an expectation generally supported, although not adequately explained, in the literature. We should expect to find an important connection between contributions and the legislative involvement of sympathetic members, especially in committee—a relationship that empirical research to date has altogether ignored.

In order to test this view of moneyed interests and congressional decision making, we investigated the participation of House members on three issues in three committees. In each case, we found solid support for our principal hypothesis: moneyed interests are able to mobilize legislators already predisposed to support the group's position. Conversely, money that a group contributes to its likely opponents has either a negligible or negative effect on their participation. While previous research on these same issues provided little evidence that PAC money purchased members' votes, it apparently did buy the marginal time, energy, and legislative resources that committee participation requires. Moreover, we found evidence that (organized) producer interests figured more prominently than (unorganized) consumer interests in the participation decisions of House committee members—both for a case in which the issue at stake evoked high district salience and one where it did not. And we found little evidence that committee members respond to the interests of unemployed workers except insofar as those interests might be represented in the activities of well-financed and well-organized labor unions. Such findings suggest several implications for our understanding of political money, interest groups, and the legislative process.

The first and most important implication is that moneyed interests *do* affect the decision-making processes of Congress, an implication that one does not easily derive from the existing political science literature on contributions. In fact, it matters most at that stage of the legislative process that matters most and for a form of legislative behavior likely to have a direct bearing on outcomes. As David Mayhew has suggested (1974, 95), parliamentary suffrage gives a member relatively little leverage over the shape of legislation, especially at the committee stage. Only a small fraction of the decisions that shape a bill ever go to a vote, either in committee or on the floor. The vast majority are made in authoring a legislative vehicle, formulating amendments, negotiating specific provisions or report language behind the scenes, developing legislative strategy, and in other activities that require substantial time, information, and energy on the part of member and staff. While such efforts by no means guarantee that a particular member will influence the final outcome, they are usually a precondition for such influence (Hall 1989).

A second and related implication of this investigation, then, is that empirical research should expand its view of the legislative purposes of political money and the other group resources that may accompany it (see also Salisbury 1984, esp. 70–72). We focus here on committee participation; but the more general implication is that group expenditures may do much more than buy votes, or they may buy votes under certain conditions and affect other forms of legislative behavior under others. Such a suggestion, of course, usually appears in the various studies that examine the relationship between contributions and floor roll calls, but it needs to be elevated from the status of footnote or parenthetic remark to a central element of future research designs. Even for a small set of issues and a single group, the legislative strategies available are several, sometimes mixed. To speculate beyond the research reported here, for instance, we believe groups allocate their various resources (1) to mobilize strong supporters not only in House committees but also on the Senate floor, in dealings with executive agencies, and in various other decision-making forums relevant to the group's interests; (2) to demobilize strong opponents; and (3) to effect the support of swing legislators. We require greater knowledge of the frequency and efficacy of such strategies, in any case, before we denigrate the role of moneyed interests in Congress, especially when the overwhelming weight of the evidence provided by Washington journalists and political insiders suggests that they matter a great deal.

Finally, the argument presented here provides a very different slant on the role of interest groups as purveyors of information in the deliberations of representative assemblies. A common defense of group lobbying activity, in fact, is that it provides ideas and information although its effect on member preferences is slight. Members (and their staffs) tend to consume information selectively, relying on sources with whom they already agree and discounting sources with whom they usually disagree (e.g., Milbrath 1963). The view that we have advanced here suggests that while this may in fact describe how such information is used, it does not render it inconsequential. In light of the extraordinary demands on each congressional office, information—gathering it; analyzing it; turning it into speeches, amendments, and bills; using it to develop legislative strategy—can be very costly. Such costs, more than anything, limit the extent to which a nominal member will be a meaningful player in the decision-making process on a particular bill. At the very least, then, money-induced activity will distort the "representativeness of deliberations," a standard that democratic theorists since John Stuart Mill have used to evaluate the legitimacy of legislative assemblies (Chamberlin and Courant 1983). But it may also affect the "representativeness of decisions." By selectively subsidizing the information costs associated with participation, groups affect the *intensity* with which their positions are promoted by their legislative agents. In short, not all preferences weigh equally in legislative deliberations; and the resources of moneyed interests at least partly determine the weights.

The extent to which such efforts are damaging to representative government, as Schattschneider claimed, depends in part on the balance of interests and resources apparent in the relevant set of groups that are organized for political action. On any given issue, the efforts of one interest to mobilize supporters in Congress may be at least partially offset by the efforts of some competing group to mobilize its own supporters; indeed, there is some evidence that such countervailing efforts occurred in the natural gas case. But for those who believe that money is an illegitimate resource in such efforts—that pluralism requires something more than a competition among moneyed interests—the results of this study can only be disturbing.

NOTES

This research was supported in part by the National Science Foundation under Grant SES-8401505. For assistance or comments at various stages of this paper, we are indebted to Severin Borenstein, John Chamberlin, Cary Coglianese, David C. King, John Kingdon, Tim McDaniel, Mike Munger, Ken Organski, Randall Ripley, Robert Salisbury, Eric Uslaner, Carl Van Horn, Jack Wright, and participants in a faculty seminar at the Institute of Public Policy Studies, University of Michigan, Ann Arbor. For assistance in collecting and coding data, we thank Nick Greifer, Ed Kutler, Gary Levenson, and Dan Polsky. An earlier version of this paper was presented at the 1989 meeting of the Midwest Political Science Association, Chicago.

1. Rothenberg (1989) finds that in the allocation of lobbying resources on the MX missile issue Common Cause did concentrate more on likely "fence straddlers." By extension, his analysis provides an excellent guide for modeling the effect of expected voting behavior on contributions. See Smith 1984 for an important formulation of this argument.

2. Kingdon found that there was no conflict in the member's "field of forces" in almost half of the important votes that members cast on the House floor. In an additional 33% of the votes all of the personal goals that were relevant to a vote pointed the member in the same direction (1981, 255). While his study was conducted before the precipitous rise of PAC contributions, Kingdon found little evidence of group influence on members' voting decisions (chap. 5).

3. In adapting our model from Hall 1987, we retained only the variables that were found to be consistently significant and collapsed the several specific leadership positions into a single dichotomous variable.

4. This assumption is especially valid for the dairy and natural gas cases, though somewhat problematic for the JPTA. Like so many of the issues that come before the House Agriculture Committee, the dairy program is a classic constituency issue. If anything, the administration's assault on the price levels intensified such interests in the minds of the legislators. Likewise, the Natural Gas Market Policy Act evoked strong sentiment among consumers, distributors, and pipelines in some states and producers in others, sentiments that were loudly communicated to their representatives in Washington (Murray 1983). The resulting regional split within the committee was noted at length in virtually every account of its deliberations (see e.g., Maraniss 1983; Murray 1983).

5. In attempting to capture the representation of constituency interests, however, we necessarily neglect constituents' preferences regarding the public goods dimensions of each of these bills. On the importance of public goods preferences to political representation, see J. Jackson and King (1989).

6. The principal grass roots campaigns in the natural gas case were conducted by the Citizen/Labor Energy Coalition (CLEC) (which conducted door-to-door efforts in a number of states) and the public utility companies (who used inserts in monthly utility bills to encourage their customers to write letters to their representatives). Both were also actively engaged in lobbying members of the Energy and Commerce Committee. (Indeed, the CLEC was one of the most vigorous in this respect; see Pressman 1983.) Neither of the two were major campaign contributors, however. The CLEC did not have an organized PAC, and of the various segments of the gas industry the utility companies contributed relatively little money. (The major gas producers, for instance, contributed more than the distributors by a factor greater than seven to one.) Similarly, there were dozens of groups active in lobbying on the Job Training Partnership Act that contributed little or nothing in the way of campaign money, including various public interest groups, state and local officials, education organizations, and the National Governors' Association (Baumer and Van Horn 1985). The correlation between contributions and other interest group activities is probably higher for the dairy stabilization case, but even here it should be fairly modest. The various dairy organizations were in fact active in getting local dairy producers to write letters and meet with their representatives during visits to the district. But such a grassroots strategy was only feasible in districts that had a significant number of dairy producers, and the correlation between district dairy production and dairy industry PAC contributions was only .09 for the period 1979–80. Likewise, while the dairy industry gave a great deal of money to some House Agriculture members and none to others, the National Milk Producers by

themselves contacted *every* committee member regarding the dairy stabilization bill, either through letters to the member's Washington office or meetings with the member or the member's staff.

7. On this point, we are especially indebted to conversations with Jack Wright.

8. Data on the first four activities were taken directly from the committee and subcommittee markup minutes and transcripts. Indexes of authorship role and behind-the-scenes participation were coded on four point scales from semistructured interviews with both minority and majority staffers who had primary responsibility for staffing the bill under study. On the collection and coding of these data, see Hall 1987, though the data-reduction technique used here loses less information than the Guttman scale scores and the informal participation indexes that were used in that analysis. The factor analysis that generated the scores retained only one factor using conventional methods, the weights assigned were similar across the three cases, and (most importantly) the ordinal ranking of the weights for each activity were precisely those hypothesized in Hall 1987. In addition to the results reported here, however, we also estimated the model using both the Guttman scales and the informal participation index as well as a simple summary of the two. These several measures of participation are all highly correlated, and various estimates of the model using them generally confirmed the findings that we report here. Problems of measurement undoubtedly remain, however; and addressing them is an important matter for future work.

9. The measure of district natural gas production was constructed from county-level data acquired directly from state departments of natural resources. Where counties were not wholly contained within a single district, the proportion of natural gas production credited to particular districts was estimated by comparing congressional district maps with the geologic surveys showing the geographic location of natural gas production within counties. The production data are for the year 1983, the year in which the Energy and Commerce Committee began consideration of the Natural Gas Market Policy Act.

10. District-level data on natural gas price changes were not immediately available, but the intrastate variations should be sufficiently small as to make the state-level data reasonable approximations of the inflation in district natural gas prices. However, there are dramatic variations in the use of natural gas from one district to the next, so that the economic effect of a given price increase on residential energy consumers may vary dramatically across districts within a state (e.g., many rural districts that depended primarily on fuel oil for home heating were virtually unaffected by major increases in the price of natural gas). Fortunately, however, district-level information about household fuel use is available. In order to create a district-level indicator of consumer interest, then, we simply multiplied the state-level price increase for 1981 82 times the percentage of households in the district that used natural gas for their home heating. State data on the average price of natural gas delivered to consumers were taken from the *Natural Gas Annual 1982* (vol. 1, Table 17) and the *Natural Gas Annual 1983* (vol. 1, Table 18). District-level data on household energy sources were taken from the U.S. Bureau of the Census 1981.

11. District-level data on CETA expenditures were calculated from *The Employment and Training Reporter* (1980), which lists the 1981 allocations to counties, cities, or other "prime sponsors" located within members' districts. In cases where a prime sponsor was located in more than one congressional district, the expenditure for that sponsor was allocated equally among the several districts in which the sponsor administered its program.

12. It is important to note, however, that we are not assuming that NFU, ADA, or any other voting index measures members' personal ideology (much less their true preferences); a number of factors combine to determine these voting patterns, ideology being only one. (See Jackson and Kingdon 1990; Carson and Oppenheimer 1984.) Rather, we simply assume that the rating summarizes members' past voting behavior, which in turn form the basis for particular groups' expectations about what positions members will take in the future. Indeed, one of the principal reasons that groups construct their own indexes is to help them distinguish between friend and foe, and raters themselves report that the ratings "have their greatest impact on the distribution of campaign funds, because they provide a simple test of support or opposition" (Fowler 1982). The NFU scores were taken from the National Farmers Union Newsletter (1982a, 1982b).

13. We measured dairy industry contributions for each member as the summary of contributions from the three main dairy PACs during the previous election cycle: Committee for Thorough Agricultural Political Education of Associated Milk Producers; Mid-America Dairymen; and Dairymen Special Political Agricultural Community Education.

14. The Moody's entry included a brief description of each business's activities that usually indicated whether it belonged primarily in one category or another. Where that description mentioned interests in more than one category, we went to the financial statements or audit summaries provided in the Moody's entry and classified businesses as producer, interstate pipeline, intrastate pipeline, or distributor according to the principal sources of their natural gas revenues. Such information permitted an unambiguous classification in almost every case. Natural gas peak associations were categorized according to the nature of the businesses they represented. In addition, some of the classifications were checked against similar classifications made by Eric Uslaner using both interview and archival data. In every case where our data overlapped, our classifications matched his (see Uslaner 1989).

15. Other groups interested in the legislation included the National Governors' Association, national education groups, city and county officials, and the various organizations that represented them, such as the National League of Cities (Baumer and Van Horn, 1985). Of these, however, only the education groups contributed money; and they tended to align with, and contribute to, the same members as organized labor. The education contributions were very small in any case, and the alternative strategy of adding them to the labor PAC total had no effect on the coefficients.

16. Included in this category were the American Business Association, the Business Industry Council, the Chamber of Commerce, the National Association of Manufacturers, and the National Federation of Independent Businesses.

17. We believe that there is far less reason a priori to believe that PAC contributions should be considered endogenous in modeling members' participation than in modeling their roll-call voting behavior. While it is likely that PACs will give disproportionately to members with important committee positions, there is little evidence to suggest that the anticipated participation of member i on some particular bill j (independent of what one would anticipate given the member's institutional position or positions, seniority, and interests—factors that are built into our model) figures prominently in PAC allocation decisions. Such calculations, at least, have been nowhere evident in the considerable political science or journalistic literature on this subject. Hence, we also estimated the equations for both cases using ordinary least squares. The parameter estimates from the ordinary least squares and two-stage least squares (2SLS) were very similar, with the exception that the magnitude of the 2SLS mobilization coefficients were somewhat smaller in the natural gas and job training cases. By presenting the 2SLS results, then, we address the potential endogeneity problem and, as it turns out, slightly bias our results against our main conclusions.

18. While the first-stage results are not relevant to our substantive interests here, they do bear on the confidence of the second-stage results and thus warrant some attention. In estimating the first stage, we adapted the contributions model from the substantial literature on the allocation strategies of national PACs (e.g., Evans 1986; Grenzke 1989b; Gopoian 1984; Grier and Munger 1989), including three variables that qualified as instruments: party, the relevant voting index, and the marginality of the district. In all three cases the first-stage results were satisfactory. The adjusted R-squared was .34 for the model of dairy industry contributions to Agriculture Committee members, .58 for the model of net producer contributions to Commerce members, and .48 for the model of net labor contributions to Education and Labor members. More importantly, in every case the coefficient on at least one of the three instruments was large, correct in sign, and statistically significant at the .05 level. Checks for multicollinearity among the independent variables in the second stage equations likewise provided little cause for concern. Regarding the appropriateness and implementation of the two-stage least squares estimation procedure, see Hanushek and Jackson 1977, chap. 9; Pindyck and Rubinfeld 1981, 328–31.

19. As a check on the results reported here, we also estimated for the effects of contributions on participation without interacting them with anticipated support or opposition, and, as our theory would predict, the effects were consistently weaker. Note, secondly, that we do not include the relevant group support score separately in the model, a variable that has proven important in estimating the effects of contributions on roll calls. Even if ideology is what the voting scores capture (see Jackson and Kingdon 1990), there is no theoretical reason to expect that liberals will be more active than conservatives (or vice versa) or for that matter that ideological moderates will be less active than either conservatives or liberals. In any case, we tested for the effect of past voting behavior on the participation of members in each case. For all three, the t-statistics for the voting score coefficients were less than .5.

REFERENCES

Arnold, R. Douglas. 1979. *Congress and the Bureaucracy: A Theory of Influence.* New Haven: Yale University Press.

Bauer, Raymond, Ithiel de Sola Pool, and Lewis A. Dexter. 1963. *American Business and Public Policy.* Chicago: Aldine & Atherton.

Baumer, Donald C., and Carl E. Van Horn. 1985. *The Politics of Unemployment.* Washington: Congressional Quarterly Press.

Berry, Jeffrey M. 1984. *The Interest Group Society.* Boston: Little, Brown.

Bureau of National Affairs, Inc. 1980. "FY 1981 CETA Allocations and Government's Grants." *The Employment and Training Reporter.* Oct. 29.

Carson, Richard A., and Joe Oppenheimer. 1984. "A Method of Estimating the Personal Ideology of Political Representatives." *American Political Science Review* 78:163–178.

Chamberlin, John R., and Paul N. Courant. 1983. "Representative Deliberations and Representative Decisions: Proportional Representation and the Borda Rule." *American Political Science Review* 77:718–733.

Chappell, Henry. 1982. "Campaign Contributions and Congressional Voting: A Simultaneous Probit-Tobit Model." *Review of Economics and Statistics* 62:77–83.

Davis, Joseph A. 1984. "House Energy Committee Approves Natural Gas Bill." *Congressional Quarterly Weekly Report* 14 April:888–889.

Denzau, Arthur, and Michael C. Munger. 1986. "Legislators and Interest Groups: How Unorganized Interests Get Represented." *American Political Science Review* 80:89–106.

Donnelly, Harrison. 1982. "Job Training Bills: No 'CETA' Revisited." *Congressional Quarterly Weekly Report* 8 May:1035.

Drew, Elizabeth. 1982. "Politics and Money." *The New Yorker* 6 December:54–149.

Etzioni, Amitai. 1984. *Capital Corruption: The New Attack on American Democracy.* New York: Harcourt, Brace, Jovanovich.

Evans, C. Lawrence. N.d. "Participation in U.S. Senate Committees." *Political Science Quarterly.* Forthcoming.

Evans, Diana. 1986. "PAC Contributions and Roll-Call Voting: Conditional Power." In *Interest Group Politics*, 2d ed., ed. Allan J. Cigler and Burdett A. Loomis. Washington, DC: Congressional Quarterly Press.

Evans, Diana. 1988. "Oil PACs and Aggressive Contribution Strategies." *Journal of Politics* 50:1047–1056.

Fenno, Richard F. 1978. *Home Style: House Members in Their Districts.* Boston: Little, Brown.

Fiorina, Morris P. 1974. *Representatives, Roll Calls, and Constituencies.* Lexington, MA: D.C. Heath.

Fowler, Linda L. 1982. "How Interest Groups Select Issues for Rating Voting Records of Members of the U.S. Congress." *Legislative Studies Quarterly* 7:401–413.

Franklin, Grace A., and Randall B. Ripley. 1984. *CETA: Politics and Policy.* Knoxville: University of Tennessee Press.

Gais, Thomas, Mark Peterson, and Jack Walker. 1984. "Interest Groups, Iron Triangles, and Representative Institutions in American National Government." *British Journal of Political Science* 14:161–185.

Gopoian, J. David. 1984. "What Makes PACs Tick? An Analysis of the Allocation Patterns of Economic Interest Groups." *American Journal of Political Science* 28:259–281.

Grenzke, Janet M. 1989a. "Shopping in the Congressional Supermarket: The Currency Is Complex." *American Journal of Political Science* 33:1–24.

Grenzke, Janet M. 1989b. "Candidate Attributes and PAC Contributions." *Western Political Quarterly* 42:245–264.

Grier, Kevin B., and Michael C. Munger. 1986. "The Impact of Legislator Attributes on Interest-Group Campaign Contributions." *Journal of Labor Research* 7:349–361.

Grier, Kevin B., and Michael C. Munger. 1989. "Committee Assignments, Constituent Preferences, and Campaign Contributions to House Incumbents." Typescript.

Hall, Richard L. 1987. "Participation and Purpose in Committee Decision Making." *American Political Science Review* 81:105–127.

Hall, Richard L. 1989. "Committee Decision Making in the Postreform Congress." In *Congress Reconsidered*, 4th ed., ed. Lawrence C. Dodd and Bruce I. Oppenheimer. Washington, DC: Congressional Quarterly Press.

Hall, Richard L., and C. Lawrence Evans. 1990. "The Power of Subcommittees." *Journal of Politics* 52:335–355.

Hanushek, Erik A., and John E. Jackson. 1977. *Statistical Methods for Social Scientists.* Orlando: Academic.

Hayes, Michael T. 1981. *Lobbyists and Legislators.* New Brunswick: Rutgers University Press.

Herndon, James F. 1982. "Access, Record, and Competition as Influences on Interest Group Contributions to Congressional Campaigns." *Journal of Politics* 44:996–1019.

Jackson, Brooks. 1988. *Honest Graft.* New York: Knopf.

Jackson, John E. 1974. *Constituencies and Leaders in Congress: Their Effects on Senate Voting Behavior.* Cambridge: Harvard University Press.

Jackson, John E., and David C. King. 1989. "Public Goods, Private Interests, and Representation." *American Political Science Review* 83:1143–1164.

Jackson, John E., and John W. Kingdon. 1990. "Ideology, Interest Group Scores, and Legislative Votes." University of Michigan. Typescript.

Jacobson, Gary C. 1980. *Money in Congressional Elections.* New Haven: Yale University Press.

Kau, James B., and Paul H. Rubin. 1982. *Congressmen, Constituents, and Contributors: Determinants of Roll Call Voting in the House of Representatives.* Boston: Martinus Nijhoff.

Kingdon, John W. 1981. *Congressmen's Voting Decisions*, 2nd ed. New York: Harper & Row.

Maitland, Ian. 1985. "Interest Groups and Economic Growth Rates." *Journal of Politics* 47:44–58.

Maraniss, David. 1983. "Power Play: Chairman's Gavel Crushes Gas Decontrol Vote." *Washington Post* 20 November:A1.

Matthews, Donald R. [1960] 1973. *U.S. Senators and Their World.* Reprint. New York: W. W. Norton.

Mayhew, David R. 1974. *Congress: The Electoral Connection.* New Haven: Yale University Press.

Milbrath, Lester M. 1963. *The Washington Lobbyists.* Chicago: Rand McNally.

Moody's Investor Service. 1983a. *Moody's Industrial Manual.* New York: Moody's Investor Service.

Moody's Investor Service. 1983b. *Moody's Public Utilities Manual.* New York: Moody's Investor Service.

Murray, Alan. 1983. "Pressure from Consumers Pushes Congress into Action on Pricing of Natural Gas." *Congressional Quarterly Weekly Report* 5 March:443–447.

National Farmers Union. 1982a. "1981 Voting Record—House." *National Farmers Union Washington Newsletter* 5 February:4–8.

National Farmers Union. 1982b. "1982 Voting Record—House." *National Farmers Union Washington Newsletter* 15 October:4–8.

Pindyck, Robert S., and Daniel L. Rubinfeld. 1981. *Econometric Models and Economic Forecasts.* 2d ed. New York: McGraw-Hill.

Pressman, Steven. 1983. "Lobbying Free-for-all Opens as Congress Begins Mark-up of National Gas Pricing Bills." *Congressional Quarterly Weekly Report*, April 23: 793–797.

Ripley, Randall B., and Grace Franklin. 1980. *Congress, the Bureaucracy, and Public Policy.* Rev. ed. Homewood, IL: Dorsey.

Rothenberg, Lawrence S. 1989. "Do Interest Groups Make a Difference? Lobbying, Constituency Influence, and Public Policy." Presented at the annual meeting of the Midwest Political Science Association, Chicago.

Salisbury, Robert H. 1984. "Interest Representation: The Dominance of Institutions." *American Political Science Review* 78:64–76.

Salisbury, Robert H., and Kenneth A. Shepsle. 1981. "U.S. Congressmen As Enterprise." *Legislative Studies Quarterly* 6:559–576.

Schattschneider, E. E. 1960. *The Semisovereign People.* Hinsdale, IL: Dryden.

Schlozman, Kay L., and John T. Tierney. 1986. *Organized Interests and American Democracy.* New York: Harper & Row.

Shepsle, Kenneth A. 1978. *The Giant Jigsaw Puzzle.* Chicago: University of Chicago.

Silberman, Jonathan, and Garey C. Durden. 1976. "Determining Legislative Preferences on the Minimum Wage: An Economic Approach." *Journal of Political Economy* 84:317–329.

Smith, Richard A. 1984. "Advocacy, Interpretation, and Influence in the U.S. Congress." *American Political Science Review* 78:44–63.

Smith, Steven S., and Christopher J. Deering. 1984. *Committees in Congress.* Washington, DC: Congressional Quarterly Press.

Stern, Phillip M. 1988. *The Best Congress Money Can Buy.* New York: Pantheon.

Uslaner, Eric M. 1989. *Shale Barrel Politics.* Stanford: Stanford University Press.

U.S. Bureau of the Census. 1981. *Fuels and Financial Characteristics of Housing Units: 1980, Congressional Districts in the 98th Congress.* Washington: GPO.

Wayman, Frank W. 1985. "Arms Control and Strategic Arms Voting in the U.S. Senate: Patterns of Change, 1967–1983." *Journal of Conflict Resolution* 29:225–251.

Wayman, Frank W., and Edward Kutler. 1985. "The Changing Politics of Oil and Gas: Ideology, Campaign Contributions, and Interests." Presented at the annual meeting of the American Political Science Association, New Orleans.

Wehr, Elizabeth. 1982a. "Dairy, Grain Proposals Draw Administration Fire." *Congressional Quarterly Weekly Report* 24 July:1751.

Wehr, Elizabeth. 1982b. "New Farm Support Plans, Food Stamp Changes Push Savings Totals Over Top." *Congressional Quarterly Weekly Report* 21 August:2050–2051.

Welch, William P. 1982. "Campaign Contributions and Legislative Voting: Milk Money and Dairy Price Supports." *Western Political Quarterly* 35:478–495.

Wilhite, Allen, and John Theilmann. 1987. "Labor PAC Contributions and Labor Legislation: A Simultaneous Logit Approach." *Public Choice* 53:267–276.

Wright, John R. 1985. "PACS, Contributions, and Roll Calls: An Organizational Perspective." *American Political Science Review* 79:400–414.

Wright, John R. 1989. "Contributions, Lobbying, and Committee Voting in the U.S. House of Representatives." University of Iowa. Typescript.

21

HUGH HECLO

ISSUE NETWORKS
AND THE EXECUTIVE ESTABLISHMENT

In the real world of Washington politics, money matters (as the previous selection clearly demonstrated). And more generally, the structure and role of "interest groups" is more complex than traditionally portrayed in much of the academic literature on the subject. In this fine essay, Hugh Heclo, a professor at George Mason University, paints a realistic picture. Policy is made through loose "networks" of professional advocacy groups, public officials, and "issue-watchers." The fluid process has both advantages and disadvantages for the capacity of the American political system to govern responsibly.

The connection between politics and administration arouses remarkably little interest in the United States. The presidency is considered more glamorous, Congress more intriguing, elections more exciting, and interest groups more troublesome. General levels of public interest can be gauged by the burst of indifference that usually greets the announcement of a new President's cabinet or rumors of a political appointee's resignation. Unless there is some White House "tie-in" or scandal (preferably both), news stories about presidential appointments are usually treated by the media as routine filler material.

This lack of interest in political administration is rarely found in other democratic countries, and it has not always prevailed in the United States. In most nations the ups and downs of political executives are taken as vital signs of the health of a government, indeed of its survival. In the United States, the nineteenth-century turmoil over one type of connection between politics and administration—party spoils—frequently overwhelmed any notion of presidential leadership. Anyone reading the history of those troubled decades is likely to be struck by the way in which political administration in Washington registered many of the deeper strains in American society at large. It is a curious switch that appointments to the bureaucracy should loom so large in the history of the nineteenth century, when the federal government did little, and be so completely discounted in the twentieth century, when government tries to do so much.

Political administration in Washington continues to register strains in American politics and society, although in ways more subtle than the nineteenth-century spoils scramble between Federalists and Democrats, Pro- and Anti-tariff forces, Nationalists and States-Righters, and so on. Unlike many other countries, the United States has never created a high level, government-wide civil service. Neither has it been favored with a political structure that automatically produces a stock of experienced political manpower for top executive positions in government.[1] How then does political administration in Washington work? More to the

[Figures and tables have been renumbered.—Eds.]

point, how might the expanding role of government be changing the connection between administration and politics?

Received opinion on this subject suggests that we already know the answers. Control is said to be vested in an informal but enduring series of "iron-triangles" linking executive bureaus, congressional committees, and interest group clienteles with a stake in particular programs. A President or presidential appointee may occasionally try to muscle in, but few people doubt the capacity of these sub-governments to thwart outsiders in the long run.

Based largely on early studies of agricultural, water, and public works policies, the iron triangle concept is not so much wrong as it is disastrously incomplete.[2] And the conventional view is especially inappropriate for understanding changes in politics and administration during recent years. Preoccupied with trying to find the few truly powerful actors, observers tend to overlook the power and influence that arise out of the configurations through which leading policy makers move and do business with each other. Looking for the closed triangles of control, we tend to miss the fairly open networks of people that increasingly impinge upon government.

To do justice to the subject would require a major study of the Washington community and the combined inspiration of a Leonard White and a James Young. Tolerating a fair bit of injustice, one can sketch a few of the factors that seem to be at work. The first is growth in the sheer mass of government activity and associated expectations. The second is the peculiar, loose-jointed play of influence that is accompanying this growth. Related to these two is the third: the layering and specialization that have overtaken the government work force, not least the political leadership of the bureaucracy.

All of this vastly complicates the job of presidential appointees both in controlling their own actions and in managing the bureaucracy. But there is much more at stake than the troubles faced by people in government. There is the deeper problem of connecting what politicians, officials, and their fellow travelers are doing in Washington with what the public at large can understand and accept. It is on this point that political administration registers some of the larger strains of American politics and society, much as it did in the nineteenth century. For what it shows is a dissolving of organized politics and a politicizing of organizational life throughout the nation.

GOVERNMENT GROWTH IN AN AGE OF IMPROVEMENT

Few people doubt that we live in a time of big government. During his few years in office, President Kennedy struggled to avoid becoming the first President with a $100 billion budget. Just seventeen years later, President Carter easily slipped into history as the first $500 billion President. Even in constant prices, the 1979 federal budget was about double that of 1960.[3] The late 1950s and the entire 1960s witnessed a wave of federal initiatives in health, civil rights, education, housing, manpower, income maintenance, transportation, and urban affairs. To these, later years have added newer types of welfare concerns: consumer protection, the environment, cancer prevention, and energy, to name only a few. Whatever today's conventional skepticism about the success of these programs, posterity will probably regard the last twenty-odd years as an extraordinarily ambitious, reform-minded period. The dominant feeling behind our age of improvement was best expressed by Adlai Stevenson in 1955 when he sensed a new willingness "to feel strongly, to be impatient, to want mightily to see that things are done better."[4]

However, we need to be clear concerning what it is that has gotten big in government. Our modern age of improvement has occurred with astonishingly little increase in the overall size of the federal executive establishment. Figure 1 traces changes in the raw materials of government: money, rules, and people from 1949 to 1977. The year 1955 represented a return to more normal times after the Korean conflict and may be taken as a reasonable baseline. Since that year national spending has risen sixfold in current dollars and has more than doubled in constant terms. Federal regulations (as indicated by pages in the *Federal Register*) have also sextupled. In the cases of both money and regulations, it was during the second Eisenhower administration that a new and expensive activism in public policy began to sweep through the national government. The landslide congressional victory by liberal Democrats in 1958, the challenge of Sputnik, the new stirrings of the civil rights movement—these and other factors created a wave of government spending and regulation that has continued to roll ever since. The force of this growth was felt at least as much in the Nixon-Ford years as in the earlier decade of New Frontier/Great Society programs under Democratic Presidents.

Yet federal employment grew hardly at all in comparison with spending and regulations (up by less than one-fifth since 1955). Despite widespread complaints about the size of government, the federal bureaucracy is entitled to join foreign aid as one of that small band of cases where close to zero-growth has been the norm for the last twenty-five years.

The paradox of expanding government and stable bureaucracy has two explanations. In purely budgetary terms, much of the increase in federal outlays has been due to higher costs of existing policies. It does not necessarily require more bureaucrats to write larger checks. Such cost increases have been especially important in the area of income maintenance programs. Federal payments to individuals (social security, medical care, veterans' pensions, unemployment insurance, and public assistance) increased from $22 billion in 1960 to $167 billion in 1977, accounting for well over half of the total increase in federal domestic spending during these years.[5] Much of this increase came not from adding new programs but from higher bills for existing programs, particularly social security. Thus at the end of 1977, when federal outlays were at $402 billion, President Carter proposed a $500 billion budget for fiscal year 1979. Of the $98 billion increase, about 90 percent was due to the higher cost of existing policies and only 10 percent to new spending recommended by the President.[6] About one-quarter of the total cost increase was due simply to income security programs.

This sort of momentum in government obviously presents serious challenges to politicians in general and to politically appointed executives in particular. These are the people who tend to feel they have a mandate to "change things, shake up the bureaucracy" and who even in the best of circumstances have only a few years in which to do so. But there is a second and at least equally important

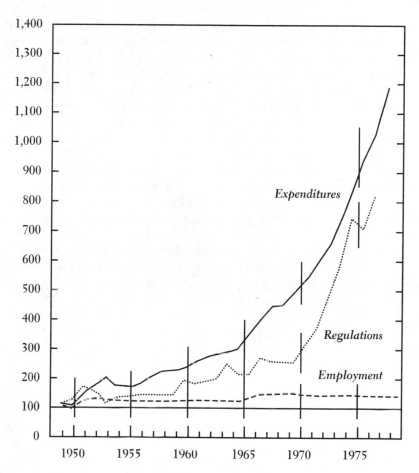

FIGURE 1. FEDERAL GOVERNMENT GROWTH: MONEY, RULES, AND PEOPLE (1949 = 100)
Note: Federal spending on income and product account. Figures are on an accrual basis and include trust account transactions with the public as well as grants-in-aid to state and local governments. Employment covers total end-of-year civilian employees in full-time, permanent, temporary, part-time, and intermittent employment in the executive branch, including the Postal Service. Regulations are indicated by numbers of pages in the *Federal Register.* *Source:* The Tax Foundation, *Facts and Figures on Government Finance,* 1977, table 20, p. 33; U.S. Office of Management and Budget, *Special Analyses, Budget of the U.S. Government,* 1979, p. 210. Figures are taken from an unpublished table compiled by the Executive Agencies Division, Office of the Federal Register, Washington, D.C. I wish to express my gratitude to this division for their cooperation in supplying information.

explanation for the stability of the national bureaucracy in an era of increased policy interventionism. This factor creates even more profound problems for government leadership.

In the main, Washington has not attempted to apply its policies by administering programs directly to the general population. It has therefore been able to avoid bureaucratic giantism. This is true in many programs classified as payments to individuals (for example, Medicare and Medicaid funds pass through large numbers of administrative middlemen), and it is especially true in several of the policy areas that have grown the fastest since the mid-1950s. One such area is investment and subsidies for the physical environment. Grants for mass transit, waste treatment plants, highways, and the like have tripled in real terms since 1960. Another area rich in indirect administration falls under the heading of social investment and services; spending for education, health care, employment training, urban development, and social services has risen more than tenfold since 1960.[7] Rather than building and staffing its own administrative facilities for these programs, the federal government has preferred to act through intermediary organizations—state governments, city halls, third party payers, consultants, contractors, and many others. Administratively, the result is that what was true during the Eisenhower administration remains true today: despite huge increases in government programs, about the only time an ordinary citizen sees a federal bureaucrat is when his mail is delivered, his taxes are audited, or a trip to the local social security office becomes necessary (unless of course an FBI agent knocks on his door).

New policies associated with our modern age of improvement have tended to promote the idea of government by remote control. Political administration in Washington is heavily conditioned by an accumulation of methods for paying the bills and regulating the conduct of intermediary organizations. This pattern is consistent with a long tradition of fragmented and decentralized administration. Moreover, it offers important political and bureaucratic advantages. Spreading cash grants among various third party payers is an important way of building support for policies, translating otherwise indivisible collective goods into terms suitable for distributive politics. Rather than having to convince everyone of the value of a clean environment, government administrators can preside over a scramble for federal funds to subsidize construction of local sewage treatment plants. Likewise, in spending for health, manpower, transportation, and so on, the federal government has sidestepped the tremendously difficult task of creating a broad national consensus for its own administered activities. It has done so by counting on third parties to crave the funds which the national government makes available to serve its purposes. Recently Charles Schultze has argued that Washington should make greater use of market incentives to meet public ends.[8] Yet as far as fiscal relations in the political marketplace are concerned, a strong case could be made that in fact the federal government has done little else.

In terms of using intermediaries to administer the new melioristic policies, the mushrooming of federal regulations has much in common with federal spending. Rather than having to work at building and policing its own delivery mechanisms, the Washington bureaucracy can use regulations and then rest content with telling other public and private bureaucracies what should be done. This has the added advantage of allowing federal policy makers to distribute not only funds but also much of the blame when things go wrong.

One might suppose that the executive establishment in Washington has put itself in an extremely comfortable position, retailing the promise of improved policies and wholesaling the administrative headaches connected with delivery. Unfortunately, life has not been so kind. People increasingly expect Washington to solve problems but not to get in anyone's way in the process. The result is that policy goals are piled on top of each other without generating any commitment to the administrative wherewithal to achieve them. Even in the depths of anti-Washington sentiment, the overwhelming majority of Americans agreed that the federal government should control inflation, prevent depressions, assure international peace, regulate private business, and also ensure that the poor are taken care of, the hungry fed, and every person assured a minimum standard of living. A comparably large majority also felt that the federal government was too "big and bureaucratic."[9] As it turns out, therefore, the executive establishment in Washington tends to get the worst of both worlds—blamed for poor delivery by its public customers and besieged with bills from its middlemen.

FRAYING AT THE CENTER

The strategy of responding to aspirations for improvement while maintaining a no-growth national administrative machine and relying on middlemen has succeeded in doing one thing. It has saved Washington policy makers from having to cope with what would otherwise have been an immense, nationwide bureaucracy. Yet far from simplifying operations, this "success" has vastly complicated the connection between administration and politics in Washington. Lacking their own electoral mandates, political administrators have always been in an ambivalent position in American government. Every ambitious new program, every clever innovation in indirect administration has merely deepened this ambivalence.

What is occurring at the national level is a peculiar "push-pull effect" on the relation between democratic politics and the executive establishment. On the one hand, government growth has pushed more and more policy concerns out of the federal government's own structure and into masses of intermediary, issue-conscious groups. On the other hand, the requirements for managing such a complex system are pulling government leadership further and further away from the nontechnical, nonspecialist understanding of the ordinary citizen and politician. It is worth looking more closely at how it is possible to be both politicizing organizational life and depoliticizing democratic leadership.

ALL JOIN IN. During 1977–1978, Harvard University hired a Washington lobbyist and joined a loose group called Friends of DNA in an effort to influence federal regulation of research into the creation of new forms of life. The same year, the former militant chairman of the Black Panther party, Bobby Seale, founded a new Washington organization to lobby for community-controlled poverty programs. And the president of the national machinists' union convened a National Energy Coalition composed of environmentalists, neighborhood organizers, and consumer advocates. Perhaps not coincidentally, forty-seven congressmen announced their retirement, citing as the major reason a lack of enjoyment in the job.

Trivial in their own right, these incidents suggest something deeper than the feeling (probably true) that exercising power is not as much fun as it used to be in the clubby days of Washington politics. As more and more puzzling, unfamiliar policy issues have been thrust on government, more and more fluid groups have been unexpectedly mobilized. As proliferating groups have claimed a stake and clamored for a place in the policy process, they have helped to diffuse the focus of political and administrative leadership.

What has happened at the subnational level of government is a striking illustration of this process. Much of the bureaucratic expansion that might otherwise have occurred nationally has taken place in state and local governments. Between 1955 and 1977 state and local public employment grew by more than two and one-half times, to 12 million people, while federal employment hovered at around 2.5 million.[10] The increased interdependence of subnational and national bureaucracies has led to the growth of what Samuel H. Beer has termed the intergovernmental lobby.[11] Those in Washington whose memories go back a generation or more can recall a time when it was something of an occasion for a governor to undertake a mission to Washington. As Senator Moynihan (who was a junior aide to Governor Averell Harriman in the 1940s) put it, "You'd spend time planning how many shirts to take. Going to Washington was a very big deal."[12] Today, not only do governors or mayors as groups have their own specialized staffs permanently stationed in Washington, but large state governments, major units within state governments, and individual cities frequently have their own Washington offices or hired representatives. In addition to umbrella organizations such as the National Governors' Conference, the Conference of State Governments, the U.S. Conference of Mayors, the National League of Cities, the National Conference of State Legislatures, and the National Association of Counties, one finds the intergovernmental lobby peopled with representatives from groups such as the New York State Association of Counties, cities such as Detroit and Boston, major counties, various state water districts, boards of regents, and so on and on and on.

Similarly, an even larger number of private and semi-private organizations have grown up as important extensions of the new federal policies. One of the enduring legacies of every reform movement in the United States—whether it was the Progressives' good government movement, Hoover's attempts at engineering voluntarism, or FDR's New Deal—has been to create new groups with a stake in the reformed processes and programs.[13] So too our own age of improvement has encouraged a blossoming of policy participants and kibitzers. In this instance (and this differentiates it somewhat from earlier periods) virtually everyone has accepted the idea that the national government in Washington is the decisive arena and will continue to be so indefinitely.

Some groups are nurtured by the government's own need for administrative help. For example, new neighborhood associations have been asked to take a major part in Washington's urban and housing programs. Or when the Consumer Product Safety Commission sets new standards for extension cords, the National Electrical Manufacturers' Association plays a major part in drawing up the new designs. Some groups are almost spontaneously called into being by what they can gain or lose from new federal policies or—perhaps just as often—the unforeseen consequences of these policies. For example, in the early 1970s Washington launched vigorous new efforts to promote grain exports. This generated not only new borrowing by farmers to expand production but also a new, militant farmers' organization (American Agriculture) when prices later fell from their export-led highs.

A key factor in the proliferation of groups is the almost inevitable tendency of successfully enacted policies unwittingly to propagate hybrid interests. The area of health care is rich in examples. Far from solidifying the established medical interests, federal funding and regulation of health care since the mid-1960s have had diverse impacts and therefore have tended to fragment what was once a fairly monolithic system of medical representation. Public policy has not only uncovered but also helped to create diverging interests among hospital associations, insurance companies, medical schools, hospital equipment manufacturers, local health planning groups, preventive medicine advocates, nonteaching research centers, and many others.[14] This does not necessarily mean that every group is in conflict with all of the others all of the time. The point is that even when government is not pursuing a deliberate strategy of divide and conquer, its activist policies greatly increase the incentives for groups to form around the differential effects of these policies, each refusing to allow any other group to speak in its name.

While nothing should necessarily be assumed about their political power, trade and professional associations offer a revealing pattern of growth. The number of such groups has grown sharply during three periods: during the First World War, the first half of the 1930s, and the Second World War. Since 1945 the total number has been continuously increasing, and in recent years more and more of these groups have found it useful to make their headquarters in Washington. During the 1970s the number of trade and professional associations headquartered in Washington surpassed that in New York for the first time, climbing to 1,800 organizations with 40,000 employees in 1977. Well over half of the nation's largest associations (those with annual budgets of over $1 million) are now located in the Washington metropolitan area.[15] This takes no account of the large number of consumer and other public interest groups that have sprouted all over the nation's capital since the early 1960s.[16]

Of course Americans' love affair with interest groups is hardly a new phenomenon. From abolitionists to abortionists there has never been a lack of issue-conscious organizations; in the 1830s, Tocqueville described how the tariff question generated an early version of local consumer groups and a national lobbying association.[17] Yet if the current situation is a mere outgrowth of old tendencies, it is so in the same sense that a 16-lane spaghetti interchange is the mere elaboration of a country crossroads. With more public policies, more groups are being mobilized and there are more complex relationships among them. Since very few policies ever seem to drop off the public agenda as more are added, congestion among those interested in various issues grows, the chances for accidental collisions increase, and the interaction tends to take on a distinctive group-life of its own in the Washington community. One scene in a recent Jacques Tati film pictures a Paris traffic circle so dense with traffic that no one can get in or out; instead, drivers spend their time socializing with each other as they drive in endless circles. Group politics in Washington may be becoming such a merry-go-round.

How these changes influence the substance of public policy processes depends on what it is that the burgeoning numbers of participants want. Obviously their wants vary greatly, but to a large extent they are probably accurately reflected in the areas of greatest policy growth since the late 1950s—programs seeking social betterment in terms of civil rights, income, housing, environment, consumer protection, and so on—what I will simply refer to as "welfare policies." The hallmark of these policies seems to reflect attitudes in the general public.[18] What is wanted is not more equal outcomes or unfair preferences. No, if there is a theme in the clamor of group politics and public policy, it is the-idea of compensation. Compensation for what? For past racial wrongs, for current overcharging of consumers, for future environmental damage. The idea of compensatory policy—that the federal government should put things right—fits equally well for the groups representing the disadvantaged (special treatment is required for truly equal opportunity to prevail) and for those representing the advantaged (any market-imposed loss can be defined as a special hardship). The same holds for newer public interest groups (government action is required to redress the impact of selfish private interests). If middle-class parents have not saved enough for college costs they should be compensated with tuition tax credits. If public buildings are inaccessible to the physically handicapped, government regulations should change that. If farmers over-invest during good times, they should be granted redress from the consequences of their actions. The old American saying "there oughtta be a law" had a negative connotation of preventing someone from getting away with something. Today the more prevalent feeling is "there oughtta be a policy," and the connotation of getting in on society's compensations is decidedly positive.

In sum, new initiatives in federal funding and regulation have infused old and new organizations with a public policy dimension, especially when such groups are used as administrative middlemen and facilitators. Moreover, the growing body of compensatory interventions by government has helped create a climate of acceptance for ever more groups to insist that things be set right on their behalf. What matters is not so much that organizations are moving to Washington as that Washington's policy problems are coming to occupy so many different facets of organizational life in the United States.

Policy as an Intramural Activity

A second tendency cuts in a direction opposite to the widening group participation in public policy. Expanding welfare policies and Washington's reliance on indirect administration have encouraged the development of specialized subcultures composed of highly knowledgeable policy-watchers. Some of these people have advanced professional degrees, some do not. What they all have in common is the detailed understanding of specialized issues that comes from sustained attention to a given policy debate.

Certain of these changes are evident in the government's own work force. Employees in the field and in Washington who perform the routine chores associated with direct administration have become less prominent. More important have become those officials with the necessary technical and supervisory skills to oversee what other people are doing. Thus the surge in federal domestic activities in the 1960s and 1970s may not have increased the overall size of the bureaucracy very much, but it did markedly expand the upper and upper-middle levels of officialdom. Compared with an 18 percent rise in total civilian employment, mid-level executive positions in the federal government (that is, supergrade and public law 313 equivalents) have increased approximately 90 percent since 1960. Some of these changes are due to a slow inflation of job titles and paper credentials that can be found in private as well as public organizations. But case studies in the 1960s suggested that most of this escalation occurring in the Washington bureaucracy could be traced to the new and expanded public programs of that decade.[19] The general effect of these policy changes has been to require more technical skills and higher supervisory levels, overlaying routine technicians with specialist engineers, insurance claims examiners with claims administrators, and so on. Approximately two-fifths of mid-level executives in the bureaucracy (grades 16–18 or the equivalent) are what might loosely be termed scientists, though frequently they are in fact science managers who oversee the work of other people inside and outside of the government.

Increasing complexity and specialization are affecting leaders in all modern organizations, even profit-oriented enterprises with stable sets of clear goals. For decision makers in government—where the policy goals have been neither stable nor clear in the last twenty years—the pressures for more expert staff assistance have become immense. This is as true for legislators as it is for public executives. President Nixon estimated that he personally saw no more than 200,000 of the 42 million pieces of paper in his own presidential materials. Recent studies of Congress estimate that the average member of the House of Representatives has, out of an eleven-hour workday, only eleven minutes to devote personally to reading and only twelve minutes in his or her own office to spend personally on writing legislation and speeches.[20] Congress, like the executive branch, has responded to the pressures by creating more specialists and topside staff. Since 1957 the total number of personal and committee staff on the Hill has climbed from 4,300 to 11,000 and over 20,000 more persons service the legislature from institutional staff positions (the General Accounting Office, Congressional Budget Office, and so on).[21] At the core of this blossoming congressional bureaucracy are bright, often remarkably young, technocrats who are almost indistinguishable from the analysts and subject matter specialists in the executive branch.

There are many straws in the wind to indicate the growing skill base of policy professionals in Washington. Executive search firms (so-called headhunters) have found a booming market in recent years, with many new firms being founded and prestigious New York organizations opening up Washington offices. One indicator of this movement, the amount of "professional opportunity" advertising in the press, now puts Washington on a par with Los Angeles and New York as an executive hunting ground for the private sector. The reason is clear. As government activities and regulations have grown, the value of policy specialists who understand the complex Washington environment has appreciated in the eyes of all of the private organizations with a stake in government activity. Another indicator is the mushrooming of new Washington law firms. Typically these firms are headed by former government officials and practice in substantive areas of law and policy that did not exist twenty years ago. Table 1 gives some idea of this trend.

TABLE 1. THE NEW WASHINGTON LAW FIRMS

Firm	Year Founded	Area of Activity	Background of Leading Partners
Beveridge, Fairbanks and Diamond	1974	environmental law	former head of Environmental Protection Agency; official in tax division of Justice Department; assistant in EPA and White House adviser on energy and environmental policy
Epstein and Becker	1972	health care	official in Health Maintenance Organization Service of Department of Health, Education, and Welfare
Blum, Parker and Nash	1977	energy, international business	associate counsel of Senate subcommittee on multinational corporations; appellate attorney in tax division of Justice Department; assistant counsel, Senate anti-trust subcommittee
Brownstein, Zeidman, Schomer and Chase	1970	housing and urban development	assistant secretary of Department of Housing and Urban Development; commissioner of Federal Housing Administration; general counsel of Small Business Administration
Lobel, Novins and Lamont	1972	consumer litigation	legislative assistant to senator; official in Justice Department; assistant counsel to Senate subcommittee on small business
Garner, Carton and Douglas	1977	defense	general counsel of Defense Department; secretary of the army
Bracewell and Patterson	1975	energy	former assistant administrator of Federal Energy Administration
Breed, Abbott and Morgan	1976	general	former solicitor of Labor Department; head of Office of Federal Contract Compliance Programs
Lane and Edson	1970	housing	general counsel of U.S. National Corporation for Housing Partnerships; former Justice Department official; former official in Department of Housing and Urban Development

Source: "The Boom in Small Law Firms," National Journal, February 4, 1978, p. 172.

Again it is tempting to borrow a term from Professor Beer and to refer to these groups of policy specialists as constituting a "professional-bureaucratic complex." Certainly there are many core groups with scientific or professional training which have carved out spheres of bureaucratic influence over health, highways, education, and so on. Likewise the familiar nexus of less professional, economic interests can still be found linking various parts of the Washington community. But the general arrangement that is emerging is somewhat different from the conventional image of iron triangles tying together executive bureaus, interest groups, and congressional committees in all-powerful alliances.

Unfortunately, our standard political conceptions of power and control are not very well suited to the loose-jointed play of influence that is emerging in political administration. We tend to look for one group exerting dominance over another, for subgovernments that are strongly insulated from other outside forces in the environment, for policies that get "produced" by a few "makers." Seeing former government officials opening law firms or joining a new trade association, we naturally think of ways in which they are trying to conquer and control particular pieces of government machinery.

Obviously questions of power are still important. But for a host of policy initiatives undertaken in the last twenty years it is all but impossible to identify clearly who the dominant actors are. Who is controlling those actions that go to make up our national policy on abortions, or on income redistribution, or consumer protection, or energy? Looking for the few who are powerful, we tend to overlook the many whose webs of influence provoke and guide the exercise of power. These webs, or what I will call "issue networks," are particularly relevant to the highly intricate and confusing welfare policies that have been undertaken in recent years.

The notion of iron triangles and subgovernments presumes small circles of participants who have succeeded in becoming largely autonomous. Issue networks, on the other hand, comprise a large number of participants with quite variable degrees of mutual commitment or of dependence on others in their environment; in fact it is almost impossible to say where a network leaves off and its environment begins. Iron triangles and subgovernments suggest a stable set of participants coalesced to control fairly narrow public programs which are in the direct economic interest of each party to the alliance. Issue networks are almost the reverse image in each respect. Participants move in and out of the networks constantly. Rather than groups united in dominance over a program, no one, as far as one can tell, is in control of the policies and issues. Any direct material interest is often secondary to intellectual or emotional commitment. Network members reinforce each other's sense of issues as their interests, rather than (as standard political or economic models would have it) interests defining positions on issues.

Issue networks operate at many levels, from the vocal minority who turn up at local planning commission hearings to the renowned professor who is quietly telephoned by the White House to give a quick "reading" on some participant or policy. The price of buying into one or another issue network is watching, reading, talking about, and trying to act on particular policy problems. Powerful interest groups can be found represented in networks but so too can individuals in or out of government who have a reputation for being knowledgeable. Particular professions may be prominent, but the true experts in the networks are those who are issue-skilled (that is, well informed about the ins and outs of a particular policy debate) regardless of formal professional training. More than mere technical experts, network people are policy activists who know each other through the issues. Those who emerge to positions of wider leadership are policy politicians—experts in using experts, victuallers of knowledge in a world hungry for right decisions.

In the old days—when the primary problem of government was assumed to be doing what was right, rather than knowing what was right—policy knowledge could be contained in the slim adages of public administration. Public executives, it was thought, needed to know how to execute. They needed power commensurate with their responsibility. Nowadays, of course, political administrators do not execute but are involved in making highly important decisions on society's behalf, and they must mobilize policy intermediaries to deliver the goods. Knowing what is right becomes crucial, and since no one knows that for sure, going through the process of dealing with those who are judged knowledgeable (or at least continuously concerned) becomes even more crucial. Instead of power commensurate with responsibility, issue networks seek influence commensurate with their understanding of the various, complex social choices being made. Of course some participants would like nothing better than complete power over the issues in question. Others seem to want little more than the security that comes with being well informed. As the executive of one new group moving to Washington put it, "We didn't come here to change the world; we came to minimize our surprises."[22]

Whatever the participants' motivation, it is the issue network that ties together what would otherwise be the contradictory tendencies of, on the one hand, more widespread organizational participation in public policy and, on the other, more narrow technocratic specialization in complex modern policies. Such networks need to be distinguished from three other more familiar terms used in connection with political administration. An issue network is a shared-knowledge group having to do with some aspect (or, as defined by the network, some problem) of public policy. It is therefore more well-defined than, first, a shared-attention group or "public"; those in the networks are likely to have a common base of information and understanding of how one knows about policy and identifies its problems. But knowledge does not necessarily produce agreement. Issue networks may or may not, therefore, be mobilized into, second, a shared-action group (creating a coalition) or, third, a shared-belief group (becoming a conventional interest organization). Increasingly, it is through networks of people who regard each other as knowledgeable, or at least as needing to be answered, that public policy issues tend to be refined, evidence debated, and alternative options worked out—though rarely in any controlled, well-organized way.

What does an issue network look like? It is difficult to say precisely, for at any given time only one part of a network may be active and through time the various connections may intensify or fade among the policy intermediaries and the executive and congressional bureaucracies. For example, there is no single health policy network but various sets of people knowledgeable and concerned about cost-control mechanisms, insurance techniques, nutritional programs, prepaid plans, and so on. At one time, those expert in designing a nationwide insurance system may seem to be operating in relative isolation, until it becomes clear that previous efforts to control costs have already created precedents that have to be accommodated in any new system, or that the issue of federal funding for abortions has laid land mines in the path of any workable plan.

The debate on energy policy is rich in examples of the kaleidoscopic interaction of changing, issue networks. The Carter administration's initial proposal was worked out among experts who were closely tied in to conservation-minded networks. Soon it became clear that those concerned with macroeconomic policies had been largely bypassed in the planning, and last-minute amendments were made in the proposal presented to Congress, a fact that was not lost on the networks of leading economists and economic correspondents. Once congressional consideration began, it quickly became evident that attempts to define the energy debate in terms of a classic confrontation between big oil companies and consumer interests were doomed. More and more policy watchers joined in the debate, bringing to it their own concerns and analyses: tax reformers, nuclear power specialists, civil rights groups interested in more jobs; the list soon grew beyond the wildest dreams of the original energy policy planners. The problem, it became clear, was that no one could quickly turn the many networks of knowledgeable people into a shared-action coalition, much less into a single, shared-attitude group believing it faced the moral equivalent of war. Or, if it was a war, it was a Vietnam-type quagmire.

It would be foolish to suggest that the clouds of issue networks that have accompanied expanding national policies are set to replace the more familiar politics of subgovernments in Washington. What they are doing is to overlay the once stable political reference points with new forces that complicate calculations, decrease predictability, and impose considerable strains on those charged with government leadership. The overlay of networks and issue politics not only confronts but also seeps down into the formerly well-established politics of particular policies and programs. Social security, which for a generation had been quietly managed by a small circle of insiders, becomes controversial and politicized. The Army Corps of Engineers, once the picturebook example of control by subgovernments, is dragged into the brawl on environmental politics. The once quiet "traffic safety establishment" finds its own safety permanently endangered by the consumer movement. Confrontation between networks and iron triangles in the Social and Rehabilitation Service, the disintegration of the mighty politics of the Public Health Service and its corps—the list could be extended into a chronicle of American national government during the last generation.[23] The point is that a somewhat new and difficult dynamic is being played out in the world of politics and administration. It is not what has been feared for so long: that technocrats and other people in white coats will expropriate the policy process, if there is to be any expropriation, it is likely to be by the policy activists, those who care deeply about a set of issues and are determined to shape the fabric of public policy accordingly.

THE TECHNOPOLS

The many new policy commitments of the last twenty years have brought about a play of influence that is many-stranded and loose. Iron triangles or other clear shapes may embrace some of the participants, but the larger picture in any policy area is likely to be one involving many other policy specialists. More than ever, policy making is becoming an intramural activity among expert issue-watchers, their networks, and their networks of networks. In this situation any neat distinction between the governmental structure and its environment tends to break down.

Political administrators, like the bureaucracies they superintend, are caught up in the trend toward issue specialization at the same time that responsibility is increasingly being dispersed among large numbers of policy intermediaries. The specialization in question may have little to do with purely professional training. Neither is it a matter of finding interest group spokesmen placed in appointive positions. Instead of party politicians, today's political executives tend to be policy politicians, able to move among the various networks, recognized as knowledge-able about the substance of issues concerning these networks, but not irretriev-ably identified with highly controversial positions. Their reputations among those "in the know" make them available for presidential appointments. Their mushiness on the most sensitive issues makes them acceptable. Neither a craft professional nor a gifted amateur, the modern recruit for political leadership in the bureaucracy is a journeyman of issues.

Approximately 200 top presidential appointees are charged with supervising the bureaucracy. These political executives include thirteen departmental secre-taries, some half a dozen nondepartmental officials who are also in the cabinet, several dozen deputy secretaries or undersecretaries, and many more commis-sion chairmen, agency administrators, and office directors. Below these men and women are another 500 politically appointed assistant secretaries, commission-ers, deputies, and a host of other officials. If all of these positions and those who hold them are unknown to the public at large, there is nevertheless no mistaking the importance of the work that they do. It is here, in the layers of public man-agers, that political promise confronts administrative reality, or what passes for reality in Washington.

At first glance, generalization seems impossible. The political executive system in Washington has everything. Highly trained experts in medicine, economics, and the natural sciences can be found in positions where there is something like guild control over the criteria for a political appointment. But one can also find the most obvious patronage payoffs; obscure commissions, along with cultural and inter-American affairs, are some of the favorite dumping grounds. There are highly issue-oriented appointments, such as the sixty or so "consumer advocates" that the Ralph Nader groups claimed were in the early Carter administration. And there are also particular skill groups represented in appointments devoid of policy content (for example, about two-thirds of the top government public rela-tions positions were filled during 1977 with people from private media organiza-tions). In recent years, the claims of women and minorities for executive positions have added a further kind of positional patronage, where it is the num-ber of positions rather than any agreed policy agenda that is important. After one year, about 11 percent of President Carter's appointees were women, mainly from established law firms, or what is sometimes referred to as the Ladies' Auxil-iary of the Old Boys' Network.

How to make sense of this welter of political executives? Certainly there is a subtlety in the arrangements by which top people become top people and deal with each other. For the fact is that the issue networks share information not only about policy problems but also about people. Rarely are high political executives people who have an overriding identification with a particular interest group or credentials as leading figures in a profession. Rather they are people with recog-nized reputations in particular areas of public policy. The fluid networks through which they move can best be thought of as proto-bureaucracies. There are subordinate and superordinate positions through which they climb from lesser to greater renown and recognition, but these are not usually within the same organization. It is indeed a world of large-scale bureaucracies but one interlaced with loose, personal associations in which reputations are established by word of mouth. The reputations in question depend little on what, in Weberian terms, would be bureaucratically rational evaluations of objective performance or on what the political scientist would see as the individual's power rating. Even less do reputations depend on opinions in the electorate at large. What matters are the assessments of people like themselves concerning how well, in the short term, the budding technopol is managing each of his assignments in and at the fringes of government.

Consider, for example, the thirteen department secretaries in Jimmy Carter's original cabinet. In theory at least, one could spin out reasons for thinking that these top political appointments would be filled by longstanding Carter loyalists, or representatives of major Democratic party factions, or recognized interest group leaders. In fact, none of these labels is an accurate characterization. One thing that stands out clearly is the continuation of a long-term trend away from relying on party politicians, others active in electoral politics, or clientele spokesmen, to fill executive positions. Nelson Polsby has concluded that at most, three members of the original Carter cabinet fell into the clientele or party political category.[24] Polsby goes on to divide the remainder into specialists and generalists, but a closer look at individual careers suggests how almost all of them—the Vances and the Califanos, the Browns and the Schlesingers—came out of or had a lasting affinity to particular issue networks.

The background of Carter's cabinet can be described in terms of movement among four great estates: academia, corporate business and the law, the government bureaucracy, and (to a lesser extent) elective politics. To represent these movements on a motionless page is difficult, but even a rough, schematic presentation of top public executives' careers reveals several outstanding features (see Table 2). Obviously no one estate is able to dominate all of the top positions. Moreover, every cabinet secretary has seen service in more than one of the major sectors. While there is movement from lower to higher positions, few people move up through the ranks of a single organization or sector in order to reach the top slots. Rather they move in hierarchies that stretch across the estates. Lower academic or business positions are parlayed into higher political appointments; lower political appointments into higher business positions; and so on.

Finally, and most importantly, all of President Carter's new cabinet secretaries had established reputations for handling leading problems that were regarded by issue-watchers as having a place on the public agenda. The secretary of interior had an outstanding record in dealing with conservation and environmental issues. The secretary of labor was a recognized expert in labor economics, particularly the problems of minorities. The secretary of health, education, and welfare had presided over the creation of the Johnson Great Society programs a decade earlier. The secretary of defense was one of the insiders in the arcane world of defense technology. The secretary of commerce had a well established reputation as an

TABLE 2. CAREER PATTERNS OF SELECTED MEMBERS OF CARTER'S FIRST CABINET

Cabinet Member	Academia	Government	Corporate Business/Law	Elective Politics
Michael Blumenthal (Treasury)	Ph.D. economics teacher 1953–1957	deputy assist. secretary 1961–1963 U.S. trade representative 1964–1967 cabinet secretary	manager 1957–1959 vice president 1959–1961 executive 1967–1972 president and chairman 1973–1976	
Harold Brown (Defense)	Ph.D. physics teacher 1947–1949 research scientist 1949–1952 laboratory manager 1952–1960 university president 1969–1977	consultant 1956–1961 director of research office 1961–1965 air force secretary 1965–1969 cabinet secretary		
Joseph Califano (Health, Education, and Welfare)	LL.B.	Judge Advocate General's Office 1955–1958 special assistant 1961–1963	law practice 1958–1961	

TABLE 2. (continued)

Cabinet Member	Academia	Government	Corporate Business/Law	Elective Politics
		general counsel 1963–1964 deputy secretary 1964–1965 presidential assistant 1965–1968	law practice 1969–1971 law firm partner 1971–1976	
		cabinet secretary		
Bob Bergland (Agriculture)		regional official 1961–1962 regional director 1963–1968	(independent farmer) (independent farmer) 1968–1970	congressman 1971–1976
		cabinet secretary		
Juanita Kreps (Commerce)	instructor 1942–1943	economist 1943–1944		
	instructor 1945–1946 Ph.D. 1948 lecturer 1952–1955 associate professor 1963–1968 dean 1969–1972 vice president 1973–1976	{ various advisory positions 1963–1976		
		cabinet secretary		
Patricia Harris (Housing and Urban Development)	L.L.B.	attorney 1960–1961		{ various part-time party positions 1960–1976
	associate dean 1962–1965	ambassador 1965–1967	law firm partner 1967–1976	
	dean 1967			
		cabinet secretary		

Note: Part-time membership on corporate boards is not included.
Source: Compiled by the author from biographies supplied by the respective cabinet secretaries' offices.

249

advocate for consumer, minority, and women's issues. And so it went. For the one new field where issues and networks were poorly formed, the Energy Department, Carter chose a respected technocrat's technocrat with a strong track record in strategic theory, defense management, and bureaucratic politics.

The emergence of the policy politicians in our national politics goes back many years, at least to the new policy commitments of the New Deal era. Policy initiatives undertaken in the last generation have only intensified the process. For example, since 1960 the selection process for presidential appointees has seen important changes.[25] Using somewhat different techniques, each White House staff has struggled to find new ways of becoming less dependent on the crop of job applicants produced by normal party channels and of reaching out to new pools of highly skilled executive manpower. The rationale behind these efforts is always that executive leadership in the bureaucracy requires people who are knowledgeable about complex policies and acceptable to the important groups that claim an interest in the ever growing number of issue areas. Not surprisingly, the policy experts within the various networks who are consulted typically end by recommending each other. Thus over half of the people President-elect Carter identified as his outside advisers on political appointments ended up in executive jobs themselves. Similarly, while candidate Carter's political manager promised to resign if establishment figures such as Cyrus Vance and Zbigniew Brzezinski were given appointments after the election, at least half of the candidate's expert foreign policy advisers (including Vance and Brzezinski) wound up in major political positions with the administration.

Historical studies tend to confirm the impression of change in the political executive system. In the past, there have generally been short-term fluctuations in a few social attributes (religion, types of school attended) that can be associated with changes in party control of the presidency. But, especially since the early 1960s, changes in party control of the White House have produced few distinctive differences in the characteristics of political appointees. Instead, the longer-term trend toward specialized policy expertise tends to wash over the short-term political fluctuations. Law, the traditional career base for generalists, has become progressively less important in filling the ranks of political executives. Academia, think tanks, and people with specialized credentials have been gaining in importance. If law itself were broken down into general versus specialized practice, the trend would probably appear even more sharply. In any event, the historical findings tentatively support the view that "there is a growing distance between electoral coalitions and governing coalitions. . . . The bases a presidential candidate needs to touch in order to win election are progressively unrelated to the bases a president needs to govern."[26]

Below the level of cabinet secretaries, the same changes in political administrators stand out even more sharply. Fifty years ago there were few political subordinates to the top executives in the departments, and scholars dismissed the career background of those who were there as a "miscellany of party assignments and political posts."[27] Today the people filling the much larger number of subordinate political executive positions are rarely partisan figures with any significant ties to party or electorate. Instead they are part of a political bureaucracy of policy specialists that sits atop and beside the permanent career bureaucracy in Washington. The key indicators for these changes are not just the obviously larger numbers of appointees. More revealing of the political bureaucracy is the growing compartmentalization by functional specialty and the increased layering of appointed executives. Figure 2 offers three snapshots of the top political manpower in one department: before the arrival of the New Deal, before the Kennedy-Johnson Great Society, and at the present time. Despite the picture that Figure 2 presents of bureaucratic expansion in political manpower, the Labor Department is actually among the smallest agencies, with a reputation for one of the leanest staff structures, in Washington.

The Agriculture Department offers another good example of change in one of the oldest and most traditional domestic departments. At one time, agricultural policies could be accounted for fairly economically in terms of general purpose farmers' organizations, particular bureaus in the Department of Agriculture, and a congressional farm bloc in legislative committees and subcommittees. Today one would have to feed into the equation not only more specialized expressions of agricultural interests (different associations for particular commodities, corporate "farmers," grass-roots family farm groups, and so on) but also environmentalists, international economic and foreign policy advocates, and civil rights, nutritional, and consumer groups. Whereas a previous agriculture secretary might have surrounded himself with a few political cronies and a clutch of Farm Bureau (or National Farmers' Union) insiders, the current secretary's inner circle is described as including "three women (one of them black), a Mexican American, an environmentalist, two economists, and a politician."[28] Within a year of his appointment the politician was gone after reported fights with one of the "women," who was also the former executive director of the Consumer Federation of America.

Of course, if appointed executives were part of a coherent political team, the larger numbers and deeper issue specialization might suggest a stronger capacity for democratic leadership in the bureaucracy. But as participants themselves often come to realize, this is not the case. Political executives' tenure in a given position is short. Their political bases of support in the electorate at large are ambiguous at best. Any mutual commitment to each other is problematic. Thus coherent political leadership in the bureaucracy—especially leadership with any ties to ordinary democratic politics—is normally at a premium. What one can count on finding in and at the fringes of every specialized part of the political bureaucracy are policy networks. It is likely to be in these that judgments about performance are made, reputations established or lost, and replacements for appointees—whoever may be the President—supplied.

THE EXECUTIVE LEADERSHIP PROBLEM

Washington has always relied on informal means of producing political leaders in government. This is no less true now than in the days when party-spoils ruled presidential appointments. It is the informal mechanisms that have changed. No

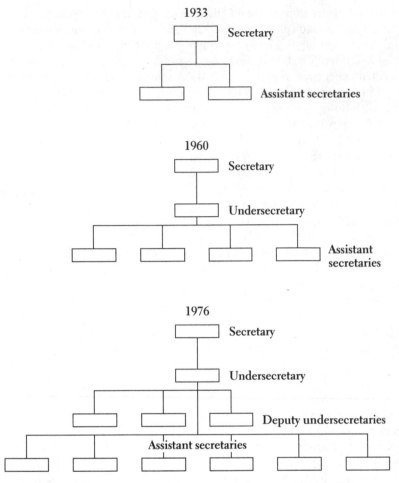

FIGURE 2. POLITICAL APPOINTEES ABOVE THE LEVEL OF BUREAU HEADS,
DEPARTMENT OF LABOR, 1933, 1960, AND 1976

Source: U.S. Congress, Senate, Committee on Civil Service, *Positions Not Under the Civil Service*, document no.
173, 72d Cong., 2d sess., January 1933, pp. 4 and 19; U.S. Congress, Senate, Committee on Post Office and Civil
Service, *United States Government Policy and Supporting Positions*, committee print, 86th Cong., 2d sess., 1960, p.
92; U.S. Congress, House, Committee on Post Office and Civil Service, *United States Government Policy and Supporting Positions*, 94th Cong., 2d sess., 1976, pp. 64–65.

doubt some of the increasing emphasis on educational credentials, professional
specialization, and technical facility merely reflects changes in society at large.
But it is also important to recognize that government activity has itself been
changing the informal mechanisms that produce political administrators. Accu-
mulating policy commitments have become crucial forces affecting the kind of
executive leadership that emerges. E. E. Schattschneider put it better when he
observed that "new policies create new politics."[29]

For many years now the list of issues on the public agenda has grown more dense as new policy concerns have been added and few dropped. Administratively, this has proliferated the number of policy intermediaries. Politically, it has mobilized more and more groups of people who feel they have a stake, a determined stake, in this or that issue of public policy. These changes are in turn encouraging further specialization of the government's work force and bureaucratic layering in its political leadership. However, the term "political" needs to be used carefully. Modern officials responsible for making the connection between politics and administration bear little resemblance to the party politicians who once filled patronage jobs. Rather, today's political executive is likely to be a person knowledgeable about the substance of particular issues and adept at moving among the networks of people who are intensely concerned about them.

What are the implications for American government and politics? The verdict cannot be one-sided, if only because political management of the bureaucracy serves a number of diverse purposes. At least three important advantages can be found in the emerging system.

First, the reliance on issue networks and policy politicians is obviously consistent with some of the larger changes in society. Ordinary voters are apparently less constrained by party identification and more attracted to an issue-based style of politics. Party organizations are said to have fallen into a state of decay and to have become less capable of supplying enough highly qualified executive manpower. If government is committed to intervening in more complex, specialized areas, it is useful to draw upon the experts and policy specialists for the public management of these programs. Moreover, the congruence between an executive leadership and an electorate that are both uninterested in party politics may help stabilize a rapidly changing society. Since no one really knows how to solve the policy puzzles, policy politicians have the important quality of being disposable without any serious political ramifications (unless of course there are major symbolic implications, as in President Nixon's firing of Attorney General Elliot Richardson).

Within government, the operation of issue networks may have a second advantage in that they link Congress and the executive branch in ways that political parties no longer can. For many years, reformers have sought to revive the idea of party discipline as a means of spanning the distance between the two branches and turning their natural competition to useful purposes. But as the troubled dealings of recent Democratic Presidents with their majorities in Congress have indicated, political parties tend to be a weak bridge.

Meanwhile, the linkages of technocracy between the branches are indeliberately growing. The congressional bureaucracy that has blossomed in Washington during the last generation is in many ways like the political bureaucracy in the executive branch. In general, the new breed of congressional staffer is not a legislative crony or beneficiary of patronage favors. Personal loyalty to the congressman is still paramount, but the new-style legislative bureaucrat is likely to be someone skilled in dealing with certain complex policy issues, possibly with credentials as a policy analyst, but certainly an expert in using other experts and their networks.

None of this means an absence of conflict between President and Congress. Policy technicians in the two branches are still working for different sets of clients with different interests. The point is that the growth of specialized policy networks tends to perform the same useful services that it was once hoped a disciplined national party system would perform. Sharing policy knowledge, the networks provide a minimum common framework for political debate and decision in the two branches. For example, on energy policy, regardless of one's position on gas deregulation or incentives to producers, the policy technocracy has established a common language for discussing the issues, a shared grammar for identifying the major points of contention, a mutually familiar rhetoric of argumentation. Whether in Congress or the executive branch or somewhere outside, the "movers and shakers" in energy policy (as in health insurance, welfare reform, strategic arms limitation, occupational safety, and a host of other policy areas) tend to share an analytic repertoire for coping with the issues. Like experienced party politicians of earlier times, policy politicians in the knowledge networks may not agree; but they understand each other's way of looking at the world and arguing about policy choices.

A third advantage is the increased maneuvering room offered to political executives by the loose-jointed play of influence. If appointees were ambassadors from clearly defined interest groups and professions, or if policy were monopolized in iron triangles, then the chances for executive leadership in the bureaucracy would be small. In fact, however, the proliferation of administrative middlemen and networks of policy watchers offers new strategic resources for public managers. These are mainly opportunities to split and recombine the many sources of support and opposition that exist on policy issues. Of course, there are limits on how far a political executive can go in shopping for a constituency, but the general tendency over time has been to extend those limits. A secretary of labor will obviously pay close attention to what the AFL-CIO has to say, but there are many other voices to hear, not only in the union movement but also minority groups interested in jobs, state and local officials administering the department's programs, consumer groups worried about wage-push inflation, employees faced with unsafe working conditions, and so on. By the same token, former Secretary of Transportation William Coleman found new room for maneuver on the problem of landings by supersonic planes when he opened up the setpiece debate between pro- and anti-Concorde groups to a wider play of influence through public hearings. Clearly the richness of issue politics demands a high degree of skill to contain expectations and manage the natural dissatisfaction that comes from courting some groups rather than others. But at least it is a game that can be affected by skill, rather than one that is predetermined by immutable forces.

These three advantages are substantial. But before we embrace the rule of policy politicians and their networks, it is worth considering the threats they pose for American government. Issue networks may be good at influencing policy, but can they govern? Should they?

The first and foremost problem is the old one of democratic legitimacy. Weaknesses in executive leadership below the level of the President have never really been due to interest groups, party politics, or Congress. The primary problem has always been the lack of any democratically based power. Political executives get their popular mandate to do anything in the bureaucracy secondhand, from either an elected chief executive or Congress. The emerging system of political technocrats makes this democratic weakness much more severe. The more closely political administrators become identified with the various specialized policy networks, the farther they become separated from the ordinary citizen. Political executives can maneuver among the already mobilized issue networks and may occasionally do a little mobilizing of their own. But this is not the same thing as creating a broad base of public understanding and support for national policies. The typical presidential appointee will travel to any number of conferences, make speeches to the membership of one association after another, but almost never will he or she have to see or listen to an ordinary member of the public. The trouble is that only a small minority of citizens, even of those who are seriously attentive to public affairs, are likely to be mobilized in the various networks.[30] Those who are not policy activists depend on the ability of government institutions to act on their behalf.

If the problem were merely an information gap between policy experts and the bulk of the population, then more communication might help. Yet instead of garnering support for policy choices, more communication from the issue networks tends to produce an "everything causes cancer" syndrome among ordinary citizens. Policy forensics among the networks yield more experts making more sophisticated claims and counterclaims to the point that the nonspecialist becomes inclined to concede everything and believe nothing that he hears. The ongoing debates on energy policy, health crises, or arms limitation are rich in examples of public skepticism about what "they," the abstruse policy experts, are doing and saying. While the highly knowledgeable have been playing a larger role in government, the proportion of the general public concluding that those running the government don't seem to know what they are doing has risen rather steadily.[31] Likewise, the more government has tried to help, the more feelings of public helplessness have grown.

No doubt many factors and events are linked to these changing public attitudes. The point is that the increasing prominence of issue networks is bound to aggravate problems of legitimacy and public disenchantment. Policy activists have little desire to recognize an unpleasant fact: that their influential systems for knowledgeable policy making tend to make democratic politics more difficult. There are at least four reasons.

COMPLEXITY. Democratic political competition is based on the idea of trying to simplify complexity into a few, broadly intelligible choices. The various issue networks, on the other hand, have a stake in searching out complexity in what might seem simple. Those who deal with particular policy issues over the years recognize that policy objectives are usually vague and results difficult to measure. Actions relevant to one policy goal can frequently be shown to be inconsistent with others. To gain a reputation as a knowledgeable participant, one must juggle all of these complexities and demand that other technocrats in the issue networks do the same.

CONSENSUS. A major aim in democratic politics is, after open argument, to arrive at some workable consensus of views. Whether by trading off one issue against another or by combining related issues, the goal is agreement. Policy activists may commend this democratic purpose in theory, but what their issue networks actually provide is a way of processing dissension. The aim is good policy—the right outcome on the issue. Since what that means is disputable among knowledgeable people, the desire for agreement must often take second place to one's understanding of the issue. Trade-offs or combinations—say, right-to-life groups with nuclear-arms-control people; environmentalists and consumerists; civil liberties groups and anti-gun controllers—represent a kind of impurity for many of the newly proliferating groups. In general there are few imperatives pushing for political consensus among the issue networks and many rewards for those who become practiced in the techniques of informed skepticism about different positions.

CONFIDENCE. Democratic politics presumes a kind of psychological asymmetry between leaders and followers. Those competing for leadership positions are expected to be sure of themselves and of what is to be done, while those led are expected to have a certain amount of detachment and dubiety in choosing how to give their consent to be governed. Politicians are supposed to take credit for successes, to avoid any appearance of failure, and to fix blame clearly on their opponents; voters weigh these claims and come to tentative judgments, pending the next competition among the leaders.

The emerging policy networks tend to reverse the situation. Activists mobilized around the policy issues are the true believers. To survive, the newer breed of leaders, or policy politicians, must become well versed in the complex, highly disputed substance of the issues. A certain tentativeness comes naturally as ostensible leaders try to spread themselves across the issues. Taking credit shows a lack of understanding of how intricate policies work and may antagonize those who really have been zealously pushing the issue. Spreading blame threatens others in the established networks and may raise expectations that new leadership can guarantee a better policy result. Vagueness about what is to be done allows policy problems to be dealt with as they develop and in accord with the intensity of opinion among policy specialists at that time. None of this is likely to warm the average citizen's confidence in his leaders. The new breed of policy politicians are cool precisely because the issue networks are hot.

CLOSURE. Part of the genius of democratic politics is its ability to find a nonviolent decision-rule (by voting) for ending debate in favor of action. All the incentives in the policy technocracy work against such decisive closure. New studies and findings can always be brought to bear. The biggest rewards in these highly intellectual groups go to those who successfully challenge accepted wisdom. The networks thrive by continuously weighing alternative courses of action on particular policies, not by suspending disbelief and accepting that something must be done.

For all of these reasons, what is good for policy making (in the sense of involving well-informed people and rigorous analysts) may be bad for democratic politics. The emerging policy technocracy tends, as Henry Aaron has said of social science research, to "corrode any simple faiths around which political coalitions ordinarily are built."[32] Should we be content with simple faiths? Perhaps not; but the great danger is that the emerging world of issue politics and policy experts will turn John Stuart Mill's argument about the connection between liberty and popular government on its head. More informed argument about policy choices may produce more incomprehensibility. More policy intermediaries may widen participation among activists but deepen suspicions among unorganized nonspecialists. There may be more group involvement and less democratic legitimacy, more knowledge and more Know-Nothingism. Activists are likely to remain unsatisfied with, and nonactivists uncommitted to, what government is doing. Superficially this cancelling of forces might seem to assure a conservative tilt away from new, expansionary government policies. However, in terms of undermining a democratic identification of ordinary citizens with their government, the tendencies are profoundly radical.

A second difficulty with the issue networks is the problem that they create for the President as ostensible chief of the executive establishment. The emerging policy technocracy puts presidential appointees outside of the chief executive's reach in a way that narrowly focused iron triangles rarely can. At the end of the day, constituents of these triangles can at least be bought off by giving them some of the material advantages that they crave. But for issue activists it is likely to be a question of policy choices that are right or wrong. In this situation, more analysis and staff expertise—far from helping—may only hinder the President in playing an independent political leadership role. The influence of the policy technicians and their networks permeates everything the White House may want to do. Without their expertise there are no option papers, no detailed data and elaborate assessments to stand up against the onslaught of the issue experts in Congress and outside. Of course a President can replace a political executive, but that is probably merely to substitute one incumbent of the relevant policy network for another.

It is, therefore, no accident that President Carter found himself with a cabinet almost none of whom were either his longstanding political backers or leaders of his party. Few if any of his personal retinue could have passed through the reputational screens of the networks to be named, for example, a secretary of labor or defense. Moreover, anyone known to be close to the President and placed in an operating position in the bureaucracy puts himself, and through him the President, in an extremely vulnerable position. Of the three cabinet members who were President Carter's own men, one, Andrew Young, was under extreme pressure to resign in the first several months. Another Carter associate, Bert Lance, was successfully forced to resign after six months, and the third, Griffin Bell, was given particularly tough treatment during his confirmation hearings and was being pressured to resign after only a year in office. The emerging system of political administration tends to produce executive arrangements in which the President's power stakes are on the line almost everywhere in terms of policy, whereas almost nowhere is anyone on the line for him personally.

Where does all this leave the President as a politician and as an executive of executives? In an impossible position. The problem of connecting politics and administration currently places any President in a classic no-win predicament. If he attempts to use personal loyalists as agency and department heads, he will be accused of politicizing the bureaucracy and will most likely put his executives in an untenable position for dealing with their organizations and the related networks. If he tries to create a countervailing source of policy expertise at the center, he will be accused of aggrandizing the Imperial Presidency and may hopelessly bureaucratize the White House's operations. If he relies on some benighted idea of collective cabinet government and on departmental executives for leadership in the bureaucracy (as Carter did in his first term), then the President does more than risk abdicating his own leadership responsibilities as the only elected executive in the national government; he is bound to become a creature of the issue networks and the policy specialists. It would be pleasant to think that there is a neat way out of this trilemma, but there is not.

Finally, there are disturbing questions surrounding the accountability of a political technocracy. The real problem is not that policy specialists specialize but that, by the nature of public office, they must generalize. Whatever an influential political executive does is done with all the collective authority of government and in the name of the public at large. It is not difficult to imagine situations in which policies make excellent sense within the cloisters of the expert issue watchers and yet are nonsense or worse seen from the viewpoint of ordinary people, the kinds of people political executives rarely meet. Since political executives themselves never need to pass muster with the electorate, the main source of democratic accountability must lie with the President and Congress. Given the President's problems and Congress's own burgeoning bureaucracy of policy specialists, the prospects for a democratically responsible executive establishment are poor at best.

Perhaps we need not worry. A case could be made that all we are seeing is a temporary commotion stirred up by a generation of reformist policies. In time the policy process may reenter a period of detumescence as the new groups and networks subside into the familiar triangulations of power.

However, a stronger case can be made that the changes will endure. In the first place, sufficient policy-making forces have now converged in Washington that it is unlikely that we will see a return to the familiar cycle of federal quiescence and policy experimentation by state governments. The central government, surrounded by networks of policy specialists, probably now has the capacity for taking continual policy initiatives. In the second place, there seems to be no way of braking, much less reversing, policy expectations generated by the compensatory mentality. To cut back on commitments undertaken in the last generation would itself be a major act of redistribution and could be expected to yield even more turmoil in the policy process. Once it becomes accepted that relative rather than absolute deprivation is what matters, the crusaders can always be counted upon to be in business.

A third reason why our politics and administration may never be the same lies in the very fact that so many policies have already been accumulated. Having to make policy in an environment already crowded with public commitments and programs increases the odds of multiple, indirect impacts of one policy on another, of one perspective set in tension with another, of one group and then another being mobilized. This sort of complexity and unpredictability creates a hostile setting for any return to traditional interest group politics.

Imagine trying to govern in a situation where the short-term political resources you need are stacked around a changing series of discrete issues, and where people overseeing these issues have nothing to prevent their pressing claims beyond any resources that they can offer in return. Imagine too that the more they do so, the more you lose understanding and support from public backers who have the long-term resources that you need. Whipsawed between cynics and true believers, policy would always tend to evolve to levels of insolubility. It is not easy for a society to politicize itself and at the same time depoliticize government leadership. But we in the United States may be managing to do just this.

NOTES

1. Hugh Heclo, *A Government of Strangers: Executive Politics in Washington* (Washington, D.C.: Brookings Institution, 1977).

2. Perhaps the most widely cited interpretations are J. Leiper Freeman, *The Political Process* (New York: Random House, 1965); and Douglass Cater, *Power in Washington* (New York: Vintage, 1964).

3. Office of Management and Budget, *The United States Budget in Brief, 1979* (Washington, D.C., 1978), p. 21.

4. Adlai E. Stevenson, quoted in James L. Sundquist, *Politics and Policy* (Washington, D.C.: Brookings Institution, 1968), p. 385.

5. Office of Management and Budget, *The Budget in Brief, 1979*, p. 21.

6. Office of Management and Budget, *Special Analyses, Budget of the United States Government, 1979* (Washington, D.C., 1978), table A-4, p. 12.

7. Charles L. Schultze, "Federal Spending: Past, Present, and Future," in Henry Owen and Charles L. Schultze, *Setting National Priorities: The Next Ten Years* (Washington, D.C.: Brookings Institution, 1976), p. 335.

8. Charles L. Schultze, *The Public Use of Private Interest* (Washington, D.C.: Brookings Institution, 1977).

9. U.S. Congress, Senate, Subcommittee on Intergovernmental Relations of the Committee on Government Operations, *Confidence and Concern: Citizens View American Government*, committee print, 93d Cong., 1st sess., 1973, part 2, pp. 111, 117, 118–119, 238.

10. Office of Management and Budget, *Special Analyses, 1979 Budget*, p. 33.

11. Samuel H. Beer, "Political Overload and Federalism," *Polity*, 10 (March 1977).

12. Unpublished talk at the Brookings Institution, June 8, 1977.

13. See for example Ellis Hawley, "Herbert Hoover and the Associative State," *Journal of American History*, June 1974; and Grant McConnell, *Private Power and American Democracy* (New York: Alfred Knopf, 1966), pp. 50, 69.

14. A similar tendency for public involvement to divide private interests occurred with earlier health initiatives in other countries. See Arnold Heidenheimer, Hugh Heclo, and Carolyn Adams, *Comparative Public Policy* (New York: St. Martin's Press, 1976).

15. Craig Colgate, Jr., ed., *National Trade and Professional Associations* (Washington, D.C.: Columbia Books, 1978).

16. For example, a statement issued by Ralph Nader on April 24, 1978, criticizing the Carter energy program included endorsements by the National Resources Defense Council Inc., Friends of the Earth Inc., the Environmental Policy Center, the Environmental Action Foundation, Environmentalists for Full Employment, the Wilderness Society, Consumer Action Now, the Sierra Club, the Environmental Defense Fund, Inc., the National Parks and Conservation Association, and the National Consumers League.

17. Alexis de Tocqueville, *Democracy in America* (New York: Harper and Row, 1966), p. 176.

18. Seymour Martin Lipset and William Schneider, "The Bakke Case: How Would It Be Decided at the Bar of Public Opinion?" *Public Opinion* (March/April 1978): pp. 41–42.

19. McKinsey and Company, Inc., "Strengthening Control of Grade Escalation" (Office of Management and Budget Archives: processed, June 1966).

20. *Washington Post*, August 28, 1977, p. 1.

21. Harrison W. Fox, Jr. and Susan Webb Hammond, *Congressional Staffs* (New York: Free Press, 1977).

22. Steven V. Roberts, "Trade Associations Flocking to Capital as U.S. Role Rises," *New York Times*, March 4, 1978, p. 44.

23. For a full account of particular cases, see for example Martha Derthick, *Policy-Making for Social Security* (Washington, D.C.: Brookings Institution, forthcoming); Daniel Mazmanian and Jeanne Nienaber, *Environmentalism, Participation and the Corps of Engineers: A Study of Organizational Change* (Washington, D.C.: Brookings Institution, 1978). For the case of traffic safety, see Jack L. Walker, "Setting the Agenda in the U.S. Senate," *British Journal of Political Science*, 7 (1977): pp. 432–445.

24. Nelson W. Polsby, "Presidential Cabinet Making," *Political Science Quarterly*, 93 (Spring 1978). Brief biographies of the original Carter cabinet are given in Congressional Quarterly, *President Carter* (Washington, D.C.: Congressional Quarterly, 1977), pp. 17–22.

25. Changes in the presidential personnel process are discussed in Hugh Heclo, *A Government of Strangers* (Washington, D.C.: Brookings Institution, 1977), pp. 89–95.

26. Kenneth Prewitt and William McAllister, "Changes in the American Executive Elite, 1930–1970," in Heinz Eulau and Moshe Czudnowski, *Elite Recruitment in Democratic Politics* (New York: Wiley, 1976), p. 127.

27. Arthur W. Macmahon and John D. Millett, *Federal Administrators* (New York: Columbia University Press, 1939), pp. 295, 302.

28. Daniel J. Baltz, "Agriculture under Bergland—Many Views, Many Directions," *National Journal*, December 10, 1977, p. 1918. For an interesting case study of the multifaceted play of influence in recent agricultural policy see I. M. Destler, *United States Foreign Economic Policy-Making* (Washington, D.C.: Brookings Institution, 1978).

29. E. E. Schattschneider, *Politics, Pressures and the Tariff* (Hamden: Archon, 1963), p. 288 (originally published 1935).

30. An interesting recent case study showing the complexity of trying to generalize about who is "mobilizable" is James N. Rosenau, *Citizenship Between Elections* (New York: Free Press, 1974).

31. Since 1964 the Institute for Social Research at the University of Michigan has asked the question, "Do you feel that almost all of the people running the government are smart people, or do you think that quite a few of them don't seem to know what they are doing?" The proportions choosing the latter view have been 28 percent (1964), 38 percent (1968), 45 percent (1970), 42 percent (1972), 47 percent (1974), and 52 percent (1976). For similar findings on public feelings of lack of control over the policy process, see U.S. Congress, Senate, Subcommittee on Intergovernmental Relations of the Committee on Government Operations, *Confidence and Concern: Citizens View American Government*, committee print, 93d Cong., 1st sess., 1973, pt. 1, p. 30. For a more complete discussion of recent trends see the two articles by Arthur H. Miller and Jack Citrin in the *American Political Science Review* (September 1974).

32. Henry J. Aaron, *Politics and the Professors* (Washington, D.C.: Brookings Institution, 1978), p. 159.

22

E. E. SCHATTSCHNEIDER

THE SCOPE AND BIAS
OF THE PRESSURE SYSTEM

In this selection from his book, The Semisovereign People *(1960), E. E. Schatt-schneider (1892–1971), a professor of political science at Wesleyan University, main-tained that organized special interests have a class bias. Hence, perhaps "90 percent of the people" cannot participate actively in the system of pressure group politics. Nonetheless, mediating institutions, such as political parties, help aggregate a welter of narrow interests and keep governance from becoming little more than the pursuit of public affairs for private advantage.*

. . . As a matter of fact, the distinction between *public and private* interests is a thoroughly respectable one; it is one of the oldest known to political theory. In the literature of the subject, the public interest refers to general or common interests shared by all or by substantially all members of the community.[1] Presumably no community exists unless there is some kind of community of interests, just as there is no nation without some notion of national interests. If it is really impossible to distinguish between private and public interests, the group theorists have produced a revolution in political thought so great that it is impossible to foresee its consequences. For this reason the distinction ought to be explored with great care.

At a time when nationalism is described as one of the most dynamic forces in the world, it should not be difficult to understand that national interests actually do exist.[2] It is necessary only to consider the proportion of the American budget devoted to national defense to realize that the common interest in national survival is a great one. Measured in dollars this interest is one of the biggest things in the world. Moreover, it is difficult to describe this interest as special. The diet on which the American leviathan feeds is something more than a jungle of disparate special interests. In the literature of democratic theory the body of common agreement found in the community is known as the "consensus," without which it is believed that no democratic system can survive.

The reality of the common interest is suggested by demonstrated capacity of the community to survive. There must be something that holds people together.

In contrast with the common interests are the special interests. The implication of this term is that these are interests shared by only a few people or a fraction of the community; they *exclude* others and may be *adverse* to them. A special interest is exclusive in about the same way as private property is exclusive. In a complex society it is not surprising that there are some interests that are shared by all or substantially all members of the community and some interests that are not shared so widely. The distinction is useful precisely because conflicting claims are made by people about the nature of their interests in controversial matters.

Perfect agreement within the community is not always possible, but an interest may be said to have become public when it is shared so widely as to be substantially universal. Thus, the difference between 99 percent agreement and perfect agreement is not so great that it becomes necessary to argue that all interests are special, that the interests of 99 percent are as special as the interests of the 1 percent. For example, the law is probably doing an adequate job of defining the public interest in domestic tranquility despite the fact that there is nearly always one dissenter at every hanging. That is, the law defines the public interest in spite of the fact that there may be some outlaws.

Since one function of theory is to explain reality, it is reasonable to add that it is a good deal easier to explain what is going on in politics by making a distinction between public and private interests than it is to attempt to explain *everything* in terms of special interests. The attempt to prove that all interests are special forces us into circumlocutions such as those involved in the argument that people have special interests in the common good. The argument can be made, but it seems a long way around to avoid a useful distinction.

What is to be said about the argument that the distinction between public and special interests is "subjective" and is therefore "unscientific"?

All discussion of interests, special as well as general, refers to the motives, desires, and intentions of people. In this sense the whole discussion of interests is subjective. We have made progress in the study of politics because people have observed some kind of relation between the political behavior of people and certain wholly impersonal data concerning their ownership of property, income, economic status, professions, and the like. All that we know about interests, private as well as public, is based on inferences of this sort. Whether the distinction in any given case is valid depends on the evidence and on the kinds of inferences drawn from the evidence.

The only meaningful way we can speak of the interests of an association like the National Association of Manufacturers is to draw inferences from the fact that the membership is a select group to which only manufacturers may belong and to try to relate that datum to what the association does. The implications, logic, and deductions are persuasive only if they furnish reasonable explanations of the facts. That is all that any theory about interests can do. It has seemed persuasive to students of politics to suppose that manufacturers do not join an association to which only manufacturers may belong merely to promote philanthropic or cultural or religious interests, for example. The basis of selection of the membership creates an inference about the organization's concerns. The conclusions drawn from this datum seem to fit what we know about the policies promoted by associations, i.e., the policies seem to reflect the exclusive interests of manufacturers. The method is not foolproof, but it works better than many other kinds of analysis and is useful precisely because special-interest groups often tend to rationalize their special interests as public interests.

Is it possible to distinguish between the "interests" of the members of the National Association of Manufacturers and the members of the American League to Abolish Capital Punishment? The facts in the two cases are not identical. First, *the members of the A.L.A.C.P. obviously do not expect to be hanged.* The membership of the A.L.A.C.P. is not restricted to persons under indictment for murder or in jeopardy of the extreme penalty. *Anybody* can join A.L.A.C.P. Its members oppose capital punishment, although they are not personally likely to benefit by the policy they advocate. The inference is therefore that the interest of the A.L.A.C.P. is not adverse, exclusive, or special. It is not like the interest of the Petroleum Institute in depletion allowances.

Take some other cases. The members of the National Child Labor Committee are not children in need of legislative protection against exploitation by employers. The members of the World Peace Foundation apparently want peace, but in the nature of things they must want peace for everyone because no group can be at peace while the rest of the community is at war. Similarly, even if the members of the National Defense League wanted defense only for themselves, they would necessarily have to work for defense for the whole country because national security is indivisible. Only a naive person is likely to imagine that the political involvements of the members of the American Bankers Association and members of the Foreign Policy Association are identical. In other words, we may draw inferences from the exclusive or the nonexclusive nature of benefits sought by organizations as well as we can from the composition of groups. The positions of these groups can be distinguished not on the basis of some subjective process, but by making reasonable inferences from verifiable facts.

On the other hand, because some special-interest groups attempt to identify themselves with the public interest it does not follow that the whole idea of the public interest is a fraud. Mr. Wilson's famous remark that what is good for General Motors is good for the country assumes that people generally do in fact desire the common good. Presumably, Mr. Wilson attempted to explain the special interest of General Motors in terms of the common interest because that was the only way he could talk to people who do not belong to the General Motors organization. *Within* the General Motors organization, discussions might be carried on in terms of naked self-interest, but a *public discussion must be carried on in public terms.*

All public discussion is addressed to the general community. To describe the conflict of special-interest groups as a form of politics means that the conflict has become generalized, has become a matter involving the broader public. In the nature of things *a political conflict among special interests is never restricted to the group most immediately interested.* Instead, it is an appeal (initiated by relatively small numbers of people) for the support of vast numbers of people who are sufficiently remote to have a somewhat different perspective on the controversy. It follows that Mr. Wilson's comment, far from demonstrating that the public interest is a fraud, proves that he thinks that the public interest is so important that even a great private corporation must make obeisance to it.

The distinction between public and special interests is an indispensable tool for the study of politics. To abolish the distinction is to make a shambles of political science by treating things that are different as if they were alike. The kind of distinction made here is a commonplace of all literature dealing with human society, but *if we accept it, we have established one of the outer limits of the subject;* we have split the world of interests in half and have taken one step toward defining the scope of this kind of political conflict.

We can now examine the second distinction, the distinction between organized and unorganized groups. The question here is not whether the distinction can be made but whether or not it is worth making. Organization has been described as "merely a stage or degree of interaction" in the development of a group.[3]

The proposition is a good one, but what conclusion do we draw from it? We do not dispose of the matter by calling the distinction between organized and unorganized groups a "mere" difference of degree because some of the greatest differences in the world are differences of degree. As far as special-interest politics is concerned the implication to be avoided is that a few workmen who habitually stop at a corner saloon for a glass of beer are essentially the same as the United States Army because the difference between them is merely one of degree. At this point we have distinction that makes a difference. The distinction between organized and unorganized groups is worth making because it ought to alert us against an analysis which begins as a general group theory of politics but ends with a defense of pressure politics as inherent, universal, permanent, and inevitable. This kind of confusion comes from the loosening of categories involved in the universalization of group concepts.

Since the beginning of intellectual history, scholars have sought to make progress in their work by distinguishing between things that are unlikely and by dividing their subject matter into categories to examine them more intelligently. It is something of a novelty, therefore, when group theorists reverse this process by discussing their subject in terms so universal that they wipe out all categories, because this is the dimension in which it is least possible to understand anything.

If we are able, therefore, to distinguish between public and private interests and between organized and unorganized groups we have marked out the major boundaries of the subject; *we have given the subject shape and scope.* We are now in a position to attempt to define the area we want to explore. Having cut the pie into four pieces, we can now appropriate the piece we want and leave the rest to someone else. For a multitude of reasons *the most likely field of study is that of the organized, special-interest groups.* The advantage of concentrating on organized groups is that they are known, identifiable, and recognizable. The advantage of concentrating on special-interest groups is that they have one important characteristic in common; they are all exclusive. This piece of the pie (the organized special-interest groups) we shall call the *pressure system.* The pressure system has boundaries we can define; we can fix its scope and make an attempt to estimate its bias.

It may be assumed at the outset that all organized special-interest groups have some kind of impact on politics. A sample survey of organizations made by the Trade Associations Division of the United States Department of Commerce in 1942 concluded that "From 70 to 100 percent (of these associations) are planning activities in the field of government relations, trade promotion, trade practices, public relations, annual conventions, cooperation with other organizations, and information services."[4]

The subject of our analysis can be reduced to manageable proportions and brought under control if we restrict ourselves to the groups whose interests in politics are sufficient to have led them to unite in formal organizations having memberships, bylaws, and officers. A further advantage of this kind of definition is, we may assume, that the organized special-interest groups are the most self-conscious, best developed, most intense and active groups. Whatever claims can be made for a group theory of politics ought to be sustained by the evidence concerning these groups, if the claims have any validity at all.

The organized groups listed in the various directories (such as *National Associations of the United States*, published at intervals by the United States Department of Commerce) and specialty yearbooks, registers, etc. and the *Lobby Index*, published by the United States House of Representatives, probably include the bulk of the organizations in the pressure system. All compilations are incomplete, but these are extensive enough to provide us with some basis for estimating the scope of the system.

By the time a group has developed the kind of interest that leads it to organize, it may be assumed that it has also developed some kind of political bias because *organization is itself a mobilization of bias in preparation for action*. Since these groups can be identified and since they have memberships (i.e., they include and exclude people), it is possible to think of the *scope* of the system.

When lists of these organizations are examined, the fact that strikes the student most forcibly is that *the system is very small*. The range of organized, identifiable, known groups is amazingly narrow; there is nothing remotely universal about it. There is a tendency on the part of publishers of directories of associations to place an undue emphasis on business organizations, an emphasis that is almost inevitable because the business community is by a wide margin the most highly organized segment of society. Publishers doubtless tend also to reflect public demand for information. Nevertheless, the dominance of business groups in the pressure system is so marked that it probably cannot be explained away as an accident of the publishing industry.

The business character of the pressure system is shown by almost every list available. *National Associations of the United States*[5] lists 1,860 business associations out of a total of 4,000 in the volume, though it refers without listing (p. VII) to 16,000 organizations of businessmen. One cannot be certain what the total content of the unknown associational universe may be, but, taken with the evidence found in other compilations, it is obvious that business is remarkably well represented. Some evidence of the over-all scope of the system is to be seen in the estimate that 15,000 national trade associations have a gross membership of about one million business firms.[6] The data are incomplete, but even if we do not have a detailed map this is the shore dimly seen.

Much more directly related to pressure politics is the *Lobby Index, 1946–1949* (an index of organizations and individuals registering or filing quarterly reports under the Federal Lobbying Act), published as a report of the House Select Committee on Lobbying Activities. In this compilation, 825 out of a total of 1,247 entities (exclusive of individuals and Indian tribes) represented business.[7] A selected list of the most important of the groups listed in the *Index* (the groups spending the largest sums of money on lobbying) published in the *Congressional Quarterly Log* shows 149 business organizations in a total of 265 listed.[8]

The business or upper-class bias of the pressure system shows up everywhere. Businessmen are four or five times as likely to write to their congressmen as manual laborers are. College graduates are far more apt to write to their congressmen than people in the lowest educational category are.[9]

The limited scope of the business pressure system is indicated by all available statistics. Among business organizations, the National Association of Manufacturers (with about 20,000 corporate members) and the Chamber of Commerce of the United States (about as large as the N.A.M.) are giants. Usually business associations are much smaller. Of 421 trade associations in the metal-products industry listed in *National Associations of the United States*, 153 have a membership of less than 20.[10] The median membership was somewhere between 24 and 50. Approximately the same scale of memberships is to be found in the lumber, furniture, and paper industries where 37.3 percent of the associations listed had a membership of less than 20 and the median membership was in the 25 to 50 range.[11]

The statistics in these cases are representative of nearly all other classifications of industry.

Data drawn from other sources support this thesis. Broadly, the pressure system has an upper-class bias. There is overwhelming evidence that participation in voluntary organizations is related to upper social and economic status; the rate of participation is much higher in the upper strata than it is elsewhere. The general proposition is well stated by Lazarsfeld:

> People on the lower SES levels are less likely to belong to any organizations than the people on high SES (Social and Economic Status) levels. (On an A and B level, we find 72 percent of these respondents who belong to one or more organizations. The proportion of respondents who are members of formal organizations decreases steadily as SES level descends until, on the D level only 35 percent of the respondents belong to any associations.)[12]

The bias of the system is shown by the fact that *even nonbusiness organizations reflect an upper-class tendency*.

Lazarsfeld's generalization seems to apply equally well to urban and rural populations. The obverse side of the coin is that large areas of the population appear to be wholly outside the system of private organization. A study made by Ira Reid of a Philadelphia area showed that in a sample of 963 persons, 85 percent belonged to no civic or charitable organization and 74 percent belonged to no occupational, business, or professional associations, while another Philadelphia study of 1,154 women showed that 55 percent belonged to no associations of any kind.[13]

A *Fortune* farm poll taken some years ago found that 70.5 percent of farmers belonged to no agricultural organizations. A similar conclusion was reached by two Gallup polls showing that perhaps no more than one third of the farmers of the country belonged to farm organizations,[14] while another *Fortune* poll showed that 86.8 percent of the low-income farmers belonged to no farm organizations.[15]

All available data support the generalization that the farmers who do not participate in rural organizations are largely the poorer ones.

A substantial amount of research done by other rural sociologists points to the same conclusion. Mangus and Cottam say, on the basis of a study of 556 heads of Ohio farm families and their wives:

> The present study indicates that comparatively few of those who ranked low on the scale of living took any active part in community organizations as members, attendants, contributors, or leaders. On the other hand, those families that ranked high on the scale of living comprised the vast majority of the highly active participants in formal group activities. . . . Fully two-thirds of those in the lower class as defined in this study were non-participants as compared with only one-tenth of those in the upper class and one-fourth of those in the middle class. . . . When families were classified by the general level-of-living index, 16 times as large a proportion of those in the upper classes as of those in the lower class were active participants. . . .[16]

Along the same line Richardson and Bauder observe, "Socio-economic status was directly related to participation."[17] In still another study it was found that "a highly significant relationship existed between income and formal participation."[18] It was found that persons with more than four years of college education held twenty times as many memberships (per one hundred persons) as did those with less than a fourth-grade education and were forty times as likely to hold office in nonchurch organizations, while persons with an income over $5,000 hold ninety-four times as many offices as persons with incomes less than $250.[19]

D. E. Lindstrom found that 72 percent of farm laborers belonged to no organizations whatever.[20]

There is a great wealth of data supporting the proposition that participation in private associations exhibits a class bias.[21]

The class bias of associational activity gives meaning to the limited scope of the pressure system, because *scope and bias are aspects of the same tendency.* The data raise a serious question about the validity of the proposition that special-interest groups are a universal form of political organization reflecting *all* interests. As a matter of fact, to suppose that everyone participates in pressure-group activity and that all interests get themselves organized in the pressure system is to destroy the meaning of this form of politics. The pressure system makes sense only as the political instrument of a segment of the community. It gets results by being selective and biased; *if everybody got into the act, the unique advantages of this form of organization would be destroyed, for it is possible that if all interests could be mobilized the result would be a stalemate.*

Special-interest organizations are most easily formed when they deal with small numbers of individuals who are acutely aware of their exclusive interests. To describe the conditions of pressure-group organization in this way is, however, to say that it is primarily a business phenomenon. Aside from a few very large organizations (the churches, organized labor, farm organizations, and veterans' organizations) the residue is a small segment of the population. *Pressure politics is essentially the politics of small groups.*

The vice of the groupist theory is that it conceals the most significant aspects of the system. The flaw in the pluralist heaven is that the heavenly chorus sings with a strong upper-class accent. Probably about 90 percent of the people cannot get into the pressure system.

The notion that the pressure system is automatically representative of the whole community is a myth fostered by the universalizing tendency of modern group theories. *Pressure politics is a selective process* ill designed to serve diffuse interests. The system is skewed, loaded, and unbalanced in favor of a fraction of a minority.

On the other hand, pressure tactics are not remarkably successful in mobilizing general interests. When pressure-group organizations attempt to represent the interests of large numbers of people, they are usually able to reach only a small segment of their constituencies. Only a chemical trace of the fifteen million Negroes in the United States belong to the National Association for the Advancement of Colored People. Only one five hundredths of 1 percent of American women belong to the League of Women Voters, only one sixteen hundredths of 1 percent of the consumers belong to the National Consumers' League, and only 6 percent of American automobile drivers belong to the American Automobile Association, while about 15 percent of the veterans belong to the American Legion.

The competing claims of pressure groups and political parties for the loyalty of the American public revolve about the difference between the results likely to be achieved by small-scale and large-scale political organization. Inevitably, the outcome of pressure politics and party politics will be vastly different.

A CRITIQUE OF GROUP THEORIES OF POLITICS

It is extremely unlikely that the vogue of group theories of politics would have attained its present status if its basic assumptions had not been first established by some concept of economic determinism. The economic interpretation of politics has always appealed to those political philosophers who have sought a single prime mover, a sort of philosopher's stone of political science around which to organize their ideas. The search for a single, ultimate cause has something to do with the attempt to explain *everything* about politics in terms of group concepts. The logic of economic determinism is to *identify the origins of conflict and to assume the conclusion.* This kind of thought has some of the earmarks of an illusion. The somnambulatory quality of thinking in this field appears also in the tendency of research to deal only with successful pressure campaigns or the willingness of scholars to be satisfied with having placed pressure groups on the scene of the crime without following through to see if the effect can really be attributed to the cause. What makes this kind of thinking remarkable is the fact that in political contests there are as many failures as there are successes. Where in the literature of pressure politics are the failures?

Students of special-interest politics need a more sophisticated set of intellectual tools than they have developed thus far. The theoretical problem involved in the search for a single cause is that all power relations in a democracy are reciprocal. Trying to find the original cause is like trying to find the first wave of the ocean.

Can we really assume that we know all that is to be known about a conflict if we understand its *origins?* Everything we know about politics suggests that a conflict is likely to change profoundly as it becomes political. It is a rare individual who can confront his antagonists without changing his opinions to some degree. Everything changes once a conflict gets into the political arena—*who* is involved, *what* the conflict is about, the resources available, etc. It is extremely difficult to predict the outcome of a fight by watching its beginning because we do not even know who else is going to get into the conflict. The logical consequence of the exclusive emphasis on the determinism of the private origins of conflict is to assign zero value to the political process.

The very expression "pressure politics" invites us to misconceive the role of special-interest groups in politics. The word "pressure" implies the use of some kind of force, a form of intimidation, something other than reason and information, to induce public authorities to act against their own best judgment. In Latham's famous statement . . . the legislature is described as a "referee" who "ratifies" and "records" the "balance of power" among the contending groups.[22]

It is hard to imagine a more effective way of saying that Congress has no mind or force of its own or that Congress is unable to invoke new forces that might alter the equation.

Actually the outcome of political conflict is not like the "resultant" of opposing forces in physics. To assume that the forces in a political situation could be diagramed as a physicist might diagram the resultant of opposing physical forces is to wipe the slate clean of all remote, general, and public considerations for the protection of which civil societies have been instituted.

Moreover, the notion of "pressure" distorts the image of the power relations involved. *Private conflicts are taken into the public arena precisely because someone wants to make certain that the power ratio among the private interests most immediately involved shall not prevail.* To treat a conflict as a mere test of the strength of the private interests is to leave out the most significant factors. This is so true that it might indeed be said that the only way to preserve private power ratios is to keep conflicts out of the public arena.

The assumption that it is only the "interested" who count ought to be re-examined in view of the foregoing discussion. The tendency of the literature of pressure politics has been to neglect the low-tension force of large numbers because it *assumes that the equation of forces is fixed at the outset.*

Given the assumptions made by the group theorists, the attack on the idea of the majority is completely logical. The assumption is that conflict is monopolized narrowly by the parties immediately concerned. There is no room for a majority when conflict is defined so narrowly. It is a great deficiency of the group theory that it has found no place in the political system for the majority. The force of the majority is of an entirely different order of magnitude, something not to be measured by pressure-group standards.

Instead of attempting to exterminate all political forms, organizations, and alignments that do not qualify as pressure groups, would it not be better to attempt to make a synthesis, covering the whole political system and finding a place for all kinds of political life?

One possible synthesis of pressure politics and party politics might be produced by *describing politics as the socialization of conflict.* That is to say, the political process is a sequence: conflicts are initiated by highly motivated, high-tension groups so directly and immediately involved that it is difficult for them to see the justice of competing claims. As long as the conflicts of these groups remain *private* (carried on in terms of economic competition, reciprocal denial of goods and services, private negotiations and bargaining, struggles for corporate control or competition for membership), no political process is initiated. Conflicts become political only when an attempt is made to involve the wider public. Pressure politics might be described as a stage in the socialization of conflict. This analysis makes pressure politics an integral part of all politics, including party politics.

One of the characteristic points of origin of pressure politics is a breakdown of the discipline of the business community. The flight to government is perpetual. Something like this is likely to happen wherever there is a point of contact between competing power systems. It is the *losers in intrabusiness conflict who seek redress from public authority. The dominant business interests resist appeals to the government.* The role of the government as the patron of the defeated private interest sheds light on its function as the critic of private power relations.

Since the contestants in private conflicts are apt to be unequal in strength, it follows that *the most powerful special interests want private settlements* because they are able to dictate the outcome as long as the conflict remains private. If A is a hundred times as strong as B he does not welcome the intervention of a third party because he expects to impose his own terms on B; he wants to isolate B. He is especially opposed to the intervention of public authority, because public authority represents the most overwhelming form of outside intervention. Thus, if $\frac{A}{B} = \frac{100}{1}$, it is obviously not to A's advantage to involve a third party a million times as strong as A and B combined. Therefore, it is the weak, not the strong, who appeal to public authority for relief. It is the weak who want to socialize conflict, i.e., to involve more and more people in the conflict until the balance of forces is changed. In the schoolyard it is not the bully but the defenseless smaller boys who "tell the teacher." When the teacher intervenes, the balance of power in the schoolyard is apt to change drastically. It is the function of public authority to *modify private power relations by enlarging the scope of conflict.* Nothing could be more mistaken than to suppose that public authority merely registers the dominance of the strong over the weak. The mere existence of public order has already ruled out a great variety of forms of private pressure. Nothing could be more confusing than to suppose that the refugees from the business community who come to Congress for relief and protection *force* Congress to do their bidding.

Evidence of the truth of this analysis may be seen in the fact that the big private interests do not necessarily win if they are involved in public conflicts with petty interests. The image of the lobbyists as primarily the agents of big business is not easy to support on the face of the record of congressional hearings, for example. The biggest corporations in the country tend to avoid the arena in which pressure

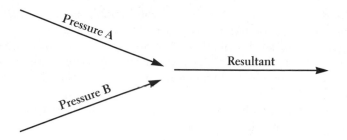

groups and lobbyists fight it out before the congressional committees. To describe this process exclusively in terms of an effort of business to intimidate congressmen is to misconceive what is actually going on.

It is probably a mistake to assume that pressure politics is the typical or even the most important relation between government and business. The pressure group is by no means the perfect instrument of the business community. What does big business want? The *winners* in intrabusiness strife want (1) to be let alone (they want autonomy) and (2) to preserve the solidarity of the business community. For these purposes pressure politics is not a wholly satisfactory device. The most elementary considerations of strategy call for the business community to develop some kind of common policy more broadly based than any special-interest group is likely to be.

The political influence of business depends on the kind of solidarity that, on the one hand, leads all business to rally to the support of *any* businessman in trouble with the government and, on the other hand, keeps internal business disputes out of the public arena. In this system businessmen resist the impulse to attack each other in public and discourage the efforts of individual members of the business community to take intrabusiness conflicts into politics.

The attempt to mobilize a united front of the whole business community does not resemble the classic concept of pressure politics. The logic of business politics is to keep peace within the business community by supporting as far as possible all claims that business groups make for themselves. The tendency is to support all businessmen who have conflicts with the government and support all businessmen in conflict with labor. In this way *special-interest politics can be converted into party policy.* The search is for a broad base of political mobilization grounded on the strategic need for political organization on a wider scale than is possible in the case of the historical pressure group. Once the business community begins to think in terms of a larger scale of political organization the Republican party looms large in business politics.

It is a great achievement of American democracy that business has been forced to form a political organization designed to win elections, i.e., has been forced to compete for power in the widest arena in the political system. On the other hand, *the power of the Republican party to make terms with business rests on the fact that business cannot afford to be isolated.*

The Republican party has played a major role in *the political organization of the business community,* a far greater role than many students of politics seem to have realized. The influence of business in the Republican party is great, but it is never absolute because business is remarkably dependent on the party. The business community is too small, it arouses too much antagonism, and its aims are too narrow to win the support of a popular majority. The political education of business is a function of the Republican party that can never be done so well by anyone else.

In the management of the political relations of the business community, the Republican party is much more important than any combination of pressure groups ever could be. The success of special interests in Congress is due less to the "pressure" exerted by these groups than it is due to the fact that Republican members of Congress are committed in advance to a general probusiness attitude. The notion that business groups coerce Republican congressmen into voting for their bills underestimates the whole Republican posture in American politics.[23]

It is not easy to manage the political interests of the business community because there is a perpetual stream of losers in intrabusiness conflicts who go to the government for relief and protection. It has not been possible therefore to maintain perfect solidarity, and when solidarity is breached the government is involved almost automatically. The fact that business has not become hopelessly divided and that it has retained great influence in American politics has been due chiefly to the over-all mediating role played by the Republican party. There has never been a pressure group or a combination of pressure groups capable of performing this function.

NOTES

1. References to the public interest appear under a variety of headings in the literature of political theory.

See G. D. H. Cole's comment on "the will of all" and the "general will," pp. xxx and xxxi of his introduction to Everyman's edition of Rousseau's *Social Contract*, London, 1913.

See Ernst Cassirer, *The Myth of the State*, Garden City, 1955, pp. 88–93, for a discussion of Plato's concept of "justice" as the end of the state in his criticism of the sophists.

See S. D. Lindsay, *The Essentials of Democracy*, Philadelphia, 1929, p. 49, for a statement regarding consensus.

2. It does not seem necessary to argue that nationalism and national interests are forces in the modern world. E. H. Carr writes about "the catastrophic growth of nationalism" in *Nationalism and After*, New York, 1945, p. 18. D. W. Brogan describes nations as "the only communities that now exist," *The American Character*, New York, 1944, p. 169. "The outstanding and distinctive characteristic of the people of the Western State System is their devotion and allegiance to the 'nations' into which they have got themselves divided," Frederick L. Schumann, *International Politics*, 3d ed., New York, 1941, p. 300. A. D. Lindsay in *The Essentials of Democracy*, Philadelphia, 1929, p. 49, has stated the doctrine of the democratic consensus as follows: "Nationality, however produced, is a sense of belonging together, involving a readiness on the part of the members of a state to subordinate their differences to it. It involves something more. It has a connection with the notion of a distinctive culture—some sort of rough ideal of the kind of common life for which the community stands, which always exists in people's minds as a rough criticism by which political proposals are to be judged. This

at least is clear, that where such common understanding and sense of belonging together either does not exist or is overshadowed by other differences, successful democracy is not really possible."

3. David Truman, *The Government Process*, New York, 1951, p. 51.

4. *National Associations of the United States*, p. xi.

5. Edited by Jay Judkins, Washington, 1949, p. viii.

6. *National Associations of the United States*, p. viii.

7. House Report No. 3197, 81st Congress, 2d Session, December 15, 1950, Washington.

8. *Congressional Quarterly Log*, week ending February 24, 1950, pp. 217 ff. Another compilation, the list of approximately one thousand associations and societies published in the *World Almanac* for 1953, reflects to a very great extent the economic, professional and leisure interests and activities of the upper economic strata of the community. Scarcely more than a dozen or so of the associations listed in the *World Almanac* can be described as proletarian in their outlook or membership.

9. *American Institute of Public Opinion*, May 29, 1946.

10. Four hundred fifty associations are listed, but figures for membership are given for only 421.

11. Membership statistics are given for only 177 of the 200 associations listed.

12. Lazarsfeld and Associates, *The People's Choice*, p. 145.

13. Reid and Ehle, "Leadership Selection in the Urban Locality Areas," *Public Opinion Quarterly* (1950) 14:262–284. See also Powell, *Anatomy of Public Opinion*, New York, 1951, pp. 180–181.

14. See Carey McWilliams, *Small Farm and Big Farm*, Public Affairs Pamphlet, No. 100.

15. *Fortune* poll, April, 1943.

16. A. R. Mangus and H. R. Cottam, *Level of Living, Social Participation, and Adjustment of Ohio Farm People*, Bulletin 624, Ohio Agricultural Experiment Station, Wooster, Ohio, September, 1941, pp. 51, 53.

Another study (of New York farmers) shows that there is a direct relation between organizational activity and the economic status of farmers. The author concludes that "the operators of farms of less than 55 acres in size are represented in only very small proportions in membership in the farm bureau and in the Dairymen's League and other cooperatives." W. A. Anderson, *The Membership of Farmers in New York Organizations*, Cornell University Agricultural Experiment Station, Ithaca, N.Y., 1937, p. 20.

17. P. D. Richardson and Ward W. Bauder, *Participation in Organized Activities in a Kentucky Rural Community*, Bulletin 598, Kentucky Agricultural Experimental Station, University of Kentucky, Lexington, Kentucky, 1953, pp. 26, 28. "The number of memberships varied directly with the socio-economic score."

18. Harold F. Kaufman, *Participation in Organized Activities in Selected Kentucky Localities*, Bulletin 528, Kentucky Agricultural Experiment Station, University of Kentucky, Lexington, 1949, p. 19.

19. Ibid., pp. 11, 12, 13, 21.

See also Mirra Komorovsky, "The Voluntary Association of Urban Dwellers," *American Sociological Review* 11:686–698, 1946.

20. *Forces Affecting Participation of Farm People in Rural Organizations*, Bulletin 423, University of Illinois Agricultural Experiment Station, 1936, p. 103.

21. "Associational participation is greatest at the top of Jonesville society and decreases on the way down the class hierarchy. The upper class belongs to the greatest number of associations, the upper-middle class next, and so on down to the lower-lower class which belongs to the least." Warner, *Democracy in Jonesville*, New York, 1949, p. 117. See also pp. 138, 140, 141, 143.

"A higher proportion of the members of the upper class belong to more associations than the members of any other class." Warner, *Jonesville*, p. 131.

"The upper and upper-middle classes are highly organized, well integrated social groups. The lower-middle and lower classes are more loosely organized and have fewer devices for maintaining their own distinctiveness in the community." Warner, *Jonesville*, p. 148. See also p. 153.

"Many organized groups touch only a few people in a community. Studies in cities reveal that 40 to 60 percent of adults are members of these organized groups if church membership is excluded. In rural communities the percentage is smaller. So when we bring in representatives from these organized groups, we should not pretend that we are getting a complete representation of the people of the community. The American practice of 'joining' is not as universal as popularly assumed."

G. W. Blackwell, "Community Analysis," *Approaches to the Study of Politics*, Roland Young, ed., Northwestern University Press, 1958, p. 306.

"Aside from church participation, most urban individuals belong to one organization or none. Low socio-economic rank individuals and middle-rank individuals, usually belong to one organization at most, and it is usually work-connected for men, child-connected for women. Only in the upper socio-economc levels is the 'joiner' to be found with any frequency. When attendance at organizations is studied, some twenty per cent of the memberships are usually 'paper' memberships." Scott Greer, "Individual Participation in Mass Society," *Approaches to the Study of Politics*, p. 332.

22. Earl Latham, *The Group Basis of Politics*, Ithaca, N.Y., 1952, pp. 35–36.

23. See *Reporter*, November 25, 1958, for story of Senator Bricker and the Ohio Right-to-Work referendum.

PART SIX

THE CONGRESS

Congress is often called the "First Branch" as it is the subject of Article I of the Constitution and because the Framers clearly thought it would be the most powerful unit of the new national government. In their view, the legislature was necessarily the center of republican government. Congress's constitutional powers are much greater than those of the president and the courts. Historically, however, the use of congressional power has varied widely. At times, Congress has taken the initiative for public policies and been the dominant branch. But at other times it has been predominantly reactive, choosing to allow the executive to be the proactive branch and responding to its proposals. Accounting for Congress's performance has been a major interest of American political scientists for more than a century.

To some extent, variation in congressional power is a product of constitutional design. In this chapter's first selection, *Federalist 51*, James Madison explains why coordinated congressional action is difficult to achieve. Madison writes

> . . . it is not possible to give to each department an equal power of self-defense. In republican government, the legislative authority necessarily predominates. The remedy for this inconveniency is to divide the legislature into different branches; and to render them, by different modes of election and different principles of action, as little connected with each other as their nature of their common functions and common dependence on the society will admit.

Madison's expectations are broadly supported by the research presented in "Constituency Influence In Congress" (1963) by Warren E. Miller and Donald E. Stokes. Reviewing different theories of legislative representation, the authors find that the strength of the relationship between a constituency's attitude and its congressional representative's roll-call votes varies by policy area. They find that members of Congress act as instructed delegates on civil rights issues; more like partisan representatives in the field of social welfare; and relatively independently of their constituencies' attitudes on matters of foreign affairs. Miller and Stokes conclude that ". . . the relation of Congressman to voter is not a simple bilateral one but is complicated by the presence of all manner of intermediaries: the local party, economic interests, the news media, racial and nationality organizations, and so forth."

In the face of these centrifugal forces, one might expect political parties to coordinate legislative action. To some extent they do. The parties play a major role in organizing each house of Congress. They choose leaders, make assignments to committees, and try to control their members on important committee and floor votes. Theoretically, a party's ability to coordinate congressional action should be greatest when it controls the presidency, Senate, and House. However, David R. Mayhew, in *Divided We Govern* (1991), observes that ". . . it does not seem to make all that much difference whether party control of the American government happens to be unified or divided." The parties serve more as "policy factions" than as "governing instruments." Why? Mayhew notes that issues may cut across parties (e.g., regional interests); government "floats in public opinion" in "waves" that are not strongly connected to political parties; and, following Miller and Stokes, "there is a deep-seated individualism among American politicians, who build and tend their own electoral bases and maintain their own relations of responsibility with electorates."

But Congress is not simply a body of individual actors. It is also an organization with a leadership structure, division of labor, and settled routines. Nelson Polsby explores "The Institutionalization of the U.S. House of Representatives" (1968). Institutionalization occurs when ". . . entry is more difficult, and turnover is less frequent," "leadership professionalizes and persists," so leaders are more likely to be chosen from within, "and the apprenticeship period lengthens." The organization also develops a complex division of labor and tends to use "automatic rather than discretionary methods for conducting its internal business." Although all the consequences of these organizational changes are neither known nor necessarily beneficial, Polsby notes that institutionalization enables the House of Representatives to succeed "in representing a large number of diverse constituents, and in legitimizing, expressing, and containing political opposition within a complex political system."

Much of the division of labor in Congress is achieved by relying on standing committees. Committees play a much more prominent role in the U.S. system than in parliamentary systems. On the surface, the committee system appears to contribute to the disaggregation of power in Congress. However, some committees are much more powerful than others, and are such a potent force in the legislative process that, at least with respect to certain issues, they may steer the rest of the legislative body.

This chapter's final reading, taken from Richard F. Fenno, Jr.'s *Congressmen in Committees* (1973), provides enduring insights into the congressional committee system. The key sections of three chapters are excerpted to provide a concise summary of his principal findings. Briefly, Fenno studied six important committees in the House of Representatives: Appropriations, Ways and Means, Interior, Post Office, Education and Labor, and Foreign Affairs. He discovered that the committees behaved differently according to the goals pursued by their members, the external political constraints placed upon them by other interested parties, and the "decision rules" adopted to accommodate these pressures and to conduct committee business. In some cases, committees developed a high degree of consensus on goals and the rules of decision making; in others, much less. For some (for instance, Education and Labor), external clientele groups were an especially salient constraint; in others (Appropriations as well as Ways and Means), the dominant imperative was to wield influence *inside* Congress. The Appropriations committee functioned in such a fashion as to ensure that the parent chamber would acquiesce to its recommendations almost routinely.

23

JAMES MADISON

FEDERALIST 51

James Madison explains the theory behind the constitutional separation of powers and how it is augmented by federalism. ". . . [T]he great security against a gradual concentration of the several powers in the same department [i.e., branch] consists of giving to those who administer each department the necessary constitutional means and personal motives to resist encroachments of the others. . . . Ambition must be made to counteract ambition." Following these principles, Congress is divided and each house is rendered ". . . by different modes of election and different principles of action, as little connected with each other as the nature of their common functions and their common dependence on the society will admit."

To what expedient, then, shall we finally resort, for maintaining in practice the necessary partition of power among the several departments as laid down in the Constitution? The only answer that can be given is that as all these exterior provisions are found to be inadequate the defect must be supplied, by so contriving the interior structure of the government as that its several constituent parts may, by their mutual relations, be the means of keeping each other in their proper places. Without presuming to undertake a full development of this important idea I will hazard a few general observations which may perhaps place it in a clearer light, and enable us to form a more correct judgment of the principles and structure of the government planned by the convention.

In order to lay a due foundation for that separate and distinct exercise of the different powers of government, which to a certain extent is admitted on all hands to be essential to the preservation of liberty, it is evident that each department should have a will of its own; and consequently should be so constituted that the members of each should have as little agency as possible in the appointment of the members of the others. Were this principle rigorously adhered to, it would require that all the appointments for the supreme executive, legislative, and judiciary magistracies should be drawn from the same fountain of authority, the people, through channels having no communication whatever with one another. Perhaps such a plan of constructing the several departments would be less difficult in practice than it may in contemplation appear. Some difficulties, however, and some additional expense would attend the execution of it. Some deviations, therefore, from the principle must be admitted. In the constitution of the judiciary department in particular, it might be inexpedient to insist rigorously on the principle: first, because peculiar qualifications being essential in the members, the primary consideration ought to be to select that mode of choice which best secures these qualifications; second, because the permanent tenure by which the appointments are held in that department must soon destroy all sense of dependence on the authority conferring them.

It is equally evident that the members of each department should be as little dependent as possible on those of the others for the emoluments annexed to their

offices. Were the executive magistrate, or the judges, not independent of the legislature in this particular, their independence in every other would be merely
nominal.

But the great security against a gradual concentration of the several powers in
the same department consists in giving to those who administer each department
the necessary constitutional means and personal motives to resist encroachments
of the others. The provision for defense must in this, as in all other cases, be made
commensurate to the danger of attack. Ambition must be made to counteract
ambition. The interest of the man must be connected with the constitutional
rights of the place. It may be a reflection on human nature that such devices
should be necessary to control the abuses of government. But what is government
itself but the greatest of all reflections on human nature? If men were angels, no
government would be necessary. If angels were to govern men, neither external
nor internal controls on government would be necessary. In framing a government which is to be administered by men over men, the great difficulty lies in
this: you must first enable the government to control the governed; and in the
next place oblige it to control itself. A dependence on the people is, no doubt,
the primary control on the government; but experience has taught mankind the
necessity of auxiliary precautions.

This policy of supplying, by opposite and rival interests, the defect of better
motives, might be traced through the whole system of human affairs, private as well
as public. We see it particularly displayed in all the subordinate distributions of
power, where the constant aim is to divide and arrange the several offices in such a
manner as that each may be a check on the other—that the private interest of every
individual may be a sentinel over the public rights. These inventions of prudence
cannot be less requisite in the distribution of the supreme powers of the State.

But it is not possible to give to each department an equal power of self-defense.
In republican government, the legislative authority necessarily predominates.
The remedy for this inconveniency is to divide the legislature into different
branches; and to render them, by different modes of election and different principles of action, as little connected with each other as the nature of their common
functions and their common dependence on the society will admit. It may even
be necessary to guard against dangerous encroachments by still further precautions. As the weight of the legislative authority requires that it should be thus
divided, the weakness of the executive may require, on the other hand, that it
should be fortified. An absolute negative on the legislature appears, at first view,
to be the natural defense with which the executive magistrate should be armed.
But perhaps it would be neither altogether safe nor alone sufficient. On ordinary
occasions it might not be exerted with the requisite firmness, and on extraordinary occasions it might be perfidiously abused. May not this defect of an absolute
negative be supplied by some qualified connection between this weaker department and the weaker branch of the stronger department, by which the latter may
be led to support the constitutional rights of the former, without being too much
detached from the rights of its own department?

If the principles on which these observations are founded be just, as I persuade
myself they are, and they be applied as a criterion to the several State constitu-

tions, and to the federal Constitution, it will be found that if the latter does not perfectly correspond with them, the former are infinitely less able to bear such a test.

There are, moreover, two considerations particularly applicable to the federal system of America, which place that system in a very interesting point of view.

First. In a single republic, all the power surrendered by the people is submitted to the administration of a single government; and the usurpations are guarded against by a division of the government into distinct and separate departments. In the compound republic of America, the power surrendered by the people is first divided between two distinct governments, and then the portion allotted to each subdivided among distinct and separate departments. Hence a double security arises to the rights of the people. The different governments will control each other, at the same time that each will be controlled by itself.

Second. It is of great importance in a republic not only to guard the society against the oppression of its rulers, but to guard one part of the society against the injustice of the other part. Different interests necessarily exist in different classes of citizens. If a majority be united by a common interest, the rights of the minority will be insecure. There are but two methods of providing against this evil: the one by creating a will in the community independent of the majority—that is, of the society itself; the other, by comprehending in the society so many separate descriptions of citizens as will render an unjust combination of a majority of the whole very improbable, if not impracticable. The first method prevails in all governments possessing an hereditary or self-appointed authority. This, at best, is but a precarious security; because a power independent of the society may as well espouse the unjust views of the major as the rightful interests of the minor party, and may possibly be turned against both parties. The second method will be exemplified in the federal republic of the United States. Whilst all authority in it will be derived from and dependent on the society, the society itself will be broken into so many parts, interests and classes of citizens, that the rights of individuals, or of the minority, will be in little danger from interested combinations of the majority. In a free government the security for civil rights must be the same as that for religious rights. It consists in the one case in the multiplicity of interests, and in the other in the multiplicity of sects. The degree of security in both cases will depend on the number of interests and sects; and this may be presumed to depend on the extent of country and number of people comprehended under the same government. This view of the subject must particularly recommend a proper federal system to all the sincere and considerate friends of republican government, since it shows that in exact proportion as the territory of the Union may be formed into more circumscribed Confederacies, or States, oppressive combinations of a majority will be facilitated; the best security, under the republican forms, for the rights of every class of citizen, will be diminished; and consequently the stability and independence of some member of the government, the only other security, must be proportionally increased. Justice is the end of government. It is the end of civil society. It ever has been and ever will be pursued until it be obtained, or until liberty be lost in the pursuit. In a society under the forms of which the stronger faction can readily unite and oppress the weaker, anarchy may as truly be said to reign as in a state of nature, where the weaker individual is not secured against the violence of the stronger; and as, in the latter state, even the stronger individuals are prompted, by the uncertainty of their condition, to submit to a government which may protect the weak as well as themselves; so, in the former state, will the more powerful factions or parties be gradually induced, by a like motive, to wish for a government which will protect all parties, the weaker as well as the more powerful. It can be little doubted that if the State of Rhode Island was separated from the Confederacy and left to itself, the insecurity of rights under the popular form of government within such narrow limits would be displayed by such reiterated oppressions of factious majorities that some power altogether independent of the people would soon be called for by the voice of the very factions whose misrule had proved the necessity of it. In the extended republic of the United States, and among the great variety of interests, parties, and sects which it embraces, a coalition of a majority of the whole society could seldom take place on any other principles than those of justice and the general good; whilst there being thus less danger to a minor from the will of a major party, there must be less pretext, also, to provide for the security of the former, by introducing into the government a will not dependent on the latter, or, in other words, a will independent of the society itself. It is no less certain than it is important, notwithstanding the contrary opinions which have been entertained, that the larger the society, provided it lie within a practicable sphere, the more duly capable it will be of self-government. And happily for the *republican cause*, the practicable sphere may be carried to a very great extent by a judicious modification and mixture of the *federal principle*.

24

WARREN E. MILLER AND DONALD E. STOKES

CONSTITUENCY INFLUENCE IN CONGRESS

To what extent and in what ways are members of the House of Representatives influenced by the attitudes of their constituents? Warren E. Miller and Donald E. Stokes empirically test the widespread assumption that representatives are influenced substantially by their constituents. They conclude that the relationship of representatives to voters is complex and influenced by a number of intermediaries, such as the media, local political parties, and interest groups. The relationship also varies among different policy arenas. Warren Miller, teaches political science at Arizona State University. Donald Stokes served for many years as dean of the Woodrow Wilson School at Princeton University.

Substantial constituency influence over the lower house of Congress is commonly thought to be both a normative principle and a factual truth of American government. From their draft constitution we may assume the Founding Fathers expected it, and many political scientists feel, regretfully, that the Framers' wish has come all too true.[1] Nevertheless, much of the evidence of constituency control rests on inference. The fact that our House of Representatives, especially by comparison with the House of Commons, has irregular party voting does not of itself indicate that Congressmen deviate from party in response to local pressure. And even more, the fact that many Congressmen *feel* pressure from home does not of itself establish that the local constituency is performing any of the acts that a reasonable definition of control would imply.

I. CONSTITUENCY CONTROL IN THE NORMATIVE THEORY OF REPRESENTATION

Control by the local constituency is at one pole of *both* the great normative controversies about representation that have arisen in modern times. It is generally recognized that constituency control is opposite to the conception of representation associated with Edmund Burke. Burke wanted the representative to serve the constituency's *interest* but not its *will*, and the extent to which the representative should be compelled by electoral sanctions to follow the "mandate" of his constituents has been at the heart of the ensuing controversy as it has continued for a century and a half.[2]

Constituency control also is opposite to the conception of government by responsible national parties. This is widely seen, yet the point is rarely connected with normative discussions of representation. Indeed, it is remarkable how little attention has been given to the model of representation implicit in the doctrine of a "responsible two-party system." When the subject of representation is broached among political scientists the classical argument between Burke and his opponents is likely to come at once to mind. So great is Burke's influence that the antithesis he proposed still provides the categories of thought used in contemporary treatments of representation despite the fact that many students of politics today would advocate a relationship between representative and constituency that fits *neither* position of the mandate-independence controversy.

The conception of representation implicit in the doctrine of responsible parties shares the idea of popular control with the instructed-delegate model. Both are versions of popular sovereignty. But "the people" of the responsible two-party system are conceived in terms of a national rather than a local constituency. Candidates for legislative office appeal to the electorate in terms of a *national* party program and leadership, to which, if elected, they will be committed. Expressions of policy preference by the local district are reduced to endorsements of one or another of these programs, and the local district retains only the arithmetical significance that whichever party can rally to its program the greater number of supporters in the district will control its legislative seat.

No one tradition of representation has entirely dominated American practice. Elements of the Burkean, instructed-delegate, and responsible party models can all be found in our political life. Yet if the American system has elements of all three, a good deal depends on how they are combined. Especially critical is the question whether different models of representation apply to different public issues. Is the saliency of legislative action to the public so different in quality and degree on different issues that the legislator is subject to very different constraints from his constituency? Does the legislator have a single generalized mode of response to his constituency that is rooted in a normative belief about the representative's role or does the same legislator respond to his constituency differently on different issues? More evidence is needed on matters so fundamental to our system.

II. AN EMPIRICAL STUDY OF REPRESENTATION

To extend what we know of representation in the American Congress the Survey Research Center of the University of Michigan interviewed the incumbent Congressman, his non-incumbent opponent (if any), and a sample of constituents in each of 116 congressional districts, which were themselves a probability sample of all districts.[3] These interviews, conducted immediately after the congressional election of 1958, explored a wide range of attitudes and perceptions held by the individuals who play the reciprocal roles of the representative relation in national government. The distinguishing feature of this research is, of course, that it sought direct information from both constituent and legislator (actual and aspiring). To this fund of comparative interview data has been added information about the roll call votes of our sample of Congressmen and the political and social characteristics of the districts they represent.

Many students of politics, with excellent reason, have been sensitive to possible ties between representative and constituent that have little to do with issues of public policy. For example, ethnic identifications may cement a legislator in the affections of his district, whatever (within limits) his stands on issues. And many Congressmen keep their tenure of office secure by skillful provision of district benefits ranging from free literature to major federal projects. In the full study of which this analysis is part we have explored several bases of constituency support that have little to do with policy issues. Nevertheless, the question how the representative should make up his mind on legislative issues is what the classical arguments over representation are all about, and we have given a central place to a comparison of the policy preferences of constituents and Representatives and to a causal analysis of the relation between the two.

In view of the electorate's scanty information about government it was not at all clear in advance that such a comparison could be made. Some of the more buoyant advocates of popular sovereignty have regarded the citizen as a kind of kibitzer who looks over the shoulder of his representative at the legislative game. Kibitzer and player may disagree as to which card should be played, but they were at least thought to share a common understanding of what the alternatives are.

No one familiar with the findings of research on mass electorates could accept this view of the citizen. Far from looking over the shoulder of their Congressmen at the legislative game, most Americans are almost totally uninformed about legislative issues in Washington. At best the average citizen may be said to have some general ideas about how the country should be run, which he is able to use in responding to particular questions about what the government ought to do. For example, survey studies have shown that most people have a general (though differing) conception of how far government should go to achieve social and economic welfare objectives and that these convictions fix their response to various particular questions about actions government might take.[4]

What makes it possible to compare the policy preferences of constituents and Representatives despite the public's low awareness of legislative affairs is the fact that Congressmen themselves respond to many issues in terms of fairly broad evaluative dimensions. Undoubtedly policy alternatives are judged in the executive agencies and the specialized committees of the Congress by criteria that are relatively complex and specific to the policies at issue. But a good deal of evidence goes to show that when proposals come before the House as a whole they are judged on the basis of more general evaluative dimensions.[5] For example, most Congressmen, too, seem to have a general conception of how far government should go in the area of domestic social and economic welfare, and these general positions apparently orient their roll call votes on a number of particular social welfare issues.

It follows that such a broad evaluative dimension can be used to compare the policy preferences of constituents and Representatives despite the low state of the public's information about politics. In this study three such dimensions have been drawn from our voter interviews and from congressional interviews and roll call records. As suggested above, one of these has to do with approval of government action in the social welfare field, the primary domestic issue of the New Deal-Fair Deal (and New Frontier) eras. A second dimension has to do with support for American involvement in foreign affairs, a latter-day version of the isolationist-internationalist continuum. A third dimension has to do with approval of federal action to protect the civil rights of Negroes.[6]

Because our research focused on these three dimensions, our analysis of constituency influence is limited to these areas of policy. No point has been more energetically or usefully made by those who have sought to clarify the concepts of power and influence than the necessity of specifying the acts *with respect to which* one actor has power or control over another.[7] Therefore, the scope or range of influence for our analysis is the collection of legislative issues falling within our three policy domains. We are not able to say how much control the local constituency may or may not have over *all* actions of its Representative, and there may well be pork-barrel issues or other matters of peculiar relevance to the district on which the relation of Congressman to constituency is quite distinctive. However, few observers of contemporary politics would regard the issues of government provision of social and economic welfare, of American involvement in world affairs, and of federal action in behalf of the Negro as constituting a trivial range of action. Indeed, these domains together include most of the great issues that have come before Congress in recent years.

In each policy domain we have used the procedures of cumulative scaling, as developed by Louis Guttman and others, to order our samples of Congressmen, of opposing candidates, and of voters. In each domain Congressmen were ranked once according to their roll call votes in the House and again according to the attitudes they revealed in our confidential interviews. These two orderings are by no means identical, nor are the discrepancies due simply to uncertainties of measurement.[8] Opposing candidates also were ranked in each policy domain according to the attitudes they revealed in our interviews. The nationwide sample of constituents was ordered in each domain, and by averaging the attitude scores of all constituents living in the same districts, whole constituencies were ranked on each dimension so that the views of Congressmen could be compared with those of their constituencies.[9] Finally, by considering only the constituents in each district who share some characteristic (voting for the incumbent, say) we were able to order these fractions of districts so that the opinions of Congressmen could be compared with those, for example, of the dominant electoral elements of their districts.

In each policy domain, crossing the rankings of Congressmen and their constituencies gives an empirical measure of the extent of policy agreement between legislator and district.[10] In the period of our research this procedure reveals very different degrees of policy congruence across the three issue domains. On questions of social and economic welfare there is considerable agreement between Representative and district, expressed by a correlation of approximately 0.3. This coefficient is, of course, very much less than the limiting value of 1.0, indicating that a number of Congressmen are, relatively speaking, more or less "liberal" than their districts. However, on the question of foreign involvement there is no discernible agreement between legislator and district whatever. Indeed, as if to emphasize the point, the coefficient expressing this relation is slightly negative (−0.09), although not significantly so in a statistical sense. It is in the domain of civil rights that the rankings of Congressmen and constituencies most nearly agree. When we took our measurements in the late 1950s the correlation of congressional roll call behavior with constituency opinion on questions affecting the Negro was nearly 0.6.

The description of policy agreement that these three simple correlations give can be a starting-point for a wide range of analyses. For example, the significance of party competition in the district for policy representation can be explored by comparing the agreement between district and Congressman with the agreement between the district and the Congressman's non-incumbent opponent. Alternatively, the significance of choosing Representatives from single-member districts by popular majority can be explored by comparing the agreement between the Congressman and his own supporters with the agreement between the Congressman and the supporters of his opponent. Taking *both* party competition and majority rule into account magnifies rather spectacularly some of the coefficients reported here. This is most true in the domain of social welfare, where attitudes both of candidates and of voters are most polarized along party lines. Whereas the correlation between the constituency majority and congressional roll call votes is nearly +0.4 on social welfare policy, the correlation of the district majority with the non-incumbent candidate is –0.4. This difference, amounting to almost 0.8, between these two coefficients is an indicator of what the dominant electoral element of the constituency gets on the average by choosing the Congressman it has and excluding his opponent from office.[11]

These three coefficients are also the starting-point for a causal analysis of the relation of constituency to representative, the main problem of this paper. At least on social welfare and Negro rights a measurable degree of congruence is found between district and legislator. Is this agreement due to constituency influence in Congress, or is it to be attributed to other causes? If this question is to have a satisfactory answer the conditions that are necessary and sufficient to assure constituency control must be stated and compared with the available empirical evidence.

III. THE CONDITIONS OF CONSTITUENCY INFLUENCE

Broadly speaking, the constituency can control the policy actions of the Representative in two alternative ways. The first of these is for the district to choose a Representative who so shares its views that in following his own convictions he does his constituents' will. In this case district opinion and the Congressman's actions are connected through the Representative's own policy attitudes. The second means of constituency control is for the Congressman to follow his (at least tolerably accurate) perceptions of district attitude in order to win re-election. In this case constituency opinion and the Congressman's actions are connected through his perception of what the district wants.[12]

These two paths of constituency control are presented schematically in Figure 1. As the figure suggests, each path has two steps, one connecting the constituency's attitude with an "intervening" attitude or perception, the other connecting this attitude or perception with the Representative's roll call behavior. Out of respect for the processes by which the human actor achieves cognitive congruence we have also drawn arrows between the two intervening factors, since the Congressman probably tends to see his district as having the same opinion as his own and also tends, over time, to bring his own opinion into line with the district's. The inclusion of these arrows calls attention to two other possible

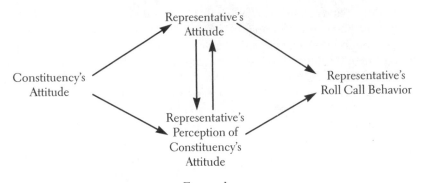

FIGURE 1
CONNECTIONS BETWEEN A CONSTITUENCY'S ATTITUDE AND ITS REPRESENTATIVE'S
ROLL CALL BEHAVIOR

influence paths, each consisting of *three* steps, although these additional paths will turn out to be of relatively slight importance empirically.

Neither of the main influence paths of Figure 1 will connect the final roll call vote to the constituency's views if either of its steps is blocked. From this, two necessary conditions of constituency influence can be stated: *first*, the Representative's votes in the House must agree substantially with his own policy views or his perceptions of the district's views, and not be determined entirely by other influences to which the Congressman is exposed; and, *second*, the attitudes or perceptions governing the Representative's acts must correspond, at least imperfectly, to the district's actual opinions. It would be difficult to describe the relation of constituency to Representative as one of control unless these conditions are met.[13]

Yet these two requirements are not sufficient to assure control. A *third* condition must also be satisfied: the constituency must in some measure take the policy views of candidates into account in choosing a Representative. If it does not, agreement between district and Congressman may arise for reasons that cannot rationally be brought within the idea of control. For example, such agreement may simply reflect the fact that a Representative drawn from a given area is likely, by pure statistical probability, to share its dominant values, without his acceptance or rejection of these ever having been a matter of consequence to his electors.

IV. EVIDENCE OF CONTROL: CONGRESSIONAL ATTITUDES AND PERCEPTIONS

How well are these conditions met in the relation of American Congressmen to their constituents? There is little question that the first is substantially satisfied; the evidence of our research indicates that members of the House do in fact vote both their own policy views and their perceptions of their constituents' views, at least on issues of social welfare, foreign involvement, and civil rights. If these two intervening factors are used to predict roll call votes, the prediction is quite successful. Their multiple correlation with roll call position is 0.7 for social welfare, 0.6 for foreign involvement, and 0.9 for civil rights; the last figure is especially persuasive. What is more, both the Congressman's own convictions and his perceptions of district opinion make a distinct contribution to his roll call behavior. In each of the three domains the prediction of roll call votes is surer if it is made from both factors rather than from either alone.

Lest the strong influence that the Congressman's views and his perception of district views have on roll call behavior appear somehow foreordained—and, consequently, this finding seem a trivial one—it is worth taking a sidewise glance at the potency of possible other forces on the Representative's vote. In the area of foreign policy, for example, a number of Congressmen are disposed to follow the administration's advice, whatever they or their districts think. For those who are, the multiple correlation of roll call behavior with the Representative's own foreign policy views and his perception of district views is a mere 0.2. Other findings could be cited to support the point that the influence of the Congressman's own preferences and those he attributes to the district is extremely variable. Yet in the House as a whole over the three policy domains the influence of these forces is quite strong.

The connections of congressional attitudes and perceptions with actual constituency opinion are weaker. If policy agreement between district and Representative is moderate and variable across the policy domains, as it is, this is to be explained much more in terms of the second condition of constituency control than the first. The Representative's attitudes and perceptions most nearly match true opinion in his district on the issues of Negro rights. Reflecting the charged and polarized nature of this area, the correlation of actual district opinion with perceived opinion is greater than 0.6, and the correlation of district attitude with the Representative's own attitude is nearly 0.4, as shown by Table 1. But the comparable correlations for foreign involvement are much smaller—indeed almost negligible. And the coefficients for social welfare are also smaller, although a detailed presentation of findings in this area would show that the Representative's perceptions and attitudes are more strongly associated with the attitude of his electoral *majority* than they are with the attitudes of the constituency as a whole.

Knowing this much about the various paths that may lead, directly or indirectly, from constituency attitude to roll call vote, we can assess their relative importance. Since the alternative influence chains have links of unequal strength, the full chains will not in general be equally strong, and these differences are of great importance in the relation of Representative to constituency. For the domain of civil rights Figure 2 assembles all the intercorrelations of the variables of our

TABLE 1. CORRELATIONS OF CONSTITUENCY ATTITUDES

	CORRELATION OF CONSTITUENCY ATTITUDE WITH	
	---	---
Policy Domain	*Representative's Perception of Constituency Attitude*	*Representative's Own Attitude*
Social welfare	.17	.21
Foreign involvement	.19	.06
Civil rights	.63	.39

Civil Rights: Intercorrelations

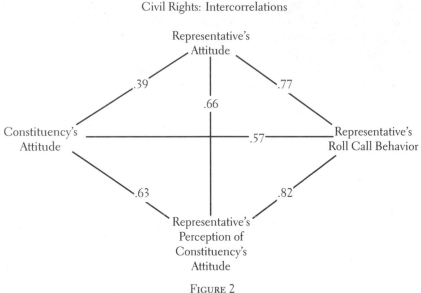

FIGURE 2

INTERCORRELATIONS OF VARIABLES PERTAINING TO CIVIL RIGHTS

system. As the figure shows, the root correlation of constituency attitude with roll call behavior in this domain is 0.57. How much of this policy congruence can be accounted for by the influence path involving the Representative's attitude? And how much by the path involving his perception of constituency opinion? When the intercorrelations of the system are interpreted in the light of what we assume its causal structure to be, it is influence passing through the Congressman's perception of the district's views that is found to be preeminently important.[14] Under the least favorable assumption as to its importance, this path is found to account for more than twice as much of the variance of roll call behavior as the paths involving the Representative's own attitude.[15] However, when this same procedure is applied to our social welfare data, the results suggest that the direct connection of constituency and roll call through the Congressman's own attitude is the most important of the alternative paths.[16] The reversal of the relative importance of the two paths as we move from civil rights to social welfare is one of the most striking findings of this analysis.

V. EVIDENCE OF CONTROL: ELECTORAL BEHAVIOR

Of the three conditions of constituency influence, the requirement that the electorate take account of the policy positions of the candidates is the hardest to match with empirical evidence. Indeed, given the limited information the average voter carries to the polls, the public might be thought incompetent to perform any task of appraisal. Of constituents living in congressional districts where there was a contest between a Republican and a Democrat in 1958, less than one in five said they had read or heard something about both candidates, and well over half conceded they had read or heard nothing about either. And these proportions are not much better when they are based only on the part of the sample, not much more than half, that reported voting for Congress in 1958. The extent of awareness of the candidates among voters is indicated in Table 2. As the table shows, even of the portion of the public that was sufficiently interested to vote, almost half had read or heard nothing about either candidate.

Just how low a hurdle our respondents had to clear in saying they had read or heard something about a candidate is indicated by detailed qualitative analysis of the information constituents *were* able to associate with congressional candidates. Except in rare cases, what the voters "knew" was confined to diffuse evaluative judgments about the candidate: "he's a good man," "he understands the problems," and so forth. Of detailed information about policy stands not more than a chemical trace was found. Among the comments about the candidates given in response to an extended series of free-answer questions, less than two percent had to do with stands in our three policy domains; indeed, only about three comments in every hundred had to do with legislative issues of *any* description.[17]

This evidence that the behavior of the electorate is largely unaffected by knowledge of the policy positions of the candidates is complemented by evidence about the forces that *do* shape the voters' choices among congressional candidates. The primary basis of voting in American congressional elections is identification with party. In 1958 only one vote in twenty was cast by persons without any sort of party loyalty. And among those who did have a party identification, only one in ten voted against their party. As a result, something like 84 percent of the vote that year was cast by party identifiers voting their usual party line. What is more, traditional party voting is seldom connected with current legislative issues. As the party loyalists in a nationwide sample of voters told us what they liked and disliked about the parties in 1958, only a small fraction of the comments (about 15 percent) dealt with current issues of public policy.[18]

Yet the idea of reward or punishment at the polls for legislative stands is familiar to members of Congress, who feel that they and their records are quite visible to their constituents. Of our sample of Congressmen who were opposed for re-election in 1958, more than four-fifths said the outcome in their districts had been strongly influenced by the electorate's response to their records and personal standing.

TABLE 2. AWARENESS OF CONGRESSIONAL CANDIDATES AMONG VOTERS, 1958

		READ OR HEARD SOMETHING ABOUT INCUMBENT[a]		
		Yes	No	
Read or Heard Something about Non-Incumbent	Yes	24	5	29
	No	25	46	71
		49	51	100%

[a] In order to include all districts where the House seat was contested in 1958 this table retains ten constituencies in which the incumbent Congressman did not seek re-election. Candidates of the retiring incumbent's party in these districts are treated here as if they were incumbents. Were these figures to be calculated only for constituencies in which an incumbent sought re-election, no entry in this four-fold table would differ from that given by more than 2 percent.

Indeed, this belief is clear enough to present a notable contradiction: Congressmen feet that their individual legislative actions may have considerable impact on the electorate, yet some simple facts about the Representative's salience to his constituents imply that this could hardly be true.

In some measure this contradiction is to be explained by the tendency of Congressmen to overestimate their visibility to the local public, a tendency that reflects the difficulties of the Representative in forming a correct judgment of constituent opinion. The communication most Congressmen have with their district inevitably puts them in touch with organized groups and with individuals who are relatively well informed about politics. The Representative knows his constituents mostly from dealing with people who *do* write letters, who *will* attend meetings, who *have* an interest in his legislative stands. As a result, his sample of contacts with a constituency of several hundred thousand people is heavily biased: even the contacts he apparently makes at random are likely to be with people who grossly overrepresent the degree of political information and interest in the constituency as a whole.

But the contradiction is also to be explained by several aspects of the Representative's electoral situation that are of great importance to the question of constituency influence. The first of these is implicit in what has already been said. Because of the pervasive effects of party loyalties, no candidate for Congress starts from scratch in putting together an electoral majority. The Congressman is a dealer in increments and margins. He starts with a stratum of hardened party voters, and if the stratum is broad enough he can have a measurable influence on his chance of survival simply by attracting a small additional element of the electorate—or by not losing a larger one. Therefore, his record may have a very real bearing on his electoral success or failure without most of his constituents ever knowing what that record is.

Second, the relation of Congressman to voter is not a simple bilateral one but is complicated by the presence of all manner of intermediaries: the local party, economic interests, the news media, racial and nationality organizations, and so forth. Such is the lore of American politics, as it is known to any political scientist. Very often the Representative reaches the mass public through these mediating agencies, and the information about himself and his record may be considerably transformed as it diffuses out to the electorate in two or more stages. As a result, the public—or parts of it—may get simple positive or negative cues about the Congressman which were provoked by his legislative actions but which no longer have a recognizable issue content.

Third, for most Congressmen most of the time the electorate's sanctions are potential rather than actual. Particularly the Representative from a safe district may feel his proper legislative strategy is to avoid giving opponents in his own party or outside of it material they can use against him. As the Congressman pursues this strategy he may write a legislative record that never becomes very well known to his constituents; if it doesn't win votes, neither will it lose any. This is clearly the situation of most southern Congressmen in dealing with the issue of Negro rights. By voting correctly on this issue they are unlikely to increase their visibility to constituents. Nevertheless, the fact of constituency influence, backed by potential sanctions at the polls, is real enough.

TABLE 3. AWARENESS OF CONGRESSIONAL CANDIDATES AMONG VOTERS
IN ARKANSAS FIFTH DISTRICT, 1958

| | | READ OR HEARD SOMETHING ABOUT HAYS | | |
		Yes	No	
Read or Heard Something about Alford	Yes	100	0	100
	No	0	0	0
		100	0	100%

That these potential sanctions are all too real is best illustrated in the election of 1958 by the reprisal against Representative Brooks Hays in Arkansas' Fifth District.[19] Although the perception of Congressman Hays as too moderate on civil rights resulted more from his service as intermediary between the White House and Governor Faubus in the Little Rock school crisis than from his record in the House, the victory of Dale Alford as a write-in candidate was a striking reminder of what can happen to a Congressman who gives his foes a powerful issue to use against him. The extraordinary involvement of the public in this race can be seen by comparing how well the candidates were known in this constituency with the awareness of the candidates shown by Table 2 [p. 289] for the country as a whole. As Table 3 indicates, not a single voter in our sample of Arkansas' Fifth District was unaware of either candidate.[20] What is more, these interviews show that Hays was regarded both by his supporters and his opponents as more moderate than Alford on civil rights and that this perception brought his defeat. In some measure, what happened in Little Rock in 1958 can happen anywhere, and our Congressmen ought not to be entirely disbelieved in what they say about their impact at the polls. Indeed, they may be under genuine pressure from the voters even while they are the forgotten men of national elections.[21]

VI. CONCLUSION

Therefore, although the conditions of constituency influence are not equally satisfied, they are met well enough to give the local constituency a measure of control over the actions of its Representatives. Best satisfied is the requirement about motivational influences on the Congressman: our evidence shows that the Representative's roll call behavior is strongly influenced by his own policy preferences and by his perception of preferences held by the constituency. However, the conditions of influence that presuppose effective communication between Congressman and district are much less well met. The Representative has very imperfect information about the issue preferences of his constituency, and the constituency's awareness of the policy stands of the Representative ordinarily is slight.

The findings of this analysis heavily underscore the fact that no single tradition of representation fully accords with the realities of American legislative politics. The American system *is* a mixture, to which the Burkean, instructed-delegate, and responsible-party models all can be said to have contributed elements. Moreover, variations in the representative relation are most likely to occur as we move from one policy domain to another. No single, generalized configuration of attitudes and perceptions links Representative with constituency but rather several distinct patterns, and which of them is invoked depends very much on the issue involved.

The issue domain in which the relation of Congressman to constituency most nearly conforms to the instructed-delegate model is that of civil rights. This conclusion is supported by the importance of the influence-path passing through the Representative's perception of district opinion, although even in this domain the sense in which the constituency may be said to take the position of the candidate into account in reaching its electoral judgment should be carefully qualified.

The representative relation conforms most closely to the responsible-party model in the domain of social welfare. In this issue area, the arena of partisan conflict for a generation, the party symbol helps both constituency and Representative in the difficult process of communication between them. On the one hand, because Republican and Democratic voters tend to differ in what they would have government do, the Representative has some guide to district opinion simply by looking at the partisan division of the vote. On the other hand, because the two parties tend to recruit candidates who differ on the social welfare role of government, the constituency can infer the candidates' position with more than random accuracy from their party affiliation, even though what the constituency has learned directly about these stands is almost nothing. How faithful the representation of social welfare views is to the responsible-party model should not be exaggerated. Even in this policy domain, American practice departs widely from an ideal conception of party government.[22] But in this domain, more than any other, political conflict has become a conflict of national parties in which constituency and Representative are known to each other primarily by their party association.

It would be too pat to say that the domain of foreign involvement conforms to the third model of representation, the conception promoted by Edmund Burke. Clearly it does in the sense that the Congressman looks elsewhere than to his district in making up his mind on foreign issues. However, the reliance he puts on the President and the Administration suggests that the calculation of where the public interest lies is often passed to the Executive on matters of foreign policy. Ironically, legislative initiative in foreign affairs has fallen victim to the very difficulties of gathering and appraising information that led Burke to argue that Parliament rather than the public ought to hold the power of decision. The background information and predictive skills that Burke thought the people lacked are held primarily by the modern Executive. As a result, the present role of the legislature in foreign affairs bears some resemblance to the role that Burke had in mind for the elitist, highly restricted *electorate* of his own day.

NOTES

1. To be sure, the work of the Federal Convention has been supplemented in two critical respects. The first of these is the practice, virtually universal since the mid-nineteenth Century, of choosing Representatives from single-member districts of limited geographic area. The second is the practice, which has also become virtually universal in our own century, of selecting party nominees for the House by direct primary election.

2. In the language of Eulau, Wahlke, et al., we speak here of the "style," not the "focus," of representation. See their "The Role of the Representative: Some Empirical Observations on the Theory of Edmund Burke," this *Review*, 53 (September, 1959): pp. 742–756. An excellent review of the mandate-independence controversy is given by Hanna Fenichel Pitkin, "The Theory of Representation" (unpublished doctoral dissertation, University of California, Berkeley, 1961). For other contemporary discussions of representation, see Alfred de Grazia, *Public and Republic* (New York, 1951), and John A. Fairlie, "The Nature of Political Representation," this *Review* 34 (April–June, 1940): pp. 236–248, 456–466.

3. The sampling aspects of this research were complicated by the fact that the study of representation was a rider midway on a four-year panel study of the electorate whose primary sampling units were not congressional districts (although there is no technical reason why they could not have been if the needs of the representation analysis had been foreseen when the design of the sample was fixed two years before). As a result, the districts in our sample had unequal probabilities of selection and unequal weights in the analysis, making the sample somewhat less efficient than an equal-probability sample of equivalent size.

It will be apparent in the discussion that follows that we have estimated characteristics of whole constituencies from our samples of constituents living in particular districts. In view of the fact that a sample of less than two thousand constituents has been divided among 116 districts, the reader may wonder about the reliability of these estimates. After considerable investigation we have concluded that their sampling error is not so severe a problem for the analysis as we had thought it would be. . . .

4. See Angus Campbell, Philip E. Converse, Warren E. Miller, and Donald E. Stokes, *The American Voter* (New York, 1960): pp. 194–209.

5. This conclusion, fully supported by our own work for later Congresses, is one of the main findings to be drawn from the work of Duncan MacRae on roll call voting in the House of Representatives. See his *Dimensions of Congressional Voting: A Statistical Study of the House of Representatives in the Eighty-First Congress* (Berkeley and Los Angeles: University of California Press, 1958). For additional evidence of the existence of scale dimensions in legislative behavior, see N. L. Gage and Ben Shimberg, "Measuring Senatorial Progressivism," *Journal of Abnormal and Social Psychology* 44 (January 1949): pp. 112–117. George M. Belknap, "A Study of Senatorial Voting by Scale Analysis" (unpublished doctoral dissertation, University of Chicago, 1951), and "A Method for Analyzing Legislative Behavior," *Midwest Journal of Political Science* 2 (1958): pp. 377–402; two other articles by MacRae, "The Role of the State Legislator in Massachusetts," *American Sociological Review* 19 (April 1954): pp. 185–194, and "Roll Call Votes and Leadership," *Public Opinion Quarterly* 20 (1956): pp. 543–558; Charles D. Farris, "A Method of Determining Ideological Groups in Congress," *Journal of Politics* 20 (1958): pp. 308–338; and Leroy N. Rieselbach, "Quantitative Techniques for Studying Voting Behavior in the U. N. General Assembly," *International Organization* 14 (1960): pp. 291–306.

6. The content of the three issue domains may be suggested by some of the roll call and interview items used. In the area of social welfare these included the issues of public housing, public power, aid to education, and government's role in maintaining full employment. In the area of foreign involvement the items included the issues of foreign economic aid, military aid, sending troops abroad, and aid to neutrals. In the area of civil rights the items included the issues of school desegregation, fair employment, and the protection of Negro voting rights.

7. Because this point has been so widely discussed it has inevitably attracted a variety of terms. Dahl denotes the acts of *a* whose performance A is able to influence as the *scope of A's* power. See

Robert A. Dahl, "The Concept of Power," *Behavioral Science* 2 (July 1957): pp. 201–215. This usage is similar to that of Harold D. Lasswell and Abraham Kaplan, *Power and Society* (New Haven: Yale University Press, 1950), pp. 71–73. Dorwin Cartwright, however, denotes the behavioral or psychological changes in P which O is able to induce as the *range of O's power*: "A Field Theoretical Conception of Power," *Studies in Social Power* (Ann Arbor: Research Center for Group Dynamics, Institute for Social Research, The University of Michigan, 1959), pp. 183–220.

8. That the Representative's roll call votes can diverge from his true opinion is borne out by a number of findings of the study (some of which are reported here) as to the conditions under which agreement between the Congressman's roll call position and his private attitude will be high or low. However, a direct confirmation that these two sets of measurements are not simply getting at the same thing is given by differences in attitude-roll call agreement according to the Congressman's sense of how well his roll call votes have expressed his real views. In the domain of foreign involvement, for example, the correlation of our attitudinal and roll call measurements was .75 among Representatives who said that their roll call votes had expressed their real views fairly well. But this correlation was only .04 among those who said that their roll call votes had expressed their views poorly. In the other policy domains, too, attitude-roll call agreement is higher among Congressmen who are well satisfied with their roll call votes than it is among Congressmen who are not.

9. During the analysis we have formed constituency scores out of the scores of constituents living in the same district by several devices other than calculating average constituent scores. In particular, in view of the ordinal character of our scales we have frequently used the *median* constituent score as a central value for the constituency as a whole. However, the ordering of constituencies differs very little according to which of several reasonable alternatives for obtaining constituency scores is chosen. As a result, we have preferred mean scores for the greater number of ranks they give.

10. The meaning of this procedure can be suggested by two percentage tables standing for hypothetical extreme cases, the first that of full agreement, the second that of no agreement whatever. For convenience, these illustrative tables categorize both Congressmen and their districts in terms of only three degrees of favor and assume for both a nearly uniform distribution across the three categories. The terms "pro," "neutral," and "con" indicate a relative rather than an absolute opinion. In Case I, full agreement, all districts relatively favorable to social welfare action have Congressmen who are so too, etc.; whereas in Case II, or that of no agreement, the ordering of constituencies is independent in a statistical sense of the ranking of Congressmen: knowing the policy orientation of a district gives no clue at all to the orientation of its Congressman. Of course, it is possible for the orders of legislators and districts to be *inversely* related, and this possibility is of some importance, as indicated below, when the policy position of non-incumbent candidates as well as incumbents is taken into account. To summarize the degree of congruence between legislators and voters, a measure of correlation is introduced. Although we have used a variety of measures of association in our analysis, the values reported in this article all refer to product moment correlation coefficients. For our hypothetical Case I a measure of correlation would have the value 1.0; for Case II, the value 0.0. When it is applied to actual data this convenient indicator is likely to have a value somewhere in between. The question is where.

Case I: Full Policy Agreement

Congressmen	Constituencies			
	Pro	Neutral	Con	
Pro	33	0	0	33
Neutral	0	34	0	34
Con	0	0	33	33
	33	34	33	100%

Correlation = 1.0

Case II: No Policy Agreement

Constituencies

Congressmen	Pro	Neutral	Con	
Pro	11	11	11	33
Neutral	11	12	11	34
Con	11	11	11	33
	33	34	33	100%

Correlation = 0.0

11. A word of caution is in order, lest we compare things that are not strictly comparable. For obvious reasons, most non-incumbent candidates have no roll call record, and we have had to measure their policy agreement with the district entirely in terms of the attitudes they have revealed in interviews. However, the difference of coefficients given here is almost as great when the policy agreement between the incumbent Congressman and his district is also measured in terms of the attitudes conveyed in confidential interviews.

12. A third type of connection, excluded here, might obtain between district and Congressman if the Representative accedes to what he thinks the district wants because he believes that to be what a representative *ought* to do, whether or not it is necessary for re-election. We leave this type of connection out of our account here because we conceive an influence relation as one in which control is not voluntarily accepted or rejected by someone subject to it. Of course, this possible connection between district and Representative is not any the less interesting because it falls outside our definition of influence or control, and we have given a good deal of attention to it in the broader study of which this analysis is part.

13. It scarcely needs to be said that demonstrating *some* constituency influence would not imply that the Representative's behavior is *wholly* determined by constituency pressures. The legislator acts in a complex institutional setting in which he is subject to a wide variety of influences. The constituency can exercise a genuine measure of control without driving all other influences from the Representative's life space.

14. We have done this by a variance-component technique similar to several others proposed for dealing with problems of this type. See especially Herbert A. Simon, "Spurious Correlation: A Causal Interpretation," *Journal of the American Statistical Association* 49 (1954): pp. 467–479; Hubert M. Blalock, Jr., "The Relative Importance of Variables," *American Sociological Review* 26 (1961): pp. 866–874; and the almost forgotten work of Sewall Wright, "Correlation and Causation," *Journal of Agricultural Research,* 20 (1920): pp. 557–585. Under this technique a "path coefficient" (to use Wright's terminology, although not his theory) is assigned to each of the causal arrows by solving a set of equations involving the correlations of the variables of the model. The weight assigned to a full path is then the product of its several path coefficients, and this product may be interpreted as the proportion of the variance of the dependent variable (roll call behavior, here) that is explained by a given path.

A special problem arises because influence may flow in either direction between the Congressman's attitude and his perception of district attitude (as noted above, the Representative may tend both to perceive his constituency's view selectively, as consistent with his own, and to change his own view to be consistent with the perceived constituency view). Hence, we have single causal model but a whole family of models, varying according to the relative importance of influence from attitude to perception and from perception to attitude. Our solution to this problem has been to calculate influence coefficients for the two extreme models in order to see how much our results could vary according to which model is chosen from our family of models. Since the systems of equations in this analysis are linear it can be shown that the coefficients we seek have their maximum and minimum values under one or the other of the limiting models. Therefore, computing any given coefficient for each of these limiting cases defines an interval in which the true value of the coefficient must lie. In fact these intervals turn out to be fairly small; our findings as to the relative importance of alternative influence paths would change little according to which model is selected.

The two limiting models with their associated systems of equations and the formulas for computing the relative importance of the three possible influence paths under each model are given below.

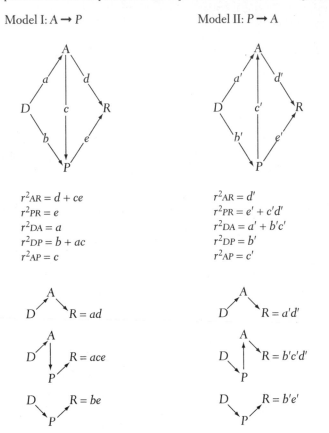

Model I: $A \to P$

$$r^2_{AR} = d + ce$$
$$r^2_{PR} = e$$
$$r^2_{DA} = a$$
$$r^2_{DP} = b + ac$$
$$r^2_{AP} = c$$

$D \nearrow^A \searrow R = ad$

$D \nearrow^A_{\big| P} \searrow R = ace$

$D \searrow_P \nearrow R = be$

Model II: $P \to A$

$$r^2_{AR} = d'$$
$$r^2_{PR} = e' + c'd'$$
$$r^2_{DA} = a' + b'c'$$
$$r^2_{DP} = b'$$
$$r^2_{AP} = c'$$

$D \nearrow^A \searrow R = a'd'$

$D \nearrow^A_{\big| P} \searrow R = b'c'd'$

$D \searrow_P \nearrow R = b'e'$

15. By "least favorable" we mean the assumption that influence goes only from the Congressman's attitude to his perception of district attitude (Model I) and not the other way round. Under this assumption, the proportions of the variance of roll call behavior accounted for by the three alternative paths, expressed as proportions of the part of the variance of roll call votes that is explained by district attitude, are these:

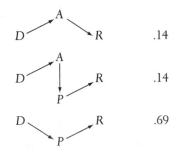

$D \nearrow^A \searrow R \qquad .14$

$D \nearrow^A_{\big| P} \searrow R \qquad .14$

$D \searrow_P \nearrow R \qquad .69$

Inverting the assumed direction of influence between the Congressman's own attitude and district attitude (Model II) eliminates altogether the effect that the Representative's attitude can have had on his votes, independently of his perception of district attitude.

16. Under both Models I and II the proportion of the variance of roll call voting explained by the influence path involving the Representative's own attitude is twice as great as the proportion explained by influence passing through his perception of district attitude.

17. What is more, the electorate's awareness of Congress as a whole appears quite limited. A majority of the public was unable to say in 1958 which of the two parties had controlled the Congress during the preceding two years. Some people were confused by the coexistence of a Republican President and a Democratic Congress. But for most people this was simply an elementary fact about congressional affairs to which they were not privy.

18. For a more extended analysis of the forces on the congressional vote, see Donald E. Stokes and Warren E. Miller, "Party Government and the Saliency of Congress," *Public Opinion Quarterly* 26 (Winter 1962): pp. 531–546.

19. For an account of this episode see Corinne Silverman, "The Little Rock Story," Inter-University Case Program series, reprinted in Edwin A. Bock and Alan K. Campbell, eds., *Case Studies in American Government* (Englewood Cliffs, 1962), pp. 1–46.

20. The sample of this constituency was limited to twenty-three persons of whom thirteen voted. However, despite the small number of cases the probability that the difference in awareness between this constituency and the country generally as the result only of sampling variations is much less than one in a thousand.

21. In view of the potential nature of the constituency's sanctions, it is relevant to characterize its influence over the Representative in terms of several distinctions drawn by recent theorists of power, especially the difference between actual and potential power, between influence and coercive power, and between influence and purposive control. Observing these distinctions, we might say that the constituency's influence is *actual* and not merely *potential* since it is the sanction behavior rather than the conforming behavior that is infrequent (Dahl). That is, the Congressman is influenced by his calculus of potential sanctions, following the "rule of anticipated reactions" (Friedrich), however oblivious of his behavior the constituency ordinarily may be. We might also say that the constituency has *power* since its influence depends partly on sanctions (Lasswell and Kaplan), although it rarely exercises *control* since its influence is rarely conscious or intended (Cartwright). In the discussion above we have of course used the terms "influence" and "control" interchangeably.

22. The factors in American electoral behavior that encourage such a departure are discussed in Stokes and Miller, loc cit.

25

DAVID R. MAYHEW

DIVIDED WE GOVERN

Since the end of World War II, the presidency and at least one house of Congress have frequently been controlled by different political parties, a phenomenon called "divided government." David R. Mayhew, a political science professor at Yale University, asks whether divided government matters in terms of the national government's performance of its core functions. He concludes that ". . . surprisingly it does not seem to make all that much difference whether party control of the American government happens to be unified or divided." This is because at the national level political parties are more like policy factions than governing instruments. Mayhew advises reformers not to channel their energies into " 'party government' schemes" because they fit neither the American constitutional design nor political experience.

. . . [A]re there . . . ways in which unified [UNI] as opposed to divided [DIV] party control might make a significant difference?

There are. In closing, five such ways will be introduced here by posing questions and speculating briefly about what their answers might be. In all instances the speculation ends in skepticism: Unified versus divided control has probably *not* made a notable difference during the postwar era. The arguments stop short of systematic analysis and are thus inconclusive. But they point to relevant kinds of evidence and, perhaps as important, they make a case that evidence is relevant. It is an empirical matter, finally, whether conditions of party control make a difference—regardless of the aspect one is considering. One really does have to look and compare over time. It is not enough, as is often done, to single out some governmental pathology of the 1970s or 1980s, note that party control was divided, set out a plausible connecting logic, and declare divided control to be the culprit.

The first question is: Even if important laws win enactment just as often under conditions of divided party control, might they not be *worse* laws? Isn't "seriously defective legislation" a likelier result?[1] That is sometimes alleged, and if true it would obviously count heavily. The subject is murky, even if kept free of ideological tests of "worseness," but the case seems to have a two-pronged logic. First, enacting coalitions under divided control, being composed of elements not "naturally" united on policy goals, might be less apt to write either clear ends or efficient means into their statutes. Second, such coalitions, absolved from unambiguous "party government" checks by the electorate down the line, might worry less about the actual effects of laws.

For an example, consider the Energy Policy and Conservation Act of 1975, which was voted by a Democratic Congress and signed by Ford but "satisfied no one."[2] It was an awkwardly stitched-together compromise; many others could be cited from times of divided control. Lack of regard for effects— namely, long-run costs—is said to have been exhibited in the immense expansion of entitlements

[Notes have been renumbered.—Eds.]

by Democratic Congresses under Nixon. Promises were just wantonly written into law.[3] In light of the savings-and-loan scandal, it may be worth noting that the Garn-St. Germain Depository Institutions Act, which has been called "perhaps the single most ill-conceived piece of domestic legislation in modern times," was enacted under divided control in 1982.[4] It took the constraints off loans that thrifts could make.

These are reasonable enough logics and instances, but the overall case is dubious. At least as convincing is the logic that enacting coalitions are hard to assemble even if party control is unified; awkwardly stitched-together compromises can occur anyway. In current scholarship, a favorite instance is the Natural Gas Policy Act of 1978—a "convoluted measure" of which "unintended consequences" have been a "hallmark" since its passage.[5] "Because assembling a centrist majority coalition in a polarized ideological conflict depended heavily on granting special favors to narrow groups, the bill created a bizarre and implausible regulatory scheme."[6] That happened in a Democratic Congress under Carter (UNI). Other instances could be cited from times of unified control.

Another consideration is that district-oriented distributive politics can intrude into lawmaking at any time. That is a particular coalition-building tendency that transcends conditions of party control. For example, the "demonstration cities" act of 1966 (UNI) began as a Johnson administration plan to fund some five to ten cities as showcases of urban reform, but the list expanded to 120 to 150 cities in order to assemble a congressional majority for passage. The result was a kind of legislative failure: no showcases, no planned experimentation, just another way of doling out small amounts of money widely.[7]

Unified party control, moreover, can foster a pathological enactment logic all its own. Anyone who witnessed the Great Society will remember Johnson's frenzied drive to pass as many bills as he could while his mandate and sizable Democratic congressional majorities lasted. It was a "politics of haste" in which "solutions were often devised and rushed into law before the problems were understood." "Pass the bill now, worry about its effects and implementation later—this was the White House strategy."[8] That strategy had its chief work-out in 1965 after the 1964 election generated a rare two-to-one Democratic edge in the House, but it figured also in 1964 as Johnson manipulated Democratic majorities in the aftershock of Kennedy's assassination. James L. Sundquist has written of that year's anti-poverty program: "Rarely has so sweeping a commitment been made to an institution so little tested and so little understood as the community action agency [the most prominent creation of the program]. And no time was accorded Congress to find out. . . . On some of the most important sections of the act, little legislative history was written or none at all."[9] Ingenious as the maneuvering to pass it might have been, the anti-poverty program was a "hastily packaged" product that, once enacted, soon lost popular and Capitol Hill support and sowed what Daniel Patrick Moynihan later termed "maximum feasible misunderstanding."[10]

As for reckless expansion of entitlements, that is a question of fact, and the record does not seem to favor unified party control. How about, for example, the expansion during the Great Society (UNI)? In fact, the enacters of Medicare and

Medicaid in 1965 greatly underestimated the long-run costs of the former and scarcely gauged those of the latter at all. "Lyndon Johnson's decision not to run for president in 1967 may have been a wiser one than he realized, for, beyond his troubles with the Vietnam War, he had helped to open the flood gates of public programs without controls. . . . Medicare and Medicaid expenditures were greatly in excess of expectations."[11] It is interesting to note the degree to which criticism of American political institutions lurches from era to era making time-bound diagnoses of what went wrong. As of the 1930s, for example, the leading kind of entitlements pathology was thought to be the veterans bonus bill enacted by a craven Congress over a right-thinking president's veto. That happened at least five times under Coolidge, Hoover, and Franklin Roosevelt between 1924 and 1936, all during times of unified party control.[12] And in the realm of savings-and-loan legislation, the Garn-St. Germain Act of 1982 was in fact the second shoe to drop. The first was the Depository Institutions and Monetary Control Act of 1980 (UNI), which raised interest rates that thrifts could pay and more than doubled federal deposit insurance to $100,000 per account. These were evidently imprudent moves.[13]

A democracy's laws, Tocqueville wrote, "are almost always defective or untimely."[14] That makes a search for "seriously defective legislation" easy. In fact, of course, a great deal of legislation is not seriously defective. At least by the tests of clear ends, effective means, and longevity, the postwar era presents such success stories as the Taft-Hartley Act of 1947, the National Defense Education Act of 1958, the Voting Rights Act of 1965, and the Food Stamp Acts of 1964 and 1970. Lawmaking can obviously work. But whatever the tests, it seems unlikely that divided party control lowers the quality of statutes. As suggestive additional evidence, one can read dozens of legislative histories by policy-area specialists and not come across judgments that it does; it if did, such analysts would probably notice.

The second question is: Even if important individual statutes can win enactment regardless of conditions of party control, how about programmatic "coherence" across statutes? Isn't that a likelier outcome under unified party control? The argument is sometimes made.[15] Confronted by this claim, one's first response is to note that "coherence" exists in the eyes of beholders, that beholders differ in what they see, and in any event, why is "coherence" necessary or desirable? Democracy, according to some leading models, can function well enough as an assortment of decentralized, unconnected incursions into public affairs. Interests, ideas, and causes disjointedly intrude into governmental processes and win victories in Charles E. Lindblom's *Intelligence of Democracy*.[16] "Minorities rule" in Robert A. Dahl's *Preface to Democratic Theory*.[17] Nothing requires the imposition or perception of any kind of cognitive order across governmental activities in general.

Still, widespread agreement does exist about the features and importance of at least two patterns of coherence across statutes, and those should be considered. One is *ideological coherence*, for which an argument might go as follows. To permit broad-ranging change of the sort recommended by ideologies that arise now and then, and to provide a graspable politics to sectors of the public who might be interested in such change, a system needs to allow ideological packaging. That is, it needs to allow, at least sometimes, the enactment of rather large collections of laws thrusting in the same ideological direction. But such packaging has already been discussed. The postwar American system has accommodated it under circumstances of both unified and divided party control—notably in the successfully enacted presidential programs of Johnson (UNI) and Reagan (DIV), and in the liberal legislative surge of 1963 through 1975–76 (UNI then DIV). Presidential programs, given their properties as drama, can probably reach the general public more effectively, but ideological surges arising from "moods" can unquestionably engage appreciable sectors of the public.

Then there is *budgetary coherence*—that is, a match between revenue and expenditure across all government programs. Whether such a match occurs is of course ultimately a matter of statutes, including appropriations bills. It goes without saying that the federal government's immense deficits have daunted and preoccupied the country's political elite as much as anything during the last decade. For some observers, the deficits have also posed a clear test of divided party control, which it has flunked. A single ruling party would have done better, the argument goes, for reasons either of ideological uniformity or electoral accountability. Lloyd N. Cutler made the latter argument in 1988: "If one party was responsible for all three power centers [House, Senate, and presidency] and produced deficits of the magnitude in which they have been produced in recent years, there would be no question of the accountability and the responsibility of that party and its elected public officials for what had happened."[18]

Is this a valid case, finally, against divided party control? That has to remain an open question, since not much scholarship has yet appeared about the history of budgeting as it may have been affected by conditions of party control; also, highly relevant events will no doubt continue to take place. But the case is considerably less compelling than it may first look. For one thing, there is evidently no statistical relation between divided party control and deficit financing over the two centuries of American national history, or more specifically since World War II.[19] That recent period includes the 1950s, it is useful to remember, when Eisenhower, who faced Democratic Congresses for six years, fought major political battles and drew much criticism from liberal intellectuals because he would *not* accept unbalanced budgets. Taking into account size of deficit or surplus, what the postwar pattern does show is a "sudden break" under Reagan.[20] Deficits "blossomed suddenly in 1981."[21] A time series of federal debt as a percentage of gross national product falls almost monotonically from 1946 through 1974, holds more or less steady until 1981, and then surges.[22] The 1980s are the problem.

An explanation that seems to fit this pre-1980 versus post-1980 experience involves not conditions of party control but rather individual presidents' policies. At least since World War II, according to Paul E. Peterson, Congress "has generally followed the presidential lead on broad fiscal policies."[23] Overall congressional appropriations—that is, for each year the total across all programs—have ordinarily come quite close to overall presidential spending requests.[24] Changes in total revenue generated by congressional tax enactments have ordinarily approximated those proposed by presidents.[25]

Sometimes these results have not come easily. It required a year to enact the Kennedy tax cut proposed in 1963 (UNI). Johnson's tax surcharge, a deficit-reduction measure proposed in August 1967 (UNI), won enactment only after ten months of deadlock and a "battle of the titans" between the president and Ways and Means chairman Wilbur Mills.[26] The encounter is instructive. At the low point, in May 1968, Johnson accused Ways and Means of "blackmail" and was reported to be "in a mood of despair, fearing that the tax bill may be dead," although "some lawmakers [were] still clinging to hope that the threatened deterioration of the U.S. economic position, domestically and internationally, will yet compel the warring politicians to compromise."[27] The basic problem was that congressional conservatives would vote for a tax increase only if it was accompanied by substantial expenditure cuts. House Republicans warned that they would not supply needed votes unless the president and a majority of House Democrats publicly backed such a package. Johnson finally capitulated. A centrist, cross-party House coalition approved a compromise plan in mid-June; many anti-tax Republicans and liberal Democrats (notably most members from the Detroit and New York City areas) opposed it.

This was a success story, of sorts. And in general, presidents have ended up winning the overall tax and spending contours they asked for, or close to them, regardless of conditions of party control.[28] Under divided control, that held true for Nixon in 1969–74, although the ultimate mix of defense as opposed to domestic spending during those years did not satisfy him.[29] It held for Eisenhower, who guarded his budgets as effectively from a Democratic spending drive in 1957–60 as he had from Republican tax-cutting pressure in 1953.[30] It finally held for Bush in the fall of 1990, when he won "the biggest deficit reduction legislation in history."[31] The circumstances were unusually adverse: A fall election approached, primary electorates had shown a surly anti-incumbent mood, a recession was setting in, and Bush had just confused the electorate and his own party by abandoning his "Read my lips" no-tax pledge of the 1988 campaign. The result came after five months of haggling, a temporary no-funds shutdown of the Washington Monument, public outcries against government disorder, and a desertion by House Republicans that shifted the final package in a Democratic direction. But a five-year $490 billion plan did pass. In a perhaps unparalleled test, during pre-war times, the generalization held in 1932 when Hoover sought a major tax increase from a Democratic House during an election year at the depth of the depression. He got it—if only after, as discussed earlier, backbench Democrats and progressive Republicans rebelled against party leaders and wrote their own brand of provisions.[32]

And the generalization held for Reagan in 1981 (DIV). Though he made unusual requests, he got largely what he asked for.[33] His basic mix of a severe tax cut, heavy cuts in domestic spending, but increased defense spending and hands off Social Security was ratified by Congress and paved the way for the deficits of the 1980s.[34] The program's enactment owed partly to Reagan's and David Stockman's inventive arithmetic, but there was support from economists. These included supply-side theorists, a fringe of the profession, but also the Reagan coalition's monetarists who had come to question the relevance of deficits to prices, income, or growth (at least in the short run).[35] This was a rationale for deficits, or at least for a lack of concern about them. True, some vigorous logrolling took place on Capitol Hill in 1981 as White House agents conceded tax breaks to advance the president's tax bill and reprieved targeted programs to enact Gramm-Latta II (the expenditure cuts).[36] Both sorts of bargaining added to future deficits. But these actions came at the margin and in the service of a cause.[37] As much as anything, Reagan's 1981 victories seem to have been a triumph of ideas—a low-tax, low-spend doctrine that at once had the backing of some respectable economists and was saleable in simple form to a mass public. Of course the effort required a good salesman.

In fiscal affairs, Paul E. Peterson and Mark Rom argue, the apt analogy is between Reagan and Franklin Roosevelt (who always faced Congresses of his own party): "Deficit politics has proven to be a winning strategy for two popular presidents, both of whom had controversial agendas that shifted American policy in a new direction." "Overall, deficit politics became a vital component of the two strongest, most dramatic presidencies of the twentieth century."[38] In both cases, deficit financing seemed to work. That is, the electorate, reacting as customary to macroeconomic indicators, rewarded the party in control of the presidency.[39] In the 1980s that meant Republican victories in 1984 and 1988 (times of prosperity) although losses in 1982 (a recession year).[40] That, in the economic sphere, is the kind of "accountability" that the American system offers.

It is entirely possible, of course, that the immense deficits of the 1980s would have been avoided if one party had controlled the government. But it is an act of faith to suppose so. Party-centered accountability would scarcely have done the trick: Nothing we know about electoral behavior suggests that American voters, whatever the circumstances of party control, will reward a government for balancing budgets. Beyond this, perhaps the key decision in conjuring up counterfactual replays of the 1980s is whether to allow the intrusion of a captivating low-tax ideology into the system. If the answer is yes, budgets come under pressure. Given that pressure, imagine for example a Republican government in control of all three branches led by Reagan, Bush, Howard Baker, Bob Dole, Robert Michel, and Newt Gingrich. Would it have balanced its budgets? Recall that much of the actual budgetary disagreement during the 1980s took place *within* the Republican party.

On the Democratic side, to envision a post-Carter ruling combination in control of all three branches is not that easy. But Democrats have not proven immune to low-tax pressure. Developments at the state level are suggestive, although, for constitutional reasons, budgetary disorder has to assume forms there other than deficits. In California, an all-Democratic government was bowled over by Proposition 13 in 1978. In Massachusetts, an all-Democratic government virtually disintegrated in 1989–90 as a result of low-tax, low-spending sentiment exhibited in opinion polls and primaries. How would a Democratic government at the national level have managed such demands? That seems to be the appropriate question. "Party government" does not provide a refuge from them.

The third question is: Doesn't government administration suffer as a result of divided party control? Doesn't exaggerated pulling and hauling between president and Congress undermine the implementation of laws and, in general, the functioning of agencies and the administration of programs? High-publicity Capitol Hill investigations, which have been discussed, are relevant to an answer, but the subject is broader than that. It is also vaguer and quite difficult to address. The strategy here will be to present a plausible case *for* an instance of such undermining of administration and then draw a historical comparison. This will scarcely exhaust the topic, but the instances to be compared are important in their own right as well as suggestive about conditions of party control in general.

The plausible instance is Congress's thrust toward "micro-managing" the executive branch in recent decades.[41] That is, Congress has greatly increased its staff who monitor administration, multiplied its days of oversight hearings, greatly expanded its use of the legislative veto (until a federal court ruled that device unconstitutional in 1983), taken to writing exceptionally detailed statutes that limit bureaucratic discretion (notably in environmental law), and tried to trim presidential power through such measures as the War Powers Act of 1973 and the Budget and Impoundment Act of 1974.[42] Whether these moves have helped or harmed the system can be argued either way, but let us stipulate for the moment that they have undermined administration.

Has "micro-management" resulted, at least partly, from divided party control of the government? That too can be argued either way. An abundant list of alternative causes includes public and congressional reaction to the Vietnam war (as conducted by both Johnson and Nixon) and the public's rising distrust of bureaucracy.[43] But let us hypothesize that divided party control is at least partly the cause. Here is the argument. Rather than appearing gradually, "micro-management" came into its own rather quickly under Nixon and Ford in the 1970s—especially during the Nixon-Ford term of 1973–76. To cite some quantitative evidence, days spent per year on congressional oversight hearings, and average number of pages per enacted law (an indicator of statutory detail), achieved *most* of the considerable increase they showed from 1961 through 1984 during just the four years of 1973–76.[44]

That was during a period of divided party control. Obviously, micro-management has not flashed on whenever party control became divided (as under Eisenhower) or flashed off whenever it became unified (as under Carter). Much of it, at least, came in under Nixon-Ford and stayed. One might say that those years saw the initiation of a "regime" of micro-management—that is, a durable set of views and institutionally located practices geared to that end. Once in place, those views and practices could survive the transition to Carter and then to Reagan. Their origin is what counts. To implicate divided party control plausibly, one has to argue that two conditions were necessary for this "micro-management regime" to come into existence. First, party control had to be divided: Congress would not have inaugurated such a regime otherwise. Second, there had to occur some unusual shock to the system such as Watergate, Nixon's conduct of the war, or simply Nixon's aggressive presidency: Divided control would not have engendered such a regime otherwise. Divided control, that is, was a necessary *part* of the causal structure that triggered the regime.[45]

That is a plausible, particular argument. Can it be generalized? The broader case would be that members of a relevant class of congressional regimes that includes the micro-management one—that is, regimes that can reasonably be alleged to undermine administration—can be expected to arise under the same circumstances. That is, they require some similar shock to the system plus a background of divided party control.

Has any other such regime ever existed? As it happens, what looks like a particularly good instance of one originated in 1938 and led a vibrant life through 1954. It was that era's "loyalty regime"—the brilliant innovation of Democratic Congressman Martin Dies of Texas, founder of the House Un-American Activities Committee. Dies pioneered a formula that carried through the Hiss, McCarran, Army-McCarthy and other investigations after the war.[46] It was a low-cost, high-publicity, committee-centered way of waging a congressional opposition against the New Deal, the Truman administration, and then Eisenhower. Its chief technique was the hearing where someone could accuse members of the executive branch of being disloyal to the United States. No one should be surprised that that evidently had a pronounced effect on administration. Beyond its effects on the targeted personnel, it could demoralize agencies, preoccupy the White House, put a chill on unorthodox policy options, and even exile whole schools of thought from the government (as with China specialists after 1949).

It seems a good bet that this loyalty regime made as much of a mark on administration—to be sure, its own kind of mark as has Congress's more recent micromanagement regime. Compare, for example, the "Who lost China?" inquiries that dogged Truman's China policy with the Boland amendments aimed at micro-managing Reagan's Central America policy. But of course the loyalty regime began, led nearly all its existence, and ended during times of unified party control.[47] Nothing is more striking than the inventiveness of the lopsidedly Democratic Congress of 1937–38. Not only did it originate HUAC—"the outstanding political show of 1938."[48] It also generated a House Rules Committee regime that, although not involved in administration, gave conservatives a cross-party location for blocking or delaying liberal legislative proposals between 1937 and 1961.[49] Under Democratic presidents, those were often White House proposals. The options of loyalty probes and Rules Committee vetoes helped to insure that, for a generation, government would proceed largely through open contention among officials operating from separate executive and congressional power bases.

The analogy here is between Congress's loyalty and micro-management regimes. The former shows at least that regimes affecting—and arguably undermining—administration *can* materialize and thrive during times of unified party control. That is the narrow claim. It does not rule out the possibility that such regimes have been less common or consequential during times of unified control—although to demonstrate that would require evidence and it is not clear what it would be. In the instances of the loyalty and micro-management regimes—and also the Rules Committee one—one credible and parsimonious account of at least their origins has nothing to do with conditions of party control.

Instead it would emphasize the extraordinary disruption caused to the system by Roosevelt and Nixon around the time they were winning landslide re-elections and entering their second terms.[50] Roosevelt forged an alliance with the new CIO, built a WPA patronage organization deployable in national elections, introduced his controversial court-packing and executive reorganization plans, and ultimately tried to purge House and Senate Democrats in the 1938 primaries.[51] Nixon conducted the Indochina war in his memorable way, hatched internal security schemes, aggressively impounded Capitol Hill appropriations, advanced a plan (which resembled Roosevelt's) to centralize control of the administrative branch, and finally brought on Watergate.[52] Given the way American politics works, it would have been surprising in either president's case if an alarmed Congress had *not* undertaken serious countermoves.

The fourth question is: Does the conduct of foreign policy suffer under divided party control? That might be a special concern, since "coordination" is often held to be central to effective foreign policymaking. Perhaps an excess of "deadlock" or "non-coordination" occurs under conditions of divided control. But of course such disorderliness, looked at from the other side as by opponents of Truman's China policy or Reagan's Central America policy, figures as a healthy exercise of checks and balances. Foreign policy is often a fighting matter at home. There does not seem to be any way around this. "Coordination," however much sense it may seem to make, does not and cannot dominate every other value.[53]

Yet once past that realization, it is not clear what standards to apply. None will be proposed here. But let the reader try the following thought experiment. Choose *any* plausible set of standards and, using them, scan through the history of American foreign policymaking since World War II. Here is a prediction of what most readers will conclude: In general, the record was no worse when the two parties shared power. Any appraisal has to accommodate or steer around, for example, the Marshall Plan, which owed to bipartisan cooperation during a time of divided control; the Kennedy-Johnson intervention in Indochina, which, whatever else may be said about it, scarcely took its shape because of a lack of coordination; Nixon's openings to China and the Soviet Union, which were maneuvered with little Capitol Hill dissent during a time of divided control; and Bush's liberation of Kuwait in 1990–91. Given just these items, many readers may agree, considerable ingenuity would be needed to concoct a verdict spanning the four and a half decades that favors unified party control. . . . the same lack of pattern appears in foreign policy areas requiring legislative action across several Congresses—foreign aid, foreign trade, and treaty ratifications. There too the record does not seem to have differed or suffered under divided control.[54]

The fifth question: Are the country's lower-income strata served less well under divided party control? One can assemble a theory that they might be, assuming for a moment that "serve" refers to direct government action rather than, say, encouragement of long-term economic growth. Separation of powers biases the American regime toward the rich, Progressive theorists used to argue at the outset of the twentieth century. The rich profit when the government does nothing, whereas the non-rich require concerted public action that can all too easily be blocked somewhere in the system's ample array of veto-points. An obvious remedy would be a constitution allowing strict majority rule.[55] But lacking that, according to a conventional argument of political science, much depends on political parties. Their distinctive role is to impose on the country's collection of government institutions a kind of order that serves majority interests. In principle, that might be done by one party embodying the views and experiences of the non-rich (a socialist sort of argument) or by two parties bidding for the votes of the non-rich (a Downsian sort of argument). Either way, unified control is needed to deliver the goods. It allows action, rules out buck-passing, fixes responsibility, permits accountability.

That is a plausible line of argument, and the Great Society as well as the New Deal might be said to bear it out. But altogether too much of the record since World War II does not. What were the origins of the "social safety net" that the Reagan administration—during a time of divided control, for what that is worth—succeeded in widening the holes of?[56] In fact, that net owed much of its weaving to the Nixon and Ford years—also a time of divided control. That period was the source of EEA and CETA jobs, expanded unemployment insurance, low-income energy assistance, post-1974 housing allowances, Pell grants for lower-income college students, greatly multiplied food-stamps assistance, a notable progressivizing of tax incidence, Supplementary Security Income for the aged, blind, and disabled, and Social Security increases that cut the proportion of aged below the poverty line from 25 percent in 1970 to 16 percent in 1974.[57] The laws just kept getting passed. The Reaganite assault against both the Great Society and the 1970s pitted era against era and mood against mood. But it did not pit divided party control against unified party control or even all that clearly Republicans against Democrats.

These five questions are not the only additional ones that might be asked about unified as opposed to divided party control.[58] This work skirts, moreover, the separate and obviously important question of whether the American system of government, with its separation-of-powers features, has been functioning adequately in recent times. Some analysts, for example John E. Chubb and Paul E. Peterson, say no: "When governments of quite different political combinations [that is, unified as well as divided control] all fail to perform effectively, it is worth considering whether the problem is the government itself and not the people or parties that run it."[59] Energy and budgetary policies have been creaking. Each of the last two decades has ended with a riveting spectacle of government inefficacy or disorder—Carter's "malaise" crisis in 1979 and Bush's budget wrangle in 1990. Otherwise, the country is faced with declining voter turnout as well as a rise in election technologies and incumbent-serving practices that seem to be delegitimizing elected officials.[60]

There is no end of taking steps to reform American political institutions, or of good reasons for it. But short of jettisoning the separation-of-powers core of the Constitution—an unlikely event—it would probably be a mistake to channel such concern into "party government" schemes. This work has tried to show that, surprisingly, it does not seem to make all that much difference whether party control of the American government happens to be unified or divided. One reason we assume it does is that "party government" plays a role in political science somewhere between a Platonic form and a grail. When we reach for it as a standard, we draw on abstract models, presumed European practice, and well-airbrushed American experience, but we seldom take a cold took at real American experience. We forget about Franklin Roosevelt's troubles with HUAC and the Rules Committee, Truman's and Kennedy's domestic policy defeats, McCarthy's square-off against Eisenhower, Johnson versus Fulbright on Vietnam, and Carter's energy program and "malaise."

Political parties can be powerful instruments, but in the United States they seem to play more of a role as "policy factions" than as, in the British case, governing instruments. A party as policy faction can often get its way even in circumstances of divided control: Witness the Taftite Republicans in 1947, congressional Democrats under Nixon, or the Reaganites in 1981. How, one might ask, were these temporary policy ascendancies greatly different from that of the Great Society Democrats in 1964–66?

To demand more of American parties—to ask that they become governing instruments—is to run them up against components of the American regime as fundamental as the party system itself. There is a strong pluralist component, for example, as evidenced in the way politicians respond to cross-cutting issue cleavages. There is a public-opinion component that political science's modern technologies do not seem to reach very well. The government floats in public opinion; it goes up and down on great long waves of it that often have little to do with parties. There is the obvious structural component—separation of powers—that brings on deadlock and chronic conflict, but also nudges officials toward deliberation, compromise, and super-majority outcomes. And there is a component of deep-seated individualism among American politicians, who build and tend their own electoral bases and maintain their own relations of responsibility with electorates. This seems to be a matter of political culture—perhaps a survival of republicanism—that goes way back. Unlike most politicians elsewhere, American ones at both legislative and executive levels have managed to navigate the last two centuries of history without becoming minions of party leaders. In this complicated, multi-component setting, British-style governing by party majorities does not have much of a chance.

NOTES

1. The term is from John B. Gilmour, "Bargaining between Congress and the President: The Bidding-Up Phenomenon" (Paper presented at the 1990 Annual Meeting of the American Political Science Association), p. 25.

2. Richard H. K. Vietor, *Energy Policy in America since 1945: A Study of Business-Government Relations* (New York: Cambridge University Press, 1984), pp. 249–258, quotation at p. 249.

3. On entitlements expansion as a growing problem of budgetary "uncontrollability" in the years around 1970, see John W. Ellwood, "The Great Exception: The Congressional Budget Process in an Age of Decentralization," chap. 14 in Lawrence C. Dodd and Bruce I. Oppenheimer, eds., *Congress Reconsidered*, 3d ed. (Washington, D.C.: Congressional Quarterly Press, 1985), pp. 322–325.

4. John Kenneth Galbraith, "The Ultimate Scandal," *New York Review of Books.* January 18, 1990, p. 16.

5. Paul J. Quirk, "Regulatory Policy Making in the New Congress: Deregulation Revisited" (Paper presented at the Conference on the New Politics of Public Policy, Brandeis University, April 1990), pp. 24–29, first quotation at p. 25; John E. Chubb, "U.S. Energy Policy: A Problem of Delegation," in Chubb and Paul E. Peterson, eds., *Can the Government Govern?* (Washington, D.C.: Brookings Institution Press, 1989), pp. 73–76, other quotations at p. 74. Technically, the Natural Gas Policy Act of 1978 was a component of the omnibus energy measure enacted that year.

6. Quirk, "Regulatory Policy Making," p. 28.

7. R. Douglas Arnold, *Congress and the Bureaucracy: A Theory of Influence* (New Haven and London: Yale University Press, 1979), pp. 165–169.

8. Doris Kearns, *Lyndon Johnson and the American Dream* (New York: Harper and Row, 1976), pp. 216–218, quotations at pp. 216, 218. "There seemed to be few among the principal officers of government who were trying to determine how the programs could be made actually to work. The standard of success was the passage of the law" (p. 218). These statements refer to the Eighty-ninth Congress, elected in 1964.

9. James L. Sundquist, *Politics and Policy: The Eisenhower, Kennedy, and Johnson Years* (Washington, D.C.: Brookings Institution Press, 1968), p. 151.

10. See Jeffrey K. Tulis, *The Rhetorical Presidency* (Princeton, N.J.: Princeton University Press, 1987), pp. 161–72, first quotation at p. 172; Daniel P. Moynihan, *Maximum Feasible Misunderstanding: Community Action in the War on Poverty* (New York: Free Press, 1969), chap. 5.

11. Odin W. Anderson, *Health Services in the United States: A Growth Enterprise since 1875* (Ann Arbor, Mich.: Health Administration Press, 1985), pp. 201–202. See also Herbert Stein, *Presidential Economics: The Making of Economic Policy* (New York: Simon and Schuster, 1985), p. 116. On Medicaid: James T. Patterson, *America's Struggle against Poverty, 1900–1985* (Cambridge: Harvard University Press, 1986), p. 169; Robert Stevens and Rosemary Stevens, *Welfare Medicine in America: A Case Study of Medicaid* (New York: Free Press, 1974), pp. 51–53, 68–69.

12. See the data in V. O. Key, Jr., "The Veterans and the House of Representatives: A Study of a Pressure Group and Electoral Morality," *Journal of Politics* 5 (1943): 28–30. See also E. Cary Brown, "Fiscal Policy in the 'Thirties: A Reappraisal," *American Economic Review* 46 (1956): 863–869.

13. According to one recent account, these statutory changes "guaranteed that the Savings and Loans . . . would engage in a binge of blue-sky financing and outright thievery." George P. Brockway, "Who Killed the Savings and Loans?" *New Leader,* September 3, 1990, p. 16. On raising the deposit insurance ceiling from $40,000 to $100,000: "No hearing was held on this move; there was no debate. It now seems clear that, at the time, most of the legislators had no idea of what they were doing." L. J. Davis, "Chronicle of a Debacle Foretold: How Deregulation Begat the S&L Scandal," *Harper's,* September 1990, p. 53.

14. Alexis de Tocqueville, *Democracy in America* (Garden City, N.Y.: Doubleday Anchor, 1969), p. 232. See also pp. 248–250.

15. See, for example, James P. Pfiffner, "Divided Government and the Problem of Governance," chap. 3 in James A. Thurber, ed., *Divided Democracy: Cooperation and Conflict between the President and Congress* (Washington, D.C.: Congressional Quarterly Press, 1991), p. 48.

16. Charles E. Lindblom, *The Intelligence of Democracy: Decision Making through Mutual Adjustment* (New York: Free Press, 1965).

17. Robert A. Dahl, *A Preface to Democratic Theory* (Chicago: University of Chicago Press, 1956), chap. 5.

18. Lloyd N. Cutler, "Some Reflections about Divided Government," *Presidential Studies Quarterly* 18 (1988): 489.

19. James E. Alt and Charles H. Stewart III, "Parties and the Deficit: Some Historical Evidence" (Paper prepared for the Conference on Political Economics, National Bureau of Economic Research, February 1990), pp. 6–7, 18–19, and tables 2 and 6.

20. Andre Modigliani and Franco Modigliani, "The Growth of the Federal Deficit and the Role of Public Attitudes," *Public Opinion Quarterly* 51 (1987): 470. "To summarize, the great deficits that began in 1982 are something altogether unparalleled in the fiscal history of the United States, except during major wars and depressions" (p. 473).

21. Paul E. Peterson, "The New Politics of Deficits," chap. 13 in John E. Chubb and Peterson, eds., *The New Direction in American Politics* (Washington, D.C.: Brookings Institution Press, 1985), pp. 365–370, quotation at p. 366.

22. Ibid., p. 369.

23. Ibid., p. 366. For a general discussion, see pp. 370–382. "Throughout the postwar period Congress has operated within a budget framework initially specified by the president. . . . However much Congress may modify the details of that policy, it seems to have accepted the executive's prerogative to define the budget's general contours" (p. 379).

24. Ibid., pp. 372–379. The data are for 1947 through 1984.

25. Ibid., pp. 380–382. "On tax matters, Congress also mainly follows the presidential lead" (p. 381). The data are for 1948 through 1984.

26. See the account in Lawrence C. Pierce, *The Politics of Fiscal Policy Formation* (Pacific Palisades, Calif.: Goodyear Publishing, 1971), pp. 7–8, 146–172, quotation at p. 146.

27. Ibid., p. 155 (first quotation); Edwin L. Dale, Jr., "Johnson Demands Increase in Taxes Despite Election," *New York Times*, May 4, 1968, p. 16 (second quotation); Norman C. Miller and Richard F. Janssen, "Tax Chances Seen Further Dimmed by Johnson Talk, But Economic Aides No Longer Fear Fiscal 'Shambles,' " *Wall Street Journal*, May 6, 1968, p. 3 (third quotation).

28. "Even during the Carter administration—when, surprisingly enough, the fiscal differences between the executive and legislative branches were the largest—congressional appropriations differed from presidential requests by less than 0.7 percent of GNP." Paul E. Peterson and Mark Rom, "Macroeconomic Policymaking: Who Is in Control?" in Chubb and Peterson, eds., *Can the Government Govern?* p. 166.

29. Peterson, "New Politics of Deficits," pp. 375, 381; Stein, *Presidential Economics*, chap. 5.

30. Herbert Stein, *The Fiscal Revolution in America* (Chicago: University of Chicago Press, 1969), chaps. 11–14; Iwan W. Morgan, *Eisenhower Versus "the Spenders": The Eisenhower Administration, the Democrats, and the Budget, 1953–60* (London: Pinter, 1990), Conclusions; Dwight D. Eisenhower, *The White House Years*, vol. 2, *Waging Peace, 1956–1961* (Garden City, N.Y.: Doubleday, 1965), pp. 377–381, 385–388.

31. David E. Rosenbaum, "House and Senate Pass Budget Bill; Bush is 'Pleased,' " *New York Times*, October 28, 1990, p. I:1.

32. See Jordan A. Schwarz, *The Interregnum of Despair: Hoover, Congress, and the Depression* (Urbana: University of Illinois Press, 1970), chap. 5. It would be interesting to do a comparative analysis of the deficit-reduction enterprises of 1932, 1968, and 1990.

33. On the Reagan tax cut: "The bill that passed cut taxes by about as much as the President had proposed. This should not have been a surprise. There is usually little Congressional motivation to cut taxes less than a President says is prudent." Stein, *Presidential Economics*, p. 272.

34. At a rhetorical level, the president did keep asking for deeper domestic spending cuts than Congress gave him in 1981, but evidently he had no better idea than anyone else where those might come from. See David A. Stockman, *The Triumph of Politics: How the Reagan Revolution Failed* (New York: Harper and Row, 1986), pp. 91–92, 128–133, 274–276, 344–346, 356–360.

35. Peterson, "New Politics of Deficits," pp. 382–397; James D. Savage, *Balanced Budgets and American Politics* (Ithaca, N.Y.: Cornell University Press, 1988), pp. 209–222; Hugh Heclo and Rudolph G. Penner, "Fiscal and Political Strategy in the Reagan Administration," chap. 2 in Fred I. Greenstein, ed., *The Reagan Presidency: An Early Assessment* (Baltimore: Johns Hopkins University Press, 1983), pp. 21–26.

36. See Stockman, *Triumph of Politics*, chaps. 8, 9; R. Douglas Arnold, *The Logic of Congressional Action* (New Haven and London: Yale University Press, 1990), pp. 208–209.

37. To draw an analogy, one of the classic exercises of congressional logrolling took place during passage of the Smoot-Hawley tariff of 1930, which, from the standpoint of the world economy, may have been the most unfortunate statute enacted by the U.S. government during the twentieth century. (Note that it passed at a time of unified party control.) But Robert Pastor has convincingly argued that, notwithstanding the logrolling, a doctrine of protectionism shared by President Hoover and congressional Republicans was essential to the act's passage. Take that away, as happened in the next important consideration of foreign trade under the Democrats in 1934, and the cross-industry logrolling disappeared also. Doctrines dominated deals. The argument here is that Reaganite ideology comparably legitimized

the logrolling of 1981. See Robert A. Pastor, *Congress and the Politics of U.S. Foreign Economic Policy, 1929–1976* (Berkeley: University of California Press, 1980), pp. 77–84. On Smoot-Hawley, see E. E. Schattschneider, *Politics, Pressures, and the Tariff: A Study of Free Private Enterprise in Pressure Politics, as Shown in the 1929–1930 Revision of the Tariff* (Hamden, Conn.: Archon Books, 1963).

38. Peterson and Rom, "Macroeconomic Policymaking," pp. 179, 180.

39. The standard source is Gerald H. Kramer, "Short-Term Fluctuations in U.S. Voting Behavior, 1896–1964," *American Political Science Review* 65 (1971): 131–143. For an analysis that covers the post–World War II era, see Robert S. Erikson, "Economic Conditions and the Presidential Vote," *American Political Science Review* 83 (1989): 567–573.

40. On the 1984 election, see D. Roderick Kiewiet and Douglas Rivers, "The Economic Basis of Reagan's Appeal," chap. 3 in Chubb and Peterson, eds., *New Direction in American Politics*; Donald R. Kinder, Gordon S. Adams, and Paul W. Gronke, "Economics and Politics in the 1984 American Presidential Election," *American Journal of Political Science* 33 (1989): 491–515.

41. The term appears in, for example, James Q. Wilson, *Bureaucracy: What Government Agencies Do and Why They Do It* (New York: Basic Books, 1989), pp. 241–244.

42. See Joel D. Aberbach, *Keeping a Watchful Eye: The Politics of Congressional Oversight* (Washington, D.C.: Brookings Institution Press, 1990), pp. 34–46; William T. Gormley, Jr., *Taming the Bureaucracy: Muscles, Prayers, and Other Strategies* (Princeton, N.J.: Princeton University Press, 1989), pp. 56–59 and chap. 8.

43. See Aberbach, *Keeping a Watchful Eye*, pp. 26–28, 39–46, 48–73, 191–193, and Gormley, *Taming the Bureaucracy*, pp. 32–35.

44. Aberbach, *Keeping a Watchful Eye*, pp. 38, 44.

45. To put it another way, and to generalize, the key causal variable is an interaction term whose components are a relevant kind of shock and the circumstance of divided party control.

46. Although 1948 through 1954 seems to have been the peak period for this regime, at least as regards the executive branch (the investigators did have other targets), HUAC also made a significant impact earlier. Between 1938 and 1947, the committee pursued alleged disloyalty in the WPA's Federal Theatre and Writers Project, the National Labor Relations Board, the National Youth Administration, the Tennessee Valley Authority, the Office of Price Administration, the Federal Communications Commission, the Office of Civil Defense, the Board of Economic Warfare, the War Production Board, and the Departments of Labor, State, and Interior. The Department of Justice came under fire for allegedly disregarding disloyalty elsewhere. See Walter Goodman, *The Committee: The Extraordinary Career of the House Committee on Un-American Activities* (New York: Farrar, Straus and Giroux, 1964), pp. 29, 35, 42–48, 55, 69–75, 100, 104–113, 124–128, 131–152, 171–172, 203–207. Almost all of this took place while the Democrats controlled both the presidency and Congress—that is, before the 1946 election. Dies chaired HUAC through 1944.

47. Or receded into insignificance if not exactly ended. No loyalty investigation had much impact on the executive branch after 1954.

48. Ibid., p. 54. On the origins of HUAC, see ibid., chaps. 1, 2; Richard Polenberg, "The Decline of the New Deal, 1937–1940" in John Braeman, Robert H. Bremner, and David Brody, eds., *The New Deal: The National Level* (Columbus: Ohio State University Press, 1975), pp. 257–258; William E. Leuchtenberg, *Franklin D. Roosevelt and the New Deal, 1932–1940* (New York: Harper and Row, 1963), pp. 280–281. "Ostensibly nonpartisan, the Dies Committee served the purposes of those who claimed that the New Deal was a Red stratagem" (p. 281). Nothing may index better the demise of the New Deal than the switch of public and media attention from La Follette's pro-union hearings in 1937 to Dies's anti-Communist investigation of 1938.

49. The Rules Committee's move into that role during 1937–38 is discussed in Patterson, *Congressional Conservatism*, pp. 53, 167–168, 176–177, 179–183, 186, 193–194, 225–229, 243–244, 247.

50. To put it another way, as earlier, the interaction term drops its divided-control component and becomes just a shock variable.

51. See for example Sidney M. Milkis, "Franklin D. Roosevelt and the Transcendence of Partisan Politics," *Political Science Quarterly* 100 (1985): 479–504.

52. Richard P. Nathan draws the analogy between Roosevelt's and Nixon's executive reorganization drives in *The Plot That Failed: Nixon and the Administrative Presidency* (New York: John Wiley and Sons, 1975), pp. 87–89.

53. For a relevant discussion, see Larry N. George, "Tocqueville's Caveat: Centralized Executive Foreign Policy and American Democracy," *Polity* 22 (1990): 419–441.

54. Foreign trade policy can be said to require its own special brand of "coherence." Often that is not forthcoming, but in one recent review of U.S. trade policy since the 1930s there is no suggestion that divided party control has caused any distinctive problems. See David B. Yoffie, "American Trade Policy: An Obsolete Bargain?" pp. 100–138 in Chubb and Peterson, eds., *Can the Government Govern?*

55. For the Progressive case, see J. Allen Smith, *The Spirit of American Government: A Study of the Constitution; Its Origin, Influence, and Relation to Democracy* (New York: Macmillan, 1907).

56. On the safety net, see for example Peter Passell, "Forces in Society, and Reaganism, Helped Dig Deeper Hole for Poor," *New York Times*, July 16, 1989, p. I:1.

57. See Patterson, *America's Struggle against Poverty*, chap. 10 (on Social Security expansion at p. 158), and pp. 197–198, 200; Timothy Conlan, *New Federalism: Intergovernmental Reform from Nixon to Reagan* (Washington, D.C.: Brookings Institution Press, 1988), pp. 81–82; R. Allen Hays, *The Federal Government and Urban Housing* (Albany: State University of New York Press, 1985), pp. 145–51; Robert X. Browning, *Politics and Social Welfare Policy in the United States* (Knoxville: University of Tennessee Press, 1986), pp. 84–90, 95, 107–114, 120–121, 141–148, 161–162. Largely at Democratic behest, shifts of tax law in a progressive direction took place under Nixon in 1969 (DIV) and also under Hoover in 1932 (DIV) and Bush in 1990 (DIV).

58. A topical one concerns appointments to the Supreme Court. At three junctures since World War II, presidents who undertook to move the Court in a liberal or conservative direction have had their appointments blocked by the Senate. Not confirmed were Johnson nominees Abe Fortas (for elevation to Chief Justice) and Homer Thornberry in 1968 (UNI), Nixon nominees Clement Haynsworth and G. Harrold Carswell in 1969–70 (DIV), and Reagan nominees Robert Bork and Douglas Ginsburg (who withdrew) in 1987 (DIV). If one takes into account who finally won the vacant positions, then in an ideological sense Johnson's campaign can be said to have failed (Warren Burger became Chief Justice), Nixon fared indifferently (the position went to Harry Blackmun), and Reagan succeeded (the position went to Anthony Kennedy).

59. John E. Chubb and Paul E. Peterson, "American Political Institutions and the Problem of Governance," in Chubb and Peterson, eds., *Can the Government Govern?* p. 1. See also Terry M. Moe, "The Politics of Bureaucratic Structure," in ibid.

60. It has been alleged that divided party control *causes* lower turnout, or at least has done so recently, by confusing voters and muffling choice. The record of the past century and a half does not bear out the idea. Note that the mid-1870s through the mid-1890s was at once the country's golden age of voter turnout and an era of usually divided government. Turnout began its twentieth-century plunge, for whatever reasons, after 1896, when party control returned to unified. See Walter Dean Burnham, "The Changing Shape of the American Political Universe," *American Political Science Review*, 59 (1965): 11.

26

NELSON W. POLSBY

THE INSTITUTIONALIZATION OF THE
U.S. HOUSE OF REPRESENTATIVES

Governmental institutions evolve and adjust over time. Nelson W. Polsby adds to our understanding of Congress by explaining how the House of Representatives was transformed from a relatively open, flexible organization to one characterized by more difficult entry, less turnover, greater professionalization, and more routinization. Institutionalization dramatically changed the way the House operates, but, as Polsby notes, its full consequences are uncertain. This selection is excerpted from Polsby's article by the same title in the American Political Science Review *(1968). Polsby teaches political science at the University of California, Berkeley.*

Most people who study politics are in general agreement, it seems to me, on at least two propositions. First, we agree that for a political system to be viable, for it to succeed in performing tasks of authoritative resource allocation, problem solving, conflict settlement, and so on, in behalf of a population of any substantial size, it must be institutionalized. That is to say, organizations must be created and sustained that are specialized to political activity.[1] Otherwise, the political system is likely to be unstable, weak, and incapable of servicing the demands or protecting the interests of its constituent groups. Secondly, it is generally agreed that for a political system to be in some sense free and democratic, means must be found for institutionalizing representativeness with all the diversity that this implies, and for legitimizing yet at the same time containing political opposition within the system.[2]

Our growing interest in both of these propositions, and in the problems to which they point, can begin to suggest the importance of studying one of the very few extant examples of a highly specialized political institution which over the long run has succeeded in representing a large number of diverse constituents, and in legitimizing, expressing, and containing political opposition within a complex political system—namely, the U.S. House of Representatives.

The focus of my attention here will be first of all descriptive, drawing together disparate strands—some of which already exist in the literature[3]—in an attempt to show in what sense we may regard the House as an institutionalized organ of government. Not all the necessary work has been done on this rather difficult descriptive problem, as I shall indicate. Secondly, I shall offer a number of speculative observations about causes, consequences, and possible lessons to be drawn from the institutionalization of the House.

The process of institutionalization is one of the grand themes in all of modern social science. It turns up in many guises and varieties: as Sir Henry Maine's discussion of the change from status to contract in the history of legal obligations,[4]

[Tables and notes have been renumbered.—Eds.]

as Ferdinand Tönnies' treatment of the shift from *Gemeinschaft* to *Gesellschaft*,[5] as Max Weber's discussion of the development of "rational-legal" modes of legitimization as an alternative to "traditional" and "charismatic" modes,[6] as Durkheim's distinction between "mechanical" and "organic" solidarity in his treatment of the consequences of the division of labor[7] and finally—dare we say finally?—as the central process at work in the unfolding of organizations that are held to obey Parkinson's Law.[8]

Such theoretical riches are bound to prove an embarrassment to the empirical researcher, since, unavoidably, in order to do his work, he must pick and choose among a host of possibilities—not those that initially may be the most stimulating, but those that seem most likely to be reflected in his data, which, perforce, are limited.[9] Thus the operational indices I am about to suggest which purport to measure empirically the extent to which the U.S. House of Representatives has become institutionalized may strike the knowledgeable reader as exceedingly crude; I invite the ingenuity of my colleagues to the task of suggesting improvements.

For the purposes of this study, let us say that an institutionalized organization has three major characteristics: 1) it is relatively well-bounded, that is to say, differentiated from its environment. Its members are easily identifiable, it is relatively difficult to become a member, and its leaders are recruited principally from within the organization. 2) The organization is relatively complex, that is, its functions are internally separated on some regular and explicit basis, its parts are not wholly interchangeable, and for at least some important purposes, its parts are interdependent. There is a division of labor in which roles are specified, and there are widely shared expectations about the performance of roles. There are regularized patterns of recruitment to roles, and of movement from role to role. 3) Finally, the organization tends to use universalistic rather than particularistic criteria, and automatic rather than discretionary methods for conducting its internal business. Precedents and rules are followed; merit systems replace favoritism and nepotism; and impersonal codes supplant personal preferences as prescriptions for behavior.

Since we are studying a single institution, the repeated use of words like "relatively" and "tends" in the sentences above refers to a comparison of the House of Representatives with itself at different points in time. The descriptive statement: "The House of Representatives has become institutionalized over time" means then, that over the life span of this institution, it has become perceptibly more bounded, more complex, and more universalistic and automatic in its internal decision making. But can we find measures which will capture enough of the meaning of the term "institutionalization" to warrant their use in an investigation of the process at work in the U.S. House of Representatives?

I. THE ESTABLISHMENT OF BOUNDARIES

One aspect of institutionalization is the differentiation of an organization from its environment. The establishment of boundaries in a political organization refers mostly to a channeling of career opportunities. In an undifferentiated organization, entry to and exit from membership is easy and frequent. Leaders emerge rapidly, lateral entry from outside to positions of leadership is quite common, and persistence of leadership over time is rare. As an organization institutionalizes, it stabilizes its membership, entry is more difficult, and turnover is less frequent. Its leadership professionalizes and persists. Recruitment to leadership is more likely to occur from within, and the apprenticeship period lengthens. Thus the organization establishes and "hardens" its outer boundaries.

Such measures as are available for the House of Representatives unmistakably show this process at work. In the eighteenth and nineteenth centuries, the turnover of Representatives at each election was enormous. Excluding the Congress of 1789, when of course everyone started new, turnover of House members exceeded fifty percent in fifteen elections—the last of which was held in 1882. In the twentieth century, the highest incidence of turnover (37.2 percent—almost double the twentieth century median) occurred in the Roosevelt landslide of 1932—a figure exceeded forty-seven times—in other words almost all the time—in the eighteenth and nineteenth centuries. As Table 1 and Figure 1 make clear, there has been a distinct decline in the rate at which new members are introduced into the House. Table 2 and Figure 2 make a similar point with data that are partially independent; they show that the overall stability of membership, as measured by the mean terms of members (total number of terms served divided by total number of Representatives) has been on the rise.

These two tables provide a fairly good indication of what has happened over the years to rank-and-file members of the House. Another method of investigating the extent to which an institution has established boundaries is to consider its leaders, how they are recruited, what happens to them, and most particularly the extent to which the institution permits lateral entry to and exit from positions of leadership.

The classic example of lateral movement—possibly the most impressive such record in American history—is of course contained in the kaleidoscopic career of Henry Clay, seventh Speaker of the House. Before his first election to the House, Clay had already served two terms in the Kentucky House of Representatives, and had been sent by the legislature to the U.S. Senate for two nonconsecutive short terms. Instead of returning to the Senate in 1811, he ran for the Lexington seat in the U.S. House and was elected. He took his seat on March 4, 1811, and eight months later was elected Speaker at the age of 34. Three years later, he resigned and was appointed a commissioner to negotiate the Treaty of Ghent with Great Britain. The next year, he returned to Congress, where he was again promptly elected Speaker. In 1820 he resigned once again and left public office for two years. But in 1823 he returned to the House, served as Speaker two more terms, and then resigned again, to become Secretary of State in John Quincy Adams' cabinet. In 1831, Clay became a freshman Senator. He remained in the Senate until 1844, when he resigned his seat. Five years later he re-entered the Senate, this time remaining until his death in 1852. Three times (in 1824, 1832, 1844) he was a candidate for president.[10]

Clay's career was remarkable, no doubt, even in a day and age when the boundaries of the House of Representatives were only lightly guarded and leadership in

TABLE 1. THE ESTABLISHMENT OF BOUNDARIES: DECLINE IN PERCENTAGE OF FIRST TERM
MEMBERS, U.S. HOUSE OF REPRESENTATIVES, 1789–1965

Congress	Year of 1st Term	% 1st Term Members	Congress	Year of 1st term	% 1st Term Members
1	1789	100.0	45	1877	46.6
2	1791	46.5	46	1879	42.3
3	1793	56.5	47	1881	31.8
4	1795	38.9	48	1883	51.5
5	1797	43.1	49	1885	38.0
6	1799	36.0	50	1887	35.6
7	1801	42.5	51	1889	38.1
8	1803	46.9	52	1891	43.8
9	1805	39.9	53	1893	38.1
10	1807	36.2	54	1895	48.6
11	1809	35.9	55	1897	37.9
12	1811	38.5	56	1899	30.1
13	1813	52.6	57	1901	24.4
14	1815	42.9	58	1903	31.3
15	1817	59.2	59	1905	21.0
16	1819	40.8	60	1907	22.5
17	1821	45.2	61	1909	19.9
18	1823	43.2	62	1911	30.5
19	1825	39.4	63	1913	34.4
20	1827	33.2	64	1915	27.2
21	1829	41.0	65	1917	16.0
22	1831	38.0	66	1919	22.7
23	1833	53.7	67	1921	23.6
24	1835	40.0	68	1923	27.1
25	1837	48.6	69	1925	16.3
26	1839	46.3	70	1927	13.3
27	1841	37.7	71	1929	17.7
28	1843	66.7	72	1931	19.0
29	1845	49.0	73	1933	37.2
30	1847	50.4	74	1935	23.4
31	1849	53.1	75	1937	22.7
32	1851	53.3	76	1939	25.5
33	1853	60.5	77	1941	17.0
34	1855	57.5	78	1943	22.9
35	1857	40.2	79	1945	15.8
36	1859	45.1	80	1947	24.1
37	1861	53.9	81	1949	22.3
38	1863	58.1	82	1951	14.9
39	1865	44.3	83	1953	19.5
40	1867	46.0	84	1955	11.7
41	1869	49.2	85	1957	9.9
42	1871	46.5	86	1959	18.2
43	1873	52.0	87	1961	12.6
44	1875	58.0	88	1963	15.2
			89	1965	20.9

Data for 1st through 68th Congresses are from Stuart A. Rice, *Quantitative Methods in Politics* (New York: Knopf, 1928), pp. 296–297. Data for 69th through 89th Congresses are calculated from *Congressional Directories*.

TABLE 2. THE ESTABLISHMENT OF BOUNDARIES: INCREASE IN TERMS SERVED BY
INCUMBENT MEMBERS OF THE U.S. HOUSE OF REPRESENTATIVES, 1789–1963

Congress	Beginning Term	Mean Terms of Service*	Congress	Beginning Term	Mean Terms of Service*
1	1789	1.00	45	1877	2.11
2	1791	1.54	46	1879	2.21
3	1793	1.64	47	1881	2.56
4	1795	2.00	48	1883	2.22
5	1797	2.03	49	1885	2.41
6	1799	2.23	50	1887	2.54
7	1801	2.25	51	1889	2.61
8	1803	2.14	52	1891	2.44
9	1805	2.36	53	1893	2.65
10	1807	2.51	54	1895	2.25
11	1809	2.71	55	1897	2.59
12	1811	2.83	56	1899	2.79
13	1813	2.31	57	1901	3.11
14	1815	2.48	58	1903	3.10
15	1817	1.93	59	1905	3.48
16	1819	2.15	60	1907	3.61
17	1821	2.23	61	1909	3.84
18	1823	2.29	62	1911	3.62
19	1825	2.42	63	1913	3.14
20	1827	2.68	64	1915	3.44
21	1829	2.55	65	1917	3.83
22	1831	2.59	66	1919	3.74
23	1833	2.15	67	1921	3.69
24	1835	2.23	68	1923	3.57
25	1837	2.13	69	1925	3.93
26	1839	2.17	70	1927	4.26
27	1841	2.30	71	1929	4.49
28	1843	1.76	72	1931	4.48
29	1845	1.90	73	1933	3.67
30	1847	2.00	74	1935	3.71
31	1849	1.92	75	1937	3.84
32	1851	1.84	76	1939	3.91
33	1853	1.69	77	1941	4.24
34	1855	1.81	78	1943	4.22
35	1857	2.04	79	1945	4.50
36	1859	2.02	80	1947	4.34
37	1861	1.83	81	1949	4.42
38	1863	1.75	82	1951	4.73
39	1865	2.00	83	1953	4.69
40	1867	2.12	84	1955	5.19
41	1869	2.04	85	1957	5.58
42	1871	2.11	86	1959	5.37
43	1873	2.07	87	1961	5.65
44	1875	1.92	88	1963	5.65

* Total number of terms served divided by total number of Representatives.

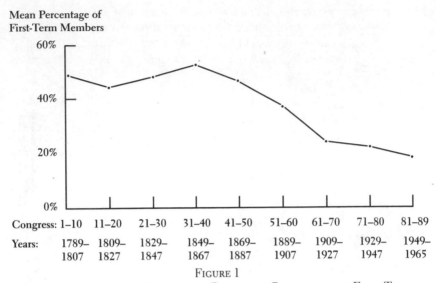

FIGURE 1

THE ESTABLISHMENT OF BOUNDARIES: DECLINE IN PERCENTAGE OF FIRST-TERM
MEMBERS, U.S. HOUSE OF REPRESENTATIVES, 1789–1965*

* Data from Table 1.

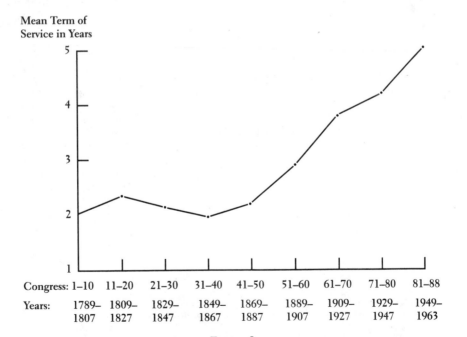

FIGURE 2

THE ESTABLISHMENT OF BOUNDARIES: INCREASE IN TERMS SERVED BY INCUMBENT
MEMBERS OF THE U.S. HOUSE OF REPRESENTATIVES, 1789–1963*

* Data from Table 2.

the House was relatively open to lateral entry. But the point to be emphasized here is that Clay's swift rise to the Speakership is only slightly atypical for the period before the turn of the twentieth century.

Table 3 demonstrates that there has been a change over time in the seniority of men selected for the Speakership. Before 1899, the mean years of service of members selected for the Speakership was six; after 1899, the mean rises steeply to twenty-six. Figure 3 . . . summarizes the gist of the finding in compact form.

Just as nineteenth-century Speakers arrived early at the pinnacle of House leadership, many left early as well and went on to other things: freshman Senators, state legislators, Cabinet members, and judges in the state courts. One became President of the U.S., one a Justice of the Supreme Court, one a Minister to Russia, one the Mayor of Auburn, New York, and one the Receiver-General of the Pennsylvania land office. Indeed, of the first twenty-seven men to be Speaker, during the first eighty-six years of the Republic, *none* died while serving in the House of Representatives. In contrast, of the last ten Speakers, six died while serving, and of course one other sits in the House today. . . .

The importance of this information about Speakers' careers is that it gives a strong indication of the development of the Speakership as a singular occupational specialty. In earlier times, the Speakership seems to have been regarded as a position of political leadership capable of being interchanged with other, comparable positions of public responsibility—and indeed a high incidence of this

TABLE 3. THE ESTABLISHMENT OF BOUNDARIES: YEARS SERVED IN CONGRESS BEFORE FIRST SELECTION AS SPEAKER

Date of Selection	Speaker	Years	Date of Selection	Speaker	Years
1789	Muhlenberg	1 or less	1861	Grow	10
1791	Trumbull	3	1863	Colfax	8
1795	Dayton	4	1869	Pomeroy	8
1799	Sedgwick	11	1869	Blaine	6
1801	Macon	10	1875	Kerr	8
1807	Varnum	12	1876	Randall	13
1811	Clay	1 or less	1881	Keifer	4
1814	Cheves	5	1883	Carlisle	6
1820	Taylor	7	1889	Reed	12
1821	Barbour	6	1891	Crisp	8
1827	Stephenson	6	1899	Henderson	16
1834	Bell	7	1903	Cannon	28
1835	Polk	10	1911	Clark	26
1839	Hunter	2	1919	Gillett	26
1841	White	6	1925	Longworth	22
1843	Jones	8	1931	Garner	26
1845	Davis	6	1933	Rainey	28
1847	Winthrop	8	1935	Byrns	25
1849	Cobb	6	1936	Bankhead	15
1851	Boyd	14	1940	Rayburn	27
1855	Banks	2	1946	Martin	22
1857	Orr	7	1962	McCormack	34
1859	Pennington	1 or less			

Mean Years of Prior
Service by Speakers

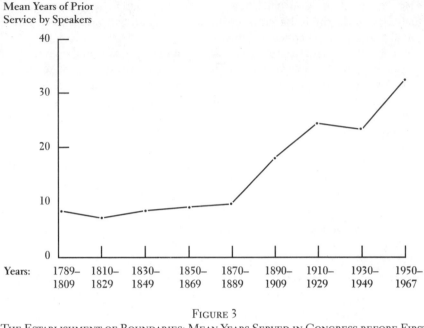

FIGURE 3
THE ESTABLISHMENT OF BOUNDARIES: MEAN YEARS SERVED IN CONGRESS BEFORE FIRST
BECOMING SPEAKER BY 20-YEAR INTERVALS*
* Data from Table 3.

sort of interchange is recorded in the careers of nineteenth century Speakers. That this sort of interchange is most unusual today suggests—as do the other data presented in this section—that one important feature in the development of the U.S. House of Representatives has been its differentiation from other organizations in the political system, a stabilization of its membership, and a growing specialization of its leaders to leadership of the House as a separate career.

The development of a specifically House leadership, the increase in the overall seniority of members, and the decrease in the influx of newcomers at any point in time have the effect not only of separating the House from other organizations in the political system, but also of facilitating the growth of stable ways of doing business within the institution, as we shall see shortly.

II. THE GROWTH OF INTERNAL COMPLEXITY

Simple operational indices of institutional complexity and universalistic-automated decision making are less easy to produce in neat and comparable time series. As for the growth of internal complexity, this is easy enough to establish impressionistically, but the most obvious quantitative measure presents a drastic problem of interpretation. The temptation is great to measure internal differentiation by simply counting the number of standing committees in each Congress.

This would produce a curiously curvilinear result, because in 1946 the number of standing committees was reduced from 48 to 19, and the number has since crept up only as far as 20.[11]

But the "streamlining," as it was called,[12] of 1946 can hardly be said to have reduced the internal differentiation of the House. On the contrary, by explicitly delineating the legislative jurisdictions of the committees, by consolidating committees with parallel and overlapping functions, by assigning committees exclusive oversight responsibilities over agencies of the executive branch, and by providing committees with expanded staff aid, the 1946 reorganization contributed to, rather than detracted from, the reliance of the House upon committees in the conduct of its business. Thus the mute testimony of the sheer numbers of committees cannot be accepted as an appropriate index of internal complexity. I shall therefore attempt a more anecdotal accounting procedure.

Briefly, the growth of internal complexity can be shown in three ways: in the growth in the autonomy and importance of committees, in the growth of specialized agencies of party leadership, and in the general increase in the provision of various emoluments and auxiliary aids to members in the form of office space, salaries, allowances, staff aid, and committee staffs.

A wholly satisfactory account of the historical development of the House committee system does not exist. But perhaps I can swiftly sketch in a number of plausible conclusions from the literature.

From the perspective of the present-day United States, the use of standing committees by Congress is scarcely a controversial issue.[13] Yet, in the beginning the House relied only very slightly upon standing committees. Instead of the present-day system, where bills are introduced in great profusion and automatically shunted to one or another of the committees whose jurisdictions are set forth in the rules, the practice in the first, and early Congresses was for subjects to be debated initially in the whole House and general principles settled upon, before they were parceled out for further action—fact-finding, detailed consideration or the proposal of a bill—to any one of four possible locations: an officer in the Executive Branch, a Committee of the Whole, a Select Committee formed *ad hoc* for the reception of a particular subject, or a standing committee. Generally, one of the alternatives to standing committees was used.

Of the First Congress, Harlow writes:

> The outstanding feature of procedure in the House was the important part played by the Committee of the Whole. Much of the business in the House of Delegates of Virginia was transacted in that way, and the Virginians were influential enough to impose their methods upon the federal House. . . . It was in Committee of the Whole that Congress worked out the first tarriff bill, and also the main outlines of such important measures as the laws organizing the executive departments. After the general principles were once determined, select committees would be appointed to work out the details, and to frame bills in accordance with the decision already agreed upon in Committee of the Whole. Considerable work was done by these select committees, especially after the first session.[14]

And Alexander says:

In the early history of the House the select committee . . . was used exclusively for the consideration of bills, resolutions, and other legislative matters.[15] As business increased and kindred subjects became scattered, however, a tendency to concentrate inaugurated a system of standing committees. It rooted itself slowly. There was an evident distrust of the centralizing influence of permanent bodies. Besides, it took important business from the many and gave it to a few, one standing committee of three or five members often taking the place of half a dozen select committees.[16]

It is difficult to disentangle the early growth of the standing committee system from concurrent developments in the party system. For as Alexander Hamilton took control of the administration of George Washington, and extended his influence toward men of like mind in Congress, the third alternative to standing committees—reference to a member of the Executive Branch—became an important device of the Federalist majority in the House.

By the winter of 1790 [Harlow writes] Hamilton was attracting attention because of his influence over Congress. . . . His ready intelligence grasped the truth at once that Jefferson spent more than ten years learning: that not even the Constitution of the United States could keep apart two such inseparable factors in government as executive and legislature.[17]

In the first two Congresses Hamilton is said to have used the Federalist caucus to guide debate in the Committee of the Whole, and also to have arranged for key financial measures to be referred directly to himself for detailed drafting.[18] This practice led, in the Second Congress, to sharp clashes with followers of Jefferson, who

made it perfectly clear that if they should ever get the upper hand in Congress, they would make short work of Hamilton, and restore to the House what they considered to be its constitutional authority over finance.[19]

The Republicans did in fact gain the upper hand in the Third Congress (elected in 1792) and they restored detailed power over finances to the Committee of the Whole. This did not work satisfactorily, however, and in the Fourth Congress a Committee on Ways and Means was formed. Harlow says:

The appointment of . . . standing committees, particularly . . . Ways and Means, was in a way a manifestation of the Republican theory of government. From their point of view, the members of the House, as the direct representatives of the voters, ought to be the mainspring of the whole system. Hitherto, the Federalists had sold their birthright by permitting the executive to take a more active part in the government than was warranted by the Constitution. The Republicans now planned to bring about the proper balance between the different branches, by broadening at once the scope of the operations of the House, and restricting the executive. It was the better to enable the House to take its assigned part that the new type of organization was worked out. Just as the heads of departments were looked upon as agents of the executive, so the committees would be considered as the agents of the House.[20]

During the presidency of Thomas Jefferson, committees were constituted and employed as agents of the President's faction in Congress which was in most matters actively led by the President himself. Binkley says:

> . . . When the House of Representatives had elected its Speaker and the committee chairmen had been appointed it was apparent to the discerning that lieutenants of the President had not appointed them, but his wishes, confidentially expressed, had determined them just as surely as if he had formally and publicly nominated them. Here was the fulfillment of Marshall's prediction that Jefferson would "embody himself in the House of Representatives."[21]

There is, however, some doubt as to Jefferson's absolute mastery over committee appointments, since it is also reported that Speaker Macon was extremely important in constituting the committees, and, in particular, in keeping John Randolph on as chairman of the Ways and Means Committee for some time after Randolph had repeatedly and violently broken with the Jefferson administration.[22]

Recently the suggestion has been made that the direct evidence is slight and contradictory that political parties in Congress went through rapid organization and differentiation in the earliest years of the Republic. This revisionist interpretation lays greater stress upon boarding house cliques, more or less sectional and more or less ideologically factional in their composition, as the heretofore neglected building blocks out of which the more conventionally partisan Congressional politics of the Jacksonian era eventually grew.[23]

But even revisionists concede to Jefferson a large influence over Congressional politics; the conventional accounts of the growth of the committee system are pretty much undisturbed by their critique. In essence, by the early years of the nineteenth century, the House committee system had passed through two distinct phases: the no-committee, Hamiltonian era, in which little or no internal differentiation within the institution was visible; and a Jeffersonian phase, in which factional alignments had begun to develop—these were exploited by the brilliant and incessant maneuverings of the President himself, who selected his lieutenants and confidants from the ranks of Congress *ad hoc*, as political requirements and opportunities dictated. During this period a small number of standing committees existed, but were not heavily relied upon. Their jurisdictions were not so securely fixed that the Speaker could not instead appoint select committees to deal with business that ought to have been sent to them.[24]

The advent of Henry Clay and the victory of the War Hawk faction in the elections of 1810 brought the committee system to its third phase. Clay for the first time used the Speaker's prerogative of appointment of members to committees independently of Presidential designs. There is some question whether Clay's appointment policies were calculated to further his policy preferences or merely his popularity (and hence his Presidential ambitions) within the factionally divided house,[25] but there seems no reason to doubt that Clay won for the Speakership a new measure of independence as a power base in the American political system. Under Clay five House committees were constituted to

oversee expenditures in executive departments, the first major institutionalization of the Congressional function of oversight. William N. Chambers writes:

> [By] 1814 the committee system had become the dominant force in the chamber.
> Thus effective power was exercised not by the President, as had been the case with Jef-
> ferson, but by factional Congressional leaders working through the speakership, the
> caucus, and the committees.[26]

For the next 100 years the committee system waxed and waned more or less
according to the ways in which committees were employed by the party or faction
that dominated the House and elected the Speaker. Figures from the latter
decades of the nineteenth century testify amply to the leeway afforded Speakers—especially new ones—in constituting committees regardless of their prior
composition.[27] In part, it was Speaker Cannon's increasing use of this prerogative
in an attempt to keep control of his fragmenting party that triggered the revolt
against his Speakership in 1910–11, and that led to the establishment of the committee system as we know it today.[28]

Under the fourth, decentralized, phase of the committee system, committees
have won solid institutionalized independence from party leaders both inside
and outside Congress. Their jurisdictions are fixed in the rules; their composition
is largely determined and their leadership entirely determined by the automatic
operation of seniority. Their work is increasingly technical and specialized, and
the way in which they organize internally to do their work is entirely at their own
discretion. Committees nowadays have developed an independent sovereignty of
their own, subject only to very infrequent reversals and modifications of their
powers by House party leaders backed by large and insistent majorities.

To a degree, the development over the last sixty years of an increasingly complex machinery of party leadership within the House cross-cuts and attenuates
the independent power of committees. Earlier, the leading faction in the House
elected the Speaker and the Speaker in turn distributed the chairmanships of key
committees to his principal allies and opponents. Thus the work of the House
was centralized to the extent that the leading faction in the House was centralized. But differences of opinion are not uncommon among qualified observers.
The Jeffersonian era, for example, is widely regarded as a high point of centralization during the nineteenth century. Harlow reports:

> From 1801 to 1808 the floor leader was distinctly the lieutenant of the executive.
> William B. Giles, who was actually referred to as "the premier, or prime minister,"
> Caesar A. Rodney, John Randolph of Roanoke, and Wilson Cary Nicholas all held that
> honorable position at one time or another. It was their duty to look after party interests
> in the House, and in particular to carry out the commands of the President. The status
> of these men was different from that of the floor leader of today . . . They were presi-
> dential agents, appointed by the executive, and dismissed at his pleasure.[29]

But another observer, a Federalist congressman quoted by Noble Cunningham, suggests that the Jeffersonian group was not at all times well organized:

The ruling faction in the legislature have not yet been able to understand each other. . . . There evidently appears much rivalry and jealousy among the leaders. S[amuel] Smith thinks his experience and great address ought to give him a preponderance in all their measures, whilst Nicholson evidently looks upon these pretensions of his colleague with contempt, and Giles thinks the first representative of the Ancient Dominion ought certainly on all important occasions to take the lead, and Johnny Randolph is perfectly astonished that his great abilities should be overlooked. There is likewise a great number of other persons who are impatient of control and disposed to revolt at any attempts at discipline.[30]

This certainly squares with the reports of Jefferson's own continued attempts, also revealed in his letters, to recruit men to the House with whom he could work.[31]

Despite Jefferson's difficulties, he was the most consistently successful of all the nineteenth century Presidents in "embodying himself in the House of Representatives." After Jefferson, the Speaker became a power in his own right; not infrequently he was a candidate for the Presidency himself, and the House was more or less organized around his, rather than the President's, political interests. There was no formal position of majority leader; the leading spokesman for the majority party on the floor was identified by personal qualities of leadership and by the favor of the Speaker (or in the Jeffersonian era, of the President) rather than by his institutional position.[32]

Later, however, the chairman of the Ways and Means Committee—a key post reserved for the chief lieutenant of the Speaker—became *de facto* floor leader, a natural consequence of his responsibilities in managing the tariff bills that were so important in nineteenth century congressional politics. Occasionally the chairman of the Committee on Appropriations was the *de facto* leader, especially during periods of war mobilization, when the power of the House in the political system was coextensive with the power of the purse.[33] In the last part of the nineteenth century, however, the Committee on Appropriations was temporarily dismantled, and the chairman of Ways and Means Committee began to receive the formal designation as party leader.

The high point of the Ways and Means chairman's power came in the aftermath of the 1910 revolt against the Speaker. The power of committee appointments was for Democrats lodged in the Ways and Means Committee. Chairman Oscar Underwood, in cooperation with President Wilson, for a time (1911–1915) eclipsed the Speaker and the committee chairmen by operating the majority party by caucus.[34]

But Underwood's successor as Chairman of Ways and Means, Claude Kitchin (majority leader 1915–1919), disapproved of Wilson's war policies; this made it cumbersome and impractical for the leader of the majority on the floor and in caucus to hold this job by virtue of what was becoming an automatic succession through seniority to the chairmanship of Ways and Means. A separation of the two roles was effected after the Democrats became the minority in 1919.[35] Ever since then, the majority leader's job has existed as a full-time position; the incumbent now holds a nominal, junior committee post but he rarely attends committee meetings. At the same time, the majority leader has become less of a

President's man, and the caucus is now dormant as an instrument of party leadership—although it now sometimes becomes a vehicle, especially at the opening of Congress, for the expression of widespread dissatisfaction by rank-and-file House members. Thus, while binding votes on policy matters have not been put through the caucus by party leaders, the Republican caucus has three times in recent years deposed party leaders and the Democratic caucus has deprived three of its members of their committee seniority.

Formally designated party whips are, like the differentiated post of majority leaders, an innovation principally of the twentieth century. The first whips date back to just before the turn of the century. In the early years, the designation seems to have been quite informal, and it is only recently that an elaborate whip system, with numerous deputies, a small staff, and formal procedures for canvassing members, has been established by both parties in the House.[36]

Thus, we can draw a contrast between the practices of recent and earlier years with respect to formal party leaders other than the Speaker:

(1) Floor leaders in the twentieth century are officially designated; in the nineteenth, they were often informally designated, indefinite, shifting or even competitive, and based on such factors as personal prestige, speaking ability, or Presidential favor.[37]

(2) Floor leaders in recent years are separated from the committee system and elected by party members; earlier they were prominent committee chairmen who were given their post by the Speaker, sometimes as a side-payment in the formation of a coalition to elect the Speaker.[38]

(3) Floor leaders today rely upon whip systems; before 1897 there were no formally designated whips.

A third indicator of the growth of internal organization is the growth of resources assigned to internal House management, measured in terms of personnel, facilities, and money. Visitors to Washington are not likely to forget the sight of the five large office buildings, three of them belonging to the House, that flank the Capitol. The oldest of these on the House side was built just after the turn of the century, in 1909, when a great many other of our indices show significant changes.

Reliable figures, past or present, on personnel assigned to the House are impossible to come by; but it is unlikely that a commentator today would agree with the observer early in this century who said:

> It is somewhat singular that Congress is one of the few legislative bodies that attempts to do its work almost entirely without expert assistance—without the aid of parliamentary counsel, without bill drafting and revising machinery and without legislative and reference agencies, and until now it has shown little inclination to regard with favor proposals looking toward the introduction of such agencies.[39]

Indeed, the only major contemporary study we have of congressional staff speaks of present "tendencies toward overexpansion of the congressional staff," and says that "Three-fourths of the committee aides interviewed" thought that professional staffs of committees were sufficiently large to handle their present work load.[40]

Needless to say, that work load has grown, and, though it is impossible to say precisely by how much, congressional staffs have grown as well. This is roughly reflected in figures that are more or less comparable over time on that portion of the legislative budget assigned to the House. These figures show the expected increases. However, except for the jump between 1945 and 1946, reflecting the new provisions for staff aid of the Legislative Reorganization Act, the changes in these figures over time are not as abrupt as is the case with other of our time series. . . . So we must regard this indicator as weak, but nevertheless pointing in the expected direction.

III. FROM PARTICULARISTIC AND DISCRETIONARY TO UNIVERSALISTIC AND AUTOMATED DECISION MAKING

The best evidence we have of a shift away from discretionary and toward automatic decision making is the growth of seniority as a criterion determining committee rank and the growth of the practice of deciding contested elections to the House strictly on the merits.

The literature on seniority presents a welter of conflicting testimony. Some commentators date the seniority system from 1910;[41] others say that seniority as a criterion for determining the committee rank of members was in use well before.[42] Woodrow Wilson's classic account of *Congressional Government* in 1884 pays tribute both to the independence of the committees and their chairmen and to the absolute discretion of the Speaker in the committee appointment process.[43] It is clear that the Speaker has no such power today. In another paper my colleagues and I present a detailed preliminary tabulation and discussion on the extent to which seniority in its contemporary meaning was followed in the selection of committee chairmen in the most recent 40 Congresses.[44] The central finding for our present purposes (summarized in Table 4) is that the seniority system—an automatic, universally applied, nondiscretionary method of selection—is now always used, but that formerly the process by which chairmen were selected was highly and later partially discretionary.

The figures for before 1911 can be interpreted as indicating the use of the Speaker's discretion in the appointment of committee chairmen. After 1911,

TABLE 4. THE GROWTH OF UNIVERSALISM: VIOLATIONS OF SENIORITY IN THE APPOINTMENT OF COMMITTEE CHAIRMEN, U.S. HOUSE OF REPRESENTATIVES, 1881–1963

Percentage of Committees on which the chairman was not selected by seniority, averaged by decades			
Congress:	47–51	52–56	57–61	62–66
Years:	1881–1889	1891–1899	1901–1909	1911–1919
Average:	60.4%	49.4%	19%	30.8%
Violations of Seniority				
Congress:	67–71	72–76	77–81	82–88
Years:	1921–1929	1931–1939	1941–1949	1951–1963
Average:	26%	23%	14%	.7%
Violations				

when committee appointment powers are vested in committees on committees, the figures principally reflect the growth of the norm that no one man should serve as chairman of more than one committee. Congressmen often sat on a large number of committees, and senior men rose to the top of more than one committee, but allowed less senior men to take the chair, much as the custom presently is in the U.S. Senate. After 1946, when the number of committees was drastically reduced, this practice died out, and a strictly automated system of seniority has asserted itself.

The settlement of contested elections on some basis other than the merits seems in earlier years to have been a common phenomenon. To this point, we can bring the testimony of a number of quotes and anecdotes, widely separated in time. Here are a few examples:

1795: A foreshadowing of future developments arose in the contested election of Joseph B. Varnum, of Massachusetts, in the Fourth Congress. This case became the focus of a struggle for power between the Federalists and the Anti-Federalists. It is an early instance of the triumph of the rule that all too often might makes right, at least in the settlement of election contests in the House of Representatives.

Varnum's election was contested on the principal ground that the Board of Selectmen of his home town (of which Board he was a member) had returned sixty votes more than there were qualified voters in the town. Since he had been elected with a certified overall plurality of eleven votes, investigation was warranted. Theodore Sedgwick, leader of the Federalists in the House, suggested that testimony be taken . . . inasmuch as the House alone had the power to compel the town clerk to produce the records containing the names of the illegal voters, if indeed any existed. Varnum, an Anti-Federalist, strongly protested against such a procedure. . . . He proposed . . . that petitioners . . . should present the names of the illegal voters, if they could do so. . . . This was impossible, since only the town clerk had access to the voting records of the town. The Anti-Federalists, who controlled the House at the time, on a party-line vote sustained Varnum's objections . . . in fact, the controlling faction even went so far as to adopt a resolution, again by a partisan vote, declaring that "the charges against [Varnum] are wholly unfounded. . . ." "Thus, amidst an outburst of derisive laughter, the incident closed like a harliquinade."[45]

1860s: I served in my second term on the Committee on Elections. . . . Election cases in the House up to that time were . . . determined entirely by party feeling. Whenever there was a plausible reason for making a contest the dominant party in the House almost always awarded the seat to the man of its own side. There is a well-authenticated story of Thaddeus Stevens, that going into the room of the Committee on Elections, of which he was a member, he found a hearing going on. He asked one of his Republican colleagues what was the point in the case. "There is not much point to it," was the answer. "They are both damned scoundrels." "Well," said Stevens, "which is the Republican damned scoundrel? I want to go for the Republican damned scoundrel."[46]

1869: All traces of a judicial character in these proceedings are fast fading away. . . . Each case is coming to be a mere partisan struggle. At the dictate of party majorities, the Committee [on Elections] must fight, not follow, the law and the evidence. . . . This tendency is so manifest . . . that it has ceased to be questioned, and is now but little resisted . . . [E]fforts . . . to hold the judgments of the Committee on Elections up above the dirty pool of party politics have encountered such bitter and unsparing denunciation, and such rebuke for treason to party fealty, that they are not likely often to be repeated.[47]

1890:   The [elections] committee usually divides on the line of party . . . and the House usually follows in the same way. . . . The decision of election cases invariably increases the party which organized the House and . . . appoints the majority of the Committee on Elections. Probably there is not an instance on record where the minority was increased by the decision of contested cases. . . . It may be said that our present method of determining election cases is . . . unjust to members and contestants and fails to secure the representation which the people have chosen.[48]

1895:   A most casual inspection of the workings of the present system of deciding election contests will show that it barely maintains the form of a judicial inquiry and that it is thoroughly tainted with the grossest partisanship. . . . When it is alleged that members of a minority do not generally contest seats, a striking tribute is paid to the partisanship of the present system.[49]

1899:   The Republican majority in this House [Fifty-sixth Congress] was reduced about fifty from the previous Congress, but before the [first] session closed, a dozen or more Democrats lost their seats in election contests, which gave the Republicans a comfortable majority with which to do business.[50]

1905:   Today it is simply a contest between two parties for political influence and the rewards of office, or sometimes a contest between the majority in the House and a constituency of the minority party . . . In the period [1865–1905, Thirty-ninth through Fifty-eighth Congresses] . . . the majority deprived itself of seats only nine times, while it deprived the minority of seats eighty-two times.[51]

A journalist writing at the beginning of the twentieth century summarizes the situation as he had encountered it over a twenty-year period:

It may be said . . . that there is no fairness whatever exercised in . . . contests for seats, especially where the majority needs the vote for party purposes. Hundreds of men have lost their seats in Congress, to which they were justly entitled upon all fair, reasonable, and legal grounds, and others put in their places for purely partisan reasons. This has always been so and doubtless will continue so. . . .[52]

In fact, it has not continued so; nowadays, contested elections are settled with much more regard to due process and the merits of the case than was true throughout the nineteenth century. By 1926, a minority member of the Committee on Elections No. 1 could say:

In the eight years I have served on Elections Committees and six years upon this Committee, I have never seen partisanship creep into that Committee but one time. There has not been any partisanship in the Committee since the distinguished gentleman from Utah became Chairman of that Committee. A Democrat was seated the last time over a Republican by this Committee, and every member of the Committee voted to seat that Democrat.[53]

This quotation suggests a method by which the development of universalistic criteria for settling contested House elections can be monitored, namely, measuring the extent to which party lines are breached in committee reports and in voting on the floor in contest cases. I have made no such study, but on the basis of the accumulated weight of contemporary reports such as I have been quoting, I predict that a time series would show strict party voting in the nineteenth century, switching to unanimity or near-unanimity, in most cases, from the early years of the twentieth century onward.

Attempts to establish legal precedents for the settlement of contested elections date from the recommendations of the Ames Committee in 1791. In 1798 a law was enacted prescribing a uniform mode of taking testimony and for compelling the attendance of witnesses. This law was required to be renewed in each Congress and was allowed to lapse in 1804. Bills embodying similar laws were proposed in 1805, 1806, 1810, 1813, and 1830. Not until 1851 was such a law passed, which provided for the gathering of testimony forming the bases of the proofs of each contestant's claim, but not for rules concerning other aspects of contested elections. More significant, however, was a clause permitting the House to set the law aside in whole or in part in specific cases, which apparently the House availed itself of with some regularity in the nineteenth century. With a few modifications this law is still in effect.[54]

The absolute number of contests shows a decrease in recent decades, as does the number of contests in relation to the number of seats. This suggests that the practice of instigating contests for frivolous reasons has passed into history; contemporary House procedures no longer hold out the hope of success for such contests.[55] Table 5 gives the figures, by decades.

There is today, certainly, no wholesale stealing of seats. If any bias exists in the system, it probably favors the protection of incumbents irrespective of party,[56] and hence (we may surmise not incidentally) the protection of the boundaries of the organization.

IV. CAUSES, CONSEQUENCES, CONCLUSIONS

It seems reasonable to conclude that one of the main long-run changes in the U.S. House of Representatives has been toward greater institutionalization. Knowing this, we may wish to ask, at a minimum, three questions: What caused it? What follows from it? What can this case tell us about the process in general? It is not from lack of space alone that our answers to each of these questions will be brief and highly speculative.

Not much, for example, is known about the causes of institutionalization. The best theoretical guess in the literature is probably Durkheim's: "The division of labor varies in direct ratio with the volume and density of societies, and, if it progresses in a continuous manner in the course of social development, it is because societies become regularly denser and generally more voluminous."[57] "Density" in at least some sense is capable of being operationalized and measured separately from its institutional consequences. For present purposes, the proposition

TABLE 5. THE GROWTH OF UNIVERSALISM: CONTESTED ELECTIONS IN THE HOUSE
BY DECADES, 1789–1964

Congress	Number of Contested Seats	Mean Seats in House for Decade	% Seats Contested Per Congress*
1– 5 (1789–1798)	16	89.8	3.56
6–10 (1799–1808)	12	126.6	1.90
11–15 (1809–1818)	16	166.4	1.92
16–20 (1819–1828)	12	202.6	1.18
21–25 (1829–1838)	11	230.0	.96
26–30 (1839–1848)	17	231.8	1.46
31–35 (1849–1858)	23	233.0	1.98
36–40 (1859–1868)	73	196.4	7.44
41–45 (1869–1878)	72	273.0	5.28
46–50 (1879–1888)	58	312.2	3.72
51–55 (1889–1898)	87	346.8	5.02
56–60 (1899–1908)	41	374.4	2.20
61–65 (1909–1918)	36	417.4	1.72
66–70 (1919–1928)	23	435.0	1.06
71–75 (1929–1938)	25	435.0	1.14
76–80 (1939–1948)	15	435.0	.68
81–85 (1949–1958)	12	435.0	.56
86–88 (1959–1964)	8	437.0	.90

* Column 2 divided by column 3, over the number of Congresses (5 except in last instance).
Sources: Dempsey op. cit., Appendix I, and George B. Galloway, *History of the U.S. House of Representatives* (House Document 246, 87th Congress, 1st session) (Washington: U.S. Government Printing Office, 1962), pp. 215–216.

can probably be rendered as follows: As the responsibilities of the national government grew, as a larger proportion of the national economy was affected by decisions taken at the center, the agencies of the national government institutionalized.[58] Another, complementary, translation of the density theorem would be that as organizations grow in size, they tend to develop internally in ways predicted by the theory of institutionalization. Size and increasing work-load seem to me in principle measurable phenomena.[59] Size alone, in fact, seems almost too easy. Until a deliberative body has some minimum amount of work to do, the necessity for interaction among its members remains slight, and, having no purpose, coordination by means of a division of labor, rule and regulations, precedents and so on, seem unlikely to develop. So a somewhat more complicated formula has to be worked out, perhaps relating the size of an organization to the amount of work it performs (e.g., number of work-days per year, number of full-time as opposed to nominal members, number of items considered, number of reports rendered) before the strength of "density" and "volume" can be tested as causes of the process of institutionalization.

A discussion of the consequences of the House's institutionalization must be equally tentative. It is hard—indeed, for the contemporary observer, impossible—to shake the conviction that the House's institutional structure does matter greatly in the production of political outcomes. A recent popular account begins:

A United States Congressman has two principal functions: to make laws and to keep laws from being made. The first of these he and his colleagues perform only with sweat, patience and a remarkable skill in the handling of creaking machinery; but the second they perform daily, with ease and infinite variety.[60]

No observer who focuses upon policy results, or who cares about the outputs of the American legislative process, fails to note the "complicated forms and diversified structure" which "confuse the vision, and conceal the system which underlies its composition."[61] All this is such settled knowledge that it seems unnecessary to mention it here. Still, it is important to stress that the very features of the House which casual observers and freshman legislators find most obtrusive are principal consequences of (among other things) the process we have been describing.[62]

It is, however, not merely the complexity or the venerability of the machinery that they notice. These, in our discussion so far, have been treated as defining characteristics rather than consequences of institutionalization. What puzzles and irks the outside observer is a partial displacement of goals, and a focus of resources upon internal processes at the expense of external demands, that come as a consequence of institutionalization. This process of displacement is, of course, well known to social theory in other settings.[63] A closer look at the general character of this displacement is bound to suggest a number of additional consequences.

For example, Representatives may find that the process of institutionalization has increased their incentives to stay within the system. For them, the displacement of resources transforms the organization from a convenient instrument for the pursuit of social policies into an end value itself, a prime source of gratification, of status and power.[64]

The increasing complexity of the division of labor presents an opportunity for individual Representatives to specialize and thereby enormously increase their influence upon a narrow range of policy outcomes in the political system at large. Considered separately, the phenomenon of specialization may strike the superficial observer as productive of narrow-minded drones. But the total impact of a cadre of specialists operating over the entire spectrum of public policies is a formidable asset for a political institution; and it has undoubtedly enabled the House to retain a measure of autonomy and influence that is quite exceptional for a twentieth century legislature.[65]

Institutionalization has, in the House, on the whole meant the decentralization of power. This has created a great many important and interesting jobs within the House, and thus increased the attractiveness of service therein as a career. Proposed reforms of Congress which seek to move toward a recentralization of Congressional power rarely consider this fact. But it is at least possible that some moves to restore discretion to the Speaker, or to centralized party agencies outside Congress, would reduce the effectiveness of Congress far below the level anticipated, because the House would come to be less valued in and of itself, its division of labor would provide less of a power base for subject matter specialists, and the incentives to stay within the organization would sharply decline.

Thus we can argue that, along with the more obvious effects of institutionalization, the process has also served to increase the power of the House within the political system and to spread somewhat more widely incentives for legislators to participate actively in policy-making.

A final possible consequence of institutionalization can be suggested: that the process tends to promote professional norms of conduct among participants. Indeed, something like these norms are built into the definition of institutionalization by some commentators.[66] But the built-in norms typically mentioned in discussions of "organization men" have to do with the segmental, ritualized interaction that characterizes organizations coordinated by hierarchical means; slightly different predictions about norms would have to be made for more decentralized, more egalitarian institutionalized legislative bodies.

In fact, there is coming to be a sizable body of literature about the norms of professional legislative conduct. Time and again, the norms of predictability, courtesy, and reciprocity are offered by professional legislators as central to the rules of the legislative game.[67] Thus, we can suggest a hypothesis that the extent to which these norms are widely applied in a legislative body is a direct function of that body's structural institutionalization. Appropriate tests can be made cross-sectionally, by comparing contemporary legislatures that vary with respect to boundary-maintenance, internal complexity, and universalistic-automated internal decision making. Historically, less satisfactory tests are possible, since a number of vagaries enter into the determination of what is recorded and what is not, and since antecedent factors may account for both structural and normative institutionalization. This makes it hard to estimate the dispersion and importance of norms of conduct.

Nevertheless, the history of the House does suggest that there has been a growth in the rather tame virtues of reciprocity, courtesy, and predictability in legislative life since the turn of the century. Clem Miller describes human relations in the House of today:

> One's overwhelming first impression as a member of Congress is the aura of friendliness that surrounds the life of a congressman. No wonder that "few die and none resign." Almost everyone is unfailingly polite and courteous. Window washers, clerks, senators—it cuts all ways. We live in a cocoon of good feeling. . . .[68]

No doubt there are breaches in the fabric of good fellowship, mostly unpublicized, but the student of Congress cannot refrain even so from comparing this testimony with the following sampling of nineteenth century congressional conduct:

> Upon resuming his seat, after having replied to a severe personal arraignment of Henry Clay, former Speaker White, without the slightest warning, received a blow in the face. In the fight that followed a pistol was discharged wounding an officer of the police. John Bell, the distinguished Speaker and statesman, had a similar experience in Committee of the Whole (1838). The fisticuffs became so violent that even the Chair would not quell it. Later in the day both parties apologized and "made their submissions." On February 6, 1845, Edward J. Black, of Georgia, "crossed over from his seat, and, coming within the bar behind Joshua R. Giddings as he was speaking, made a pass at the back of his head with a cane. William H. Hammett, of Mississippi, threw his arms round Black and bore him off as he would a woman from a fire. . . ."

When Reuben M. Whitney was before a committee of investigation in 1837, Bailie Peyton, of Tennessee, taking offense at one of his answers, threatened him fiercely, and when he rose to claim the committee's protection, Mr. Peyton, with due and appropriate profanity, shouted: "You shan't say one word while you are in this room; if you do I will put you to death." The chairman, Henry A. Wise, added: "Yes; this insolence is insufferable." As both these gentlemen were armed with deadly weapons, the witness could hardly be blamed for not wanting to testify before the committee again.

"These were not pleasant days," writes Thomas B. Reed. "Men were not nice in their treatment of each other."[69]

Indeed they were not: Nineteenth century accounts of Congressional behavior abound in passages like these. There is the consternation of members who put up with the presence on the floor of John Randolph's hunting dogs.[70] There is the famous scene on May 22, 1851, when Representative Preston Brooks of South Carolina entered the U.S. Senate and beat Senator Charles Sumner senseless with a cane,[71] and the record contains accounts of more than one such occasion:

When Matthew Lyon, of Kentucky, spat in his face, [Roger] Griswold [of Connecticut, a member 1795–1805] stiffened his arm to strike, but remembering where he was, he coolly wiped his cheek. But after the House by its vote failed to expel Lyon, he "beat him with great violence," says a contemporary chronicle, "using a strong walking-stick."[72]

With all the ill will that the heat of battle sometimes generates currently, the House has long since left behind the era of guns and dogs, canings and fisticuffs, that occupied so much of the nineteenth century scene. No doubt this reflects general changes in manners and morals, but it also reflects a growth in the value of the House as an institution capable of claiming the loyalty and good behavior of its members.[73] The best test of the hypothesis, to be sure, remains the cross-sectional one. If American state legislatures, for example, can be found to differ significantly with respect to structural institutionalization, they may also be found to vary concomitantly with respect to the application of the norms of professional legislative life.[74]

Finally, the study of the institutionalization of the House affords us a perspective from which to comment upon the process in general. First, as to its reversibility. Many of our indicators show a substantial decay in the institutional structure of the House in the period surrounding the Civil War. In sheer numbers, the House declined from 237 members in the Congress of 1859 to 178 in the Congress of 1861; not until a decade later did the House regain its former strength. Frivolous contests for seats reached a height in this period, and our rank-and-file boundary measures reflect decay as well. It may be true, and it is certainly amusing, that the strength of the British Admiralty grows as the number of ships declines;[75] but that this illustrates an inflexibly narcissistic law of institutional growth may be doubted. As institutions grow, our expectations about the displacement of resources inward do give us warrant to predict that they will resist decay, but the indications of curve-linearity in our present findings give us ample warning that institutions are also continuously subject to environmental influence and their power to modify and channel that influence is bound to be less than all-encompassing.

Some of our indicators give conditional support for a "take-off" theory of modernization. If one of the stigmata of the take-off to modernity is the rapid development of universalistic, bounded, complex institutional forms, the data presented here lend this theory some plausibility.[76] This "big bang" seems to come in the 1890–1910 period, on at least some of the measures.

In conclusion, these findings suggest that increasing hierarchical structure is not a necessary feature of the institutionalization process. Organizations other than bureaucracies, it seems clear, also are capable of having natural histories which increase their viability in the modern world without forcing them into uniformly centralized patterns of authority.

NOTES

1. A good recent summary of literature bearing on this point as it applies to the study of political development may be found in Samuel P. Huntington, "Political Development and Political Decay," *World Politics* 17 (April, 1965). 386–430.

2. Robert A. Dahl speaks of "the three great milestones in the development of democratic institutions—the right to participate in governmental decisions by casting a vote, the right to be represented, and the right of an organized opposition to appeal for votes against the government in elections and in parliament." In enumerating these three great achievements of democratic government, Dahl also implies that they are embodied principally in three main institutions: parties, elections, and legislatures: Robert A. Dahl (ed.), *Political Oppositions in Western Democracies* (New Haven and London: Yale University Press, 1966), p. xi. See also William Nisbet Chambers, "Party Development and the American Mainstream," especially pp. 18–19, in Chambers and Walter Dean Burnham (eds.), *The American Party Systems: Stages of Political Development* (New York: Oxford, 1967).

3. See for example, Nelson W. Polsby, "Congressional Research and Congressional Data: A Preliminary Statement" (mimeo) delivered at the Conference on Congressional Research, sponsored by the Inter-university Consortium for Political Research and the Social Science Research Council at the Brookings Institution, Washington, D.C., April 3–4, 1964; H. Douglas Price, "The Congressman and the Electoral Arena" (mimeo, 1964); and T. Richard Witmer, "The Aging of the House," *Political Science Quarterly* 79 (December, 1964): 526–541.

4. Sir Henry Summer Maine, *Ancient Law* (London: John Murray, 1908), pp. 220–325.

5. Ferdinand Tönnies, *Community and Society (Gemeinschaft und Gesellschaft)* (East Lansing: Michigan State University Press, 1957). See, in particular, the introductory commentary by Charles P. Loomis and John C. McKinney, "The Application of Gemeinschaft and Gesellschaft as Related to Other Typologies," ibid., pp. 12–29.

6. Max Weber, *The Theory of Social and Economic Organization* (Glencoe: Free Press, 1947), pp. 328ff.

7. Emile Durkheim, *The Division of Labor in Society* (Glencoe: Free Press, 1947).

8. C. Northcote Parkinson, *Parkinson's Law* (Boston: Houghton Mifflin, 1957).

9. The only successful modern attempt I am aware of that employs a classical theory of institutionalization in an empirical study of something other than a bureaucracy is Harold W. Pfautz's "Christian Science: The Sociology of a Social Movement and Religious Group" (unpublished Ph.D. dissertation, Department of Sociology, University of Chicago, 1954). See also Harold W. Pfautz, "The Sociology of Secularization: Religious Groups," *American Journal of Sociology* 41 (September, 1955):

121–128, and Pfautz, "A Case Study of an Urban Religious Movement: Christian Science" in E. W. Burgess and D. J. Bogue (eds.), *Contributions to Urban Sociology* (Chicago and London: University of Chicago Press, 1963), pp. 284–303.

10. On Clay, see Bernard Mayo, *Henry Clay: Spokesman of the New West* (Boston: Houghton Mifflin, 1937); Glyndon G. Van Deusen, *The Life of Henry Clay* (Boston: Little, Brown, 1937); Mary Parker Follett, *The Speaker of the House of Representatives* (New York: Longman's, Green, 1896), pp. 69–82; and Booth Mooney, *Mr. Speaker* (Chicago: Follett, 1964), pp. 21–48.

11. The combined totals of standing committees and subcommittees might be a better guide; but reliable information about subcommittees only exists for the most recent two decades.

12. I believe the word is George Galloway's. See *Congress at the Crossroads* (New York: Crowell, 1946), p. 340.

13. It certainly is, on the other hand, in the present-day United Kingdom, where purely legislative committees are regarded as a threat to the cohesion of the national political parties because they would give the parliamentary parties special instruments with which they could develop independent policy judgments and expertise and exercise oversight over an executive which is, after all, not formally constituted as an entity separate from Parliament. Thus committees can be construed as fundamentally inimical to unified Cabinet government. For an overview see Bernard Crick, *The Reform of Parliament* (Garden City: Doubleday Anchor, 1965); *The Political Quarterly* 36 (July-September, 1965); and Andrew Hill and Anthony Whichelow, *What's Wrong with Parliament?* (Harmondsworth: Penguin, 1964), esp. pp. 64–82. See also a most illuminating essay by Robert C. Fried on the general conditions under which various political institutions (including legislatures) are strong or weak within their political systems: *Comparative Political Institutions* (New York: Macmillan, 1966), esp. p. 31.

14. Ralph V. Harlow, *The History of Legislative Methods in the Period Before 1825* (New Haven: Yale, 1917), pp. 127–128. See also Joseph Cooper, "Jeffersonian Attitudes Toward Executive Leadership and Committee Development in the House of Representatives 1789–1829," *Western Political Quarterly* 18 (March, 1965): 45–63; and Cooper, "Congress and Its Committees in the Legislative Process" (unpublished Ph.D. dissertation, Department of Government, Harvard University, 1960), pp. 1–65.

15. On changes in the use of select committees, Lauros G. McConachie says: "Business of the earlier Houses went to hosts of select committees. At least three hundred and fifty were raised in the Third Congress. A special committee had to be formed for every petty claim. A bill founded on the report of one small committee had to be recommended to, or carefully drafted by, yet another committee. But the decline in the number of these select committees was strikingly rapid. In twenty years, at the Congress of 1813–1815 with its three war sessions, it had fallen to about seventy": *Congressional Committees* (New York: Crowell, 1898), p. 124. See also Galloway, op. cit., p. 88.

16. DeAlva Stanwood Alexander, *History and Procedure of the House of Representatives* (Boston: Houghton-Mifflin, 1916), p. 228.

17. Harlow, op. cit., pp. 141.

18. Ibid., pp. 120–150.

19. Ibid., p. 151.

20. Ibid., pp. 157–158.

21. Wilfred E. Binkley, *President and Congress* (New York: Vintage, 1962), p. 64.

22. Of Randolph's initial appointment as chairman of the Ways and Means Committee, in the Seventh Congress, Noble Cunningham writes: "in view of the close friendship of [Speaker] Macon and Randolph, it is unlikely that Jefferson had any influence in the choice of Randolph as Chairman of the Ways and Means Committee": *Jeffersonian Republicans in Power* (Chapel Hill: University of North Carolina Press, 1963), p. 73. See also Henry Adams, *John Randolph* (Boston: Houghton-Mifflin, 1886), pp. 54–55, 123–165ff; and Adams, *History of the United States of America During the Administrations of Thomas Jefferson and James Madison* (New York: Boni, 1930), Vol. III, p. 128.

23. This interpretation is the brilliant achievement of James S. Young in *The Washington Community: 1800–1828* (New York: Columbia University Press, 1966). It harmonizes with Richard P. McCormick's notion of a series of historically discrete American party systems. See McCormick, *The Second American Party System* (Chapel Hill: University of North Carolina Press, 1966).

24. See Wilfred Binkley, "The President and Congress," *Journal of Politics* 11 (February 1949): 65–79.

25. See Young, op. cit., pp. 131–135.

26. William Nisbet Chambers, *Political Parties in a New Nation* (New York: Oxford, 1963), p. 194.

27. See Nelson W. Polsby, Miriam Gallaher and Barry Spencer Rundquist, "The Growth of the Seniority System in the Selection of Committee Chairman in the U.S. House of Representatives" (mimeo., October, 1967).

28. Ibid. Chang-wei Chiu says, "The power of appointing committees by the Speaker was a real issue in the attempts to reform the House. In the eyes of the insurgents no change would be of any real and permanent value to the country if that change did not take away from the Speaker the power of appointing standing committees": *The Speaker of The House of Representatives Since 1896* (New York: Columbia University Press, 1928), pp. 71–72.

29. Harlow, op. cit., p. 176.

30. Cunningham, op. cit., p. 74. The quotation is from a letter from Roger Griswold to John Rutledge, December 14, 1801.

31. See Jefferson's letters to Barnabas Bidwell and Wilson Cary Nicholas cited in ibid., pp. 89–92. Also Henry Adams, *History*, op. cit., Vol. III, pp. 166–171.

32. Randall Ripley, in his forthcoming Brookings study, *Party Leadership in the House of Representatives* (mimeo, 1966) says: "The Majority leader did not become a separate and consistently identifiable party figure until some time around the turn of the century." Ripley also discusses the indeterminancy of the minority leadership in the mid-19th century. Of an earlier period (1800–1828) Young (op. cit., pp. 126–127) writes: "Party members elected no leaders, designated no functionaries to speak in their behalf or to carry out any legislative task assignments. The party had no whips, no seniority leaders. There were no committees on committees, no steering committees, no policy committees: none of the organizational apparatus that marks the twentieth-century congressional parties. . . ." On pp. 127–130 Young argues that although there were a number of party leaders in the House, there was no fixed majority leader. "[W]hile the names of Randolph, Giles, Nicholas and Rodney appear more frequently, at least twenty Republican legislators in the eight years of Jefferson's administration are either explicitly identified as leaders in the documentary record or are associated with activities strongly suggesting a role of presidential spokesmanship" (p. 130).

33. From 1865–1869, for example, Thaddeus Stevens left the chairmanship of Ways and Means (a post he had held from 1861–1865) to become chairman of the new Committee on Appropriations. See Samuel W. McCall, *Thaddeus Stevens* (Boston: Houghton-Mifflin, 1899), pp. 259–260. McCall says, oddly, that at the time the Appropriations Committee was not very important, but this is hard to credit. From 1895–1899, Joseph G. Cannon was floor leader and chairman of Appropriations. See Edward T. Taylor, *A History of the Committee on Appropriations* (House Document 299, 77th Congress, 1st Session) (Washington, Government Printing Office, 1941).

34. See George Rothwell Brown, *The Leadership of Congress* (Indianapolis: Bobbs Merrill, 1922), pp. 174–177, 183–184; Oscar King Davis, "Where Underwood Stands," *Outlook* (December 23, 1911): 197–201. At p. 199: "Every move Mr. Underwood has made, every bill he has brought forward, he first submitted to a caucus. . . . Not until the last man had had his say was the vote taken that was to bind them all to united action in the House. Every time that vote has been either unanimous or nearly so, and invariably it has approved Mr. Underwood." See also Binkley, "The President and Congress," op. cit., p. 72.

35. See Ripley, op. cit.; Hasbrouck, op. cit., p. 94; and Alex M. Arnett, *Claude Kitchin and the Wilson War Policies* (Boston: Little, Brown, 1937), pp. 42, 71–72, 75–76, 88–89 and passim.

36. See Randall B. Ripley, "The Party Whip Organization in the United States House of Representatives" this *Review*, 58 (September, 1964): pp. 561–576.

37. See, e.g., Alexander, op. cit., pp. 111–114. "[W]ith very few exceptions, the really eminent debaters . . . were in the Senate; otherwise, MacDuffie [who served 1821–1834], Chief of the Hotspurs, could scarcely have justified his title to floor leader," p. 114.

38. Ibid., p. 110: "In selecting a floor leader the Speaker often names his party opponent."

39. James W. Garner, "Executive Participation in Legislation as a Means of Increasing Legislative Efficiency," *Proceedings of the American Political Science Association at its Tenth Annual Meeting* (Baltimore: Waverly Press, 1914), p. 187.

40. Kenneth Kofmehl, *Professional Staffs of Congress* (Lafayette, Indiana: Purdue University Press, 1962), pp. 97–99. The quotation is at p. 99. Kofmehl presents a short, nonquantitative historical

sketch of the growth of committee staffs on pp. 3–5. See also Samuel C. Patterson "Congressional Committee Professional Staffing: Capabilities and Constraints," a paper presented at the Planning Conference of the Comparative Administration Group, Legislative Services Project, Planting Fields, New York, December 8–10, 1967; and Lindsay Rogers "The Staffing of Congress" *Political Science Quarterly* 56 (March, 1941): pp. 1–22.

41. George B. Galloway, op. cit., p. 187; George Goodwin, Jr., "The Seniority System in Congress" this *Review* 53 (June, 1959): p. 417.

42. Chiu, op. cit., pp. 68–72; James K. Pollock, Jr., "The Seniority Rule in Congress," *North American Review* 222 (1925): pp. 235, 236; Asher Hinds, "The Speaker of the House of Representatives," this *Review* 3 (May, 1909): pp. 160–161.

43. Woodrow Wilson, *Congressional Government* (New York: Meridian Books, 1956) (First edition, 1884). See, for example, on pp. 85–86: "The Speaker is expected to constitute the Committees in accordance with his own political views . . . [and he] generally uses his powers as freely and imperatively as he is expected to use them. He unhesitatingly acts as the legislative chief of his party, organizing the Committees in the interest of this or that policy, not covertly or on the sly, as one who does something of which he is ashamed, but openly and confidently, as one who does his duty. . . ." Compare this with p. 82: "I know not how better to describe our form of government in a single phrase than by calling it a government by the chairmen of the Standing Committees of Congress. This disintegrate ministry, as it figures on the floor of the House of Representatives, has many peculiarities. In the first place, it is made up of the elders of the assembly; for, by custom, seniority in congressional service determines the bestowal of the principal chairmanships. . . ."

44. Polsby, Gallaher, and Rundquist, op. cit.

45. John Thomas Dempsey, "Control by Congress over the Seating and Disciplining of Members" (unpublished Ph.D. dissertation, The University of Michigan, 1956), pp. 50–51. The final quotation is from Alexander, op. cit., p. 315.

46. George F. Hoar, *Autobiography of Seventy Years* (New York: Scribner, 1903), Vol. I, p. 268. Hoar claims that during the time he served on the Elections Committee in the Forty-second Congress (1871–73), contested elections were settled on the merits.

47. Henry L. Dawes, "The Mode of Procedure in Cases of Contested Elections," *Journal of Social Science* (No. 2, 1870): 56–68. Quoted passages are at p. 64. Dempsey, op. cit., pp. 83–84, identifies Dawes as a one-time chairman of the House Committee on Elections. See also C. H. Rammelkamp, "Contested Congressional Elections," *Political Science Quarterly* 20 (Sept., 1905): pp. 434–435.

48. Thomas B. Reed, "Contested Elections," *North American Review* 151 (July, 1890): pp. 112–120. Quoted passages are at pp. 114 and 117. See also Alexander, op. cit., p. 323.

49. Report from Elections Committee No. 3, Mr. McCall, chairman, quoted in Rammelkamp, op. cit., p. 435.

50. O. O. Stealey, *Twenty Years in the Press Gallery* (New York: published by the author, 1906), p. 147.

51. Rammelkamp, op. cit., pp. 421–442. Quoted passages are from pp. 423 and 434.

52. Stealey, op. cit., p. 147.

53. Quoted in Paul De Witt Hasbrouck, *Party Government in the House of Representatives* (New York: Macmillan, 1927), p. 40.

54. See U.S., *Revised Statutes of the United States*, Title II, Ch. 8, Sections 105–130, and Dempsey, op. cit., pp. 55–60. For indications of attempts to routinize the process of adjudication by setting up general criteria to govern House disposition of contested elections, see two 1933 cases: Gormley vs. Goss (House Report 893, 73rd Congress; see also 78 *Congressional Record*, pp. 4035, 7087, April 20, 1934) and Chandler vs. Burnham (House Report 1278, 73rd Congress; see also 78 *Congressional Record*, pp. 6971, 8921, May 15, 1934).

55. On the relatively scrupulous handling of a recent contest see Richard H. Rovere, "Letter from Washington," *New Yorker* (October 16, 1965), 233–244. Rovere (at p. 243) identifies criteria governing the report on the 1965 challenge by the Mississippi Freedom Democratic Party to the entire Mississippi House delegation in the following passage: ". . . the majority could find no way to report favorably [on the challenge] without, as it seemed to them, abandoning due process and their constitutional responsibilities. Neither, for that matter, could the minority report, which went no further than to urge continued study."

56. See, e.g., the assignment of burden of proof in Gormley vs. Goss and Chandler vs. Burnham, loc. cit.

57. Durkheim, op. cit., p. 262. Durkheim in turn cites Comte as describing this mechanism. Weber's notion, that the central precondition for the development of bureaucratic institutions is the money economy, strikes me as less interesting and less plausible. See H. H. Gerth and C. Wright Mills (eds.), *From Max Weber: Essays in Sociology* (N.Y.: Oxford University Press, 1946), pp. 204–209. See, however, Weber's comment (p. 211): "It is obvious that technically the great modern state is absolutely dependent upon a bureaucratic basis. The larger the state, and the more it is or the more it becomes a great power state, the more unconditionally is this the case."

58. Cf. Young, op. cit., pp. 252–253, who seems to put great stress on public attitudes and local political organization as causes of the growth in the influence of the central government.

59. George Galloway's *History of the U.S. House of Representatives*, 87th Congress, 1st Session, House Document No. 246 (Washington: U.S. Government Printing Office, 1962), pp. 215–216, has a convenient scorecard on the size and party composition of the House for the first 87 Congresses. Mere size has been found to be an indifferent predictor of the internal complexity of bureaucratic organizations. See Richard H. Hall, J. Eugene Haas and Norman J. Johnson, "Organizational Size, Complexity, and Formalization," *American Sociological Review* 32 (December, 1967): 903–912.

60. Robert Bendiner, *Obstacle Course on Capitol Hill* (N.Y.: McGraw-Hill, 1964), p. 15.

61. Woodrow Wilson, op. cit., p. 57.

62. This is not to say, however, that the policy output of the House is exclusively determined by its level of institutionalization. The 88th, 89th and 90th Congresses all represent more or less equivalent levels of institutionalization, yet their policy outputs varied greatly. Nevertheless if the casual observer asked why it took thirty years, more or less, to get the New Deal enacted in the House, and what sorts of strategies and circumstances made the legislative output of the 89th Congress possible, answers would have to refer quite extensively to structural properties of the institution.

63. See, e.g., Peter M. Blau, *The Dynamics of Bureaucracy* (Chicago: University of Chicago Press, 1955), passim; Philip Selznick, *TVA and the Grass Roots* (Berkeley: University of California Press, 1953), esp. pp. 250ff.

64. See Philip Selznick, *Leadership in Administration* (Evanston: Row, Peterson, 1957).

65. This position disagrees with Sidney Hyman, "Inquiry into the Decline of Congress," *New York Times Magazine*, January 31, 1960. For the argument that 20th century legislatures are on the whole weak see David B. Truman, "The Representative Function in Western Systems," in Edward H. Buehrig (ed.), *Essays in Political Science* (Bloomington: Indiana University Press, 1966), pp. 84–96; Truman, *The Congressional Party* (New York: Wiley, 1954), pp. 1–10; Truman, "Introduction: The Problem and Its Setting," in Truman (ed.), *The Congress and America's Future* (Englewood Cliffs, N.J.: Prentice-Hall, 1965), pp. 1–4. For the beginning of an argument that the U.S. Congress may be an exception, see Nelson W. Polsby, *Congress and the Presidency* (Prentice-Hall, 1964), pp. 2, 31–32, 47–115.

66. See Weber, op. cit., p. 69, pp. 330–334; and Gerth and Mills, op. cit., pp. 198–204.

67. See, for example, Donald Matthews, "The Folkways of the U.S. Senate," this *Review* 53 (December, 1959): 1064–1089; John C. Wahlke, Heinz Eulau, William Buchanan, and Leroy C. Ferguson, *The Legislative System* (New York: Wiley, 1962), pp. 141–169; Alan Kornberg, "The Rules of the Game in the Canadian House of Commons," *The Journal of Politics*, 26 (May, 1964): pp. 358–380; Ralph K. Huitt, "The Outsider in The Senate," this *Review*, 55 (September, 1961): pp. 566–575; Nicholas A. Masters, "Committee Assignments in The House of Representatives," this *Review*, 55 (June, 1961): pp. 345–357; Richard F. Fenno, Jr., "The House Appropriations Committee as a Political System: The Problem of Integration," this *Review*, 56 (June, 1962): pp. 310–324.

68. Clem Miller, *Member of the House* (John W. Baker, ed.) (New York: Scribner, 1962), p. 93. See also pp. 80–81 and 119–122.

69. Alexander, op. cit., pp. 115–116. The internal quotations are from John Quincy Adams' *Diary* and from an article by Reed in the *Saturday Evening Post*, December 9, 1899.

70. Mayo, op. cit., p. 424; William Parkes Cutler and Julia Perkins Cutler (eds.), *Life, Journals and Correspondence of Reverend Manasseh Cutler* (Cincinnati: Robert Clark and Co., 1888), Vol. II, pp. 186–189.

71. A motion to expel Brooks from the House for this act was defeated; but soon thereafter Brooks resigned anyway. He was subsequently reelected to fill the vacancy caused by his resignation. See

Biographical Directory of The American Congress, 1774–1961 (Washington: Government Printing Office, 1961), p. 604.

72. Alexander, op. cit., pp. 111–112. Other instances of flagrant misbehavior are chronicled in Ben Perley Poore, *Perley's Reminiscences of Sixty Years in the National Metropolis* (Philadelphia: Hubbard, 1886), Vol. I, pp. 394–395; and William Plumer, *Memorandum of Proceedings in the United States Senate* (Everett Somerville Brown, ed.) (New York: Macmillan, 1923), pp. 269–276.

73. A report on decorum in the 19th Century House of Commons suggests that a corresponding toning down has taken place, although Commons was palpably a good bit less unruly to start with. Says an ecstatic commentator, "Like so much else that is good in the institutions of Parliament, the behaviour of the House has grown straight, or, like a river, purified itself as it flowed": Eric Taylor, *The House of Commons at Work* (Baltimore: Penguin, 1961), pp. 85–87. Anthony Barker says: "The close of the 19th Century has been described by Lord Campion as the ending of informality and the beginning of rigid government responsibility for policy in the procedures of the House of Commons": " 'The Most Important And Venerable Function': A Study of Commons Supply Procedure," *Political Studies* 13 (February, 1965): p. 45.

74. Perhaps secondary analysis comparing the four states (California, New Jersey, Tennessee, Ohio) in the Wahlke, Eulau, Buchanan, and Ferguson study (op. cit.) will yield an acceptable test of the hypothesis. This study has good information on the diffusion of legislative norms; it is less strong on structural data, but these might be relatively easy to gather.

75. Parkinson, op. cit., p. 39.

76. The growth of political institutions does not play a particularly important part in the interpretation offered by W. W. Rostow in *The Stages of Economic Growth* (Cambridge: Cambridge University Press, 1960), see, e.g., pp. 18–19, but these may afford at least as good support for his theory as some of the economic indicators he proposes.

27

RICHARD F. FENNO, JR.

CONGRESSMEN IN COMMITTEES

The following excerpt is drawn from several chapters of Richard F. Fenno, Jr.'s book Congressmen in Committees *(1973). In this pathbreaking study of a half-dozen standing committees in the House of Representatives, Fenno discovered that committees differ importantly in their organizational goals, institutional autonomy, responsiveness to external environments, and success rates on the House floor. Fenno's analysis suggests how in-depth studies of committees (and presumably other legislative units) can enrich our understanding of Congress. Fenno is a professor of political science at the University of Rochester.*

. . . We have begun our committee analysis by trying to find out what the individual members of each committee want for themselves from their present committee service. And we have found three quite different patterns, each of which gives special prominence to one of the three basic goals of House members. Furthermore, we found a remarkable consensus on goals among each committee's membership, a discovery that has persuaded us to ground our analysis here. Moreover, each of the three goals (and this was more fortuitous than planned) is the consensual one for two of our six committees. Appropriations and Ways and Means are populated mostly by influence-oriented members; Interior and Post Office are populated mostly by re-election-oriented members; Education and Labor and Foreign Affairs are populated mostly by policy-oriented members. Such modal characterizations are admittedly oversimplifications. But they do have sufficient validity to serve as a basis for predicting gross similarities and differences in committee behavior. Assuming that members will work in committee to achieve their stated goals, committees with similar goal patterns should display important similarities in behavior, and committees with different goal patterns should display important differences in behavior. More specifically, these similarities and differences should appear with respect to decision-making processes and decisions. But even such rudimentary predictions as these will hold only when "all other things are equal." And we know enough about committees to know that such a condition does not obtain. Most important, perhaps, we know that each committee works in a somewhat different environment. We need, therefore, to add this key variable to the analysis.

. . . The question now arises: how far do committee patterns that are based on members' goals correspond to committee patterns based on environmental constraints? That is, do committees whose members have similar goals operate in similar environments? The answer to both questions, we would now have to conclude is: "a little, but not much."

The two committees with distinctively influence-oriented members are also the two committees with the parent chamber as the most prominent environmental element. Similarly, the two committees whose members are re-election-oriented are also the two committees for which clientele groups are the most prominent environmental element. This is what we mean by "a little." On the other hand, for each of these two pairs of committees, there are some marked dissimilarities in environment. The policy coalitions facing Ways and Means are more complex and more partisan than those facing Appropriations. And the policy coalitions facing Interior are more complex and more pluralistic than those facing Post Office. In terms of their environments, the influence-oriented and re-election-oriented committees are as much unlike as they are like one another.

The environments of the two policy-oriented committees have almost nothing in common. The policy coalitions facing Education and Labor are more complex than those confronting Foreign Affairs. The environment of Foreign Affairs most closely resembles that of Post Office in its monolithic character. And the environment of Education and Labor most nearly resembles that of Ways and Means in its partisan character. Overall, within each pair of committees, one committee seems to confront a distinctly more complex, more pluralistic policy coalition than the other. The policy environment of Ways and Means is more complex than that of Appropriations, that of Interior more complex than Post Office, and that of Education and Labor more complex than Foreign Affairs. As we move to describe committee behavior, we might expect it to be more difficult to predict the behavior of a committee operating in a complex environment than that of a committee, composed of members with the same goals, subject to a relatively simple set of constraints.

What seems most striking, in answering our earlier question, is the degree to which the environments of our pairs differ from one another. None of our three pairs, alike in member goals, is wholly alike with regard to the environment. We conclude, therefore, that the environmental variable is a largely *independent* one. It is not possible to predict the characteristics of a committee's environment by knowing only its members' goals. Nor is it possible to predict the goals simply by knowing the environment. Each variable can be expected to make an independent contribution in explaining a committee's behavior. And each must be investigated carefully. We do not mean there is no relationship between member goals and environmental constraints. The small degree of interconnection we have noted indicates that there are some linkages. And we would certainly expect that for any given committee, a change in one variable might produce a change in the other. But, clearly, each must be given independent weight throughout the analysis which follows.

. . . We have viewed the committee environment in terms of the influence outsiders have on committee members. But if one is searching for the antecedents of these external constraints, one finds that the subject of the policy and its associated characteristics must be given a central place. We have compared the relative prominence of four categories of interested outsiders. But we have found, again and again, that similarities and, more often, differences in their interest and prominence are related to the policy area itself. Our idea of "policy coalition" is intended to acknowledge the importance of policy subjects, without, at the same time, making them an independent variable of the analysis. Some readers will probably wish we had done just that—developed a classification of policy subjects and/or policy characteristics to serve as major independent variables. Those who feel this way should be encouraged to try. There is nothing in this study to challenge and much to confirm Capitol Hill wisdom that committee differences are related to policy differences. From the foregoing analysis, one might suggest that such policy characteristics as their importance to the parent institution, their salience, and their fragmentation would be useful categories. But we have chosen to compare committees at one level removed from their policy subjects because to do so helps us to advance the argument we have been making. We have given special emphasis to the goals of committee members; it is more in keeping with that emphasis to consider the environment in terms of people actively applying constraints to the members. From this perspective, policy subjects become important primarily because of the outsiders that take an interest in them and, hence, in the committee. It is obviously necessary to know about policy characteristics in order to locate the crucially important outsiders. But it is the outsiders that interest us most in this analysis . . .

On every committee the members try to accommodate their personal goals to important environmental expectations and to embody this accommodation in broad, underlying guidelines for decision making. No two committees, it appears, will produce the same set of guiding premises. One explanation is, of course, that no two committees share the same set of member goals and the same set of environmental constraints. Another explanation might be that no two committees deal with the same area of policy. For, once again, we find differences among our variables related to differences in policy subject. In this chapter as in the previous one, however, we have conducted our analysis at one level removed from policy subjects. We have been interested, here, in the *perceptions* that each committee's members have of their policy area — on the assumption that members' behavior is based on members' perceptions of policy subjects and not on the objective characteristics of the policies themselves. At least we would argue this way until such time as a satisfactory categorization of policy subjects could be made from which one could deduce members' perceptions. For now, we might simply underscore the value of knowing: that Appropriations members perceive their subject matter to be nonideological, while Education and Labor members perceive their subject matter to be ideological; that Ways and Means members think of their business as freighted with consequences, while Post Office members think of their business as inconsequential; that Interior members view their policy area as specific and detailed, while Foreign Affairs members see theirs as general and vague. These differences in perceptions of subject matter help to account for differences in the decision-making processes of the committees. For example, the perceptions of subject matter held by Appropriations, Ways and Means, and Interior are more conducive to developing and sustaining expertise as a basis for decision making than are the perceptions held by the other three committees.

Despite the uniqueness of each committee's decision rules, two interesting patterns did emerge — interesting because both of them distinguish Appropriations, Ways and Means, and Interior on the one hand from Education and Labor, Foreign Affairs, and Post Office on the other. Each of the first three committees has achieved a consensus on its decision rules; each of the latter three committees has not. Furthermore, the decision rules of the first three committees are all, in one way or another, oriented toward insuring success on the House floor; the decision rules of the latter three are not. By *floor success*, we mean to include *both* House members' reactions to the content of a committee's decisions and House members' reactions to the committee as a decision-making collectivity. Obviously, the explanation for the two patterns—in terms of members' goals, environmental constraints, and strategic problems—differs within and across the two clusters of committees. We have tried to supply committee-by-committee explanations as we went along.

It may be that the two patterns are related. The more a committee concerns itself about floor success, the more likely it is, perhaps, to come to agreement on an operative set of decision rules. Or, perhaps, the greater its agreement on decision rules, the more likely will a committee enjoy success on the floor. Or it may be that the two patterns are not connected at all. Starting with the observation, however, we can ask whether the three high-consensus, House-oriented committees will display different decision-making processes from those of the three low-consensus, non-House-oriented committees. . . .

We have tried to demonstrate . . . that each committee's internal decision-making processes are shaped by its members' goals, by the constraints placed upon the members by interested outside groups, and by the strategic premises that members adopt in order to accommodate their personal goals to environmental constraints. One overall comparative dimension suggested by the independent variables of the analysis involves the relative impact of the members themselves and of external groups on decision-making processes. We might think of the dimension as *decision-making autonomy*. The greater the relative influence of the members, the more autonomous the committee; the greater the relative influence of outside groups, the less autonomous the committee. Making only the grossest kinds of distinctions, it appears that Ways and Means, Appropriations, and Interior are more autonomous decisionmakers than Foreign Affairs, Education and Labor, and Post Office. That is, members of the first three committees have a more independent influence on their own decision-making processes than do the members of the second three. For Ways and Means, we might mention the restraints on partisanship and the leadership of Wilbur Mills; for Appropriations, there are the specialization and internal influence of its subcommittees; for Interior, there are its participatory democracy and the leadership of Wayne Aspinall. The sources of committee autonomy are not always the same, but the result—a marked degree of internal, member control of decision making—is the same. With the other three committees, it is the environmental impact on decision making that seems most noteworthy. For Foreign Affairs, it is executive domination; for Education and Labor, it is the permeation of partisan policy coalitions; for Post Office, it is clientele domination. The three more autonomous committees emphasize expertise in decision making more than the three less autonomous ones, suggesting that perception of subject matter is related to decision-making processes.

The clustering of committees with regard to decision-making autonomy parallels the clustering noted in the last chapter, based on some similarities and differences in the committees' decision rules. Appropriations, Ways and Means, and Interior have, in common, and consensus on decision rules, a House-oriented set of decision rules, and decision-making autonomy. The three characteristics are probably closely interrelated. But the main thrust of our argument would be that the first two contribute to the third. When a committee's members agree on what they should do, they are more likely to be able to control their own decision making than when they cannot agree on what to do. When a committee's decision rules are oriented toward success (i.e., winning plus respect and confidence) on the House floor, the committee will have a greater desire to establish its operating independence than when its strategies are not especially concerned with floor success. House members, we recall, *want* their committees to be relatively autonomous, relatively expert decision makers. They are more likely, therefore, to follow and to respect committees that can demonstrate some political and intellectual independence of outside, non-House groups. Whether or not distinguishing the two clusters of committees will, in turn, help us to differentiate and explain committee decisions is a question we will keep in mind as we turn to a discussion of that subject . . .

We have presented evidence to demonstrate that committee decisions do, indeed, follow those decision rules that each committee's members have devised to accommodate their personal goals to the constraints of their environment. That is, a committee's decisions are explainable in terms of its members' goals, the constraints of its environment, its decision strategies, and—to a lesser, refining degree, perhaps—by its decision-making processes. Enough evidence has been mustered, we hope, to lend strength to the line of argument we have pursued. We have not, of course, *proven* anything, for we have not tried very determinedly to muster a contrary body of evidence. Those who find themselves resisting our selective use of evidence are invited to provide counterexamples and to fashion another line of argument. We hope that what we have presented will seem worth that kind of further development and testing.

To the degree that a committee's decisions follow its decision rules, committee members and the most interested outside groups should be reasonably satisfied with committee performance. For those rules are, after all, an effort to accommodate the views of each. We have not found a measure of satisfaction that would allow us to describe and compare amounts of internal and/or external satisfaction. But we have detected varying degrees of it. For member satisfaction, a necessary condition would seem to be committee *activity*. No member goal can be achieved without some minimal level of activity. Post Office members' dissatisfaction arose because that Committee slipped below an acceptable level of activity; it "wasn't doing anything." Foreign Affairs has simmered with dissatisfaction because its members have felt they "weren't doing enough." Both would have been satisfied with increased activity. The other committees have been active. For Education and Labor members, indeed, their increased activity was the basis for their newly found satisfaction in the Powell years.

Members of our other three committees require an additional condition for their satisfaction. They feel the need to make an *independent* contribution to decision making. Especially, they want to feel a measure of independence relative to the executive branch—in both an institutional and a policy sense. They want to preserve autonomous decision-making processes and they want to develop substantive expertise. When they do achieve such independence, they develop a psychological feeling of group identity, which further strengthens their independence. Ways and Means, Appropriations, and Interior members' satisfaction, then, seems to be based on both their *activity* and their *independence*. During the period studied, these three committees maintained a higher and steadier level of satisfaction with their own performance than did the three other committees.

It is hard to generalize about the conditions of satisfaction for the groups comprising the environment. Perhaps it is enough to remind ourselves, again, that individual committees face quite varied sets of environmental constraints. For two of our committees, the institutional constraints of the parent chamber are most important. House expectations call for a balance between autonomous and responsive decision making. And, so far, Ways and Means and Appropriations seem to have maintained a balance satisfactory to House leaders and House majorities. For the other four, the policy coalitions of their environments are more important. But dominance in those policy coalitions varies, so that the expectations confronting the four committees also vary. The executive-led coalition confronting Foreign Affairs wants legitimation plus assessments of political feasibility. The clientele-led coalitions facing Interior and Post Office want access to members plus sympathetic committee member spokesmen. The party-led coalitions facing Education and Labor want all these things plus a partisanship that will abet victory at the polls. How can we compare levels of satisfaction across such diverse expectations? Is the executive branch more satisfied with the legitimation it gets than clientele groups are with the spokesmanship they get? All we can say is that the leaders of each coalition do seem pretty well satisfied with the committees that interest them—the executive with Foreign Affairs, the postal employees with Post Office, all but the preservationist groups with Interior, the Democrats and Republicans with Education and Labor.

Looking across the six committees, some of the gross similarities and difference noted earlier do appear to carry through to their decisions. That is, Ways and Means, Appropriations, and Interior remain strikingly similar to one another and strikingly different from Education and Labor, Foreign Affairs, and Post Office. The three committees with a consensus on House-oriented decision rules do seem to be more successful on the House floor than the three committees whose decision rules are not House-oriented. Members of the same three, more autonomous committees express a greater overall satisfaction with their committee's decision processes and decisions than do the members of the three less autonomous committees with theirs. And from the autonomy and satisfaction of the first three flows a sense of corporate identity and corporate pride that is missing in the three less autonomous, less satisfied committees. On the other hand, the decisions of our three less autonomous committees seem to bring relatively greater satisfaction to interested and influential environmental groups than do the decisions of our three more autonomous committees. Education and Labor, Foreign Affairs, and Post Office are more permeable and, hence, relatively more responsive to the wishes of people outside the Congress than are Ways and Means, Appropriations, and Interior.

Utilizing these *relative* distinctions, we find two types of House committees. One type is identified by the House orientation of its decision rules, the autonomy of its decision-making processes, its emphasis on committee expertise, its success on the House floor, its members' sense of group identity, and the relatively higher ratio of member to nonmember satisfaction with its performance. The other type is identified by its extra-House-oriented decision rules, the permeability of its decision-making processes, the de-emphasis on committee expertise, its lack of success on the House floor, the absence of any feeling of group identification, and the relatively higher ratio of nonmember to member satisfaction with its performance.

Since no committee falls completely into one category or the other, we probably should think of these as "ideal types" toward which committees tend—a *corporate* type, on the one hand, and a *permeable* type, on the other. Committees of the corporate type tend to be more influential but less responsive than permeable committees. Permeable committees tend to be more responsive but less influential than corporate committees. Ways and Means, Appropriations and Interior come closest to the corporate type of committee. Education and Labor, Foreign Affairs, and Post Office come closest to the permeable type of committee. And, we might add, all Senate committees tend toward the permeable category. There are no corporate committees in the Senate.

PART SEVEN

THE PRESIDENCY

The American presidency is paradoxical. The Constitution's Framers anticipated that Congress would be the dominant branch of government. They sought to provide the presidency with enough power to maintain its independence from the legislature and to act as a check on it, but not so much as to pose the threat of overwhelming it or undermining representative government. The first reading in this chapter, Alexander Hamilton's *Federalist* 69, explains the balance the Framers sought in creating the presidency.

The Framers' careful crafting notwithstanding, the presidency became the focal point of American politics and the symbol of national power during the New Deal, World War II, and the Cold War. The public and the Congress looked to the president for leadership in domestic and foreign policy initiatives, budgetary and administrative direction, and national defense.

As the presidency became a dominant institution in the political system, political scientists increasingly tried to develop a better understanding of presidential power. With the exception of the Twenty-Second Amendment (1951), which limits the president's tenure to two terms, the constitutional provisions for the presidency have remained static. Yet, not only has the overall power of the office grown, recent presidents have had remarkably different levels of success in employing it. What is presidential power? What accounts for it? What accounts for its successful use? These are among the many questions experts on the presidency seek to answer.

Aaron Wildavsky's "The Two Presidencies," originally published in 1966, offers a broad framework for analyzing presidential power. Wildavsky argues that the presidency has operated differently in two realms—domestic affairs and foreign policy. The president was far more powerful in the latter arena than in the domestic sphere. But the nature of politics and policy making in the two arenas also differs. In Wildavsky's words, "The President's normal problem with domestic policy is to get congressional support for the programs he prefers. In foreign affairs, in contrast, he can almost always get support for policies that he believes will protect the nation—but his problem is to find a viable policy." The stakes, too, vary greatly: "Few failures in domestic policy, Presidents soon realize could have as disastrous consequences as any one of dozens of mistakes in the international arena." As a result, at least when the stakes are high, "foreign policy concerns tend to drive out domestic policy."

Wildavsky's analysis explained some of the variations in presidential power, at least until the end of the Cold War. But why are some presidents more powerful than others and why has the presidency become larger than its constitutional provisions anticipated? In "The Power to Persuade," Richard Neustadt argues that formal powers are insufficient for presidential performance. Ultimately, presidential power is the power to *persuade.* In Neustadt's words, "Presidential 'powers' may be inconclusive when a president commands, but always remain relevant as he persuades." For Neustadt, "The power to persuade is the power to bargain." His analysis explores the advantages and limitations of the presidential bargaining position. Neustadt emphasizes that the vantage points available to the presidency are of particular importance in enhancing the president's persuasive abilities.

Charles O. Jones's "Separating to Govern" (1997) analyzes the impact of the separation of powers—between the executive and the legislature—on presidential power. Jones shows that even within the framework of one term, a president can face markedly different Congresses, especially in terms of the composition of the House of Representatives. Consequently, " . . . any one period of presidential service may be characterized by change. There may, in fact, be *more than one presidency per president,* if defined in terms of the political and policy advantages available to the incumbent in working with Congress." The president's ability to persuade varies because it is easier to bargain with a supportive Congress than an unsupportive one, and support will normally vary among policy issues.

The power to persuade is affected by policy arenas and constitutional and institutional arrangements. The president is an individual. Each one brings a unique personality, set of experiences, ability, and style to the office. Presidents will have personal qualities that contribute to success, failure, or—most likely—both. In her conclusion to *Lyndon Johnson and the American Dream* (1976), Doris Kearns (now Goodwin) tackles the very difficult problem of ". . . framing questions that might enable us to understand better the relationship between leaders and the qualities of leadership, events and historical circumstances, and institutional structure." Her analysis is confined to President Johnson, but her deep understanding of his political career and personality yields important insights about the presidency and problems of fit between the individual and the office. In particular, she notes that the qualities that make for leadership in one context may not serve well in another. Additionally, she is concerned that a presidential penchant for secrecy may move "the presidential institution outside the [constitutional] framework itself."

28

ALEXANDER HAMILTON

FEDERALIST 69

This sixty-ninth Federalist Paper *explains the constitutional design of the presidency. In it Alexander Hamilton emphasizes the variety of limitations on presidential power and the extent to which presidential actions will depend on congressional participation, particularly by the Senate.*

To the People of the State of New York:

I proceed now to trace the real characters of the proposed Executive, as they are marked out in the plan of the convention. This will serve to place in a strong light the unfairness of the representations which have been made in regard to it.

The first thing which strikes our attention is, that the executive authority, with few exceptions, is to be vested in a single magistrate. This will scarcely, however, be considered as a point upon which any comparison can be grounded; for if, in this particular, there be a resemblance to the king of Great Britain, there is not less a resemblance to the Grand Seignior, to the khan of Tartary, to the Man of the Seven Mountains, or to the governor of New York.

That magistrate is to be elected for *four* years; and is to be reëligible as often as the people of the United States shall think him worthy of their confidence. In these circumstances there is a total dissimilitude between *him* and a king of Great Britain, who is an *hereditary* monarch, possessing the crown as a patrimony descendible to his heirs forever; but there is a close analogy between *him* and a governor of New York, who is elected for *three* years, and is reëligible without limitation or intermission. If we consider how much less time would be requisite for establishing a dangerous influence in a single State, than for establishing a like influence throughout the United States, we must conclude that a duration of *four* years for the Chief Magistrate of the Union is a degree of permanency far less to be dreaded in that office, than a duration of *three* years for a corresponding office in a single State.

The President of the United States would be liable to be impeached, tried, and, upon conviction of treason, bribery, or other high crimes or misdemeanors, removed from office; and would afterwards be liable to prosecution and punishment in the ordinary course of law. The person of the king of Great Britain is sacred and inviolable; there is no constitutional tribunal to which he is amenable; no punishment to which he can be subjected without involving the crisis of a national revolution. In this delicate and important circumstance of personal responsibility, the President of Confederated America would stand upon no better ground than a governor of New York, and upon worse ground than the governors of Virginia and Delaware.

[Notes have been renumbered. —Eds.]

The President of the United States is to have power to return a bill, which shall have passed the two branches of the legislature, for reconsideration; but the bill so returned is to become a law, if upon that reconsideration, it be approved by two thirds of both houses. The king of Great Britain, on his part, has an absolute negative upon the acts of the two houses of Parliament. The disuse of that power for a considerable time past does not affect the reality of its existence; and is to be ascribed wholly to the crown's having found the means of substituting influence to authority, or the art of gaining a majority in one or the other of the two houses, to the necessity of exerting a prerogative which could seldom be exerted without hazarding some degree of national agitation. The qualified negative of the President differs widely from this absolute negative of the British sovereign; and tallies exactly with the revisionary authority of the council of revision of this State, of which the governor is a constituent part. In this respect the power of the President would exceed that of the governor of New York, because the former would possess, singly, what the latter shares with the chancellor and judges; but it would be precisely the same with that of the governor of Massachusetts, whose constitution, as to this article, seems to have been the original from which the convention have copied.

The President is to be the "commander-in-chief of the army and navy of the United States, and of the militia of the several States, when called into the actual service of the United States. He is to have power to grant reprieves and pardons for offences against the United States, *except in cases of impeachment*; to recommend to the consideration of Congress such measures as he shall judge necessary and expedient; to convene, on extraordinary occasions, both houses of the legislature, or either of them, and, in case of disagreement between them *with respect to the time of adjournment*, to adjourn them to such time as he shall think proper; to take care that the laws be faithfully executed; and to commission all officers of the United States." In most of these particulars, the power of the President will resemble equally that of the king of Great Britain and of the governor of New York. The most material points of difference are these:—*First*. The President will have only the occasional command of such part of the militia of the nation as by legislative provision may be called into the actual service of the Union. The king of Great Britain and the governor of New York have at all times the entire command of all the militia within their several jurisdictions. In this article, therefore, the power of the President would be inferior to that of either the monarch or the governor. *Secondly*. The President is to be commander-in-chief of the army and navy of the United States. In this respect his authority would be nominally the same with that of the king of Great Britain, but in substance much inferior to it. It would amount to nothing more than the supreme command and direction of the military and naval forces, as first General and admiral of the Confederacy; while that of the British king extends to the *declaring* of war and to the *raising* and *regulating* of fleets and armies,—all which, by the Constitution under consideration, would appertain to the legislature.[1] The governor of New York, on the other hand, is by the constitution of the State vested only with the command of its militia and navy. But the constitutions of several of the States expressly declare their governors to be commanders-in-chief, as well of the army as navy; and it may well be a question, whether those of New Hampshire and Massachusetts, in particular, do not, in this instance, confer larger powers upon their respective governors, than could be claimed by a President of the United States. *Thirdly.* The power of the President, in respect to pardons, would extend to all cases, *except those of impeachment.* The governor of New York may pardon in all cases, even in those of impeachment, except for treason and murder. Is not the power of the governor, in this article, on a calculation of political consequences, greater than that of the President? All conspiracies and plots against the government, which have not been matured into actual treason, may be screened from punishment of every kind, by the interposition of the prerogative of pardoning. If a governor of New York, therefore, should be at the head of any such conspiracy, until the design had been ripened into actual hostility he could insure his accomplices and adherents an entire impunity. A President of the Union, on the other hand, though he may even pardon treason, when prosecuted in the ordinary course of law, could shelter no offender, in any degree, from the effects of impeachment and conviction. Would not the prospect of a total indemnity for all the preliminary steps be a greater temptation to undertake and persevere in an enterprise against the public liberty, than the mere prospect of an exemption from death and confiscation, if the final execution of the design, upon an actual appeal to arms, should miscarry? Would this last expectation have any influence at all, when the probability was computed, that the person who was to afford that exemption might himself be involved in the consequences of the measure, and might be incapacitated by his agency in it from affording the desired impunity? The better to judge of this matter, it will be necessary to recollect, that, by the proposed Constitution, the offence of treason is limited "to levying war upon the United States, and adhering to their enemies, giving them aid and comfort"; and that by the laws of New York it is confined within similar bounds. *Fourthly.* The President can only adjourn the national legislature in the single case of disagreement about the time of adjournment. The British monarch may prorogue or even dissolve the Parliament. The governor of New York may also prorogue the legislature of this State for a limited time; a power which, in certain situations, may be employed to very important purposes.

The President is to have power, with the advice and consent of the Senate, to make treaties, provided two thirds of the senators present concur. The king of Great Britain is the sole and absolute representative of the nation in all foreign transactions. He can of his own accord make treaties of peace, commerce, alliance, and of every other description. It has been insinuated, that his authority in this respect is not conclusive, and that his conventions with foreign powers are subject to the revision, and stand in need of the ratification, of Parliament. But I believe this doctrine was never heard of, until it was broached upon the present occasion. Every jurist[2] of that kingdom, and every other man acquainted with its Constitution, knows, as an established fact, that the prerogative of making treaties exists in the crown in its utmost plentitude; and that the compacts entered into by the royal authority have the most complete legal validity and perfection, independent of any other sanction. The Parliament, it is true, is sometimes seen employing itself in altering the existing laws to conform them to the stipulations in a new

treaty; and this may have possibly given birth to the imagination, that its coöpera-
tion was necessary to the obligatory efficacy of the treaty. But this parliamentary
interposition proceeds from a different cause: from the necessity of adjusting
a most artificial and intricate system of revenue and commercial laws, to the
changes made in them by the operation of the treaty; and of adapting new provisions and precautions to the new state of things, to keep the machine from running into disorder. In this respect, therefore, there is no comparison between
the intended power of the President and the actual power of the British sovereign. The one can perform alone what the other can do only with the concurrence of a branch of the legislature. It must be admitted, that, in this instance,
the power of the federal Executive would exceed that of any State Executive.
But this arises naturally from the sovereign power which relates to treaties. If
the Confederacy were to be dissolved, it would become a question whether the
Executives of the several States were not solely invested with that delicate and
important prerogative.

The President is also to be authorized to receive ambassadors and other public
ministers. This, though it has been a rich theme of declamation, is more a matter
of dignity than of authority. It is a circumstance which will be without consequence in the administration of the government; and it was far more convenient
that it should be arranged in this manner, than that there should be a necessity of
convening the legislature, or one of its branches, upon every arrival of a foreign
minister, though it were merely to take the place of a departed predecessor.

The President is to nominate, and, *with the advice and consent of the Senate*, to
appoint ambassadors and other public ministers, judges of the Supreme Court,
and in general all officers of the United States established by law, and whose
appointments are not otherwise provided for by the Constitution. The king of
Great Britain is emphatically and truly styled the fountain of honor. He not only
appoints to all offices, but can create offices. He can confer titles of nobility at
pleasure; and has the disposal of an immense number of church preferments.
There is evidently a great inferiority in the power of the President, in this particular, to that of the British king; nor is it equal to that of the governor of New York, if
we are to interpret the meaning of the constitution of the State by the practice
which has obtained under it. The power of appointment is with us lodged in a
council, composed of the governor and four members of the Senate, chosen by
the Assembly. The governor *claims*, and has frequently *exercised*, the right of
nomination, and is *entitled* to a casting vote in the appointment. If he really has
the right of nominating, his authority is in this respect equal to that of the President, and exceeds it in the article of the casting vote. In the national government,
if the Senate should be divided, no appointment could be made; in the government of New York, if the council should be divided, the governor can turn the
scale, and confirm his own nomination.[3] If we compare the publicity which must
necessarily attend the mode of appointment by the President and an entire
branch of the national legislature, with the privacy in the mode of appointment
by the governor of New York, closeted in a secret apartment with at most four,
and frequently with only two persons; and if we at the same time consider how
much more easy it must be to influence the small number of which a council of

appointment consists, than the considerable number of which the national Senate would consist, we cannot hesitate to pronounce that the power of the chief magistrate of this State, in the disposition of offices, must, in practice, be greatly superior to that of the Chief Magistrate of the Union.

Hence it appears that, except as to the concurrent authority of the President in the article of treaties, it would be difficult to determine whether that magistrate would in the aggregate, possess more or less power than the Governor of New York. And it appears yet more unequivocally, that there is no pretence for the parallel which has been attempted between him and the king of Great Britain. But to render the contrast in this respect still more striking, it may be of use to throw the principal circumstances of dissimilitude into a closer group.

The President of the United States would be an officer elected by the people for *four* years; the king of Great Britain is a perpetual and *hereditary* prince. The one would be amenable to personal punishment and disgrace; the person of the other is sacred and inviolable. The one would have a *qualified* negative upon the acts of the legislative body; the other has an *absolute* negative. The one would have a right to command the military and naval forces of the nation; the other, in addition to this right, possesses that of *declaring* war, and of *raising* and *regulating* fleets and armies by his own authority. The one would have a concurrent power with a branch of the legislature in the formation of treaties; the other is the *sole possessor* of the power of making treaties. The one would have a like concurrent authority in appointing to offices; the other is the sole author of all appointments. The one can confer no privileges whatever: the other can make denizens of aliens, noblemen of commoners: can erect corporations with all the rights incident to corporate bodies. The one can prescribe no rules concerning the commerce or currency of the nation; the other is in several respects the arbiter of commerce, and in this capacity can establish markets and fairs, can regulate weights and measures, can lay embargoes for a limited time, can coin money, can authorize or prohibit the circulation of foreign coin. The one has no particle of spiritual jurisdiction; the other is the supreme head and governor of the national church! What answer shall we give to those who would persuade us that things so unlike resemble each other? The same that ought to be given to those who tell us that a government, the whole power of which would be in the hands of the elective and periodical servants of the people, is an aristocracy, a monarchy, and a despotism.

NOTES

1. A writer in a Pennsylvania paper, under the signature of Tamony, has asserted that the king of Great Britain owes his prerogative as commander-in-chief to an annual mutiny bill. The truth is, on the contrary, that his prerogative, in this respect, is immemorial, and was only disputed, "contrary to all reason and precedent," as Blackstone, vol. i, page 262, expresses it, by the Long Parliament of Charles I.; but by the statute the 13th of Charles II., chap. 6, it was declared to be in the king alone,

for that the sole supreme government and command of the militia within his Majesty's realms and dominions, and of all forces by sea and land, and of all forts and places of strength, ever was and is the undoubted right of his Majesty and his royal predecessors, kings and queens of England, and that both or either house of Parliament cannot nor ought to pretend to the same.

2. Vide Blackstone's "Commentaries," vol.i., p. 257.

3. Candor, however, demands an acknowledgment that I do not think the claim of the governor to a right of nomination well founded. Yet it is always justifiable to reason from the practice of a government, till its propriety has been constitutionally questioned. And independent of this claim, when we take into view the other considerations, and pursue them through all their consequences, we shall be inclined to draw much the same conclusion.

29

AARON WILDAVSKY

THE TWO PRESIDENCIES

Presidents play different roles as they manage domestic affairs on the one hand, and make defense and foreign policy on the other. At times, according to Aaron Wildavsky (1930–1993), the distinction between these arenas is so great that there are really two presidencies. Although this selection was first published in 1966 and historical events since that time have changed the context, a good deal of Wildavsky's analysis remains relevant. Presidents continue to have different opportunities, political problems, and constraints in the domestic and international domains for many of the reasons discussed here. Wildavsky taught public policy and political science at the University of California, Berkeley for most of his career.

The United States has one President, but it has two presidencies; one presidency is for domestic affairs, and the other is concerned with defense and foreign policy. Since World War II, Presidents have had much greater success in controlling the nation's defense and foreign policies than in dominating its domestic policies. Even Lyndon Johnson has seen his early record of victories in domestic legislation diminish as his concern with foreign affairs grows.

What powers does the President have to control defense and foreign policies and so completely overwhelm those who might wish to thwart him?

The President's normal problem with domestic policy is to get congressional support for the programs he prefers. In foreign affairs, in contrast, he can almost always get support for policies that he believes will protect the nation—but his problem is to find a viable policy.

Whoever they are, whether they begin by caring about foreign policy like Eisenhower and Kennedy or about domestic policies like Truman and Johnson, Presidents soon discover they have more policy preferences in domestic matters than in foreign policy. The Republican and Democratic parties possess a traditional roster of policies, which can easily be adopted by a new President—for example, he can be either for or against Medicare and aid to education. Since existing domestic policy usually changes in only small steps, Presidents find it relatively simple to make minor adjustments. However, although any President knows he supports foreign aid and NATO, the world outside changes much more rapidly than the nation inside—Presidents and their parties have no prior policies on Argentina and the Congo. The world has become a highly intractable place with a whirl of forces we cannot or do not know how to alter.

THE RECORD OF PRESIDENTIAL CONTROL

It takes great crises, such as Roosevelt's hundred days in the midst of the depression, or the extraordinary majorities that Barry Goldwater's candidacy willed to Lyndon Johnson, for Presidents to succeed in controlling domestic policy. From the end of the 1930's to the present (what may roughly be called the modern era), Presidents have often been frustrated in their domestic programs. From 1938, when conservatives regrouped their forces, to the time of his death, Franklin Roosevelt did not get a single piece of significant domestic legislation passed. Truman lost out on most of his intense domestic preferences, except perhaps for housing. Since Eisenhower did not ask for much domestic legislation, he did not meet consistent defeat, yet he failed in his general policy of curtailing governmental commitments. Kennedy, of course, faced great difficulties with domestic legislation.

In the realm of foreign policy there has not been a single major issue on which Presidents, when they were serious and determined, have failed. The list of their victories is impressive: entry into the United Nations, the Marshall Plan, NATO, the Truman Doctrine, the decisions to stay out of Indochina in 1954 and to intervene in Vietnam in the 1960's, aid to Poland and Yugoslavia, the test-ban treaty, and many more. Serious setbacks to the President in controlling foreign policy are extraordinary and unusual.

Table 1, compiled from the Congressional Quarterly Service tabulation of presidential initiative and congressional response from 1948 through 1964, shows that Presidents have significantly better records in foreign and defense matters than in domestic policies. When refugees and immigration—which Congress considers primarily a domestic concern—are removed from the general foreign policy area, it is clear that Presidents prevail about 70 percent of the time in defense and foreign policy, compared with 40 percent in the domestic sphere.

WORLD EVENTS AND PRESIDENTIAL RESOURCES

Power in politics is control over governmental decisions. How does the President manage his control of foreign and defense policy? The answer does not reside in the greater constitutional power in foreign affairs that Presidents have possessed since the founding of the Republic. The answer lies in the changes that have taken place since 1945.

TABLE 1. CONGRESSIONAL ACTION ON PRESIDENTIAL PROPOSALS FROM 1948–1964

	CONGRESSIONAL ACTION		
Policy Area	% Pass	% Fail	Number of Proposals
Domestic policy (natural resources, labor, agriculture, taxes, etc.)	40.2	59.8	2499
Defense policy (defense, disarmament, manpower, misc.)	73.3	26.7	90
Foreign policy	58.5	41.5	655
Immigration, refugees	13.2	86.0	129
Treaties, general foreign relations, State Department, foreign aid	70.8	29.2	445

Source: Congressional Quarterly Service, Congress and the Nation, 1945–1964 (Washington, 1965).

The number of nations with which the United States has diplomatic relations has increased from 53 in 1939 to 113 in 1966. But sheer numbers do not tell enough; the world has also become a much more dangerous place. However remote it may seem at times, our government must always be aware of the possibility of nuclear war.

Yet the mere existence of great powers with effective thermonuclear weapons would not, in and of itself, vastly increase our rate of interaction with most other nations. We see events in Assam or Burundi as important because they are also part of a larger worldwide contest, called the cold war, in which great powers are rivals for the control or support of other nations. Moreover, the reaction against the blatant isolationism of the 1930's has led to a concern with foreign policy that is worldwide in scope. We are interested in what happens everywhere because we see these events as connected with larger interests involving, at the worst, the possibility of ultimate destruction.

Given the overriding fact that the world is dangerous and that small causes are perceived to have potentially great effects in an unstable world, it follows that Presidents must be interested in relatively "small" matters. So they give Azerbaijan or Lebanon or Vietnam huge amounts of their time. Arthur Schlesinger, Jr., wrote of Kennedy that "in the first two months of his administration he probably spent more time on Laos than on anything else." Few failures in domestic policy, Presidents soon realize, could have as disastrous consequences as any one of dozens of mistakes in the international arena.

The result is that foreign policy concerns tend to drive out domestic policy. Except for occasional questions of domestic prosperity and for civil rights, foreign affairs have consistently higher priority for Presidents. Once, when trying to talk to President Kennedy about natural resources, Secretary of the Interior Stewart Udall remarked, "He's imprisoned by Berlin."

The importance of foreign affairs to Presidents is intensified by the increasing speed of events in the international arena. The event and its consequences follow closely on top of one another. The blunder at the Bay of Pigs is swiftly followed by the near catastrophe of the Cuban missile crisis. Presidents can no longer count on passing along their most difficult problems to their successors. They must expect to face the consequences of their actions—or failure to act—while still in office.

Domestic policy-making is usually based on experimental adjustments to an existing situation. Only a few decisions, such as those involving large dams, irretrievably commit future generations. Decisions in foreign affairs, however, are often perceived to be irreversible. This is expressed, for example, in the fear of escalation or the various "spiral" or "domino" theories of international conflict.

If decisions are perceived to be both important and irreversible, there is every reason for Presidents to devote a great deal of resources to them. Presidents have to be oriented toward the future in the use of their resources. They serve a fixed term in office, and they cannot automatically count on support from the populace, Congress, or the administrative apparatus. They have to be careful, therefore, to husband their resources for pressing future needs. But because the consequences of events in foreign affairs are potentially more grave, faster to manifest themselves, and less easily reversible than in domestic affairs, Presidents are more willing to use up their resources.

THE POWER TO ACT

Their formal powers to commit resources in foreign affairs and defense are vast. Particularly important is their power as Commander-in-Chief to move troops. Faced with situations like the invasion of South Korea or the emplacement of missiles in Cuba, fast action is required. Presidents possess both the formal power to act and the knowledge that elites and the general public expect them to act. Once they have committed American forces, it is difficult for Congress or anyone else to alter the course of events. The Dominican venture is a recent case in point.

Presidential discretion in foreign affairs also makes it difficult (though not impossible) for Congress to restrict their actions. Presidents can use executive agreements instead of treaties, enter into tacit agreements instead of written ones, and otherwise help create *de facto* situations not easily reversed. Presidents also have far greater ability than anyone else to obtain information on developments abroad through the Departments of State and Defense. The need for secrecy in some aspects of foreign and defense policy further restricts the ability of others to compete with Presidents. These things are all well known. What is not so generally appreciated is the growing presidential ability to *use* information to achieve goals.

In the past Presidents were amateurs in military strategy. They could not even get much useful advice outside of the military. As late as the 1930's the number of people outside the military establishment who were professionally engaged in the study of defense policy could be numbered on fingers. Today there are hundreds of such men. The rise of the defense intellectuals has given the President of the United States enhanced ability to control defense policy. He is no longer dependent on the military for advice. He can choose among defense intellectuals from the research corporations and the academies for alternative sources of advice. He can install these men in his own office. He can play them off against each other or use them to extend spheres of coordination.

Even with these advisers, however, Presidents and Secretaries of Defense might still be too bewildered by the complexity of nuclear situations to take action — unless they had an understanding of the doctrine and concept of deterrence. But knowledge of doctrine about deterrence has been widely diffused; it can be picked up by any intelligent person who will read books or listen to enough hours of conversation. Whether or not the doctrine is good is a separate question; the point is that civilians can feel they understand what is going on in defense policy. Perhaps the most extraordinary feature of presidential action during the Cuban missile crisis was the degree to which the Commander-in-Chief of the Armed Forces insisted on controlling even the smallest moves. From the positioning of ships to the methods of boarding, to the precise words and actions to be taken by individual soldiers and sailors, the President and his civilian advisers were in control.

Although Presidents have rivals for power in foreign affairs, the rivals do not usually succeed. Presidents prevail not only because they may have superior resources but because their potential opponents are weak, divided, or believe that they should not control foreign policy. Let us consider the potential rivals—the general citizenry, special interest groups, the Congress, the military, the so-called military-industrial complex, and the State Department.

COMPETITORS FOR CONTROL OF POLICY

THE PUBLIC. The general public is much more dependent on Presidents in foreign affairs than in domestic matters. While many people know about the impact of social security and Medicare, few know about politics in Malawi. So it is not surprising that people expect the President to act in foreign affairs and reward him with their confidence. Gallup Polls consistently show that presidential popularity rises after he takes action in a crisis—whether the action is disastrous as in the Bay of Pigs or successful as in the Cuban missile crisis. Decisive action, such as the bombing of oil fields near Haiphong, resulted in a sharp (though temporary) increase in Johnson's popularity.

The Vietnam situation illustrates another problem of public opinion in foreign affairs: it is extremely difficult to get operational policy directions from the general public. It took a long time before any sizable public interest in the subject developed. Nothing short of the large scale involvement of American troops under fire probably could have brought about the current high level of concern. Yet this relatively well developed popular opinion is difficult to interpret. While a majority appear to support President Johnson's policy, it appears that they could easily be persuaded to withdraw from Vietnam if the administration changed its line. Although a sizable majority would support various initiatives to end the war, they would seemingly be appalled if this action led to Communist encroachments elsewhere in Southeast Asia. (See "The President, the Polls, and Vietnam" by Seymour Martin Lipset, *Trans-Action*, Sept./Oct. 1966.)

Although Presidents lead opinion in foreign affairs, they know they will be held accountable for the consequences of their actions. President Johnson has maintained a large commitment in Vietnam. His popularity shoots up now and again in the midst of some imposing action. But the fact that a body of citizens do not like the war comes back to damage his overall popularity. We will support your initiatives, the people seem to say, but we will reserve the right to punish you (or your party) if we do not like the results.

SPECIAL INTEREST GROUPS. Opinions are easier to gauge in domestic affairs because, for one thing, there is a stable structure of interest groups that covers virtually all matters of concern. The farm, labor, business, conservation, veteran, civil rights, and other interest groups provide cues when a proposed policy affects them. Thus people who identify with these groups may adopt their views. But in foreign policy matters the interest group structure is weak, unstable, and thin rather than dense. In many matters affecting Africa and Asia, for example, it is hard to think of well-known interest groups. While ephemeral groups arise from

time to time to support or protest particular policies, they usually disappear when
the immediate problem is resolved. In contrast, longer-lasting elite groups like
the Foreign Policy Association and Council on Foreign Relations are composed
of people of diverse views; refusal to take strong positions on controversial matters
is a condition of their continued viability.

The strongest interest groups are probably the ethnic associations whose members have strong ties with a homeland, as in Poland or Cuba, so they are rarely activated simultaneously on any specific issue. They are most effective when most
narrowly and intensely focused—as in the fierce pressure from Jews to recognize
the state of Israel. But their relatively small numbers limit their significance to
Presidents in the vastly more important general foreign policy picture—as continued aid to the Arab countries shows. Moreover, some ethnic groups may conflict
on significant issues such as American acceptance of the Oder-Neisse line separating Poland from what is now East Germany.

THE CONGRESS. Congressmen also exercise power in foreign affairs. Yet they are
ordinarily not serious competitors with the President because they follow a self-
denying ordinance. They do not think it is their job to determine the nation's
defense policies. Lewis A. Dexter's extensive interviews with members of the Senate Armed Services Committee, who might be expected to want a voice in defense
policy, reveal that they do not desire for men like themselves to run the nation's
defense establishment. Aside from a few specific conflicts among the armed services which allow both the possibility and desirability of direct intervention, the
Armed Services Committee constitutes a sort of real estate committee dealing
with the regional economic consequences of the location of military facilities.

The congressional appropriations power is potentially a significant resource,
but circumstances since the end of World War II have tended to reduce its effectiveness. The appropriations committees and Congress itself might make their
will felt by refusing to allot funds unless basic policies were altered. But this has
not happened. While Congress makes its traditional small cuts in the military
budget, Presidents have mostly found themselves warding off congressional
attempts to increase specific items still further.

Most of the time, the administration's refusal to spend has not been seriously
challenged. However, there have been occasions when individual legislators or
committees have been influential. Senator Henry Jackson in his campaign (with
the aid of colleagues on the Joint Committee on Atomic Energy) was able to gain
acceptance for the Polaris weapons system and Senator Arthur H. Vandenberg
played a part in determining the shape of the Marshall Plan and so on. The few
congressmen who are expert in defense policy act, as Samuel P. Huntington says,
largely as lobbyists with the executive branch. It is apparently more fruitful for
these congressional experts to use their resources in order to get a hearing from
the executive than to work on other congressmen.

When an issue involves the actual use or threat of violence, it takes a great deal
to convince congressmen not to follow the President's lead. James Robinson's
tabulation of foreign and defense policy issues from the late 1930's to 1961 (Table
2) shows dominant influence by Congress in only one case out of seven—the

TABLE 2. CONGRESSIONAL INVOLVEMENT IN FOREIGN AND DEFENSE POLICY DECISIONS

Issue	Congressional Involvement (High, Low, None)	Initiator (Congress or Executive)	Predominate Influence (Congress or Executive)	Legislation or Resolution (Yes or No)	Violence at Stake (Yes or No)	Decision Time (Long or Short)
Neutrality Legislation, the 1930's	High	Exec.	Cong.	Yes	No	Long
Lend-Lease, 1941	High	Exec.	Exec.	Yes	Yes	Long
Aid to Russia, 1941	Low	Exec.	Exec.	No	No	Long
Repeal of Chinese Exclusion, 1943	High	Cong.	Cong.	Yes	No	Long
Fullbright Resolution, 1943	High	Cong.	Cong.	Yes	No	Long
Building the Atomic Bomb, 1944	Low	Exec.	Exec.	Yes	Yes	Long
Foreign Services Act of 1946	High	Exec.	Exec.	Yes	No	Long
Truman Doctrine, 1947	High	Exec.	Exec.	Yes	No	Long
The Marshall Plan, 1947–48	High	Exec.	Exec.	Yes	No	Long
Berlin Airlift, 1948	None	Exec.	Exec.	No	Yes	Long
Vandenberg Resolution, 1948	High	Exec.	Cong.	Yes	No	Long
North Atlantic Treaty, 1947–49	High	Exec.	Exec.	Yes	No	Long
Korean Decision, 1950	None	Exec.	Exec.	No	Yes	Short
Japanese Peace Treaty, 1952	High	Exec.	Exec.	Yes	No	Long
Bohlen Nomination, 1953	High	Exec.	Exec.	Yes	No	Long
Indo-China, 1954	High	Exec.	Cong.	No	Yes	Short
Formosan Resolution, 1955	High	Exec.	Exec.	Yes	Yes	Long
International Finance Corporation, 1956	Low	Exec.	Exec.	Yes	No	Long
Foreign Aid, 1957	High	Exec.	Exec.	Yes	No	Long
Reciprocal Trade Agreements, 1958	High	Exec.	Exec.	Yes	No	Long
Monroney Resolution, 1958	High	Cong.	Cong.	Yes	No	Long
Cuban Decision, 1961	Low	Exec.	Exec.	No	Yes	Long

Source: James A. Robinson, Congress and Foreign Policymaking (Homewood, Illinois, 1962).

1954 decision not to intervene with armed force in Indochina. In that instance President Eisenhower deliberately sounded out congressional opinion and, finding it negative, decided not to intervene—against the advice of Admiral Radford, chairman of the Joint Chiefs of Staff. This attempt to abandon responsibility did not succeed, as the years of American involvement demonstrate.

THE MILITARY. The outstanding feature of the military's participation in making defense policy is their amazing weakness. Whether the policy decisions involve the size of the armed forces, the choice of weapons systems, the total defense budget, or its division into components, the military have not prevailed. Let us take budgetary decisions as representative of the key choices to be made in defense policy. Since the end of World War II the military has not been able to achieve significant (billion dollar) increases in appropriations by their own efforts. Under Truman and Eisenhower defense budgets were determined by what Huntington calls the remainder method: the two Presidents estimated revenues, decided what they could spend on domestic matters, and the remainder was assigned to defense. The usual controversy was between some military and congressional groups supporting much larger expenditures while the President and his executive allies refused. A typical case, involving the desire of the Air Force to increase the number of groups of planes is described by Huntington in the *The Common Defense:*

> The FY [fiscal year] 1949 budget provided 48 groups. After the Czech coup, the Administration yielded and backed an Air Force of 55 groups in its spring rearmament program. Congress added additional funds to aid Air Force expansion to 70 groups. The Administration refused to utilize them, however, and in the gathering economy wave of the summer and fall of 1948, the Air Force goal was cut back again to 48 groups. In 1949 the House of Representatives picked up the challenge and appropriated funds for 58 groups. The President impounded the money. In June, 1950, the Air Force had 48 groups.

The great increases in the defense budget were due far more to Stalin and modern technology than to the military. The Korean War resulted in an increase from 12 to 44 billions and much of the rest followed Sputnik and the huge costs of missile programs. Thus modern technology and international conflict put an end to the one major effort to subordinate foreign affairs to domestic policies through the budget.

It could be argued that the President merely ratifies the decisions made by the military and their allies. If the military and/or Congress were united and insistent on defense policy, it would certainly be difficult for Presidents to resist these forces. But it is precisely the disunity of the military that has characterized the entire postwar period. Indeed, the military have not been united on any major matter of defense policy. The apparent unity of the Joint Chiefs of Staff turns out to be illusory. The vast majority of their recommendations appear to be unanimous and are accepted by the Secretary of Defense and the President. But this facade of unity can only be achieved by methods that vitiate the impact of the recommendations. Genuine disagreements are hidden by vague language that commits no one to anything. Mutually contradictory plans are strung together so everyone appears to get something, but nothing is decided. Since it is impossible to agree on really important matters, all sorts of trivia are brought in to make a record of agreement. While it may be true, as Admiral Denfield, a former Chief of Naval Operations, said, that "On nine-tenths of the matters that come before them the Joint Chiefs of Staff reach agreement themselves," the vastly more important truth is that "normally the *only* disputes are on strategic concepts, the size and composition of forces, and budget matters."

MILITARY-INDUSTRIAL. But what about the fabled military-industrial complex? If the military alone is divided and weak, perhaps the giant industrial firms that are so dependent on defense contracts play a large part in making policy.

First, there is an important distinction between the questions "Who will get a given contract?" and "What will our defense policy be?" It is apparent that different answers may be given to these quite different questions. There are literally tens of thousands of defense contractors. They may compete vigorously for business. In the course of this competition, they may wine and dine military officers, use retired generals, seek intervention by their congressmen, place ads in trade journals, and even contribute to political campaigns. The famous TFX controversy—should General Dynamics or Boeing get the expensive contract?—is a larger than life example of the pressures brought to bear in search of lucrative contracts.

But neither the TFX case nor the usual vigorous competition for contracts is involved with the making of substantive defense policy. Vital questions like the size of the defense budget, the choice of strategic programs, massive retaliation vs. a counter-city strategy, and the like were far beyond the policy aims of any company. Industrial firms, then, do not control such decisions, nor is there much evidence that they actually try. No doubt a precipitous and drastic rush to disarmament would meet with opposition from industrial firms among other interests. However, there has never been a time when any significant element in the government considered a disarmament policy to be feasible.

It may appear that industrial firms had no special reason to concern themselves with the government's stance on defense because they agree with the national consensus on resisting communism, maintaining a large defense establishment, and rejecting isolationism. However, this hypothesis about the climate of opinion explains everything and nothing. For every policy that is adopted or rejected can be explained away on the grounds that the cold war climate of opinion dictated what happened. Did the United States fail to intervene with armed force in Vietnam in 1954? That must be because the climate of opinion was against it. Did the United States send troops to Vietnam in the 1960's? That must be because the cold war climate demanded it. If the United States builds more missiles, negotiates a testban treaty, intervenes in the Dominican Republic, fails to intervene in a dozen other situations, all these actions fit the hypothesis by definition. The argument is reminiscent of those who defined the Soviet Union as permanently hostile and therefore interpreted increases of Soviet troops as menacing and decreases of troop strength as equally sinister.

If the growth of the military establishment is not directly equated with increasing military control of defense policy, the extraordinary weakness of the professional soldier still requires explanation. Huntington has written about how major military leaders were seduced in the Truman and Eisenhower years into believing that they should bow to the judgment of civilians that the economy could not stand much larger military expenditures. Once the size of the military pie was accepted as a fixed constraint, the military services were compelled to put their major energies into quarreling with one another over who should get the larger share. Given the natural rivalries of the military and their traditional acceptance of civilian rule, the President and his advisers—who could claim responsibility for the broader picture of reconciling defense and domestic policies—had the upper hand. There are, however, additional explanations to be considered.

The dominant role of the congressional appropriations committee is to be guardian of the treasury. This is manifested in the pride of its members in cutting the President's budget. Thus it was difficult to get this crucial committee to recommend even a few hundred million increase in defense; it was practically impossible to get them to consider the several billion jump that might really have made a difference. A related budgetary matter concerned the planning, programming, and budgeting system introduced by Secretary of Defense McNamara. For if the defense budget contained major categories that crisscrossed the services, only the Secretary of Defense could put it together. Whatever the other debatable consequences of program budgeting, its major consequence was to grant power to the secretary and his civilian advisers.

The subordination of the military through program budgeting is just one symptom of a more general weakness of the military. In the past decade the military has suffered a lack of intellectual skills appropriate to the nuclear age. For no one has (and no one wants) direct experience with nuclear war. So the usual military talk about being the only people to have combat experience is not very impressive. Instead, the imaginative creation of possible future wars—in order to avoid them—requires people with a high capacity for abstract thought combined with the ability to manipulate symbols using quantitative methods. West Point has not produced many such men.

THE STATE DEPARTMENT. Modern Presidents expect the State Department to carry out their policies. John F. Kennedy felt that State was "in some particular sense 'his' department." If a Secretary of State forgets this, as was apparently the case with James Byrnes under Truman, a President may find another man. But the State Department, especially the Foreign Service, is also a highly professional organization with a life and momentum of its own. If a President does not push hard, he may find his preferences somehow dissipated in time. Arthur Schlesinger fills his book on Kennedy with laments about the bureaucratic inertia and recalcitrance of the State Department.

Yet Schlesinger's own account suggests that State could not ordinarily resist the President. At one point, he writes of "the President, himself, increasingly the day-to-day director of American foreign policy." On the next page, we learn that "Kennedy dealt personally with almost every aspect of policy around the globe.

He knew more about certain areas than the senior officials at State and probably called as many issues to their attention as they did to his." The President insisted on his way in Laos. He pushed through his policy on the Congo against strong opposition with the State Department. Had Kennedy wanted to get a great deal more initiative out of the State Department, as Schlesinger insists, he could have replaced the Secretary of State, a man who did not command special support in the Democratic party or in Congress. It may be that Kennedy wanted too strongly to run his own foreign policy. Dean Rusk may have known far better than Schlesinger that the one thing Kennedy did not want was a man who might rival him in the field of foreign affairs.

Schlesinger comes closest to the truth when he writes that "the White House could always win any battle it chose over the [Foreign] Service; but the prestige and proficiency of the Service limited the number of battles any White House would find it profitable to fight." When the President knew what he wanted, he got it. When he was doubtful and perplexed, he sought good advice and frequently did not get that. But there is no evidence that the people on his staff came up with better ideas. The real problem may have been a lack of good ideas anywhere. Kennedy undoubtedly encouraged his staff to prod the State Department. But the President was sufficiently cautious not to push so hard that he got his way when he was not certain what that way should be. In this context Kennedy appears to have played his staff off against elements in the State Department.

The growth of a special White House staff to help Presidents in foreign affairs expresses their need for assistance, their refusal to rely completely on the regular executive agencies, and their ability to find competent men. The deployment of this staff must remain a presidential prerogative, however, if its members are to serve Presidents and not their opponents. Whenever critics do not like the existing foreign and defense policies, they are likely to complain that the White House staff is screening out divergent views from the President's attention. Naturally, the critics recommend introducing many more different viewpoints. If the critics could maneuver the President into counting hands all day ("on the one hand and on the other"), they would make it impossible for him to act. Such a viewpoint is also congenial to those who believe that action rather than inaction is the greatest present danger in foreign policy. But Presidents resolutely refuse to become prisoners of their advisers by using them as other people would like. Presidents remain in control of their staff as well as of major foreign policy decisions.

HOW COMPLETE IS THE CONTROL?

Some analysts say that the success of Presidents in controlling foreign policy decisions is largely illusory. It is achieved, they say, by anticipating the reactions of others, and eliminating proposals that would run into severe opposition. There is some truth in this objection. In politics, where transactions are based on a high degree of mutual interdependence, what others may do has to be taken into account. But basing presidential success in foreign and defense policy on anticipated reactions suggests a static situation which does not exist. For if Presidents propose only those policies that would get support in Congress, and Congress opposes them only when it knows that it can muster overwhelming strength, there would never be any conflict. Indeed, there might never be any action.

How can "anticipated reaction" explain the conflict over the policies like the Marshall Plan and the test-ban treaty in which severe opposition was overcome only by strenuous efforts? Furthermore, why doesn't "anticipated reaction" work in domestic affairs? One would have to argue that for some reason presidential perception of what would be successful is consistently confused on domestic issues and most always accurate on major foreign policy issues. But the role of "anticipated reactions" should be greater in the more familiar domestic situations, which provide a backlog of experience for forecasting, than in foreign policy with many novel situations such as the Suez crisis or the Rhodesian affair.

Are there significant historical examples which might refute the thesis of presidential control of foreign policy? Foreign aid may be a case in point. For many years, Presidents have struggled to get foreign aid appropriations because of hostility from public and congressional opinion. Yet several billion dollars a year are appropriated regularly despite the evident unpopularity of the program. In the aid programs to Communist countries like Poland and Yugoslavia, the Congress attaches all sorts of restrictions to the aid, but Presidents find ways of getting around them.

What about the example of recognition of Communist China? The sentiment of the country always has been against recognizing Red China or admitting it to the United Nations. But have Presidents wanted to recognize Red China and been hamstrung by opposition? The answer, I suggest, is a qualified "no." By the time recognition of Red China might have become a serious issue for the Truman administration, the war in Korea effectively precluded its consideration. There is no evidence that President Eisenhower or Secretary Dulles ever thought it wise to recognize Red China or help admit her to the United Nations. The Kennedy administration viewed the matter as not of major importance and, considering the opposition, moved cautiously in suggesting change. Then came the war in Vietnam. If the advantages for foreign policy had been perceived to be much higher, then Kennedy or Johnson might have proposed changing American policy toward recognition of Red China.

One possible exception, in the case of Red China, however, does not seem sufficient to invalidate the general thesis that Presidents do considerably better in getting their way in foreign and defense policy than in domestic policies.

THE WORLD INFLUENCE

The forces impelling Presidents to be concerned with the widest range of foreign and defense policies also affect the ways in which they calculate their power stakes. As Kennedy used to say, "Domestic policy . . . can only defeat us; foreign policy can kill us."

It no longer makes sense for Presidents to "play politics" with foreign and defense policies. In the past, Presidents might have thought that they could gain by prolonged delay or by not acting at all. The problem might disappear or be passed on to their successors. Presidents must now expect to pay the high costs themselves if the world situation deteriorates. The advantages of pursuing a policy that is viable in the world, that will not blow up on Presidents or their fellow citizens, far outweigh any temporary political disadvantages accrued in supporting an initially unpopular policy. Compared with domestic affairs, Presidents engaged in world politics are immensely more concerned with meeting problems on their own terms. Who supports and opposes a policy, though a matter of considerable interest, does not assume the crucial importance that it does in domestic affairs. The best policy Presidents can find is also the best politics.

The fact that there are numerous foreign and defense policy situations competing for a President's attention means that it is worthwhile to organize political activity in order to affect his agenda. For if a President pays more attention to certain problems he may develop different preferences; he may seek and receive different advice; his new calculations may lead him to devote greater resources to seeking a solution. Interested congressmen may exert influence not by directly determining a presidential decision, but indirectly by making it costly for a President to avoid reconsidering the basis for his action. For example, citizen groups, such as those concerned with a change in China policy, may have an impact simply by keeping their proposals on the public agenda. A president may be compelled to reconsider a problem even though he could not overtly be forced to alter the prevailing policy.

In foreign affairs we may be approaching the stage where knowledge is power. There is a tremendous receptivity to good ideas in Washington. Most anyone who can present a convincing rationale for dealing with a hard world finds a ready audience. The best way to convince Presidents to follow a desired policy is to show that it might work. A man like McNamara thrives because he performs; he comes up with answers he can defend. It is, to be sure, extremely difficult to devise good policies or to predict their consequences accurately. Nor is it easy to convince others that a given policy is superior to other alternatives. But it is the way to influence with Presidents. For if they are convinced that the current policy is best, the likelihood of gaining sufficient force to compel a change is quite small. The man who can build better foreign policies will find Presidents beating a path to his door.

30

RICHARD E. NEUSTADT

THE POWER TO PERSUADE

The first edition of Presidential Power *(1960), a study of the Truman and Eisenhower administrations, received national attention and served to alert the incoming president, John F. Kennedy, of the limitations of presidential power. In subsequent editions, Richard E. Neustadt, a professor of government at Harvard University, updated and expanded the original analysis to cover additional presidents. His analysis shows that presidents cannot simply rely on the formal authority of their office and partisan loyalties for effective leadership. They must know how to persuade and cajole other government actors, interest groups, and the public to support presidential initiatives. The following excerpt is from the 1976 edition of* Presidential Power.

The limits on command suggest the structure of our government. The constitutional convention of 1787 is supposed to have created a government of "separated powers." It did nothing of the sort. Rather, it created a government of separated institutions *sharing* powers.[1] "I am part of the legislative process," Eisenhower often said in 1959 as a reminder of his veto.[2] Congress, the dispenser of authority and funds, is no less part of the administrative process. Federalism adds another set of separated institutions. The Bill of Rights adds others. Many public purposes can only be achieved by voluntary acts of private institutions; the press, for one, in Douglass Cater's phrase, is a "fourth branch of government."[3] And with the coming of alliances abroad, the separate institutions of a London, or a Bonn, share in the making of American policy.

What the Constitution separates our political parties do not combine. The parties are themselves composed of separated organizations sharing public authority. The authority consists of nominating powers. Our national parties are confederations of state and local party institutions, with a headquarters that represents the White House, more or less, if the party has a president in office. These confederacies manage presidential nominations. All other public offices depend upon electorates confined within the states.[4] All other nominations are controlled within the states. The president and congressmen who bear one party's label are divided by dependence upon different sets of voters. The differences are sharpest at the stage of nomination. The White House has too small a share in nominating congressmen, and Congress has too little weight in nominating presidents for party to erase their constitutional separation. Party links are stronger than is frequently supposed, but nominating processes assure the separation.[5]

The separateness of institutions and the sharing of authority prescribe the terms on which a president persuades. When one man shares authority with another, but does not gain or lose his job upon the other's whim, his willingness to act upon the urging of the other turns on whether he conceives the action right for him. The essence of a president's persuasive task is to convince such men that what the White House wants of them is what they ought to do for their sake and on their authority.

Persuasive power, thus defined, amounts to more than charm or reasoned argument. These have their uses for a president, but these are not the whole of his resources. For the men he would induce to do what he wants done on their own responsibility will need or fear some acts by him on his responsibility. If they share his authority, he has some share in theirs. Presidential "powers" may be inconclusive when a president commands, but always remain relevant as he persuades. The status and authority inherent in his office reinforce his logic and his charm.

Status adds something to persuasiveness; authority adds still more. When Truman urged wage changes on his secretary of commerce while the latter was administering the steel mills, he and Secretary Sawyer were not just two men reasoning with one another. Had they been so, Sawyer probably would never have agreed to act. Truman's status gave him special claims to Sawyer's loyalty, or at least attention. In Walter Bagehot's charming phrase "no man can *argue* on his knees." Although there is no kneeling in this country, few men—and exceedingly few cabinet officers—are immune to the impulse to say "yes" to the president of the United States. It grows harder to say "no" when they are seated in his oval office at the White House, or in his study on the second floor, where almost tangibly he partakes of the aura of his physical surroundings. In Sawyer's case, moreover, the president possessed formal authority to intervene in many matters of concern to the secretary of commerce. These matters ranged from jurisdictional disputes among the defense agencies to legislation pending before Congress and, ultimately, to the tenure of the secretary, himself. There is nothing in the record to suggest that Truman voiced specific threats when they negotiated over wage increases. But given his *formal* powers and their relevance to Sawyer's other interests, it is safe to assume that Truman's very advocacy of wage action conveyed an implicit threat.

A president's authority and status give him great advantages in dealing with the men he would persuade. Each "power" is a vantage point for him in the degree that other men have use for his authority. From the veto to appointments, from publicity to budgeting, and so down a long list, the White House now controls the most encompassing array of vantage points in the American political system. With hardly an exception, the men who share in governing this country are aware that at some time, in some degree, the doing of *their* jobs, the furthering of *their* ambitions, may depend upon the president of the United States. Their need for presidential action, or their fear of it, is bound to be recurrent if not actually continuous. Their need or fear is his advantage.

A president's advantages are greater than mere listing of his "powers" might suggest. The men with whom he deals must deal with him until the last day of his term. Because they have continuing relationships with him, his future, while it lasts, supports his present influence. Even though there is no need or fear of him today, what he could do tomorrow may supply today's advantage. Continuing relationships may convert any "power," any aspect of his status, into vantage points in almost any case. When he induces other men to do what he wants done, a president can trade on their dependence now *and* later.

The president's advantages are checked by the advantages of others. Continuing relationships will pull in both directions. These are relationships of mutual dependence. A president depends upon the men he would persuade; he has to reckon with his need or fear of them. They too will possess status, or authority, or both, else they would be of little use to him. Their vantage points confront his own; their power tempers his.

Persuasion is a two-way street. Sawyer, it will be recalled, did not respond at once to Truman's plan for wage increases at the steel mills. On the contrary, the secretary hesitated and delayed and only acquiesced when he was satisfied that publicly he would not bear the onus of decision. Sawyer had some points of vantage all his own from which to resist presidential pressure. If he had to reckon with coercive implications in the president's "situations of strength," so had Truman to be mindful of the implications underlying Sawyer's place as a department head, as steel administrator, and as a cabinet spokesman for business. Loyalty is reciprocal. Having taken on a dirty job in the steel crisis, Sawyer had strong claims to loyal support. Besides, he had authority to do some things that the White House could ill afford. Emulating Wilson, he might have resigned in a huff (the removal power also works two ways). Or emulating Ellis Arnall, he might have declined to sign necessary orders. Or, he might have let it be known publicly that he deplored what he was told to do and protested its doing. By following any of these courses Sawyer almost surely would have strengthened the position of management, weakened the position of the White House, and embittered the union. But the whole purpose of a wage increase was to enhance White House persuasiveness in urging settlement upon union and companies alike. Although Sawyer's status and authority did not give him the power to prevent an increase outright, they gave him capability to undermine its purpose. If his authority over wage rates had been vested by a statute, not by revocable presidential order, his power of prevention might have been complete. So Harold Ickes demonstrated in the famous case of helium sales to Germany before the Second World War.[6]

The power to persuade is the power to bargain. Status and authority yield bargaining advantages. But in a government of "separated institutions sharing powers," they yield them to all sides. With the array of vantage points at his disposal, a president may be far more persuasive than his logic or his charm could make him. But outcomes are not guaranteed by his advantages. There remain the counter pressures those whom he would influence can bring to bear on him from vantage points at their disposal. Command has limited utility; persuasion becomes give-and-take. It is well that the White House holds the vantage points it does. In such a business any president may need them all—and more.

This view of power as akin to bargaining is one we commonly accept in the sphere of congressional relations. Every textbook states and every legislative session demonstrates that save in times like the extraordinary Hundred Days of 1933—times virtually ruled out by definition at mid-century—a president will often be unable to obtain congressional action on his terms or even to halt action he opposes. The reverse is equally accepted: Congress often is frustrated by the president. Their formal powers are so intertwined that neither will accomplish very much, for very long, without the acquiescence of the other. By the same token, though, what one demands, the other can resist. The stage is set for that great game, much like collective bargaining, in which each seeks to profit from the other's needs and fears. It is a game played catch-as-catch-can, case by case. And everybody knows the game, observers and participants alike.

The concept of real power as a give-and-take is equally familiar when applied to presidential influence outside the formal structure of the federal government. The Little Rock affair may be extreme, but Eisenhower's dealings with the governor—and with the citizens—become a case in point. Less extreme but no less pertinent is the steel seizure case with respect to union leaders, and to workers, and to company executives as well. When he deals with such people a president draws bargaining advantage from his status or authority. By virtue of their public places or their private rights they have some capability to reply in kind.

In spheres of party politics the same thing follows, necessarily, from the confederal nature of our party organizations. Even in the case of national nominations a president's advantages are checked by those of others. In 1944 it is by no means clear that Roosevelt got his first choice as his running mate. In 1948 Truman, then the president, faced serious revolts against his nomination. In 1952 his intervention from the White House helped assure the choice of Adlai Stevenson, but it is far from clear that Truman could have done as much for any other candidate acceptable to him.[7] In 1956 when Eisenhower was president, the record leaves obscure just who backed Harold Stassen's effort to block Richard Nixon's renomination as vice-president. But evidently everything did not go quite as Eisenhower wanted, whatever his intentions may have been.[8] The outcomes in these instances bear all the marks of limits on command and of power checked by power that characterize congressional relations. Both in and out of politics these checks and limits seem to be quite widely understood.

Influence becomes still more a matter of give-and-take when presidents attempt to deal with allied governments. A classic illustration is the long unhappy wrangle over Suez policy in 1956. In dealing with the British and the French before their military intervention, Eisenhower had his share of bargaining advantages but no effective power of command. His allies had their share of counter pressures, and they finally tried the most extreme of all: action despite him. His pressure then was instrumental in reversing them. But had the British government been on safe ground *at home*, Eisenhower's wishes might have made as little difference after intervention as before. Behind the decorum of diplomacy—which was not very decorous in the Suez affair—relationships among allies are not unlike relationships among state delegations at a national convention. Power is persuasion and persuasion becomes bargaining. The concept is familiar to everyone who watches foreign policy.

In only one sphere is the concept unfamiliar: the sphere of executive relations. Perhaps because of civics textbooks and teaching in our schools, Americans instinctively resist the view that power in this sphere resembles power in all others. Even Washington reporters, White House aides, and congressmen are not immune to the illusion that administrative agencies comprise a single structure, "the" executive branch, where presidential word is law, or ought to be. Yet we have seen . . . that when a president seeks something from executive officials his persuasiveness is subject to the same sorts of limitations as in the case of congressmen, or governors, or national committeemen, or private citizens, or foreign governments. There are no generic differences, no differences in kind and only sometimes in degree. The incidents preceding the dismissal of MacArthur and the incidents surrounding seizure of the steel mills make it plain that here as elsewhere influence derives from bargaining advantages; power is a give-and-take.

Like our governmental structure as a whole, the executive establishment consists of separated institutions sharing powers. The president heads one of these; cabinet officers, agency administrators, and military commanders head others. Below the departmental level, virtually independent bureau chiefs head many more. Under mid-century conditions, federal operations spill across dividing lines on organization charts; almost every policy entangles many agencies; almost every program calls for interagency collaboration. Everything somehow involves the president. But operating agencies owe their existence least of all to one another—and only in some part to him. Each has a separate statutory base; each has its statutes to administer; each deals with a different set of subcommittees at the Capitol. Each has its own peculiar set of clients, friends, and enemies outside the formal government. Each has a different set of specialized careerists inside its own bailiwick. Our Constitution gives the president the "take-care" clause and the appointive power. Our statutes give him central budgeting and a degree of personnel control. All agency administrators are responsible to him. But they *also* are responsible to Congress, to their clients, to their staffs, and to themselves. In short, they have five masters. Only after all of those do they owe any loyalty to each other.

"The members of the cabinet," Charles G. Dawes used to remark, "are a president's natural enemies." Dawes had been Harding's budget director, Coolidge's vice-president, and Hoover's ambassador to London; he also had been General Pershing's chief assistant for supply in the First World War. The words are highly colored, but Dawes knew whereof he spoke. The men who have to serve so many masters cannot help but be somewhat the "enemy" of any one of them. By the same token, any master wanting service is in some degree the "enemy" of such a servant. A president is likely to want loyal support but not to relish trouble on his doorstep. Yet the more his cabinet members cleave to him, the more they may need help from him in fending off the wrath of rival masters. Help, though, is synonymous with trouble. Many a cabinet officer with loyalty ill-rewarded by his lights and help withheld, has come to view the White House as innately hostile to department heads. Dawes' dictum can be turned around.

A senior presidential aide remarked to me in Eisenhower's time: "If some of these cabinet members would just take time out to stop and ask themselves 'What would I want if I were president?', they wouldn't give him all the trouble he's been having." But even if they asked themselves the question, such officials often could not act upon the answer. Their personal attachment to the president is all too often overwhelmed by duty to their other masters.

Executive officials are not equally advantaged in their dealings with a president. Nor are the same officials equally advantaged all the time. Not every officeholder can resist like a MacArthur, or like Arnall, Sawyer, Wilson, in a rough descending order of effective counter pressure. The vantage points conferred upon officials by their own authority and status vary enormously. The variance is heightened by particulars of time and circumstance. In mid-October 1950, Truman, at a press conference, remarked of the man he had considered firing in August and would fire the next April for intolerable insubordination:

> Let me tell you something that will be good for your souls. It's a pity that you . . . can't understand the ideas of two intellectually honest men when they meet. General MacArthur . . . is a member of the Government of the United States. He is loyal to that Government. He is loyal to the President. He is loyal to the President in his foreign policy. . . . There is no disagreement between General MacArthur and myself. . . .[9]

MacArthur's status in and out of government was never higher than when Truman spoke those words. The words, once spoken, added to the general's credibility thereafter when he sought to use the press in his campaign against the president. And what had happened between August and October? Near-victory had happened, together with that premature conference on *post*-war plans, the meeting at Wake Island.

If the bargaining advantages of a MacArthur fluctuate with changing circumstances, this is bound to be so with subordinates who have at their disposal fewer "powers," lesser status, to fall back on. And when officials have no "powers" in their own right, or depend upon the president for status, their counter pressure may be limited indeed. White House aides, who fit both categories, are among the most responsive men of all, and for good reason. As a director of the budget once remarked to me,

> Thank God I'm here and not across the street. If the President doesn't call me, I've got plenty I can do right here and plenty coming up to me, by rights, to justify my calling him. But those poor fellows over there, if the boss doesn't call them, doesn't ask them to do something, what *can* they do but sit?

Authority and status so conditional are frail reliances in resisting a president's own wants. Within the White House precincts, lifted eyebrows may suffice to set an aide in motion; command, coercion, even charm aside. But even in the White House a president does not monopolize effective power. Even there persuasion is akin to bargaining. A former Roosevelt aide once wrote of cabinet officers:

> Half of a President's suggestions, which theoretically carry the weight of orders, can be safely forgotten by a Cabinet member. And if the President asks about a suggestion a second time, he can be told that it is being investigated. If he asks a third time, a wise Cabinet officer will give him at least part of what he suggests. But only occasionally, except about the most important matters, do Presidents ever get around to asking three times.[10]

The rule applies to staff as well as to the cabinet, and certainly has been applied *by* staff in Truman's time and Eisenhower's.

Some aides will have more vantage points than a selective memory. Sherman Adams, for example, as the assistant to the president under Eisenhower, scarcely deserved the appellation "White House aide" in the meaning of the term before his time or as applied to other members of the Eisenhower entourage. Although Adams was by no means "chief of staff" in any sense so sweeping—or so simple— as press commentaries often took for granted, he apparently became no more dependent on the president than Eisenhower on him. "I need him," said the president when Adams turned out to have been remarkably imprudent in the Goldfine case, and delegated to him even the decision on his own departure.[11] This instance is extreme, but the tendency it illustrates is common enough. Any aide who demonstrates to others that he has the president's consistent confidence and a consistent part in presidential business will acquire so much business on his own account that he becomes in some sense independent of his chief. Nothing in the Constitution keeps a well-placed aide from converting status into power of his own, usable in some degree even against the president—an outcome not unknown in Truman's regime or, by all accounts, in Eisenhower's.

The more an officeholder's status and his "powers" stem from sources independent of the president, the stronger will be his potential pressure *on* the president. Department heads in general have more bargaining power than do most members of the White House staff; but bureau chiefs may have still more, and specialists at upper levels of established career services may have almost unlimited reserves of the enormous power which consists of sitting still. As Franklin Roosevelt once remarked:

> The Treasury is so large and far-flung and ingrained in its practices that I find it is almost impossible to get the action and results I want—even with Henry [Morgenthau] there. But the Treasury is not to be compared with the State Department. You should go through the experience of trying to get any changes in the thinking, policy, and action of the career diplomats and then you'd know what a real problem was. But the Treasury and the State Department put together are nothing compared with the Na-a-vy. The admirals are really something to cope with—and I should know. To change anything in the Na-a-vy is like punching a feather bed. You punch it with your right and you punch it with your left until you are finally exhausted, and then you find the damn bed just as it was before you started punching.[12]

[Three pages of original text omitted at this point.]

The essence of a president's persuasive task with congressmen and everybody else *is to induce them to believe that what he wants of them is what their own appraisal of their own responsibilities requires them to do in their interest, not his.* Because men may differ in their views on public policy, because differences in outlook stem from differences in duty—duty to one's office, one's constituents, oneself—that task is bound to be more like collective bargaining than like a reasoned argument among philosopher kings. Overtly or implicitly, hard bargaining has characterized all illustrations offered up to now. This is the reason why: persuasion deals in the coin of self-interest with men who have some freedom to reject what they find counterfeit.

NOTES

1. The reader will want to keep in mind the distinction between two senses in which the word *power* is employed. When I have used the word (or its plural) to refer to formal constitutional, statutory, or customary authority, it is either qualified by the adjective "formal" or placed in quotation marks as "power(s)." Where I have used it in the sense of effective influence upon the conduct of others, it appears without quotation marks (and always in the singular). Where clarity and convenience permit, *authority* is substituted for "power" in the first sense and *influence* for power in the second sense.

2. See, for example, his press conference of July 22, 1959, as reported in the *New York Times* for July 23, 1959.

3. See Douglass Cater, *The Fourth Branch of Government* (Boston: Houghton Mifflin, 1959).

4. With the exception of the vice-presidency, of course.

5. See David B. Truman's illuminating study of party relationships in the 81st Congress, *The Congressional Party* (New York: Wiley, 1959), especially chaps. 4, 6, and 8.

6. As secretary of the interior in 1939, Harold Ickes refused to approve the sale of helium to Germany despite the insistence of the State Department and the urging of President Roosevelt. Without the secretary's approval, such sales were forbidden by statute. See *The Secret Diaries of Harold L. Ickes*, vol. 2 (New York: Simon and Schuster, 1954), especially pp. 391–393, 396–399. See also Michael J. Reagan, "The Helium Controversy" in the forthcoming case book on civil-military relations prepared for the Twentieth Century Fund under the editorial direction of Harold Stein.

In this instance the statutory authority ran to the secretary as a matter of *his* discretion. A president is unlikely to fire cabinet officers for the conscientious exercise of such authority. If the president did so, their successors might well be embarrassed both publicly and at the Capitol were they to reverse decisions previously taken. As for a president's authority to set aside discretionary determinations of this sort, it rests, if it exists at all, on shaky legal ground not likely to be trod save in the gravest of situations.

7. Truman's *Memoirs* indicate that having tried and failed to make Stevenson an avowed candidate in the spring of 1952, the president decided to support the candidacy of Vice-President Barkley. But Barkley withdrew early in the convention for lack of key northern support. Though Truman is silent on the matter, Barkley's active candidacy nearly was revived during the balloting, but the forces then aligning to revive it were led by opponents of Truman's Fair Deal, principally southerners. As a practical matter, the president could not have lent his weight to *their* endeavors and could back no one but Stevenson to counter them. The latter's strength could not be shifted, then, to Harriman or Kefauver. Instead the other northerners had to be withdrawn. Truman helped withdraw them. But he had no other option. See Memoirs by Harry S. Truman, vol. 2, *Years of Trial and Hope* (Garden City: Doubleday, 1956, copr. 1956 Time Inc.), pp. 495–496.

8. The reference is to Stassen's public statement of July 23, 1956, calling for Nixon's replacement on the Republican ticket by Governor Herter of Massachusetts, the later secretary of state. Stassen's statement was issued after a conference with the president. Eisenhower's public statements on the vice-presidential nomination, both before and after Stassen's call, permit of alternative inferences: either that the president would have preferred another candidate, provided this could be arranged without a showing of White House dictation, or that he wanted Nixon on condition that the latter could show popular appeal. In the event, neither result was achieved. Eisenhower's own remarks lent strength to rapid party moves which smothered Stassen's effort. Nixon's nomination thus was guaranteed too quickly to appear the consequence of popular demand. For the public record on this matter see reported statements by Eisenhower, Nixon, Stassen, Herter, and Leonard Hall (the Republican national chairman) in the *New York Times* for March 1, 8, 15, 16; April 27; July 15, 16, 25–31; August 3, 4, 17, 23, 1956. See also the account from private sources by Earl Mazo in *Richard Nixon: A Personal and Political Portrait* (New York: Harper, 1959), pp. 158–187.

9. Stenographic transcript of presidential press conference, October 19, 1950, on file in the Truman Library at Independence, Missouri.

10. Jonathan Daniels, *Frontier on the Potomac* (New York: Macmillan, 1946), pp. 31–32.

11. Transcript of presidential press conference, June 18, 1958, in *Public Papers of the Presidents: Dwight D. Eisenhower*, 1958 (Washington: The National Archives, 1959), p. 479. In the summer of 1958, a congressional investigation into the affairs of a New England textile manufacturer, Bernard Goldfine, revealed that Sherman Adams had accepted various gifts and favors from him (the most notoriety attached to a vicuña coat). Adams also had made inquiries about the status of a Federal Communications Commission proceeding in which Goldfine was involved. In September 1958, Adams was allowed to resign. The episode was highly publicized and much discussed in that year's congressional campaigns.

12. As reported in Marriner S. Eccles, *Beckoning Frontiers* (New York: Knopf, 1951), p. 336.

31

CHARLES O. JONES

SEPARATING TO GOVERN:
THE AMERICAN WAY

"The president is not the presidency. The presidency is not the government." As an institution, the American presidency is embedded in a governmental structure that separates power among branches and levels of government and enables voters ". . . to roam freely across independently chosen bodies, putting a Democrat here, a Republican there—having it both ways through the layers of government, which themselves are interdependent." Consequently, a single president may face remarkably different political circumstances as membership in the Senate and House of Representatives changes during his years in office. Charles O. Jones, a political science professor at the University of Wisconsin, Madison, argues that critics of the American system of "separating to govern" are incorrect in claiming that it inevitably produces stalemates and would be improved by relying on more unified, responsible political parties to overcome constitutional divisions.

In his reflections entitled *Two Hundred Million Americans in Search of a Government,* the straight-talking political scientist E. E. Schattschneider observed that "Democracy is a political system for those people who are not too sure that they are right."[1] As it happened, Schattschneider spent much of his professional career urging American political parties to state what was right and proposing reforms to enable them to be effective. But I like his depiction of American democracy for a reason that would displease him. I consider it a clear statement of the rationale for a separated system of governing, one characterized by the competing legitimacies that logically interfere with the capacity of political parties to do what Schattschneider and others judged to be right.

The American system of separated institutions does not show well. It invites criticism and reform, both of which are functional for its operation. There is, in fact, continual tension between what many analysts want to see in governing and what they are likely to get with separationism. Most perspectives on the American national government are based on the classic responsible-party, presidency-centered model. In this perspective, political parties should be prepared to overcome constitutional separation, primarily through presidential leadership. What many such analysts have in mind, of course, is the clarity and elegance of the British political system. If the United States could just form a government, responsibility would surely follow. When the government acted correctly, it would be rewarded; when it did wrong, it would be punished. Lloyd Cutler, a man with substantial experience as a counselor to presidents, is an articulate advocate of this viewpoint:

> In parliamentary terms, one might say that under the U.S. Constitution it is not now feasible to "form a Government." The separation of powers between the legislative and

[Tables and figures have been renumbered.—Eds.]

executive branches, whatever its merits in 1793, has become a structure that almost guarantees stalemate today. . . .

Although the enactment of legislation takes only a simple majority of both Houses, that majority is very difficult to achieve. Any part of the president's legislative program may be defeated, or amended into an entirely different measure, so that the legislative record of any presidency may bear little resemblance to the overall program the president wanted to carry out.

. . . because we do not form a Government, we have no overall program at all. We cannot fairly hold the President accountable for the success or failure of his overall program, because he lacks the constitutional power to put that program into effect.[2]

Inconvenient factual errors undercut this analysis. First and foremost, it simply is not correct that stalemate is guaranteed within the separated system. A president may, indeed, find that his proposals are not ratified in form and in turn by the House and Senate. But lawmaking does proceed. Whether or not a government is formed in Cutler's terms, landmark legislation is enacted. What of the New Deal? the Great Society? the Great Tax Cut of 1981? Those are outstanding cases of a President having his way, no doubt pleasing the advocates of party government if not dedicated separationists.

SPLIT PARTISAN CONTROL

The great worry for these advocates, however, remains the penchant of American voters for returning split-party government—a president of one party with the other party having majorities in one or both houses of Congress. A system of disconnected or independent elections, deemed essential for the purity of the separation of powers, does lack a structural feature for ensuring partisan unity.

As it happened historically, the frequency of split-party results during the latter half of the nineteenth century (occurring 45 percent of the time, 1856–1900) abated substantially during the first half of the twentieth (occurring just 13 percent of the time, 1900–1946). That development, along with conditions facilitating the strong presidencies of Woodrow Wilson and Franklin D. Roosevelt, unquestionably encouraged the champions of party government. At long last, the American system was maturing. We would have government!

Imagine the discontent among these advocates when split-party government reemerged as a common pattern during the latter half of the twentieth century. However difficult it is to form a government (in Cutler's terms) when one party wins all three elected branches, it is well-nigh impossible with the two parties sharing power in the separated system. Stalemate is said to be the result.

Scholars of comparative political systems agree with the advocates of party government regarding the probability of stalemate in what they label "presidentialism." Thus, for example, Arend Lijphart cites deadlock as a disadvantage to presidential government. "The problem of executive-legislative conflict, which may turn into 'deadlock' and 'paralysis,' is the inevitable result of the co-existence of two independent organs that presidential government creates and that may be in disagreement. When disagreement between them occurs, there is no institutional method of resolving it."[3]

The stalemate or gridlock scenario is logical enough, I suppose, for those believing that it is necessary to "form a government" in the parliamentary way. After all, how is there to be lawmaking if the prime minister and cabinet are of one party and the House of Commons or the Diet or the Storting another? It does not necessarily follow as an outcome within a separated system, however. After all, what is the measure of stalemate? Surely it is not just the failure of the president to have his way. No one can believe that a system of independently derived and constitutionally mixed institutions would automatically and consistently accede one to the other.

What, then, is the test of stalemate or gridlock? The production of major legislation is a defensible indicator. If no laws are passed, there is gridlock; if laws are passed, the system is not gridlocked. David R. Mayhew of Yale University has examined exactly that issue in his book *Divided We Govern*. He first created an elaborate two-wave process for identifying major legislation, then simply took a look. He found that major legislation is enacted by both single- and split-party governments.

In fact there are no significant differences in the post–World War II period — an average of 12.8 major acts passed during single-party Congresses, an average of 11.7 major acts passed during split-party Congresses.[4] It is of particular note that three Congresses tie for the highest production of major legislation (at twenty-two each): the 89th (Johnson's first full Congress), the 91st (Nixon's first), and the 93d (Nixon's third—completed by Ford). Most analysts would have predicted that the 89th Congress would be included; few would have identified the Nixon Congresses as being in that group.

It is true, of course, that different political combinations will produce different *solutions* to the same public problems. There are differences in the policy goals and representation of interests between the two political parties. But having variable policy outcomes dependent on the configurations of political control is not stalemate—at least by the ordinary understanding of the term.

There is more that is questionable about the party-government perspective. The much-admired parliamentary systems do not all provide responsibility as advertised. I make mention of the Japanese system since it has been so prominent in the news in recent years. What exactly is the public accountability of a multiparty coalition government? Are not the compromises that are displayed publicly in a separated system often developed in less public settings in a coalitional government? How are the voters to determine responsibility in a government that includes socialists and conservatives? Who exactly is accountable for what? One report on 1995 local electoral defeats for the ruling coalition noted that

> The results raise new doubts about whether [Prime Minister] Murayama and his governing coalition, a marriage of convenience between Socialists and conservatives, can stay in office for the rest of the year. The 70-year-old prime minister has been savaged recently for inaction on major national problems, and members of his own coalition seem to be moving away from him.[5]

Lloyd Cutler yearns for a president to form a government "with a legislative majority which takes the responsibility for governing." But it seems that there is no magical formula for that happening in any system. Or that, having taken action, a government will necessarily invite being held responsible. Forming majority coalitions in the American political system is extremely demanding. The effort to do so is unceasing, since one coalition does not necessarily hold for the next issue. What is required, therefore, are "the skills of political management," not the transformation of the system.[6] I turn next to a review of the post–World War II experience to illustrate the range of skills required for governing, with special emphasis on the challenge of leadership facing the president.

SEPARATED INSTITUTIONS COMPETING
FOR SHARES OF POWER

The results of disconnected elections are difficult to read, even if they are endlessly fascinating to me and my colleagues. Voters are given various forms of expression to vent even contradictory moods and opinions. The vote in a parliamentary or strong-presidential system is quite efficient, but it carries a heavy weight. Once delivered, it triggers a process of government building, at least for the political side of government. But in a separated and federalized system, voters can roam freely across independently chosen bodies, putting a Democrat here, a Republican there—having it both ways through the layers of government, which are themselves interdependent. We do not really have elections in the parliamentary sense. We have political *fairs*, in which many contestants go home winners. And voters like it that way if we are to believe the polls, not to mention the frequency of their ticket splitting.

Attention here is directed to the national level. It is worth recalling, however, that a program proposed by a Democratic president, and altered by a cross-party coalition in Congress in which the Republicans serve as a majority, may then be administered by a Republican governor and legislature, to deal with problems in a city with a Democratic mayor and council. Political parties are organizations of convenience for facilitating policy action in the separated system. They are not free-standing entities.

Consider the ballot itself and the scheduling of elections (as associated with term lengths). The ballot provides the choices. Its exact form is determined by the states, where various arrangements have been tried over the decades either to encourage or discourage party voting. Scheduling was once the province of the states, but the many inconveniences caused by differing election times led Congress to set a uniform date, the first Tuesday after the first Monday in November. Even with that change, however, variable term-limits preserved and enhanced separationism.

A freshly elected president may be encouraged by congressional election results that produce a majority of his party in the House of Representatives and the Senate. He may even have the short-term advantage of a perception among these new members that he had something to do with their election or reelection, though such views are not common. Yet House members are no sooner elected than they must begin to think about reelection, which, if they have a challenger in the primary election, may be only eighteen to twenty months away. Moreover, at the point of their reelection, the president will not be on the ballot; in fact, there is no national election as such at the midterm, just national results.

Presidents vary in their willingness to participate in these midterm elections, since active involvement may invite the interpretation of having been defeated. Besides, the record of the president's party at midterm is not encouraging: an average loss of thirty seats during the post–World War II period, with a range of four to fifty-five seats. On just three occasions did the number fall below ten — for Kennedy in 1962, Reagan in 1986 (his second term), and Bush in 1990 (when Republicans had just 175 seats to start).

Scheduling for Senate elections is substantially more perverse from the president's perspective. Imagine that a president won overwhelmingly and that his party gained seats in the Senate, thus inviting the identification of a coattail effect (e.g., 1980). First, just one-third of the senators are up for reelection at the point of his triumph (a group that was itself elected six years earlier and may represent a skewed party split).[7] Second, those elected may indeed be grateful if they believe the president had a positive influence on their win. But their reelection bid comes in six years, at the midterm of the president's second administration (if there is to be a second administration). On what basis does the president have an electoral hold on those few senators who might have thought he was an asset for their election? They will never again see him on their ballot.

The next one-third will be elected at the midterm of the president's first administration and will be up for reelection at the point at which the president's stay in office will have ended (with the two-term limitation). The final one-third will be elected on the president's reelection and may also profit in the best of all possible political worlds from the president's coattails. But their term carries forward to the midterm of the next president. And the last senatorial election in a two-term presidency produces a class that is up for reelection with the new president six years hence (see Figure 1).

There is more. As noted, voters have ample opportunities to split their vote, and they do. The result has been frequent split-party governments in the post–World War II era, as voters have become comfortable electing Republican presidents and Democratic Houses, Senates, or both. Of all electoral college votes cast in presidential elections from 1948 to 1992, 63 percent were awarded to Republican presidential candidates (who won seven of twelve elections, six by electoral college landslides). Yet Democrats held majorities in the House of Representatives for a record forty years, 1954–1994, and in the Senate for a period of twenty-six years, 1954–1980. Prior to 1994, Republicans held House majorities just three times and Senate majorities six times in the postwar period.

Three newly elected Republican presidents (Nixon, Reagan, and Bush) and three reelected Republican presidents (Eisenhower, Nixon, and Reagan) faced Democratic majorities in one or both houses. One Republican (Eisenhower) and one Democrat (Clinton) watched their parties' majorities disappear at midterm.

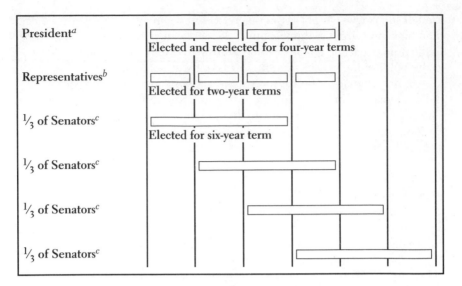

FIGURE 1

ELECTORAL TIME LINE: PRESIDENT (TWO-TERM), REPRESENTATIVES, AND SENATORS

a. Since 1951 and the ratification of the Twenty-Second Amendment, presidents are limited to two terms. In this century, only six presidents have been elected to second terms (FDR to four); only four completed their two terms (FDR completed three).

b. The president's party typically loses seats in the midterm election (with just one exception in this century—1934). Major losses were experienced in 1910 (57), 1914 (59), 1922 (75), 1938 (71), 1946 (55), 1958 (47), 1966 (47), 1974 (43), 1994 (52).

c. Note that no group of senators elected during these eight years again runs with the president on the ballot!

And one takeover president for each party (Truman and Ford) faced opposition majorities in Congress.

The point is clear enough. Elections do not automatically produce unity, even when one party wins both branches, and certainly not when the parties share control of three elected branches—the presidency, the House of Representatives, and the Senate. Building supportive coalitions is continuous, involving as it does a constant effort to convince representatives and senators that what the president wants is in their own best interests, or vice versa. All of that is demanding work on the part of political and legislative strategists, since very few members of either chamber will view their political and electoral fates as closely connected with that of the president.

It seems apparent, therefore, that a strictly partisan strategy for building coalitions is often inapt. Instead, presidents and congressional party leaders must devise cross-party strategies for two quite different legislative bodies—the House and Senate. Reforms that seek to strengthen party discipline and unity falter in the face of an electoral and representational system that fosters copartisan, cross-partisan, and bipartisan lawmaking. I understand that it is difficult for the "form a government!" advocates to accept, but the American political system relegates political party to a facilitating, not an assertive or controlling, role.

MANY PRESIDENCIES

There is an understandable practice of marking historical periods by presidents, for example, the Roosevelt, Eisenhower, or Reagan era. And though we may label presidents as strong or weak, we seldom do more than identify the whole period of service as their presidency. I do acknowledge that dividing history by the presidents who serve is a convenience. But it also follows in the separated system that any one period of presidential service may be characterized by change. There may, in fact, be *more than one presidency per president,* if defined in terms of the political and policy advantages available to the incumbent in working with Congress.

I have classified each president in the past hundred years by his political advantages upon entering office, at midterm, and, for six presidents, on reelection (see Table 1). After that, I first examined four-year terms of service, noting the stability and change of advantages following the presidential and midterm elections (see Table 2). The range is from huge advantages (a landslide presidential election combined with substantial congressional majorities) to weak minority status (a president facing formidable opposition-party majorities in Congress). The results of this analysis show the following:

1. Relatively few presidents sustain substantial advantages over a four-year period. In fact, there are only three clear cases: Franklin Roosevelt's first and second terms, and the one full term of Theodore Roosevelt.
2. Four presidents had relatively stable advantages over four years—two with moderate political status, two with weak status (their party being in a minority in Congress).
3. Two administrations maintained moderate advantages through four years, but the presidents changed (McKinley to Roosevelt; Kennedy to Johnson).
4. Most common are modest or substantial changes in advantages as a result of midterm elections. Sixteen of the presidencies fall into this classification, with eight demonstrating modest but notable shifts and eight demonstrating substantial shifts from one Congress to the next.

What of the reelected presidents? Do any maintain stable advantages through two terms (eight years)? There are but six reelected presidents in this century, four of whom completed two terms (Roosevelt completed three). McKinley and Franklin Roosevelt had the most stable presidencies for two full terms—McKinley with moderate advantages throughout (though succeeded by Theodore Roosevelt in 1901), Franklin Roosevelt with huge advantages in his first two terms. Franklin Roosevelt's second two terms were less impressive, eventually resulting in an opposition-party Congress after Harry Truman became president. The three reelected Republicans in the post–World War II years, Eisenhower, Nixon (succeeded by Ford), and Reagan, demonstrate somewhat similar patterns— mostly a stable set of limited advantages until the second midterm election, when the Democrats strengthened their hold on Congress. Finally, Woodrow Wilson's presidencies display a steady decline in advantages from large to moderate to small to minority status (see Table 3).

TABLE 1. PRESIDENTS' POLITICAL ADVANTAGES, 1896–1996, AT PRESIDENTIAL
AND MIDTERM ELECTIONS

President	EV	PV	House 1	House 2	Senate 1	Senate 2	PRESIDENT'S OVERALL POLITICAL ADVANTAGES[a]	
							1st Cong.	2d Cong.
McK1	Mod.	Small	Mod.	Small	Small	Mod.	Mod.	Mod.
McK2→TR	Mod.	Small	Mod.	Small	Large	Large	Mod.+	Mod.
TR	Large	Large	Large	Mod.	Huge	Huge	Large+	Large
WHT	Mod.	Small	Mod.	Min.	Large	Small	Mod.	Small–
WW1	Huge	Min.[b]	Huge	Small	Small	Mod.	Large	Mod.
WW2	Small	Min.	Min.[c]	Min.	Mod.	Min.	Small	Min.
WGH→CC	Large	Huge	Huge	Small	Small	Mod.	Large	Mod.
CC	Large	Mod.	Mod.	Small	Mod.	Small	Mod.	Small
HH	Huge	Large	Large	Min.[d]	Mod.	Small	Large	Small
FDR1	Huge	Large	Huge	Huge	Large	Huge	Huge	Huge
FDR2	Huge	Huge	Huge	Large	Huge	Huge	Huge	Huge
FDR3	Huge	Mod.	Large	Small	Huge	Mod.	Large	Mod.
FDR4→HST	Huge	Mod.	Mod.	Min.	Mod.	Min.	Mod.	Min.
HST	Small	Small[e]	Large	Small	Mod.	Small	Mod.	Small
DDE1	Huge	Mod.	Small	Min.	Small	Min.	Mod.–	Min.+
DDE2	Huge	Large	Min.	Min.–	Min.	Min.–	Min.+	Min.–
JFK→LBJ	Small	Min.	Large	Mod.	Large	Large	Mod.	Mod.
LBJ	Huge	Huge	Huge	Mod.	Huge	Large	Huge	Large
RMN1	Small	Min.[f]	Min.	Min.	Min.	Min.	Min.	Min.
RMN2→GRF	Huge	Huge	Min.	Min.–	Min.	Min.–	Min.+	Min.–
JEC	Small	Small	Huge	Large	Large	Mod.	Mod.	Mod.
RWR1	Huge	Small[g]	Min.	Min.–	Small	Small	Mod.	Mod.–
RWR2	Huge	Huge	Min.	Min.	Small	Min.	Mod.	Min.
GHWB	Large	Mod.	Min.	Min.–	Min.	Min.	Min.	Min.
WJC	Mod.	Min.[h]	Mod.	Min.	Mod.	Min.	Mod.	Min.

KEY TO COLUMN HEADS AND SCALE RANGES

EV = Electoral college vote: 50–59 percent = Small; 60–69 percent = Moderate (Mod.); 70–79 percent = Large, 80 percent and above = Huge.

PV = Popular vote: Less than 50 percent = Minority (Min.); 50–52 percent = Small; 53–55 percent = Moderate (Mod.); 56–58 percent = Large; 59 percent and above = Huge.

House 1 = 1st Congress of an administration; House 2 = 2d Congress of an administration.

Senate 1 = 1st Congress of an administration; Senate 2 = 2d Congress of an administration.

House and Senate ranges are defined by percentages of seats held by president's party: Less than 50 percent = Minority (Min.); 50–54 percent = Small; 55–59 percent = Moderate (Mod.); 60–64 percent = Large; 65 percent and above = Huge. A plus or minus symbol indicates the top or bottom region of the range it follows.

a. Takes into account both electoral advantages and the margin of seats held by the president's party in Congress.

b. There was a third candidate, Theodore Roosevelt.

c. The Democrats failed to elect a majority in 1916, but Progressives voted with the Democrats to organize the House.

d. The Republicans elected a majority in 1930, but several died before the opening of Congress, enabling the Democrats to organize.

e. There was a third-party candidate, Strom Thurmond.

f. There was a third-party candidate, George Wallace.

g. There was an independent candidate, John Anderson.

h. There was an independent candidate, H. Ross Perot.

TABLE 2. STABILITY AND CHANGE IN THE POLITICAL
ADVANTAGE OF PRESIDENCIES, 1896–1996

Advantages	*Presidents in Category*	*Number of Presidencies[a]*
Stable—Substantial advantages		
Huge→Huge	FDR1, FDR2	1
Large plus→Large	TR	1
Stable—Moderate advantages		
Moderate→Moderate	McK1, JEC	2
Stable—Few advantages		
Minority→Minority	RMN1, GHWB	2
Stable advantage, change in presidents		
Moderate plus→Moderate	McK2→TR	2
Moderate→Moderate	JFK→LBJ	2
Changing—Modest shift (variable advantages)		
Huge→Large	LBJ	2
Large→Moderate	WW1, WGH→CC, FDR3	7
Moderate→Moderate minus	RWR1	2
Moderate→Small	CC, HST	4
Small→Minority	WW2	2
Changing—Substantial shift (variable advantages)		
Large→Small minus	HH	2
Moderate→Small minus	WHT	2
Moderate→Minority	FDR4→HST, RHR2, WJC	7
Moderate minus→Minority	DDE1	2
Minority plus→Minority minus	DDE2, RMN2→GRF	5
Total		45

a. A presidency for these purposes is defined as one in which there has been a change in advantage or in president.
Source: Compiled by the author, based on data in Table 1.

In summary, a system of separated elections produces an ever-shifting coalitional base. The numbers change for presidents and Congresses every two years. If we count presidencies as suggested earlier—that is, those cases where there are marked differences in advantages and/or a change in presidents—then I count forty-five presidencies for the eighteen presidents who have served during these hundred years, 1896–1996. One can understand such circumstances why the "form a government" advocates are distressed. Short of major constitutional restructuring, however, individual presidents, congressional party leaders, committee chairs, and other decision makers need to accommodate the realities of the separated system if we are to make law.

STABILITY IN CONGRESS

Frequent elections and variable terms do not necessarily equate with instability in Congress. Instead, these characteristics pose a challenge for the president

TABLE 3. STABILITY AND CHANGE IN POLITICAL ADVANTAGE FOR REELECTED PRESIDENTS, 1896–1996 (RANKED FROM MOST STABLE TO LEAST)

President	Stability and Change
McKinley[a]	Moderate→Moderate→Moderate plus→Moderate
F.D. Roosevelt[b]	Huge→Huge→Huge→Huge→Large→Moderate→Moderate→Minority
Eisenhower	Moderate minus→Minority plus→Minority plus→Minority minus
Reagan	Moderate→Moderate minus→Moderate→Minority
Nixon[c]	Minority→Minority→Minority plus→Minority minus
Wilson	Large→Moderate→Small→Minority

a. Succeeded by Theodore Roosevelt in 1901.
b. Succeeded by Harry Truman in 1945.
c. Succeeded by Gerald Ford in 1974.
Source: Compiled by author, based on data in Table 1.

for the reasons stated earlier, that is, member allegiance to separate constituencies. The president might conceivably gain an edge, however, if there were high turnover, amateurism, and short memories. No such luck. The House and Senate have come to be increasingly professional, career oriented, and institutionalized. They are repositories of policy knowledge and experience. They have developed a well-articulated committee structure that serves as home base to private and governmental clienteles. And they have created an elaborate staff apparatus that more than matches that immediately available to the White House, albeit not as hierarchically organized.

Consider these facts. Incumbent return remains high in the House of Representatives, typically over 90 percent. By design, Senate incumbent return is 67 percent, to which is added whatever number is reelected (typically somewhat lower than for the House). The average length of service of members during the post–World War II period has typically been about ten years each for the House and Senate. The average for presidents in that same time is half that number.

The president might realize a leadership advantage if congressional leaders changed with each change in presidents. Again, no such luck. The House and Senate act independently in choosing leaders; any change with presidents is purely coincidental. In recent decades, only the Carter administration could take advantage of new party leadership in both the House and Senate coincident with the president's taking office. Alas, as a professed and dedicated outsider, President Carter was not even in a position to view the change as an asset.

Typically, party and committee leaders serve in accordance with the internal politics and traditions of each body. The average service of the two principal House party leaders for 1945–1985 was 9.1 years;[8] of the Senate leaders, 6.3 years. Major committee chairs also have had lengthy service, in some cases carrying through several presidents: Carl Hayden, fourteen years as chair of the Senate Appropriations Committee; Russell Long, sixteen years as chair of the Senate Finance Committee; George Mahon, fifteen years as chair of House Appropriations; Wilbur Mills, seventeen years as chair of House Ways and Means.[9]

Professional staff has expanded significantly in the past two decades. Each member has been given additional staff, many of whom are then dispatched to the state or district to aid in perfecting a representational style that will be approved at election time. Committee staffs have become not-so-small bureaucracies, some of which operate outside the orbit of daily congressional politics. New support agencies have been created—the Congressional Budget Office and the Office of Technology Assessment; others, like the Congressional Research Service, have been greatly expanded.[10]

The House and Senate are separate lawmaking enterprises fully prepared by reason of institutional and membership continuity and of professional capability to participate widely in national policymaking. An unusually vigorous term-limitation movement has recently emerged to challenge the whole concept of a career-oriented legislature. The group has had a significant impact: Several members have limited themselves, and freshman classes have demanded more participation, unwilling to accede to the seniority principle that advises them to wait their turn. Term-limit proposals actually reached the House floor for debate during the 1995 hundred-day legislative blitz, though none received the necessary two-thirds majority. Yet, perhaps most important, the term of service of committee chairs was limited to six years by a change in the rules of the House of Representatives.

Are these changes, including term limits, likely to encourage the formation of a "government"? There is no reason to believe that they will. These are not changes designed to alter the separation of institutions or reduce the competition for shared powers. The term-limited Republican freshmen of the 104th Congress appear to be as devoted to controlling affairs in competition with the president as were the Democratic chairmen of the 100th Congress (Reagan's last)—perhaps more so.

POLICY ERAS

All too often, political scientists discuss institutions devoid of their vital role in the lawmaking and policymaking processes.[11] Yet the separated system exists to act authoritatively on public problems. And so presidents, representatives, and senators, along with their respective staffs, spend much of the working day on substantive issues—many of which are a consequence of laws they passed earlier. Further, these issues are central to how the institutions are organized and how the work gets scheduled. Substantive policy issues permeate a capital, in the physical presence of buildings with names like Department of Agriculture and legislative rooms designated as Committee on Armed Services, as well as in the talk that mostly centers on what to do about what has been done in the past.

Presidents and Congresses work within an agenda orientation that is naturally associated with broad policy developments. Until 1981, we observed a familiar cycle of expansion and consolidation. Government expanded to meet new needs, followed by periods of consolidation wherein the principal effort was to make government more effective in administering new programs (often through reorganization and regulation). The periods of expansion were during the Wilson, Franklin Roosevelt, and Johnson presidencies, each of which was succeeded by consolidation.

In 1980, a president—Ronald Reagan—was elected who judged that government was the problem, not the solution. He questioned whether it was appropriate to make government work better, if to work at all was inimical to the public interest. So for the first time, there was a serious effort to install a contractive agenda. Two approaches were tried. The first was programmatic: seeking to cut back, eliminate, or devolve various federal programs. The second was fiscal: seeking to reduce taxes, thereby starving the revenue side so as to prevent enactment of new programs and to force serious evaluation of existing programs.

The first, program cutbacks, was only marginally successful, given strong opposition from clienteles. The result was great pressure for another kind of solution, that is, increasing taxes again so as to avoid escalating debt and to provide more latitude in policymaking. Taxes were raised several times during the Reagan presidency, but it fell to George Bush publicly to rescind his "no new taxes" pledge. And still the deficits rose, greatly complicating incremental adjustments in existing programs.

During the Reagan and Bush presidencies, it became apparent that serious contraction of government programs simply was not possible.[12] Cutting back lacked political support, and therefore the agenda was dominated by fiscal issues—mostly finding new revenues so as to reduce the deficit. And then along came Newt Gingrich and the "Contract with America." The Democrats were correct in associating the contract with Reaganism. It is the unfinished business of the contractive agenda, that is, serious reduction of government spending as a means for reducing the deficit.

As a result, the version of the separated system following the 1994 elections had these features: a policy-ambitious Democratic president with weak status, a highly energized Republican House of Representatives, a competitive Republican Senate with several presidential candidates, all tackling an intricate contractive agenda. My final thoughts are about these intriguing and historic circumstances, starting with President Clinton's first two years.

PRESIDENT CLINTON AND THE SEPARATED SYSTEM

Bill Clinton fits with the weakest of the presidents in this century in terms of his political capital on entering office. He won with a minority of the popular vote, 43 percent, and a moderate electoral vote count. There are no coattails, perceived or real, for 43 percent presidents. In fact, Democrats suffered a net loss of House seats in 1992 and failed to gain the hoped-for sixty-seat majority in the Senate, so as to be able to break filibusters.

Why Clinton won at all is relevant to his policy status once in office. Clinton emphasized change in the people who would serve, in the style of leadership, and in the policies enacted. But it is far from certain that his election carried with it an open-ended mandate for dramatic change. The "form a government" analysts were predictably pleased with the results, since the Democrats won all three elected branches. Here is how one such advocate viewed the results:

If the government cannot succeed in the present configuration, when can it possibly ever succeed? . . . the stars are really aligned right for the next four years.

The country has finally gotten back to unified government. For the first time in twelve years, somebody is going to be responsible. . . . Now the day of buck passing and blame shifting is over.[13]

Another interpretation, one derived from a separationist perspective, might have gone something like this. Many Reagan voters in 1984 and Bush voters in 1988 were displeased with President Bush's performance. The change they desired was for him to leave the White House. Had they had a chance to vote for Ronald Reagan again, they probably would have done so. Even then, a substantial number of this group voted for Ross Perot, not Bill Clinton.[14] There was no mandate for new social programs, including a national health-care plan.

Bill Clinton was instead authorized by reason of his election to use the presidency to persuade Congress and the public of the correctness of his policy views. But there was no escaping the Reagan legacy of debt or the unfinished contractive agenda, for which there was continuing public support. And the charge to the president in a separated system is to fit himself into the permanent government so as to be a credible participant, perhaps a leader. As noted earlier, very few presidents enter with huge advantages, and few maintain those advantages through their term. By this reading, President Clinton needed to compensate for his weaknesses to take full advantage of his constitutional status in the separated system.

What are those weaknesses? Presumably, they are not in campaigning, where he excelled.[15] Instead, he had limitations related to the fact that he was a governor from a small state located at a distance from Washington. He had never held a position in the federal government. While governor, he had worked with a Democratic legislature, seldom ever having to take Republicans into account. Like most governors, he lacked experience with foreign and national security matters. He was an admitted "policy wonk," who found it difficult to concentrate on a few issues. Wishing to please, he frequently engaged in hyperbole, promising more than could conceivably be delivered. Also, the governorship of Arkansas is not a huge management job. Thus Bill Clinton lacked direct experience in forming (and accommodating) to an elaborately articulated staff. "He wouldn't know good staff work if he saw it," was how one member of the Clinton administration expressed it.[16]

What did the new president then do by way of compensating? He relied on his presumed strength—campaigning—instead of overcoming his weaknesses. He did not form an effective staff. He did not work with Republicans, who would be needed for support of his proposals, particularly in the Senate. He postponed foreign and national security issues so as to emphasize domestic concerns (with the exception of early announcements on Haiti, later altered, and the promise of an executive order ending the ban on gays in the military, not fulfilled). He issued a laundry list of proposals, promising early action on very complicated pieces of legislation, most notably health-care and welfare reform.

How effective has his campaigning style been? First, some facts. In his first twenty months in office, he traveled to 150 places, making 203 official appearances, exclusive of travel to Camp David, to Arkansas, to foreign countries, and to vacation sites.[17] He is our most traveled president, exceeding even George Bush, who loved to fly in Air Force One. And Clinton's travel was associated primarily with the selling of public policy proposals. Approximately one-quarter of the travel of Bush and Reagan was for party and candidate fund-raising events. As Clinton's political adviser, Mandy Grunwald, reportedly explained it: "It's a bank shot, what you say to the American people bounces back to the Congress."[18]

Unfortunately, there is limited evidence that this "going public" strategy worked very well in the first two years. One measure might be the public approval ratings. Did they rise with the president's domestic travel? They did not. His quarterly approval ratings in the Gallup poll exceeded 50 percent just twice in the first twenty months in office. And the rating was lowest in the seventh and last quarter for that period. Another measure would be a favorable response among the public to his policy priorities, most notably health-care reform. Again the evidence shows the reverse to be the case; support for his plan declined steadily following his presentation in a special message to Congress in the fall of 1993.

A more substantive measure of presidential success is the passage of major legislation. Three kinds of legislation were enacted in his first year: (1) those bills already in the legislative pipeline, having been vetoed by President Bush (e.g., family leave, motor voter, a waiting period for handgun purchase); (2) the "big ticket" items—the economic plan and NAFTA; and (3) special Clinton initiatives such as lifting the ban on homosexuals in the military, the National Service Act (or "Americorps"), and the "reinventing government" proposals. These accomplishments are significant by Mayhew's count of major legislation[19]—nearly equal to Carter's first year, less than Kennedy's, less than half of what passed in Johnson's first year as an elected president, but markedly more than most Republican presidents with the exception of Nixon.

Can they be said to have been enacted because of the "bank shot"? That would be a difficult argument. The first group passed quickly because they were essentially congressional Democratic initiatives. The second group did not go so well: the economic stimulus plan was defeated in the Senate, the budget reconciliation package passed by a tie-breaking vote from the vice-president in the Senate and by a two-vote margin in the House, and NAFTA was a Bush administration carryover enacted with Republican support. The third set was more purely the president's, but, in fact, was not frequently discussed in his many travels (National Service being mentioned most often).[20] Whatever the explanation, President Clinton could be justifiably pleased with the legislative product in his first year, particularly given his weak political status. And he was rewarded by judgments that he "and the 103d Congress broke through the legislative gridlock that has gripped Washington in recent decades. . . ."[21]

There would be no such plaudits at the end of the second year. The campaign approach to governing continued, with the president taking to the road to sell his program. But there were few positive parallel developments that could contribute to producing a strong legislative record. Major proposals came to produce the congressional equivalent of a logjam at the end of the session, thus granting the Republicans the advantage allowed by the filibuster, at no political cost to them. Among the casualties was Clinton's health-care proposal, his principal priority. But the list was long of those measures postponed or killed.

The count of major legislation enacted at the end of the session was small; by Mayhew's count, the fewest major bills passed for any elected president in his second year during the postwar period.[22] And the judgments by analysts were harsh: "This will go into the record books as perhaps the worst Congress—least effective, most destructive, nastiest—in 50 years."[23]

PRESIDENT CLINTON AND THE NEW CONGRESS

The 1994 congressional midterm elections were historic in many respects. No elected first-term Democratic president in this century had experienced loss of both houses of Congress. The win for the House Republicans produced their first majority in forty years, a record length of time in the minority. And having a serious party platform such as the "Contract with America" is unprecedented for midterm elections.

Thus, one can sympathize with the president's political and policy predicament. There were no obvious analogies. The opposition Republicans were extraordinarily energized to assume leadership. Media analysts interpreted the results as constituting a mandate for the House Republicans and a major defeat for the president. And White House political strategists seemingly had failed to prepare a worst-case scenario, leaving a garrulous president virtually speechless.

The consequence was the most unusual, even peculiar, first three months of a congressional session in history. It is unusual for the House of Representatives to set the agenda. It is unusual for either house to produce legislation during the first three months. It is unusual to maintain strong party discipline in Congress. It is unusual for party leaders to manage the House of Representatives in competition with committee chairs. It is unusual for junior members to be a driving force on legislation. Yet all of these things happened. Here are some of the measures of the activity in the House of Representatives during the hundred days:[24]

Hours in sessions:	531
Measures passed:	124
Recorded votes:	302

By comparison, the busier-than-usual first three months of the 103d Congress had been markedly less active by these measures. The 80th Congress, which is sometimes used for comparison, was somnolent (two roll-call votes in the House, seven in the Senate; no completed legislation). Republican Party unity in the House was likewise phenomenal in these first hundred days. *Congressional Quarterly* identified thirty-three votes incorporating the "Contract with America." House Republicans averaged 98 percent unity on these votes.[25] Republicans had perfect unity on sixteen of the thirty-three votes and attracted a majority of Democrats on sixteen of the thirty-three.

Here then was a most interesting case of a presidential-congressional partnership in the first year, disintegrating due to minority party obstruction in the second year, and then being transformed into congressional domination as a result of surprising election results and the rarity of a midterm party platform, inviting a concocted identification of a mandate for the new Speaker of the House. During the election, one of the president's closest political advisers, Paul Begala, reportedly had revealed that "there is not a night I don't thank God for the contract [with America]."[26] No doubt by April the Contract had come to be a nightly event somewhat more disturbing of sleep for Begala and his client.

I begin my book on the presidency with these sentences: "The president is not the presidency. The presidency is not the government."[27] It is equally true that the Speaker is not the House of Representatives, and the House of Representatives is not the government. Gingrich's hundred days differ significantly from Roosevelt's, in that the Democrats won the presidency, House, and Senate in 1932, at the point of the greatest domestic crisis in the twentieth century. Franklin Roosevelt had authority virtually to act as he thought best. By contrast, and substantially as a result of his own political ingenuity, Newt Gingrich had an opening to move his program through one chamber of a bicameral Congress.

Senate Republicans had not committed themselves to the Contract and, in any event, are part of an institution designed to be more deliberative. They were led by Bob Dole (R–Kans.), a person with ten years' experience as a floor leader (two in the majority) and a leading candidate for the Republican presidential nomination in 1996. He could be expected to act cautiously for institutional and political reasons. Therefore, the Senate would not be expected to act quickly, though it was fully engaged too on the early work necessary to cope with a broad range of Republican initiatives.

What, then, of the president's position under conditions of congressional preponderance? A president with limited domestic policy goals, such as George Bush, or one whose goals have been achieved, such as Ronald Reagan, may adapt rather well to those circumstances. Content to concentrate on foreign and national security issues, such presidents employ the veto to curb congressional excesses and participate in domestic initiatives where political gain is to be realized.

In the case of Bill Clinton, however, this formula was more problematic. First, he is a restless, policy-ambitious chief executive, not one comfortable in responding to the initiatives of others. He is also personally ambitious: he wants to be a great president. But relying on the veto is reactive not active. Further, the Republicans appropriated many of his issues—tax cuts, welfare reform, line-item veto, governmental reform, relief for the states, even health-care reform—in essence forcing him to redefine his goals within the context of their legislation. Then, as it happens, his anxiety during the first two years to avoid gridlock resulted in his not having vetoed any bills—a modern record. Therefore he had to create a credible veto threat as a means of regaining influence in lawmaking.

President Clinton's virtual exclusion from action on Capitol Hill through much of 1995 provided time for him and his staff to devise a strategy for regaining political status. As revealed in a series of speeches during the first months of 1995, the strategy contained the following tenets:

1. Associate the president with the change seemingly demanded by the voters. Argue that the 1994 results represent a continuation of the mandate for change designated as a consequence of the 1992 election.
2. Remind the public that the president was there first with many of the issues of the "Contract with America"—tax cuts, welfare reform, relief for the states, reducing the deficit—and thus he can be cooperative where possible.
3. Reveal that the president's proposals are more humane, that they represent improving government, not destroying it. Thus he will identify the limits of devolution to the states, measuring proposals by their adverse effects on various clienteles.
4. Search for high profile issues subject to executive order, where congressional action is not required.
5. Threaten the veto primarily as a means for identifying the president's position. Avoid being too specific prior to more explicit Senate action for strategic reasons.
6. State a "no politics as usual" position—getting it right is more important than being reelected.
7. Take full advantage of the uniquely presidential status in foreign and national security issues, as well as national disasters or crises.

Later dubbed "triangulation," the strategy was designed to position the president as the moderate, one who accepted many of the goals of the "Contract with America" (which had, after all, been market tested), but served to protect the beneficiaries of programs whose growth was to be slowed.

The strategy was skillfully executed. Particularly striking was the exercise of the veto. President Clinton rejected major appropriations bills, the debt limit extension, and a massive budget reconciliation package. One risky consequence was the shutting down of the government. As it happened, congressional Republicans were judged by most Americans to be responsible for this unpopular action. Their leaders were no match for Clinton's campaigning style with the public. The president was still not a major player in formulating policy—the agenda continued to be set on Capitol Hill—but he had reestablished himself as a force to be reckoned with.

One final point in regard to the president's status. There have been but three presidents reelected in the postwar period—all Republicans (Eisenhower, Nixon, and Reagan), all three reelected by landslides, all three returned with Democratic congressional majorities in one house or two. Successful cross-party coalition building can be rewarded at the polls. The trick for President Clinton was to receive credit or even to share credit with congressional Republicans for positive legislative achievements, while avoiding the blame for unpopular reductions in the growth of spending. By the time Congress recessed in August 1996, President Clinton had accomplished precisely those goals.

THE SEPARATED SYSTEM

A separated system necessarily operates through a series of approximations. One of the casualties is the swift formulation and implementation of the best solution. Instead, the competition among institutions takes time. It fosters a melding toward the middling rather than the adoption of one or another version of perfection. And so critics who believe they know the answers—who are "right," in Schattschneider's terms—are understandably frustrated by a system in which they have access but over which they lack control.

At present, the agenda includes a series of basic questions on what government should do, on which government should do it, and on the capacity of the private sphere to solve public problems. This debate should not and will not be settled by one party or one institution—and surely not in a hundred days. Governing is real-life speculation. Some systems work with "clean" theories—the most pristine of which have been shown to be very wrong. The separated system is "unclean." It promotes access, propagates legitimacy, and disperses accountability, yet compels agreement. It cannot be made to work simply.

NOTES

1. E. E. Schattschneider, *Two Hundred Million Americans in Search of a Government* (New York: Holt, Rinehart, and Winston, 1969), 53.

2. Lloyd N. Cutler, "To Form a Government," *Foreign Affairs* 59 (Fall 1980): 127–128.

3. Arend Lijphart, "Introduction," in *Parliamentary versus Presidential Government*, ed. Arend Lijphart (New York: Oxford University Press, 1992), 15.

4. David R. Mayhew, *Divided We Govern, Party Control, Lawmaking, and Investigations, 1946–1990* (New Haven: Yale University Press, 1991), 76. Keith Krehbiel approaches this issue differently but with a similar conclusion, that "gridlock occurs in divided and unified government alike." "Institutional and Partisan Sources of Gridlock: A Theory of Divided and Unified Government," forthcoming in the *Journal of Theoretical Politics*, 1996. George C. Edwards III, Andrew Barrett, and Jeffrey Peake show that divided government has an impact on legislation that fails if the administration is in opposition. "The Legislative Impact of Divided Government: What *Failed* to Pass in Congress?" paper presented at the annual meeting of the American Political Science Association, Chicago, 1995.

5. T. R. Reid, "Japanese Coalition Parties Dealt Setback," *Washington Post*, April 10, 1995, A15.

6. Thomas E. Mann and Norman J. Ornstein make this point in a comment on Cutler's article, noting that "the recent deadlocks or failures of policy initiatives [that so concerned Cutler] have been as much failures of political will and skill as anything else." *Foreign Affairs* 59 (Winter 1980/1981): 418.

7. For example, in 1994 the Democrats held 56 percent of the Senate seats, yet had 63 percent of the one-third up for reelection (22 of 35 seats). Having the same ratio of seats held to those up for reelection is pure coincidence.

8. The count is based on who led the party either as Speaker or minority leader. Thus Sam Rayburn and Joseph Martin traded places twice in the immediate postwar period but served as principal leaders of their respective parties throughout.

9. It is also the case that most committee chairs previously served as major subcommittee chairs. As an extreme case, Jamie Whitten (D–Miss.) first served as an appropriations subcommittee chair in 1949, then the committee chair in 1979, finally stepping down in 1991.

10. The Republicans reduced staff and eliminated the Office of Technology Assessment when they won majority status in the 104th Congress.

11. An argument made in Charles O. Jones, "A Way of Life and Law," *American Political Science Review* 89 (March 1995): 1–9.

12. For details, see David Stockman, *The Triumph of Politics: Why the Reagan Revolution Failed* (New York: Harper & Row, 1986).

13. James L. Sundquist, ed., *Beyond Gridlock? Prospects for the Clinton Years and After* (Washington, D.C.: Brookings Institution, 1993), 25.

14. Estimates vary on how many Reagan-Bush voters chose Perot. One exit poll had 56 percent of Perot voters having voted for Bush in 1988 (17 percent for Dukakis). *American Enterprise,* January/February 1993, 94. A Democratic Leadership Council study found that "roughly 70 percent of those over age 30 . . . supported either Ronald Reagan or Bush during the 1980s" (as reported in the *Washington Post* July 8, 1993, A1). The National Election Study found that 24.3 percent of 1988 Bush voters chose Clinton in 1992, while 21.8 percent chose Perot. Herb Asher, "The Perot Campaign," in *Democrat's Feast: Elections in America,* ed. Herbert F. Weisberg (Chatham, N.J.: Chatham House, 1995), 171.

15. The evidence of success is actually rather limited. He did not receive a majority of the vote in any state, and it was Ross Perot's vote that surged at the end of the campaign, not Bill Clinton's. Further, in the 1994 election, Clinton campaigned vigorously during the final days, primarily along a northern tier of states. He visited nineteen places, making twenty-nine appearances. Republicans won all eight governor's races in these states (a net gain of three), as well as realizing a net gain of three Senate and sixteen House seats.

16. Private conversation.

17. Travel during this time is reported in detail in Charles O. Jones, "Campaigning to Govern: The Clinton Style," in *The Clinton Presidency: First Appraisals,* ed. Colin Campbell and Bert A. Rockman (Chatham, N.J.: Chatham House, 1996), 30–32.

18. As reported in Bob Woodward, *The Agenda: Inside the Clinton White House* (New York: Simon and Schuster, 1994), 141. Woodward offers evidence that the political consultants often won out over Howard Paster, the congressional liaison chief.

19. Mayhew's count for Clinton in the first year is seven: the deficit package, NAFTA, family leave, motor voter, national service, college loans, and the Brady bill. David R. Mayhew, "Clinton, the 103d Congress, and Unified Party Control: What Are the Lessons?" paper presented at a conference honoring Stanley Kelley Jr., Princeton University, October 27–28, 1995, table 3.

20. See Jones, "Campaigning to Govern," table 1.5, 32.

21. Helen Dewar et al., "Dust Clears on a Fruitful Legislative Year," *Washington Post,* November 28, 1993, A1.

22. Mayhew counts just four pieces of legislation. "Clinton, the 103d Congress," table 3.

23. "Perhaps the Worst Congress," *Washington Post,* October 7, 1994, A24. Others noted the return of gridlock. "Gridlock's Political Price," *New York Times,* October 9, 1994, 14.

24. Cited in Norman Ornstein, "The GOP Revolution," *Roll Call,* September 11, 1995, B38.

25. Calculated from votes listed in *Congressional Quarterly Weekly Report,* April 8, 1995, 1006.

26. *New York Times,* September 28, 1994, A20.

27. Charles O. Jones, *The Presidency in a Separated System* (Washington, D.C.: Brookings Institution, 1994), 1.

32

DORIS KEARNS

LYNDON JOHNSON
AND THE AMERICAN DREAM

The American presidency differs from other political institutions, such as the bureau-
cracy or political parties, in that it has a uniquely personal dimension. The individual
who is president and the office of the presidency become intertwined. Doris Kearns
(Goodwin), a Harvard professor, explores the interaction between Lyndon Johnson's
personal qualities and the institutional aspects of the presidency. Her analysis relies
on the richness of an in-depth case study of a fascinating president to develop a more
complete understanding of the presidency. This selection is from the "General Con-
clusions" to her brilliant political biography of Johnson, Lyndon Johnson and the
American Dream *(1976).*

GENERAL CONCLUSIONS

Lyndon Johnson's public career, with the exception of a single election defeat, was one of uninterrupted and unparalleled success in the accumulation of power and—although with less consistency—in the use of power to achieve practical results. This implies that varied repositories of public authority share common elements of structure, which are, moreover, relatively resistant to rapid historical change. Our examination of Johnson's leadership proved to be a study not only of particular institutions but of attributes and vulnerabilities which are common to several institutions, and which, therefore, probably derive from the more comprehensive institutional processes of politics and government.

I offer these general observations more by way of suggestion than conclusion, but useful, perhaps, in framing questions that might enable us to understand better the relationship between leaders and the qualities of leadership, events and historical circumstances, and institutional structure. I offer these as only a few possibilities. The reader hopefully will see many more.

First: Different institutions reward different qualities—although what constitutes "reward" depends not only on the institution but upon the nature of the individual leader's ambitions. Neither John Kennedy nor Richard Nixon wanted to become a great Senate leader; to them the Senate was a useful platform, though not the only one possible, to advance their careers. Of equal importance, the abilities and characteristic modes of conduct of both men kept them from attempting to become powerful Senate leaders, and would have kept them from accomplishing such an objective.

Johnson, on the other hand, in psychic nature, modes of conduct, and natural abilities, possessed all the qualifications required by the structure in the Senate as it existed at a particular moment for becoming an enormously powerful leader. The institution rewarded his qualities, and that reward was the object of his ambitions.

Of course, he, too, had higher aspirations. But his qualities, forms of conduct, the demands and fears that were an aspect of his nature seemed to foreclose other routes. He had to depend, as he always had, upon effective performance—which meant controlling his institutional environment. He was further restrained by the fact that this performance not only was his means of advancing his ambition but was also an end in itself, and he was not capable of risking it for actions that might seem to enhance his chances for more significant power in another institution.

In fact, the qualities the Senate rewarded were not adapted to the institutional process of presidential nomination nor, probably, to that of presidential election, for it was unlikely that Johnson could have moved from Majority Leader to election as President on his own.

Not only do institutions reward different qualities, but their demands are often contradictory. The same qualities and capacities that make success probable in one setting may be inconsistent with success in another setting. Johnson was fortunate that conditions in 1964 and 1965 permitted him to use many of the abilities and qualities with which he had mastered the legislative process to conduct his Presidency with some success. However, when circumstances changed, these capacities proved ill-suited to the Presidency, which was a vastly different institution. He could not lead or inspire the nation by secret deals; he did not understand foreign policy; he could not deal with conflicts taking place in a setting where he could not establish personal detailed knowledge of the problems and the participants; and the same search for control that gave such force and direction to his legislative career caused him now to move toward coercive action and to transform the executive branch into a personal instrument, and a weapon for concealing facts and policies from other branches of government and the people.

Of course, Johnson was unique, as was his career. However, that career suggests that many of the qualities that make for success in the legislative branch—compromise, avoidance of conflict, secrecy, the effort to submerge personal responsibility for success or failure in a collective body, the vision of law as the end of the process, etc.—may be contradictory to those required for effective national leadership: indeed, that a career in the legislative process may inculcate modes of behavior or strengthen existing qualities inconsistent with the nature of the presidential institution. This conjecture, which I believe to be true, is of special importance at a time when the Congress has become a significant platform for presidential candidates.

However, it demonstrates that fact that talent for public life is not a unity, but that there are distinct, often contradictory, talents, which are relevant to success in one area of public life and not in another. This is important in assessing not only whether a leader is likely to achieve his ambitions in a particular setting, but—more significantly—whether his leadership is likely to benefit or damage the country.

Second: Johnson demonstrated hitherto unsuspected powers in the executive branch. There was, as many have observed, a growing evolution toward concentration of power in that branch. However, Johnson did not merely continue this evolution. He gave it a new dimension. Previous evolution had rested on changing circumstances, e.g., federal intervention in economic policy and problems of public welfare, the growing significance of foreign policy, the size of the defense establishment, involvement in war, etc. For the most part, this expanding power was exercised with the knowledge and acquiescence of Congress and the informed public. Johnson discovered that the resources of the Presidency allowed him to conceal much of the exercise of power; that presidential authority could be exerted on the basis of undisclosed information and the private interpretation of information; indeed, that in many cases even presidential actions and decisions could be concealed. Of course, the effects of many such decisions would eventually become visible, thus revealing the decision itself. But not all. Moreover, concealment of the decision-making process shut out the opportunity for public discussion that is an essential part of the institutional process in our representative democracy. Johnson's actions became known because they were directed toward public goals, their objectives were of a public nature, and, hence, their effects would inevitably be revealed. Nixon illustrated how this power of concealment could be used for other kinds of objectives so that the probability of continuing concealment was increased. The development or discovery of a capacity to exercise substantial executive power in secret is not simply an increase in the power of the Presidency; it represents a change in the relationship of institutions within the constitutional framework, a change which, in some part, has the potential of moving the presidential institution outside the framework itself.

Third: This aspect of institutional change, developed under Johnson, and reinforced by the fate of the Nixon administration, suggests that the most effective checks on presidential power are not the committees that form the constitutional system of "checks and balances." They are the media and public opinion, catalyzed, in Johnson's case, by the presidential primaries. In both administrations these nongovernmental institutions were more effective restraints on presidential actions and usurpations than established governmental institutions.

Fourth: Johnson's career also helps to reaffirm the significance, probably the necessity, of consensus politics to effective presidential leadership. Historically, the only exceptions have been under special conditions—depression under Roosevelt, shifts and growth of population under Jackson—which produced large popular majorities whose interests were opposed to those protected by the dominant structure of economic and political power. Jefferson, after all, moved to placate the Federalists, even at the cost of disappointing some of his Republican followers, while Theodore Roosevelt took steps to placate his business supporters even while establishing a reputation as a trust buster. Johnson, however, showed that consensus could be a foundation for an extensive program of domestic reform even at a time when there were no serious class hostilities nor any economic crisis. That accomplishment requires a modification of what is meant by "consensus," or, rather, a recognition that the term is susceptible to different definitions. Eisenhower's consensus consisted of the fact that a large popular majority was satisfied with his policies, and no substantial proportion of the population was urging him in another direction. Under Johnson as well, there was no significant movement for domestic reform (with the exception, for a time, of the civil rights movement). He himself was the initiating force. Admittedly, the absence of serious division, and favorable economic conditions, made it possible for him to initiate such a program. However, he also saw that consensus did not require him to marshal public enthusiasm and support. He would achieve consensus among groups of special interests and concerns, usually organized and with identifiable leaders, who could influence congressional action directly. And each program required a different kind of appeal to different kinds of groups. By persuading religious and educational associations, he could remove obstacles to a program for aiding education. Certain programs of public welfare required union support and the willingness of business groups to, at least, withdraw opposition. Thus, in a manner similar to the way in which he imposed his will in the Senate, he constructed a consensus from an assembly of particular groups and interests, most of them led by individuals with whom he could deal directly. He created an interlocking web of services and obligations. Finally, many were willing to support particular programs about which they had reservations because they believed that, on the whole, Johnson's program was good for them and for the country. It was a pluralistic consensus, an agreement among groups of limited, often contradictory interests. This consensus, Johnson knew, would shape the actions of Congress. Popular support, that other form of consensus, would be a consequence of achievement, not its source.

We cannot determine, however, the extent to which Johnson had developed a method for public action that can be applied in other situations, and how much its effectiveness depended upon his unique qualities and capacities. And of course, events during the last years of his administration showed that even a consensus built on majority support and the desire for action cannot survive serious public divisions.

Fifth: Johnson's career also provides further evidence that the basic qualities of a leader do not change when he assumes new and larger responsibilities. It is more a metaphor than an accurate description to say, for example, that a man "grows" in office. Of course, individuals do learn from experience—some better than others, and some become more skillful. But basic abilities, ambitions grounded on inner needs, modes of conduct, and inclinations of behavior are deeply and permanently embedded. It may be that these qualities cannot be displayed in a particular setting, or are not suited to achievement within a particular institutional framework and/or under certain historical conditions; yet in another place they can be the basis of accomplishments and actions that others would not have anticipated. One thinks of Truman. Or it may be that the widened constituency of the Presidency allows a broadening of goals. Yet, while Johnson's landslide victory did stretch his aspirations, it did not change the essential elements of his behavior. Even his possession of the most powerful office in the country did not diminish his need to extend control or increase his capacity to deal with certain kinds of conflict or resistance. All his newly acquired ability to command did not reduce his drive to coerce. And under the right conditions, these qualities, which many had seen in him previously, were bound to emerge. And just as great office could magnify, if not change, his strength, so it could disastrously extend the consequences of his flaws. So, too, we discovered that the new Nixon was the old Nixon with much more power.

Therefore the best evidence of what can be expected of a candidate for high office—especially the Presidency—can better be found in an examination of his pattern of activity at other stages of his public life than in his statements or goals, and particularly in situations of stress, when he was confronted with difficult decisions that were bound to affect his ambitions, his leadership, and his concept of himself.

Sixth: The dilemma of the modern Presidency is not as simple as the contemporary talk of the imperial President suggests. Admittedly, the presidential institution has widened in power, as has the capacity of the President to concentrate that power in his own hands—a consequence less of tyranny than of the steady weakening of the various institutions designed to check the President—the Cabinet, the Congress, and the party. But the same centralization of resources that allows an almost unconstrained initiation of policies in some areas (the making of war and peace) and the exercise of almost unilateral authority in others (the dropping of bombs) incapacitates implementation of both domestic and foreign programs and eventually weakens the President's ability to lead. With a weakened Cabinet, the President has less chance of controlling his vast bureaucracy; with a shattered party and diminished Congress, he is unable to command that restrained public support essential for the continued viability of both his policies and his leadership. Thus the concentration of resources is at once enabling and constricting; the analytical problem is to understand not only where the President is too strong but also where he is too weak; to delineate what is meant by strong and weak and to describe the curious relationship between the two.

Seventh: The President's ability to focus national attention upon his every word and deed—which is made possible, and almost inescapable, by the nature of the national media—is a source of both power and illusion. And the same can be said of the enlarged White House staff and the use of a technological apparatus unparalleled in history. For five years, between 1963 and 1968, Lyndon Johnson dominated public life in Washington to such an extent that the Cabinet was *his* Cabinet, the Great Society *his* program, the Congress *his* instrument. With every technological innovation at his disposal, he could tape his own television shows, tell his pilots ten thousand miles away where and when to bomb, talk with the Soviet Premier on a moment's notice, and fly around the world in less than two days. But the man in the center when things are good remains in the center when things go bad, and the resources technology provides are often illusory, substituting the sense of control for real control. Thus the war in Vietnam became Lyndon Johnson's war; he personally was dropping the bombs, disrupting the economy, making prices rise, setting back the progress of black and poor. Obviously, neither image—villain or hero—is valid; historical circumstances and institutional conditions were vital to both success in the Great Society and failure in Vietnam. And this understanding is of more than intellectual interest, for exaggeration of the President's personal powers (both self-induced and media propelled) is an inevitable source of frustration as the President's actions invariably fall short of expectations, producing a destructive cycle for the man, the office, and the nation.

PART EIGHT

THE BUREAUCRACY

Public bureaucracies are central to contemporary politics and governance in the United States. Civil servants and appointed political executives at all levels of government implement public policies. They transform laws and judicial decisions into action. But bureaucratic agencies are no longer thought of as mere transmission belts between policymakers and the public. The agencies are also deeply involved in setting the public policy agenda, as well as formulating, evaluating, and revising public policy. Many agencies combine legislative, executive, and judicial functions. They make rules that have the force of law, enforce them, and adjudicate their application.

Agencies vary greatly in their missions, powers, size, structure, and relation to the chief executive. However, most embody the core characteristics of bureaucratic organization: specialization (a division of labor) for efficiency; hierarchy for coordination and accountability; formalization (reliance on written rules and procedures) to establish precise jurisdictions and responsibilities; impersonality for processing cases efficiently and for treating like cases alike; and recruitment and promotion on the basis of some conception of merit to assure that civil servants are qualified for their jobs and protected from partisan manipulation. Although these organizational features are intended to make bureaucracies efficient and economical, they sometimes have the opposite effect, causing them to become rule-bound, oriented towards procedures rather than results, and plodding.

Bureaucracy may be the most misunderstood part of American government. The development of large-scale, politically powerful federal agencies was not envisioned by the Framers. Consequently, the constitutional provisions regarding them are rudimentary. Though we sometimes think in terms of a monolithic entity, "the bureaucracy," it is really composed of diverse departments, agencies, commissions, boards, corporations, and other arrangements. We are accustomed to viewing these as part of the executive branch, but Congress has a great deal of authority over them—for their missions, budget, size, procedures, and powers. From a constitutional perspective, independent regulatory commissions, such as the Federal Trade Commission, may not even be considered part of the executive branch. In recent years the federal courts have also played an important role in overseeing and regulating the agencies.

The selections in this chapter address fundamental political questions posed by the development of government bureaucracies. James Q. Wilson's "The

Bureaucracy Problem" succinctly analyzes the complexity of public bureaucracy: "There is not one bureaucracy problem, there are several, and the solution to each is in some degree incompatible with the solution to every other." We want control and accountability, equity, efficiency, responsiveness, and fiscal integrity. But there are trade-offs among them and different constituencies for them.

Herbert Kaufman explains why public agencies are thought to generate too much red tape. He departs from the conventional view that bureaucrats themselves are the sole source of rules and regulations. Instead, "all of us together produce it." "Each constraint is the product of a fairly small number of claimants. But there are so many of us, and such a diversity of interests among us, that modest individual demands result in great stacks of official paper and bewildering procedural mazes."

In the broadest sense, both Wilson and Kaufman agree that our bureaucracy and red tape problems are a product of our particular constitutional democracy.

33

JAMES Q. WILSON

THE BUREAUCRACY PROBLEM

Regardless of one's position on the political spectrum, the federal bureaucracy is problematic. The "bureaucracy problem" is how to achieve simultaneously acceptable levels of accountability, equity, efficiency, political responsiveness, and fiscal integrity in federal agencies. In practice, these objectives are often mutually inconsistent. James Q. Wilson is professor emeritus at the University of California, Los Angeles. "The Bureaucracy Problem" was published in The Public Interest *in 1967.*

The federal bureaucracy, whose growth and problems were once only the concern of the Right, has now become a major concern of the Left, the Center, and almost all points in between. Conservatives once feared that a powerful bureaucracy would work a social revolution. The Left now fears that this same bureaucracy is working a conservative reaction. And the Center fears that the bureaucracy isn't working at all.

Increasing federal power has always been seen by conservatives in terms of increasing *bureaucratic* power. If greater federal power merely meant, say, greater uniformity in government regulations—standardized trucking regulations, for example, or uniform professional licensing practices—a substantial segment of American businessmen would probably be pleased. But growing federal power means increased discretion vested in appointive officials whose behavior can neither be anticipated nor controlled. The behavior of state and local bureaucrats, by contrast, can often be anticipated *because* it can be controlled by businessmen and others.

Knowing this, liberals have always resolved most questions in favor of enhancing federal power. The "hacks" running local administrative agencies were too often, in liberal eyes, the agents of local political and economic forces—businessmen, party bosses, organized professions, and the like. A federal bureaucrat, because he was responsible to a national power center and to a single President elected by a nationwide constituency, could not so easily be bought off by local vested interests; in addition, he would take his policy guidance from a President elected by a process that gave heavy weight to the votes of urban, labor, and minority groups. The New Deal bureaucrats, especially those appointed to the new, "emergency" agencies, were expected by liberals to be free to chart a radically new program and to be competent to direct its implementation.

It was an understandable illusion. It frequently appears in history in the hopes of otherwise intelligent and far-sighted men. Henry II thought his clerks and scribes would help him subdue England's feudal barons; how was he to know that in time they would become the agents of Parliamentary authority directed at stripping the king of his prerogatives? And how were Parliament and its Cabinet ministers, in turn, to know that eventually these permanent undersecretaries would become an almost self-governing class whose day-to-day behavior would become virtually immune to scrutiny or control? Marxists thought that Soviet bureaucrats would work for the people, despite the fact that Max Weber had pointed out why one could be almost certain they would work mostly for themselves. It is ironic that among today's members of the "New Left," the "Leninist problem"—i.e., the problem of over-organization and of self-perpetuating administrative power—should become a major preoccupation.

This apparent agreement among polemicists of the Right and Left that there is a bureaucracy problem accounts, one suspects, for the fact that non-bureaucratic solutions to contemporary problems seem to command support from both groups. The negative income tax as a strategy for dealing with poverty is endorsed by economists of such different persuasions as Milton Friedman and James Tobin, and has received favorable consideration among members of both the Goldwater brain trust and the Students for Democratic Society. Though the interests of the two groups are somewhat divergent, one common element is a desire to scuttle the social workers and the public welfare bureaucracy, who are usually portrayed as prying busybodies with pursed lips and steel-rimmed glasses ordering midnight bedchecks in public housing projects. (Police officers who complain that television makes them look like fools in the eyes of their children will know just what the social workers are going through.)

Now that everybody seems to agree that we ought to do something about the problem of bureaucracy, one might suppose that something would get done. Perhaps a grand reorganization, accompanied by lots of "systems analysis," "citizen participation," "creative federalism," and "interdepartmental coordination." Merely to state this prospect is to deny it.

There is not one bureaucracy problem, there are several, and the solution to each is in some degree incompatible with the solution to every other. First, there is the problem of accountability or control—getting the bureaucracy to serve agreed-on national goals. Second is the problem of equity—getting bureaucrats to treat like cases alike and on the basis of clear rules, known in advance. Third is the problem of efficiency—maximizing output for a given expenditure, or minimizing expenditures for a given output. Fourth is the problem of responsiveness—inducing bureaucrats to meet, with alacrity and compassion, those cases which can never be brought under a single national rule and which, by common human standards of justice or benevolence, seem to require that an exception be made or a rule stretched. Fifth is the problem of fiscal integrity—properly spending and accounting for public money.

Each of these problems mobilizes a somewhat different segment of the public. The problem of power is the unending preoccupation of the President and his staff, especially during the first years of an administration. Equity concerns the lawyers and the courts, though increasingly the Supreme Court seems to act as if it thinks its job is to help set national goals as a kind of auxiliary White House. Efficiency has traditionally been the concern of businessmen who thought, mistakenly, that an efficient government was one that didn't spend very much money. (Of late, efficiency has come to have a broader and more accurate meaning as an optimal relationship between objectives and resources: Robert McNamara has shown that an "efficient" Department of Defense costs a lot more money than an "inefficient" one; his disciples are now carrying the message to all parts of a skeptical federal establishment.) Responsiveness has been the concern of individual citizens and of their political representatives, usually out of wholly proper motives, but sometimes out of corrupt ones. Congress, especially, has tried to retain some power over the bureaucracy by intervening on behalf of tens of thousands of immigrants, widows, businessmen, and mothers-of-soldiers, hoping that the collective effect of many individual interventions would be a bureaucracy that, on large matters as well as small, would do Congress's will. (Since Congress only occasionally has a clear will, this strategy only works occasionally.) Finally, fiscal integrity—especially its absence—is the concern of the political "outs" who want to get in and thus it becomes the concern of "ins" who want to keep them out.

Obviously the more a bureaucracy is responsive to its clients—whether those clients are organized by radicals into Mothers for Adequate Welfare or represented by Congressmen anxious to please constituents—the less it can be accountable to presidential directives. Similarly, the more equity, the less responsiveness. And a preoccupation with fiscal integrity can make the kind of program budgeting required by enthusiasts of efficiency difficult, if not impossible.

Indeed, of all the groups interested in bureaucracy, those concerned with fiscal integrity usually play the winning hand. To be efficient, one must have clearly stated goals, but goals are often hard to state at all, much less clearly. To be responsive, one must be willing to run risks, and the career civil service is not ordinarily attractive to people with a taste for risk. Equity is an abstraction, of concern for the most part only to people who haven't been given any. Accountability is "politics," and the bureaucracy itself is the first to resist that (unless, of course, it is the kind of politics that produces pay raises and greater job security). But an absence of fiscal integrity is welfare chiseling, sweetheart deals, windfall profits, conflict of interest, malfeasance in high places—in short, corruption. Everybody recognizes *that* when he sees it, and none but a few misguided academics have anything good to say about it. As a result, fiscal scandal typically becomes the standard by which a bureaucracy is judged (the FBI is good because it hasn't had any, the Internal Revenue Service is bad because it has) and thus the all-consuming fear of responsible executives.

If it is this hard to make up one's mind about how one wants the bureaucracy to behave, one might be forgiven if one threw up one's hands and let nature take its course. Though it may come to that in the end, it is possible—and important—to begin with a resolution to face the issue squarely and try to think through the choices. Facing the issue means admitting what, in our zeal for new programs, we usually ignore: *There are inherent limits to what can be accomplished by large hierarchical organizations.*

The opposite view is more often in vogue. If enough people don't like something, it becomes a problem; if the intellectuals agree with them, it becomes a crisis; any crisis must be solved; if it must be solved, then it can be solved—and creating a new organization is the way to do it. If the organization fails to solve the problem (and when the problem is a fundamental one, it will almost surely fail), then the reason is "politics," or "mismanagement," or "incompetent people," or "meddling," or "socialism," or "inertia."

Some problems cannot be solved and some government functions cannot, in principle, be done well. Notwithstanding, the effort must often be made. The rule of reason should be to try to do as few undoable things as possible. It is regrettable, for example, that any country must have a foreign office, since none can have a good one. The reason is simple: it is literally impossible to have a "policy" with respect to *all* relevant matters concerning *all* foreign countries, much less a consistent and reasonable policy. And the difficulty increases with the square of the number of countries, and probably with the cube of the speed of communications. The problem long ago became insoluble and any sensible Secretary of State will cease trying to solve it. He will divide his time instead between *ad hoc* responses to the crisis of the moment and appearances on Meet the Press.

The answer is not, it must be emphasized, one of simply finding good people, though it is at least that. Most professors don't think much of the State Department, but it is by no means clear that a department made up only of professors would be any better, and some reason to believe that it would be worse. One reason is that bringing in "good outsiders," especially good outsiders from universities, means bringing in men with little experience in dealing with the substantive problem but many large ideas about how to approach problems "in general." General ideas, no matter how soundly based in history or social science, rarely tell one what to do tomorrow about the visit from the foreign trade mission from Ruritania or the questions from the Congressional appropriations subcommittee.

Another reason is that good people are in very short supply, even assuming we knew how to recognize them. Some things literally cannot be done—or cannot be done well—because there is no one available to do them who knows how. *The supply of able, experienced executives is not increasing nearly as fast as the number of problems being addressed by public policy.* All the fellowships, internships, and "mid-career training programs" in the world aren't likely to increase that supply very much, simply because the essential qualities for an executive—judgment about men and events, a facility for making good guesses, a sensitivity to political realities, and an ability to motivate others—are things which, if they can be taught at all, cannot be taught systematically or to more than a handful of apprentices at one time.

This constraint deserves emphasis, for it is rarely recognized as a constraint at all. Anyone who opposed a bold new program on the grounds that there was nobody around able to run it would be accused of being a pettifogger at best and a reactionary do-nothing at worst. Everywhere except in government, it seems, the scarcity of talent is accepted as a fact of life. Nobody (or almost nobody) thinks seriously of setting up a great new university overnight, because anybody familiar with the university business knows that, for almost any professorship one would want to fill, there are rarely more than five (if that) really top-flight people in the country, and they are all quite happy—and certainly well-paid—right where they are. Lots of new business ideas don't become profit-making realities because good business executives are both hard to find and expensive to hire. The government—at least publicly—seems to act as if the supply of able political executives were infinitely elastic, though people setting up new agencies will often admit privately that they are so frustrated and appalled by the shortage of talent that the only wonder is why disaster is so long in coming. Much would be gained if this constraint were mentioned to Congress *before* the bill is passed and the hopes aroused, instead of being mentioned afterward as an excuse for failure or as a reason why higher pay scales for public servants are an urgent necessity. "Talent is Scarcer Than Money" should be the motto of the Budget Bureau.

If administrative feasibility is such a critical issue, what can be done about it? Not a great deal. If the bureaucracy problem is a major reason why so many programs are in trouble, it is also a reason why the problem itself cannot be "solved." But it can be mitigated—though not usually through the kinds of expedients we are fond of trying: Hoover Commissions, management studies, expensive consultants, co-ordinating committees, "czars," and the like. The only point at which very much leverage can be gained on the problem *is when we decide what it is we are trying to accomplish*. When we define our goals, we are implicitly deciding how much, or how little, of a bureaucracy problem we are going to have. A program with clear objectives, clearly stated, is a program with a fighting chance of coping with each of the many aspects of the bureaucracy problem. Controlling an agency is easier when you know what you want. Equity is more likely to be assured when over-all objectives can be stated, at least in part, in general rules to which people in and out of the agency are asked to conform. Efficiency is made possible when you know what you are buying with your money. Responsiveness is never easy or wholly desirable; if every person were treated in accordance with his special needs, there would be no program at all. (The only system that meets the responsiveness problem squarely is the free market.) But at least with clear objectives we would know what we are giving up in those cases when responsiveness seems necessary, and thus we would be able to decide how much we are willing to tolerate. And fiscal integrity is just as easy to insure in a system with clear objectives as in one with fuzzy ones; in the former case, moreover, we are less likely to judge success simply in terms of avoiding scandal. We might even be willing to accept a little looseness if we knew what we were getting for it.

The rejoinder to this argument is that there are many government functions which, by their nature, can never have clear objectives. I hope I have made it obvious by now that I am aware of that. We can't stop dealing with foreign nations just because we don't know what we want; after all, they may know what *they* want, and we had better find out. My argument is advanced, not as a panacea—there is no way to avoid the problem of administration—but as a guide to choice in those cases where choice is open to us, and as a criterion by which to evaluate proposals for coping with the bureaucracy problem.

Dealing with poverty—at least in part—by giving people money seems like an obvious strategy. Governments are very good at taking money from one person and giving it to another; the goals are not particularly difficult to state; measures are available to evaluate how well we are doing in achieving a predetermined income distribution. There may be many things wrong with this approach, but administrative difficulty is not one of them. And yet, paradoxically, it is the last approach we will probably try. We will try everything else first—case work, counseling, remedial education, community action, federally financed mass protests to end "alienation," etc. And whatever else might be said in their favor, the likelihood of smooth administration and ample talent can hardly be included.

Both the White House and the Congress seem eager to do something about the bureaucracy problem. All too often, however, the problem is described in terms of "digesting" the "glut" of new federal programs—as if solving administrative difficulties had something in common with treating heartburn. Perhaps those seriously concerned with this issue will put themselves on notice that they ought not to begin with the pain and reach for some administrative bicarbonate of soda; they ought instead to begin with what was swallowed and ask whether an emetic is necessary. *Coping with the bureaucracy problem is inseparable from rethinking the objectives of the programs in question.* Administrative reshuffling, budgetary cuts (or budgetary increases), and congressional investigation of lower-level boondoggling will not suffice and are likely, unless there are some happy accidents, to make matters worse. Thinking clearly about goals is a tough assignment for a political system that has been held together in great part by compromise, ambiguity, and contradiction. And if a choice must be made, any reasonable person would, I think, prefer the system to the clarity. But now that we have decided to intervene in such a wide range of human affairs, perhaps we ought to reassess that particular trade-off.

34

HERBERT KAUFMAN

RED TAPE

Public agencies are often criticized for their "red tape." The term was apparently coined in response to the nineteenth-century practice of binding official documents with red ribbons. It is currently used as a generic reference to cumbersome, laborious, time-consuming, or bewildering administrative processes. But much red tape is the product of our collective desire for government that is compassionate and representative. For instance, it is used to protect people from each other, alleviate distress, and forestall disruptions, as well as to promote due process, administrative effectiveness, and open government. Herbert Kaufman has been a leading scholar of public organizations for more than three decades. Now retired, he taught political science at Yale University and was for many years a senior fellow in the Governmental Studies Program at the Brookings Institution.

In suggesting that responsibility for the massive outpouring of government requirements and restraints decried as red tape is widely shared, I do not mean to imply that we manufacture red tape deliberately. For the most part, we do so without realizing it. That we do so inadvertently, however, does not alter the facts about the origins of the outpouring. All of us together produce it.

Every restraint and requirement originates in somebody's demand for it. Of course, each person does not will them all; on the contrary, even the most broadly based interest groups are concerned with only a relatively small band of the full spectrum of government activities, and most interest groups are narrowly specialized rather than broadly based. So each constraint is the product of a fairly small number of claimants. But there are so many of us, and such a diversity of interests among us, that modest individual demands result in great stacks of official paper and bewildering procedural mazes.

Let me illustrate this contention by reviewing the effects of just two properties we have tried to infuse into our government: compassion and representativeness. Each of these is a cluster of attributes, not a single simple trait. And they are only two such clusters among many. But they account for a storm of complaints about red tape.

HOW COMPASSION SPAWNS RED TAPE

If the government were not driven to protect us from injury, for example, there would be many fewer governmental constraints and complicated procedures in our society. I exclude "common crimes" and the administration of criminal justice from this discussion—not because they are conceptually or practically distinct from other kinds of official prohibitions and obligations, but because, for obscure reasons, they are not usually regarded as red tape,[1] and because, in any event, they fall chiefly within the jurisdiction of the states rather than the federal government. The remaining protections are still vast, for the federal government tries in so many ways to prevent harm from befalling us.

Protecting People from Each Other

Take the relations between buyers and sellers. For a long time, these were left largely to negotiations between the parties to each transaction; the government had little to do with them. They were not *entirely* unregulated by public authority, the courts being available to parties aggrieved by deception or other injury. For the most part, though, remedies could be sought only after damages had been inflicted or at least only when damages were imminent. Hence the warning that it was up to the buyer to beware. The government took no responsibility for the buyer's well-being.

Today, the government is deeply involved in trying to prevent injuries *before* they occur. People demanded its protection for many reasons—the marketplace worked too imperfectly to shield them from harm by venal or careless producers and distributors, the courts were uneconomic instruments of redress for individuals whose damages were of small monetary value, the amount of technical knowledge required to choose sensibly among the innumerable products offered for sale came to exceed what most of us could master, agreements between buyers and sellers began to impinge more and more heavily on persons not party to the negotiations or to the bargains struck, and social values changed as industrial society proved fertile soil for new philosophies. In response to the demands for governmental intervention provoked by these developments, the government interceded in more and more buyer-seller relations.

It has attempted, for instance, to assure the purity of food and the safety of drugs.[2] It has attempted to prevent false and misleading advertising.[3] It has attempted to reduce dangers from hazardous substances and products of all kinds.[4] It has attempted to improve the safety of passengers in public and private transportation.[5] These are just a few of the programs to raise the minimum standards of selected goods and services. Buyers still have to beware; the public programs fall short of absolute guarantees. But they illustrate how the generous impulses of the government give rise to all sorts of controls.

A host of agencies were created to perform these functions, including the Food and Drug Administration, the Federal Trade Commission, the Consumer Products Safety Commission, the National Transportation Safety Board, inspection services of the Department of Agriculture, and safety divisions in the Interstate Commerce Commission, the Coast Guard, and the Federal Aviation Agency. For each one, pages of statutes brought it into existence, set its mandate, and defined its powers. Each agency discharges its responsibilities through volumes of administrative rules and regulations, orders addressed to individual people and firms, and adjudications of disputed decisions and orders, many of which are reached in courtlike proceedings. For these purposes, each agency has its forms for applications and collecting data, and each issues its own procedural directives. Some agencies have licensing powers, most have powers of inspection, a few have powers of summary action to deal with emergencies.[6] Today, therefore, buyer-seller relations once ignored by the government are modified and controlled by hosts of official specifications and by the public administrative officers and employees who enforce them.

Beyond question, one consequence of all these measures has been to multiply by a large factor the number of governmental constraints people encounter in day-to-day life. Also beyond question, the measures can be traced to entreaties for the protection of people unable to protect themselves in the modern world. This is not to say that every response has been exactly what the petitioners expected or that every response has been a smashing success. But it is from such demands for governmental intercession and from the convergence of political necessity and genuine concern for innocent victims that the avalanche of government paper often springs.

Buyer-seller relations are only one of the broad areas in which the government has been impelled to intervene. It is also a party to relations between employers and employees and between unions and union members,[7] universities and students,[8] bankrupts and their creditors,[9] tenants and landlords,[10] shippers and carriers,[11] state and local governments and their residents,[12] banks and depositors,[13] investors and issuers and underwriters of securities,[14] lenders and borrowers,[15] researchers and human research subjects,[16] even animal handlers and animals,[17] among many others. It is involved in relations between competing firms of all kinds, both to limit excessive competition for markets and resources and to preserve competition where it is threatened.[18] It is concerned with prices and rates,[19] the quality of goods and services,[20] safety,[21] and equal rights under law.[22] Every interposition is a response to a cry for help from some group unable to defend its interests by itself. And every one entails as much legislation, administrative procedure and action, and litigation as does intervention in buyer-seller relations. In this sense, much of the great volume of governmental requirements and prohibitions that we encounter on all sides owes its existence to the government's endeavors to keep some people from being hurt by other people.

Alleviating Distress

The government has also responded to pleas for assistance from people buffeted not so much by their fellows as by forces over which they have no control. For a long time, many of these unfortunates were left to the mercy of their families and neighbors, of private charities, of local units of government, or simply of fate; the federal government assumed almost no responsibility for them. But the scale and character of hardship in modern industrial society overwhelmed the traditional instrumentalities of aid. Political pressure, humanitarian impulses, guilt, pity, and other sentiments built up. The federal government could not ignore them; it moved in to help.

Seamen were treated as "wards" of the government early in the nation's history,[23] as Indians were later.[24] Assistance to veterans and their families was likewise begun many years ago.[25] Later, there were also federal services for children, for the aged, the blind, the disabled, retired workers, the poor, and others.[26] Relief for the victims of natural disasters—floods, droughts, storms, earthquakes—was routinized.[27]

Unemployment compensation was federally encouraged and financed by federal grants to tide the unemployed over hard times.[28] The list goes on and on; the federal government has heeded many calls for help.

The government's generosity, incidentally, is not confined to the destitute and the handicapped. Subsidies to farmers and certain industries relieve the hardships of these groups, some of whom would otherwise be forced out of business by foreign competition or adverse economic conditions.[29] State and local governments have also been helped by federal grants-in-aid and revenue sharing.[30] Programs on behalf of these beneficiaries are frequently justified in economic rather than moral terms—the supports presumably enable important functions to continue and also preserve the jobs these functions create. But welfare programs for the poor may be similarly defended on economic grounds, for they shore up purchasing power and thus provide job-sustaining, production-maintaining markets. The philosophical differences between services to various target populations are quite narrow. *All* these services come about because people and organizations in distress seek federal contributions to alleviate their pain, and the federal government, for a mixture of pragmatic and idealistic reasons, answers the calls.

The moment a government program for a specified group gets started, legislation and administrative directives and court battles proliferate. It is essential to define who is in the group and who is not. The amounts of benefits and the criteria for determining who in the group is eligible for which amount must be established. Procedures for requesting benefits, for processing such applications, for distributing the benefits, and for settling disputes with applicants over their entitlements have to be set up. Preparations must be made to defend actions in court and to justify them to legislators representing disappointed constituents. In short, because each decision in a grant program is tailored to the situation of each recipient, the administering agencies are compelled to issue a multitude of guidelines and to construct elaborate machinery to accomplish their ends.

Consider a couple of illustrations from social security. The statute provides for "mother's insurance benefits." A number of conditions must be met for a woman to qualify, including one that she have "in her care a child of the deceased worker under age 18 or disabled who is entitled to child's insurance benefits." But what does "in her care" mean? Some women apply even though they are not living with the child in question; must the mother and child be living together? Is living together proof that the child is in her care? Does legal right to the child's care and custody by itself establish eligibility? Nearly two pages of regulations have been promulgated to answer questions of this kind for all foreseeable contingencies in connection with this single phrase. ("In her care" means that she exercises "parental control and responsibility for the welfare and care" of the child, or performs "personal services" for a child eighteen or over who is mentally incompetent.[31] Parental control and responsibility, in turn, mean "supervising the child's activities and participating in the important decisions about the child's physical and mental needs."[32] Performing personal services means "services [with illustrations listed] performed for a child other than any routine household services which are performed for any adult member of a household."[33] Parental control and responsibility may be exercised indirectly, with mother and child apart, but for specified lengths of time and for specific purposes, such as the child being away at school.[34] Mere legal right to a child's care and custody does not in itself constitute parental care and responsibility.[35] Indeed, there is a whole section illustrating situations in which a mother is deemed *not* to have a child in her care.[36]) It is necessary to go on at such length and in such detail because thousands of employees of the Social Security Administration must make judgments on tens of thousands of claims encompassing all sorts of different circumstances. Only precise, specific guidelines can assure common treatment of like cases. Otherwise, programs for alleviating distress on an individual basis lose all consistency.

Similarly, the statutory provisions for disability payments under the social security program are amplified by a large body of administrative regulations. Disability is defined in the legislation as "inability to engage in any substantial gainful activity by reason of any medically determinable physical or mental impairment which can be expected to result in death or has lasted or can be expected to last for a continuous period of not less than 12 months."[37] But it takes fifteen pages of specifications of symptoms, clinical signs, and laboratory findings for the musculoskeletal system, special sense organs, respiratory system, cardiovascular system, digestive system, genitourinary system, hemic and lymphatic system, skin, endocrine system, multiple body systems, neurological problems, mental disorders, and malignant neoplastic diseases to describe the kinds of impairments within the statutory standard.[38] Indeed, even when the statute is quite specific ("'blindness' means central visual acuity of 20/200 or less in the better eye with the use of a correcting lens. An eye which is accompanied by a limitation in the fields of vision such that the widest diameter of the visual field subtends an angle no greater than 20 degrees shall be considered for the purposes of this paragraph as having a central visual acuity of 20/200 or less"[39]), it may require elaboration. In the case of blindness, administrative regulations prescribe the tests to be used in determining visual acuity—for instance, for an eye with a lens, the "usual perimetric methods, utilizing a 3 mm. white disc target at a distance of 330 mm. under illumination of not less than 7 foot-candles," according to a prescribed table of central visual efficiency and a chart showing the normal field of vision and the method of computing percentage of field efficiency.[40] In this fashion, the Social Security Administration tries to make sure that the same criteria of eligibility are applied everywhere.

Obviously, the program could be run with far fewer specifications and requirements. One consequence, however, would be the award of benefits to people whom Congress and the program administrators never intended to support and the denial of benefits to many they wanted to reach. Once a program of tailor-made assistance gets started, it is not likely to attain its announced objectives unless it is laid out in great detail. Humane goals thus add to the paper blizzard.

Forestalling Systemic Disruptions

Another way in which the federal government strives to prevent pain and hardship from afflicting people is by heading off systemic breakdowns. Industrial systems are composed of such specialized and interdependent subsystems that a failure of any subsystem inevitably slows or stops other subsystems, and the repercussions spread through the whole society. If the subsystem is an especially important one—transportation, energy, agriculture, or a basic industry like steel production—the results can be catastrophic. Many federal interventions in the economy, with their accompanying mounds of laws and regulations, are brought on by the resolve to shield people from the suffering that would ensue.

Hence the programs and agencies to prevent work stoppages caused by labor-management and interunion disputes,[41] to manage the economy when inflation or deflation threatens its stability,[42] to prevent the waste and destruction of natural resources and to assure a steady supply of vital materials from abroad,[43] to deter aggression against this country and its friends by potential foes,[44] to assist other nations striving for economic and political development and stability,[45] and to encourage and facilitate the peaceful resolution of international conflicts that could explode into worldwide crises.[46] Even leaders whose personal preference might be to stay aloof from such involvements cannot ignore the demands and expectations of the people generally, or of powerful groups among them, that the government do something about such dangers. The government will therefore almost always do something—maybe something that proves unwise in retrospect, but in any case, something—to forestall events and practices that could disrupt the system under which we live.

Of course, the programs launched to provide this security increase the size of the government and the number and complexity of government operations and procedures. Think of the number of agencies set up to work for the objectives just mentioned: the Department of Labor, the National Labor Relations Board, the National Mediation Board, the Federal Mediation and Conciliation Service, the Department of the Interior, the Environmental Protection Agency, the Federal Energy Administration, the Energy Research and Development Administration, the Department of Commerce, the Department of State, the Agency for International Development, the Export-Import Bank, the Department of Defense, the Central Intelligence Agency, and many others. If we were willing to take greater risks with the very existence of our economic and political systems, we would undoubtedly enjoy less government, smaller government, and simpler government—provided, that is, we had any government at all. Perhaps we have opted for excessive caution. But the suffering from systemic breakdowns evidently is so much less acceptable than the controls and procedures set up to prevent them that we prefer the certain constraints and annoyances to the possibility of even temporary disruption.

Compassion and Expedience

In suggesting that there is compassion behind governmental policies intended to protect people from one another, help the victims of events that overwhelm them, and keep the system from breaking down or being smashed, I don't mean to rule out the political expediency of these policies. The careers, reputations, even the jobs of government officers and employees depend on the maintenance of order and continuity in the polity; if substantial numbers of people—even if they are only a minority—are disaffected and rebellious or if the society cannot function or defend itself, the institutions of government may be overturned, sweeping the leaders out. And even if the institutions survive, the leaders will be replaced if they appear indifferent to the pains and fears of the public. So it is in the self-interest of officials to respond to people's expressions of distress and anxiety. Compassion and expediency thus converge to produce the proliferation of government requirements, prohibitions, and labyrinthine procedures.

REPRESENTATIVENESS AND ITS CONSEQUENCES

Despite governmental solicitude, distrust of government is a deeply ingrained tradition in America. Consequently, the growth of government stimulates fear in the people even though the growth came about in response to demands for protection and assistance from the people themselves. Americans worry about the dangers of tyranny or at least of official arrogance. And they are uneasy about the possibility that the vast impersonal machinery of government, with its endless obscure activities and powers, will be turned from its public purposes to private advantage by powerful private interests or crooks in its ranks or outside. That is, Americans assert a need to be protected *from* the government as well as by it, and they recognize a need to protect it from those who would despoil it.

The representativeness of the government is a safeguard against such abuses. If all interests are represented in the government's decision-making processes and if its decisions are not skewed by resources or methods employed only by a small set of interests, it is less likely to be tyrannical, arbitrary, dishonest, or extensively victimized. So steps have been taken to assure representativeness.

Unfortunately, like so many other unexceptionable objectives, this one too brings procedural complications, substantive constraints, paperwork, and additional agencies in its wake. How these undesired characteristics are brought about by the quest for representativeness is best explained by examining some of the specific tactics employed in that quest. Efforts to guarantee due process, rationality in decisionmaking, the integrity of every decision, and taxation with representation illustrate clearly what happens.

Due Process

Preservation of due process, for instance, obliges officials to give people affected by governmental actions a fair chance to get their views on official decisions registered so that their interests are not overlooked or arbitrarily overridden by those in power. Actions judged to be in violation of these requirements may be nullified.

The desire for fairness adds to the practices and constraints commonly regarded as red tape. Take the Administrative Procedure Act as an example.[47] Enacted in 1946, it is a legally binding codification and summary of procedural fairness requirements governing administrative agencies. It applies to agency rules ("the whole or any part of any agency statement of general or particular applicability and future effect"), orders ("the whole or any part of the final disposition . . . of any agency in any matter other than rule making but including licensing"), and licenses ("the whole or part of any agency permit, certificate, approval, registration, charter, membership, statutory exemption or other form of permission"), and to the processes by which each of these decisions is reached and promulgated.[48]

To ensure that people are not kept in the dark about who is responsible for the decisions about rules, orders, and licenses, by what authority the decisions are issued, the exact wording of the decisions, and how and where to protest unfavorable decisions, the statute includes a section on public information commanding agencies to "separately state and currently publish in the Federal Register" descriptions of central and field organization, including delegations of authority; "statements of the general course and methods by which its functions are channeled and determined," including formal or informal procedures and forms and instructions; and substantive rules plus statements of general policy or interpretations adopted by the agencies. They must also "publish or, in accordance with published rule, make available to public inspection all final opinions or orders in the adjudication of cases." Matters of record must, in accordance with published rules, be made available to "persons properly and directly concerned."[49]

Another section of the law, on rule making, requires also that "general notice of proposed rule making shall be published in the *Federal Register*," and that each agency "shall afford interested persons an opportunity to participate in the rule making" through written submissions "with or without opportunity to present the same orally." All relevant submissions must be considered by the decisionmakers, and rules adopted must contain "a concise general statement of their basis and purpose." Any interested person must be accorded "the right to petition for the issuance, amendment, or repeal of a rule."[50]

Small wonder, then, that the *Federal Register* and the *Code of Federal Regulations* fill shelf after shelf in library stacks.

The act also specifies how various proceedings must be conducted. A section on adjudication directs that persons entitled to notice of an agency hearing be given timely information about all the relevant details of the pending matter. The times and places of hearings must be set "with due regard . . . for the convenience and necessity of the parties or their representatives." Agencies must give all interested parties a chance for "the submission and consideration of facts, arguments, offers of settlement, or proposals of adjustment," and, if no agreement is reached, a chance for a hearing.[51]

The management of hearings is spelled out in detail, with particulars on the powers of presiding officers, the taking of evidence (including the right to cross-examine), and the character of the official record. Decisions by subordinates are authorized, but appeal to "the agency" (i.e., its highest officers) is permitted, and the procedures for appeal are explicitly described. Decisions must include "findings and conclusions, as well as the reasons or basis therefor, upon all the material issues of fact, law, or discretion presented on the record." Agencies are directed to appoint "as many qualified and competent examiners [now called administrative law judges] as may be necessary" for these purposes.[52]

Finally, "Any person suffering legal wrong because of any agency action, or adversely affected or aggrieved by such action . . . shall be entitled to judicial review thereof." Review proceedings and the scope of court jurisdiction are defined.[53]

Here, then, are some of the reasons for the elaborateness and deliberateness of administrative procedures in federal agencies. To be sure, were there no Administrative Procedure Act, agencies would not cavalierly trample the rights of their clients; other statutes, judicial precedents, political pressures, and generally accepted standards of equity would keep them in check. But the act unquestionably compelled them to formalize and elaborate their procedures to a greater degree than they otherwise would.

Special due-process guarantees cover employees of the government.[54] Superiors cannot hire and fire subordinates at will, punish them freely, or even unrestrainedly assign them to functions or locations. Civil service laws and regulations, collective bargaining agreements, and, more recently, judicial interpretations of the first amendment to the Constitution,[55] not to mention political realities, circumscribe the superiors, and aggrieved employees may seek formal review of actions affecting them. At least some of the slowness, awkwardness, and intricacy of federal administration can be traced to the protection of the rights of people who work for the government.

A society less concerned about the rights of individuals in government and out might well be governed with a much smaller volume of paper and much simpler and faster administrative procedures than are typical of governance in this country. Americans have adopted a different mix.

Representation, Rationality, and Administrative Effectiveness

Participation of relevant interests in decisionmaking, one of the principal ways of achieving due process, is an end in itself. At the same time, it contributes to another widely shared value, rationality in decisionmaking. Rationality, in turn, is both an end in itself and a means to another value, administrative effectiveness. The simultaneous pursuit of all these objectives generates still more of the practices and requirements reviled as red tape.

Rationality here refers to consideration of all reasonable alternatives and their effects when choices must be made. It also refers to the logical consistency of decisions, to the elimination of inexplicable and unjustifiable discrepancies among them, and to the avoidance of embarrassing contradictions.

Lack of comprehensiveness in weighing alternatives can reduce rationality and effectiveness in several ways. It may result in selection of a course of action inferior to other available options. It may eventuate in decisions that powerful public agencies and political leaders, excluded from the process of deciding, cannot support. It may produce policies offensive to a segment of the community capable of offering strong resistance and even of overturning them. In short, wisdom, teamwork, and compliance may suffer from the failure to take into account everything and everybody that reasonably could be taken into account in arriving at a policy position.

Lack of consistency can reduce rationality and effectiveness in similar ways. The work of one agency may end up negating the labors of another. The discovery by some people that other people in the same position fare better because different agencies or regional offices handle identical problems in different ways may lead to noncompliance, litigation, and even political upheavals. Indeed, inconsistent requirements may force citizens to violate some legal mandates in order to comply with others, which means that one or more programs will fall short of their announced goals. In any event, disclosure of such cases makes those in power look ludicrous.

Government procedures were therefore designed to avert these doleful possibilities by facilitating interest-group participation in official decisions to a greater extent than would be dictated by concern for fairness alone. This makes it harder to reach policy decisions. But giving every interested party a voice in official decisions increases the likelihood that no feasible option will be overlooked, that no important consequence of any feasible option will be forgotten or unperceived, that conflicts and contradictions will be brought to light and resolved, and that the policies ultimately emerging from such broadly reviewed deliberations will enjoy a higher degree of voluntary compliance on the part of the public than policies fashioned in ignorance of public attitudes and expectations. Presumably, such policies will also be maximally fair because nobody's rights are likely to be trampled under these conditions. Whether they are more just or not, however, they are said to enjoy better hope of success than policies formulated in isolation or secrecy. It is in this sense that they are called more rational and effective.

Some of the methods of increasing group participation are time-honored.[56] One is to designate agencies to be spokesmen for specific groups; at the departmental level, for example, the Departments of Labor, Agriculture, and Commerce were so conceived, but there are also many single-constituency agencies at the bureau level and among the so-called independent bodies, such as the Veterans' Administration. Other long-standing methods include selecting agency staffs from the clientele served or regulated and reserving places on administrative and advisory boards for representatives of such interests. Occasionally, a private interest may be virtually clothed with public authority. These practices are often assailed for giving too much weight to special interests as against the public interest, and their efficacy in furthering the cause of justice and rationality has been sharply questioned. Hidden motives may indeed underlie some of them. All the same, they doubtless do result in decisions different from the ones public officials would reach if nongovernmental groups had no part in official decisionmaking. That is why they were invented and why they endure.

More recently, interest-group representation has been pressed into new areas. In the war against poverty, particularly, the federal government insisted that federally assisted local antipoverty agencies include the poor and ethnic minorities in their governing boards, while some revenue sharing programs require evidence of local participation in the drafting of applications for federal funds.[57]

Old or new, the methods of interest-group representation generate more directives and controls, more steps in the forging of governmental policies, more bargaining before decisions are reached, and more postdecision litigation than would otherwise develop. Fairness, comprehensiveness, and community acceptance of policy decisions obviously rate higher than administrative simplicity and speed.

Increased participation in governmental decisions by external groups is matched by procedures to make sure that every administrative unit *inside* the government also contributes its special knowledge, point of view, and sympathy for its clientele to the final product. One method is compulsory clearance of pending decisions with every relevant organizational unit whose jurisdiction touches on the matters under consideration; the Secretary of Housing and Urban Development, for instance, is forbidden by the Housing and Community Development Act of 1974 to make community development grants "unless the application therefor has been submitted for review and comment to an areawide agency under procedures established by the President,"[58] while the State Department, according to one report, has developed clearance to such a high art that as many as twenty-seven signatures may be required on an instruction to an ambassador before it is sent.[59] Another method is to require studies and written reports on various "impacts" of proposed policies; environmental impact statements are now mandatory prerequisites for official action affecting the environment, inflation impact statements must accompany draft legislation, rules, and regulations proposed by executive branch agencies, and similar statements about the consequences of pending measures for the public's paperwork burdens, for the costs of doing business, and for family life have been proposed.[60] Still another method is to place separate organizations under a common command with authority to compel coordination.[61] All these devices are internal counterparts of external-group representation and are defended with the same arguments: fewer vital considerations are neglected, less opposition and evasion are engendered.

Opinions about the effectualness of these practices vary. But even if they accomplish all that is claimed for them, there is a cost in "red tape." They multiply the paper flow inside the system or the paperwork demands on the public or both. They make the government slow and ponderous, thus reducing the vigor of policy execution. They increase expenses. Sometimes unknowingly or unwillingly, but often deliberately, we pay these costs to get the asserted benefits even if the costs are certain and the benefits in doubt.

Keeping Government Public

Similarly, we try to do whatever is necessary to keep the government from turning into an instrumentality of private profit for those in its employ or those with private fortunes at their disposal.

The temptations facing the government work force are varied and enormous. They handle hundreds of billions of dollars in revenues, in expenditures (paychecks, retirement benefits, payments for supplies and services, rent, subsidies, tax refunds, etc.), and in vast quantities of removable property, from postage stamps and office equipment to vehicles and electronic gear. Without exceedingly tight controls, nobody would ever know if one government employee took a little here, another stole a little there, and a third pocketed a bit somewhere else. Public moneys would thus be diverted from their intended uses to the enrichment of dishonest public servants. Even if no individual defalcation were large, the collective effect could be massive.[62] And without controls, unfortunately, the scale of the average individual offense would doubtless be substantial.

Public officers and employees are also tempted by opportunities to sell their official discretion and information.[63] Historically, the letting of government contracts, the sale or gift of government land, and the disposition of government-owned resources were riddled with corruption of this kind as government agents were bribed to overlook wholesale perversions of the law. Indeed, some inspectors and law-enforcement officers and tax collectors in all fields have occasionally been induced to disregard violations, withhold reports to higher levels, or at least reduce charges against offenders. They have also been persuaded to certify that products of substandard quality meet legal specifications and that extravagant tax deductions are valid. They have been paid to leak confidential information enabling their corrupters to beat out competitors in the marketplace or in bidding for government contracts, or even allowing foreign governments to gain an advantage over our own.

They have also been tempted by the opportunities to extort payments.[64] Permits can be delayed, licenses held up, deliberations protracted, proceedings prolonged, unless rewards are offered. Inspectors can charge violations by the score if their requests for payoffs are rejected. At one time, government workers were fired if they did not contribute to the political party in power, and parties routinely attracted people to toil for them free by holding out the hope of eventual government employment as compensation.

We have attempted to suppress such practices. Many of them, such as bribery, have been declared crimes, but criminal penalties deter only if there is a good chance that the forbidden acts will be detected. Corrupt bargains, however, are difficult to detect. We have therefore gone beyond deterrence; we have tried, by elaborate procedural safeguards, to make the commission of these acts almost impossible. These tactics are executed through torrents of laws and regulations and cumbersome procedures; it is sometimes said the prevention costs more than the ailment. But our attitude toward public property is typified by the comments of a famous economist ordinarily inclined to reject costs that exceed benefits in dollar terms: "The Office of Management and Budget *should* spend $20 to prevent the theft of $1 of public funds."[65] Not only are public property and public discretion held to have a special moral status; they occupy a special political position because abusing them eats away at the foundations of representative government. So we are willing to put up with a lot to safeguard their integrity.

The controls on accounting and financial management therefore abound,[66] as do the statutes and regulations on personnel administration,[67] on government contracting and procurement,[68] on property management,[69] on data processing,[70] on privacy and freedom of information.[71] There are watchdogs who watch watchdogs watching watchdogs. The Treasury, the Office of Management and Budget, and the General Accounting Office stand guard over fiscal matters, along with departmental and bureau financial officers. The Civil Service Commission and departmental and bureau personnel administrators are the guardians of the personnel system. The General Services Administration maintains surveillance over purchasing and property, the Privacy Protection Commission over privacy and freedom of information laws. Though every agency has its own legal counsel, only the Department of Justice (with a few exceptions) represents the government in court.

Administrators of line agencies chafe at these restraints, the paperwork they inflict, the time and frustrations they add to the routine business of government. Chances are that most of the public knows little about them, though anyone who does business with the government doubtless learns quickly. Much of the often-satirized clumsiness, slowness, and complexity of government procedures is merely the consequence of all these precautions. Things would be simpler and faster if we were not resolved to block abuses that turn public goods to private profit.

A private redirection of government occurs also when rich people and organizations successfully use their wealth to determine who gets office or what the officeholders do. Such uses of wealth were not held illegal or immoral in the past; they were taken for granted. But the disparities in wealth in the society give to the rich an advantage in selecting leaders and controlling official behavior out of all proportion to their numbers. These inequalities conflict with the ideal that each individual should carry as nearly as possible the same political weight as every other individual. We have therefore taken steps to reduce them. That is why there are laws that limit contributions to political parties and candidates, set ceilings on political campaign expenditures, grant public funds to eligible parties for their nominating and electoral functions, and establish agencies to administer and police these laws.[72] It is also why we oblige lobbyists to register and to disclose their finances[73] and why there are a constitutional amendment and legislation forbidding denial of the right to vote for nonpayment of poll taxes or other taxes.[74]

Most of these requirements bring in their train a good deal of red tape for those to whom they apply. They mean people and organizations that used to act without reference to the government at all have to read statutes and regulations, prepare applications, file reports, keep records, appeal unfavorable decisions, and in other ways accommodate themselves to public officials and employees. Many constraints of this sort directly affect only a small percentage of the population. All together, however, they touch large numbers of us. In this way, high idealism precipitates the requirements and prohibitions, the twists and turns in the governmental maze, that contribute to the luxuriant growth of government red tape.

Taxation with Representation

One area in which a noble ideal has resulted in almost *universal* discontent with the voluminousness and complications of government requirements is taxation. Taxation without representation is odious to Americans in principle. Taxation with representation, however, may make for a greater profusion of elaborate and incomprehensible statutes and regulations than one would find in an autocratic system.

For everyone has a finger in the making of our tax policy. Not with perfect equality, of course; differences in influence and in concern are substantial. Directly or indirectly, however, most interests have some impact on tax decisions. In a society as diversified as ours, that means a lot of fingers.

Indeed, our society is so complex that even an absolute autocrat would have trouble keeping the tax system simple; the economic situations of taxpayers vary so much that only a sophisticated system would be likely to produce large public revenues without devastating large sectors of the economy. Furthermore, taxes are not only instruments for raising money; they are also employed for management of the economy. They can be lowered to encourage certain kinds of activity or to assist growth in certain regions, and raised for the opposite purpose. Increased at strategic times, they can, all other things remaining the same, combat inflationary tendencies; decreased, other things unchanged, they can spur the economy. When all these effects are factored into a tax system, it takes a great deal of legislative and administrative elaboration to make it work.

In a diversified and democratic polity, the system gets still more elaborate as each set of interests strives to shift as much of the tax burden from its own shoulders as it can. Battles may be fought over broad policy issues—sales versus income taxes, the degree of progressivity of income tax schedules, business versus personal income liabilities, payroll taxes versus other methods of financing. Equally important for the complexity of the tax system and the difficulties of complying with its requirements, however, are the large reductions in taxes that some groups enjoy because of relatively small changes in tax laws and regulations. Such provisions often go unnoticed by all who are not affected by them. If they are observed, the observers may agree to withhold opposition and publicity in return for support of their own special advantages. Obscure parts of long technical legislative bills and administrative regulations thus make their way routinely through the policymaking machinery. That is why proposals that begin as comprehensive tax reform usually end up as "Christmas-tree" law—law containing a gift for nearly everyone. Nobody would argue that the results are models of equity and rationality. Certainly, they are far from simple, brief, and symmetrical.[75] Everybody grumbles.

The shortcomings of taxation with representation were probably not fully anticipated by those who struggled for it. Had they been able to see what lay ahead, however, they probably would still have opted for it, shortcomings and all.

DIVERSITY, DISTRUST, AND DEMOCRACY

Americans' insistence on compassionate and representative government thus contributes to the enormous output of requirements and prohibitions and the elaborateness of procedures so characteristic of our political system. Compassion and representativeness are not the only values we pursue, of course; they do not account for the *total* volume of paper and *all* the procedural complexities. We also set great store by efficiency, expertness, vigorous leadership, freedom to do as we please and to be let alone, stability, strength, and other things. Exploring the multifarious effects of only two broad values, however, illustrates how the things we treasure and demand lead to the curtailments of freedom of action, the burdens and inconveniences, and the delays we decry. If these are the consequences of just two values, though they are sweeping ones, imagine the combined impact of all of them.

Were we a less differentiated society, the blizzard of official paper might be less severe and the labyrinths of official processes less tortuous. Had we more trust in one another and in our public officers and employees, we would not feel impelled to limit discretion by means of lengthy, minutely detailed directives and prescriptions or to subject public and private actions to check after check. If our polity were less democratic, imperfect though our democracy may be, the government would not respond as readily to the innumerable claims on it for protection and assistance. Diversity, distrust, and democracy thus cause the profusion of constraints and the unwieldiness of the procedures that afflict us. It is in this sense that we bring it on ourselves.

NOTES

1. Alvin W. Gouldner, "Red Tape as a Social Problem," in Robert K. Merton and others, eds., *Reader in Bureaucracy* (Free Press, 1952), p. 411.

2. 21 U.S.C. (1970).

3. 15 U.S.C. §§52–56, 64, 68a–f, 69a–i, 70a–g (1970); 18 U.S.C. §709 (1970).

4. 15 U.S.C. chs. 26, 30, 36.

5. For safety regulation of civil aeronautics, see 49 U.S.C. ch. 20, subch. VI (1970); for ship and boat safety, see 46 U.S.C. ch. 15 (1970), ch. 33 (Supp. IV, 1974); for motor vehicle and highway safety, see 15 U.S.C. ch. 38, and 23 U.S.C. ch. 4 (1970); for railroad safety, see 45 U.S.C. ch. 13 (1970). These statutes and the supplementary administrative regulations issued under their provisions do not comprehend all relevant safety requirements and precautions, but they illustrate this kind of compassionate concern of the federal government.

6. For a survey of the types of adjudicatory actions performed by administrative agencies, see Dalmas H. Nelson, *Administrative Agencies of the U.S.A.* (Wayne State University Press, 1964).

7. 29 U.S.C. chs. 4C, 7–9, 14, 15 (1970), chs. 17–18 (Supp. IV, 1974); 42 U.S.C. ch. 21, subch. VI (1970 and Supp. IV, 1974).

8. For example, the Department of Health, Education, and Welfare issued regulations forbidding colleges and universities to discriminate against women in admissions, financial aid, vocational and academic counseling, and athletics; Nancy Hicks, *New York Times*, June 4, July 19, 1975. Some college administrators protested the growing federal involvement in higher education; Judith Cummings, ibid., November 12 and 16, 1975.

9. 11 U.S.C. chs. 6, 8 (1970).

10. 42 U.S.C. §§3604, 3613 (1970).

11. 49 U.S.C. §§3(1), (2), (3); 20(11), (12); 908; and ch. 4.

12. By statute, public facilities and public education are to be desegregated; 42 U.S.C. §§2000b, 2000c(6) (1970). Also, no program or activity receiving federal financial assistance may discriminate on the ground of race, color, or national origin; 42 U.S.C. §2000d. Federal courts have also held that the Constitution requires correction of gross numerical inequalities in electoral districts at all levels of government; Robert G. Dixon, Jr., *Democratic Representation* (Oxford University Press, 1968).

13. 12 U.S.C. §§371a, b (1970). These provisions apply only to banks that are members of the Federal Reserve System.

14. 15 U.S.C. ch. 2A. See also chs. 2B-1, 2D.

15. 15 U.S.C. ch. 41; 12 U.S.C. ch. 27 (Supp. IV, 1974).

16. 45 C.F.R. pt. 46 (1976).

17. 7 U.S.C. ch. 54 (1970).

18. See, for example, Marle Fainsod, Lincoln Gordon, and Joseph C. Palamountain, Jr., *Government and the American Economy*, 3d ed. (Norton, 1959), pts. 3–5; Alfred E. Kahn, *The Economics of Regulation* (Wiley, 1970), vol. 2, chap. 5.

19. In addition to the types of controls described in the two books cited in n. 18, there is a wide range of controls on financial committees; see President's Commission on Financial Structure and Regulation, *Report* (GPO, 1972).

20. See, for example, consumer protections in 15 U.S.C. ch. 47. Also, the safety regulations under the laws identified in n. 5, above, include standards and requirements for operators of certain vehicles in interstate commerce and certain repair and training services; see, for example, 14 C.F.R. ch. 1, subchs. D, G, H (1977). On the other hand, see Kahn, *Economics of Regulation*, pp. 21–25, for an argument that quality of service is often ignored.

21. In addition to the safety provisions described in n. 5, above, see Occupational Safety and Health Act, 29 U.S.C. ch. 15 (1970).

22. 42 U.S.C. §§2000e–2000e(17) (1970); 29 U.S.C. ch. 14 (1970).

23. Special legislation governing the rights and duties of seamen go all the way back to the first Congress; 1 Stat. 131. The legislation on the subject has now grown to substantial proportions; 46 U.S.C. ch. 18 (1970).

24. Wilfred E. Binkley and Malcolm C. Moos, *A Grammar of American Politics* (Knopf, 1949), p. 681. The special status of Indians apparently came about because they were considered "conquered nations to whom the United States owed protection under its signed treaties": Sar A. Levitan and William B. Johnston, *Indian Giving* (Johns Hopkins University Press, 1975), p. 5. For this and other reasons, the government's solicitude seemed to Indians more oppressive than protective. Nevertheless, the Indians are among the first groups for whom a special agency was established and special services maintained; see Alan L. Sorkin, *American Indians and Federal Aid* (Brookings Institution, 1971).

25. President's Commission on Veterans' Pensions, *Staff Report No. 1: The Historical Development of Veterans' Benefits in the United States*, prepared for the House Committee on Veterans' Affairs, 84:2 (GPO, 1956).

26. Gilbert Y. Steiner, *Social Insecurity* (Rand McNally, 1966), *The State of Welfare* (Brookings Institution, 1971), and *The Children's Cause* (Brookings Institution, 1976), chap. 1.

27. Disaster Relief Act of 1970, 84 Stat. 1744. See also "Disaster Assistance," *1975/76 United States Government Manual*, p. 813.

28. William Haber and Merrill G. Murray, *Unemployment Insurance in the American Economy* (Richard D. Irwin, 1966), chaps. 2, 6, 7.

29. *1969 Listing of Operating Federal Assistance Programs Compiled During the Roth Study*, H. Doc. 91-177, 91:1 (GPO, 1969), describes 1,315 aid programs.

30. Such aid programs serve many purposes besides providing support; see V. O. Key, *The Administration of Federal Grants to the States* (Public Administration Service, 1937), pp. 1–26; Committee on Federal Grants-in-Aid, Council of State Governments, *Federal Grants-in-Aid* (CSG, 1949), pp. 42–43; Walter W. Heller and Joseph A. Pechman, "Questions and Answers on Revenue Sharing," in *Revenue Sharing and Its Alternatives: What Future for Fiscal Federalism?* Hearings before the Subcommittee on Fiscal Policy of the Joint Economic Committee, 90:1 (GPO, 1967), pp. 111–117 (Brookings Reprint 135). Beyond question, however, helping state and local governments meet their obligations to their citizens and creditors is one of the major objectives.

31. 20 C.F.R. pt. 404.342 (1976).

32. 20 C.F.R. pt. 404.345.

33. 20 C.F.R. pt. 404.344.

34. 20 C.F.R. pts. 404.347, 404.348.

35. 20 C.F.R. pt. 404.343(a)(2).

36. 20 C.F.R. pt. 404.349.

37. 20 C.F.R. pt. 404.1501(a)(i).

38. 20 C.F.R. pt. 404, subpt. P, appendix.

39. 42 U.S.C. §416(i)(1)(B) (1970).

40. Ibid., table 2, n. 1.

41. The agencies set up for this purpose include the Federal Labor Relations Council, the Federal Mediation and Conciliation Service, the Federal Service Impasses Panel, the National Labor Relations Board, the National Mediation Board, and of course the Department of Labor; *1975/76 United States Government Manual*, p. 817.

42. The Economic Policy Council, the Council on International Economic Policy, the President's Economic Policy Board, the United States International Trade Commission, the Council on Wage and Price Stability, the Council of Economic Advisers, the Federal Reserve System, elements of the Departments of the Treasury and Commerce, and others; ibid., p. 814.

43. For illustrations, see the agencies listed in ibid. under "Agriculture and Agricultural Programs" (p. 811), "Conservation" (p. 812), "Electric Power" (p. 814), "Energy" (pp. 814–815), "Environmental Protection" (p. 815), "Fish and Fisheries" (p. 815), "Flood Control" (p. 815), "Forest and Forest Products" (p. 816), "Imports and Exports" (p. 817), "Land" (p. 817), "Mining" (p. 819), "Nuclear Energy" (p. 819), "Oceans" (p. 819), "Oil" (p. 819), "Pollution" (p. 820), "Recreation" (p. 820), "Tariffs" (p. 821), "Textiles" (p. 822), "Tobacco and Tobacco Products" (p. 822), "Trade" (p. 822), "Water and Waterways" (pp. 822–823), and "Wildlife" (p. 823).

44. This includes not only the Departments of Defense and State, but all the international defense organizations to which the United States belongs, the intelligence-gathering agencies, the Arms Control and Disarmament Agency, and the emergency preparedness programs throughout the government; ibid., "Defense, National," p. 813, and "Emergency Preparedness," p. 814. See also n. 45, below.

45. To get an idea of the varieties of programs of this kind, see *The Foreign Assistance Program: Annual Report* [of the President] *to the Congress for Fiscal Year 1971.*

46. In addition to unilateral mediation efforts by the Secretary of State and other representatives of the President, the United States belongs to more than two dozen multilateral international organizations of a nonmilitary character; *1975/76 United States Government Manual*, pp. 653–664.

47. 60 Stat. 237; now incorporated, as amended, in 5 U.S.C. ch. 5, subch. II, and ch. 7 (1970 and Supp. IV, 1974).

48. 5 U.S.C. §551 (1970 and Supp. IV, 1974).

49. 5 U.S.C. §552 (1970 and Supp. IV, 1974).

50. 5 U.S.C. §553 (1970 and Supp. IV, 1974).

51. 5 U.S.C. §554 (1970).

52. 5 U.S.C. §556 (1970).

53. 5 U.S.C. §701–06 (1970).

54. 5 U.S.C. chs. 33, 35, 71–77 (1970); 5 C.F.R. (1977).

55. *Elrod v. Burns*, 452 U.S. 909 (1976).

56. Avery Leiserson, "Interest Groups in Administration," in Fritz Morstein Marx, ed., *Elements of Public Administration* (Prentice-Hall, 1946).

57. Joseph A. Kershaw, *Government against Poverty* (Brookings Institution 1970), pp. 45–47; and Herbert Kaufman, "Administrative Decentralization and Political Power," *Public Administration Review*, vol. 29 (January–February 1969), pp. 3–15. For the provisions for citizen participation in community development grant applications, see 42 U.S.C. §5304(a)(6) (Supp. IV, 1974). See also the steps taken by the Secretary of Health, Education, and Welfare, to increase the public's role in the formulation of departmental regulations; Eric Wentworth, *Washington Post*, July 25, 1976.

58. 42 U.S.C. §5304(c) (Supp. IV, 1974).

59. Terence Smith, "Foreign Policy: Ebbing of Power at the State Department," *New York Times*, January 17, 1971; cited in John H. Esterline and Robert B. Black, *Inside Foreign Policy* (Mayfield Publishing, 1975), p. 60, footnote.

60. The guidelines for environmental impact statements are in 40 C.F.R. pt. 1500 (1976). Inflation impact statements are mandated in Executive Order 11821 (November 27, 1974), as extended by Executive Order 11949 (December 31, 1976). The proposal for paperwork impact findings is in *The Federal Paperwork Burden*, S. Rept. 93–125, 93:1 (1973), pp. 69–71. The case for family impact statements is advanced in Sheila B. Kamerman, *Developing a Family Impact Statement*, An Occasional Paper from the Foundation for Child Development (New York: FCD, May 1976). A plan for economic impact statements describing the costs that would be imposed on business by proposed administrative

regulations reportedly provoked controversy among top government officials; David Burnham, *New York Times*, May 9, 1977.

61. Hierarchy is probably the oldest axiom of organization; see Exodus 19:25. It is usually justified on grounds of coordination; for example, see Leonard D. White, *Introduction to the Study of Public Administration*, 4th ed. (Macmillan, 1955), pp. 38–39; and Herbert A. Simon, Donald W. Smithburg, and Victor A. Thompson, *Public Administration* (Knopf, 1950), pp. 130–133. When reorganizers speak of "streamlining" administration, they usually mean grouping agencies in larger collectivities under a single command, the way the armed services, once separate from each other, were gathered under the Department of Defense.

62. Some indication of possible scale is provided by the experience of retail stores. Despite $2 billion spent annually for security, stores lost almost $6 billion to thieves, and experts estimated that three-quarters of all thefts were committed by employees; *U.S. News & World Report* (June 16, 1975), p. 28. The National Retail Merchants Association offered a somewhat lower estimate, but one still in excess of a billion dollars a year taken by employees; *Newsweek* (November 24, 1975), pp. 103, 107.

63. Not a year goes by without at least a few such cases coming to light. In 1974, for example, the Supreme Court upheld the conviction of a former immigration officer for accepting bribes (and for other crimes) while in office (Warren Weaver, Jr., *New York Times*, February 26); a congressman pleaded guilty to charges of accepting fees while in office to represent a company in dealings with federal agencies from which it was seeking favorable decisions (Arnold H. Lubasch, *NYT*, October 2); and a former import specialist with the Customs Bureau went to prison after pleading guilty to accepting gifts from art galleries (*NYT*, October 5). In 1975, a high-ranking officer of the Small Business Administration was arrested for accepting bribes and other offenses (*NYT*, April 12); seven employees of the Immigration and Naturalization Service were convicted of a series of crimes, including encouraging and assisting illegal entry into the country and drug smuggling (*NYT*, October 5, 1974, and M. A. Farber, *NYT*, April 27, 1975); another INS officer pleaded guilty to taking bribes to give permanent status to aliens working as waiters in restaurants, including three owned by the defendant (Donald Janson, *NYT*, July 1; and *NYT*, November 27); a retired collection officer of the Internal Revenue Service was indicted for soliciting and receiving bribes for favors to taxpayers (Max H. Siegel, *NYT*, October 25); a Federal Energy Administration official was arrested for requesting a bribe from a coal brokerage company to reverse a decision (*NYT*, November 7); and a financial aid officer in the Department of Health, Education, and Welfare resigned under congressional investigation for alleged acceptance of bribes to approve student loans to a chain of vocational education schools accused of cheating both students and the federal government of student aid funds (Nancy Hicks, *NYT*, November 20). In 1976, an assistant secretary of the Department of Housing and Urban Development resigned at the request of the President while under investigation for exploring future job possibilities with firms doing business with his department (Philip Shabecoff, *NYT*, January 29); the President withdrew his nominee for assistant secretary of the Air Force when it was disclosed that the nominee had been promised a job by a major defense contractor after the end of his government service (*NYT*, March 26); contract officers in the Department of Defense were found to have taken favors from contractors ("U.S. Government Employees and Officials, Ethics in Office," *New York Times Index*, entry for July 5); and Defense Department meat inspectors admitted to a congressional committee that they took bribes from meat suppliers to misgrade meat sold to the military (Morton Mintz, *Washington Post*, May 7, and Spencer Rich, *Washington Post*, May 11). The list, unfortunately, is lengthy.

64. For example, a former agent of the Alcohol, Tobacco, and Firearms Bureau was indicted for extortion (*New York Times*, June 15, 1974), and a quality-assurance specialist of the General Services Administration was convicted of exacting kickbacks for contracts (ibid., January 8, 1976).

65. Arthur M. Okun, *Equality and Efficiency: The Big Tradeoff* (Brookings Institution, 1975), p. 60.

66. See, for example, 31 U.S.C. chs. 1A, 2, 10, 18 (1970); 4 C.F.R. (1977); and the entries under "Accounts and Accounting" in the General Index, U.S.C.S. (Lawyer's Ed., 1973). There are also many internal documents governing financial management, such as the Federal Management Circulars of the Office of Management and Budget; see 34 C.F.R. ch. 1 (1976). Among the executive departments and agencies of the federal government (not including government corporations and certain quasi-governmental bodies), 286 accounting systems subject to approval by the Comptroller General are currently in use; *[Sixth] Report by the Comptroller General of the United States on the Status, Progress, and Problems in Federal Agency Accounting during Fiscal Year 1975*, pp. 1–5.

67. 5 U.S.C. pts. II, III (1970); 5 C.F.R. pts. 1–1300, 1501 (1977). In addition to nearly 300 pages of legislation and over 400 pages of rules and regulations applicable to the whole government, each agency has its own personnel manual.

68. 41 U.S.C. (1970); 41 C.F.R. subtitles A, B (1976).

69. 40 U.S.C. chs. 3, 4, 6, 10, 11, 12, 14, 15, 16 (1970); 41 C.F.R. subtitle C (1976).

70. 40 U.S.C. §759; 34 C.F.R. pt. 281 (1976); 41 C.F.R. pt. 101–132.

71. 88 Stat. 1561, 1896; 1 C.F.R. pts. 430, 431 (1977). For regulations issued by individual agencies under these statutes, see C.F.R. Index (1977), "Information Availability" and "Privacy Act." Administration of privacy requirements, now a responsibility of the Privacy Protection Commission, was originally assigned to the Office of Management and Budget, which issued a 111-page set of guidelines to instruct agencies on how to comply; Linda Charlton, *New York Times,* July 8, 1975.

72. For a full collection of all the relevant statutory provisions, see *Federal Election Campaign Laws,* compiled by the Federal Election Commission, 1976. See also 2 U.S.C. ch. 8 (1970); C.F.R. Index (1976), "Political Activity" and "Political Candidates"; and 41 Fed. Reg. 35932–76 (August 25, 1976).

73. 2 U.S.C. ch. 8A.

74. Twenty-Fourth Amendment. See also 42 U.S.C. §1973h (1970) for enforcing legislation.

75. See, for instance, the Tax Reform Act of 1976, 90 Stat. 1520, which runs for more than 400 pages. The Internal Revenue Code as a whole, Title 26 of the U.S.C. (1970), goes on for more than 1,000 double-columned pages. The administrative regulations governing internal revenue, Title 26 of the C.F.R. (1976), occupy fourteen volumes and thousands of pages.

PART NINE

THE JUDICIARY

The Constitution is central to American political culture. It authorizes, organizes, and constrains the exercise of governmental power. It also serves as a guide to the formulation and implementation of public policy. In some contexts, the Constitution provides moral and ethical guidance as well. A governmental practice that much of the public considers unfair may be attacked as a violation of due process, equal protection, or some other constitutional right.

Ever since Tocqueville's time, political analysts have noted an American tendency to "constitutionalize" political discourse, that is to discuss politics and policy in terms of the Constitution. Examples include affirmative action, drug testing, and regulation of abortion. Misconduct in office by judges or presidents is discussed in terms of the meaning of "high crimes and misdemeanors" in the Constitution's impeachment clause.

American constitutionalism bestows great power on the judiciary, especially the Supreme Court. As far back as its decision in *Marbury v. Madison* (1803), the Court established its authority to review the constitutionality of acts of Congress and, therefore, to void acts that are deemed "unconstitutional." As the Court explained in the portion of *Marbury* included in this section, "it is emphatically the province and duty of the judicial department to say what the law is" and "an act of the legislature, repugnant to the Constitution, is void." The power to rule that laws, governmental practices, administrative regulations, treaties, and other official acts do or don't conform to the Constitution is called judicial review. It enables the judiciary continually to define the Constitution and presumably to protect its integrity.

As the nation's highest court, the Supreme Court gives specific meaning to the Constitution's broad clauses and thereby adapts it to an ever changing society. To be sure, the justices will typically look to the Framers' intent and wisdom, but some cases involve phenomena that no one living in the eighteenth century could possibly have foreseen or considered.

Because Americans look to the Constitution for political guidance and the Supreme Court is the definitive interpreter of what government may do constitutionally, the Court is extraordinarily influential. However, institutionally the judiciary is in tension with the basic concept of representative government because justices and judges are appointed, rather than elected, and can be removed only through impeachment. For the Framers, the antimajoritarian implications of the judiciary were both a virtue and a concern. It could protect minorities' property and civil liberties against tyrannical majorities. But it could also frustrate governmental responsiveness to the public. As with so much of the of the constitutional design, the Framers sought balance by placing a number of checks on the judicial branch.

The Supreme Court's size, budget, and much of its jurisdiction are established by legislation, not by the Constitution itself. The Court heads the federal judiciary, but all other federal courts are established by law and subject to reorganization by statute. For the most part, the Supreme Court and judiciary as a whole must rely on the executive branch to enforce their decisions. As Alexander Hamilton argued in the *Federalist 78*, which is reprinted in this section, "The judiciary . . . has no influence over either the sword or the purse; no direction either of the strength or of the wealth of the society, and can take no active resolution whatever. It may truly be said to have neither FORCE nor WILL but merely judgment."

It follows that the judiciary's power will be most secure when its judgment is considered correct and legitimate by political officials and the public or significant groups within it. This has important consequences for the Supreme Court as a political institution. First, the Court is often acutely aware of potential opposition to its decisions. For example, in *Roe v. Wade* (1973), another case included in this section, the Court began by acknowledging its "awareness of the sensitive and emotional nature of the abortion controversy, of the vigorous opposing views, even among physicians, and of the deep and seemingly absolute convictions that the subject inspires." Second, even when deciding constitutional matters for the first time, the Court will often present its judgment as compelled by the Framers' intent, the text's wording, and past interpretations. Thus, in *Roe*, the Court claimed it was resolving "the issue by constitutional measurement, free of emotion and of predilection." In *Marbury*, Chief Justice John Marshall affirmed the power of judicial review, which is not mentioned in the Constitution as if that power had been part of the constitutional design. Finally, the Court may assert that new knowledge requires an updating of constitutional interpretation. In *Brown v. Board of Education* (1954), the Court noted that "whatever may have been the extent of psychological knowledge" when laws requiring racial segregation were held constitutional in the 1890s, their interference with the Fourteenth Amendment's guarantee of equal protection of the laws "is amply supported by modern authority."

The selections in this section highlight key features of the Supreme Court as a governmental institution and its roles in the political system. We begin with Edward S. Corwin's "The 'Higher Law' Background of American Constitutional Law" (1928). Corwin relies on the history of Western jurisprudence to explain why Americans often define political and policy questions in constitutional terms. He concludes that the supremacy of the Constitution in American politics cannot be attributed solely to that document's origins and ratification. Rather, he suggests, the Constitution's special place in American political life is due to its content, its "embodiment of an essential and unchanging justice." It is to these elemental principles that generation after generation of American public officials are accountable.

Federalist 78 is a remarkable essay. It anticipated the development of judicial review by more than a decade. It also foresaw the problems inherent in providing this power to unelected officials holding what are essentially lifetime appointments. Hamilton rationalized the nondemocratic character of the judiciary as follows: "Whoever attentively considers the different departments of power must perceive that, in a government in which they are separated from each other, the judiciary, will always be the least dangerous to the political rights of the Constitution; because it will be least in capacity to annoy or injure them."

Walter Murphy, in "Marshalling the Court" (1964), adds a major dimension by explaining how justices are policymakers who seek to promote their policy preferences rationally. Murphy analyzes the strategies a policy-oriented judge might use "to influence his colleagues with as little expenditure of time and energy as possible" to gain their support for a policy position. Drawing broadly on Supreme Court history, Murphy considers the strengths and weaknesses of a variety of tactics available to such a judge. In the process, he describes much of the politicking that goes on among the justices.

Martin Shapiro's "The Presidency and the Federal Courts" (1981) focuses on the judiciary's antimajoritarian qualities. He notes that whereas the public has come to look to the president for leadership and coordination of much governmental activity, "the power of the nonelected branch to interfere in our individual lives and set our national priorities" may "reduce the president's options in domestic policy to the vanishing point." Moreover, judicial involvement in public policy "plays a substantial role in the fragmentation of political authority." Shapiro reviews the development of a more activist federal judiciary and suggests that "the president's best defense is to seize the initiative in proclaiming values, but to avoid the rhetoric of rights that invites both judicial intervention and policy rigidity."

The section is completed by abridged versions of four Supreme Court decisions. *Marbury* is essential to understanding the logic of judicial review. *Brown* illustrates Corwin's premise that there is a "higher law" background of constitutional interpretation and also shows how the Court may update the Constitution in the face of political and social change. *Roe* remains controversial. To its supporters, *Roe* is like *Brown* in that it declares a right that is rooted in fundamental fairness. For them, a public policy that requires a pregnant woman involuntarily to carry her fetus to term is a deep invasion of personal liberty. Opponents criticize *Roe* as an exercise of blatant judicial excess with literally murderous consequences.

The final case, *Korematsu v. U.S.* (1944), forces one to consider the limits of constitutional protection and judicial power. It deals with the relocation of citizens and aliens of Japanese descent to internment camps during World War II. The Supreme Court's majority opinion expresses great deference to the president's executive orders and the military's assertions that the actions were necessary for national security. The dissenting justices viewed the exclusion and relocation as without constitutional justification. Justice Robert Jackson's dissent squarely laments the courts' weakness: "The existence of a military power resting on force, so vagrant, so centralized, so necessarily heedless of the individual, is an inherent threat to liberty. But I would not lead people to rely on this Court for a review that seems to me wholly delusive. . . . If the people ever let command of the war power fall into irresponsible and unscrupulous hands, the courts wield no power equal to its restraint."

35

EDWARD S. CORWIN

THE "HIGHER LAW" BACKGROUND
OF AMERICAN CONSTITUTIONAL LAW

Why do Americans revere the Constitution? Edward S. Corwin (1878–1963), a Princeton University professor, argued that ". . . the legality of the Constitution, its supremacy, and its claim to be worshipped, alike find common standing ground on the belief in a law superior to the will of human governors." This superior, or higher, law embodies ". . . certain principles of right and justice which are entitled to prevail of their own intrinsic excellence. . . . They are eternal and immutable." For all its limitations, the Constitution is founded on such a concept of "transcendental justice." A key consequence is that higher law is not the product of will or power, but of "discovery and declaration"—much as American courts have historically developed constitutional law. "The 'Higher Law' Background of American Constitutional Law" was originally published in the 1928–1929 Harvard Law Review

Theory is the most important part of the dogma of the law, as the architect is the most important man who takes part in the building of a house.

Collected Legal Papers, OLIVER WENDELL HOLMES

The Reformation superseded an infallible Pope with an infallible Bible; the American Revolution replaced the sway of a king with that of a document. That such would be the outcome was not unforeseen from the first. In the same number of *Common Sense* which contained his electrifying proposal that America should declare her independence from Great Britain, [Thomas] Paine urged also a "Continental Conference," whose task he described as follows:

The conferring members being met, let their business be to frame a Continental Charter, or Charter of the United Colonies; (answering to what is called the Magna Charta of England) fixing the number and manner of choosing members of congress and members of assembly . . . and drawing the line of business and jurisdiction between them: (always remembering, that our strength is continental, not provincial) securing freedom and property to all men . . . with such other matter as it is necessary for a charter to contain. . . . But where, say some, is the King of America? Yet that we may not appear to be defective even in earthly honors, let a day be solemnly set apart for proclaiming the charter; let it be brought forth placed in the divine law, the word of God; let a crown be placed thereon, by which the world may know, that so far as we approve of monarchy, that in America the law is King.[1]

This suggestion, which was to eventuate more than a decade later in the Philadelphia Convention, is not less interesting for its retrospection than it is for its prophecy.

In the words of the younger Adams, "the Constitution itself had been extorted from the grinding necessity of a reluctant nation"[2]; yet hardly had it gone into operation than hostile criticism of its provisions not merely ceased but gave place to "an undiscriminating and almost blind worship of its principles"[3]—a worship which continued essentially unchallenged till the other day. Other creeds have waxed and waned, but "worship of the Constitution" has proceeded unabated.[4] It is true that the Abolitionists were accustomed to stigmatize the Constitution as "an agreement with Hell," but their shrill heresy only stirred the mass of Americans to renewed assertion of the national faith. Even Secession posed as loyalty to the *principles* of the Constitution and a protest against their violation, and in form at least the constitution of the Southern Confederacy was, with a few minor departures, a studied reproduction of the instrument of 1787. For by far the greater reach of its history, Bagehot's appraisal of the British monarchy is directly applicable to the Constitution: "The English Monarchy strengthens our government with the strength of religion."[5]

The fact that its adoption was followed by a wave of prosperity no doubt accounts for the initial launching of the Constitution upon the affections of the American people. Travelling through various parts of the United States at this time, Richard Bland Lee found "fields a few years ago waste and uncultivated filled with inhabitants and covered with harvests, new habitations reared, contentment in every face, plenty on every board. . . ." "To produce this effect," he continued, "was the intention of the Constitution, and it has succeeded." Indeed it is possible that rather too much praise was lavished upon the Constitution on this score: "It has been usual with declamatory gentlemen," complained the astringent Maclay, "in their praises of the present government, by way of contrast, to paint the state of the country under the old (Continental) congress, as if neither wood grew nor water ran in America before the happy adoption of the new Constitution"; and a few years later, when the European turmoil at once assisted, and by contrast advertised, our own blissful state, Josiah Quincy voiced a fear that "we have grown giddy with good fortune, attributing the greatness of our prosperity to our own wisdom, rather than to a course of events, and a guidance over which we had no influence."[6]

But while the belief that it drew prosperity in its wake may explain the beginning of the worship of the Constitution, it leaves a deeper question unanswered. It affords no explanation why this worship came to ascribe to the Constitution the precise virtues it did as an efficient cause of prosperity. To answer this question we must first of all project the Constitution against a background of doctrinal tradition which, widespread as European culture, was at the time of the founding of the English colonies especially strong in the mother country, though by the irony of history it had become a century and a half later the chief source of division between mother country and colonies.

It is customary nowadays to ascribe the *legality* as well as the *supremacy* of the Constitution—the one is, in truth, but the obverse of the other—exclusively to the fact that, in its own phraseology, it was "ordained" by "the people of the United States." Two ideas are thus brought into play. One is the so-called "positive" conception of law as a general expression merely for the particular commands of a human lawgiver, as a series of acts of human will[7]; the other is that the highest possible source of such commands, because the highest possible embodiment of human will, is "the people." The same two ideas occur in conjunction in the oft-quoted text of Justinian's *Institutes:* "Whatever has pleased the prince has the force of law, since the Roman people by the *lex regia* enacted concerning his *imperium,* have yielded up to him all their power and authority."[8] The sole difference between the Constitution of the United States and the imperial legislation justified in this famous text is that the former is assumed to have proceeded immediately from the people, while the latter proceeded from a like source only mediately.

The attribution of supremacy to the Constitution on the ground solely of its rootage in popular will represents, however, a comparatively late outgrowth of American constitutional theory. Earlier the supremacy accorded to constitutions was ascribed less to their putative source than to their supposed content, to their embodiment of an essential and unchanging justice. The theory of law thus invoked stands in direct contrast to the one just reviewed. *There are,* it is predicated, *certain principles of right and justice which are entitled to prevail of their own intrinsic excellence, altogether regardless of the attitude of those who wield the physical resources of the community. Such principles were made by no human hands; indeed, if they did not antedate deity itself, they still so express its nature as to bind and control it. They are external to all Will as such and interpenetrate all Reason as such. They are eternal and immutable. In relation to such principles, human laws are, when entitled to obedience save as to matters indifferent, merely a record or transcript, and their enactment and act not of will or power but one of discovery and declaration.*[9] The Ninth Amendment of the Constitution of the United States, in stipulating that "the enumeration of certain rights in this Constitution shall not prejudice other rights not so enumerated," illustrates this theory perfectly except that the principles of transcendental justice have been here translated into terms of personal and private rights. The relation of such rights, nevertheless, to governmental power is the same as that of the principles from which they spring and which they reflect. They owe nothing to their recognition in the Constitution — such recognition was necessary if the Constitution was to be regarded as complete.

Thus the *legality* of the Constitution, its *supremacy,* and its claim to be worshipped, alike find common standing ground on the belief in a law superior to the will of human governors. Certain questions arise: Whence came this idea of a "higher law?" How has it been enabled to survive, and in what transformations? What special forms of it are of particular interest for the history of American constitutional law and theory? By what agencies and as a result of what causes was it brought to America and wrought into the American system of government? . . .

NOTES

1. Paine, *Political Writings* (1837) 45–46.
2. Adams, *Jubilee Discourse on the Constitution* (1839) 55.
3. Woodrow Wilson, *Congressional Government* (13th ed. 1898) 4.
4. On the whole subject, see 1 Von Holst, *Constitutional History* (1877) c. 2; Schechter, *Early History of the Tradition of the Constitution* (1915) 9 *American Political Science Review* 707 *et seq.*

5. Bagehot, *English Constitution* (2d ed., 1952) 39. "The monarchy by its religious sanction now confirms all our political order. . . . It gives . . . a vast strength to the entire constitution, by enlisting on its behalf the credulous obedience of enormous masses." Ibid. 43–44.

6. Schechter, supra note 4, at 720–721.

7. Bentham, as quoted in Holland, *Elements of Jurisprudence* (12th ed. 1916) 14. For further definitions of "positive law," see ibid. 22–23; Willoughby, *Fundamental Concepts of Public Law* (1924) c. 10.

8. *Institutes* 1, 2, 6: "Quod principi placuit, legis habet vigorem, cum lege regia quae de ejus imperio lata est, populus ei et in eum, omne imperium suum et potestatem concessit." The source is Ulpian, *Dig.* I, 4, 1. The Romans always regarded the people as the source of the legislative power. "Lex est, quod populus Romanus senatorie magistratu interrogante, veluti Consule, constituebat." *Institutes* 1, 2, 4. During the Middle Ages the question was much debated whether the *lex regia* effected an absolute alienation (*translatio*) of the legislative power to the Emperor, or was a revocable delegation (*cessio*). The champions of popular sovereignty at the end of this period, like Marsiglio of Padua in his *Defensor Pacis*, took the latter view. See Gierke, *Political Theories of the Middle Ages* (Maitland's tr. 1922) 150, notes 158, 159.

9. For definitions of law incorporating this point of view, see Holland, op. cit. supra note 7, at 19–20, 32–36. Cf. 1 Blackstone, *Commentaries*, Intro.

36

ALEXANDER HAMILTON

FEDERALIST 78

In Federalist 78, Alexander Hamilton explains the benefits of the Constitution's provisions for the judiciary. He notes that the judiciary will be the "least dangerous" branch because it has "neither FORCE nor WILL but merely judgment." Hamilton observes that the constitutional scheme implies that the courts will have the power of judicial review.

We proceed now to an examination of the judiciary department of the proposed government.

In unfolding the defects of the existing Confederation, the utility and necessity of a federal judicature have been clearly pointed out. It is the less necessary to recapitulate the considerations there urged as the propriety of the institution in the abstract is not disputed; the only questions which have been raised being relative to the manner of constituting it, and to its extent. To these points, therefore, our observation shall be confined.

The manner of constituting it seems to embrace these several objects: 1st. The mode of appointing the judges. 2nd. The tenure by which they are to hold their places. 3rd. The partition of the judiciary authority between different courts and their relations to each other.

First. As to the mode of appointing the judges: this is the same with that of appointing the officers of the Union in general and has been so fully discussed in the two last numbers that nothing can be said here which would not be useless repetition.

Second. As to the tenure by which the judges are to hold their places: this chiefly concerns their duration in office, the provisions for their support, the precautions for their responsibility.

According to the plan of the convention, all judges who may be appointed by the United States are to hold their offices *during good behavior;* which is conformable to the most approved of the State constitutions, and among the rest, to that of this State. Its propriety having been drawn into question by the adversaries of that plan is no light symptom of the rage for objection which disorders their imaginations and judgments. The standard of good behavior for the continuance in office of the judicial magistracy is certainly one of the most valuable of the modern improvements in the practice of government. In a monarchy it is an excellent barrier to the despotism of the prince; in a republic it is a no less excellent barrier to the encroachments and oppressions of the representative body. And it is the best expedient which can be devised in any government to secure a steady, upright, and impartial administration of the laws.

Whoever attentively considers the different departments of power must perceive that, in a government in which they are separated from each other, the judiciary, from the nature of its functions, will always be the least dangerous to the political rights of the Constitution; because it will be least in a capacity to annoy or injure them. The executive not only dispenses the honors but holds the sword of the community. The legislature not only commands the purse but prescribes the rules by which the duties and rights of every citizen are to be regulated. The judiciary, on the contrary, has no influence over either the sword or the purse; no direction either of the strength or of the wealth of the society, and can take no active resolution whatever. It may truly be said to have neither FORCE nor WILL but merely judgment; and must ultimately depend upon the aid of the executive arm even for the efficacy of its judgments.

This simple view of the matter suggests several important consequences. It proves incontestably that the judiciary is beyond comparison the weakest of the three departments of power;[1] that it can never attack with success either of the other two; and that all possible care is requisite to enable it to defend itself against their attacks. It equally proves that though individual oppression may now and then proceed from the courts of justice, the general liberty of the people can never be endangered from that quarter; I mean so long as the judiciary remains truly distinct from both the legislature and the executive. For I agree that "there is no liberty if the power of judging be not separated from the legislative and executive powers."[2] And it proves, in the last place, that as liberty can have nothing to fear from the judiciary alone, but would have everything to fear from its union with either of the other departments; that as all the effects of such a union must ensue from a dependence of the former on the latter, notwithstanding a nominal and apparent separation; that as, from the natural feebleness of the judiciary, it is in continual jeopardy of being overpowered, awed, or influenced by its co-ordinate branches; and that as nothing can contribute so much to its firmness and independence as permanency in office, this quality may therefore be justly regarded as an indispensable ingredient in its constitution, and, in a great measure, as the citadel of the public justice and the public security.

The complete independence of the courts of justice is peculiarly essential in a limited Constitution. By a limited Constitution, I understand one which contains certain specified exceptions to the legislative authority; such, for instance, as that it shall pass no bills of attainder, no *ex post facto* laws, and the like. Limitations of this kind can be preserved in practice no other way than through the medium of courts of justice, whose duty it must be to declare all acts contrary to the manifest tenor of the Constitution void. Without this, all the reservations of particular rights or privileges would amount to nothing.

Some perplexity respecting the rights of the courts to pronounce legislative acts void, because contrary to the Constitution, has arisen from an imagination that the doctrine would imply a superiority of the judiciary to the legislative power. It is urged that the authority which can declare the acts of another void must necessarily be superior to the one whose acts may be declared void. As this doctrine is of great importance in all the American constitutions, a brief discussion of the grounds on which it rests cannot be unacceptable.

There is no position which depends on clever principles than that every act of a delegated authority, contrary to the tenor of the commission under which it is exercised, is void. No legislative act, therefore, contrary to the Constitution, can be valid. To deny this would be to affirm that the deputy is greater than his principal; that the servant is above his master; that the representatives of the people are superior to the people themselves; that men acting by virtue of powers may do not only what their powers do not authorize, but what they forbid.

If it be said that the legislative body are themselves the constitutional judges of their own powers and that the construction they put upon them is conclusive upon the other departments it may be answered that this cannot be the natural presumption where it is not to be collected from any particular provisions in the Constitution. It is not otherwise to be supposed that the Constitution could intend to enable the representatives of the people to substitute their *will* to that of their constituents. It is far more rational to suppose that the courts were designed to be an intermediate body between the people and the legislature in order, among other things, to keep the latter within the limits assigned to their authority. The interpretation of the laws is the proper and peculiar province of the courts. A constitution is, in fact, and must be regarded by the judges as, a fundamental law. It therefore belongs to them to ascertain its meaning as well as the meaning of any particular act proceeding from the legislative body. If there should happen to be an irreconcilable variance between the two, that which has the superior obligation and validity ought, of course, to be preferred; or, in other words, the Constitution ought to be preferred to the statute, the intention of the people to the intention of their agents.

Nor does this conclusion by any means suppose a superiority of the judicial to the legislative power. It only supposes that the power of the people is superior to both, and that where the will of the legislature, declared in its statutes, stands in opposition to that of the people, declared in the Constitution, the judges ought to be governed by the latter rather than the former. They ought to regulate their decisions by the fundamental laws rather than by those which are not fundamental.

This exercise of judicial discretion in determining between two contradictory laws is exemplified in a familiar instance. It not uncommonly happens that there are two statutes existing at one time, clashing in whole or in part with each other and neither of them containing any repealing clause or expression. In such a case, it is the province of the courts to liquidate and fix their meaning and operation. So far as they can, by any fair construction, be reconciled to each other, reason and law conspire to dictate that this should be done; where this is impracticable, it becomes a matter of necessity to give effect to one in exclusion of the other. The rule which has obtained in the courts for determining their relative validity is that the last in order of time shall be preferred to the first. But this is a mere rule of construction, not derived from any positive law but from the nature and reason of the thing. It is a rule not enjoined upon the courts by legislative provision but adopted by themselves, as consonant to truth and propriety, for the direction of their conduct as interpreters of the law. They thought it reasonable that between the interfering acts of an *equal* authority that which was the last indication of its will should have the preference.

But in regard to the interfering acts of a superior and subordinate authority of an original and derivative power, the nature and reason of the thing indicate the converse of that rule as proper to be followed. They teach us that the prior act of a superior ought to be preferred to the subsequent act of an inferior and subordinate authority; and that accordingly, whenever a particular statute contravenes the Constitution, it will be the duty of the judicial tribunals to adhere to the latter and disregard the former.

It can be of no weight to say that the courts, on the pretense of a repugnancy, may substitute their own pleasure to the constitutional intentions of the legislature. This might as well happen in the case of two contradictory statutes; or it might as well happen in every adjudication upon any single statute. The courts must declare the sense of the law; and if they should be disposed to exercise WILL instead of JUDGMENT, the consequence would equally be the substitution of their pleasure to that of the legislative body. The observation, if it proved anything, would prove that there ought to be no judges distinct from that body.

If, then, the courts of justice are to be considered as the bulwarks of a limited Constitution against legislative encroachments, this consideration will afford a strong argument for the permanent tenure of judicial offices, since nothing will contribute so much as this to that independent spirit in the judges which must be essential to the faithful performance of so arduous a duty.

This independence of the judges is equally requisite to guard the Constitution and the rights of individuals from the effects of those ill humors which the arts of designing men, or the influence of particular conjunctures, sometimes disseminate among the people themselves, and which, though they speedily give place to better information, and more deliberate reflection, have a tendency, in the meantime, to occasion dangerous innovations in the government, and serious oppressions of the minor party in the community. Though I trust the friends of the proposed Constitution will never concur with its enemies[3] in questioning that fundamental principle of republican government which admits the right of the people to alter or abolish the established Constitution whenever they find it inconsistent with their happiness; yet it is not to be inferred from this principle that the representatives of the people, whenever a momentary inclination happens to lay hold of a majority of their constituents incompatible with the provisions in the existing Constitution would, on that account, be justifiable in a violation of those provisions; or that the courts would be under a greater obligation to connive at infractions in this shape than when they had proceeded wholly from the cabals of the representative body. Until the people have, by some solemn and authoritative act, annulled or changed the established form, it is binding upon themselves collectively, as well as individually; and no presumption, or even knowledge of their sentiments, can warrant their representatives in a departure from it prior to such an act. But it is easy to see that it would require an uncommon portion of fortitude in the judges to do their duty as faithful guardians of the Constitution, where legislative invasions of it had been instigated by the major voice of the community.

But it is not with a view to infractions of the Constitution only that the independence of the judges may be an essential safeguard against the effects of occasional ill humors in the society. These sometimes extend no farther than to the injury of the private rights of particular classes of citizens, by unjust and partial laws. Here also the firmness of the judicial magistracy is of vast importance in mitigating the severity and confining the operation of such laws. It not only serves to moderate the immediate mischiefs of those which may have been passed but it operates as a check upon the legislative body in passing them; who, perceiving that obstacles to the success of an iniquitous intention are to be expected from the scruples of the courts, are in a manner compelled, by the very motives of the injustice they meditate, to qualify their attempts. This is a circumstance calculated to have more influence upon the character of our governments than but few may be aware of. The benefits of the integrity and moderation of the judiciary have already been felt in more States than one; and though they may have displeased those whose sinister expectations they may have disappointed, they must have commanded the esteem and applause of all the virtuous and disinterested. Considerate men of every description ought to prize whatever will tend to beget or fortify that temper in the courts; as no man can be sure that he may not be tomorrow the victim of a spirit of injustice, by which he may be a gainer today. And every man must now feel that the inevitable tendency of such a spirit is to sap the foundations of public and private confidence and to introduce in its stead universal distrust and distress.

That inflexible and uniform adherence to the rights of the Constitution, and of individuals, which we perceive to be indispensable in the courts of justice, can certainly not be expected from judges who hold their offices by a temporary commission. Periodical appointments, however regulated, or by whomsoever made, would, in some way or other, be fatal to their necessary independence. If the power of making them was committed either to the executive or legislature there would be danger of an improper complaisance to the branch which possessed it; if to both, there would be an unwillingness to hazard the displeasure of either; if to the people, or to persons chosen by them for the special purpose, there would be too great a disposition to consult popularity to justify a reliance that nothing would be consulted but the Constitution and the laws.

There is yet a further and a weighty reason for the permanency of the judicial offices which is deducible from the nature of the qualifications they require. It has been frequently remarked with great propriety that a voluminous code of laws is one of the inconveniences necessarily connected with the advantages of a free government. To avoid an arbitrary discretion in the courts, it is indispensable that they should be bound down by strict rules and precedents which serve to define and point out their duty in every particular case that comes before them; and it will readily be conceived from the variety of controversies which grow out of the folly and wickedness of mankind that the records of those precedents must unavoidably swell to a very considerable bulk and must demand long and laborious study to acquire a competent knowledge of them. Hence it is that there can be but few men in the society who will have sufficient skill in the laws to qualify them for the stations of judges. And making the proper deductions for the ordinary depravity of human nature, the number must be still smaller of those who unite the requisite integrity with the requisite knowledge. These considerations apprise us that the government can have no great option between fit characters; and that a temporary duration in office which would naturally discourage such characters from quitting a lucrative line of practice to accept a seat on the bench would have a tendency to throw the administration of justice into hands less able and less well qualified to conduct it with utility and dignity. In the present circumstances of this country and in those in which it is likely to be for a long time to come, the disadvantages on this score would be greater than they may at first sight appear; but it must be confessed that they are far inferior to those which present themselves under the other aspects of the subject.

Upon the whole, there can be no room to doubt that the convention acted wisely in copying from the models of those constitutions which have established *good behavior* as the tenure of their judicial offices, in point of duration; and that so far from being blamable on this account, their plan would have been inexcusably defective if it had wanted this important feature of good government. The experience of Great Britain affords an illustrious comment on the excellence of the institution.

NOTES

1. The celebrated Montesquieu, speaking of them, says: "Of the three powers above mentioned, the judiciary is next to nothing."—*Spirit of Laws*, vol. 1, page 186.

2. *Idem*, page 181.

3. Vide, *Protest of the Minority of the Convention of Pennsylvania*, Martin's speech, etc.

37

WALTER F. MURPHY

MARSHALLING THE COURT

What strategies are available to a policy-oriented Supreme Court justice who wants to obtain the support of a majority of justices for his or her position? Walter F. Murphy, whose work greatly expands our understanding of judicial behavior, identifies and analyzes several possible tactics: persuasion on the merits, increasing personal regard, use of sanctions, and bargaining. Justices who find themselves in a minority with no chance of prevailing at the moment, may seek to build a bloc with other dissenters in the hope that their position will win in the future. Professor Murphy teaches political science at Princeton University. "Marshalling the Court" originally appeared as Chapter 3 in his book Elements of Judicial Strategy (1964).

Since he shares decision-making authority with eight other judges, the first problem that a policy-oriented justice would confront is that of obtaining at least four, and hopefully eight, additional votes for the results he wants and the kinds of opinions he thinks should be written in cases important to his objectives. Moreover, because he faces other problems as well, he must try to influence his colleagues with as little expenditure of time and energy as possible.

His initial step would be to examine the situation on the Court. In general three sets of conditions may obtain. There may be complete coincidence of interest with the other Justices, or at least with the number of associates he feels is necessary to attain his aim. Second, the interests of the other Justices, or a majority of them, may be indifferent to his objective. Third, the interests of his colleagues may be in opposition to his own. Since there are varying degrees of coincidence, indifference, and opposition, each represents a range rather than a pin-pointed position. The coincidence may be such that the justice need only bring the facts or implications of a specific situation to the attention of his colleagues, or it may be so imperfect that the term coincidence can be used only in the sense of an analogy. Under the latter circumstances, the justice may have to do a great deal of persuading to convince his colleagues that their objectives are not incongruous and that it is important to their interests that they support his suggestions.

Indifference may be, as one might assume, the situation in which attempts to exercise influence would be most necessary and would pay the biggest dividends; but influence could also have a major effect where interests were in opposition. Where the opposition was intense a justice might still be able to lessen its impact on his policy aims by decreasing its intensity. Where the opposition was mild, a justice might conceivably convince his associates that they were mistaken, or he might offer a concession in another area which they valued more highly in exchange for a concession here.

Influence, of course, does not simply come into existence. It is the result of interaction among human beings, of their individual interests, values, and concepts of

[Notes have been renumbered. — Eds.]

what moral rules, if any, ought to be controlling, and of their different perceptions of the situations in which they are operating. A policy-oriented Justice must therefore want to know what factors predispose one actor to respond positively to the suggestions, wishes, requests, or commands of another. Where actors are behaving rationally in terms of their particular goals, the question, "What shall I gain if I do *x* because actor A suggests, wishes, requests, or commands it?" is crucial. Personal esteem can also be important in gauging reactions, and it is often tied to self-interest. We tend to like those whose actions have benefited us in the past, to interpret as beneficial the actions of those whom we like, and, in turn, to help those whom we like. In addition, we frequently find ourselves liking another person for no apparent reason at all. In the process of reacting favorably to the suggestions of those we like, we may be unconsciously reckoning on intangible as well as tangible gains, such as an increase in affection. The desire to be loved seems as important as it is widespread in our society. Furthermore, once our affections have become attached to another person, whether or not because of rational considerations, what Pepitone has called "facilitative distortion" may set in.[1] That is, we tend to attribute to persons to whom we are emotionally drawn the virtues and talents we would like them to have.

Thus, in disposing an actor to respond positively to the attempts at influence by another actor, personal esteem may merge with professional esteem—respect for judgment, knowledge, or skills—in that we might see those whom we like as having somewhat more of these qualities than they perhaps possess. Self-interest, as has already been indicated, may also be involved in professional evaluations. It is easier to esteem the abilities of those whose previous actions have been beneficial to one's own interests than to esteem the abilities of those whose actions have been harmful or indifferent. This is not to deny that such respect may be based on purely professional standards, largely apart from interest or affection, and still influence our decisions. In addition, such respect, no matter how generated, can lead to influence insofar as it operates as an economizing device. An actor might conclude that "A is an expert in this field, and I am not. The cost of becoming an expert is so high that I find it more efficient to follow than to become an expert myself."

The concept of "oughtness" also plays a role in disposing an actor to respond to the suggestions of another. One might react positively or negatively to a suggestion because one feels that because of broad moral precepts or because of one's particular role in society, one should or should not perform such an act. In a more specific fashion, when he is a member of an institutional hierarchy, an actor might feel that he ought to carry out the wishes of those further up the hierarchy than he, at least in those matters relating to the superiors' areas of authority. Fear, too, can be a significant factor in determining influence. The question, "What reprisals shall I be risking if I do not do *x* at actor A's suggestion?" is central to any rational process of decisionmaking. And, in politics, sanctions can take forms ranging all the way from a decrease in affection to physical violence.

Since the Justices are largely equal in authority, an appeal by one Justice to his position on the Court is not likely to be an effective means of increasing influence with his associates, except perhaps in those few fields in which tradition has given the Chief Justice certain prerogatives. The Justices, however, are not equal in intellectual ability, in perspicacity, learning, legal craftsmanship, persuasive talents, energy, determination, ambition, or social skills; nor do they hold each other in equal personal and professional esteem. Thus a Justice has considerable opportunity to try to exercise influence over his colleagues. He could attempt to appeal to their interests—to convince them that their interests would gain from furthering his interests or that their interests would suffer injury if they opposed his; to increase or create and then appeal to their personal and professional esteem for him; and to appeal to their concepts of duty and moral obligation.

The peculiar formal rules and informal norms of the Court would allow a Justice to operate under one or more of several simple strategies to exploit each of these possible appeals. First, he might try by force of his intellect and will to convince his colleagues not only that what he wanted was in the best interests of themselves, the Court, the country, humanity, or whatever other goals they might wish to foster, but also that it was morally incumbent upon them to act in the fashion he was proposing.

Second, a Justice might plan so to endear himself to the other Justices that they would be reluctant to vote against him in matters he considered to be vital. Conversely, he might try to capitalize on fear rather than affection and try to bludgeon his colleagues into agreement by threatening them with use of the sanctions available to him. Fourth, he might conclude that the only viable way to come near achieving his goal would be to negotiate: to compromise with those who were less intensively opposed to his policies. Last, he might decide that the best way of securing approval of his policies would be to secure new men for the Court, men whose interests would coincide closely with his own.

Taken alone, none of these simple strategies seems very promising. Occasionally a giant like Marshall can dominate the Court, but the great Chief Justice was blessed with several cooperative colleagues as well as with a magnificent sense of statecraft. As Justice Johnson explained to Jefferson:[2]

> While I was on our state-bench I was accustomed to delivering seriatim opinions . . . and was not a little surprised to find our Chief Justice in the Supreme Court delivering all the opinions in cases in which he sat, even in some instances when contrary to his own judgment and vote. But I remonstrated in vain; the answer was he is willing to take the trouble and it is a mark of respect to him. I soon found out however the real cause. Cushing was incompetent. Chase could not be got to think or write—Patterson [*sic*] was a slow man and willingly declined the trouble, and the other two judges [Marshall and Bushrod Washington] you know are commonly estimated as one judge. . . .

On the other hand, it is difficult to imagine any judge, even a Marshall, dominating men like Johnson, Taney, Field, Miller, Bradley, Brewer, Harlan, Holmes, Hughes, Brandeis, Sutherland, Van Devanter, Cardozo, or Stone. It is equally difficult to imagine any Justice getting passive acquiescence, for any length of time, on important and controversial issues from a Court composed of Justices as brilliant, individualistic, and strong-willed as Black, Douglas, Frankfurter, and Jackson.

Similarly, Supreme Court Justices are as unlikely to be swayed by personal esteem alone as solely by the threat of sanctions being applied against them.

Bargaining, too, hardly seems to be the golden key to success, unless accompanied by high personal or professional esteem, some measure of coincidence or indifference of interests, and, perhaps, by some fear of the application of sanctions.

Last, staffing the Court with men whose interests coincided with the policy-oriented Justice's would undoubtedly be very effective. It would depend, however, on (1) the Justice's being gifted with better vision than most Presidents have had in foreseeing how future judges would behave once securely on the bench, (2) enough vacancies occurring to permit a favorable majority to be formed, (3) the President and the general political environment allowing the Justice to play the chief role in the appointing process. The necessity of all three conditions happening simultaneously is a severe limitation on the practicality of sole reliance on this strategy.

It is obvious that in most circumstances a Justice would be far more prudent to pursue a mixed strategy employing some elements of each of these simple approaches—so obvious in fact that the only real question is what blend should be adopted. Without knowing the specific policy involved and the exact moment of time in the Court's history, one can only formulate some general considerations.

First would be the personality of the Justice himself. Realization of the major sources of influence potential might, for instance, induce a Justice who inclines to rely on hard intellectual argument on the merits of an issue to the neglect of considerations of the feelings, interests, and moral concepts of those with whom he is debating to pay more attention to the social amenities, so that his ideas will find a more receptive audience. Conversely, a recognition of influence potential should move every Justice toward diligent attention to the craftsmanship of his profession. By the time he comes to the Court, however, a Justice's personality is so formed that even a strong-willed man probably cannot completely remold himself. It would have been impossible, for example, for Taft to have become a scholar and to have awed the conference with his legal erudition. At another extreme is the kind of man whom Justice Jackson once described: "You must go to war with him if you disagree."[3] While Jackson was hardly a disinterested critic of the particular justice to whom he was referring, his characterization does fit a common personality type. It is improbable that any amount of effort could turn such a man into the warm, sensitive, forgiving sort of person who refuses to press an intellectual advantage or who smilingly overlooks personal affronts.

An effective, policy-oriented Justice must be able to assess with a considerable degree of objectivity his own strengths and his weaknesses and, while trying to make adjustments to minimize the latter, concentrate on exploiting his major abilities. Choosing an ally with complementary talents is one way of maximizing potentials. Taft, for instance, knew that he had a rare social skill, but he was also keenly aware of his intellectual limitations. He complained to his family on several occasions that his colleagues would "humiliate" him in conference discussion,[4] and he was struck by the contrast between his own and Van Devanter's grasp of the intricacies of the Court's business. As the Chief Justice told his son, "The familiarity with the practice and the thoroughness of examination in certain cases that Van Devanter is able to give makes him a most valuable member of the Court and makes me feel quite small, and as if it would be better to have the matter run by him alone. . . ." Taft, however, had no intention of letting another man even appear to run the office which had been his life-long ambition. Instead he shrewdly utilized Van Devanter's immense learning to improve his own opinions, to supply technical knowledge at conference, and to advise on the numerous political affairs in which the Chief Justice was constantly getting involved. Meanwhile Taft continued to make full use of his own sensitivity to the feelings of others and the personal esteem in which other justices held him. As he told his son, he would be "content to aid in the deliberation when there is a difference of opinion."[5]

What mixture of appeals, threats, and offers to compromise would be effective would also depend in large part on the character of the justice's colleagues. Indeed, a somewhat different combination might have to be devised in dealing with each member of the Court. It would be far easier, though not necessarily very profitable, to bargain with a born negotiator like Brandeis than with a lone wolf like Douglas; easier to reason with an open-minded judge like Holmes than with a man like Peckham, whose major premise, so one Justice remarked, was "God damn it";[6] easier to play on charm with a genial character like Taft or Sherman Minton than with a waspish, suspicious McReynolds; easier to dominate a Justice who has ceased to care about his work than a man who, like most Justices, is fully committed to the Court's operations.

The ideal strategic formula would also be affected by the nature of the policy itself and the kinds of cases relating to that policy which the Court was receiving, what the policy meant in terms of existing legal doctrine and the commitments thereto not only of the Justices but also of the demands and supports from other government officials and powerful interest groups. One or more such factors would certainly be significant in determining the kinds of stimuli to which each of the justices would respond in a positive manner. Moreover, the general political situation would be a key element in a Justice's capacity to influence the appointment of new members of the Court.

I. TACTICS

Once he has decided on a strategic plan to secure a majority within the Court—and integrated that plan into his larger scheme to meet the other obstacles in his path—a Justice would have to consider the tactics open to him to carry out his efforts to persuade on the merits of his policy choice, to capitalize on personal regard, to bargain, to threaten, and if possible to have a voice in the selection of new personnel.

Persuasion on the Merits

To date all the Justices have been lawyers, and whatever the status of their technical knowledge when appointed, their work, their friends, their critics, their pride, and their clerks have forced most of them to become competent and usually highly competent lawyers. Traditional overemphasis on the logical element in judicial decision-making has been ridiculed by Legal Realists. Yet, while it is true that the work of courts revolves around basically subjective value judgments, judgments conditioned by all sorts of subconscious drives shaped in part by childhood experiences, no evidence has yet been adduced to show that judges decide cases through some automatic operation of emotional prejudices. To a significant extent judges can and do weigh such factors as legal principles and precedents and well thought-out ideas of proper public policy.

Furthermore, judges can be persuaded to change their minds about specific cases as well as about broad public policies, and intellectual persuasion can play an important role in such shifts. As Robert Jackson once commented from the bench: "I myself have changed my opinion after reading the opinions of the other members of this Court. And I am as stubborn as most. But I sometimes wind up not voting the way I voted in conference because the reasons of the majority didn't satisfy me."[7] An examination of the notes of conference discussions which Justice Murphy filed with his papers and the memoranda in this and in other collections of judicial papers show that time and again positions first taken at conference are changed as other Justices bring up new arguments. Perhaps most convincing in demonstrating the impact of intellectual factors are the numerous instances on record in which the Justice assigned the opinion of the Court has reported back to the conference that additional study had convinced him that he and the rest of the majority had been in error. A few examples will have to suffice:

When, in May, 1922, Taft circulated his opinion in *Hill v. Wallace*, he attached a statement summarizing the history of the Court's handling of the dispute:[8]

> . . . we voted first that there was equitable jurisdiction by a vote of 7 to 1, Justice Brandeis voting "No" and Justice Holmes being doubtful. On the question of whether [the congressional statute regulating trading in grain futures] could be sustained as a taxing act, the vote stood 7 to 1, Justice McKenna casting the negative vote, and Justice Brandeis not voting. Later we took a vote as to whether the act could be sustained as a regulation of interstate commerce. At first, by a vote of 5–4, it was held that it could not be so sustained. Later there was a change, and by a vote of 5 to 3, Justice Brandeis not voting, its validity as a regulation of interstate commerce was sustained.

Taft then pointed out that he had changed his mind and asked the Court to go along with him. "On a close examination of the case, the law and the record, I have reached the conclusion that the law is invalid as a taxing law and that it can not be sustained as a valid regulation of interstate commerce." When the opinion came down three days later, the statute was declared unconstitutional as a taxing act, under the authority of the Child Labor Tax Case. The vote was 8–1, with Brandeis agreeing in a separate opinion that the statute was unconstitutional but doubting that the plaintiffs had standing to sue.

In March, 1945, a majority of the Court voted in conference to affirm the conviction under the Sherman Act of several employers and union officials who had conspired to raise wages and prices by trying to monopolize the lumber business in the San Francisco Bay area.[9] The opinion of the Court was assigned to Justice Black. On May 2, 1945, however, Black circulated an opinion reversing the convictions. He explained that further study had convinced him that the trial judge had improperly interpreted the Norris–La Guardia Act.[10]

Black may have been persuaded, but his colleagues were not, at least not immediately, The case was twice set down for reargument on the construction of the Norris–La Guardia Act, and the decision did not finally come down until March 10, 1947. The vote to reverse was 5–3, Justice Jackson not participating. As the senior majority Justice, Black, possibly as a means of conciliation, assigned the opinion to Reed rather than to himself; and Reed held that the trial judge's charge to the jury had been erroneous under the Norris–La Guardia Act and ordered a new trial.

As every serious scholar has recognized, the openness of many Justices to logical persuasion on the merits points up the importance of professional skills to a policy-oriented Justice. It is almost trite to note that if a Justice is able to mass legal precedents and history to bolster an intellectually and morally defensible policy and can present his arguments in a convincing manner, he stands an excellent chance of picking up votes. Indeed, without this kind of approach it is extremely unlikely that a Justice will significantly influence any of his colleagues, although, because they have found the necessary evidence themselves or because of their own policy predilections, they may vote in the way he wishes.

As in all phases of human activity, eloquence and charm would be valuable additions to professional competence. One might suspect that Hughes's opening remarks to the conference when the troublesome issue of a compulsory flag salute was first discussed increased the predisposition of the other Justices to accept his reasoning. "I come up to this case," Justice Murphy recorded the Chief Justice as saying, "like a skittish horse to a brass band."[11]

It does not follow, to be sure, that all or even four Justices would be open to persuasion on the policy which the Justice wanted adopted. Certainly a Justice coming to the bench after 1941 would have received reactions no more favorable than bored yawns had he urged the Court to resume its role as defender of laissez faire. Thus a Justice would also have to consider exploiting the vulnerability of any of his colleagues to non- or extra-rational arguments. He would probably feel it unethical to appeal to the strong personal dislike of one Justice for another, though there may have been occasions when such an appeal would have been effective.

Less distasteful would be an appeal to loyalty to the Court as an institution, though it would normally be possible for a Justice to utilize this argument fully only when he was in the majority and was trying to pick up additional votes or was trying to get a majority to agree to an institutional opinion in preference to a seriatim expression of views. Similarly, in situations where the Justice feels that the general political environment requires unanimity, he might play on the isolation of a would-be dissenter.

Hirabayashi v. United States provides one example of a combination of such tactics. After reading a draft of Stone's opinion for the Court sustaining the conviction of a Nisei for violating the curfew imposed by the military on all West Coast Japanese Americans—an opinion which ducked the more serious question of the constitutionality of the evacuation and internment aspects of the program—Justice Murphy began writing a dissent. Hearing of this, Frankfurter sent him a plea to close ranks with his colleagues:[12]

Please, Frank, with your eagerness for the austere functions of the Court and your desire to do all that is humanly possible to maintain and enhance the *corporate* reputation of the Court, why don't you take the initiative with the Chief Justice in getting him to take out everything that either offends you or that you would want to express more irenically.

Even after an exchange of several other notes, Murphy remained adamant, and he circulated a blistering opinion branding the whole Nisei program as "utterly inconsistent with our ideals and traditions" and "at variance with the principles for which we are fighting."[13] Frankfurter read Murphy's protest in horror, and he immediately wrote another impassioned plea:[14]

Of course I shan't try to dissuade you from filing a dissent in that case — not because I do not think it highly unwise but because I think you are immovable. But I would like to say two things to you about the dissent: (1) it has internal contradictions which you ought not to allow to stand, and (2) do you really think it is conducive to the things you care about, including the great reputation of this Court, to suggest that everybody is out of step except Johnny, and more particularly that the Chief Justice and seven other Justices of this Court are behaving like the enemy and thereby playing into the hands of the enemy?

Murphy was apparently moved at least to second thoughts about the possible implications of what he was doing. Within a few days he had switched his vote and had modified his dissent into a concurrence, though one which still expressed concern over the "melancholy resemblance" between United States treatment of the Nisei and Nazi treatment of the Jews.

Shortly after Stone came to the bench, Taft tried to use this sort of approach with him. When Stone was considering a dissent in an important labor case,[15] the Chief Justice wrote him: "My dear Brother Stone: I am quite anxious, as I am sure we all are, that the continuity and weight of our opinions on important questions of law should not be broken any more than we can help by dissents. . . ." Holmes and Brandeis, Taft went on, had originally dissented from the line of cases on which the instant decision was based and would doubtless grasp at any minute distinction to persist in their opposition to established law. "With respect to those judges who have come to the Court since these decisions were rendered, I am sure it is not their purpose to depart from what has been declared to be accepted law."[16] Stone gave in to the extent of writing only a concurring opinion.

A few years later McReynolds used the same kind of argument in an unsuccessful effort to dissuade Stone from what was becoming a pronounced tendency to dissent. McReynolds wrote:[17]

Please don't think me presumptuous. Certainly I do not mean to be. All of us get into a fog now and then, as I know so well from my own experience. Won't you "Stop, Look, and Listen"? In my view, we have one member [Brandeis?] who is consciously boring from within. Of course, you have no such purpose, but you may unconsciously aid his purpose. At least do think twice on a subject — three times indeed. If the Court is broken down, then there will be rejoicing in certain quarters. I cannot think that the last three dissents which you have sent me will aid you, the law or the Court. Give the matter another thought.

A Justice might appeal to other emotions, for example, patriotism in cases involving issues of national security. In *Ex parte Quirin*, the Justices were unanimous in their conclusion that the government could try captured Nazi saboteurs in military tribunals rather than in regularly constituted civil courts, but they could not agree on an opinion explaining why such trials were constitutional. After the Chief Justice had circulated three different drafts of an opinion without securing full assent, one of the other members of the Court sent a long memorandum to all of his colleagues. He began by pointing out that most of the discussion was now approaching mere quibbling about words, since the Justices were agreed that the only real point of difference, the extent to which Congress could bind the President as Commander-in-Chief, should not be decided. As the clearest way of explaining his own views, the Justice offered a dialogue between himself and the saboteurs, a dialogue in which he rejected their claims out of hand, describing them as "damned scoundrels" who were attempting to create a conflict between the President and Congress which would continue long "after your bodies will be rotting in lime." At the conclusion of the dialogue, the Justice again spoke directly to his brethren:[18]

> Some of the very best lawyers I know are now in the Solomon Island battle, some are seeing service in Australia, some are subchasers in the Atlantic, and some are on the various air fronts. It requires no poet's imagination to think of their reflections if the unanimous result reached by us in these cases should be expressed in opinions which would black out agreement in result and reveal internecine conflict about the manner of stating that result. I know some of these men very, very intimately. I think I know what they would deem to be the governing canons of constitutional adjudication in a case like this. And I almost hear their voices were they to read more than a single opinion in this case. They would say something like this but in language hardly becoming a judge's tongue: "What in hell do you fellows think you are doing? Haven't we got enough of a job trying to lick the Japs and Nazis without having you fellows on the Court dissipate thoughts and feelings and energies of the folks at home by stirring up a nice row as to who has what power . . . ? Haven't you got any more sense than to get people by the ear on one of their favorite American pastimes—abstract constitutional discussions? . . . Just relax and don't be too engrossed in your own interests in verbalistic conflicts because the inroads on energy and national unity that such conflict inevitably produces, is a pastime we had better postpone until peacetime."

Stone, too, was hard at work trying to woo the doubtful Justices by means of what he described as "patient negotiations."[19] Eventually the opinion which came down was unanimous.

Increasing Personal Regard

Some people are blessed with a warmth and a sincerity that immediately attract other human beings. It is improbable that even a sophisticated version of a

Dale Carnegie course, whether or not self-taught, could build up anything approaching the personal magnetism that such people have by nature. Observance of the simple rules of human courtesy and thoughtfulness, however, can do much to keep interpersonal relations on a plane where a meaningful exchange of ideas is possible.

When a new Justice comes to the Court, an older colleague might try to charm his junior brother. A gracious letter of welcome may make the new Justice more disposed to trust another's judgment or at least more disposed to compromise without rancor. When Wiley Rutledge was appointed, Felix Frankfurter, who along with Stone had been reported as working for Learned Hand's promotion,[20] wrote the new Justice:[21]

> You are, I am sure, much too wise a man to pay any attention to gossip, even when it is printed. And so I depart from a fixed rule of mine—which Lincoln's life has taught me—not to contradict paragraphs. I do so not because I think for a moment that the silly statement that I am "opposed to" you for a place on this Court has found any lodgment in your mind but to emphasize it as a striking illustration of sheer invention parading as information. The fact of the matter is that the opposite of that baseless statement could much more plausibly be asserted.

Three years earlier, when Frankfurter's nomination was confirmed by the Senate, Hughes, despite the fact that his work on the Court had been sharply criticized by Frankfurter, immediately wrote a welcoming note:[22]

> Let me extend to you a warm welcome to collaboration in our work—for which you are so exceptionally qualified. We need you and I trust you will be able to take your seat at the opening of our next session on January 30th. If there is anything that I can do to aid in making your arrangements here, command me.
>
> With kindest regards, and looking forward with the greatest of pleasure to the renewal, in this relation, of the association with you that I had when you were with the Department of Justice many years ago. . . .

Once on the Court, the freshman Justice, even if he has been a state or lower federal court judge, moves into a strange and shadowy world. An occasional helping hand—a word of advice about procedure and protocol, a warning about personal idiosyncrasies of colleagues, or the trustworthiness of counsel—can be helpful and appreciated. Particularly if a new Justice comes to Washington in mid-term, aid in securing clerical assistance and law clerks can be a means of establishing good will—with the new Justice as well as with his staff.

The new Justice may also feel it necessary to establish warm social relations with his brethren. When he first came to the Court, Justice Stone asked several of his associates for pictures of themselves. At the end of his first few months on the Court, one Justice sent Hughes this note: "I don't want to leave without telling you how forbearing and generous you have been to this fledgling judge and what an inspiration it has been to work under your chieftainship."[23] After his first year on the bench, that Justice again told Hughes of his great esteem:[24]

Perhaps this day [Hughes's birthday] I may say to your face what I have several times—to my wife and to a few of my intimate friends—said behind your back: that no one could have welcomed me more generously to the Court than you did, nor have sustained a spirit of generosity and considerateness toward a very junior Brother in those day-to-day joint labors which, because of the inevitable difference of opinion, test and give the quality to, the relations between men.

No outside student of the work of the Court could be unaware of the intrinsic authority with which you have exercised your Chief Justiceship. But only one who has been privileged to sit under your chief[tainship] can possibly appreciate the sweep and impact of resources and fruitful traditions and creative energy with which you lead the Court. Of your complete dedication to its function in our national life it would be almost humorously impertinent to speak.

Notations on slip opinions provide another avenue of social access. A large ego seems to be a prerequisite of political success, and large egos bruise easily—though the exigencies of American politics probably sift out most of those people with slow recuperative powers. In any event, a judicial opinion represents considerable labor, and it would be a rare man who did not enjoy appreciation of his intellectual off-spring. Remarks on slip opinions are frequently glowing in their praise. Holmes could be as charmingly eloquent in his editorial comments as in his other writing. He told Taft in 1921, "I cling to my preceptor's hand and follow him through the dark passages to the light."[25] Stone received his full share of such encomia. On the back of the draft of the opinion in *United States v. Darby*, Douglas wrote: "I heartily agree. This has the master's real touch!" Frankfurter added: "This is a grand plum pudding. There are so many luscious plums in it that it's invidious to select. But I especially rejoice over (1) the way you buried *Hammer v. Dagenhart* and (2) your definitive exposure of the empty hobgoblin of the 10th Amendt. It's a superb job." On the back of Stone's dissent in *Cloverleaf Butter Co. v. Patterson*, Frank Murphy said: "This seems to me the finest kind of writing and it is sound too."

After Hughes had finished his opinion in the Minnesota Rate Cases (1913), Justice Lamar sent him a note: ". . . It is a great opinion and will stand as one of the greatest in our records. Your success ought to be compensation for your days and weeks and months of unceasing labor. . . . I congratulate you most sincerely and heartily on having written an opinion which not only sustains the particular rights of the states and of the United States but, will be a landmark in the history of the Court."[26] A week later Justices Day and Lurton wrote Mrs. Hughes: "Your husband has done a great work this day, the effects of which will be beneficially felt for generations to come. Congratulations."[27] Certainly such comments make for an easier exchange of views than remarks like McReynolds' about an opinion of which he did not approve: "This statement makes me sick."[28]

Similarly, suggestions for changes in opinion should be made with tender regard for the feelings of the writer. Stone, for example, wrote Douglas about the latter's opinion[29] in a 1942 term case:[30]

I have gone over your opinion in this case with some care, and I congratulate you on your lucid and penetrating analysis and the great thoroughness with which you have done a difficult job. If Justice Brandeis could read it he would be proud of his successor.

Stone then quietly added to these gallantries a single-spaced typewritten page of suggestions for revision.

When a Justice has won a fight over a decision, he may be well advised to offer the olive branch to the loser, knowing that today's opponent will often be tomorrow's ally. After their failure to agree in the first Flag Salute case, Frankfurter wrote Stone a gentle note: "Though we read the scales differently in weighing these 'imponderables,' I cannot but feel confident that our scales are the same. In any event our ways do not part and we care no differently for the only things that give dignity to man—the things of the spirit."[31]

A somewhat different way for a Justice to build up a reservoir of good will for later use would be to accede frequently to the majority, and to let the majority know that although acquiescence goes against his better judgment, he is stifling his doubts for the sake of harmony. As Pierce Butler once wrote on the back of one of Stone's slip opinions:[32]

> I voted to reverse. While this sustains your conclusion to affirm, I still think reversal would be better. But I shall in silence acquiesce. Dissents seldom aid in the right development or statement of the law. They often do harm. For myself I say: "Lead us not into temptation."

Sutherland, too, let Stone know his real feelings. In 1930 he commented: "I was inclined the other way, but I think no one agreed with me. I, therefore, yield my not very positive views to those of the majority."[33] In 1932 he told Stone: "I voted the other way, but I have acquiesced in other outrages and probably shall in this. Shall let you know Saturday, though I should like more time to forget."[34] Three years later, he noted on the back of the *Alaska Packers* opinion: "Probably bad — but only a small baby. Let it go."[35] As handed down, all three decisions were unanimous. Hughes, too, on occasion abstained from dissenting. As he commented on a 1939 slip opinion: "I choke a little at swallowing your analysis, still I do not think it would serve any useful purpose to expose my views."[36]

If such concessions as these are made on issues which a Justice does not think important—or on which he would have been in a small minority anyway—he has lost very little and may have put himself in an excellent position to win reluctant votes from colleagues on other issues. Certiorari voting supplies an opportunity for such tactics. The Court's rules require a vote of four Justices to bring up a case, but where one or two members feel strongly about granting certiorari in a case, another Justice—providing the final decision in the litigation is not likely to affect detrimentally his cause—can capitalize on the situation by graciously saying something to the effect that he is willing to defer to the judgment of the minority.

Members of the Court should be sufficiently sophisticated to take praise and apparent deference from colleagues no more seriously than do most senators. Judges are usually mature, educated, and experienced men, long accustomed to recognizing and thwarting efforts to smoothtalk them into favors.[37] It would be rare for a Justice to succumb to flattery to the extent of changing his vote on a case he thought important. Yet, as has already been pointed out, friendship and the social amenities, especially when coupled with genuine intellectual respect, can play an important auxiliary role in the judicial process insofar as they help determine with whom a Justice is more apt to interact and with whom he will probably continue to negotiate even after an impasse has seemingly been reached.

When Stone first came to the Court, he was, as Taft thought, fundamentally a conservative. Within a very few years, however, Stone had joined Holmes and Brandeis in what the Chief Justice considered "radical" constitutional opinions. In part this change reflected Stone's capacity for intellectual growth, but the warm and stimulating companionship of Holmes and to a lesser extent Brandeis may also have been a decisive factor. As Thomas Reed Powell, a long-time confidant of Stone, commented, it was "respect and liking for Holmes and Brandeis that turned him from his earlier attitudes."[38] On the other hand, Stone probably had slight intellectual respect for Taft. This fact, coupled with McReynolds' bigoted attitude toward Brandeis as well as his continual carping at Stone's opinions,[39] did little to keep the new Justice in the conservative camp.

Stone's change of viewpoint may be an unusual case. Probably more typical is that of the Justice who finds it easier to compromise with a colleague who has shown him respect and consideration than with an associate who has been coldly formal or even impolite. Holmes and Sutherland had very different views of the judicial function,[40] but they were able to work together in making mutual accommodations much more easily than, for example, Brandeis and McReynolds. Conversely, lack of rapport can severely limit opportunities for influencing the Court's work. The relations between McReynolds and Clarke were even more strained than between McReynolds and Brandeis, and as Clarke once told Taft, "I never deign—or dare—to make suggestions to McReynolds, J., as to his opinions."[41]

Use of Sanctions

The two major sanctions which a Justice can use against his colleagues are his vote and his willingness to write opinions which will attack a doctrine the minority or majority wishes to see adopted. The effectiveness of the first sanction usually depends on the closeness of the vote, though there may be special situations, as with Brandeis in the Child Labor Tax Case, where a particular Justice's vote will greatly increase the impact of the arguments of one side or the other, or where, as in the school segregation cases, the general political environment in which the Court functions makes unanimity or near unanimity extraordinarily desirable.

The effectiveness of the second sanction depends largely on the literary and forensic skill of the particular judge. A threat of a separate opinion from one Justice may be a matter hardly worth considering where the vote is not close, while a similar threat from a Johnson, a Field, a Bradley, a Harlan, a Brandeis, or a Black may menace both one's intellectual pride and policy objectives.

A Justice may employ sanctions which are even stronger—and more dangerous—than these. In 1893, Justice Field took what might be termed extreme measures against Justice Gray. After reading Field's dissent in *Fong Yue Ting v. United States,* Gray changed a sentence in his opinion for the majority. Feeling this modification took some of the sting out of his dissent, Field wrote Chief Justice Fuller that if Gray did not restore the sentence as originally written, he—Field—would add a footnote to his opinion explaining that Gray had corrected his error under fire. Gray consulted with the Chief Justice and backed down, leaving the sentence as originally written.[42]

McReynolds expressed his displeasure over Justice Clarke's votes and opinions in a more systematically unpleasant fashion. When he was Attorney General, McReynolds had been instrumental in getting Clarke appointed to the district bench; and when Clarke was promoted to the Supreme Court, McReynolds thought the new Justice should follow his benefactor's ultra-conservative constitutional philosophy. Clarke, however, went his own individual and sometimes erratic way; but, in his first few years on the Court, he tended to side more with Holmes and Brandeis than with McReynolds on constitutional cases. As a result, McReynolds cut off all pleasant social relations with Clarke, meting out only curt sarcasm to him.

Similarly, but in one swift blow, Justice Jackson lashed out at Justice Black in 1946. Roosevelt had promised Jackson—or led Jackson to think that he had promised—to promote him to the chief justiceship when Stone stepped down, but Stone outlived Roosevelt by eleven months. When Stone died, Jackson was at Nürnberg finishing his work as chief American prosecutor of the Nazi war criminals, and he heard rumors that Black and his friends were feverishly lobbying against his promotion. Infuriated, Jackson cabled a long letter to the chairmen of the House and Senate judiciary committees, charging that Black had made "public threats to the President" to resign if Jackson were appointed Chief Justice. Jackson then offered a detailed explanation of the feud between himself and Black, accusing Black of "bullying" tactics and of dealings of questionable propriety in sitting in a case argued by a former law partner.[43]

Like massive retaliation, the threat of airing disputes in public is effective to the extent that it is never actually applied. Its use may embarrass one's adversary, but even a threat to use it may enrage him to the point of total alienation as far as future consultation or compromise is concerned. More important—since, if the Justice employing such a sanction were acting rationally, he would not make the threat unless relations with the target Justice had already reached a hopeless point—public use or threats of sanctions may damage the Court's prestige and so weaken its institutional power and thereby the Justice's ability to use that power for his own ends. McReynolds' tactics were only slightly less dangerous. In fact his shabby treatment of his brethren did become known outside the Court, though not with a dramatic effect comparable to that achieved by Jackson in his Nürnberg cable. On the other hand, McReynolds' tactics may have been the most successful of the three for Clarke resigned in 1922.[44] He claimed that he was bored with "the trifling character of judicial work,"[45] but Taft, who had been an appalled witness to the feud between Clarke and McReynolds, felt sure that the real reason was McReynolds.[46]

Ridicule can be a lethal weapon in undermining the professional esteem in which an opposing Justice is held, although it is also a most dangerous device in that it will undoubtedly provoke the man against whom it is directed, and its clumsy use can engender sympathy for the target Justice even among those who disagree with him on the merits of a case. Occasionally, however, a Justice may accept these risks, as did the author of the following memorandum.[47]

> Mr. Justice — — —, concurring.
> I greatly sympathize with the essential purpose of my Brother . . . 's dissent. His roundabout and turgid legal phraseology is a *cri de cœur*. "Would I were back in the Senate," he means to say, "so, that I could put on the statute books what really ought to be there. But here I am, cast by Fate into a den of judges devoid of the habits of legislators, simple fellows who have a crippling feeling that they must enforce the laws as Congress wrote them and not as they ought to have been written. . . ."

Bargaining

Bargaining is most likely to occur when men agree on some matters, disagree on others, and still feel that further agreement would be profitable. Where the disputants are of approximately equal authority, they must, if persuasion has failed and force is not a feasible alternative, either turn to bargaining or reconcile themselves to loss of the advantages which they would accrue from compromising over the remaining points of difference. Disputants in posts of political authority who fail to achieve some sort of *modus vivendi* will frequently find that the problem at hand will be solved by other actors—with perhaps no profit and some loss to the original disputants or to their policy goals.

For Justices, bargaining is a simple fact of life. Despite conflicting views on literary style, relevant precedents, procedural rules, and substantive policy, cases have to be settled and opinions written; and no opinion may carry the institutional label of the Court unless five Justices agree to sign it. In the process of judicial decision-making, much bargaining may be tacit, but the pattern is still one of negotiation and accommodation to secure consensus. Thus how to bargain wisely—not necessarily sharply—is a prime consideration for a Justice who is anxious to see his policy adopted by the Court. A Justice must learn not only how to put pressure on his colleagues but how to gauge what amounts of pressure are sufficient to be "effective" and what amounts will overshoot the mark and alienate another judge. In many situations a Justice has to be willing to settle for less than he wants if he is to get anything at all. As Brandeis once remarked, the "great difficulty of all group action, of course, is when and what concession to make."[48]

To bargain effectively, one must have something to trade and also a sanction to apply if the offer is rejected or if there is a renege on a promise. The personal honor of the Justices minimizes the possibility of a renege in the usual sense of the term, but under existing Supreme Court practice a Justice is free to change his vote—and perhaps the disposition of a case—up to the minute the decision is announced in the courtroom. Beyond this, he may even change his position and vote for a rehearing and a reversal if such a petition is filed after a case has been decided. Equally important, he may shift his doctrinal position the next time the basic issue is before the Court.

The most significant items a Justice has to offer in trade are his vote and his concurrence in an opinion. Conversely, as the last section pointed out, threats to change a vote or to write a separate opinion, dissenting or concurring, are the sanctions most generally available to a Justice. When the Court is sharply divided any Justice can wield great influence. In 1889 Justice Gray deftly pressured Miller:[49]

> After a careful reading of your opinion in *Shotwell v. Moore*, I am very sorry to be compelled to say that the first part of it (especially in the passage which I have marked in the margin) is so contrary to my convictions, that I fear, unless it can be a good deal tempered, I shall have to deliver a separate'opinion on the lines of the enclosed memorandum.
>
> I am particularly troubled about this, because, if my scruples are not removed, and Justices Field, Bradley and Lamar adhere to their dissent, your opinion will represent only four judges, half of those who took part in the case.

Faced with the defection of one of his narrow majority, Miller had little choice but to adopt Gray's views.

It is also clear that where the Court is closely divided an uncommitted justice has great bargaining advantages, advantages which a deeply committed Justice might assume by appearing unsure. During the Court's deliberations over the Meadowmoor Dairies case in 1941,[50] a review of a state court injunction against picketing in a labor dispute which had been fraught with violence, Justice Murphy was toying with the idea of writing a separate opinion. His law clerk, however, sent him a lucid argument against such a course. Noting that Frankfurter had already circulated a draft of an opinion for the majority and Black and Reed had prepared separate dissents, the clerk advised that "the better and more effective approach is now to take advantage of your eminently strategic position. All three will try to woo you. Wouldn't it be better to work out your own views? Then pick the opinion that comes the closest. Then start work (à la Stone) on that." In closing, the clerk reminded his Justice of the importance of his vote to the various factions: "The name of Murphy in this case means much. It adds great weight to the opinion bearing it since you wrote Thornhill.* I'd act accordingly."[51]

Murphy consented to this game of watchful waiting. While disapproving of the emotional overtones of both Black's and Frankfurter's opinions, he considered Frankfurter's the better approach and decided to "improve" that opinion. In a few days he received the following memorandum from Frankfurter:[52]

> 1. You know how eager I have been—and am—to have our Milk opinion reflect your specifically qualified expert views. You also know how anxious I am to add not one extra word, and especially not to say anything that is absolutely avoidable by way of

---

* *Thornhill v. Alabama* (1940), and its companion case, *Carlson v. California* (1940), held for the first time that picketing was a form of free speech protected by the First and Fourteenth Amendments—a doctrine which the Court was later to qualify, but which typified at the time the spirit of the "new" Court.

creating a heated atmosphere. So here is my effort to translate the various suggestions into terms that would fit into, and truly strengthen, our opinion.

2. *Of course* I am open for any further suggestion. . . .

3. I am sending this to you, and not circulating it to others.

The final decision, which provoked one of Black's most eloquent protests, sustained the injunction against picketing. The opinion of the Court, however, stressed that the justification for this decision lay in the context of violence—the burnings, beatings, bombings, and shootings in which the picketing had taken place. Frankfurter's opinion specifically stated: "We do not qualify the Thornhill and Carlson decisions. We reaffirm them." Then he quoted Murphy's opinion in the Thornhill case to show the basic consistency between the two decisions.

All intra-Court bargaining takes place with the understanding that if the opinion writer ignores the suggestions which his colleagues scribble on slip opinions, he risks the disintegration of his majority. The threat to pull out normally need not be expressed, though some Justices have preferred to be very explicit about their intentions. Stone, for example, once wrote Frankfurter:[53]

> If you wish to write, placing the case on the ground which I think tenable and desirable, I shall cheerfully join you. If not, I will add a few observations for myself.

Only slightly less direct was the note, attached to a draft of a concurring opinion, which Stone sent Roberts:

> I doubt if we are very far apart in the Cantwell case, but in order that you might get exactly my views, I have written them out and enclosed them herewith.
>
> If you feel that you could agree with me, I think you would find no difficulty in making some changes in your opinion which would make it unnecessary for me to say anything.

While it is probably true that accommodation within the Court more often prevents a majority from splintering into concurring faction's, compromise can also serve to mute dissent. In either case the threat of a separate opinion may create a bargaining situation in which both minority and majority may gain something. Fearing that publication of a dissent or concurrence might cause the author of the prevailing opinion to make his pronouncements more rigid or perhaps draw attention to and emphasize an "erroneous" ruling, a minority Justice might reason that it would be more prudent to suppress his disagreement if he can win concessions from the majority.

Justice Johnson had the opportunity to explain one such occasion, *Sturges v. Crowninshield,* and to live to see a new majority erode the disputed policy. As he later wrote: "The Court was, in that case, greatly divided in their views of the doctrine, and the judgment partakes as much of a compromise as of a legal adjudication. The minority thought it better to yield something than risk the whole."[54] Other judges may not be so fortunate. "Silence under such circumstances," Alexander Bickel has pointed out, "is a gamble. . . . The risk is that if the birth is successful, silence will handicap one's future opposition. For one is then chargeable with parenthood. . . . Brandeis was to face the dilemma more than once. Instinct, a craftsman's inarticulable feel, which must largely govern action in such a matter, dictated now one choice, now the other."[55]

Publication of a dissent and *circulation within the Court* of a separate opinion serve two different functions. The latter is essentially at effort to resolve conflict within the Court by persuading, in one fashion or another, other Justices. The former is basically an attempt to shift the arena of combat. Having lost in the Court, a dissenting opinion is, as Cardozo said, an appeal to history, particularly to future judges.[56] But a dissent can be more. Whether the author intends it or not, a dissent can become an appeal to contemporaries—to members of Congress, to the President and executive officials, to lower court judges, to the bar or other interest groups, or to the public at large—to change the decision of the majority. As Frankfurter explained to Murphy in discussing a dissent in *Harris v. United States*:[57]

> This a protest opinion—a protest at the Bar of the future—but also an effort to make the brethren realize what is at stake. Moreover, a powerful dissent in a case like that is bound to have an effect on the lower courts as well as on the officers of the law, just as a failure to speak out vigorously against what the Court is doing will only lead to further abuse. And so in order to impress our own brethren, the lower courts, and enforcement officers, it seems to me vital to make the dissent an impressive document.

Although dissent is a cherished part of the common law tradition, a Justice who persistently refuses to accommodate his views to those of his colleagues may come to be regarded as an obstructionist. A Justice whose dissents become levers for legislative or administrative action reversing judicial policies may come to be regarded as disloyal to the bench. It is possible that either appraisal would curtail his influence with his associates. Even in his despair over the course of constitutional adjudication after Marshall's death, Justice Story thought this consideration limited the frequency with which he could dissent. He told Chancellor Kent that he would stay on the bench and continue to express his—and Marshall's—opinions, "But I shall naturally be silent on many occasions from an anxious desire not to appear contentious, or dissatisfied, or desirous of weakening the [word unclear] influence of the court."[58] Some years earlier, when Story's constitutional philosophy had been ascendant, Justice Johnson explained to Jefferson that he had found that one had to be wary of writing separate opinions "or become such a cypher in our consultations as to effect no good at all."[59]

At this time we lack sufficient empirical knowledge about the norms of intra-Court behavior to know how far a Justice would have to go in writing separate opinions before alienating his associates. It is possible that a reputation for writing dissents which result in favorable legislative and/or executive action might actually increase the Justice's bargaining power. A Justice who tried to build up such a reputation would have to be aware that, damage to personal relations within the Court aside, frequent appeals, especially if they were successful, to other branches of government or to public opinion to change what the Court was doing could severely injure the prestige of the Court and thus the Justice's chances of utilizing judicial power to achieve his own goals.

A justice has to be concerned also about the attention outside the Court which his dissents will gain. As in all aspects of life, overexposure can lead to boredom. Stone explained this to Karl Llewellyn: "You know, if I should write in every case where I do not agree with some of the views expressed in the opinions, you and all my other friends would stop reading them."[60]

Another factor which might prod a minority Justice into accepting compromise is psychological. Most people experience anxiety when they find themselves in sharp disagreement with a group with whom they are intimately associated. Supreme Court Justices tend to be highly independent and individualistic men, but they may not be completely immune to this distaste for isolation. Their professional socialization—especially their legal training and the accepted norms of judicial behavior—to some extent encourages judges to express their own views, but only to some extent. This socialization to some extent encourages a judge to strive for harmony and teamwork with his colleagues.

The strength of this tug toward agreement will vary according to the Justice's reliance on the Court as a reference group, and this reliance in turn will largely be a function of the personal and professional esteem in which he holds his colleagues. Where another reference group, either outside the Court or in the minority on the Court, is equally or more important to the Justice than the Court majority and where his views are applauded by that other group, he is very likely to be more persistent in asserting his views. Stone's reference group of law school professors such as John Bassett Moore, Edwin Borchard, Thomas Reed Powell, Herman Oliphant, Karl Llewellyn, and Felix Frankfurter made it easier for him to maintain his position in the old Court, as did his friendship with Holmes and Brandeis and later Cardozo.

By recognizing the existence of this tug toward agreement and the factors which affect it, a Justice might be better able to control it in himself and able to use it to his advantage. Where a Justice is one of a minority group on the Court, his friends in academic life—and many Justices have had close ties with major universities, either through their previous careers or their law clerks—might build themselves into a reference group for the minority by writing encouraging letters and publishing laudatory articles about the minority's work. When the Justice is in the majority he might further isolate the minority by having his friends write critical articles, or he might try to cut the minority off from access to their academic connections.[61] More simply, where he thought the Court was the other Justices' reference group, he might stress loyalty to the Court as an institution and the implications of isolation from the majority, as Frankfurter did with Murphy in *Hirabayashi*.

On the other hand, there are factors which push the majority Justices, especially the opinion writer, to accept accommodation. An eloquent, tightly-reasoned dissent can be an upsetting force. Stone's separate opinions during the thirties pointed up more sharply the folly of the conservative Justices than did any of the attacks on the Court by elected politicians. The majority may thus find it profitable to mute criticism from within the Court by giving in on some issues. The Justice who has been assigned the task of writing the opinion of the Court may see himself as a broker adjusting the interests of his associates as well as of himself. His problems, of course, are dynamic rather than static. By making a change in an opinion to pick up one vote he may lose another. Moreover, by compromising and incorporating several different lines of reasoning in his opinion he may expose himself to even more damaging dissent, as Hughes did in the Minnesota Moratorium case.[62]

Most important, a Justice would want to avoid having to water down his policy to the point where it ceased to be an operational doctrine—though it is possible that emasculation may be the only alternative to an outright rejection of his policy by the majority. As Stone wrote a colleague about the draft opinion in *Hirabayashi*: "I am anxious as far as I reasonably can to meet the views of my associates, but it seems to me that if I accepted your suggestions very little of the structure of my opinion would be left, and that I should lose most of my adherents. It seems to me, therefore, that it would be wiser for me to stand by the substance of my opinion and for you to express our views in your concurrence as you have already done."[63]

The opinion writer can apply some sort of marginal analysis to the alternatives he confronts. His minimum need—his essential need—is for four additional votes if he is to speak with the institutional authority of the Court. Thus, given the high value of these first four votes, he should rationally be willing to pay a relatively high price in accommodation to secure them. Once majority acquiescence has been obtained, the marginal value of any additional vote declines perceptibly, as would the price which all opinion writer should be willing to pay. However, the marginal value of another vote is never zero, though the asking price may exceed its real value and may have to be rejected. In the judicial process a 5–4 decision emphasizes the strength of the losing side and may encourage resistance and evasion. The greater the majority, the greater the appearance of certainty and the more likely a decision will be accepted and followed in similar cases. One hesitates to imagine how much more difficult implementation of the school segregation decisions would be had there been a four or three or even a two judge minority willing to claim in public that "separate but equal" was a valid constitutional doctrine.

A further bargaining complication may arise when a Justice who at first noted his dissent is persuaded that the majority is right, and, like many converts, is willing to take a firmer stand than some of the original believers with whom the opinion writer has had to negotiate. Here the opinion writer faces a most delicate choice between publication of a more forceful assertion of the doctrine which he is advocating and potential alienation of one or more relatively lukewarm members of his coalition who may view strengthening the majority opinion as a breach of faith or at least cause for a separate statement of views.

There is also the question of with whom to bargain. If a Justice were in the minority and trying to lessen the damage the majority opinion would do to the chances of achieving his objective, the obvious person whom he would have to influence would be the Justice assigned the task of writing the opinion of the Court. It would not, however, always be necessary to approach the opinion writer directly. The minority Justice might exploit his social relations with a Justice who was also on close terms with the opinion writer and have that third Justice act as an intermediary. Then, too, if the opinion writer were handling a particularly controversial case or were the kind of person who put a very high value on unanimity, it might be most prudent for the minority Justice to wait to be approached rather than make the first overtures himself. The same sort of considerations would apply to a majority Justice who wished the Court to issue a stronger statement than he thought the opinion writer would draft.

If a Justice were in the minority and trying to pick up an extra vote to give the appearance of more solidity to his protest or to turn his minority into a majority, or if the author of the opinion of the Court were attempting to increase his majority, the obvious colleague to approach—again directly or through an intermediary—would be one who had expressed some uncertainty during or after conference or whose voting record indicated ambiguous commitment to the side with which he had actually voted. Having attended the conference and having talked probably with several colleagues in private, a Justice would normally have a good idea of who might be wavering. To give himself the greatest possible advantage in such situations, he might even have one of his staff construct Guttman scales of the voting records of all the members of the Court, though with his intimate day-to-day knowledge of his colleagues' behavior it is not likely that this sort of formal analysis would be of great value.

The writer of the majority opinion who wished to squelch a dissent might also have the option of contacting the dissenter directly or working through an intermediary or, if he strongly suspected that the dissent was being circulated merely for bargaining purposes, of sitting back and waiting to be approached. Probably the most ticklish situation, from the point of view of interpersonal relations, in which a Justice might find himself is when he is with the majority but not writing the majority opinion, and he fears that the opinion writer is about to win over a dissenter by conceding more than the value of the additional vote. Under such circumstances, a Justice would have to proceed most cautiously in order to avoid the twin perils of appearing to be a busybody interfering at every stage of the negotiations and at the other extreme of sulking behind the threat of writing a separate concurrence. Either course might annoy the opinion writer to the extent that he would give up the chance of having that Justice's vote and make even greater concessions to win the former dissenter.

A Case Study in Persuasion

Goldman v. United States provides an excellent example of the use of several different kinds of persuasion within the Court. Under review was a conviction of three lawyers for conspiring to violate the Bankruptcy Act. Federal agents, with the co-operation of the building superintendent, entered the office of one of the defendants and installed a listening device. The apparatus failed to work, but the agents, who occupied the adjacent office, utilized a detectaphone—an instrument which can amplify the sound of voices talking on the other side of a wall—and transcribed several incriminating conversations.

At the Saturday conference[64] of the Court in early February, 1942, Chief Justice Stone said that he found the law hazy; it allowed some invasions of privacy but not others. The vice of this sort of eavesdropping, he thought, was that it was totally unrestrained. The federal agents had not asked for a warrant; in fact, if they had merely been searching for evidence, it was unlikely that they would have been able to show the probable cause necessary to obtain a warrant. While he did not think the case was "dead open and shut," he leaned toward reversal. Roberts and Reed took a strong position to affirm. Roberts candidly stated that he did not believe the Fourth Amendment had been intended to prevent police snooping, and Reed felt that the situation was completely covered by *Olmstead v. United States*, the famous wiretapping case of 1928. Frankfurter sharply challenged both Roberts' interpretation of the Constitution and Reed's faith in *Olmstead* as a viable precedent, but the conference voted 5–3 to affirm, with Justice Jackson not participating.

As the senior majority Justice, Roberts assigned himself the task of writing the opinion. He held that use of the detectaphone did not violate the Federal Communications Act, nor, under the doctrine of *Olmstead*, did it contravene the Fourth Amendment. He also stated that whatever trespass the agents had committed in installing the unsuccessful listening device did not make inadmissible any evidence later obtained through the detectaphone. For the dissenters Stone undertook to write an opinion, and Murphy gave general directions to guide his clerk in preparing a second dissent.

Stone quickly drafted his opinion; and by February 27, he had incorporated some minor suggestions by Frankfurter. At this point the draft read:[65]

> Had a majority of the Court been willing at this time to overrule the *Olmstead* case, we would have been happy to join them. But as they have declined to do so, and as we think this case is indistinguishable in principle from *Olmstead*'s, we have no occasion to repeat here the dissenting views [of Holmes, Brandeis, and Butler] in that case with which we agree.
>
> Both courts below found that the trespass by the Government officers in locating the dictaphone did not aid materially in the use of the detectaphone. Hence it is unnecessary to consider whether the use of the detectaphone, if aided by the trespass, would constitute a violation of the Fourth Amendment. The Government did not deny that it would, and we explicitly dissociate ourselves from the declaration in the opinion [of the Court] that it would not.

When Roberts read the second paragraph of Stone's opinion, he agreed to modify what he had said about the trespass and substantially adopted Stone's phrasing: "Both courts below have found that the trespass did not aid materially in the use of the detectaphone. Since we accept these concurrent findings, we need not consider a contention based on a denial of their verity." Having achieved this minor victory, Stone dropped the second paragraph of his opinion.

Meanwhile, when the Chief Justice's opinion came to Murphy's office, his clerk sent it on to the Justice with a report that he had just had a visit from one of Stone's clerks who told him that Frankfurter was champing at the bit to write a searing dissent. The Chief Justice, however, was convinced that it was wiser for the minority to take a beating now without putting up a public fight on *Olmstead*, lest that case become even more entrenched as the survivor of two great battles within the Court. Murphy's clerk added as a countervailing consideration that perhaps Brandeis' arguments in favor of privacy should be repeated every so often.[66]

Murphy may have remembered—he had made lengthy notes during the discussion of the case among the Justices—that at the conference Stone had suggested that *Olmstead* might be overruled, but had not pressed the point; he had also suggested that the two cases could be distinguished. Moreover, the Chief Justice had admitted that historically, many different kinds of invasions of privacy had been allowed under the Fourth Amendment.[67] Perhaps because of this recollection Murphy was unsure that Stone was fully committed to overturning *Olmstead*. In any event, he continued work on his own dissent. On March 5, Frankfurter, who by now had been won over to Stone's strategy of avoiding open conflict, tried to dissuade Murphy:[68]

> You have heard my views expressed in Conference, and I am afraid somewhat fiercely, on wiretapping, and you must, therefore, know that I am as uncompromising on that subject as you are, feeling as you do that the issue goes to the very essence of a civilized society. Like you, therefore, I will not yield an inch on my convictions and would accede to no compromising expression of them.
>
> But I do not see that any "compromise" is involved in the way in which the C. J. has formulated dissent from the majority opinion. Of course each man's phrasing has its own distinctive quality, but so far as the substance of the matter goes, I certainly could not dream of improving on what Brandeis and Holmes said in the *Olmstead* case. And so it seems to me that an unequivocal announcement that we would overrule the *Olmstead* case and adopt as our own the views expressed by the dissenters in that case, is an unswerving and unqualified adoption of these views and a reaffirmation of them. And to do it in the way in which the Chief Justice proposes has for me the quality of Doric eloquence. Simplicity and austerity are sometimes the most emphatic way of conveying an idea to the world.

In closing his letter, Frankfurter added a plea for solidarity:

> For the three of us to speak in different language would imply a difference of opinion amongst us. That would attenuate the moral strength of our position. I hope very much, therefore, that it will commend itself to you to have the three of us speak with one voice and in the way in which the C. J. has proposed.

Murphy, however, stuck to his own plan and circulated a long and eloquent dissent, asserting that government officers had committed a palpable invasion of the defendants' privacy in violation of explicit prohibitions of the Fourth Amendment. In his opinion, he referred to the federal agents as "overzealous officials," and castigated their action as "debasing to government." When he received his copy, Frankfurter made only a few small suggestions and concluded; "You have not only expressed your convictions but you have expressed them, if I may say so, well."[69]

On April 6, after Murphy's dissent was circulated, Justice Jackson, who had been Attorney General when the Goldman prosecution was conducted, sent a memorandum to all members of the Court. Jackson said that in light of Murphy's remarks he felt it necessary to file an opinion to explain his own non-participation in the case:[70]

By Mr. Justice Jackson

As notation of my disqualification without more would create uncertain implications as to my responsibility for the questionable conduct of the investigation, it is desirable to state the precise facts which lead to my non-participation.

Thirteen days after I was commissioned as Attorney General of the United States this indictment was found. While the prosecution was determined upon and prepared and the detectaphone recordings in question were made prior to my entrance into office and under rules, regulations, and practices of the Attorney General that I found in force, the prosecution was continued under my official responsibility. Under these circumstances it seemed appropriate to refrain from judicial action in the case.

Since he had been Attorney General before Jackson and since, therefore, the action which he was so bitterly criticizing had been conducted under his own official responsibility—though probably without his personal knowledge—Murphy was put in a squeeze. The squeeze was made even tighter because, although the matter was ultimately one for the judgment of each Justice, there was doubt—and Jackson's opinion drew attention to the doubt—that a former Attorney General should hear a case on the bench which was prosecuted under his auspices. The same day as Jackson circulated his opinion, Murphy contacted him and indicated a willingness to reconsider his remarks.[71] Jackson immediately seized the opportunity to seal a bargain. In a letter which began "My dear Frank," he offered a full statement of his feelings:[72]

This case presents a new question of law on which difference of opinion is to be expected and upon which it is conceivable that one's attitude as a prosecutor and as a judge might differ. However, the Department of Justice under several Attornies General has assumed the law to be as the Court now holds it to be. Even so, any Attorney General was empowered to impose further limitations on investigative methods if he thought good morals or good government required it. None of us did so. . . .

But any discomfort of my own is small compared with the position of those who served under both of us and who looked to us—not as much as they should have, perhaps—for guidance and supervision. . . . My grievance is only academic compared to the gravity of putting words such as I have quoted ["overzealous officials"; action "debasing to government"] into the mouth of every criminal lawyer in the United States to be hurled at the Government as quotations from a former Attorney General and a Present Justice, when it attempts to use evidence the Court now holds to be its legal right. . . .

In his next to the last paragraph, Jackson further tightened the squeeze on Murphy by withdrawing his opinion:

Now that you know how I feel in the matter, I shall leave the result to your own good judgment. Whatever you do, I think the interests of the Court would not be served by carrying the matter to the public. I commit myself not to do that in order to leave you free of any pressures in the matter except those of your own strong sense of justice.

As the final turn of the screw, Jackson noted in his closing sentence: "I am sending a copy of this to the Chief Justice and to our associates so that they may know the way the matter stands."

Murphy was left with no real choice. He might have been able to answer Jackson's argument about how his remarks would reflect on officials of the Department of Justice, past or future; but Jackson's withdrawal of his own opinion and his announcement of this fact to the Court had put Murphy in a position where he had to compromise. In effect, Jackson opened the door to negotiation and then shoved Murphy through it. Murphy's published opinion excused the Department of Justice from any deliberate wrongdoing:

> On the basis of the narrow, literal construction of the search and seizure clause of the Fourth Amendment adopted in Olmstead v. United States, Government officials could well believe that activities of the character here involved did not contravene the constitutional mandate. But for my part, I think that the Olmstead Case was wrong.

Co-Option

It would be much easier for a Justice to vote and join in opinions with a judge whose policy goals were identical or very similar to his own than with a colleague with contrary aims. It is possible, under the sort of favorable political circumstances discussed earlier . . . , for a policy-oriented Justice to exert influence in the executive process and to have a voice in choosing a new colleague, a colleague who, hopefully, will agree with him on decisions and opinions important to his policy goals. Gratitude, especially if it were coupled with deep intellectual respect, might play a role in increasing the helping Justice's influence with the new appointee, but its role would probably be minor. As Presidents have often painfully learned, gratitude is usually a weak emotion in judges who have what amounts to life tenure. Although gratitude might make social relations easier, certainly it would not be comparable in effect to a basic agreement on policy.

Many members of the Court have become embroiled in appointment politicking. Miller,[73] Fuller,[74] and Brown[75] tried it with varying degrees of success, but the most systematic efforts along these lines were made by William Howard Taft.[76] Probably no judge ever came to the Bench with a clearer conception of the "proper" role of the individual Justice within the Court or the "proper" role of the Court in the American political system than Taft. "Teamwork" was the Chief Justice's overriding value in intra-Court relations, and he saw the protection of property rights through the Fifth and Fourteenth Amendments as the Court's principal task.

Since Harding had promised Sutherland the first place on the Court, Taft had little to do with the former Senator's appointment—except perhaps in a negative way in that both Taft and Sutherland had been candidates for the chief justiceship. The center chair had been Taft's avowed lifelong ambition, and Sutherland, so Harding said, was "crazy" for the office.[77] Taft gave a broad hint about his alert interest in the appointing process when, after his own selection, he wrote a gracious letter to George Sutherland expressing the hope that Sutherland would soon join him on the bench. "Our views," the new Chief Justice noted, "are very much alike and it is important that they prevail."[78]

When Justice Day retired, Taft, knowing that Harding was not committed to any candidate, began to work feverishly to find a suitable nominee. After failing to interest John W. Davis, the Chief Justice and Van Devanter decided that "Pierce Butler is our man."[79] Taft then opened an intensive campaign to bring off the nomination. He called on the President and wrote him several letters lavishly praising Butler and criticizing other candidates. The Chief Justice also carried on a lengthy correspondence with Butler, giving him news on events in Washington and plying him with advice on how to advance his cause. Taft's suggestions included not only the best way for Butler to deploy his political assets but also how to exploit his religious assets as well. The Chief Justice believed that Harding wanted to appoint a Catholic (Justice McKenna was expected to retire soon); Taft also knew that Archbishop Hayes of New York was pushing Judge Martin Manton of the United States Circuit Court of Appeals for the Second Circuit. To counter this activity, Taft urged Butler to line up the Catholic hierarchy in the Middle West. Butler protested that he abhorred the thought of involving clergymen in politics, but he did supply the names of one cardinal, two archbishops, and three bishops, plus the bishops in the archdiocese of St. Paul, with whom Harding could consult.

After Harding nominated Butler, the Chief Justice switched his attention to the Senate and once again gave Butler detailed advice on which senators were important and how they might be approached. Taft talked with his own friends on Capitol Hill and arranged a quick judiciary committee meeting to approve the nomination.

When Pitney retired—with an assist from Taft in getting special legislation through Congress allowing full retirement benefits, despite the fact that Pitney had not yet reached the statutory retirement age—the Chief Justice once again plunged into the appointments maelstrom. Several candidates with impressive reputations were under consideration for this vacancy, and the Chief Justice consulted with a number of people, including the President, the Attorney General, and the chairman of the finance committee of the Republican National Committee. For Harding's benefit, Taft gave a rundown on each of the people under consideration. He conceded that Judge Cuthbert Pound of the New York Court of Appeals "has some ability and experience," but that he had shown a preference for dissent over "teamwork" and "solidarity." Judge Frederick Crane, a colleague of Pound, was a popular man. Although not a lawyer of "the greatest ability . . . he would probably be preferable to Pound." Taft dismissed Chief Justice Robert Von Moschzisker of Pennsylvania as an accident—in Pennsylvania the chief justiceship rotated according to seniority, and the judges ahead of Von Moschzisker had died rather promptly. "He is a politician more than a judge."[80] (With his brother Taft was more candid: Von Moschzisker took too broad a view of the police power and state control over the uses of private property.)[81]

Cardozo, Taft continued in his letter to Harding, "is the best judge in New York. . . . [He] is a Jew and a Democrat. I don't think he would always side with Brandeis, but he is what they call a progressive judge." Learned Hand was described as "an able judge and a hard worker. I appointed him . . . but he turned out to be a wild Roosevelt man [in 1912] and a Progressive, and though on the Bench, he went into the campaign. If promoted to our Bench, he would almost certainly herd with Brandeis and be a dissenter. I think it would be risking too much to appoint him."[82]

Taft had many kind words for U.S. District Judge William Grubb, a Yale classmate of Horace Taft; but the Chief Justice's highest praise was reserved for Judge Charles Hough of the U.S. Circuit Court of Appeals. Despite several personal pleas by Taft and his use of intermediaries, Harding refused to appoint Hough because he thought the judge too old. Later, in the course of a conversation with the Chief Justice, Harry Daugherty suggested the name of Edward T. Sanford, U.S. District Judge in Tennessee. Taft jumped at the suggestion and was soon strenuously supporting Sanford. The Chief Justice admitted to a friend that Sanford was not "the strongest man but I so much prefer him to Pound or Crane or the Chief Justice of Pennsylvania that I would now be glad to have him appointed."[83] How much Harding's final decision was due to Taft, or to Daugherty, or to other political considerations will probably never be known, but once again the men whom Taft had opposed were kept off the bench and one of his candidates, although not his first choice, was appointed.

When McKenna retired—also with Taft's assistance, this time in the form of a positive suggestion to the Justice that he was too infirm to perform his duties in a satisfactory manner[84]—the Chief Justice once more took part in choosing a colleague. He visited Coolidge and claimed to have "rather forced" the President to appoint Stone.[85] Fourteen years later, when Stone heard of Taft's statement, he said he doubted that Taft had been influential with Coolidge or that Coolidge had needed anyone to recommend his Attorney General to him.[86] Taft, however, persisted in asserting responsibility for Stone's selection even after he became convinced that he had made a serious error in the choice.[87]

Stone, in turn, played a major part in Cardozo's nomination. Taking advantage of his close relationship with Hoover, Stone introduced Cardozo to the President. As Stone recalled the incident, "I seized the opportunity to make the President acquainted with the kind of a judge he ought to appoint and prefaced the call by expatiating on that topic at some length."[88] On several later occasions Stone reminded Hoover of Cardozo's fitness[89] and strongly recommended him when Holmes retired. Hoover, however, wavered, fearing to offend the Senate by having three New York men (Stone and Hughes were also from New York) and two Jews (Brandeis was still on the bench) on the Court.

Stone then took a bold course of action:[90]

> I was apprehensive lest a selection should be made which would emphasize the Court's conservative tendencies, and feeling that they were already over-emphasized, I feared that great harm might result and that some sort of an explosion would occur not unlike that which actually took place after the decisions in the A.A.A. case and the *Tipaldo Women's Wage* case. In a conversation with President Hoover intended to emphasize both the importance of the appointment and Judge Cardozo's fitness I intimated to him that if he feared criticism because of the addition of a New York man to the Court when there were two other New Yorkers already there, I would be willing to retire from the Court. Later, in conversation with Senator Wagner, who was then about to discuss the matter with President Hoover, I made the same suggestion.

It is impossible to determine whether Stone was merely trying to put additional pressure on Hoover or was really tired of the frustrations of judicial work.[91] Other men and forces were also at work in the appointment and Stone never claimed full—or even much—credit, though when the nomination was announced Frankfurter wired him: "The country is your debtor for your decisive help in achieving a great national good."*[92]

Undoubtedly there have been many other instances of Justices working for or against the appointment of specific men. Van Devanter and Butler acted as intermediaries for the Attorney General in sounding out Charles Evans Hughes for the chief justiceship in 1930.[93] In the light of Attorney General Mitchell's long friendship with Pierce Butler, it is not improbable that Butler was acting as more than a passive instrument of the Hoover administration.

Some judicial efforts have been successful, others may not have been. Hughes later endorsed Mitchell for Holmes's chair but the nomination went to Cardozo. Frankfurter, and to a lesser extent Stone, worked for Learned Hand's promotion to the High Bench in 1942, but F. D. R. reacted against what he felt was too heavy pressure and chose Wiley Rutledge instead. Some Justices, like Taft or Stone or perhaps Butler, have been in all excellent position to influence appointments; other Justices have not. But, since most members of the Court come to the bench only after extensive political experience,[94] the average Justice must be aware of the informal as well as the formal channels through which influence can be exerted. Most important, it is quite clear that if a Justice wishes to enter the appointing process—and is able to do so—he can make ideology a prime factor in determining who will receive his support.

Although many Justices are in a position where they can affect appointments, it does not necessarily follow that any particular Justice will always, often, or even ever have a voice in the selection of other members of the Court. Nor does it mean that those Justices who can exert influence will choose to do so. There are dangers in participating in the political processes, and a judge may reasonably conclude in many situations that, all questions of ethics aside, the risk of high costs in possible requests for a *quid pro quo* from executive officials is not worth the benefit that may be derived.[95] This sort of assessment is especially likely to occur when the Justice has good reason to believe that the administration will select the "right" kind of man without assistance from the bench.

II. BLOC FORMATION

When it is impossible for a Justice to secure in the foreseeable future majority endorsement of his policy, he has to make a different kind of assessment of strategic plans and tactical maneuvers. In general he would have under such circumstances three major alternatives:

---

*It should be noted that Justice Frankfurter later changed his mind. In a letter to me of Sept. 27, 1961, he stated that he had come to believe that the "decisive help" had been supplied by Senators Borah and Watson.

a) Going along with the majority, trying to minimize through bargaining the damage done by the majority's refusal to accept "true" doctrine or its acceptance of "false" doctrine.

b) Dissenting alone or with whoever will join him in a particular case.

c) Trying to form a minority group of justices into a voting bloc, at least for purposes of one set of issues.

Alternative *a* may offer the greatest advantages, but only if the members of the majority are willing to compromise. It may happen that they would feel sufficiently secure to refuse to make any significant concessions, thus leaving a policy-oriented Justice with a real choice only between alternatives *b* and *c*. Alternative *b* is cheap in terms of the expenditure of some kinds of resources, since, by playing the role of a lone wolf, the Justice would avoid many of the costs in time, energy, and purity of doctrine involved in arriving at a group decision. On the other hand, this alternative may entail high opportunity costs, forgoing as it does many of the tactics which might gain one, two, or three additional votes to support a particular set of views. There may also be the opportunity cost of winning a particular case, since a bloc of four Justices has thirty-one out of thirty-two chances of winning any vote, and a three-judge bloc has approximately seven out of eight chances—*providing that the votes of the other Justices are distributed randomly.* This condition, of course, is extremely unlikely to obtain; but while the chances of winning are vastly less in the real world than such statistics indicate, the chances would still be far better if the minority Justices stuck together and hoped to pick up the additional vote or two needed, than if they divided among themselves according to the nuances of peculiar cases.

Alternative *c* is not always the better choice, despite its potential advantages. Where there is considerable disagreement among the minority Justices on basic issues, the costs of alternative *c* will be high in terms of doctrinal purity as well as in the time and energy needed to come to a group decision. Conversely, since the opportunity costs of alternative *b* in such a situation would be quite low, it would probably be the more rational choice, at least as measured in short-run gains. On the other hand, where there is a high level of agreement among the minority Justices, the group decision-making and doctrinal costs of alternative *c* will be relatively low and the opportunity costs of *b* relatively high, making *c* the preferable choice.

Even assuming a situation in which *c*, the establishment of a bloc, is the more profitable course, it is improbable that any justice could "form" a bloc among his colleagues. What he could very possibly do is to discover similar outlooks and voting tendencies among his brethren and then use his social and intellectual skills to reinforce ideological affinities and bring about a measure of co-ordination to individual behavior patterns. Most of the tactics discussed in other sections of this chapter would be applicable to bloc "formation." Quite relevant would be another stratagem, the "rump conference"—a device used by Taft as Chief Justice and Stone as an Associate Justice. Taft would occasionally call together Van Devanter and several of his other friends for Sunday afternoon meetings at his home. There the group would thrash over some of the more difficult cases and opinions so that they could present a united front to the rest of the Court. Some years later, to thwart what he thought was Hughes's overefficient disposal of business, Stone held Friday evening meetings at his home to hammer out in advance the important issues scheduled to be taken up at the next day's conference.

Maintaining the group morale needed to keep a bloc together would be a very trying task. A finely developed capacity for moral leadership would be essential where the majority was united and determined in its position. As Samuel Miller explained after the legal tender controversy, "marshalling my forces and keeping up their courage against a domineering Chief, and a party in court who have been accustomed to carry everything their own way, has been such a strain on my brain and nervous system as I never wish to encounter again."[96] Minimum requirements for minority bloc leadership would be a capacity to communicate hope, plus a readiness to compromise—and to do so quickly and amiably—with other bloc members, as well as to accede to the wishes of other bloc members on issues the Justice did not think especially important.

On the other hand, bloc unanimity insofar as published votes and opinions are concerned need be neither an absolute rule nor even necessarily a wise policy. One of the tactics of a bloc should be to conceal as far as possible the fact of its existence, lest other Justices feel it vital to their interests to form a counterbloc and so perhaps nullify the advantages of the first bloc. Thus it might be more prudent if on some, perhaps many, issues, the bloc members vote against each other or at least concur in separate opinions.

Camouflage can be facilitated in several ways. First, if there are some issues coming before the Court which all members of the bloc consider trivial, the members can agree to open or pitched battle among themselves as a smokescreen. Such divisions can also be arranged where the bloc has lost or where it has a majority which is sufficiently large that defection of one or more of its members will not change the decision of the Court. Separate opinions in these kinds of cases can be based on technical grounds so as both to mask the existence of the bloc and to enhance individual Justices' reputations as skilled craftsmen who are sticklers for procedural niceties.

Third, while it would generally be unwise for bloc members to vote to grant certiorari in cases on which they will be outvoted on the merits, it might help conceal the bloc's existence if the members sometimes vote to bring up a dispute which threatens to push one of the bloc's policies beyond the point where bloc members feel it should go. It would have been shrewd, for instance, for the libertarians on the Roosevelt Court to vote to review *Chaplinsky v. New Hampshire*. In that case a Jehovah's Witness who had called a local police officer a "goddamned Fascist" and a "damned racketeer" was claiming the protection of the First Amendment—an extension of free speech which none of the Court's libertarians was then willing to support. Similarly, it might be tactically clever for those Justices on the Warren Court who strongly favor workingmen's claims under the Federal Employers' Liability Act to vote to bring up some cases in which they can, in good conscience, decide for the employer. Indeed, one student[97] of the Court has suggested that this might have been done in *Herdman v. Pennsylvania R. R. Co.* (1957).

It is improbable that any or all of these stratagems could long conceal either from other Justices or from scholars the existence of a cohesive bloc. Nevertheless, since even a gain in time of a term or two could be important in gaining votes in particular cases for the bloc members, efforts at camouflage may well be worth the effort.

Bloc formation may be equally attractive to a Justice in the majority as to a Justice in the minority, though the addition of each new bloc member tends to increase the number of doctrinal adjustments that have to be made as well as the difficulties of obtaining group agreement. The profit of keeping a majority together, however, may far outweigh these extra costs. Moreover, minority bloc formation, like defense in war, would only be thought of as a temporary measure. The primary aim of a policy-oriented Justice's operations within the Court would be to secure a majority for his policy, and minority bloc formation is, at most, only an expedient step toward that end.

The primacy of this objective means, most obviously, that the Justice would be ready to woo any colleague likely to vote with the bloc in a particular case. It also means that a Justice would have to be very subtle in his planning. Where the votes required to achieve a majority *on a decision* are available but serious questions about over-all policy are present, the Justice would have to persuade the bloc members to avoid taking a doctrinaire line either in conference discussion or in opinion writing. The most prudent approach might well be to discuss the case and write the opinion on relatively narrow grounds, hoping that if several such decisions follow each other over a period of years the underlying doctrine will evolve naturally and not prematurely frighten an undecided Justice into rejecting the logical conclusions of the premises he has been accepting. It requires very delicate judgment to decide whether it is better to move when five votes are secured or to play for time, to settle for an immediate but limited victory or wait until a sixth or a seventh vote can be picked up—and risk that the majority could also be lost in the interval—before announcing a controversial principle as the justification of a decision. If the slower approach is adopted, when the Justice does decide to try to persuade the bloc members to move, two arguments will be available to defend the newly captured position: first, the substantive reasons behind the principle and second, an appeal to *stare decisis*, that touchstone of judicial virtue and regularity.

A policy-oriented Justice would also have to plan antibloc tactics. If he perceived opposing members of the Court uniting on some issues, he would have to utilize this information to bring together a countergroup or to break down the unity of the opposing group. One possible method of accomplishing the latter task would be to press, both in conference discussions and in written opinions, arguments on which he knew the bloc members disagreed. Stone told Roosevelt that Hughes was particularly adept at using this maneuver against the liberals on the old Court. When a difference of opinion was apparent among the liberals, the Chief Justice would, so Roosevelt recounted to Harold Ickes, "get his big toe in and widen the cleavage."[98] Whether or not Stone's or Roosevelt's or Ickes' judgment and memory were affected by the bitterness of the Court fight over the New Deal, the statistical fact remains that, from whatever motivation, Hughes was apt to assign opinions of the Court to liberals when they were divided among themselves and to conservatives when that group was split.[99]

III. THE SPECIAL CASE OF THE CHIEF JUSTICE

So far this discussion has treated all Justices as equal in authority if not in power and influence. But the Chief Justice, while usually thought of by his colleagues only as *primus inter pares*, does have some authority which other members of the Court do not possess. He presides in open Court and at conference. He speaks first at the conference and votes last. When in the majority he assigns the opinion of the Court. By a tradition built up since Hughes's time, the Chief Justice circulates a "special list" of petitions for certiorari which he thinks should be denied without conference discussion. Although any Justice may have a petition taken off this list, such action is not often requested. While only indirectly affecting his relations with other Justices, the Chief Justice is expected to make the appointments to staff positions for the entire Court—the clerk, the marshal, the director of the Administrative Office of United States Courts, and so on—with each Justice having the right to appoint his own personal staff.

Justice Miller claimed that the Chief Justice has no more authority than his colleagues care to give him.[100] But, if, as some of the studies of formal groups indicate, there is an expectation that a titular leader will exert both task and social leadership, it would follow that the Chief Justice generally has an initial psychological advantage over any Associate Justice in a struggle for influence within the Court—though this advantage may be indecisive and short-lived. The Chief Justice, Taft wrote shortly before he assumed the office, "is the head of the Court, and while his vote counts but one in the nine, he is, if he be a man of strong and persuasive personality, abiding convictions, recognized by learning and statesmanlike foresight, expected to promote team-work by the Court, so as to give weight and solidarity to its opinions."[101]

Presiding at conference gives the Chief an opportunity to exercise task leadership by stating his views first on cases and, as Hughes usually did, selecting the issues to be discussed. So, too, at oral argument the Chief Justice may take advantage of his presiding office to give direction to the lines of reasoning which counsel will explore. As presiding officer he may also exert social leadership. He may have the Court dispose of the less controversial decisions before taking up those more likely to cause dissension. By tackling these simpler items first a higher degree of harmony can be established, and this harmony might carry over and protect later discussion from personal rancor. If and when arguments begin to get heated, the Chief may use his authority to ease tension, either by cutting off debate or soothing hurt feelings. Hughes would often end a discussion which was threatening to get out of hand by saying, "Brethren, the only way to settle this is to vote."[102] When Melville W. Fuller was Chief Justice, Holmes once interrupted Justice Harlan's statement of his views with a caustic, "That won't wash!" Harlan, never noted for avoiding a fight, reddened, but Fuller quickly broke in: "But I keep scrubbing away, scrubbing away," using his hands as if rubbing clothes on a washboard. The laughter that ensued allowed the Justices to get back to their work without a bitter exchange of words.[103]

An astute Chief Justice can also utilize his opinion-assigning power to increase his influence on the Court. When in agreement with the majority, the Chief

Justice can assign the opinion to the most moderate member, hoping that his mild statement of the doctrine might prevent defections or even gain adherents. The Chief may even assign the opinion to a wavering Justice, hoping that this task—if not further reflection and research—will strengthen the Justice's resolve and perhaps sway the minority. Alternately, the Chief Justice may use the opinion-assigning power to reward his coalition within the Court. He can assign the opinions in interesting and important cases to those Justices who tend to vote with him, leaving the dregs for those who vote against him on issues he thinks important. This authority may also be used as a means of encouraging an elderly or failing colleague to retire. Chief Justice Fuller withheld opinions from old Justice Field to help nudge him off the bench, and Taft tried the same tactic with McKenna.

The advantages of the opinion-assigning power are augmented by the fact that the Chief Justice votes last in conference. Thus, before he finally commits himself, he knows where each Justice stands—at least for the present—and which side will most probably win. If his own views are going to be in the minority, he can vote with the majority and retain the opinion-assigning authority. He may keep the opinion himself—as apparently John Marshall sometimes did—and so do a minimum of damage to his own deeply felt values. Or the Chief may assign the opinion to the majority Justice whose views are closest to his own. It is worth noting in this regard that during his first nine terms as Chief Justice (1930–38), Hughes officially registered only 23 dissents in 1,382 cases decided by full opinion.

There is an additional potential source of power for the Chief Justice which is usually overlooked by students of the Court. If, in fact, the so-called paradox of voting or the problem of cyclical majorities does occur on the Court, the Chief Justice in his capacity as presiding officer has a unique opportunity to exploit the situation. The voting paradox might take place in a decision-making body where more than two alternatives—as in complex litigation—were available to the group, and where each actor has different and transitive choice preferences. For preferences to be transitive an actor who prefers alternative *a* to alternative *b* and alternative *b* to alternative *c*, must also prefer *a* to *c*. The voting paradox may occur where.

Actor I prefers *a* to *b*, *b* to *c*, and *a* to *c*.
Actor II prefers *b* to *c*, *c* to *a*, and *b* to *a*.
Actor III prefers *c* to *a*, *a* to *b*, and *c* to *b*.

Here two actors prefer alternative *a* to alternative *b*, and two prefer *b* to *c*, but two also prefer *c* to *a*. Thus each alternative is actually opposed by a majority, although the rules of voting used by most decision-making groups, whether by accident or by some unconscious design, will usually conceal the existence of the paradox and result in a majority choice.

This cyclical problem has been recognized at least since Condorcet, and in recent years a number of economists and a few political scientists have explored more fully its implications for public-policy formulation. One of the most important implications for the power of the Chief Justice is Duncan Black's conclusion that, where the paradox does occur, the time at which a given alternative is put to the vote is crucial in determining its acceptance or rejection, since most rules for voting would provide an opportunity for expression of second choices.[104] The internal procedures of the Court are sufficiently loose so that the Chief Justice might manipulate rather easily the order in which issues were voted on and thus change the outcome.

For example, assume that in discussing a case the Justices divide in support of three alternatives: *a*, *b*, and *c*. Alternative *a* might well be a decision to affirm the entire judgment under review; alternative *b* could be a decision to affirm one part of the judgment and to reverse a second part; alternative *c* could be a decision to reverse both issues before the Court. Conference discussion has brought out that the division is:

> Prefer *a*: Chief Justice and Justices 1, 2, 3 (Group I).
> Prefer *b*: Justice 4 (Group II).
> Prefer *c*: Justices 5, 6, 7, 8 (Group III).

The conference discussion has also brought out the following preference rankings:

> Group I prefers *a* to *b*, *b* to *c*, and *a* to *c*.
> Group II prefers *b* to *a*, *a* to *c*, and *b* to *c*.
> Group III prefers *c* to *b*, *b* to *a*, and *c* to *a*.

The Chief Justice knows that the first alternative voted on, whichever it is, will be defeated, and on the next vote supporters of the defeated alternative will have an opportunity to express their second choice. Thus he suggests a vote first on *b*, which is, of course, defeated by 8–1. Next he puts his own preference, alternative *a*, to a vote, and it carries 5–4 since Justice 4 prefers *a* to *c*. If, however, the Chief Justice had first put *a* to a vote, it would have been defeated and *b* would have become the winner if the Group I Justices next voted their second choice.

Neither singularly nor together do these special powers insure the Chief Justice sufficient influence to persuade the other Justices to endorse his policy goals. Much of his initial advantage is postulated on the belief that his accepted, i.e., legitimate, role is one of leadership. This may or may not be true. It would not be too much to say that the severe and efficient Hughes did dominate the conference.[105] Only rarely were matters discussed which he did not want brought up, and the Justice who dared debate with the Chief usually found himself in a very painful position since Hughes came into the conference armed both with heavily marked volumes of the U.S. Reports and a photographic memory. He also had a keen sense of humor, though he used it infrequently. Nevertheless, apparently no other member of the Court had the temerity to try to exert social leadership.

When Stone succeeded Hughes, it is not unlikely that the Associate Justices had come to expect the Chief to act both as a task and a social leader. But Stone did not play either role, at least not in a fashion comparable to that of either of his immediate predecessors. Since he had felt frustrated by Hughes's methods, the new Chief Justice refused to cut off discussion—indeed, he joined in angry wrangling with his associates, something which Hughes considered beneath his station. Long, acrimonious harangues, which often stretched from Saturday until Wednesday, marked the Stone conferences.[106]

Harlan Stone held the center chair for five years, and his legacy to his successor was in all probability a changed concept in the minds of the Associate Justices of the Chief Justice's role. Thus if Vinson, assuming he had had the desire as well as the intellectual ability and social charm, had tried to return to the kind of leadership which Hughes had exerted, he might well have alienated his associates by violating their expectations of his proper role. It is quite possible that for the immediate future Stone destroyed any aura of legitimacy surrounding the Chief Justice's position of leadership within the Court. This does not mean, of course, that such an aura could not be re-created. Hughes, for example, built up an expectation of task leadership which Taft never exercised, and he did so with Van Devanter, the old task leader, still on the bench. John Marshall, of course, had to start with even less of a tradition than did Hughes and for almost twenty-five years achieved a degree of success which startled and dismayed his enemies.

Even where an expectation of leadership by the Chief Justice has been inherited or built up, the advantages conferred are not necessarily decisive. Like that of any Associate Justice, the influence of the Chief is materially affected by the caliber of his colleagues as well as by their willingness to let him select the issues to be discussed at conference and oral argument. Both friendly and critical students of Marshall's reign agree that after 1825 he pretty well lost control over his Court as younger and more energetic men with different policy ideas replaced the older Justices.[107] Hughes exploited his authority with superb skill, yet he could not prevent his Court from splintering into angry factions or keep some of his colleagues from engaging in a wasted and almost suicidal war against the twentieth century. Nor could Hughes's great talents conceal the drastic nature of the reversal which the High Bench executed when it capitulated to the New Deal—though he was largely successful in masking the extent of his own vacillating course during the period 1935–37.[108]

The Chief Justice's advantage vis-à-vis his colleagues of voting last varies with the seniority of the individual Justice. A knowledge of the Chief's voting record and of his tentative views on the case at bar can give the senior Associate Justice an accurate idea of the Chief Justice's true feelings. Thus, since seven Justices have voted before him, the senior Associate Justice is also in a good position to adopt deceptive poses similar to those open to the Chief Justice. He may vote with the majority and hope that the Chief (if he, too, is with the majority) will pick him to write the Court's opinion, or that the Chief Justice will dissent and leave him the authority of assigning the opinion writer. To lesser extents down the seniority list, similar opportunities are open to other Associate Justices.

Any advantage to the Chief Justice when—or if—the voting paradox occurs depends on his ability immediately to recognize the situation and to discern the preference schedules of the other Justices. Second, the Chief Justice's advantage depends on a Justice's—or several Justices'—willingness to vote his second preference rather than to insist stubbornly on going on record for his first choice, no matter what the Court decides or cannot decide. Third, since any Justice is free to change his vote after conference and since bargaining is always possible, exploitation of the voting paradox can never insure that the Chief Justice will still have a majority when the decision is finally announced. Last, his advantage here also depends on the other Justices being unaware of the situation, lest they demand strict adherence to a particular order of voting.

In short, the chief justiceship supplies numerous opportunities to exert influence; it offers no guaranty that the incumbent can utilize these opportunities to achieve his policy goals. When the votes are tallied, the Chief's counts no more than that of any associate.

IV. PROFESSIONAL REPUTATION

This chapter has tended to emphasize opportunities within the Court for persuasion by negotiation and accommodation. There are also situations in which a Justice should not compromise except on inconsequential details. The ethical reasons which sometimes necessitate this sort of stand will be discussed in chapter vii. At this point it is sufficient merely to note that a Justice may be unable in conscience to dilute his views or keep them to himself. What should be brought out here is that a concern for professional reputation may make such all occasional stand strategically wise and perhaps even necessary.

To make the most of having to share decision-making authority with eight other men, a Justice would have to be willing generally to compromise—unless, of course, he found himself in the very unusual position of being in a strong majority in all cases, or at least all cases which he considered significant—assuming that his colleagues were men of comparable skill, learning, and intelligence. On the other hand, a Justice who was always ready to give in, to accept a half-loaf, could by that very fact weaken his bargaining position. If he habitually accommodated himself to others on all issues, his colleagues might well cease to take him seriously. To maintain the respect of the Court, a Justice would have to use some sanctions at various times. In a similar fashion, Franklin Roosevelt was anxious to veto legislation to prevent congressmen from thinking him soft. It is hardly a novel observation that a successful policy-maker must be feared as well as loved.

NOTES

1. Albert Pepitone, "Motivational Effects in Social Perception," 3 *Human Relations* 57, 71–75 (1950).

2. Quoted in Donald Morgan, *Justice William Johnson* (Columbia: University of South Carolina Press, 1954), pp. 181–182.

3. Quoted in Eugene Gerhart, *America's Advocate: Robert H. Jackson* (Indianapolis: Bobbs-Merrill, Inc., 1958), p. 274.

4. William Howard Taft to Robert A. Taft, January 25, 1925, and October 23, 1927; William Howard Taft Papers, Library of Congress.

5. Taft to Robert A. Taft, October 23, 1927, ibid.

6. Holmes made this remark to Felix Frankfurter. It is quoted in Alexander Bickel, *The Unpublished Opinions of Mr. Justice Brandeis* (Cambridge, Mass.: Belknap Press of Harvard University Press, 1957), p. 164.

7. Quoted in Alan Westin, *The Anatomy of a Constitutional Law Case* (New York: Macmillan Co., 1958), pp. 123–124.

8. Memorandum of Taft to the other Justices, May 12, 1922, Taft Papers. The memorandum was addressed to all members of the Court except John Clarke. Since the U.S. Reports do not note that Clarke did not participate, the omission was probably due to an oversight by the Chief Justice's secretary.

9. *United Brotherhood of Carpenters v. United States* (1947).

10. Black to members of the conference, May 2, 1945, Harlan Fiske Stone Papers, Library of Congress.

11. Box 4, *West Virginia v. Barnette* file, Frank Murphy Papers, Michigan Historical Collections, Ann Arbor, Mich. The Murphy Papers used in this book are arranged in boxes by terms of the Court, with each case having a separate file or set of files. The Taft Papers are arranged chronologically, with no topical order whatever. The Stone Papers are arranged in several different ways. Some correspondence is contained in files organized according to person; other correspondence and slip opinions are filed according to term; and some files are arranged by subject matter.

12. Frankfurter to Murphy, June 5, 1943, Box 4, Hirabayashi file, Murphy Papers.

13. Draft opinion, ibid.

14. June 10, 1943, ibid.

15. *Bedford Cut Stone Co. v. Journeymen Stone Cutters* (1927).

16. Taft to Stone, Jan. 26, 1927, the Stone and Taft Papers. For a full treatment of the incident, see Alpheus T. Mason, *Harlan Fiske Stone: Pillar of the Law* (New York: Viking Press, 1956), pp. 255–260.

17. The letter is dated only April 2, but Stone's reply is dated April 3, 1930, Stone Papers.

18. Box 4, Ex parte Quirin file, Murphy Papers. Although this memorandum was initialed and the style is unmistakable, I think the Justice who wrote it would prefer to remain anonymous.

19. Stone to Roger Nelson, Nov. 30, 1942, Stone Papers. Mason, op. cit., chap. xxxix, presents a detailed account of the way the case was handled.

20. The reports were correct, but Stone had endorsed other candidates as well. See my "In His Own Image," *1961 Supreme Court Review* 159, 191 n. Charles C. Burlingham blamed Stone's failure to support only Hand as the reason for Roosevelt's appointment of Rutledge, C. C. Burlingham file, the Oral History Project, Columbia University, p. 23. The truth is somewhat different or at least more complex. As will be mentioned later in the text, F. D. R. reacted against the heavy pressure to appoint Hand, pressure which the President told a friend he could trace back to a member of the Court.

21. Frankfurter to Rutledge, November 6, 1942, Stone Papers.

22. Hughes to Frankfurter, January 18, 1939, Charles Evans Hughes Papers, Library of Congress.

23. Frankfurter to Hughes, June 5, 1939, ibid.

24. Frankfurter to Hughes, February 24, 1940, ibid.

25. *Yazoo & Miss. V. Rr. v. Clarksdale* (1921); quoted in David Danelski, "The Chief Justice and the Supreme Court" (Ph.D. diss., University of Chicago, 1961), p. 179.

26. Lamar to Hughes, June 3, 1913, Hughes Papers.

27. Day to Mrs. Hughes, June 9, 1913, ibid. There is a similar letter of the same date in the Hughes Papers from Lurton to Mrs. Hughes.

28. Quoted in Merlo Pusey, *Charles Evans Hughes* (New York: Macmillan Co., 1951), II, 671.

29. *Institutional Investors v. Chi., Milwaukee, St. Paul & Pac. Rr.* (1943).

30. Feb. 20, 1943, Stone Papers.

31. The note is dated only "Friday." From its place in the Stone Papers, I judge the year to be 1940.

32. The Malcomb Baxter (1928), Stone Papers. The final decision was unanimous.

33. *Broad River Power Co. v. South Carolina* (1930), ibid.

34. *Lamb v. Schmidt* (1932), ibid.

35. *Alaska Packers Ass'n. v. Industrial Accident Comm'n* (1935), ibid.

36. Quoted in Danelski, "The Influence of the Chief Justice in the Decisional Process," in Murphy and Pritchett, *Courts, Judges, and Politics*, p. 506.

37. Holmes, of course, once commented that "Judges are apt to be naif, simple-minded men"; and, he added, "they need something of Mephistopheles." "Law and the Court" (1913), reprinted in Max Lerner (ed.), *The Mind and Faith of Justice Holmes* (New York: Random House, Inc., 1943), p. 390.

38. Quoted in Mason, *Harlan Fiske Stone*, p. 254.

39. Few of Stone's early opinions escaped criticism from McReynolds, criticism of a kind which can best be described as "picky." In McReynolds' defense, however, it should be said that he believed—though he was not always able to translate his belief into practice—that a judicial opinion should say no more than was absolutely necessary to decide a specific case. "When a judge fully appreciates that every unnecessary word in an opinion hurts it, he may be relied upon to write with good effect. But when vanity, or an itch to throw off new and striking phrases and shine in the books, troubles him, his outgivings are apt to be noxious." McReynolds to Judge Hollzer, August 31, 1933, James C. McReynolds Papers, Alderman Library, University of Virginia. McReynolds felt (quite correctly) that Stone often put more into his opinions than the cases demanded.

40. See Joel Francis Paschal, *Mr. Justice Sutherland: A Man against the State* (Princeton, N.J.: Princeton University Press, 1951), pp. 115–116, for a discussion of the pleasant exchange of views which was always possible between Holmes and Sutherland and between Brandeis and Sutherland.

41. Clarke to Taft, undated memorandum, ca. 1922, Taft Papers.

42. The story is told in Willard L. King, *Melville Weston Fuller* (New York: Macmillan Co., 1950), pp. 185–186.

43. For an account sympathetic to Jackson, read Gerhart, *America's Advocate*, chap. xv; for an account sympathetic to Black, see John P. Frank, *Mr. Justice Black: The Man and His Opinions* (New York: A. A. Knopf, 1948), chap. vii.

44. Justice Jackson once remarked privately that the unpleasantness in personal relations within the Court during the forties made him seriously consider resigning.

45. Clarke to Taft, September 12, 1922, Taft Papers.

46. Taft to Warren G. Harding, September 5, 1922, ibid.

47. This memorandum is filed in the Stone Papers. I would suspect that, as with the Quirin memorandum cited in note 19, the Justice would prefer to remain anonymous. Moreoever, unlike the Quirin memorandum, this one is not initialed, so it may not have been written by the purported author.

48. Quoted in Bickel, *Unpublished Opinions of Mr. Justice Brandeis*, p. 18.

49. Quoted in Charles Fairman, *Mr. Justice Miller and the Supreme Court 1862–1890* (Cambridge, Mass.: Harvard University Press, 1939), p. 320.

50. *Milkwagon Drivers Union v. Meadowmoor Dairies* (1941).

51. Law clerk to Murphy, February 2, 1941, Box 2, Meadowmoor Dairies file, Murphy Papers.

52. Frankfurter to Murphy, February 7, 1941, ibid.

53. January 20, 1941, Stone Papers.

54. *Ogden v. Saunders* (1827).

55. Bickel, op. cit., p. 30.

56. B. N. Cardozo, "Law and Literature," 14 *Yale Review* 699, 715–716 (1925). Charles Evans Hughes made much the same comment in his book *The Supreme Court of the United States* (New York: Columbia University Press, 1928), p. 68.

57. February 15, 1947, Box 8, Harris file, Murphy Papers.

58. The letter is published in Charles Fairman, "The Retirement of Federal Judges," 51 *Harvard Law Review* 397, 412–414 (1938).

59. Quoted in Morgan, *Justice William Johnson*, p. 182.

60. February 4, 1935, Stone Papers.

61. Taft thought that Brandeis was supported by a "claque" of liberal professors who wrote for law reviews. Taft to W. L. Phelps, May 30, 1927, Taft Papers. More recently, other Justices have sometimes been alleged to have used their law-school connections to reward friends and punish enemies, or at least to carry on a fight from the conference room or the pages of the U.S. Reports to the pages of law reviews.

62. *Home Building & Loan Ass'n v. Blaisdell* (1934). Mason, *Harlan Fiske Stone*, pp. 360–365 has a full account of the intra-Court negotiations here.

63. Stone to Douglas, June 9, 1943, Stone Papers.

64. The following summary of the conference is from the notes which Murphy took. Box 2, Goldman file, Murphy Papers. While Murphy's conference notes are often quite extensive and sometimes use quotation marks, these documents must, of course, be used with great care. I have not quoted directly from them, except for a few phrases or an occasional sentence which seem likely to have struck the ear of a listener. I have used them as relatively accurate summaries where, as here, they are supported by other evidence. I should add here that I was fortunate in that Professor J. Woodford Howard of Duke University, an expert on Frank Murphy, was in Ann Arbor when I was going through the Murphy Papers. Without Professor Howard's help I would never have been able to decipher much of Murphy's scrawl.

65. The draft is filed in the Stone Papers.

66. Box 2, Goldman file, Murphy Papers.

67. Conference notes, ibid.

68. March 5, 1942, Stone Papers.

69. Frankfurter to Murphy, April 3, 1942, Goldman file, Murphy Papers.

70. This draft is in both the Stone and Murphy Papers.

71. So Jackson noted in his letter to Murphy of April 6, 1942; the original is in the Murphy Papers and a carbon in the Stone Papers.

72. Ibid.

73. Fairman, *Mr. Justice Miller and the Supreme Court 1862–1890*, pp. 349–368, 370–371, 381, 429.

74. King, *Melville Weston Fuller*, pp. 180–181.

75. Ibid.

76. For studies of Taft's activities in the appointing process and the criteria which he applied, see my "In His Own Image," 1961 *Supreme Court Review* 159; and "Chief Justice Taft and the Lower Court Bureaucracy," 24 *Journal of Politics* 453 (1962). David Danelski, *A Supreme Court Justice Is Appointed* (New York: Random House, 1964), has an intricately detailed examination of the appointment of Pierce Butler.

77. Taft's old friend and former White House Press Secretary, Gus Karger, wrote Taft that Harding had told him this. Karger to Taft, May 25, 1921, Taft Papers.

78. Taft to Sutherland, July 2, 1921, George Sutherland Papers, Library of Congress.

79. Taft to Van Devanter, October 27, 1922, Taft Papers.

80. Taft to Harding, December 4, 1922, ibid.

81. Taft to Henry W. Taft, January 6, 1923, ibid.

82. Taft to Harding, December 4, 1922, ibid.

83. Taft to Henry W. Taft, January 16, 1923, ibid.

84. Taft left a remarkable memorandum describing the background to and the actual discussion with McKenna about his resignation; see my "In His Own Image," loc. cit.

85. Taft to Robert A. Taft, July 2, 1925, Taft Papers.

86. See Mason, *Harlan Fiske Stone*, p. 184.

87. Taft to Horace Taft, June 8, 1928, Taft Papers.

88. Stone to G. Helman, May 29, 1939, Stone Papers.

89. Stone to B. Shein, February 3, 1942, ibid. As other possibilities Stone also mentioned Newton D. Baker and Learned Hand. Stone to R. Hale, February 15, 1932, ibid.

90. Stone to G. Helman, November 30, 1939, ibid.

91. In 1939 Stone, disclaiming any altruism in offering to resign, said that he would not have been sorry to leave the Court because "I felt mine was a voice crying in the wilderness so far as the tendencies of the Court were concerned, and I had numerous opportunities to do worthwhile things." Stone to G. Helman, ibid. In 1929, less than three years before the Cardozo nomination, Stone faced no less opposition on the Court—indeed Hughes and Roberts were not as conservative as Taft and Sanford had been—but he turned down several opportunities to leave the bench for lucrative private practice as well as offers to become Secretary of State and head of the National Law Reform Committee. These persistent refusals do not appear to indicate an anxiousness to throw off the cares of the Court. On the other hand, Stone had ambitions to become Chief Justice and his name had been frequently mentioned as Taft's successor. Hughes's appointment to the center chair may well have dampened Stone's enthusiasm for judicial work.

92. February 15, 1932, ibid.

93. Pusey, *Charles Evans Hughes*, II, pp. 650–651.

94. John Schmidhauser, "The Justices of the Supreme Court: A Collective Portrait," 3 *Midwest Journal of Political Science* 1 (1959).

95. Taft, for instance, was asked several favors by politicians whose aid he had sought. See my "In His Own Image," loc. cit.

96. Fairman, *Mr. Justice Miller and the Supreme Court 1862–1890*, p. 171.

97. Glendon Schubert, *Quantitative Analysis of Judicial Behavior* (New York: Free Press, 1959), pp. 246–247.

98. *The Secret Diaries of Harold L. Ickes* (New York: Simon & Schuster, Inc., 1954), II, 552.

99. See Danelski, "The Assignment of Court's Opinions by the Chief Justice" (paper presented to the 1960 meetings of the Midwest Conference of Political Scientists).

100. Charles Fairman, "John Marshall and the American Judicial Tradition," in W. Melville Jones (ed.), *Chief Justice John Marshall: A Reappraisal* (Ithaca, N.Y.: Cornell University Press, 1956), p. 94.

101. Draft of a tribute to Edward D. White, ca. May 1921, Taft Papers.

102. Pusey, op. cit., II, p. 676.

103. King, *Melville Weston Fuller*, p. 290.

104. Black, op. cit., p. 40. Actually Black is more specific than I have indicated. He says: "When the ordinary committee procedure is in use, the later any resolution enters the voting, the greater its chances of adoption." Timing is obviously important, but I think that Black's phrasing sets too rigid a rule.

105. For Hughes's manner of presiding over the Court, see Mason, *Harlan Fiske Stone*, pp. 788–790; Pusey, op. cit., II, pp. 672–678; Felix Frankfurter, "Chief Justices I Have Known," 39 *Virginia Law Review* 883 (1953); Edwin McElwain, "The Business of the Supreme Court as Conducted by Chief Justice Hughes," 63 *Harvard Law Review* 5 (1949).

106. For Stone's concept of his role as Chief Justice, see Mason, *Harlan Fiske Stone*, chap. xlvii. Sociological research has documented the commonsense observation of most people who have had to do committee work: too much time spent in group discussion lowers satisfaction with the final decision. Similar research, however, contradicts the actual occurrence in the Stone Court—that is, several sociologists claim that free discussion increases group coalescence, whereas the effect on the Stone Court was increased division and dissension. See the literature cited in Bass, *Leadership, Psychology, and Organizational Behavior*, pp. 131–132.

107. Albert J. Beveridge, *The Life of John Marshall* (Boston: Houghton Mifflin Co., 1916–1919), IV, 480 ff., 512–514, 585; Charles G. Haines, *The Supreme Court in American Government and Politics, 1789–1835* (Berkeley: University of California Press, 1944), pp. 579 ff. Cf. William W. Crosskey, "Mr. Chief Justice Marshall," in Allison Dunham and Philip Kurland (eds.), *Mr. Justice* (Chicago: University of Chicago Press, 1956).

108. See Charles Hendel, *Charles Evans Hughes and the Supreme Court* (New York: King's Crown Press, 1951), p. 279. Pusey, op. cit., II, pp. 770–772, does not believe that Hughes did change. Pusey's reasoning and evidence, however, have been demolished by Alpheus Mason in "Charles Evans Hughes: An Appeal to the Bar of History," 6 *Vanderbilt Law Review* 1 (1952). Cf. John P. Roche, *Courts and Rights* (New York: Random House, Inc., 1961), p. 94: "Like General Douglas MacArthur, Hughes never retreated—he firmly advanced to the rear. . . ."

38

MARTIN M. SHAPIRO

THE PRESIDENCY AND THE FEDERAL COURTS

During the 1960s and 1970s, judicial restraint in policymaking gave way to greater activism. This created a problem for presidential leadership because the judiciary — particularly the Supreme Court — became heavily involved in setting the national policy agenda, reviewing the executive branch, strengthening legal rights, and indirectly distributing resources. Martin Shapiro, who teaches law at the University of California, Berkeley, advises presidents to respond by being especially cautious in making appointments to the federal judiciary.

Political scientists generally accept that recent presidents have been losing control over executive agencies and budget decisions. The current wisdom is that presidential power—certainly in the domestic arena—is seriously constrained by the existence of "iron triangles," or alliances between Congress, an agency, and an interest group. This may be so. But an equally important development has been less widely recognized, and that is the increasingly active participation of the courts in policymaking since the early 1960s.

The courts have been steadily reducing the discretionary power of executive agencies and rewriting their regulations. At the same time, a new iron triangle has appeared consisting of agency, court, and interest group. Congress initiates the triangle by creating a statutory right, but then it withdraws. The triangle perpetuates itself. The president is effectively excluded from its policy actions, since he has almost no influence over judges (once appointed) as contrasted with his power over members of congressional subcommittees. Just as a president faces a mass of past spending commitments that obligate much of his budgetary resources, he now faces an increasing number of statutorily created rights which arm the courts to obligate even more commitments and to mandate that the executive branch pursue implementation policies that run counter to those it favors.

The president now faces courts which are his rival in agenda setting and in the formulation of public goals and values. How did this happen, and what can he do to protect his authority?

POLITICAL SUASION AND JUDICIAL POWER

A new president faces not only political institutions but also contemporary attitudes about those institutions. This is nowhere more important than for the Supreme Court. Deprived of direct control over both the purse and the sword, the Court's political effectiveness depends largely on voluntary compliance with its commands by other political institutions and by the people. Historically, the Supreme Court has suffered more than the other two branches from problems of legitimacy. If the meaning of our Constitution were absolutely clear and the Court simply acted to enforce it, then the Court's actions would be perfectly legitimate. If the Constitution had no fixed meanings, so that the Supreme Court simply wrote its own policy preferences into the Constitution as it went along, then its actions would be perfectly illegitimate. But because the Constitution has some fixity and some flexibility, and because actions of the justices mix law and policy, the Supreme Court has always lived in a state of uncertain legitimacy. Americans have always asked how much the president and Congress should govern, but they have not questioned their right to govern. There is no more characteristic question of American political discourse, however, than the question of whether the Court should govern at all.

There is a New Deal theory of the Supreme Court just as there are New Deal theories of the presidency and Congress, and like those theories it has honorable roots. The three theories are, of course, interdependent. New Deal proponents of the strong presidency argued that the president, rather than Congress, should act as chief lawmaker because the presidency was more unified and because it more truly represented the national majority will. At the same time, a New Deal school of judicial self-restraint was busy subordinating the Supreme Court to Congress. If the Court's judgments on the constitutionality of federal legislation merely substituted judicial policy preferences for legislative ones, then the Court ought to stop reviewing and to leave policy decision to Congress . . .

While New Deal commentators never openly put the two streams of thought together, the political arithmetic was clear. Congress ought to defer to the lawmaking of the president. The Supreme Court ought to defer to the lawmaking of Congress. Therefore, the Supreme Court ought to defer to the president. QED. The only legitimate role for the Supreme Court was that of whipping the state legal systems into line with the Constitution and federal statutes . . .

This attitude predominated during the presidencies of Roosevelt, Truman, and Eisenhower. A chink in the New Deal theory, however, allowed the Supreme Court to reemerge as a rival to and manipulator of the presidency. For if the Court were still free to whip the states into line, it might whip them into a different line or require different modes of whipping than the president would have chosen.

Eisenhower's experience with Little Rock is instructive. Clearly, at the time of *Brown v. Board of Education* (347 U.S. 483 [1954]) there was a national majority against Jim Crow laws, but it was a marginal majority both in breadth and depth of sentiment—not the kind of majority that would find expression through Congress or the presidency. Once the Supreme Court had put the new anti–Jim Crow policy in place, however, the president's power stakes changed rapidly. Because his military background had led to "man on horseback" fears, Eisenhower was particularly reluctant to use the military to enforce the law. Yet he found himself using the army to do the Supreme Court's bidding—a bidding for which he had no great personal enthusiasm. He did so because the Court had built a coalition that he could not resist. It had added the constituency which believed that the law must be obeyed to the constituency which believed that Jim Crow was a national disgrace. He need not have sent troops to end Jim Crow. He had no choice but to send troops to enforce the Constitution as interpreted by the Court (see Wilkinson 1978).

The New Deal theory of judicial restraint did not die with *Brown v. Board of Education* and Little Rock. Indeed, it continued to flourish in the academy long after the Warren Court had passed it by. Nevertheless, it became increasingly difficult to insist that the Court could and should do nothing when it was doing a great deal and when much of what it was doing seemed good. President Nixon could still seize upon judicial self-restraint as a campaign issue—both intellectually alive and emotionally appealing—but it is unlikely that any president or presidential candidate will be able to do so in the near future.

JUDICIAL ACTIVISM

In part, of course, the decline of judicial self-restraint as a political slogan results from the change from the Warren to the Burger Court. The Burger Court is less given to dramatic gestures. Yet this is not the whole story. Even in the bitter controversy over the Burger Court's abortion decisions, the "pro-life" forces have never asserted that the Court had no right to make public policy, only that the Court made an immoral policy.

The major new fact about the Supreme Court is that there has been a fundamental change in the predominant conception of its appropriate role. While some remnants of New Deal theory remain, there is now a strong consensus that the Court should *either* support minority interests not adequately represented elsewhere in the political process *or* defend fundamental public values (Choper 1980; Fiss 1979, pp. 1–58; Ely 1980). Whichever way judicial activism is justified, it reduces the New Deal role of the president. It was Roosevelt who was supposed to protect minorities; Roosevelt, not his Court, who announced the Four Freedoms.

Today's most fashionable school of constitutional thought argues that one great purpose of government is to provide an arena in which men and women can come together to debate and thus create public values. The courts are ideal for this, every bit as good as Congress and the presidency. Indeed, they are better, because the reasoned argument and elaboration of litigational procedures are particularly good vehicles for ethical/political discourse . . .

This new school of thought may be seen as part of the contemporary revolt of the intellectuals against popular majorities. For it asserts that public values are best discovered, not by the messy processes of politics, but by a group of Harvard and Yale lawyers arguing with one another according to a ritual that only they understand in front of a judge drawn from their own ranks.

From a slightly different perspective, the new movement can be seen as part of the rights fetishism that has become a principal tool of the left for extracting what it wants from the political system no matter what the majority or its elected representatives want (see, e.g., Michelman 1969, pp. 7–56). When an interest—what somebody wants—is transformed into a right, it goes to the head of the line. The normal political process by which legislatures and agencies establish priorities among competing interests are set aside. Thus if a court decides that mental patients in state hospitals have a right to treatment, more state money must be spent on psychiatrists even if the state legislature would have preferred to spend the money on fire inspectors. The principal problem that judges pose for other politicians is that recently they have been using their rights-declaring powers liberally and thus asserting ultimate, even if only sporadically exercised, control over the distributional politics that are the focus of the legislative process.

Political executives confronted with their own unpopularity often take comfort in the widespread disparagement of legislatures. It has become a commonplace that many congressmen seek reelection by campaigning against Congress . . . The creation of judicial rights is another form of that disdain. For when a court converts an interest into a right, it is declaring that it does not trust the legislature to be fair. The ultimate defense of judicial rights creation is the belief that if some people in a society are being badly treated, someone must step in if the legislature fails to do so. While forty years ago the someone was typically thought to be the president, today the most frequently nominated someone is the judge . . .

It would be excessive to suggest that judges have replaced elected officials as our dominant political leaders or that presidential leadership has been replaced by Supreme Court leadership. The president's problem is that the courts may create rights which bring issues to the fore that he might prefer not to confront—desegregation, school busing, abortion. By creating rights, the courts set themselves up as rivals with the president in national agenda setting. Moreover, the particular charm of rights creation is that it can ignore the relational aspects of politics and treat each right as totally independent. As a result, the ability to create rights encourages the single-issue politics that are so troublesome to presidents who are necessarily concerned with coalition building. The Supreme Court can and does promote single-issue movements, leaving the president to deal with them.

STATUTORY RIGHTS

Courts today participate vigorously in announcing values, establishing priorities, and setting agendas, all of which in the days of the Imperial Presidency seemed to be increasingly the preserve of the executive branch. But to appreciate the dynamics of executive/judicial interaction, we must go beyond judicial rights creation to the legislative process. While the Supreme Court has dramatically announced new constitutional rights like the "right" to abortion, Congress has also added to our law an amazing new assortment of statutory rights.

During the Roosevelt administration it became the habit of Congress to pass very broadly worded statutes delegating large chunks of its lawmaking power either directly to the president, to exercise by executive order, or to the federal agencies, to be exercised by administrative regulations. Many of these regulations amounted to major pieces of legislation. The Supreme Court has long since approved such delegations to the executive branch[1] and has held that its regulations have the same force of law as statutes enacted by Congress itself.[2]

In New Deal days such delegation followed the New Deal theory of separation of powers. Congress was deferring to the executive branch, and the Supreme Court was nominally deferring to Congress but was actually deferring to the presidency. Delegation was an unmixed blessing to the president, however, only for so long as certain conditions were met. First, the president had to control the bureaucracy. Second, the delegations had to create wide-ranging administrative discretion rather than vesting legal rights in individuals. A statute that says agency X may do whatever it pleases to alleviate problem Y strengthens the president if he controls agency X. A statute that says agency X is entitled to enforce the right Y of citizen Z may delegate wide rule-making power to the agency. It also enables citizen Z to make demands upon the agency, no matter what the president wants. Third, the delegation had to be unreviewable by the courts. Where delegation is accompanied by active judicial review, then, even if he controls the agency the president must share the lawmaking power with the courts that do the reviewing. For whatever the pretense, judicial review of agency lawmaking amounts to judicial participation in lawmaking.

All three conditions for presidential control have been eroded. President Roosevelt enjoyed a suddenly enormously expanded bureaucracy staffed largely by people attracted to Washington by the promise of the New Deal. Presidents since Eisenhower have faced an entrenched New Deal bureaucracy. Thus, delegation of lawmaking power to the agencies has strengthened another rival to presidential authority.

At the same time, Congress and the courts have interacted to produce a shift from administrative discretion to statutory rights. A 1940 statute called the "National Transportation Policy" may provide the ultimate New Deal model of administrative discretion. This act simply empowered the Interstate Commerce Commission to regulate modes of transportation "so . . . as to . . . preserve the inherent advantages of each; to promote . . . efficient service and foster sound economic conditions." In more recent years, however, Congress has tended to conceive the task of solving massive social and economic problems in terms of creating statutory rights vested in individuals, with broad delegations to administrative agencies to implement those rights. For instance, the Education for Handicapped Children Act invests handicapped children with a right to an adequate education and their parents with a right to participate in determining their education. It goes on to delegate to the agency broad discretion to write regulations defining standards of adequacy as well as processes necessary to ensure participation.

Rights are not negotiable. Faced with a handicapped child who has a right to an adequate education, we are unlikely to say that any education that the president says is adequate is adequate or that some bureaucrat should have the discretion to decide that injured athletes rather than handicapped children should have first crack at the hydrotherapy equipment. Rights—whether statutory or constitutional—are assertions of absolute entitlement.

A mere change in statutory rhetoric from agency discretion to citizens' rights would not, in itself, greatly limit the discretion of the executive branch. But the change in rhetoric *plus* the growth of judicial review has done so. In the late 1930s and 1940s the Supreme Court was not only busy providing constitutional legitimacy for vast delegations of congressional lawmaking power to the executive branch, but was also working hard to construct a theory under which administrators wielding that power would be insulated from judicial review. The Court argued that the executive branch constituted a reservoir of technical expertise upon which most administrative decisions depended. It followed that judges, who were not experts, should defer to the decisions of administrators, who were. This general doctrine was supplemented by a special doctrine which called for judicial deference to administrators even in the one area in which it might be argued that judges were the most expert: questions of the meaning of the delegating statute. Even though freeing agencies to interpret these statutes as they pleased would enable them to expand their powers indefinitely, the Supreme Court held that such regulations had the same force of law as if Congress itself had enacted them. The courts would not review them, and the agencies became the final authority on questions of the legal meaning of the statutory provisions under which they operated.[3]

During the 1960s and 1970s, however, their insulation from judicial review broke down. Led by the District of Columbia and 2nd Circuits, judges began to challenge the expertise of the agencies, sometimes directly, but mostly by procedural indirection. The courts came to hold that the agencies must listen to all sides of questions and that failure to do so, and to provide a record proving that they had done so, would lead to judicial invalidation of their regulations.[4] Under the guise of inspecting whether the agency had followed consultative procedures, judges came more and more to second-guess agency policy decisions and to at least delay those they didn't like. At the same time, standing doctrines were liberalized so that not only were courts more willing to review, but also more people were enabled to ask for review. Despite some unease,[5] the Supreme Court has basically accepted this trend. So while the doctrine that agency regulations have the force of law has not changed, courts have again set themselves up as rival interpreters of the congressional language under which the agencies' delegated lawmaking powers are exercised . . .

This change in the courts' behavior has been seconded by Congress. Many recent statutes delegating lawmaking authority require agencies to engage in the kinds of elaborate consultative procedures that the courts have been requiring. And many of those same statutes give rights to individuals and allow them to vindicate those rights in court.

THE NEW IRON TRIANGLE

What does all this mean for the president? The original New Deal delegations increased his power because they gave full policy discretion to agencies that he controlled. Today the president exercises less control over the federal agencies; the agencies have less discretion in that they cannot refuse to implement statutorily created rights, and the courts have triumphantly reentered the policy arena.

Congressionally created individual rights have been rigidified through agency regulations and judicial review to the point of constraining the president's discretion in vast areas of federal regulation. In addition, networks — "iron triangles" — of congressional subcommittee, executive bureau, and interest group alliances make their own public policy and resist outside control. Now there is the new triangle, consisting of agency, court, and interest group, which is bringing about a new diminution of presidential authority.

Congress or the courts or both give the interest group standing to lobby the agency and the courts. The agency knows that, unless it satisfies the group, the group will sue, thus increasing the cost and delaying the implementation of the proposed policy. The agency also knows that unless it anticipates the policy views of the courts, the judges will find some way to reverse or at least delay the proposed policy if a suit takes place. The interest group knows that the cheapest thing to do is to persuade the agency. It also knows that, if properly approached, courts may strengthen its statutory entitlements, thus providing a stronger base for negotiation with the agency. And the courts know that all they can do is to increase the time and money costs to the agency, which can eventually win if it is willing to pay those costs. The courts also know that if they attempt to build a barrier to some agency policy by announcing a statutory right debarring it, Congress may reverse them. It follows that the agencies, interest groups, and courts live by mutual accommodation over relatively long periods of time, effectively excluding the president.

The new triangle is worse for the president than the old. An alert president might discover ways to reward or punish individual members of the congressional subcommittee involved. He could reward or punish the agency at budget time. And most interest groups would prefer presidential patronage to presidential animosity. But there is little he can do for—or to—the federal judges who now participate in the "administration" of statutes.

A brief example will illustrate these points. In the Age Discrimination Act of 1975 Congress prohibited discrimination on the basis of age in all federally assisted programs. It also provided several broadly worded exceptions to the prohibition which allow "reasonable" use of age as a criterion in assigning jobs and benefits. As Peter Schuck . . . has pointed out in his illuminating case study of the statute, it looks toward two policy goals: bettering the social and economic status of the aged and improving economic efficiency. It creates specific statutory rights for the aged and delegates lawmaking power to the Department of Labor to effectuate them. Because the two goals conflict, and the trade-offs between them are not clearly specified in the statute, the Department of Labor has enormous discretion in writing the real law—its own detailed regulations. In doing so, however, it must follow the protracted procedures required by the courts. Moreover, once the regulations are enacted, aged people who feel they do not adequately protect their rights as established by the statute will challenge them in court. Courts may or may not be tempted into writing their own version of the statute. Congress having acted, the law on age discrimination is now being written. It will take a long time to write, and it will be the product of a great deal of discretion. But almost none of that discretion will be wielded by the president.

THE PRESIDENT'S RESOURCES

In summary, the president now faces a Supreme Court which rivals his authority in formulating public goals and values and in agenda setting. And in formulating values, the Court often contributes to the single-issue politics that make it difficult for the president to form and lead a winning national coalition. Furthermore, the Court has the power to implicate the president in the achievement of the goals *it* chooses, thus diverting presidential energies and creating expectations about presidential performance that the president may be unable to satisfy. The Supreme Court and the other federal courts have also returned to a major role in day to day, detailed lawmaking. That return has helped to create an agency/interest group/court triangle which dominates much of the routine decision-making of government and is largely impervious to presidential intervention.

What resources does the president command to meet his judicial rivals? Unfortunately for him, the answer is more than enough resources to meet the micro problems and almost none to meet the macro developments I have just outlined. Compared to these macro phenomena, the various points of microtension between president and Supreme Court which appear so dramatically to threaten his power are really trivial.

The microlevel problems are "point" problems that tend to come to a head in a single case or a short series of cases which bring to constitutional issue the legitimacy of some particular claim of presidential authority. The batting average of the presidency in such disputes is high. The president's massive constitutional authority has been increased rather than decreased by successive Supreme Court decisions, even those of the Nixon years. In these areas, the president is fully armed with the executive mystique and has the power both to fine-tune his claims to the political exigencies and to adopt alternative means of achieving his goals (Scigliano 1972).

It is one of the small ironies of history that a Republican president, Nixon, was smashed in the process of attempting to push the New Deal theory of the presidency to its logical extreme. His insistence on the absolute power to impound funds appropriated by Congress and to be the sole judge of when the exigencies of national security required him to exercise an executive privilege to withhold whatever information he pleased from Congress, the courts, and the people was met by an alliance of Congress and the courts. Nevertheless, the presidency emerged with legal recognition of both the impoundment power and executive privilege, recognition that had not existed before. Similarly, President Nixon suffered congressional refusal to accept two consecutive presidential nominations to the Supreme Court, but the appointment power remained firmly in his hands. The Nixon administration was repulsed in an attempt to restrain publication of the Pentagon Papers in the name of national security, but the security classification system is still with us . . .

At the macro level, the causes of the president's problems are beyond his control. The increase in judicial willingness to intervene in administrative lawmaking was caused by a basic increase in judicial self-confidence resulting from changing public attitudes toward technocratic government. As Americans lost faith in the technocrat, the judge emerged as the lay hero riding forth to curb his arbitrary power. Because American attitudes toward technocracy are fundamentally ambivalent, we may shortly experience another swing in favor of the expert and a consequent decline in judicial activity. But there is little that any given president can do to bring this about except, perhaps, to learn that denouncing the bureaucracy strengthens the hands of judges.

On another front, however, each new president can contribute something to an increase in presidential discretion. Presidents have probably already learned that massive congressional delegations of lawmaking power to the bureaucracy are not necessarily delegations to them. They must also recognize that massive congressional creations of new statutory rights obligate administrative resources just as massive spending programs obligate financial resources. And along with the obligation come higher levels of judicial intervention. To counter this, the president can be careful about the kinds of legislation he proposes. A bill authorizing the federal government to spend X billion to improve education for the handicapped has far different consequences for presidential authority than one that gives the handicapped a right to adequate education and requires the Department of Education to write regulations sustaining that right. Presidents can control spending far more readily than rights once they have been let loose in the rights triangle. Presidents must learn to draft their statutes so as to promise government programs, not to guarantee legal rights. The movement toward rights legislation has been so strong, however, that any given president seems likely to make only limited headway against it.

What about the power of appointment? This is a very weak resource. As recent history shows, the voting of justices on matters of immediate constitutional concern to the president does not depend on who appointed them. No president is likely to be so insightful about the two mysteries of human personality and future events as to appoint just the right person for just those constitutional issues of presidential power that will arise during his term . . .

Nor is a president likely to find appointees who exactly share his value preferences. Justices appointed because they are tough on crime or pro-busing will turn out to have values different from his in other areas such as welfare or presidential power or economic regulation.

Even more important, the new iron triangle does not depend on the Supreme Court alone, but also on certain key courts of appeal and district courts. In many areas of law, appointments to the District of Columbia and 2nd Circuits are as crucial as those to the Supreme Court. Nevertheless, when so many judges sitting for life share judicial power, no single president's appointments make much immediate difference. There is no doubt that the five Democratic terms after 1932 filled the federal bench with judges whose ideology made the judicial activism of the 1960s and 1970s possible, but no single president could have achieved that result, nor did presidents Roosevelt and Truman intend the results they achieved.

Presidents ought to take their judicial appointments seriously as an opportunity to influence long-range policy directions and perhaps to have a more immediate impact on one or two areas of policymaking with which they are particularly concerned. The appointment power can do little, however, to bring the judicial rivals of the president to heel.

We must conclude that the federal judiciary plays a substantial role in the fragmentation of political authority that confronts the president. From time to time it can and does seize the initiative from him in setting the issue agenda and proclaiming dominant values. And it can and does participate in the mass of low-level incremental decision-making that fixes most of the policies of government in channels that the president can do little about. Should we continue to pile up statutes that mandate legal duties to public and private authorities and assign rights to individuals and groups to obtain judicial enforcement of those mandates, we will not only greatly increase the power of the nonelected branch to interfere in our individual lives and set our national priorities, but we will arrive at a stage of legal overkill that will reduce the president's options in a domestic policy to the vanishing point. The president's best defense is to seize the initiative in proclaiming values, but to avoid the rhetoric of rights that invites both judicial intervention and policy rigidity.

NOTES

1. *Amalgamated Meat Cutters v. Connally*, 337 F. Supp. 737 (D.D.C. 1971).
2. *Mourning v. Family Publications Services, Inc.*, 411 U.S. 356 (1973).
3. Idem.
4. This development is traced in detail in Davis 1976.
5. See *Vermont Yankee Nuclear Power Corp. v. Natural Resources Defense Council*, 435 U.S. 519 (1978).

SOURCES

Abraham, Henry. *Justices and Presidents* (New York: Oxford Press, 1974).

Choper, Jesse H. "The Alienated Voter," *Taxing and Spending* (Oct./Nov., 1980).

Davis, Kenneth C. *Discretionary Justice in Europe and America* (Urbana: University of Illinois Press, 1976).

Ely, John Hart. *Democracy and Distrust: A Theory of Judicial Review* (Cambridge, Mass.: Harvard University Press, 1980).

Fenno, Richard F., Jr. *Homestyle: House Members in Their Districts* (Boston: Little Brown, 1978).

Fisher, Louis. *The Constitution between Friends: Congress, the President, and the Law* (New York: St. Martin's, 1978).

Fiss, Owen. "The Forms of Justice," *Harvard Law Review* 93 (1979).

Freedman, James O. *Crisis and Legitimacy: The Administrative Process and American Government* (Cambridge: Cambridge University Press, 1978).

Hand, Learned. *The Bill of Rights* (Cambridge, Mass.: Harvard University Press, 1958).

Horowitz, Donald. *Courts and Social Policy* (Washington, D.C.: Brookings Institution, 1977).

Mendelson, Wallace. *Justices Black and Frankfurter: Conflict on the Court* (Chicago: University of Chicago Press, 1961).

Michelman, Frank. "On Protecting the Poor through the Fourteenth Amendment," *Harvard Law Review* 83 (1969).

Schmidhauser, John. *Supreme Court as Final Arbiter in Federal State Relations* (Chapel Hill: University of North Carolina Press, 1958).

Schuck, Peter. "The Graying of Civil Rights Law: The Age Discrimination Act of 1975," *Yale Law Journal* 89 (1979).

Scigliano, Robert. *The Supreme Court and the Presidency* (New York: Free Press, 1972).

Stewart, Richard. "The Reformation of American Administrative Law," *Harvard Law Review* 88 (1975).

Tribe, Lawrence. "Puzzling Persistence of Progress-Based Constitutional Theories," *Yale Law Journal* 89 (1980).

Wilkinson, J. Harvie. *From Brown to Bakke: The Supreme Court and School Integration, 1954-1978* (New York: Oxford Press, 1978).

39

MARBURY v. MADISON (1803)

Just before leaving office in 1801, President John Adams appointed William Marbury to the post of justice of the peace for the District of Columbia. However, in the presidential transition, Marbury failed to receive his commission—a legal document enabling him to exercise the authority of that position. After taking office, the new secretary of state, James Madison, refused to deliver the commission and was sued by Marbury. The technical issue before the Supreme Court involved section 13 of the Judiciary Act of 1789. The section authorized the Court to issue writs of mandamus (that is, a command to a public official to carry out a specific action, such as giving Marbury his commission). The act also augmented the Supreme Court's "original jurisdiction," as established by the Constitution, by providing that such cases can be initiated in the Court, rather than heard by it on appeal only. The case presented the Court with a serious dilemma. On one hand, Marbury was legally entitled to his commission. On the other hand, there was a very real prospect that for partisan reasons Madison would ignore the Court's order to deliver it, thereby injuring the Court's prestige and standing. Chief Justice John Marshall's brilliant solution was to declare that the Court had no power to issue the writ because the Judiciary Act's expansion of its original jurisdiction was unconstitutional. Thus, while claiming it was powerless to help Marbury and avoiding confrontation with the executive branch, the Court nonetheless successfully established its fundamental power of judicial review.

Mr. Chief Justice Marshall delivered the opinion of the Court:

At the last term on the affidavits then read and filed with the clerk, a rule was granted in this case, requiring the secretary of state to show cause why a *mandamus* should not issue, directing him to deliver to William Marbury his commission as a justice of the peace for the county of Washington, in the District of Columbia.

No cause has been shown, and the present motion is for a *mandamus*. The peculiar delicacy of this case, the novelty of some of its circumstances, and the real difficulty attending the points which occur in it, require a complete exposition of the principles on which the opinion to be given by the Court is founded.

These principles have been, on the side of the applicant, very ably argued by the bar. In rendering the opinion of the Court, there will be some departure in form, though not in substance, from the points stated in that argument.

In the order in which the Court has viewed this subject, the following questions have been considered and decided.

1st. Has the applicant a right to the commission he demands?

2d. If he has a right, and that right has been violated, do the laws of his country afford him a remedy?

3d. If they do afford him a remedy, is it a *mandamus* issuing from this Court?

The first object of inquiry is,

Has the applicant a right to the commission he demands? . . .

It is . . . decidedly the opinion of the Court, that when a commission has been signed by the president, the appointment is made; and that the commission is complete when the seal of the United States has been affixed to it by the secretary of state.

Where an officer is removable at the will of the executive, the circumstance which completes his appointment is of no concern; because the act is at any time revocable; and the commission may be arrested, if still in the office. But when the officer is not removable at the will of the executive, the appointment is not revocable, and cannot be annulled. It has conferred legal rights which cannot be resumed.

The discretion of the executive is to be exercised, until the appointment has been made. But having once made the appointment, his power over the office is terminated, in all cases where, by law, the officer is not removable by him. The right to the office is then in the person appointed, and he has the absolute unconditional power of accepting or rejecting it.

Mr. Marbury, then, since his commission was signed by the president, and sealed by the secretary of state, was appointed; and as the law creating the office, gave the officer a right to hold for five years, independent of the executive, the appointment was not revocable, but vested in the officer legal rights, which are protected by the laws of his country.

To withhold his commission, therefore, is an act deemed by the Court not warranted by law, but violative of a vested legal right.

This brings us to the second inquiry; which is,

If he has a right, and that right has been violated, do the laws of this country afford him a remedy?

The very essence of civil liberty certainly consists in the right of every individual to claim the protection of the laws, whenever he receives an inquiry. One of the first duties of government is to afford that protection. . . .

The government of the United States has been emphatically termed a government of laws, and not of men. It will certainly cease to deserve this high appellation, if the laws furnish no remedy for the violation of a vested legal right.

If this obloquy is to be cast on the jurisprudence of our country, it must arise from the peculiar character of the case.

It behooves us, then, to inquire whether there be in its composition any ingredient which shall exempt it from legal investigation, or exclude the injured party from legal redress. . . .

Is it in the nature of the transaction? Is the act of delivering or withholding a commission to be considered as a mere political act, belonging to the executive department alone, for the performance of which entire confidence is placed by our Constitution in the supreme executive; and for any misconduct respecting which, the injured individual has no remedy? That there may be such cases is not to be questioned; but that every act of duty, to be performed in any of the great departments of government, constitutes such a case, is not to be admitted. . . .

It follows, then, that the question, whether the legality of an act of the head of a department be examinable in a court of justice or not, must always depend on the nature of that act.

If some acts be examinable, and others not, there must be some rule of law to guide the court in the exercise of its jurisdiction.

In some instances, there may be difficulty in applying the rule to particular cases; but there cannot, it is believed, be much difficulty in laying down the rule.

By the Constitution of the United States, the president is invested with certain important political powers, in the exercise of which he is to use his own discretion, and is accountable only to his country in his political character and to his own conscience. To aid him in the performance of these duties, he is authorized to appoint certain officers, who act by his authority, and in conformity with his orders.

In such cases, their acts are his acts; and whatever opinion may be entertained of the manner in which executive discretion may be used, still there exists, and can exist, no power to control that discretion. The subjects are political. They respect the nation, not individual rights, and being intrusted to the executive, the decision of the executive is conclusive. The application of this remark will be perceived by adverting to the act of Congress for establishing the department of foreign affairs. This officer, as his duties were prescribed by that act, is to conform precisely to the will of the president. He is the mere organ by whom that will is communicated. The acts of such an officer, as an officer, can never be examinable by the courts.

But when the legislature proceeds to impose on that officer other duties; when he is directed peremptorily to perform certain acts; when the rights of individuals are dependent on the performance of those acts; he is so far the officer of the law; is amenable to the laws for his conduct; and cannot at his discretion sport away the vested rights of others.

The conclusion from this reasoning is, that where the heads of departments are the political or confidential agents of the executive, merely to execute the will of the president, or rather to act in cases in which the executive possesses a constitutional or legal discretion, nothing can be more perfectly clear than that their acts are only politically examinable. But where a specific duty is assigned by law, and individual rights depend upon the performance of that duty, it seems equally clear that the individual who considers himself injured, has a right to resort to the laws of his country for a remedy. . . .

It is, then, the opinion of the Court,

1st. That by signing the commission of Mr. Marbury, the president of the United States appointed him a justice of peace for the county of Washington, in the District of Columbia; and that the seal of the United States, affixed thereto by the secretary of state, is conclusive testimony of the verity of the signature, and of the completion of the appointment, and that the appointment conferred on him a legal right to the office for the space of five years.

2dly. That, having this legal title to the office, he has a consequent right to the commission; a refusal to deliver which is a plain violation of that right, for which the laws of his country afford him a remedy.

It remains to be inquired whether,

3dly. Is he entitled to the remedy for which he applies?

This depends on — 1st. The nature of the writ applied for; and 2dly. The power of this court.

The nature of the writ. . . .

This writ, if awarded, would be directed to an officer of government, and its mandate to him would be, to use the words of Blackstone, "to do a particular thing therein specified, which appertains to his office and duty, and which the court has previously determined, or at least supposes, to be consonant to right and justice." Or, in the words of Lord Mansfield, the applicant, in this case, has a right to execute an office of public concern, and is kept out of possession of that right.

These circumstances certainly concur in this case.

Still, to render the *mandamus* a proper remedy, the officer to whom it is to be directed, must be one to whom, on legal principles, such writ may be directed; and the person applying for it must be without any other specific and legal remedy.

With respect to the officer to whom it would be directed.

The intimate political relation subsisting between the president of the United States and the heads of departments, necessarily renders any legal investigation of the acts of one of those high officers peculiarly irksome, as well as delicate; and excites some hesitation with respect to the propriety of entering into such investigation. Impressions are often received without much reflection or examination, and it is not wonderful that in such a case as this the assertion, by an individual, of his legal claims in a court of justice, to which claims it is the duty of that court to attend, should at first view be considered by some, as an attempt to intrude into the cabinet, and to intermeddle with the prerogatives of the executive.

It is scarcely necessary for the court to disclaim all pretentions to such jurisdiction. An extravagance, so absurd and excessive, could not have been entertained for a moment. The province of the court is, solely, to decide on the rights of individuals, not to inquire how the executive, or executive officers, perform duties in which they have a discretion. Questions in their nature political, or which are, by the Constitution and laws, submitted to the executive, can never be made in this Court.

But, if this be not such a question; if, so far from being an intrusion into the secrets of the cabinet, it respects a paper which, according to law, is upon record, and to a copy of which the law gives a right, on the payment of ten cents; if it be no intermeddling with a subject over which the executive can be considered as having exercised any control; what is there in the exalted station of the officer, which shall bar a citizen from asserting, in a court of justice, his legal rights, or shall forbid a court to listen to the claim, or to issue a *mandamus* directing the performance of a duty, not depending on executive discretion, but on particular acts of Congress, and the general principles of law?

. . . [W]here [the head of a department] is directed by law to do a certain act affecting the absolute rights of individuals, in the performance of which he is not placed under the particular direction of the president, and the performance of which the president cannot lawfully forbid, and therefore is never presumed to have forbidden; as for example to record a commission, or a patent for land, which has received all the legal solemnities; or to give a copy of such record; in such cases, it is not perceived on what ground the courts of the country are further excused from the duty of giving judgment that right be done to an injured individual, than if the same services were to be performed by a person not the head of a department. . . .

This, then, is a plain case for a *mandamus*, either to deliver the commission, or a copy of it from the record; and it only remains to be inquired,

Whether it can issue from this Court.

The act to establish the judicial courts of the United States authorizes the Supreme Court "to issue writs of *mandamus* in cases warranted by the principles and usages of law, to any courts appointed, or persons holding office, under the authority of the United States."

The secretary of state, being a person holding an office under the authority of the United States, is precisely within the letter of the description, and if this court is not authorized to issue a writ of *mandamus* to such an officer, it must be because the law is unconstitutional, and therefore absolutely incapable of conferring the authority, and assigning the duties which its words purport to confer and assign.

The Constitution vests the whole judicial power of the United States in one Supreme Court, and such inferior courts as Congress shall, from time to time, ordain and establish. This power is expressly extended to all cases arising under the laws of the United States; and, consequently, in some form, may be exercised over the present case; because the right claimed is given by a law of the United States.

In the distribution of this power it is declared that "the Supreme Court shall have original jurisdiction in all cases affecting ambassadors, other public ministers and consuls, and those in which a state shall be a party. In all other cases, the Supreme Court shall have appellate jurisdiction."

It has been insisted, at the bar, that as the original grant of jurisdiction, to the Supreme and inferior courts, is general, and the clause, assigning original jurisdiction to the Supreme Court, contains no negative or restrictive words, the power remains to the legislature, to assign original jurisdiction to that Court in other cases than those specified in the article which has been recited, provided those cases belong to the judicial power of the United States.

If it had been intended to leave it in the discretion of the legislature to apportion the judicial power between the supreme and inferior courts according to the will of that body, it would certainly have been useless to have proceeded further than to have defined the judicial power, and the tribunals in which it should be vested. The subsequent part of the section is mere surplusage, is entirely without meaning, if such is to be the construction. If Congress remains at liberty to give this Court appellate jurisdiction, where the Constitution has declared their jurisdiction shall be original; and original jurisdiction where the Constitution has declared it shall be appellate; the distribution of jurisdiction, made in the Constitution, is form without substance.

Affirmative words are often, in their operation, negative of other objects than those affirmed; and in this case, a negative or exclusive sense must be given to them, or they have no operation at all.

It cannot be presumed that any clause in the Constitution is intended to be without effect; and, therefore, such a construction is inadmissible, unless the words require it.

If the solicitude of the convention, respecting our peace with foreign powers, induced a provision that the Supreme Court should take original jurisdiction in cases which might be supposed to affect them; yet the clause would have proceeded no further than to provide for such cases, if no further restriction on the powers of Congress had been intended. That they should have appellate jurisdiction in all other cases, with such exceptions as Congress might make, is no restriction; unless the words be deemed exclusive of original jurisdiction. . . .

To enable this court, then, to issue a *mandamus*, it must be shown to be an exercise of appellate jurisdiction, or to be necessary to enable them to exercise appellate jurisdiction. . . .

It is the essential criterion of appellate jurisdiction, that it revises and corrects the proceedings in a cause already instituted, and does not create that cause. Although, therefore, a *mandamus* may be directed to courts, yet to issue such a writ to an officer for the delivery of a paper, is in effect the same as to sustain an original action for that paper, and, therefore, seems not to belong to appellate but to original jurisdiction. Neither is it necessary in such a case as this, to enable the Court to exercise its appellate jurisdiction.

The authority, therefore, given to the Supreme Court, by the act establishing the judicial courts of the United States, to issue writs of *mandamus* to public officers, appears not to be warranted by the Constitution; and it becomes necessary to inquire whether a jurisdiction so conferred can be exercised.

The question, whether an act, repugnant to the Constitution, can become the law of the land, is a question deeply interesting to the United States; but happily, not of an intricacy proportioned to its interest. It seems only necessary to recognize certain principles, supposed to have been long and well established, to decide it.

That the people have an original right to establish, for their future government, such principles, as, in their opinion, shall most conduce to their own happiness is the basis on which the whole American fabric has been erected. The exercise of this original right is a very great exertion; nor can it, or ought it, to be frequently repeated. The principles, therefore, so established, are deemed fundamental. And as the authority from which they proceed is supreme, and can seldom act, they are designed to be permanent.

This original and supreme will organizes the government, and assigns to different departments their respective powers. It may either stop here, or establish certain limits not to be transcended by those departments.

The government of the United States is of the latter description. The powers of the legislature are defined and limited; and that those limits may not be mistaken, or forgotten, the Constitution is written. To what purpose are powers limited, and to what purpose is that limitation committed to writing, if these limits may, at any time, be passed by those intended to be restrained? The distinction between a government with limited and unlimited powers is abolished, if those limits do not confine the persons on whom they are imposed, and if acts prohibited and acts allowed, are of equal obligation. It is a proposition too plain to be contested, that the Constitution controls any legislative act repugnant to it; or, that the legislature may alter the Constitution by an ordinary act.

Between these alternatives there is no middle ground. The Constitution is either a superior paramount law, unchangeable by ordinary means, or it is on a level with ordinary legislative acts, and, like other acts, is alterable when the legislature shall please to alter it.

If the former part of the alternative be true, then a legislative act contrary to the Constitution is not law: if the latter part be true, then written constitutions are absurd attempts, on the part of the people, to limit a power in its own nature illimitable.

Certainly all those who have framed written constitutions contemplate them as forming the fundamental and paramount law of the nation, and, consequently, the theory of every such government must be, that an act of the legislature, repugnant to the Constitution, is void.

This theory is essentially attached to a written Constitution, and is, consequently, to be considered, by this Court, as one of the fundamental principles of our society. It is not therefore to be lost sight of in the further consideration of this subject.

If an act of the legislature, repugnant to the Constitution, is void, does it, notwithstanding its invalidity, bind the courts, and oblige them to give it effect? Or, in other words, though it be not law, does it constitute a rule as operative as if it was a law? This would be to overthrow in fact what was established in theory; and would seem, at first view, an absurdity too gross to be insisted on. It shall, however, receive a more attentive consideration.

It is emphatically the province and duty of the judicial department to say what the law is. Those who apply the rule to particular cases, must of necessity expound and interpret that rule. If two laws conflict with each other, the courts must decide on the operation of each.

So if a law be in opposition to the Constitution; if both the law and the Constitution apply to a particular case, so that the court must either decide that case conformably to the law, disregarding the Constitution; or conformably to the Constitution, disregarding the law; the court must determine which of these conflicting rules governs the case. This is of the very essence of the judicial duty.

If, then, the courts are to regard the Constitution, and the Constitution is superior to any ordinary act of the legislature, the Constitution, and not such ordinary act, must govern the case to which they both apply.

Those, then, who controvert the principle that the Constitution is to be considered, in court, as a paramount law, are reduced to the necessity of maintaining that courts must close their eyes on the Constitution, and see only the law.

This doctrine would subvert the very foundation of all written constitutions. It would declare that an act which, according to the principles and theory of our government, is entirely void, is yet, in practice, completely obligatory. It would declare that if the legislatures shall do what is expressly forbidden, such act, notwithstanding the express prohibition, is in reality effectual. It would be giving to the legislature a practical and real omnipotence, with the same breath which professes to restrict their powers within narrow limits. It is prescribing limits, and declaring that those limits may be passed at pleasure.

That it thus reduces to nothing what we have deemed the greatest improvement on political institutions, a written constitution, would of itself be sufficient, in America, where written constitutions have been viewed with so much reverence, for rejecting the construction. But the peculiar expressions of the Constitution of the United States furnish additional arguments in favour of its rejection.

The judicial power of the United States is extended to all cases arising under the Constitution.

Could it be the intention of those who gave this power, to say that in using it the Constitution should not be looked into? That a case arising under the Constitution should be decided without examining the instrument under which it arises?

This is too extravagant to be maintained.

In some cases, then, the Constitution must be looked into by the judges. And if they can open it at all, what part of it are they forbidden to read or to obey?

There are many other parts of the Constitution which serve to illustrate this subject.

It is declared that "no tax or duty shall be laid on articles exported from any state." Suppose a duty on the export of cotton, of tobacco, or of flour; and a suit instituted to recover it. Ought judgment to be rendered in such a case? Ought the judges to close their eyes on the Constitution, and only see the law?

The Constitution declares "that no bill of attainder or *ex post facto* law shall be passed."

If, however, such a bill should be passed, and a person should be prosecuted under it; must the Court condemn to death those victims whom the Constitution endeavors to preserve?

"No person," says the Constitution, "shall be convicted of treason unless on the testimony of two witnesses to the same overt act, or on confession in open court."

Here the language of the Constitution is addressed especially to the courts. It prescribes, directly for them, a rule of evidence not to be departed from. If the legislature should change that rule, and declare one witness, or a confession out of court, sufficient for conviction, must the constitutional principle yield to the legislative act?

From these, and many other selections which might be made, it is apparent, that the framers of the Constitution contemplated that instrument as a rule for the government of courts, as well as of the legislature.

Why otherwise does it direct judges to take an oath to support it? This oath certainly applies in an especial manner, to their conduct in their official character. How immoral to impose it on them, if they were to be used as the instruments, and the knowing instruments, for violating what they swear to support! . . .

It is also not entirely unworthy of observation, that in declaring what shall be the *supreme* law of the land, the *Constitution* itself is first mentioned; and not the laws of the United States generally, but those only which shall be made in *pursuance* of the Constitution, have that rank.

Thus, the particular phraseology of the Constitution of the United States confirms and strengthens the principle, supposed to be essential to all written constitutions, that a law repugnant to the Constitution is void; and that courts, as well as other departments, are bound by the instrument.

The rule must be

                                                Discharged.

40

BROWN v. BOARD OF EDUCATION (1954)

A unanimous Supreme Court declared that laws or governmental regulations provid-
ing for racially segregated public schools violate the equal protection clause of the
Fourteenth Amendment. This is true even if all the "tangible" factors, such as physical
plant, curricula, and teachers' salaries, are equal. Separating African-American chil-
dren "from others of similar age and qualifications solely because of their race gener-
ates a feeling of inferiority as to their status in the community that may affect their
hearts and minds in a way unlikely ever to be undone." Consequently, "[s]eparate
educational facilities are inherently unequal."

Mr. Chief Justice Warren delivered the opinion of the Court:

These cases come to us from the states of Kansas, South Carolina, Virginia, and Delaware. They are premised on different facts and different local conditions, but a common legal question justifies their consideration together in this consolidated opinion.

In each of the cases, minors of the Negro race, through their legal representatives, seek the aid of the courts in obtaining admission to the public schools of their community on a nonsegregated basis. In each instance, they had been denied admission to schools attended by white children under laws requiring or permitting segregation according to race. This segregation was alleged to deprive the plaintiffs of the equal protection of the laws under the Fourteenth Amendment. . . .

The plaintiffs contend that segregated public schools are not "equal" and cannot be made "equal," and that hence they are deprived of the equal protection of the laws. Because of the obvious importance of the question presented, the Court took jurisdiction. Argument was heard in the 1952 term, and reargument was heard this term on certain questions propounded by the Court.

Reargument was largely devoted to the circumstances surrounding the adoption of the Fourteenth Amendment in 1868. It covered exhaustively consideration of the amendment in Congress, ratification by the states, then existing practices in racial segregation, and the views of proponents and opponents of the amendment. This discussion and our own investigation convince us that, although these sources cast some light, it is not enough to resolve the problem with which we are faced. At best, they are inconclusive. The most avid proponents of the post-War amendments undoubtedly intended them to remove all legal distinctions among "all persons born or naturalized in the United States." Their opponents, just as certainly, were antagonistic to both the letter and the spirit of the amendments and wished them to have the most limited effect. What others in Congress and the state legislatures had in mind cannot be determined with any degree of certainty.

In the first cases in this Court construing the Fourteenth Amendment, decided shortly after its adoption, the Court interpreted it as proscribing all state-imposed discriminations against the Negro race. The doctrine of "separate but equal" did not make its appearance in this Court until 1896 in the case of *Plessy v. Ferguson* involving not education but transportation. American courts have since labored with the doctrine for over half a century. In this Court, there have been six cases involving the "separate but equal" doctrine in the field of public education. In *Cumming v. County Board of Education* and *Gong Lum v. Rice* the validity of the doctrine itself was not challenged. In more recent cases, all on the graduate school level, inequality was found in that specific benefits enjoyed by white students were denied to Negro students of the same educational qualifications. *Missouri ex rel. Gaines v. Canada, Sipuel v. Oklahoma, Sweatt v. Painter, McLaurin v. Oklahoma State Regents.* In none of these cases was it necessary to reexamine the doctrine to grant relief to the Negro plaintiff. And in *Sweatt v. Painter* the Court expressly reserved decision on the question whether *Plessy* should be held inapplicable to public education.

In the instant cases, that question is directly presented. Here . . . there are findings below that the Negro and white schools involved have been equalized, or are being equalized, with respect to buildings, curricula, qualifications and salaries of teachers, and other "tangible" factors. Our decision, therefore, cannot turn on merely a comparison of these tangible factors in the Negro and white schools involved in each of the cases. We must look instead to the effect of segregation itself on public education.

In approaching this problem, we cannot turn the clock back to 1868 when the amendment was adopted, or even to 1896 when *Plessy* was written. We must consider public education in the light of its full development and its present place in American life throughout the nation. Only in this way can it be determined if segregation in public schools deprives these plaintiffs of the equal protection of the laws.

Today, education is perhaps the most important function of state and local governments. Compulsory school attendance laws and the great expenditures for education both demonstrate our recognition of the importance of education to our democratic society. It is required in the performance of our most basic public responsibilities, even service in the armed forces. It is the very foundation of good citizenship. Today it is a principal instrument in awakening the child to cultural values, in preparing him for later professional training, and in helping him to adjust normally to his environment. In these days, it is doubtful that any child may reasonably be expected to succeed in life if he is denied the opportunity of an education. Such an opportunity, where the state has undertaken to provide it, is a right which must be made available to all on equal terms.

We come then to the question presented: Does segregation of children in public schools solely on the basis of race, even though the physical facilities and other "tangible" factors may be equal, deprive the children of the minority group of equal educational opportunities? We believe that it does.

In *Sweatt, supra,* in finding that a segregated law school for Negroes could not provide them equal educational opportunities, this Court relied in large part on "those qualities which are incapable of objective measurement but which make for greatness in a law school." In *McLaurin* the Court, in requiring that a Negro admitted to a white graduate school be treated like all other students, again resorted to intangible considerations: ". . . his ability to study, to engage in discussions and exchange views with other students, and, in general, to learn his profession." Such considerations apply with added force to children in grade and high schools. To separate them from others of similar age and qualifications solely because of their race generates a feeling of inferiority as to their status in the community that may affect their hearts and minds in a way unlikely ever to be undone. The effect of this separation on their educational opportunities was well stated by a finding in the Kansas case by a court which nevertheless felt compelled to rule against the Negro plaintiffs: "Segregation of white and colored children in public schools has a detrimental effect upon the colored children. The impact is greater when it has the sanction of the law; for the policy of separating the races is usually interpreted as denoting the inferiority of the Negro group. A sense of inferiority affects the motivation of a child to learn. Segregation with the sanction of law, therefore, has a tendency to retard the educational and mental development of Negro children and to deprive them of some of the benefits they would receive in a racially integrated school system." Whatever may have been the extent of psychological knowledge at the time of *Plessy*, this finding is amply supported by modern authority. Any language in *Plessy* contrary to this finding is rejected.

We conclude that in the field of public education the doctrine of "separate but equal" has no place. Separate educational facilities are inherently unequal. Therefore, we hold that the plaintiffs and other similarly situated for whom the actions have been brought are, by reason of the segregation complained of, deprived of the equal protection of the laws guaranteed by the Fourteenth Amendment. . . .

41

ROE v. WADE (1973)

By a vote of 7–2, the Supreme Court held for the first time that the ". . . right of privacy, whether it be founded in the Fourteenth Amendment's concept of personal liberty and restrictions upon state action, as we feel it is, or, as the District Court determined, in the Ninth Amendment's reservation of rights to the people, is broad enough to encompass a woman's decision whether or not to terminate her pregnancy." The decision notes, however, that because this privacy right is not absolute, it may be subject to governmental regulation under appropriate circumstances.

Mr. Justice Blackmun delivered the opinion of the Court:

This Texas federal appeal and its Georgia companion, *Doe v. Bolton, post,*. p. 179, present constitutional challenges to state criminal abortion legislation. The Texas statutes under attack here are typical of those that have been in effect in many States for approximately a century. The Georgia statutes, in contrast, have a modern cast, and are a legislative product that, to an extent at least, obviously reflects the influences of recent attitudinal change, of advancing medical knowledge and techniques, and of new thinking about an old issue.

We forthwith acknowledge our awareness of the sensitive and emotional nature of the abortion controversy, of the vigorous opposing views, even among physicians, and of the deep and seemingly absolute convictions that the subject inspires. One's philosophy, one's experiences, one's exposure to the raw edges of human existence, one's religious training, one's attitudes toward life and family and their values, and the moral standards one establishes and seeks to observe, are all likely to influence and to color one's thinking and conclusions about abortion.

In addition, population growth, pollution, poverty, and racial overtones tend to complicate and not to simplify the problem.

Our task, of course, is to resolve the issue by constitutional measurement, free of emotion and of predilection. We seek earnestly to do this, and, because we do, we . . . have inquired into, and in this opinion place some emphasis upon, medical and medical-legal history and what that history reveals about man's attitudes toward the abortion procedure over the centuries. . . .

I

The Texas statutes . . . make it a crime to "procure an abortion," as therein defined, or to attempt one, except with respect to "an abortion procured or attempted by medical advice for the purpose of saving the life of the mother." Similar statutes are in existence in a majority of the States.

Texas first enacted a criminal abortion statute in 1854. . . . This was soon modified into language that has remained substantially unchanged to the present time. . . . The final article in each of these compilations provided the same exception, as does the present Article 1196, for an abortion by "medical advice for the purpose of saving the life of the mother." . . .

V

The principal thrust of appellant's attack on the Texas statutes is that they improperly invade a right, said to be possessed by the pregnant woman, to choose to terminate her pregnancy. Appellant would discover this right in the concept of personal "liberty" embodied in the Fourteenth Amendment's due process clause; or in personal, marital, familial, and sexual privacy said to be protected by the Bill of Rights or its penumbras, *see Griswold v. Connecticut*, 381 U.S. 479 (1965); *Eisenstadt v. Baird*, 405 U.S. 438 (1972); *id.* at 460 (WHITE, J., concurring in result); or among those rights reserved to the people by the Ninth Amendment, *Griswold v. Connecticut*, 381 U.S. at 486 (Goldberg, J., concurring). Before addressing this claim, we feel it desirable briefly to survey, in several aspects, the history of abortion, for such insight as that history may afford us, and then to examine the state purposes and interests behind the criminal abortion laws.

VI

It perhaps is not generally appreciated that the restrictive criminal abortion laws in effect in a majority of States today are of relatively recent vintage. Those laws, generally proscribing abortion or its attempt at any time during pregnancy except when necessary to preserve the pregnant woman's life, are not of ancient or even of common law origin. Instead, they derive from statutory changes effected, for the most part, in the latter half of the 19th century.

1. *Ancient attitudes.* These are not capable of precise determination. We are told that, at the time of the Persian Empire, abortifacients were known, and that criminal abortions were severely punished. We are also told, however, that abortion was practiced in Greek times as well as in the Roman Era, and that "it was resorted to without scruple." The Ephesian, Soranos, often described as the greatest of the ancient gynecologists, appears to have been generally opposed to Rome's prevailing free-abortion practices. He found it necessary to think first of the life of the mother, and he resorted to abortion when, upon this standard, he felt the procedure advisable. Greek and Roman law afforded little protection to the unborn. If abortion was prosecuted in some places, it seems to have been based on a concept of a violation of the father's right to his offspring. Ancient religion did not bar abortion.

2. *The Hippocratic Oath.* What then of the famous Oath that has stood so long as the ethical guide of the medical profession and that bears the name of the great Greek (460(?)–377(?) B.C.), who has been described . . . as the Father of Medicine, the "wisest and the greatest practitioner of his art," and the "most important and most complete medical personality of antiquity," who dominated the medical schools of his time, and who typified the sum of the medical knowledge of the past? The Oath varies somewhat according to the particular translation, but in any translation the content is clear:

I will give no deadly medicine to anyone if asked, nor suggest any such counsel; and in like manner, I will not give to a woman a pessary to produce abortion,

or

I will neither give a deadly drug to anybody if asked for it, nor will I make a suggestion to this effect. Similarly, I will not give to a woman an abortive remedy.

Although the Oath is not mentioned in any of the principal briefs in this case or in *Doe v. Bolton, post,* p. 179, it represents the apex of the development of strict ethical concepts in medicine, and its influence endures to this day. Why did not the authority of Hippocrates dissuade abortion practice in his time and that of Rome? The late Dr. Edelstein provides us with a theory: The Oath was not uncontested even in Hippocrates' day; only the Pythagorean school of philosophers frowned upon the related act of suicide. Most Greek thinkers, on the other hand, commended abortion, at least prior to viability. *See* Plato, Republic, V, 461; Aristotle, Politics, VII, 1335b 25. For the Pythagoreans, however, it was a matter of dogma. For them, the embryo was animate from the moment of conception, and abortion meant destruction of a living being. The abortion clause of the Oath, therefore, "echoes Pythagorean doctrines," . . . and "[i]n no other stratum of Greek opinion were such views held or proposed in the same spirit of uncompromising austerity."

Dr. Edelstein then concludes that the Oath originated in a group representing only a small segment of Greek opinion, and that it certainly was not accepted by all ancient physicians. He points out that medical writings down to Galen (A.D. 130–200) "give evidence of the violation of almost every one of its injunctions." But with the end of antiquity, a decided change took place. Resistance against suicide and against abortion became common. The Oath came to be popular. The emerging teachings of Christianity were in agreement with the Pythagorean ethic. The Oath "became the nucleus of all medical ethics," and "was applauded as the embodiment of truth." Thus, suggests Dr. Edelstein, it is "a Pythagorean manifesto, and not the expression of an absolute standard of medical conduct."

This, it seems to us, is a satisfactory and acceptable explanation of the Hippocratic Oath's apparent rigidity. It enables us to understand, in historical context, a long-accepted and revered statement of medical ethics.

3. *The common law.* It is undisputed that, at common law, abortion performed before "quickening"—the first recognizable movement of the fetus *in utero,* appearing usually from the 16th to the 18th week of pregnancy—was not an indictable offense. The absence of a common law crime for pre-quickening abortion appears to have developed from a confluence of earlier philosophical, theological, and civil and canon law concepts of when life begins. These disciplines variously approached the question in terms of the point at which the embryo or fetus became "formed" or recognizably human, or in terms of when a "person" came into being, that is, infused with a "soul" or "animated." A loose consensus evolved in early English law that these events occurred at some point between conception and live birth. This was "mediate animation." Although Christian theology

and the canon law came to fix the point of animation at 40 days for a male and 80 days for a female, a view that persisted until the 19th century, there was otherwise little agreement about the precise time of formation or animation. There was agreement, however, that, prior to this point, the fetus was to be regarded as part of the mother, and its destruction, therefore, was not homicide. . . .

Whether abortion of a quick fetus was a felony at common law, or even a lesser crime, is still disputed. . . . [W]hile most American courts ruled, in holding or dictum, that abortion of an unquickened fetus was not criminal under their received common law, others followed Coke in stating that abortion . . . of a quick fetus was a "misprision," a term they translated to mean "misdemeanor." That their reliance on Coke on this aspect of the law was uncritical and, apparently in all the reported cases, dictum (due probably to the paucity of common law prosecutions for post-quickening abortion), makes it now appear doubtful that abortion was ever firmly established as a common law crime even with respect to the destruction of a quick fetus.

4. *The English statutory law.* England's first criminal abortion statute, Lord Ellenborough's Act, . . . came in 1803. It made abortion of a quick fetus, §1, a capital crime, but, in §2, it provided lesser penalties for the felony of abortion before quickening, and thus preserved the "quickening" distinction. This contrast was continued in the general revision of 1828. . . . It disappeared, however, together with the death penalty, in 1837, . . . and did not reappear in the Offenses Against the Person Act of 1861, . . . that formed the core of English anti-abortion law until the liberalizing reforms of 1967. In 1929, the Infant Life (Preservation) Act, . . . came into being. Its emphasis was upon the destruction of "the life of a child capable of being born alive." It made a willful act performed with the necessary intent a felony. It contained a proviso that one was not to be . . . found guilty of the offense

> unless it is proved that the act which caused the death of the child was not done in good faith for the purpose only of preserving the life of the mother. . . .

Recently, Parliament enacted a new abortion law. This is the Abortion Act of 1967. The Act permits a licensed physician to perform an abortion where two other licensed physicians agree (a)

> that the continuance of the pregnancy would involve risk to the life of the pregnant woman, or of injury to the physical or mental health of the pregnant woman or any existing children of her family, greater than if the pregnancy were terminated,

or (b)

> that there is a substantial risk that, if the child were born it would suffer from such physical or mental abnormalities as . . . to be seriously handicapped.

The Act also provides that, in making this determination, "account may be taken of the pregnant woman's actual or reasonably foreseeable environment." It also permits a physician, without the concurrence of others, to terminate a pregnancy where he is of the good faith opinion that the abortion "is immediately necessary to save the life or to prevent grave permanent injury to the physical or mental health of the pregnant woman."

5. *The American law.* In this country, the law in effect in all but a few States until mid-19th century was the preexisting English common law. Connecticut, the first State to enact abortion legislation, adopted in 1821 that part of Lord Ellenborough's Act that related to a woman "quick with child." The death penalty was not imposed. Abortion before quickening was made a crime in that State only in 1860. In 1828, New York enacted legislation that, in two respects, was to serve as a model for early anti-abortion statutes. First, while barring destruction of an unquickened fetus as well as a quick fetus, it made the former only a misdemeanor, but the latter second-degree manslaughter. Second, it incorporated a concept of therapeutic abortion by providing that an abortion was excused if it

> shall have been necessary to preserve the life of such mother, or shall have been advised by two physicians to be necessary for such purpose.

By 1840, when Texas had received the common law, only eight American States . . . had statutes dealing with abortion. It was not until after the War Between the States that legislation began generally to replace the common law. Most of these initial statutes dealt severely with abortion after quickening, but were lenient with it before quickening. Most punished attempts equally with completed abortions. While many statutes included the exception for an abortion thought by one or more physicians to be necessary to save the mother's life, that provision soon disappeared, and the typical law required that the procedure actually be necessary for that purpose. Gradually, in the middle and late 19th century, the quickening distinction disappeared from the statutory law of most States and the degree of the offense and the penalties were increased. By the end of the 1950s, a large majority of the jurisdictions banned abortion, however and whenever performed, unless done to save or preserve the life of the mother. The exceptions, Alabama and the District of Columbia, permitted abortion to preserve the mother's health. Three States permitted abortions that were not "unlawfully" performed or that were not "without lawful justification," leaving interpretation of those standards to the courts. In the past several years, however, a trend toward liberalization of abortion statutes has resulted in adoption, by about one-third of the States, of less stringent laws, . . .

It is thus apparent that, at common law, at the time of the adoption of our Constitution, and throughout the major portion of the 19th century, abortion was viewed with less disfavor than under most American statutes currently in effect. Phrasing it another way, a woman enjoyed a substantially broader right to terminate a pregnancy than she does in most States today. At least with respect to the early stage of pregnancy, and very possibly without such a limitation, the opportunity . . . to make this choice was present in this country well into the 19th century.

Even later, the law continued for some time to treat less punitively an abortion procured in early pregnancy.

6. *The position of the American Medical Association.* The anti-abortion mood prevalent in this country in the late 19th century was shared by the medical profession. Indeed, the attitude of the profession may have played a significant role in the enactment of stringent criminal abortion legislation during that period.

An AMA Committee on Criminal Abortion was appointed in May, 1857. It presented its report, . . . to the Twelfth Annual Meeting. That report observed that the Committee had been appointed to investigate criminal abortion "with a view to its general suppression." It deplored abortion and its frequency and it listed three causes of "this general demoralization":

> The first of these causes is a widespread popular ignorance of the true character of the crime—a belief, even among mothers themselves, that the foetus is not alive till after the period of quickening.
> The second of the agents alluded to is the fact that the profession themselves are frequently supposed careless of foetal life. . . .
> The third reason of the frightful extent of this crime is found in the grave defects of our laws, both common and statute, as regards the independent and actual existence of the child before birth, as a living being. These errors, which are sufficient in most instances to prevent conviction, are based, and only based, upon mistaken and exploded medical dogmas. With strange inconsistency, the law fully acknowledges the foetus *in utero* and its inherent rights, for civil purposes; while personally and as criminally affected, it fails to recognize it, . . . and to its life as yet denies all protection. . . .

The Committee then offered, and the Association adopted, resolutions protesting "against such unwarrantable destruction of human life," calling upon state legislatures to revise their abortion laws and requesting the cooperation of state medical societies "in pressing the subject". . . .

. . . In [1967], the Committee on Human Reproduction urged the adoption of a stated policy of opposition to induced abortion except when there is "documented medical evidence" of a threat to the health or life of the mother, or that the child "may be born with incapacitating physical deformity or mental deficiency," or that a pregnancy "resulting from legally established statutory or forcible rape or incest may constitute a threat to the mental or physical health of the patient," two other physicians "chosen because of their recognized professional competence have examined the patient and have concurred in writing," and the procedure "is performed in a hospital accredited by the Joint Commission on Accreditation of Hospitals." The providing of medical information by physicians to state legislatures in their consideration of legislation regarding therapeutic abortion was "to be considered consistent with the principles of ethics of the American Medical Association." This recommendation was adopted by the House of Delegates. . . .

In 1970, after the introduction of a variety of proposed resolutions and of a report from its Board of Trustees, a reference committee noted "polarization of the medical profession on this controversial issue"; division among those who had testified; a difference of opinion among AMA councils and committees; "the remarkable shift in testimony" in six months, felt to be influenced "by the rapid changes in state laws and by the judicial decisions which tend to make abortion more freely available;" and a feeling "that this trend will continue." On June 25, 1970, the House of Delegates adopted preambles and most of the resolutions pro posed by the reference committee. The preambles emphasized "the best interests of the patient," "sound clinical judgment," and "informed patient consent," in contrast to "mere acquiescence to the patient's demand." The resolutions asserted that abortion is a medical procedure that should be performed by a licensed physician in an accredited hospital only after consultation with two other physicians and in conformity with state law, and that no party to the proce dure should be required to violate personally held moral principles. . . . The AMA Judicial Council rendered a complementary opinion.

7. *The position of the American Public Health Association.* In October, 1970, the Executive Board of the APHA adopted Standards for Abortion Services. These were five in number:

> a. Rapid and simple abortion referral must be readily available through state and local public . . . health departments, medical societies, or other nonprofit organiza- tions.
> b. An important function of counseling should be to simplify and expedite the pro- vision of abortion services; it should not delay the obtaining of these services.
> c. Psychiatric consultation should not be mandatory. As in the case of other spe- cialized medical services, psychiatric consultation should be sought for definite indica- tions, and not on a routine basis.
> d. A wide range of individuals from appropriately trained, sympathetic volunteers to highly skilled physicians may qualify as abortion counselors.
> e. Contraception and/or sterilization should be discussed with each abortion patient.

> . . . Among factors pertinent to life and health risks associated with abortion were three that "are recognized as important":
> a. the skill of the physician,
> b. the environment in which the abortion is performed, and above all
> c. the duration of pregnancy, as determined by uterine size and confirmed by men- strual history. . . .

It was said that "a well-equipped hospital" offers more protection

> to cope with unforeseen difficulties than an office or clinic without such resources. . . . The factor of gestational age is of overriding importance.

Thus, it was recommended that abortions in the second trimester and early abor- tions in the presence of existing medical complications be performed in hospitals as inpatient procedures. For pregnancies in the first trimester, abortion in the hospital with or without overnight stay "is probably the safest practice." An abor- tion in an extramural facility, however, is an acceptable alternative "provided arrangements exist in advance to admit patients promptly if unforeseen complications develop." Standards for an abortion facility were listed. It was said that, at present, abortions should be performed by physicians or osteopaths who are licensed to practice and who have "adequate training." . . .

VII

Three reasons have been advanced to explain historically the enactment of criminal abortion laws in the 19th century and to justify their continued existence.

It has been argued occasionally that these laws were the product of a Victorian social concern to discourage illicit sexual conduct. Texas, however, does not advance this justification in the present case, and it appears that no court or commentator has taken the argument seriously. The appellants and *amici* contend, moreover, that this is not a proper state purpose at all and suggest that, if it were, the Texas statutes are overbroad in protecting it, since the law fails to distinguish between married and unwed mothers.

A second reason is concerned with abortion as a medical procedure. When most criminal abortion laws were first enacted, the procedure was a hazardous one for the woman. This was particularly true prior to the development of antisepsis. . . . Even after 1900, and perhaps until as late as the development of antibiotics in the 1940's, standard modern techniques such as dilation and curettage were not nearly so safe as they are today. Thus, it has been argued that a State's real concern in enacting a criminal abortion law was to protect the pregnant woman, that is, to restrain her from submitting to a procedure that placed her life in serious jeopardy.

Modern medical techniques have altered this situation. Appellants and various *amici* refer to medical data indicating that abortion in early pregnancy, that is, prior to the end of the first trimester, although not without its risk, is now relatively safe. Mortality rates for women undergoing early abortions, where the procedure is legal, appear to be as low as or lower than the rates for normal childbirth. Consequently, any interest of the State in protecting the woman from an inherently hazardous procedure, except when it would be equally dangerous for her to forgo it, has largely disappeared. Of course, important state interests in the areas of health and medical standards do remain. . . . [T]he risk to the woman increases as her pregnancy continues. Thus, the State retains a definite interest in protecting the woman's own health and safety when an abortion is proposed at a late stage of pregnancy.

The third reason is the State's interest—some phrase it in terms of duty—in protecting prenatal life. Some of the argument for this justification rests on the theory that a new human life is present from the moment of conception. The State's interest and general obligation to protect life then extends, it is argued, to prenatal life. Only when the life of the pregnant mother herself is at stake, balanced against the life she carries within her, should the interest of the embryo or fetus not prevail. Logically, of course, a legitimate state interest in this area need not stand or fall on acceptance of the belief that life begins at conception or at some other point prior to live birth. In assessing the State's interest, recognition may be given to the less rigid claim that as long as at least potential life is involved, the State may assert interests beyond the protection of the pregnant woman alone. . . .

Parties challenging state abortion laws have sharply disputed in some courts the contention that a purpose of these laws, when enacted, was to protect prenatal life. Pointing to the absence of legislative history to support the contention, they claim that most state laws were designed solely to protect the woman. Because medical advances have lessened this concern, at least with respect to abortion in early pregnancy, they argue that with respect to such abortions the laws can no longer be justified by any state interest. There is some scholarly support for this view of original purpose. The few state courts called upon to interpret their laws in the late 19th and early 20th centuries did focus on the State's interest in protecting the woman's health, rather than in preserving the embryo and fetus. Proponents of this view point out that in many States, including Texas, by statute or judicial interpretation, the pregnant woman herself could not be prosecuted for self-abortion or for cooperating in an abortion performed upon her by another. They claim that adoption of the "quickening" distinction through received common . . . law and state statutes tacitly recognizes the greater health hazards inherent in late abortion and impliedly repudiates the theory that life begins at conception. . . .

VIII

The Constitution does not explicitly mention any right of privacy. In a line of decisions, however, . . . the Court has recognized that a right of personal privacy, or a guarantee of certain areas or zones of privacy, does exist under the Constitution. In varying contexts, the Court or individual Justices have, indeed, found at least the roots of that right in the First Amendment, . . . in the Fourth and Fifth Amendments, . . . in the penumbras of the Bill of Rights, . . . in the Ninth Amendment, . . . or in the concept of liberty guaranteed by the first section of the Fourteenth Amendment. . . . These decisions make it clear that only personal rights that can be deemed "fundamental" or "implicit in the concept of ordered liberty". . . are included in this guarantee of personal privacy. They also make it clear that the right has some extension to activities relating to marriage, . . . procreation, . . . contraception, . . . family relationships, . . . and childrearing and education. . . .

This right of privacy, whether it be founded in the Fourteenth Amendment's concept of personal liberty and restrictions upon state action, as we feel it is, or, as the District Court determined, in the Ninth Amendment's reservation of rights to the people, is broad enough to encompass a woman's decision whether or not to terminate her pregnancy. The detriment that the State would impose upon the pregnant woman by denying this choice altogether is apparent. Specific and direct harm medically diagnosable even in early pregnancy may be involved. Maternity, or additional offspring, may force upon the woman a distressful life and future. Psychological harm may be imminent. Mental and physical health may be taxed by child care. There is also the distress, for all concerned, associated with the unwanted child, and there is the problem of bringing a child into a family already unable, psychologically and otherwise, to care for it. In other cases, as in this one, the additional difficulties and continuing stigma of unwed motherhood may be involved. All these are factors the woman and her responsible physician necessarily will consider in consultation.

On the basis of elements such as these, appellant and some *amici* argue that the woman's right is absolute and that she is entitled to terminate her pregnancy at whatever time, in whatever way, and for whatever reason she alone chooses. With this we do not agree. Appellant's arguments that Texas either has no valid interest at all in regulating the abortion decision, or no interest strong enough to support any limitation upon the woman's sole determination, are unpersuasive. The . . . Court's decisions recognizing a right of privacy also acknowledge that some state regulation in areas protected by that right is appropriate. As noted above, a State may properly assert important interests in safeguarding health, in maintaining medical standards, and in protecting potential life. At some point in pregnancy, these respective interests become sufficiently compelling to sustain regulation of the factors that govern the abortion decision. The privacy right involved, therefore, cannot be said to be absolute. In fact, it is not clear to us that the claim asserted by some *amici* that one has an unlimited right to do with one's body as one pleases bears close relationship to the right of privacy previously articulated in the Court's decisions. The Court has refused to recognize an unlimited right of this kind in the past. . . .

We, therefore, conclude that the right of personal privacy includes the abortion decision, but that this right is not unqualified, and must be considered against important state interests in regulation. . . .

Where certain "fundamental rights" are involved, the Court has held that regulation limiting these rights may be justified only by a "compelling state interest," . . . and that legislative enactments must be narrowly drawn to express only the legitimate state interests at stake. . . .

In the recent abortion cases, . . . courts have recognized these principles. Those striking down state laws have generally scrutinized the State's interests in protecting health and potential life, and have concluded that neither interest justified broad limitations on the reasons for which a physician and his pregnant patient might decide that she should have an abortion in the early stages of pregnancy. Courts sustaining state laws have held that the State's determinations to protect health or prenatal life are dominant and constitutionally justifiable.

IX

The Constitution does not define "person" in so many words. Section 1 of the Fourteenth Amendment contains three references to "person." The first, in defining "citizens," speaks of "persons born or naturalized in the United States." The word also appears both in the Due Process Clause and in the Equal Protection

Clause. "Person" is used in other places in the Constitution: in the listing of qualifications for Representatives and Senators, Art. I, §2, cl. 2, and §3, cl. 3; in the Apportionment Clause, Art. I, §2, cl. 3; in the Migration and Importation provision, Art. I, §9, cl. 1; in the Emolument Clause, Art. I, §9, cl. 8; in the Electors provisions, Art. II, §1, cl. 2, and the superseded cl. 3; in the provision outlining qualifications for the office of President, Art. II, §1, cl. 5; in the Extradition provisions, Art. IV, §2, cl. 2, and the superseded Fugitive Slave Clause 3; and in the Fifth, Twelfth, and Twenty-second Amendments, as well as in §§2 and 3 of the Fourteenth Amendment. But in nearly all these instances, the use of the word is such that it has application only post-natally. None indicates, with any assurance, that it has any possible pre-natal application.

All this, together with our observation, *supra*, that, throughout the major portion of the 19th century, prevailing legal abortion practices were far freer than they are today, persuades us that the word "person," as used in the Fourteenth Amendment, does not include the unborn. This is in accord with the results reached in those few cases where the issue has been squarely presented. . . .

This conclusion, however, does not of itself fully answer the contentions raised by Texas, and we pass on to other considerations.

B. The pregnant woman cannot be isolated in her privacy. She carries an embryo and, later, a fetus, if one accepts the medical definitions of the developing young in the human uterus. . . . The situation therefore is inherently different from marital intimacy, or bedroom possession of obscene material, or marriage, or procreation, or education. . . . As we have intimated above, it is reasonable and appropriate for a State to decide that, at some point in time another interest, that of health of the mother or that of potential human life, becomes significantly involved. The woman's privacy is no longer sole and any right of privacy she possesses must be measured accordingly.

Texas urges that, apart from the Fourteenth Amendment, life begins at conception and is present throughout pregnancy, and that, therefore, the State has a compelling interest in protecting that life from and after conception. We need not resolve the difficult question of when life begins. When those trained in the respective disciplines of medicine, philosophy, and theology are unable to arrive at any consensus, the judiciary, at this point in the development of man's knowledge, is not in a position to speculate as to the answer. . . .

It should be sufficient to note briefly the wide divergence of thinking on this most sensitive and difficult question. There has always been strong support for the view that life does not begin until live birth. . . . As we have noted, the common law found greater significance in quickening. Physicians and their scientific colleagues have regarded that event with less interest and have tended to focus either upon conception, upon live birth, or upon the interim point at which the fetus becomes "viable," that is, potentially able to live outside the mother's womb, albeit with artificial aid. Viability is usually placed at about seven months (28 weeks) but may occur earlier, even at 24 weeks. The Aristotelian theory of "mediate animation," that held sway throughout the Middle Ages and the Renaissance in Europe, continued to be official Roman Catholic dogma until the 19th century, despite opposition to this "ensoulment" theory from those in the

Church who would recognize the existence of life from the moment of conception. The latter is now, of course, the official belief of the Catholic Church. As one brief *amicus* discloses, this is a view strongly held by many non-Catholics as well, and by many physicians. Substantial problems for precise definition of this view are posed, however, by new embryological data that purport to indicate that conception is a "process" over time, rather than an event, and by new medical techniques such as menstrual extraction, the "morning-after" pill, implantation of embryos, artificial insemination, and even artificial wombs.

In areas other than criminal abortion, the law has been reluctant to endorse any theory that life, as we recognize it, begins before live birth, or to accord legal rights to the unborn except in narrowly defined situations and except when the rights are contingent upon live birth. For example, the traditional rule of tort law denied recovery for prenatal injuries even though the child was born alive. That rule has been changed in almost every jurisdiction. In most States, recovery is said to be permitted only if the fetus was viable, or at least quick, when the injuries were sustained, though few . . . courts have squarely so held. In a recent development, generally opposed by the commentators, some States permit the parents of a stillborn child to maintain an action for wrongful death because of prenatal injuries. Such an action, however, would appear to be one to vindicate the parents' interest and is thus consistent with the view that the fetus, at most, represents only the potentiality of life. Similarly, unborn children have been recognized as acquiring rights or interests by way of inheritance or other devolution of property, and have been represented by guardians *ad litem*. Perfection of the interests involved, again, has generally been contingent upon live birth. In short, the unborn have never been recognized in the law as persons in the whole sense.

X

In view of all this, we do not agree that, by adopting one theory of life, Texas may override the rights of the pregnant woman that are at stake. We repeat, however, that the State does have an important and legitimate interest in preserving and protecting the health of the pregnant woman, whether she be a resident of the State or a nonresident who seeks medical consultation and treatment there, and that it has still *another* important and legitimate interest in protecting the potentiality of human life. These interests are separate and distinct. Each grows in substantiality as the woman approaches . . . term and, at a point during pregnancy, each becomes "compelling."

With respect to the State's important and legitimate interest in the health of the mother, the "compelling" point, in the light of present medical knowledge, is at approximately the end of the first trimester. This is so because of the now-established medical fact . . . that, until the end of the first trimester mortality in abortion may be less than mortality in normal childbirth. It follows that, from and after this point, a State may regulate the abortion procedure to the extent that the regulation reasonably relates to the preservation and protection of maternal health. Examples of permissible state regulation in this area are requirements as to the qualifications of the person who is to perform the abortion; as to the licensure of that person; as to the facility in which the procedure is to be performed, that is, whether it must be a hospital or may be a clinic or some other place of less-than-hospital status; as to the licensing of the facility; and the like.

This means, on the other hand, that, for the period of pregnancy prior to this "compelling" point, the attending physician, in consultation with his patient, is free to determine, without regulation by the State, that, in his medical judgment, the patient's pregnancy should be terminated. If that decision is reached, the judgment may be effectuated by an abortion free of interference by the State.

With respect to the State's important and legitimate interest in potential life, the "compelling" point is at viability. This is so because the fetus then presumably has the capability of meaningful life outside the mother's womb. State regulation protective of fetal life after viability thus has both logical and biological justifications. If the State is interested in protecting fetal life after viability, it may go so far as to proscribe abortion . . . during that period, except when it is necessary to preserve the life or health of the mother.

Measured against these standards, . . . the Texas Penal Code, in restricting legal abortions to those "procured or attempted by medical advice for the purpose of saving the life of the mother," sweeps too broadly. The statute makes no distinction between abortions performed early in pregnancy and those performed later, and it limits to a single reason, "saving" the mother's life, the legal justification for the procedure. The statute, therefore, cannot survive the constitutional attack made upon it here. . . .*

---

* Several concurring and dissenting opinions were filed.—Eds.

42

KOREMATSU v. UNITED STATES (1944)

Pursuant to an act of Congress and a variety of executive and military orders, American citizens and resident aliens of Japanese descent were excluded from living in certain designated "military areas" during World War II and involuntarily confined to internment camps. Korematsu, a native-born U.S. citizen, was convicted specifically of failing to leave such a military area—a place where he had lived his entire life. His only means of legal exit would have been to report to the military authorities for internment. The Supreme Court upheld the constitutionality of the exclusionary order on the basis that Congress had authorized the program to protect national security during a period of war. Three dissenting opinions condemned the exclusion-internment program for its damage to fundamental constitutional values and principles. Eventually, in the 1990s, the U.S. government formally apologized to the persons of Japanese ancestry to whom the regulations had applied.

Mr. Justice Black delivered the opinion of the Court:

The petitioner, an American citizen of Japanese descent, was convicted in a federal district court for remaining in San Leandro, California, a "Military Area," contrary to Civilian Exclusion Order No. 34 of the Commanding General . . . of the Western Command, U.S. Army, which directed that, after May 9, 1942, all persons of Japanese ancestry should be excluded from that area. No question was raised as to petitioner's loyalty to the United States. The Circuit Court of Appeals affirmed,[1] and the importance of the constitutional question involved caused us to grant certiorari.

It should be noted, to begin with, that all legal restrictions which curtail the civil rights of a single racial group are immediately suspect. That is not to say that all such restrictions are unconstitutional. It is to say that courts must subject them to the most rigid scrutiny. Pressing public necessity may sometimes justify the existence of such restrictions; racial antagonism never can.

In the instant case, prosecution of the petitioner was begun by information charging violation of an Act of Congress, of March 21, 1942, . . . which provides that

. . . whoever shall enter, remain in, leave, or commit any act in any military area or military zone prescribed, under the authority of an Executive order of the President, by the Secretary of War, or by any military commander designated by the Secretary of War, contrary to the restrictions applicable to any such area or zone or contrary to the order of the Secretary of War or any such military commander, shall, if it appears that he knew or should have known of the existence and extent of the restrictions or order and that his act was in violation thereof, be guilty of a misdemeanor and upon conviction shall be liable to a fine of not to exceed $5,000 or to imprisonment for not more than one year, or both, for each offense.

[Notes have been renumbered.—Eds.]

Exclusion Order No. 34, which the petitioner knowingly and admittedly violated, was one of a number of military orders and proclamations, all of which were substantially . . . based upon Executive Order No. 9066. . . . That order, issued after we were at war with Japan, declared that

> the successful prosecution of the war requires every possible protection against espionage and against sabotage to national defense material, national defense premises, and national defense utilities. . . .

One of the series of orders and proclamations, a curfew order, which, like the exclusion order here, was promulgated pursuant to Executive Order 9066, subjected all persons of Japanese ancestry in prescribed West Coast military areas to remain in their residences from 8 P.M. to 6 A.M. As is the case with the exclusion order here, that prior curfew order was designed as a "protection against espionage and against sabotage." In *Hirabayashi v. United States*, . . . we sustained a conviction obtained for violation of the curfew order. The Hirabayashi conviction and this one thus rest on the same 1942 Congressional Act and the same basic executive and military orders, all of which orders were aimed at the twin dangers of espionage and sabotage.

The 1942 Act was attacked in the *Hirabayashi* case as an unconstitutional delegation of power; it was contended that the curfew order and other orders on which it rested were beyond the war powers of the Congress, the military authorities, and of the President, as Commander in Chief of the Army, and, finally, that to apply the curfew order against none but citizens of Japanese ancestry amounted to a constitutionally prohibited discrimination solely on account of race. To these questions, we gave the serious consideration which their importance justified. We upheld the curfew order as an exercise of the power of the government to take steps necessary to prevent espionage and sabotage in an area threatened by Japanese attack.

In the light of the principles we announced in the *Hirabayashi* case, we are unable to conclude that it was beyond the war power of Congress and the Executive to exclude . . . those of Japanese ancestry from the West Coast war area at the time they did. True, exclusion from the area in which one's home is located is a far greater deprivation than constant confinement to the home from 8 P.M. to 6 A.M. Nothing short of apprehension by the proper military authorities of the gravest imminent danger to the public safety can constitutionally justify either. But exclusion from a threatened area, no less than curfew, has a definite and close relationship to the prevention of espionage and sabotage. The military authorities, charged with the primary responsibility of defending our shores, concluded that curfew provided inadequate protection and ordered exclusion. They did so, as pointed out in our *Hirabayashi* opinion, in accordance with Congressional authority to the military to say who should, and who should not, remain in the threatened areas.

In this case, the petitioner challenges the assumptions upon which we rested our conclusions in the *Hirabayashi* case. He also urges that, by May, 1942, when Order No. 34 was promulgated, all danger of Japanese invasion of the West Coast had disappeared. After careful consideration of these contentions, we are compelled to reject them.

Here, as in the *Hirabayashi* case, *supra*, at p. 99,

> . . . we cannot reject as unfounded the judgment of the military authorities and of Congress that there were disloyal members of that population, whose number and strength could not be precisely and quickly ascertained. We cannot say that the war-making branches of the Government did not have ground for believing that, in a critical hour, such persons could not readily be isolated and separately dealt with, and constituted a menace to the national defense and safety which demanded that prompt and adequate measures be taken to guard against it.

Like curfew, exclusion of those of Japanese origin was deemed necessary because of the presence of an unascertained number of disloyal members of the group, most of . . . whom we have no doubt were loyal to this country. It was because we could not reject the finding of the military authorities that it was impossible to bring about an immediate segregation of the disloyal from the loyal that we sustained the validity of the curfew order as applying to the whole group. In the instant case, temporary exclusion of the entire group was rested by the military on the same ground. The judgment that exclusion of the whole group was, for the same reason, a military imperative answers the contention that the exclusion was in the nature of group punishment based on antagonism to those of Japanese origin. That there were members of the group who retained loyalties to Japan has been confirmed by investigations made subsequent to the exclusion. Approximately five thousand American citizens of Japanese ancestry refused to swear unqualified allegiance to the United States and to renounce allegiance to the Japanese Emperor, and several thousand evacuees requested repatriation to Japan.[2]

We uphold the exclusion order as of the time it was made and when the petitioner violated it. . . . In doing so, we are not unmindful of the hardships imposed by it upon a large group of American citizens. . . . But hardships are part of war, and war is an aggregation of hardships. All citizens alike, both in and out of uniform, feel the impact of war in greater or lesser measure. Citizenship has its responsibilities, as well as its privileges, and, in time of war, the burden is always heavier. Compulsory . . . exclusion of large groups of citizens from their homes, except under circumstances of direst emergency and peril, is inconsistent with our basic governmental institutions. But when, under conditions of modern warfare, our shores are threatened by hostile forces, the power to protect must be commensurate with the threatened danger.

It is argued that, on May 30, 1942, the date the petitioner was charged with remaining in the prohibited area, there were conflicting orders outstanding, forbidding him both to leave the area and to remain there. Of course, a person cannot be convicted for doing the very thing which it is a crime to fail to do. But the outstanding orders here contained no such contradictory commands.

There was an order issued March 27, 1942, which prohibited petitioner and others of Japanese ancestry from leaving the area, but its effect was specifically limited in time "until and to the extent that a future proclamation or order should so permit or direct." . . . That "future order," the one for violation of which petitioner was convicted, was issued May 3, 1942, and it did "direct" exclusion from the area of all persons of Japanese ancestry before 12 o'clock noon, May 9; furthermore, it contained a warning that all such persons found in the prohibited area would be liable to punishment under the March 21, 1942, Act of Congress. Consequently, the only order in effect touching the petitioner's being in the area on May 30, 1942, the date specified in the information against him, was the May 3 order which prohibited his remaining there, and it was that same order which he stipulated in his trial that he had violated, knowing of its existence. There is therefore no basis for the argument that, on May 30, 1942, he was subject to punishment, under the March 27 and May 3 orders, whether he remained in or left the area.

It does appear, however, that, on May 9, the effective date of the exclusion order, the military authorities had . . . already determined that the evacuation should be effected by assembling together and placing under guard all those of Japanese ancestry at central points, designated as "assembly centers," in order

> to insure the orderly evacuation and resettlement of Japanese voluntarily migrating from Military Area No. 1, to restrict and regulate such migration.

Public Proclamation No. 4. . . . And on May 19, 1942, eleven days before the time petitioner was charged with unlawfully remaining in the area, Civilian Restrictive Order No. 1, . . . provided for detention of those of Japanese ancestry in assembly or relocation centers. It is now argued that the validity of the exclusion order cannot be considered apart from the orders requiring him, after departure from the area, to report and to remain in an assembly or relocation center. The contention is that we must treat these separate orders as one and inseparable; that, for this reason, if detention in the assembly or relocation center would have illegally deprived the petitioner of his liberty, the exclusion order and his conviction under it cannot stand.

We are thus being asked to pass at this time upon the whole subsequent detention program in both assembly and relocation centers, although the only issues framed at the trial related to petitioner's remaining in the prohibited area in violation of the exclusion order. Had petitioner here left the prohibited area and gone to an assembly center, we cannot say, either as a matter of fact or law, that his presence in that center would have resulted in his detention in a relocation center. Some who did report to the assembly center were not sent to relocation centers, but were released upon condition that they remain outside the prohibited zone until the military orders were modified or lifted. This illustrates that they pose different problems, and may be governed by different principles. The lawfulness of one does not necessarily determine the lawfulness of the others. This is made clear . . . when we analyze the requirements of the separate provisions of the separate orders. These separate requirements were that those of Japanese ancestry (1) depart from the area; (2) report to and temporarily remain in an assembly center; (3) go under military control to a relocation center, there to remain for an indeterminate period until released conditionally or unconditionally by the military authorities. Each of these requirements, it will be noted, imposed distinct duties in connection with the separate steps in a complete evacuation program. Had Congress directly incorporated into one Act the language of these separate orders, and provided sanctions for their violations, disobedience of any one would have constituted a separate offense. . . . There is no reason why violations of these orders, insofar as they were promulgated pursuant to Congressional enactment, should not be treated as separate offenses. . . .

Since the petitioner has not been convicted of failing to report or to remain in an assembly or relocation center, we cannot in this case determine the validity of those separate provisions of the order. It is sufficient here for us to pass upon the order which petitioner violated. To do more would be to go beyond the issues raised, and to decide momentous questions not contained within the framework of the pleadings or the evidence in this case. It will be time enough to decide the serious constitutional issues which petitioner seeks to raise when an assembly or relocation order is applied or is certain to be applied to him, and we have its terms before us.

Some of the members of the Court are of the view that evacuation and detention in an Assembly Center were inseparable. After May 3, 1942, the date of Exclusion . . . Order No. 34, Korematsu was under compulsion to leave the area not as he would choose, but via an Assembly Center. The Assembly Center was conceived as a part of the machinery for group evacuation. The power to exclude includes the power to do it by force if necessary. And any forcible measure must necessarily entail some degree of detention or restraint, whatever method of removal is selected. But whichever view is taken, it results in holding that the order under which petitioner was convicted was valid.

It is said that we are dealing here with the case of imprisonment of a citizen in a concentration camp solely because of his ancestry, without evidence or inquiry concerning his loyalty and good disposition towards the United States. Our task would be simple, our duty clear, were this a case involving the imprisonment of a loyal citizen in a concentration camp because of racial prejudice. Regardless of the true nature of the assembly and relocation centers—and we deem it unjustifiable to call them concentration camps, with all the ugly connotations that term implies—we are dealing specifically with nothing but an exclusion order. To cast this case into outlines of racial prejudice, without reference to the real military dangers which were presented, merely confuses the issue. Korematsu was not excluded from the Military Area because of hostility to him or his race. He was excluded because we are at war with the Japanese Empire, because the properly constituted military authorities feared an invasion of our West Coast and felt constrained to take proper security measures, because they decided that the military urgency of the situation demanded that all citizens of Japanese ancestry be segregated from the West Coast temporarily, and, finally, because Congress, reposing its confidence in this time of war in our military leaders—as inevitably it must—determined that they should have the power to do just this. There was evidence of disloyalty on the part of some, the military authorities considered that the need for . . . action was great, and time was short. We cannot—by availing ourselves of the calm perspective of hindsight—now say that, at that time, these actions were unjustified.

Affirmed.

Jackson, J., Dissenting

Mr. Justice Jackson, dissenting.

Korematsu was born on our soil, of parents born in Japan. The Constitution makes him a citizen of the United States by nativity, and a citizen of California by . . . residence. No claim is made that he is not loyal to this country. There is no suggestion that, apart from the matter involved here, he is not law-abiding and well disposed. Korematsu, however, has been convicted of an act not commonly a crime. It consists merely of being present in the state whereof he is a citizen, near the place where he was born, and where all his life he has lived.

Even more unusual is the series of military orders which made this conduct a crime. They forbid such a one to remain, and they also forbid him to leave. They were so drawn that the only way Korematsu could avoid violation was to give himself up to the military authority. This meant submission to custody, examination, and transportation out of the territory, to be followed by indeterminate confinement in detention camps.

A citizen's presence in the locality, however, was made a crime only if his parents were of Japanese birth. Had Korematsu been one of four—the others being, say, a German alien enemy, an Italian alien enemy, and a citizen of American-born ancestors, convicted of treason but out on parole—only Korematsu's presence would have violated the order. The difference between their innocence and his crime would result, not from anything he did, said, or thought, different than they, but only in that he was born of different racial stock.

Now, if any fundamental assumption underlies our system, it is that guilt is personal and not inheritable. Even if all of one's antecedents had been convicted of treason, the Constitution forbids its penalties to be visited upon him, for it provides that "no attainder of treason shall work corruption of blood, or forfeiture except during the life of the person attainted." But here is an attempt to make an otherwise innocent act a crime merely because this prisoner is the son of parents as to whom he had no choice, and belongs to a race from which there is no way to resign. If Congress, in peacetime legislation, should . . . enact such a criminal law, I should suppose this Court would refuse to enforce it.

But the "law" which this prisoner is convicted of disregarding is not found in an act of Congress, but in a military order. Neither the Act of Congress nor the Executive Order of the President, nor both together, would afford a basis for this conviction. It rests on the orders of General DeWitt. And it is said that, if the military commander had reasonable military grounds for promulgating the orders, they are constitutional, and become law, and the Court is required to enforce them. There are several reasons why I cannot subscribe to this doctrine.

It would be impracticable and dangerous idealism to expect or insist that each specific military command in an area of probable operations will conform to conventional tests of constitutionality. When an area is so beset that it must be put under military control at all, the paramount consideration is that its measures be successful, rather than legal. The armed services must protect a society, not merely its Constitution. The very essence of the military job is to marshal physical force, to remove every obstacle to its effectiveness, to give it every strategic advantage. Defense measures will not, and often should not, be held within the limits that bind civil authority in peace. No court can require such a commander in such circumstances to act as a reasonable man; he may be unreasonably cautious and exacting. Perhaps he should be. But a commander, in temporarily focusing the life of a community on defense, is carrying out a military program; he is not making law in the sense the courts know the term. He issues orders, and they may have a certain authority as military commands, although they may be very bad as constitutional law.

But if we cannot confine military expedients by the Constitution, neither would I distort the Constitution to approve all that the military may deem expedient. That is . . . what the Court appears to be doing, whether consciously or not. I cannot say, from any evidence before me, that the orders of General DeWitt were not reasonably expedient military precautions, nor could I say that they were. But even if they were permissible military procedures, I deny that it follows that they are constitutional. If, as the Court holds, it does follow, then we may as well say that any military order will be constitutional, and have done with it.

The limitation under which courts always will labor in examining the necessity for a military order are illustrated by this case. How does the Court know that these orders have a reasonable basis in necessity? No evidence whatever on that subject has been taken by this or any other court. There is sharp controversy as to the credibility of the DeWitt report. So the Court, having no real evidence before it, has no choice but to accept General DeWitt's own unsworn, self-serving statement, untested by any cross-examination, that what he did was reasonable. And thus it will always be when courts try to look into the reasonableness of a military order.

In the very nature of things, military decisions are not susceptible of intelligent judicial appraisal. They do not pretend to rest on evidence, but are made on information that often would not be admissible and on assumptions that could not be proved. Information in support of an order could not be disclosed to courts without danger that it would reach the enemy. Neither can courts act on communications made in confidence. Hence, courts can never have any real alternative to accepting the mere declaration of the authority that issued the order that it was reasonably necessary from a military viewpoint.

Much is said of the danger to liberty from the Army program for deporting and detaining these citizens of Japanese extraction. But a judicial construction of the due process clause that will sustain this order is a far more . . . subtle blow to liberty than the promulgation of the order itself. A military order, however unconstitutional, is not apt to last longer than the military emergency. Even during that period, a succeeding commander may revoke it all. But once a judicial opinion rationalizes such an order to show that it conforms to the Constitution, or rather rationalizes the Constitution to show that the Constitution sanctions such an order, the Court for all time has validated the principle of racial discrimination in criminal procedure and of transplanting American citizens. The principle then lies about like a loaded weapon, ready for the hand of any authority that can bring forward a plausible claim of an urgent need. Every repetition imbeds that principle more deeply in our law and thinking and expands it to new purposes. All who observe the work of courts are familiar with what Judge Cardozo described as "the tendency of a principle to expand itself to the limit of its logic."[1] A military commander may overstep the bounds of constitutionality, and it is an incident. But if we review and approve, that passing incident becomes the doctrine of the Constitution. There it has a generative power of its own, and all that it creates will be in its own image. Nothing better illustrates this danger than does the Court's opinion in this case.

It argues that we are bound to uphold the conviction of Korematsu because we upheld one in *Hirabayashi v. United States*, . . . when we sustained these orders insofar as they applied a curfew requirement to a citizen of Japanese ancestry. I think we should learn something from that experience.

In that case, we were urged to consider only the curfew feature, that being all that technically was involved, because it was the only count necessary to sustain Hirabayashi's conviction and sentence. We yielded, and the Chief Justice guarded the opinion as carefully as language . . . will do. He said:

> Our investigation here does not go beyond the inquiry whether, in the light of all the relevant circumstances preceding and attending their promulgation, the challenged orders and statute *afforded a reasonable basis for the action taken in imposing the curfew.*

320 U.S. at 101.

> We decide only the issue as we have defined it—we decide only that the *curfew order*, as applied, and at the time it was applied, was within the boundaries of the war power.

320 U.S. at 102. And again: "It is unnecessary to consider whether or to what extent *such findings would support orders differing from the curfew order*" [italics supplied]. However, in spite of our limiting words, we did validate a discrimination on the basis of ancestry for mild and temporary deprivation of liberty. Now the principle of racial discrimination is pushed from support of mild measures to very harsh ones, and from temporary deprivations to indeterminate ones. And the precedent which it is said requires us to do so is *Hirabayashi*. The Court is now saying that, in *Hirabayashi*, we did decide the very things we there said we were not deciding. Because we said that these citizens could be made to stay in their homes during the hours of dark, it is said we must require them to leave home entirely, and if that, we are told they may also be taken into custody for deportation, and, if that, it is argued, they may also be held for some undetermined time in detention camps. How far the principle of this case would be extended before plausible reasons would play out, I do not know.

I should hold that a civil court cannot be made to enforce an order which violates constitutional limitations even if it is a reasonable exercise of military authority. The courts can exercise only the judicial power, can apply only law, and must abide by the Constitution, or they cease to be civil courts and become instruments of military policy. . . .

Of course, the existence of a military power resting on force, so vagrant, so centralized, so necessarily heedless of the individual, is an inherent threat to liberty. But I would not lead people to rely on this Court for a review that seems to me wholly delusive. The military reasonableness of these orders can only be determined by military superiors. If the people ever let command of the war power fall into irresponsible and unscrupulous hands, the courts wield no power equal to its restraint. The chief restraint upon those who command the physical forces of the country, in the future as in the past, must be their responsibility to the political judgments of their contemporaries and to the moral judgments of history.

My duties as a justice, as I see them, do not require me to make a military judgment as to whether General DeWitt's evacuation and detention program was a reasonable military necessity. I do not suggest that the courts should have attempted to interfere with the Army in carrying out its task. But I do not think they may be asked to execute a military expedient that has no place in law under the Constitution. I would reverse the judgment and discharge the prisoner.

NOTES

Black, J., Lead Opinion

1. 140 F.2d 289.

2. Hearings before the Subcommittee on the National War Agencies Appropriation Bill for 1945, Part 11, 608–726; Final Report, Japanese Evacuation from the West Coast, 1942, 309–327; Hearings before the Committee on Immigration and Naturalization, House of Representatives, 78th Cong., 2d sess., on H.R. 2701 and other bills to expatriate certain nationals of the United States, pp. 37–42, 49–58.

Jackson, J., Dissenting

1. Nature of the Judicial Process, p. 51.

PART TEN

THE POLICY PROCESS

A public policy is a governmental course of action addressing matters of economic, political, or social concern. There are policies on the environment, defense, occupational safety and health, agriculture, labor relations, electoral campaign financing, civil rights, controlled substances, the family, and almost anything one can think of. Most of the activity described and analyzed in the previous chapters on elections and political parties, interest groups, Congress, the presidency, the bureaucracy, and the judiciary is aimed at establishing and implementing public policies. Policies are the main products or outputs of the political system.

That American national policy making will be messy is virtually ensured by the constitutional separation of powers, electoral terms of office, and federalism. Policies tend to be the outcome of political compromise, piecemeal adjustments, temporary coalitions, and partial solutions. Often they conflict with one another. They may be internally incoherent as well.

Critics and reformers, sometimes seeking to emulate private sector models, typically favor more rational, comprehensive, and goal-oriented policy making. In their view, public policy making should incorporate the following sequential steps. First, clear, realistic, specific objectives are established; next all possible means or techniques for achieving the objectives are presented; then, an optimal course of action is selected, based on systematic examination of all the possible results and costs of each approach. The entire exercise is driven by the rational application of expert knowledge to problem solving. Radical departures from past practices may be considered and implemented as new policies are adopted or older ones are "reengineered."

This *rational-comprehensive* model has intuitive appeal and is sometimes actually followed. In most cases, however, public policies develop in ways that differ radically from the rational-comprehensive approach. Each of the four selections in this section partially explains why.

The chapter from John W. Kingdon's book *Agendas, Alternatives, and Public Policies* (1984) considers "why some subjects rise on governmental agendas while other subjects are neglected, and why people in and around government pay serious attention to some alternatives at the expense of others." Kingdon points to the importance of problem recognition, politics, and the particular participants concerned with having a policy. He concludes that agenda setting does not follow the rational-comprehensive prescriptions: ". . . [P]articipants do not first identify problems and then seek solutions for them; indeed, advocacy of solutions often precedes the highlighting of problems to which they become attached. Agendas are not first set and then alternatives generated; instead, alternatives must be advocated for a long period before a short-run opportunity presents itself on an agenda."

In 1959, Charles E. Lindblom depicted the real world's alternative to the rational-comprehensive model. He called it "the science of 'muddling through.'" This approach involves "successive limited comparisons" of potential steps in which means and ends are not distinct, analysis is limited and not necessarily driven by theory, and the test of a "good" policy is agreement by the participants rather than an objective measure such as cost-effectiveness. The model is both descriptive and prescriptive. In practice, policymakers tend to use it because they lack the necessary time, inclination, expertise, information, ability, or consensus on goals to use the rational-comprehensive approach. Lindblom views it as good prescription because ". . . it will be superior to any other decision-making method available for complex problems in many circumstances, certainly superior to a futile attempt at superhuman comprehensiveness."

When a wide variety of public policies are made separately by muddling through there is a risk that their cumulative result or impact will be unanticipated or perverse. Such "disjointed incrementalism" is a real possibility. However, Edward Banfield's "Influence and the Public Interest" (1961) suggests that the risk is reduced when "[n]othing of importance is done . . . without its first being discovered what interests will be affected and how they will be affected and without the losses that will accrue to some being weighed carefully against the gains that will accrue to others." Policy that seems to comprise little more than an assemblage of segmental decisions and marginal adjustments, in fact, may be a product of the continual pulling and hauling of competing interests whose diverse preferences are being appropriately reconciled.

There are political benefits to the fact that the actions of government in a pluralistic polity are seldom prescribed by a central decisionmaker with an explicit goal (or set of goals). In the conclusion to his fascinating book on public decisions in Chicago, Banfield emphasizes that legitimate public policy must weigh sensitively the disparate values of a variety of interested parties. Comprehensive planners—even the most enlightened and scrupulous ones, supported by the most elaborate cost-benefit studies—risk weighting the competing values arbitrarily when they impose their own judgment. Policies shaped not through "central decisions" but by spontaneous mutual accommodations among the affected interests are more likely to reflect just "social choices."

To say that policy making in the United States seldom resembles the rational-comprehensive model is not to suggest that it is *uniformly* incremental, disjointed, and given to irrational compromise. Much seems to depend on the nature of the policy issue in question. In "Distribution, Regulation, Redistribution: The Functions of Government" (1964), Theodore J. Lowi made an influential effort to classify comprehensively the styles of politics associated with differing types of policies. Lowi suggests that distributive, regulatory, and redistributive policies evoke distinctive types of participation, decision making, and implementation. Additional types of policies could be added to the model, but Lowi's key insight that *policies inform politics* provides the basis of a framework for studying the application of rational-comprehensiveness, muddling through, hybrids, and other decision-making approaches.

43

JOHN W. KINGDON

AGENDA SETTING

Why do some subjects rise on governmental agendas while other subjects are neglected? According to John W. Kingdon, the answer is because (1) they are recognized as part of an important problem; (2) they are emphasized in the politics of the day, such as a national mood or elections, and/or (3) they are put forward by a visible cluster of policy advocates, who attract significant media attention. "A complete linkage of all three streams—problems, policies, and politics—into a single package . . . dramatically enhances the odds that a subject will become firmly fixed on a decision agenda." Kingdon taught political science at the University of Michigan. This selection is taken from his pathbreaking book, Agendas, Alternatives, and Public Policies *(1984).*

This book has considered why some subjects rise on governmental agendas while other subjects are neglected, and why people in and around government pay serious attention to some alternatives at the expense of others. The book is not about how presidents, members of Congress, or other authoritative figures make their final decisions. Instead, we have been occupied with understanding why participants deal with certain issues and neglect others. This chapter summarizes and ties together what we have learned.

Two major predecision processes have occupied us: agenda setting and alternative specification. A governmental agenda is a list of subjects to which officials are paying some serious attention at any given time. Thus an agenda-setting process narrows the set of subjects that could conceivably occupy their attention to the list on which they actually do focus. Obviously, there are agendas within agendas. They range from highly general agendas, such as the list of items occupying the president and his immediate inner circle, to rather specialized agendas, including the agendas of such subcommunities as biomedical research or waterway transportation. Subjects that do not appear on a general agenda may be very much alive on a specialized agenda.

The process of alternative specification narrows the large set of possible alternatives to that set from which choices actually are made. This distinction between agenda and alternatives proves to be very useful analytically, and we have returned to it repeatedly.

Why do some subjects rise on agendas while others are neglected? Why do some alternatives receive more attention than others? Some of our answers to these questions concentrate on participants: We uncover who affects agendas and alternatives, and why they do. Other answers explore the processes through which these participants affect agendas and alternatives. We have conceived of three streams of processes: problems, policies, and politics. People recognize problems, they generate proposals for public policy changes, and they engage in such political activities as election campaigns and pressure group lobbying. Each participant—president, members of Congress, civil servants, lobbyists, journalists, academics, etc. — can in principle be involved in each process (problem recognition, proposal formation, and politics). Policy is not the sole province of analysts, for instance, nor is politics the sole province of politicians. In practice, though, participants usually specialize in one or another process to a degree. Academics are more involved in policy formation than in politics, for instance, and parties are more involved in politics than in drafting detailed proposals. But conceptually, participants can be seen as different from processes.

Each of the participants and processes can act as an impetus or as a constraint. As an impetus, the participant or process boosts a subject higher on an agenda, or pushes an alternative into more active consideration. A president or congressional committee chair, for instance, decides to emphasize a subject. Or a problem is highlighted because a disaster occurs or because a well-known indicator changes. As a constraint, the participant or process dampens consideration of a subject or alternative. Vigorous pressure group opposition to an item, for instance, moves it down the list of priorities or even off the agenda. As an administration emphasizes its priorities, for another example, it limits people's ability to attend to other subjects. Concerns over budgetary costs of an item can also make its serious consideration quite unlikely.

AGENDA SETTING

How are governmental agendas set? Our answer has concentrated on three explanations: problems, politics, and visible participants.

Problems

Why do some problems come to occupy the attention of governmental officials more than other problems? The answer lies both in the means by which those officials learn about conditions and in the ways in which conditions become defined as problems. As to means, we have discussed indicators, focusing events, and feedback. Sometimes, a more or less systematic indicator simply shows that there is a condition out there. Indicators are used to assess the magnitude of the condition (e.g., the incidence of a disease or the cost of a program), and to discern changes in a condition. Both large magnitude and change catch officials' attention. Second, a focusing event—a disaster, crisis, personal experience, or powerful symbol—draws attention to some conditions more than to others. But such an event has only transient effects unless accompanied by a firmer indication of a problem, by a preexisting perception, or by a combination with other similar events. Third, officials learn about conditions through feedback about the operation of existing programs, either formal (e.g., routine monitoring of costs or program evaluation studies) or informal (e.g., streams of complaints flowing into congressional offices).

There is a difference between a condition and a problem. We put up with all kinds of conditions every day, and conditions do not rise to prominent places on policy agendas. Conditions come to be defined as problems, and have a better chance of rising on the agenda, when we come to believe that we should do something to change them. People in and around government define conditions as problems in several ways. First, conditions that violate important values are transformed into problems. Second, conditions become problems by comparison with other countries or other relevant units. Third, classifying a condition into one category rather than another may define it as one kind of problem or another. The lack of public transportation for handicapped people, for instance, can be classified as a transportation problem or as a civil rights problem, and the treatment of the subject is dramatically affected by the category.

Problems not only rise on governmental agendas, but they also fade from view. Why do they fade? First, government may address the problem, or fail to address it. In both cases, attention turns to something else, either because something has been done or because people are frustrated by failure and refuse to invest more of their time in a losing cause. Second, conditions that highlighted a problem may change—indicators drop instead of rise, or crises go away. Third, people may become accustomed to a condition or relabel a problem. Fourth, other items emerge and push the highly placed items aside. Finally, there may simply be inevitable cycles in attention; high growth rates level off, and fads come and go.

Problem recognition is critical to agenda setting. The chances of a given proposal or subject rising on an agenda are markedly enhanced if it is connected to an important problem. Some problems are seen as so pressing that they set agendas all by themselves. Once a particular problem is defined as pressing, whole classes of approaches are favored over others, and some alternatives are highlighted while others fall from view. So policy entrepreneurs invest considerable resources bringing their conception of problems to officials' attention, and trying to convince them to see problems their way. The recognition and definition of problems affect outcomes significantly.

Politics

The second family of explanations for high or low agenda prominence is in the political stream. Independently of problem recognition or the development of policy proposals, political events flow along according to their own dynamics and their own rules. Participants perceive swings in national mood, elections bring new administrations to power and new partisan or ideological distributions to Congress, and interest groups of various descriptions press (or fail to press) their demands on government.

Developments in this political sphere are powerful agenda setters. A new administration, for instance, changes agendas all over town as it highlights its conceptions of problems and its proposals, and makes attention to subjects that are not among its high priorities much less likely. A national mood that is perceived to be profoundly conservative dampens attention to costly new initiatives, while a more tolerant national mood would allow for greater spending. The opposition of a powerful phalanx of interest groups makes it difficult—not impossible, but difficult—to contemplate some initiatives.

Consensus is built in the political stream by bargaining more than by persuasion. When participants recognize problems or settle on certain proposals in the policy stream, they do so largely by persuasion. They marshal indicators and argue that certain conditions ought to be defined as problems, or they argue that their proposals meet such logical tests as technical feasibility or value acceptability. But in the political stream, participants build consensus by bargaining—trading provisions for support, adding elected officials to coalitions by giving them concessions that they demand, or compromising from ideal positions to positions that will gain wider acceptance.

The combination of national mood and elections is a more potent agenda setter than organized interests. Interest groups are often able to block consideration of proposals they do not prefer, or to adapt to an item already high on a governmental agenda by adding elements a bit more to their liking. They less often initiate considerations or set agendas on their own. And when organized interests come into conflict with the combination of national mood and elected politicians, the latter combination is likely to prevail, at least as far as setting an agenda is concerned.

Visible Participants

Third, we made a distinction between visible and hidden participants. The visible cluster of actors, those who receive considerable press and public attention, include the president and his high-level appointees, prominent members of Congress, the media, and such elections-related actors as political parties and campaigners. The relatively hidden cluster includes academic specialists, career bureaucrats, and congressional staffers. We have discovered that the visible cluster affects the agenda and the hidden cluster, affects the alternatives. So the chances of a subject rising on a governmental agenda are enhanced if that subject is pushed by participants in the visible cluster and dampened if it is neglected by those participants. The administration—the president and his appointees—is a particularly powerful agenda setter, as are such prominent members of Congress as the party leaders and key committee chairs.

At least as far as agenda setting is concerned, elected officials and their appointees turn out to be more important than career civil servants or participants outside of government. To those who look for evidences of democracy at work, this is an encouraging result. These elected officials do not necessarily get their way in specifying alternatives or implementing decisions, but they do affect agendas rather substantially. To describe the roles of various participants in agenda setting, a fairly straightforward top-down model, with elected officials at the top, comes surprisingly close to the truth.

ALTERNATIVE SPECIFICATION

How is the list of potential alternatives for public policy choices narrowed to the ones that actually receive serious consideration? There are two families of answers: (1) Alternatives are generated and narrowed in the policy stream; and (2) Relatively hidden participants, specialists in the particular policy area, are involved.

Hidden Participants: Specialists

Alternatives, proposals, and solutions are generated in communities of specialists. This relatively hidden cluster of participants includes academics, researchers, consultants, career bureaucrats, congressional staffers, and analysts who work for interest groups. Their work is done, for instance, in planning and evaluation or budget shops in the bureaucracy or in the staff agencies on the Hill.

These relatively hidden participants form loosely knit communities of specialists. There is such a community for health, for instance, which includes analogous subcommunities for more specialized areas like the direct delivery of medical services and the regulation of food and drugs. Some of these communities, such as the one for transportation, are highly fragmented, while others are more tightly knit. Each community is composed of people located throughout the system and potentially of very diverse orientations and interests, but they all share one thing: their specialization and acquaintance with the issues in that particular policy area.

Ideas bubble around in these communities. People try out proposals in a variety of ways: through speeches, bill introductions, congressional hearings, leaks to the press, circulation of papers, conversations, and lunches. They float their ideas, criticize one another's work, hone and revise their ideas, and float new versions. Some of these ideas are respectable, while others are out of the question. But many, many ideas are possible and are considered in some fashion somewhere along the line.

The Policy Stream

The generation of policy alternatives is best seen as a selection process, analogous to biological natural selection. In what we have called the policy primeval soup, many ideas float around, bumping into one another, encountering new ideas, and forming combinations and recombinations. The origins of policy may seem a bit obscure, hard to predict and hard to understand or to structure.

While the origins are somewhat haphazard, the selection is not. Through the imposition of criteria by which some ideas are selected out for survival while others are discarded, order is developed from chaos, pattern from randomness. These criteria include technical feasibility, congruence with the values of community members, and the anticipation of future constraints, including a budget constraint, public acceptability, and politicians' receptivity. Proposals that are judged infeasible—that do not square with policy community values, that would cost more than the budget will allow, that run afoul of opposition in either the mass or specialized publics, or that would not find a receptive audience among elected politicians—are less likely to survive than proposals that meet these standards. In the process of consideration in the policy community, ideas themselves are important. Pressure models do not completely describe the process. Proposals are evaluated partly in terms of their political support and opposition, to be sure, but partly against logical or analytical criteria as well.

There is a long process of softening up the system. Policy entrepreneurs do not leave consideration of their pet proposals to accident. Instead, they push for consideration in many ways and in many forums. In the process of policy development, recombination (the coupling of already-familiar elements) is more important than mutation (the appearance of wholly new forms). Thus entrepreneurs, who broker people and ideas, are more important than inventors. Because recombination is more important than invention, there may be "no new thing under the sun" at the same time that there may be dramatic change and innovation. There is change, but it involves the recombination of already-familiar elements.

The long softening-up process is critical to policy change. Opportunities for serious hearings . . . pass quickly and are missed if the proposals have not already gone through the long gestation process before the window opens. The work of floating and refining proposals is not wasted if it does not bear fruit in the short run. Indeed, it is critically important if the proposal is to be heard at the right time.

COUPLING AND WINDOWS

The separate streams of problems, policies, and politics each have lives of their own. Problems are recognized and defined according to processes that are different from the ways policies are developed or political events unfold. Policy proposals are developed according to their own incentives and selection criteria, whether or not they are solutions to problems or responsive to political considerations. Political events flow along on their own schedule and according to their own rules, whether or not they are related to problems or proposals.

But there come times when the three streams are joined. A pressing problem demands attention, for instance, and a policy proposal is coupled to the problem as its solution. Or an event in the political stream, such as a change of administration, calls for different directions. At that point, proposals that fit with that political event, such as initiatives that fit with a new administration's philosophy, come to the fore and are coupled with the ripe political climate. Similarly, problems that fit are highlighted, and others are neglected.

Decision Agendas

A complete linkage combines all three streams—problems, policies, and politics—into a single package. Advocates of a new policy initiative not only take advantage of politically propitious moments but also claim that their proposal is a solution to a pressing problem. Likewise, entrepreneurs concerned about a particular problem search for solutions in the policy stream to couple to their problem, then try to take advantage of political receptivity at certain points in time to push the package of problem and solution. At points along the way, there are partial couplings: solutions to problems, but without a receptive political climate; politics to proposals, but without a sense that a compelling problem is being solved; politics and problems both calling for action, but without an available alternative to advocate. But the complete joining of all three streams dramatically enhances the odds that a subject will become firmly fixed on a decision agenda.

Governmental agendas, lists of subjects to which governmental officials are paying serious attention, can be set solely in either problems or political streams, and solely by visible actors. Officials can pay attention to an important problem, for instance, without having a solution to it. Or politics may highlight a subject, even in the absence of either problem or solution. A decision agenda, a list of subjects that is moving into position for an authoritative decision, such as legislative enactment or presidential choice, is set somewhat differently. The probability of an item rising on a decision agenda is dramatically increased if all three elements—problem, policy proposal, and political receptivity—are linked in a single package. Conversely, partial couplings are less likely to rise on decision agendas. Problems that come to decisions without solutions attached, for instance, are not as likely to move into position for an authoritative choice as if they did have solutions attached. And proposals that lack political backing are less likely to move into position for a decision than ones that do have that backing.

A return to our case studies . . . illustrates these points. With aviation deregulation, awareness of problems, development of proposals, and swings of national mood all proceeded separately in their own streams. Increasingly through the late 1960s and early 1970s, people became convinced that the economy contained substantial inefficiencies to which the burdens of government regulation contributed. Proposals for deregulation were formed among academics and other specialists, through a softening-up process that included journal articles, testimony, conferences, and other forums. In the 1970s, politicians sensed a change in national mood toward increasing hostility to government size and intrusiveness. All three of the components, therefore, came together at about the same time. The key to movement was the coupling of the policy stream's literature on deregulation with the political incentive to rein in government growth, and those two elements with the sense that there was a real, important, and increasing problem with economic inefficiency.

The waterway user charge case illustrates a similar coupling. A proposal, some form of user charge, had been debated among transportation specialists for years. The political stream produced an administration receptive to imposing a user charge. This combination of policy and politics was coupled with a problem—the necessity, in a time of budget stringency, to repair or replace aging facilities like Lock and Dam 26. Thus did the joining of problem, policy, and politics push the waterway user charge into position on a decision agenda.

By contrast, national health insurance during the Carter years did not have all three components joined. Proponents could argue that there were real problems of medical access, though opponents countered that many of the most severe problems were being addressed through Medicare, Medicaid, and private insurance. The political stream did produce a heavily Democratic Congress and an administration that favored some sort of health insurance initiative. It seemed for a time that serious movement was under way. But the policy stream had not settled on a single, worked-up, viable alternative from among the many proposals floating around. The budget constraint, itself a severe problem, and politicians' reading of the national mood, which seemed to be against costly new initiatives, also proved to be too much to overcome. The coupling was incomplete, and the rise of national health insurance on the agenda proved fleeting. Then the election of Ronald Reagan sealed its fate, at least for the time being.

Success in one area contributes to success in adjacent areas. Once aviation deregulation passed, for instance, government turned with a vengeance to other deregulation proposals, and passed several in short order. These spillovers, as we have called them, occur because politicians sense the payoff in repeating a successful formula in a similar area, because the winning coalition can be transferred, and because advocates can argue from successful precedent. These spillovers are extremely powerful agenda setters, seemingly bowling over even formidable opposition that stands in the way.

Policy Windows

An open policy window is an opportunity for advocates to push their pet solutions or to push attention to their special problems. Indeed, advocates in and around government keep their proposals and their problems at hand, waiting for these opportunities to occur. They have pet solutions, for instance, and wait for problems to float by to which they can attach their solutions, or for developments in the political stream that they can use to their advantage. Or they wait for similar opportunities to bring their special problems to the fore, such as the appearance of a new administration that would be concerned with these problems. That administration opens a window for them to bring greater attention to the problems about which they are concerned.

Windows are opened by events in either the problems or political streams. Thus there are problem windows and political windows. A new problem appears, for instance, creating an opportunity to attach a solution to it. Or such events in the political stream as turnover of elected officials, swings of national mood, or vigorous lobbying might create opportunities to push some problems and proposals to the fore and dampen the chances to highlight other problems and proposals.

Sometimes, windows open quite predictably. Legislation comes up for renewal on a schedule, for instance, creating opportunities to change, expand, or abolish certain programs. At other times, windows open quite unpredictably, as when an airliner crashes or a fluky election produces an unexpected turnover in key decision makers. Predictable or unpredictable, open windows are small and scarce. Opportunities come, but they also pass. Windows do not stay open long. If a chance is missed, another must be awaited.

The scarcity and the short duration of the opening of a policy window create a powerful magnet for problems and proposals. When a window opens, problems and proposals flock to it. People concerned with particular problems see the open window as their opportunity to address or even solve these problems. Advocates of particular proposals see the open window as the opportunity to enact them. As a result, the system comes to be loaded down with problems and proposals. If participants are willing to invest sufficient resources, some of the problems can be resolved and some of the proposals enacted. Other problems and proposals drift away because insufficient resources are mobilized.

Open windows present opportunities for the complete linkage of problems, proposals, and politics, and hence opportunities to move packages of the three joined elements up on decision agendas. One particularly crucial coupling is the link of a solution to something else. Advocates of pet proposals watch for developments in the political stream that they can take advantage of, or try to couple their solution to whatever problems are floating by at the moment. Once they have made the partial coupling of proposal to either problem or politics, they attempt to join all three elements, knowing that the chances for enactment are considerably enhanced if they can complete the circle. Thus they try to hook packages of problems and solutions to political forces, packages of proposals and political incentives to perceived problems, or packages of problems and politics to some proposal taken from the policy stream.

ENTREPRENEURS

Policy entrepreneurs are people willing to invest their resources in return for future policies they favor. They are motivated by combinations of several things: their straightforward concern about certain problems, their pursuit of such self-serving benefits as protecting or expanding their bureaucracy's budget or claiming credit for accomplishment, their promotion of their policy values, and their simple pleasure in participating. We have encountered them at three junctures: pushing their concerns about certain problems higher on the agenda, pushing their pet proposals during a process of softening up the system, and making the couplings we just discussed. These entrepreneurs are found at many locations; they might be elected officials, career civil servants, lobbyists, academics, or journalists. No one type of participant dominates the pool of entrepreneurs.

As to problems, entrepreneurs try to highlight the indicators that so importantly dramatize their problems. They push for one kind of problem definition rather than another. Because they know that focusing events can move subjects higher on the agenda, entrepreneurs push to create such things as personal viewings of problems by policy makers and the diffusion of a symbol that captures their problem in a nutshell. They also may prompt the kinds of feedback about current governmental performance that affect agendas: letters, complaints, and visits to officials.

As to proposals, entrepreneurs are central to the softening-up process. They write papers, give testimony, hold hearings, try to get press coverage, and meet endlessly with important and not-so-important people. They float their ideas as trial balloons, get reactions, revise their proposals in the light of reactions, and float them again. They aim to soften up the mass public, specialized publics, and the policy community itself. The process takes years of effort.

As to coupling, entrepreneurs once again appear when windows open. They have their pet proposals or their concerns about problems ready, and push them at the propitious moments. In the pursuit of their own goals, they perform the function for the system of coupling solutions to problems, problems to political forces, and political forces to proposals. The joining of the separate streams described earlier depends heavily on the appearance of the right entrepreneur at the right time. In our case study of Health Maintenance Organizations . . . , Paul

Ellwood appeared on the scene to link his pet proposal (HMOs) to the problem of medical care costs and to the political receptivity created by the Nixon administration casting about for health initiatives. The problems and political streams had opened a window, and Ellwood cleverly took advantage of that opportunity to push his HMO proposal, joining all three streams in the process.

The appearance of entrepreneurs when windows are open, as well as their more enduring activities of trying to push their problems and proposals into prominence, are central to our story. They bring several key resources into the fray: their claims to a hearing, their political connections and negotiating skills, and their sheer persistence. An item's chances for moving up on an agenda are enhanced considerably by the presence of a skillful entrepreneur, and dampened considerably if no entrepreneur takes on the cause, pushes it, and makes the critical couplings when policy windows open.

CONCLUSION

The ideas we have explored in the pages of this book have a few important properties which it is appropriate to highlight as we draw to a close. These properties fall into two general categories: the differences between our model of these processes and other notions, and the places of randomness and pattern.

Other Notions

The ideas developed in this book are quite unlike many other theories that could have captured our attention. For example, events do not proceed neatly in stages, steps, or phases. Instead, independent streams that flow through the system all at once, each with a life of its own and equal with one another, become coupled when a window opens. Thus participants do not first identify problems and then seek solutions for them; indeed, advocacy of solutions often precedes the highlighting of problems to which they become attached. Agendas are not first set and then alternatives generated; instead, alternatives must be advocated for a long period before a short-run opportunity presents itself on an agenda. Events do not necessarily proceed in similar order in several different case studies; instead, many things happen separately in each case, and become coupled at critical points.

Other notions have elements of truth, and do describe parts of the processes, but they are incomplete. A pressure model, for instance, does describe parts of the political stream, but ideas are as important as pressure in other parts of the processes. Agenda items do not necessarily start in a larger systemic or public arena and transfer to a formal or governmental agenda; indeed, the flow is just as often in the reverse direction. . . . [A] concentration on origins does not take us very far because ideas come from many locations, nobody has a monopoly on leadership or prescience, and tracing origins involves an infinite regress. We were drawn to the importance of combinations rather than single origins, and to a climate of receptivity that allows ideas to take off. . . . [W]e portrayed comprehensive-rational and incremental models as incomplete. Participants sometimes do approach their decisions quite comprehensively and decide quite rationally, but the larger process is less tidy. Incrementalism does describe the slow process of generating alternatives, and often does describe small legislative and bureaucratic changes stretching over many years, but does not describe agenda change well. Thus, in addition to arguing for one way of looking at the policy formation world, we have argued what the world does *not* look like.

On Randomness and Pattern

We still encounter considerable doses of messiness, accident, fortuitous coupling, and dumb luck. Subjects sometimes rise on agendas without our understanding completely why. We are sometimes surprised by the couplings that take place. The fortuitous appearance or absence of key participants affect outcomes. There remains some degree of unpredictability.

Yet it would be a grave mistake to conclude that the processes explored in this book are essentially random. Some degree of pattern is evident in three fundamental sources: processes within each stream, processes that structure couplings, and general constraints on the system.

First, processes operating within each stream limit randomness. Within the problems stream, not every problem has an equal chance of surfacing. Those conditions that are not highlighted by indicators, focusing events, or feedback are less likely to be brought to the attention of governmental officials than conditions that do have those advantages. Furthermore, not all conditions are defined as problems. Conditions that do not conflict with important values or that are placed in an inappropriate category are less likely to be translated into problems than conditions that are evaluated or categorized appropriately. In the policy stream, not every proposal surfaces. Selection criteria make patterns out of initial noise. Proposals that meet such standards as technical feasibility, value acceptability, public acquiescence, politicians' receptivity, and budgetary stringency are more likely to survive than those that fail to meet such standards. In the political stream, not every environment or event is equally likely. Some groups lack the resources that others have, some swings of national mood (e.g., to socialism) are unlikely, and some types of turnover of elected officials are more likely than others.

Second, some couplings are more likely than others. Everything cannot interact with everything else. For one thing, the timing of an item's arrival in its stream affects its ability to be joined to items in other streams. A window may open, for instance, but a solution may not be available at that time in the policy stream, so the window closes without a coupling of solution to problem or politics. Or a proposal may be ready in the policy stream, but the political conditions are not right for it to be pushed, again limiting the coupling possibilities. In addition to timing, germaneness limits the coupling possibilities. Not all solutions have an equal possibility of being discussed with all problems. Instead, participants have some sense of what would constitute an appropriate solution to a problem. There is some room for different solutions being hooked to a given problem or different problems being hooked to a given solution, but participants also set some limits on the appropriate couplings. Finally, the appearance of a skillful entrepreneur enhances the probability of a coupling. Potential couplings without entrepreneurs are less likely because they fail for lack of someone willing to invest resources in them.

Third, there are various constraints on the system, limits that provide a basic structure within which the participants play the games we have described.[1] The political stream provides many of these constraints. Participants sense some boundaries that are set on their actions by the mood of the mass public, and narrower boundaries set by the preferences of specialized publics and elected politicians. As I have argued elsewhere, governmental officials sense these limits and believe they must operate within them.[2] The budget imposes constraints as well. Costly proposals are not likely to be addressed in times of economic contraction or budget stringency, but might be more likely to receive attention in more robust times. Various rules of procedure, including the constitution, statutes, prescribed jurisdictions, precedents, customary decision-making modes, and other legal requirements, all impose structures on the participants. Finally, the scarcity of open windows constrains participants. They compete for limited space on agendas, and queue up for their turn. Even the selection criteria used by specialists in the policy stream anticipate these constraints.

These various types of pattern—dynamics internal to each stream, limits on coupling possibilities, and more general constraints—help us understand why some items never rise on policy agendas. [Earlier I] set forth several such items in health and transportation in the late 1970s. Some of them, such as long-term care and mental health, remained low, not because participants would not recognize real problems there but because they had little sense for alternatives that might be available as solutions. Some agenda items, such as buses, did not have powerful constituencies behind them in the political stream and failed to receive attention for lack of such advocates. Items such as rail nationalization failed because of powerful opposition. Others were not prominent on health and transportation agendas because systems of specialization and jurisdiction limited their movement. Items like direct delivery of medical care and food and drug regulation were indeed high on certain specialized agendas, but not on the larger health agenda. Finally, some items like environmental impact and transportation safety had been prominent earlier, but were played out by the time of these interviews, according to dynamics we explored when examining why problems fade. Thus this study helps to understand not only the appearance of some items on agendas, but also the failure of other items to appear.

Finally, it should be noted that all of our ideas are probabilistic. I have tried to adhere to such formulations as "the chances are improved or lessened" and "these events are more likely than others." In describing these processes, hard-and-fast rules and the specification of conditions that *must* be met seem less fruitful than a quotation of odds. Constraints, for instance, are not absolutes. Instead, they are conditions that make some events highly unlikely and other events more likely to occur. They do impose structure on the system, but it is structure that still allows room for some gray areas and some unpredictability. A budget constraint, for instance, is subject to some interpretation in the light of knowledge gaps and participants' values, but its operation still does make attention to some proposals at some points in time highly unlikely.

Thus we have made some progress in understanding the vague and imprecise phenomena we wanted to understand at the beginning of our journey. To the extent that our vision is still obscured, the world itself may be somewhat opaque. But further research and thinking beyond what is presented in this book may also allow us to see more clearly.

NOTES

1. For a good discussion of constraints, see Roger W. Cobb and Charles D. Elder, "Communications and Public Policy," in Dan Nimmo and Keith Sanders, eds., *Handbook of Political Communications* (Beverly Hills, Calif.: Sage, 1981), pp. 402–408.

2. John W. Kingdon, *Congressmen's Voting Decisions*, 2d ed. (New York: Harper and Row, 1981), Chapter 12.

44

CHARLES E. LINDBLOM

THE SCIENCE OF "MUDDLING THROUGH"

How are policy decisions made? Charles E. Lindblom argues that public administra-
tors tend to use the method of "successive limited comparisons" so that policy change
is incremental (the "branch" or "muddling through" approach). Administrative theo-
rists, on the other hand, often advocate a rational-comprehensive approach (or the
"root" method) in which all plausible policy alternatives are thoroughly analyzed
before any choices are made. Lindblom, a professor of political science at Yale Univer-
sity, noted that despite its counterintuitive qualities, "muddling through" has distinct
advantages over rational comprehensiveness. "The Science of 'Muddling Through'"
was originally published in Public Administration Review *in 1959.*

Suppose an administrator is given responsibility for formulating policy with
respect to inflation. He might start by trying to list all related values in order of
importance, e.g., full employment, reasonable business profit, protection of
small savings, prevention of a stock market crash. Then all possible policy outcomes could be rated as more or less efficient in attaining a maximum of these
values. This would of course require a prodigious inquiry into values held by
members of society and an equally prodigious set of calculations on how much
each value is equal to how much of each other value. He could then proceed to
outline all possible policy alternatives. In a third step, he could undertake systematic comparison of his multitude of alternatives to determine which attains the
greatest amount of values.

In comparing policies, he would take advantage of any theory available that
generalized about classes of policies. In considering inflation, for example, he
would compare all policies in the light of the theory of prices. Since no alternatives are beyond his investigation, he would consider strict central control and
the abolition of all prices and markets on the one hand and elimination of all
public controls with reliance completely on the free market on the other, both in
the light of whatever theoretical generalizations he could find on such hypothetical economies.

Finally, he would try to make the choice that would in fact maximize his values.

An alternative line of attack would be to set as his principal objective, either
explicitly or without conscious thought, the relatively simple goal of keeping
prices level. This objective might be compromised or complicated by only a few
other goals, such as full employment. He would in fact disregard most other
social values as beyond his present interest, and he would for the moment not
even attempt to rank the few values that he regarded as immediately relevant.
Were he pressed, he would quickly admit that he was ignoring many related values and many possible important consequences of his policies.

As a second step, he would outline those relatively few policy alternatives that
occurred to him. He would then compare them. In comparing his limited number of alternatives, most of them familiar from past controversies, he would not

ordinarily find a body of theory precise enough to carry him through a comparison of their respective consequences. Instead he would rely heavily on the record of past experience with small policy steps to predict the consequences of similar steps extended into the future.

Moreover, he would find that the policy alternatives combined objectives or values in different ways. For example, one policy might offer price level stability at the cost of some risk of unemployment; another might offer less price stability but also less risk of unemployment. Hence, the next step in his approach—the final selection—would combine into one the choice among values and the choice among instruments for reaching values. It would not, as in the first method of policy-making, approximate a more mechanical process of choosing the means that best satisfied goals that were previously clarified and ranked. Because practitioners of the second approach expect to achieve their goals only partially, they would expect to repeat endlessly the sequence just described, as conditions and aspirations changed and as accuracy of prediction improved.

BY ROOT OR BY BRANCH

For complex problems, the first of these two approaches is of course impossible. Although such an approach can be described, it cannot be practiced except for relatively simple problems and even then only in a somewhat modified form. It assumes intellectual capacities and sources of information that men simply do not possess, and it is even more absurd as an approach to policy when the time and money that can be allocated to a policy problem is limited, as is always the case. Of particular importance to public administrators is the fact that public agencies are in effect usually instructed not to practice the first method. That is to say, their prescribed functions and constraints—the politically or legally possible—restrict their attention to relatively few values and relatively few alternative policies among the countless alternatives that might be imagined. It is the second method that is practiced.

Curiously, however, the literatures of decision-making, policy formulation, planning, and public administration formalize the first approach rather than the second, leaving public administrators who handle complex decisions in the position of practicing what few preach. For emphasis I run some risk of overstatement. True enough, the literature is well aware of limits on man's capacities and of the inevitability that policies will be approached in some such style as the second. But attempts to formalize rational policy formulation—to lay out explicitly the necessary steps in the process—usually describe the first approach and not the second.[1]

The common tendency to describe policy formulation even for complex problems as though it followed the first approach has been strengthened by the attention given to, and success enjoyed by, operations research, statistical decision theory, and systems analysis. The hallmarks of these procedures, typical of the first approach, are clarity of objective, explicitness of evaluation, a high degree of comprehensiveness of overview, and, wherever possible, quantification of values for mathematical analysis. But these advanced procedures remain largely the appropriate techniques of relatively small-scale problem-solving where the total number of variables to be considered is small and value problems restricted. Charles Hitch, head of the Economics Division of RAND Corporation, one of the leading centers for application of these techniques, has written:

> I would make the empirical generalization from my experience at RAND and elsewhere that operations research is the art of sub-optimizing, i.e., of solving some lower-level problems, and that difficulties increase and our special competence diminishes by an order of magnitude with every level of decision making we attempt to ascend. The sort of simple explicit model which operations researchers are so proficient in using can certainly reflect most of the significant factors influencing traffic control on the George Washington Bridge, but the proportion of the relevant reality which we can represent by any such model or models in studying, say, a major foreign-policy decision, appears to be almost trivial.[2]

Accordingly, I propose in this paper to clarify and formalize the second method, much neglected in the literature. This might be described as the method of *successive limited comparisons*. I will contrast it with the first approach, which might be called the rational-comprehensive method.[3] More impressionistically and briefly—and therefore generally used in this article—they could be characterized as the branch method and root method, the former continually building out from the current situation, step-by-step and by small degrees; the latter starting from fundamentals anew each time, building on the past only as experience is embodied in a theory, and always prepared to start completely from the ground up.

Let us put the characteristics of the two methods side by side in simplest terms.

Rational-Comprehensive (Root)
1a. Clarification of values or objectives distinct from and usually prerequisite to empirical analysis of alternative policies
2a. Policy-formulation is therefore approached through means-end analysis: First the ends are isolated, then the means to achieve them are sought.
3a. The test of a "good" policy is that it can be shown to be the most appropriate means to desired ends.
4a. Analysis is comprehensive; every important relevant factor is taken into account.
5a. Theory is often heavily relied upon.

Assuming that the root method is familiar and understandable, we proceed directly to clarification of its alternative by contrast. In explaining the second, we shall be describing how most administrators do in fact approach complex questions, for the root method, the "best" way as a blueprint or model, is in fact not workable for complex policy questions, and administrators are forced to use the method of successive limited comparisons.

INTERTWINING EVALUATION AND EMPIRICAL ANALYSIS (1B)

The quickest way to understand how values are handled in the method of successive limited comparisons is to see how the root method often breaks down in *its* handling of values or objectives. The idea that values should be clarified, and in advance of the examination of alternative policies, is appealing. But what happens when we attempt it for complex social problems? The first difficulty is that on many critical values or objectives, citizens disagree, congressmen disagree, and public administrators disagree. Even where a fairly specific objective is prescribed for the administrator, there remains considerable room for disagreement on sub-objectives. Consider, for example, the conflict with respect to locating public housing, described in Meyerson and Banfield's study of the Chicago Housing Authority[4] — disagreement which occurred despite the clear objective of providing a certain number of public housing units in the city. Similarly conflicting are objectives in highway location, traffic control, minimum wage administration, development of tourist facilities in national parks, or insect control.

Successive Limited Comparisons (Branch)

1b. Selection of value goals and empirical analysis of the needed action are not distinct from one another but are closely intertwined.

2b. Since means and ends are not distinct, means-end analysis is often inappropriate or limited.

3b. The test of a "good" policy is typically that various analysts find themselves directly agreeing on a policy (without their agreeing that it is the most appropriate means to an agreed objective).

4b. Analysis is drastically limited:
 i) Important possible outcomes are neglected.
 ii) Important alternative potential policies are neglected.
 iii) Important affected values are neglected.

5b. A succession of comparison greatly reduces or eliminates reliance on theory.

Administrators cannot escape these conflicts by ascertaining the majority's preference, for preferences have not been registered on most issues; indeed, there often *are* no preferences in the absence of public discussion sufficient to bring an issue to the attention of the electorate. Furthermore, there is a question of whether intensity of feeling should be considered as well as the number of persons preferring each alternative. By the impossibility of doing otherwise, administrators often are reduced to deciding policy without clarifying objectives first.

Even when an administrator resolves to follow his own values as a criterion for decisions, he often will not know how to rank them when they conflict with one another, as they usually do. Suppose, for example, that an administrator must relocate tenants living in tenements scheduled for destruction. One objective is to empty the buildings fairly promptly, another is to find suitable accommodation for persons displaced, another is to avoid friction with residents in other areas in which a large influx would be unwelcome, another is to deal with all concerned through persuasion if possible, and so on.

How does one state even to himself the relative importance of these partially conflicting values? A simple ranking of them is not enough; one needs ideally to know how much of one value is worth sacrificing for some of another value. The answer is that typically the administrator chooses—and must choose—directly among policies in which these values are combined in different ways. He cannot first clarify his values and then choose among policies.

A more subtle third point underlies both the first two. Social objectives do not always have the same relative values. One objective may be highly prized in one circumstance, another in another circumstance. If, for example, an administrator values highly both the dispatch with which his agency can carry through its projects *and* good public relations, it matters little which of the two possibly conflicting values he favors in some abstract or general sense. Policy questions arise in forms which put to administrators such a question as: Given the degree to which we are or are not already achieving the values of dispatch and the values of good public relations, is it worth sacrificing a little speed for a happier clientele, or is it better to risk offending the clientele so that we can get on with our work? The answer to such a question varies with circumstances.

The value problem is, as the example shows, always a problem of adjustments at a margin. But there is no practicable way to state marginal objectives or values except in terms of particular policies. That one value is preferred to another in one decision situation does not mean that it will be preferred in another decision situation in which it can be had only at great sacrifice of another value. Attempts to rank or order values in general and abstract terms so that they do not shift from decision to decision end up by ignoring the relevant marginal preferences. The significance of this third point thus goes very far. Even if all administrators had at hand an agreed set of values, objectives, and constraints, and an agreed ranking of these values, objectives, and constraints, their marginal values in actual choice situations would be impossible to formulate.

Unable consequently to formulate the relevant values first and then choose among policies to achieve them, administrators must choose directly among alternative policies that offer different marginal combinations of values. Somewhat paradoxically, the only practicable way to disclose one's relevant marginal values even to oneself is to describe the policy one chooses to achieve them. Except roughly and vaguely, I know of no way to describe—or even to understand—what my relative evaluations are for, say, freedom and security, speed and accuracy in governmental decisions, or low taxes and better schools than to describe my preferences among specific policy choices that might be made between the alternatives in each of the pairs.

In summary, two aspects of the process by which values are actually handled can be distinguished. The first is clear: evaluation and empirical analysis are intertwined; that is, one chooses among values and among policies at one and the same time. Put a little more elaborately, one simultaneously chooses a policy to attain certain objectives and chooses the objectives themselves. The second aspect is related but distinct: the administrator focuses his attention on marginal or incremental values. Whether he is aware of it or not, he does not find general formulations of objectives very helpful and in fact makes specific marginal or incremental comparisons. Two policies, X and Y, confront him. Both promise the same degree of attainment of objectives *a, b, c, d,* and *e.* But X promises him somewhat more of *f* than does Y, while Y promises him somewhat more of *g* than does X. In choosing between them, he is in fact offered the alternative of a marginal or incremental amount of f at the expense of a marginal or incremental amount of g. The only values that are relevant to his choice are these increments by which the two policies differ; and, when he finally chooses between the two marginal values, he does so by making a choice between policies.[5]

As to whether the attempt to clarify objectives in advance of policy selection is more or less rational than the close intertwining of marginal evaluation and empirical analysis, the principal difference established is that for complex problems the first is impossible and irrelevant, and the second is both possible and relevant. The second is possible because the administrator need not try to analyze any values except the values by which alternative policies differ and need not be concerned with them except as they differ marginally. His need for information on values or objectives is drastically reduced as compared with the root method; and his capacity for grasping, comprehending, and relating values to one another is not strained beyond the breaking point.

RELATIONS BETWEEN MEANS AND ENDS (2B)

Decision-making is ordinarily formalized as a means-ends relationship: means are conceived to be evaluated and chosen in the light of ends finally selected independently of and prior to the choice of means. This is the means-ends relationship of the root method. But it follows from all that has just been said that such a means-ends relationship is possible only to the extent that values are agreed upon, are reconcilable, and are stable at the margin. Typically, therefore, such a means-ends relationship is absent from the branch method, where means and ends are simultaneously chosen.

Yet any departure from the means-ends relationship of the root method will strike some readers as inconceivable. For it will appear to them that only in such a relationship is it possible to determine whether one policy choice is better or worse than another. How can an administrator know whether he has made a wise or foolish decision if he is without prior values or objectives by which to judge his decisions? The answer to this question calls up the third distinctive difference between root and branch methods: how to decide the best policy.

THE TEST OF "GOOD" POLICY (3B)

In the root method, a decision is "correct," "good," or "rational" if it can be shown to attain some specified objective, where the objective can be specified without simply describing the decision itself. Where objectives are defined only through the marginal or incremental approach to values described above, it is still sometimes possible to test whether a policy does in fact attain the desired objectives; but a precise statement of the objectives takes the form of a description of the policy chosen or some alternative to it. To show that a policy is mistaken one cannot offer an abstract argument that important objectives are not achieved; one must instead argue that another policy is more to be preferred.

So far, the departure from customary ways of looking at problem-solving is not troublesome, for many administrators will be quick to agree that the most effective discussion of the correctness of policy does take the form of comparison with other policies that might have been chosen. But what of the situation in which administrators cannot agree on values or objectives, either abstractly or in marginal terms? What then is the test of "good" policy? For the root method, there is no test. Agreement on objectives failing, there is no standard of "correctness." For the method of successive limited comparisons, the test is agreement on policy itself, which remains possible even when agreement on values is not.

It has been suggested that continuing agreement in Congress on the desirability of extending old age insurance stems from liberal desires to strengthen the welfare programs of the federal government and from conservative desires to reduce union demands for private pension plans. If so, this is an excellent demonstration of the ease with which individuals of different ideologies often can agree on concrete policy. Labor mediators report a similar phenomenon: the contestants cannot agree on criteria for settling their disputes but can agree on specific proposals. Similarly, when one administrator's objective turns out to be another's means, they often can agree on policy.

Agreement on policy thus becomes the only practicable test of the policy's correctness. And for one administrator to seek to win the other over to agreement on ends as well would accomplish nothing and create quite unnecessary controversy.

If agreement directly on policy as a test for "best" policy seems a poor substitute for testing the policy against its objectives, it ought to be remembered that objectives themselves have no ultimate validity other than they are agreed upon. Hence agreement is the test of "best" policy in both methods. But where the root method requires agreement on what elements in the decision constitute objectives and on which of these objectives should be sought, the branch method falls back on agreement wherever it can be found.

In an important sense, therefore, it is not irrational for an administrator to defend a policy as good without being able to specify what it is good for.

NON-COMPREHENSIVE ANALYSIS (4B)

Ideally, rational-comprehensive analysis leaves out nothing important. But it is impossible to take everything important into consideration unless "important" is so narrowly defined that analysis is in fact quite limited. Limits on human intellectual capacities and on available information set definite limits to man's capacity to be comprehensive. In actual fact, therefore, no one can practice the rational-comprehensive method for really complex problems, and every administrator faced with a sufficiently complex problem must find ways drastically to simplify.

An administrator assisting in the formulation of agricultural economic policy cannot in the first place be competent on all possible policies. He cannot even comprehend one policy entirely. In planning a soil bank program, he cannot successfully anticipate the impact of higher or lower farm income on, say, urbanization—the possible consequent loosening of family ties, possible consequent eventual need for revisions in social security and further implications for tax problems arising out of new federal responsibilities for social security and municipal responsibilities for urban services. Nor, to follow another line of repercussions, can he work through the soil bank program's effects on prices for agricultural products in foreign markets and consequent implications for foreign relations, including those arising out of economic rivalry between the United States and the U.S.S.R.

In the method of successive limited comparisons, simplification is systematically achieved in two principal ways. First, it is achieved through limitation of policy comparisons to those policies that differ in relatively small degree from policies presently in effect. Such a limitation immediately reduces the number of alternatives to be investigated and also drastically simplifies the character of the investigation of each. For it is not necessary to undertake fundamental inquiry into an alternative and its consequences; it is necessary only to study those respects in which the proposed alternative and its consequences differ from the status quo. The empirical comparison of marginal differences among alternative policies that differ only marginally is, of course, a counterpart to the incremental or marginal comparison of values discussed above.[6]

Relevance as Well as Realism

It is a matter of common observation that in Western democracies public administrators and policy analysts in general do largely limit their analyses to incremental or marginal differences in policies that are chosen to differ only incrementally. They do not do so, however, solely because they desperately need some way to simplify their problems; they also do so in order to be relevant. Democracies change their policies almost entirely through incremental adjustments. Policy does not move in leaps and bounds.

The incremental character of political change in the United States has often been remarked. The two major political parties agree on fundamentals; they offer alternative policies to the voters only on relatively small points of difference. Both parties favor full employment, but they define it somewhat differently; both favor the development of water power resources, but in slightly different ways; and both favor unemployment compensation, but not the same level of benefits. Similarly, shifts of policy within a party take place largely through a series of relatively small changes, as can be seen in their only gradual acceptance of the idea of government responsibility for support of the unemployed, a change in party positions beginning in the early 30's and culminating in a sense in the Employment Act of 1946.

Party behavior is in turn rooted in public attitudes, and political theorists cannot conceive of democracy's surviving in the United States in the absence of fundamental agreement on potentially disruptive issues, with consequent limitation of policy debates to relatively small differences in policy.

Since the policies ignored by the administrator are politically impossible and so irrelevant, the simplification of analysis achieved by concentrating on policies that differ only incrementally is not a capricious kind of simplification. In addition, it can be argued that, given the limits on knowledge within which policy-makers are confined, simplifying by limiting the focus to small variations from present policy makes the most of available knowledge. Because policies being considered are like present and past policies, the administrator can obtain information and claim some insight. Non-incremental policy proposals are therefore typically not only politically irrelevant but also unpredictable in their consequences.

The second method of simplification of analysis is the practice of ignoring important possible consequences of possible policies, as well as the values attached to the neglected consequences. If this appears to disclose a shocking shortcoming of successive limited comparisons, it can be replied that, even if the exclusions are random, policies may nevertheless be more intelligently formulated than through futile attempts to achieve a comprehensiveness beyond human capacity. Actually, however, the exclusions, seeming arbitrary or random from one point of view, need be neither.

Achieving a Degree of Comprehensiveness

Suppose that each value neglected by one policy-making agency were a major concern of at least one other agency. In that case, a helpful division of labor would be achieved, and no agency need find its task beyond its capacities. The shortcomings of such a system would be that one agency might destroy a value either before another agency could be activated to safeguard it or in spite of another agency's efforts. But the possibility that important values may be lost is present in any form of organization, even where agencies attempt to comprehend in planning more than is humanly possible.

The virtue of such a hypothetical division of labor is that every important interest or value has its watchdog. And these watchdogs can protect the interests in their jurisdiction in two quite different ways: first, by redressing damages done by other agencies; and second, by anticipating and heading off injury before it occurs.

In a society like that of the United States in which individuals are free to combine to pursue almost any possible common interest they might have and in which government agencies are sensitive to the pressures of these groups, the system described is approximated. Almost every interest has its watchdog. Without claiming that every interest has a sufficiently powerful watchdog, it can be argued that our system often can assure a more comprehensive regard for the values of the whole society than any attempt at intellectual comprehensiveness.

In the United States, for example, no part of government attempts a comprehensive overview of policy on income distribution. A policy nevertheless evolves, and one responding to a wide variety of interests. A process of mutual adjustment among farm groups, labor unions, municipalities and school boards, tax authorities, and government agencies with responsibilities in the fields of housing, health, highways, national parks, fire, and police accomplishes a distribution of income in which particular income problems neglected at one point in the decision process become central at another point.

Mutual adjustment is more pervasive than the explicit forms it takes in negotiation between groups; it persists through the mutual impacts of groups upon each other even where they are not in communication. For all the imperfections and latent dangers in this ubiquitous process of mutual adjustment, it will often accomplish an adaptation of policies to a wider range of interests than could be done by one group centrally.

Note, too, how the incremental pattern of policy-making fits with the multiple pressure pattern. For when decisions are only incremental—closely related to known policies—it is easier too for one group to anticipate the kind of moves another might make and easier for it to make correction for injury already accomplished.[7]

Even partisanship and narrowness, to use pejorative terms, will sometimes be assets to rational decision-making, for they can doubly insure that what one agency neglects, another will not; they specialize personnel to distinct points of view. The claim is valid that effective rational coordination of the federal administrator, if possible to achieve at all, would require an agreed set of values[8]—if "rational" is defined as the practice of the root method of decision-making. But a high degree of administrative coordination occurs as each agency adjusts its policies to the concerns of the other agencies in the process of fragmented decision-making I have just described.

For all the apparent shortcomings of the incremental approach to policy alternatives with its arbitrary exclusion coupled with fragmentation, when compared to the root method, the branch method often looks far superior. In the root method, the inevitable exclusion of factors is accidental, unsystematic, and not defensible by any argument so far developed, while in the branch method the exclusions are deliberate, systematic, and defensible. Ideally, of course, the root method does not exclude; in practice it must.

Nor does the branch method necessarily neglect long-run considerations and objectives. It is clear that important values must be omitted in considering policy, and sometimes the only way long-run objectives can be given adequate attention is through the neglect of short-run considerations. But the values omitted can be either long-run or short-run.

SUCCESSION OF COMPARISONS (5B)

The final distinctive element in the branch method is that the comparisons, together with the policy choice, proceed in a chronological series. Policy is not made once and for all; it is made and re-made endlessly. Policy-making is a process of successive approximation to some desired objectives in which what is desired itself continues to change under reconsideration.

Making policy is at best a very rough process. Neither social scientists, nor politicians, nor public administrators yet know enough about the social world to avoid repeated error in predicting the consequences of policy moves. A wise policy-maker consequently expects that his policies will achieve only part of what he hopes and at the same time will produce unanticipated consequences he would have preferred to avoid. If he proceeds through a *succession* of incremental changes, he avoids serious lasting mistakes in several ways.

In the first place, past sequences of policy steps have given him knowledge about the probable consequences of further similar steps. Second, he need not attempt big jumps toward his goals that would require predictions beyond his or anyone else's knowledge, because he never expects his policy to be a final resolution of a problem. His decision is only one step, one that if successful can quickly be followed by another. Third, he is in effect able to test his previous predictions as he moves on to each further step. Lastly, he often can remedy a past error fairly quickly—more quickly than if policy proceeded through more distinct steps widely spaced in time.

Compare this comparative analysis of incremental changes with the aspiration to employ theory in the root method. Man cannot think without classifying, without subsuming one experience under a more general category of experiences. The attempt to push categorization as far as possible and to find general propositions which can be applied to specific situations is what I refer to with the word "theory." Where root analysis often leans heavily on theory in this sense, the branch method does not.

The assumption of root analysis is that theory is the most systematic and economical way to bring relevant knowledge to bear on a specific problem. Granting the assumption, an unhappy fact is that we do not have adequate theory to apply to problems in any policy area, although theory is more adequate in some areas—monetary policy, for example—than in others. Comparative analysis, as in the branch method, is sometimes a systematic alternative to theory.

Suppose an administrator must choose among a small group of policies that differ only incrementally from each other and from present policy. He might aspire to "understand" each of the alternatives—for example, to know all the consequences of each aspect of each policy. If so, he would indeed require theory. In fact, however, he would usually decide that, *for policy-making purposes*, he need know, as explained above, only the consequences of each of those aspects of the policies in which they differed from one another. For this much more modest aspiration, he requires no theory (although it might be helpful, if available), for he can proceed to isolate probable differences by examining the differences in consequences associated with past differences in policies, a feasible program because he can take his observations from a long sequence of incremental changes.

For example, without a more comprehensive social theory about juvenile delinquency than scholars have yet produced, one cannot possibly understand the ways in which a variety of public policies—say on education, housing, recreation, employment, race relations, and policing—might encourage or discourage delinquency. And one needs such an understanding if he undertakes the comprehensive overview of the problem prescribed in the models of the root method. If, however, one merely wants to mobilize knowledge sufficient to assist in a choice among a small group of similar policies—alternative policies on juvenile court procedures, for example—he can do so by comparative analysis of the results of similar past policy moves.

THEORISTS AND PRACTITIONERS

This difference explains—in some cases at least—why the administrator often feels that the outside expert or academic problem-solver is sometimes not helpful and why they in turn often urge more theory on him. And it explains why an administrator often feels more confident when "flying by the seat of his pants" than when following the advice of theorists. Theorists often ask the administrator to go the long way round to the solution of his problems, in effect ask him to follow the best canons of the scientific method, when the administrator knows that the best available theory will work less well than more modest incremental comparisons. Theorists do not realize that the administrator is often in fact practicing a systematic method. It would be foolish to push this explanation too far, for sometimes practical decision-makers are pursuing neither a theoretical approach nor successive comparisons, not any other systematic method.

It may be worth emphasizing that theory is sometimes of extremely limited helpfulness in policy-making for at least two rather different reasons. It is greedy for facts; it can be constructed only through a great collection of observations. And it is typically insufficiently precise for application to a policy process that moves through small changes. In contrast, the comparative method both economizes on the need for facts and directs the analyst's attention to just those facts that are relevant to the fine choices faced by the decision-maker.

With respect to precision of theory, economic theory serves as an example. It predicts that an economy without money or prices would in certain specified ways misallocate resources, but this finding pertains to an alternative far removed from the kind of policies on which administrators need help. On the other hand, it is not precise enough to predict the consequences of policies restricting business mergers, and this is the kind of issue on which the administrators need help. Only in relatively restricted areas does economic theory achieve sufficient precision to go far in resolving policy questions; its helpfulness in policy-making is always so limited that it requires supplementation through comparative analysis.

SUCCESSIVE COMPARISON AS A SYSTEM

Successive limited comparisons is, then, indeed a method or system; it is not a failure of method for which administrators ought to apologize. None the less, its imperfections, which have not been explored in this paper, are many. For example, the method is without a built-in safeguard for all relevant values, and it also may lead the decision-maker to overlook excellent policies for no other reason than that they are not suggested by the chain of successive policy steps leading up to the present. Hence, it ought to be said that under this method, as well as under some of the most sophisticated variants of the root method—operations research, for example—policies will continue to be as foolish as they are wise.

Why then bother to describe the method in all the above detail? Because it is in fact a common method of policy formulation, and is, for complex problems, the principal reliance of administrators as well as of other policy analysts.[9] And because it will be superior to any other decision-making method available for complex problems in many circumstances, certainly superior to a futile attempt at superhuman comprehensiveness. The reaction of the public administrator to the exposition of method doubtless will be less a discovery of a new method than a better acquaintance with an old. But by becoming more conscious of their practice of this method, administrators might practice it with more skill and know when to extend or constrict its use. (That they sometimes practice it effectively and sometimes not may explain the extremes of opinion on "muddling through," which is both praised as a highly sophisticated form of problem-solving and denounced as no method at all. For I suspect that in so far as there is a system in what is known as "muddling through," this method is it).

One of the noteworthy incidental consequences of clarification of the method is the light it throws on the suspicion an administrator sometimes entertains that a consultant or adviser is not speaking relevantly and responsibly when in fact by all ordinary objective evidence he is. The trouble lies in the fact that most of us approach policy problems within a framework given by our view of a chain of successive policy choices made up to the present. One's thinking about appropriate policies with respect, say, to urban traffic control is greatly influenced by one's knowledge of the incremental steps taken up to the present. An administrator enjoys an intimate knowledge of his past sequences that "outsiders" do not share, and his thinking and that of the "outsider" will consequently be different in ways that may puzzle both. Both may appear to be talking intelligently, yet each may find the other unsatisfactory. The relevance of the policy chain of succession is even more clear when an American tries to discuss, say, antitrust policy with a Swiss, for the chains of policy in the two countries are strikingly different and the two individuals consequently have organized their knowledge in quite different ways.

If this phenomenon is a barrier to communication, an understanding of it promises an enrichment of intellectual interaction in policy formulation. Once the source of difference is understood, it will sometimes be stimulating for an administrator to seek out a policy analyst whose recent experience is with a policy chain different from his own.

This raises again a question only briefly discussed above on the merits of like-mindedness among government administrators. While much of organization theory argues the virtues of common values and agreed organizational objectives, for complex problems in which the root method is inapplicable, agencies will want among their own personnel two types of diversification: administrators whose thinking is organized by reference to policy chains other than those familiar to most members of the organization and, even more commonly, administrators whose professional or personal values or interests create diversity of view (perhaps coming from different specialties, social classes, geographical areas) so that, even within a single agency, decision-making can be fragmented and parts of the agency can serve as watchdogs for other parts.

NOTES

1. James G. March and Herbert A. Simon similarly characterize the literature. They also take some important steps, as have Simon's recent articles, to describe a less heroic model of policy-making. See *Organizations* (John Wiley and Sons, 1958), p. 137.

2. "Operations Research and National Planning—A Dissent," 5 *Operations Research* 718 (October, 1957). Hitch's dissent is from particular points made in the article to which his paper is a reply; his claim that operations research is for low-level problems is widely accepted.

For examples of the kind of problems to which operations research is applied, see C. W. Churchman, R. L. Ackoff and E. L. Arnoff, *Introduction to Operations Research* (John Wiley and Sons, 1957); and J. F. McCloskey and J. M. Coppinger (eds.), *Operations Research for Management*, Vol. II (Johns Hopkins Press, 1956).

3. I am assuming that administrators often make policy and advise in the making of policy and am treating decision-making and policy-making as synonymous for purposes of this paper.

4. Martin Meyerson and Edward C. Banfield, *Politics, Planning and the Public Interest* (Free Press, 1955).

5. The line of argument is, of course, an extension of the theory of market choice, especially the theory of consumer choice, to public policy choices.

6. A more precise definition of incremental policies and a discussion of whether a change that appears "small" to one observer might be seen differently by another is to be found in my "Policy Analysis," 48 *American Economic Review* 298 (June, 1958).

7. The link between the practice of the method of successive limited comparisons and mutual adjustment of interests in a highly fragmented decision-making process adds a new facet to pluralist theories of government and administration.

8. Herbert Simon, Donald W. Smithburg, and Victor A. Thompson, *Public Administration* (Alfred A. Knopf, 1950), p. 434.

9. Elsewhere I have explored this same method of policy formulation as practiced by academic analysts of policy ("Policy Analysis," 48 *American Economic Review* 298 [June 1958]). Although it has been here presented as a method for public administrators, it is no less necessary to analysts more removed from immediate policy questions, despite their tendencies to describe their own analytical efforts as though they were the rational-comprehensive method with an especially heavy use of theory. Similarly, this same method is inevitably resorted to in personal problem-solving, where means and ends are sometimes impossible to separate, where aspirations or objectives undergo constant development, and where drastic simplification of the complexity of the real world is urgent if problems are to be solved in the time that can be given to them. To an economist accustomed to dealing with the marginal or incremental concept in market processes, the central idea in the method is that both evaluation and empirical analysis are incremental. Accordingly I have referred to the method elsewhere as "the incremental method."

45

EDWARD C. BANFIELD

INFLUENCE AND THE PUBLIC INTEREST

How are decisions on salient community interests made? Basing his analysis on six case studies of policy making in Chicago, Edward C. Banfield concludes that decisions resemble "social choices" or "mixed" decisions in which relevant preferences are weighed through a pluralist bargaining process. "Social choices" are more likely to yield policy outcomes that truly reflect the public interest than are "central decisions" made by a solitary public official or manager acting independently of other interested parties. Banfield's analysis is a classic exposition, and intellectual defense, of the pluralist policy process. Banfield was a professor in the Department of Government at Harvard University for most of his career. This selection is taken from his book Political Influence *(1961).*

Some will say that a political system such as has been described here can rarely produce outcomes that are in the public interest. If actions profoundly affecting the city's development are based not on comprehensive planning but on compromises patched up among competing parochial interests, if political heads are less concerned with the content of policy than with maintaining a voting alliance between the machine-controlled inner city and the suspicious suburbs and if the possessors of great private fortunes and the heads of big corporations cannot, despite all their talk of "civic responsibility," act concertedly for public ends — if all this be the case, then Chicago's future welfare depends (some will say) not so much upon the processes of government as upon that special providence that is reserved for fools and drunkards.

The great defect of the Chicago political system (those who take this view will say) is that it does not provide sufficient central direction. There are many special interests on the scene, each of which looks after itself and cares only incidentally, if at all, for the welfare of the community as a whole. Action in public matters is largely a by-product of the struggles of these special interests for their own advantage. What is needed (the critics will conclude) is a central public authority which will survey the entire metropolitan scene, form a comprehensive, internally consistent conception of what must be done for the good of the whole, and then carry that conception into effect without compromise. This is what the advocates of "planning" and "efficient metropolitan organization" have in mind.

It seems clear that there is a tension between the nature of the political system, on the one hand, and the requirements of planning — of comprehensiveness and consistency in policy — on the other. In part, this tension arises from the decentralization so characteristic of the Chicago political system; despite the trend of recent years toward formal centralization and despite the extensive informal arrangements for overcoming decentralization, no one is in a position to survey the city — much less the metropolitan area — as a whole and to formulate and carry out a comprehensive policy. (Mayor Daley, despite his great power as boss, can do little even in the city proper without at least tacit support from the governor.) In part, too, the tension arises from a general premise of our political culture: the belief that self-government consists, not in giving or withholding consent at infrequent intervals on matters of general principle, but rather in making influence felt in the day-to-day conduct of the public business. So long as particular interests can prevent the executive from carrying out his policy, or so long as they can place hazards and delays in the way of his carrying it out, they can demand concessions from him as the price of allowing him to act. It is the necessity of constantly making such concessions—of giving everyone something so as to generate enough support to allow of any action at all—that makes government policy so lacking in comprehensiveness and consistency.

The tendency in the United States has long been towards strengthening the executive: in Chicago as elsewhere the formal centralization of executive power is much greater than it was a decade or two ago. It seems highly unlikely, however, that this strengthening will go far enough in the forseeable future to change the essential character of the system. Chicagoans, like other Americans, want their city's policies to be comprehensive and consistent. But they also want to exercise influence in making and carrying out these policies; they want to be able to force the government to bargain with them when its policy threatens particular interests of theirs. It will be a long time, probably, before they will be willing to sacrifice as much of the second end as would be necessary to achieve the first. The tension between the nature of the system and the requirements of planning is, for all practical purposes, ineradicable.

This conclusion would be discouraging if it were perfectly clear that a comprehensive and consistent policy is necessarily better (i.e., more productive of "welfare" or "the public interest") than one which is not. We are apt to take for granted that this is the case. We are apt to suppose that a "correct" or "consistent" policy must be the product of a mind (or minds) which has addressed itself to a "problem," and, by a conscious search, "found" or "constructed" a "solution." Most of our study of political and administrative matters proceeds on the assumption that all of the elements of a problem must be brought together within the purview of some single mind (whether of a person or team) and that the task of organization is partly to assemble the elements of the problem. The more complicated the matter, the more obvious it seems that its solution must depend upon the effort of a mind which perceives a "problem" and deliberately seeks a "solution."

It will be convenient to make a fundamental distinction between "central decision," and "social choice." Both are processes by which selections are made among the action possibilities open to some group or public. A *central decision* is in some sense purposeful or deliberate: it is made by someone (leader, chairman, mayor, planning commission, council, committee of the whole, etc.) who, in making the selection, is trying (although perhaps ineffectually) to realize some intention for the group. From the standpoint of this decision-maker, the selection of an action, or course of action, for the group represents a "solution" to a "problem." A *social choice*, on the other hand, is the accidental by-product of the actions of two or more actors—"interested parties," they will be called—who have no common intention and who make their selections competitively or without regard to each other. In a social-choice process, each actor seeks to attain his own ends; the aggregate of all actions—the situation produced by all actions together—constitutes an outcome for the group, but it is an outcome which no one has planned as a "solution" to a "problem." It is a "resultant" rather than a "solution."

It may seem to be common sense that because it is the product of intention, indeed of conscious and deliberate problem-solving, a central decision is much more likely to "work" than is a social choice. The social choice is, after all, an "accident": it was not designed to serve the needs or wishes of the group, whereas the central decision *was* so designed.

And yet, despite the presumptions of common sense, it may be that under certain circumstances the competition of forces which do not aim at a common interest produces outcomes which are more "workable," "satisfactory," or "efficient" than any that could be contrived by a central decision-maker consciously searching for solutions in the common interest. Charles E. Lindblom has observed that while it is customary to think of the analysis of a policy problem as going on in the mind of one man or of a small group of men, it can also be seen as a social process. "Fragmentation" of analysis (i.e., analysis that goes on among many individuals or groups, each of whom approaches the problem from his distinctive and limited point of view) may be an aid to the correct weighting of values in a choice.

> Just how does the weighting take place in fragmentation? Not, I have suggested, in any one analyst's mind, nor in the minds of members of a research team, nor in the mind of any policy-maker or policy-making group. The weighting does not take place until actual policy decisions are made. At that time, the conflicting views of individuals and groups, each of whom have been concerned with a limited set of values, are brought to bear upon policy formulation. Policies are set as a resultant of such conflict, not because some one policy making individual or group achieves an integration but because the pulling and hauling of various views accomplishes finally some kind of decision, probably different from what any one advocate of the final solution intended and probably different from what any one advocate could comfortably defend by reference to his own limited values. The weighing or aggregation is a political process, not an intellectual process.

The evidence of the cases presented here makes it plausible to search for some such underlying logic not obvious to common sense. For if the outcomes alone of these cases are considered—that is, if the outcomes are considered apart from the seemingly "irrational" way in which they were reached—one might conclude that the political system is remarkably effective. It is impossible, of course, to come to any conclusion on this without making a large number of highly subjective judgments—not only judgments about values, but about facts and probabilities as well. Admitting this, the writer conjectures that most reasonable people who put themselves in the role of "statesman" and consider carefully all of the relevant circumstances will conclude that the outcomes are by no means indefensible. For himself, the writer can say that they are essentially what he would have favored had he been making "decisions." In every case, it seems to him "wrong" reasons (i.e., reasons which were irrelevant, illogical, or improper as a basis of a "decision" in the public interest) were controlling, but in every case these "wrong" reasons led to outcomes that were essentially "right" or "sound."

Others may not agree. But it is only necessary to establish that "obviously wrong" reasons led to outcomes that are "not obviously wrong" in order to raise the question: are such outcomes "lucky accidents" or is there some principle at work—an "invisible hand"—that leads a choice process to a result better than anyone intends?

The case for central decision rests upon the assumption that it is possible for a competent and disinterested decision-maker to find in any situation a value premise that uniquely determines the content of the public interest. If there existed several incompatible but equally desirable courses of action, a decision-maker would obviously have to employ some "arbitrary" procedure—e.g., flipping a coin, consulting his own or someone else's personal tastes, or assessing the relatives influence of the interests having a stake in the matter—in order to arrive at the decision. But the assumption of administration-minded or planning-minded persons is that this embarrassing situation seldom arises. A competent and well-intentioned decision-maker, so they suppose, can usually find in the situation some premise that clearly ought to rule. The problem of good government, therefore, is to put into office men who will look for the proper premise and use it when they find it (i.e., who seek the public interest rather than private or party advantage) and who have the technical competence necessary to apply the premise correctly in the particular circumstances.

This assumption is wrong. No matter how competent and well-intentioned, a decision-maker can never make an important decision on grounds that are not in some degree arbitrary or non-logical. He must select from among incompatible alternatives each of which is preferable in terms of a different but defensible view of the public interest. If there is a single "ultimate" value premise to which all of the lesser ones are instrumental, if its meaning is unambiguous in the concrete circumstances, and if he can know for sure which lesser premise is most instrumental to the attainment of the ultimate one, he can, indeed, make his decision in an entirely technical and non-arbitrary way. But these conditions can seldom be met, and when they can be, the matter is not "important" and usually does not require "decision." Matters come before high officials for decision precisely when it is not clear which value premises ought to be invoked, what the premises imply concretely, or what is most instrumental to their achievement. If such questions do not arise, the matter does not present itself as a "problem" at all.

In the Branch Hospital case, for example, there were at least three defensible value premises, each of which implied an altogether different decision: (a) "relieve overcrowding expeditiously" implied expanding on the West Side where a site was available; (b) "improve service" implied building on the South Side in proximity to the service area; and (c) "eliminate racial discrimination" implied not building at all in order to put pressure on the private hospitals. There was no higher premise to which each of these stood in an instrumental relationship and by which they could be judged. (There were slogans, of course, like "the greatest good of the greatest number," but these meant nothing concretely.) Clearly, then, the decision could not be made on technical or non-arbitrary grounds.

In such cases, where the decision-maker must select among alternatives without having any "higher" value premise by which to judge their relative importance, he must, wittingly or unwittingly, employ a criterion which has nothing to recommend it except use and wont or professional acceptance (e.g., "this is the way it is done in standard professional practice") or which expresses only his own (or someone else's) tastes or advantage, or else he must enact in imagination a choice process, imputing preference scales to the interested parties and striking, on their behalf, that compromise which he thinks "fair," productive of the most satisfaction, or the best reflection of the distribution of influence.

Thus, for example, a city-planning technician faced with the competing value premises of the Branch Hospital dispute and seeing no "higher" premise by which to decide the claims of the "lesser" ones, would, following the usual professional practice, gather a great deal of factual information on the distribution of potential hospital users, travel time, the optimal size of hospitals, etc., and then in all likelihood "find in the data" some reason—e.g., economy of travel time—for putting the hospital on the South Side. The chances are that the planner would not be as sensitive to the value, "relieve overcrowding expeditiously," as to the professionally sanctioned one, "minimize cross traffic." And it is very likely that the value, "eliminate racial discrimination," would not occur to him at all or that, if it did, it would not seem to him to be an appropriate ultimate criterion. If it were expressly called to his attention, he might even say that it is a "political" factor which should not be allowed to influence the decision.

There is likely to be a systematic bias in a technician's choice of value premises. He will, it seems plausible to suppose, minimize the importance of those elements of the situation that are controversial, intangible, or problematic. He will favor those value premises upon the importance of which there is general agreement (e.g., travel time), and he will ignore or underrate those that are controversial or not conventionally defined (e.g., eliminating racial discrimination); he will favor those that can be measured, especially those that can be measured in money terms (e.g., the cost of transportation), and he will ignore or underrate those that are intangible and perhaps indefinable as well (e.g., the mood of a neighborhood); he will favor those that are associated with reliable predictions about the factual situation (e.g., the premise of accessibility is associated with relatively reliable predictions about population movements and consumer behavior), and he will ignore or underrate those that are associated with subjective judgments of probability (e.g., that it will be harder to get political approval for a South Side site).

In a social-choice process, by contrast, there is a single ultimate criterion: the distribution of influence. The importance accorded to each alternative in a choice process depends, then, upon the relative amount of influence exercised on its behalf.

This may appear to be a highly inappropriate criterion in most situations. There are, however, a number of things that can be said in its favor:

1. The distribution of influence may be viewed as the outcome (as of a given moment) of a continuing "game" which has been going on under rules that a majority of the players have been free to change at any time. That the rules are as

they are implies that they seem fair, over the long run, to most of the players. Accordingly, the outcome at any particular time is also fair, even though some players are losing. A player exerts himself to win only because winners receive rewards that are not given to losers. If, therefore, the winners have no more weight in a choice than do the losers—i.e., if the criterion does not reflect the distribution of influence—they will have that much less incentive to enter the game and to fight hard to win it. If the game is, on the whole, good for the society, it is foolish to reduce the incentive to play it. In other words, a society that wants people to exert themselves to get influence must not limit, unnecessarily, opportunities to exercise it once it has been obtained.

2. A criterion which reflects the distribution of influence also reflects, although roughly, the intensity with which the competing values are held. This is so because the choice process takes into account "real" influence, i.e., not the ability of each participant to modify the behavior of others, but the ability *which each sees fit to expend, out of his limited stock, for the sake of the particular value in question.* In the Fort Dearborn case, for example, the opponents had less influence than the Sponsors in the sense that if all had exerted themselves to the utmost, the Sponsors would have had their way. But the opponents were more intensely moved. Accordingly, they exercised a larger part of their influence potential than did the Sponsors. To the extent that the process was one of bargaining, it registered a compound of influence and intensity of interest. If it is considered appropriate to maximize "total satisfaction" of those whose views are taken into account, then it is essential to have some indication of how intensely each value is held. The choice mechanism forces each bargainer to give up something (the amount of influence he "spends"); this something can therefore be taken as a measure of the value to him of what he seeks. (If the influence distribution is "incorrect," the measure will of course be, to that extent, "wrong." But, as was maintained in the paragraph above, there is some reason to assume that the distribution is "correct.")

3. The character of the influence exercised may afford additional grounds for considering the distribution of influence to be an appropriate criterion. In one situation or set of situations, influence may consist of "forcing others to do one's will even when that will is anti-social." In another it may consist of "persuading others on reasonable grounds to accept a view of the common interest." There are circumstances in which one can exercise influence only by being (or seeming to be) intelligently concerned with the common good ("by main force of being right"). So far as this is the case in a given society or situation, the criterion of influence has further justification.

The appropriateness of the criterion of influence is, however, only one aspect of the larger question, namely, the appropriateness of the social-choice process as a whole. It would be a point in favor of the choice process and a point against the decision process if it could be shown that while neither is clearly undesirable as a procedure for selecting an ultimate criterion, the former is more likely to bring all relevant considerations to the fore and to give them the attention they deserve.

There is indeed much reason to think that this is the case. A decisionmaker, even one of long experience and great capacity, is not likely, when an issue first arises, to be fully aware of all the interests that are at stake in it or of the importance that is attached to each interest by those who hold it. He gets this information (except with regard to the most obvious matters) only as the interested parties themselves bring it to his attention. The effort an interested party makes to put its case before the decision-maker will be in proportion to *the advantage to be gained from a favorable outcome multiplied by the probability of influencing the decision.* Thus, no matter how high the stakes, an interested party will invest no effort at all in putting its case before a decision-maker who cannot be influenced. On the other hand, if there is a virtual certainty that the decision can be influenced, an interested party will have incentive to expend, in the effort to influence the decision, almost all of what may be gained from a favorable decision.

If the decisionmaker is surely going to make the decision on purely public grounds, the possibilities of influencing him are relatively small. The interested party may present the facts of its case in the best possible light. It may argue that the public interest is to be understood in this way rather than that. But it cannot go much further than this. It cannot do more than try to persuade. In some cases the probability of success by persuasion may be sufficient to induce it to put forth a considerable effort. In others, however, its effort will be perfunctory because it knows that the decisionmaker will pay little attention. In still others, it will make no effort at all because it knows that the decisionmaker is not open to persuasion.

If, on the other hand, the official is open to influence by other means than persuasion, the probability of influencing the outcome may be vastly increased. If, indeed, it is possible, by a large enough expenditure of influence, virtually to compel him to select the favored alternative, then the incentive to make the effort is limited only by the advantage to be had from its success. In these circumstances, the affected interests will almost literally bring their cases "forcibly to the attention of" the official.

In a system of government in which the possibility of influencing outcomes is great, a vast amount of effort is spent by very able people in the attempt to do so. This expenditure of effort has some socially valuable results. It leads to the production of more information about the various alternatives and to a clarification of the values that are involved. Not only are the officials compelled to take into account more than they otherwise would, but the interests themselves are brought to examine their own and each other's positions with great care. Of course, in an instance where there exists some obviously appropriate and concretely meaningful value criterion upon which it is apparent, once the information is all at hand, that the official's decision ought to turn, the ability of an interested party to force the official to decide by some other criterion introduces error into the selection process. The argument here, however, is that such criteria almost never exist in matters of importance, and that when they do not exist, it is socially desirable that interested parties have incentive to vigorously assert value principles which will compete with those necessarily arbitrary ones (e.g., professional use and wont) which officials, wittingly or unwittingly, must fall back upon.

In a political system in which there exists no possibility whatever of influencing an outcome by an exercise of power (as distinguished from persuasion), it is unlikely that an interested party whose value position is not widely accepted as a plausible ultimate basis of decision will exert itself to put that position forward. Berry and Calloway, for example, would probably not have appeared upon the scene in the Branch Hospital dispute if the Chicago political system had been such as to make clear that the decision would be entirely in the hands of planners or technically minded people; but had they not exerted themselves, it is likely that the "race" position would have been entirely overlooked or given little weight. (The Welfare Council's planners, it will be remembered, virtually ignored it.) A "decision" reached without the racial aspects of the matter having been taken fully into account would have been deficient, although it might well have *seemed* (the deficiency not being called to anyone's attention) more "rational" than the social choice that was actually made.

In summary, then, it has been maintained: (1) that when, as is the case in important matters, there exists no concretely unambiguous criterion which clearly ought to rule, the distribution of "real" influence, as revealed in competitive exercises of influence, may be the appropriate criterion; and (2) that a selection process (or political system) which allows of the exercise of power other than that of persuasion by affected interests produces a wider canvas of policy alternatives and a more thorough scrutiny of each alternative than does a process which allows the affected interests only the opportunity to persuade. A corollary of these propositions is that the "rationality" of the process in which only persuasion is possible (i.e., the decision process) is often a simplification secured by overlooking or radically undervaluing some alternatives.

The social-choice process, however, suffers from at least two inherent limitations of great importance:

1. It takes into account only such ends as actors of influence see fit to assert, and it weights these ends according to the amount of influence behind them and without regard to their intrinsic value. In many circumstances, the distribution of influence may be an entirely inappropriate criterion. There may be ends which are not asserted in the choice process at all or which are asserted only weakly (e.g., ends which pertain to the community "as a whole") but which nevertheless ought to determine the outcome, ought to enter into it along with the ends which are asserted by influentials, or ought to serve as criteria by which the appropriateness and relative value of these and other ends are established.

2. There may exist an outcome which represents the "greatest total benefit" of the parties to the choice process but which is not likely to be found if each party seeks only his own advantage. There may, for example, be two ways in which A can attain his end equally well and between which he is indifferent. One of these ways may be advantageous to B and the other disadvantageous to him. A may not perceive the opportunity to increase total satisfaction by acting so as to benefit B; even if he does perceive it, he may have no incentive to act upon it.

It is a disadvantage of the choice process that no one has either an incentive to devise "greatest total benefit" solutions or the information about the preferences scales of the various interested parties that would be needed in order to do so.

In the Branch Hospital dispute, an arrangement whereby the county paid its clients' hospital bills in full, gave them freedom of choice in hospitals, and offered subsidies for expansion of those private hospitals which agreed not to discriminate might have represented a "greatest total benefit" solution. (It would presumably have suited both the left and the right wings of the Negro community, and the white hospitals as well.) But this solution was not likely to be devised by any of the parties to the struggle; each was too much committed to the solution implied by its own ends to look for one which would serve the ends of all.

The distribution of influence may be such as to paralyze action altogether. (In only two of the six cases described in the book—the Exhibition Hall and the Welfare Merger—was a course of action carried out as planned by its proponents; in the other cases, the outcomes were essentially the checking of action.) This tendency to paralyze action is sometimes regarded as a defect of the choice process. In certain circumstances it may be, of course. But from a general standpoint, there is no presumption that "inaction" represents a less desirable outcome than "action."

Certainly, a social-choice process is not always to be preferred to a central-decision process. Which is more appropriate will depend upon the circumstances of the case, especially the following: (*a*) the complexity of the policy problem to be solved, including especially the number of elements that must somehow be taken into account or weighted (and thus the amount of conflict in the situation) and the time and other resources that can be employed in looking for a solution; the more complicated the problem, the stronger the case for the choice mechanism; (*b*) the visibility of the factual and value elements that should be taken into account; where there is reason to believe that all relevant values (and their intensities) are not known, the play of influence should be allowed in order to assist their being made known; (*c*) the presence or absence of an appropriate "ultimate" criterion which is sufficiently definite in meaning to afford a basis for selection among the competing values that are instrumental to it; where such a criterion exists, a decision process is indicated, and the play of influence on the decision-maker is clearly undesirable; and (*d*) the appropriateness of one or another procedural criterion (e.g., that the settlement should reflect the distribution of influence, that it should accord with professional use and wont, that it should be "fair"); if the distribution of influence, or the bases upon which influence rests, are clearly undesirable, and if a decisionmaker can be expected to employ procedural criteria which are *not* clearly undesirable, there is, of course, a presumption in favor of the decision process.

The discussion so far will have suggested the possibility of a selection process which combines features of both central decision and social choice and which therefore has some advantages (or, it could also be, disadvantages) of both. In a *mixed decision-choice* process, there are two or more interested parties each of whom seeks its own advantage without regard to any common intention. But there is also on the scene a central decisionmaker who intervenes in the selection process to perform one or more of the following functions:

1. The central decisionmaker may regulate the selection process so that "public values" are achieved or, negatively, not disregarded. He may, in the first place, decide whether the matter is one in which only the self-regarding ends of the interested parties should be taken into account (i.e., whether they are the only relevant value stuff) or whether they are corporate ends or "public values" that ought to be

taken into account instead of, or along with, the self-regarding ends of the interested parties. He decides, in other words, whether selections ought to be made by social choice, central decision, or a mixed process. If he decides either that only "public values" or only "self-regarding ends" are relevant, the process then ceases to be "mixed": it becomes either central decision or social choice. But he may decide that what is appropriate is an aggregation of both public values *and* self-regarding ends—an aggregation in which certain public values and certain self-regarding ends are given greater or lesser weight. (He may, for example, decide that the matter is one in which a "qualified individualist" conception of the public interest is appropriate, and, accordingly, he may disregard "tastes" of "private-spirited" persons while giving great weight to the "settled convictions" of "public-spirited" persons.) Thus, the selection may be made through a social-choice process, but through a social-choice process *which operates within a limiting framework laid down by central direction.* The outcome of such a process is therefore both a "resultant" (from the standpoint of the interested parties) and a "solution" (from the standpoint of the central decisionmaker, who decided which interested parties should be allowed to enter the process, how their ends should be weighted, and what importance should be accorded to "public values").

2. The central decisionmaker may coordinate the activities of the interested parties in order to help them find positions optimal in terms of their (self-regarding) ends—i.e., positions such that no possible reallocation would make anyone better off without making others worse off. The central decisionmaker keeps track of external economies and diseconomies, which are not visible to the interested parties, and he watches for "saddle-points." He may, for example, guide the interested parties to a greater total "welfare" merely by supplying information (e.g., he may know that A is indifferent as between states x and y, whereas B much prefers state y; by pointing out that someone will gain and no one will lose by choosing state y, he increases welfare), or he may be the agent through which interpersonal comparisons of welfare are made or other agreed-upon rules are applied (e.g., if state x would mean great gains to A and small losses to B, he may intervene to impose the loss on B).

3. The central decisionmaker merely records the relative influence exercised by the competing interested parties. In this case, he is merely an environment which facilitates the working out of a social-choice process. The interested parties make their influence known by putting pressure upon him; his action is entirely in response to these pressures (he is a weathervane, responding equally to all the breezes that blow), and it constitutes the resultant of the selection process.

In the first two of these three roles—but not in the third—the central decisionmaker may eliminate inconsistences and anomalies from the outcome. Therefore, in these two types of mixed process the outcomes are both resultants (they are this insofar as they are the unintended product of competition among interested parties) and at the same time solutions (they are this insofar as they are the product of an intention—that of the central decisionmaker).

It will be seen that the Chicago political system is of the type that has been called "mixed decision-choice." It has, therefore, in principle, and to a large extent in practice, the advantages of both polar types—social choice and central decision. In the writer's view, in its general features it is a reasonably close approximation of the logical model that is preferable.

One great advantage of social choice is that it involves a thorough canvas of all the elements—both the factual and the value elements—in a selection situation. The better their opportunities to influence an outcome, the more carefully will interested parties examine a situation for its effect on them, and the more vigorously will they assert their interests when they have identified them. In Chicago the opportunities to exercise influence are great enough to call into play the best abilities of many extremely able people. Nothing of importance is done in Chicago without its first being discovered what interests will be affected and how they will be affected and without the losses that will accrue to some being weighed carefully against the gains that will accrue to others. It is easy for Americans to take this kind of thing for granted, but there are cities—London, for example—where great decisions are made with little understanding of the consequences for those interests which are not plainly visible to the decisionmakers.

Another great advantage of social choice is that, where there exists no concretely meaningful criterion of the public interest and where, accordingly (whether they realize it or not), central decision-makers must employ some standard (e.g., professional use and wont) that is essentially arbitrary, the competition of interested parties supplies a criterion—the distribution of "real" influence— which may be both generally acceptable and, since it puts a premium upon effort to acquire influence, serviceable to the society. In the cases reported here, there were not, in the writer's opinion, criteria from which central decisionmakers could have obtained clear directions with regard to the main questions. (There was not, for example, any way by which a central decisionmaker could have known whether "racial justice" or some other general end ought to be made decisive in the Branch Hospital dispute.) There being no "public values" which obviously ought to be decisive, the distribution of real influence was, it seems to the writer, as defensible a basis for decisions as any other. This judgment is strengthened by the character of the influence that is exercised in Chicago. For the most part, as previous chapters have shown, the interested parties in Chicago find it hard to take positions which cannot be defended in terms of some conception of the public interest.

The advantages of central decision are that the central decisionmaker can assert the supremacy of "public values" and can find the outcome that is "best for all." On the Chicago scene there is, to be sure, no one central decisionmaker who can do this in all of the most important matters. The mayor and the governor, whose tacit collaboration is essential in anything of importance, are required by the logic of their positions to disagree. Antagonism between mayor and governor, Democrat and Republican, Cook County and downstate, is the very basis of the political system. (Even in the rare intervals when the governor is a Democrat, the antagonism is not removed, for even then the Senate is dominated by downstate and is almost sure to be Republican.) There is, nevertheless, an important element of central decision in the Chicago system. The governor, the mayor, and the president of the County Board are all in positions to assert the supremacy of "public values" and, in general, to regulate the workings of the social-choice process. Although their practice is to let the social-choice process work itself out with as little interference from them as possible, each of them has in some matters the power to impose a settlement when he thinks doing so is necessary. Sometimes, as in the Fort Dearborn Project case, a political head's intervention is a conspicuous feature of the situation. At other times, a political head merely registers the influence exerted by the competing interests. (In the Branch Hospital dispute, this seemed for a long while to be Ryan's main function; in the end, however, he intervened to patch up a last-minute compromise without which all parties would have been worse off. Some observers were left with the suspicion that the clash of interests in that affair was not as important as it seemed—that it was, in fact, nothing but a public show staged by Ryan to justify a decision he had reached long before on the basis of his view of "public values.")

That the mixed decision-choice process, as it works in Chicago, takes more time to produce an outcome than, presumably, a central decision process would take and that the outcome, when reached, is likely to be a stalemate cannot, of course, be held against it. Time spent discovering and evaluating the probable consequences of a proposal is not necessarily wasted; and if in the end nothing is done, or not much is done, that may be because it is in the public interest to do little or nothing.

46

THEODORE J. LOWI

DISTRIBUTION, REGULATION, REDISTRIBUTION: THE FUNCTIONS OF GOVERNMENT

Does politics make policy or does policy drive politics? Theodore J. Lowi was among the first political scientists to stress the two-way relationship between political process and public policies. While politics informs policy, policy also shapes politics. Lowi considers three generic categories of public policy: distributive, regulatory, and redistributive. Each generates distinctive political dynamics. Lowi teaches political science at Cornell University. This excerpt was originally published in World Politics *in 1964.*

In the long run, all governmental policies may be considered redistributive, because in the long run some people pay in taxes more than they receive in services. Or, all may be thought regulatory because, in the long run, a governmental decision on the use of resources can only displace a private decision about the same resource or at least reduce private alternatives about the resource. But politics works in the short run, and in the short run certain kinds of government decisions can be made without regard to limited resources. Policies of this kind are called "distributive," a term first coined for nineteenth-century land policies, but easily extended to include most contemporary public land and resource policies; rivers and harbors ("pork barrel") programs; defense procurement and research and development programs; labor, business, and agricultural "clientele" services; and the traditional tariff. Distributive policies are characterized by the ease with which they can be disaggregated and dispensed unit by small unit, each unit more or less in isolation from other units and from any general rule. "Patronage" in the fullest meaning of the word can be taken as a synonym for "distributive." These are policies that are virtually not policies at all but are highly individualized decisions that only by accumulation can be called a policy. They are policies in which the indulged and the deprived, the loser and the recipient, need never come into direct confrontation. Indeed, in many instances of distributive policy, the deprived cannot as a class be identified, because the most influential among them can be accommodated by further disaggregation of the stakes.

Regulatory policies are also specific and individual in their impact, but they are not capable of the almost infinite amount of disaggregation typical of distributive policies. Although the laws are stated in general terms ("Arrange the transportation system artistically." "Thou shalt not show favoritism in pricing."), the impact of regulatory decisions is clearly one of directly raising costs and/or reduc-

[Tables have been renumbered. — Eds.]

ing or expanding the alternatives of private individuals ("Get off the grass!" "Produce kosher if you advertise kosher!"). Regulatory policies are distinguishable
from distributive in that in the short run the regulatory decision involves a direct
choice as to who will be indulged and who deprived. Not all applicants for a single television channel or an overseas air route can be propitiated. Enforcement of
an unfair labor practice on the part of management weakens management in its
dealings with labor. So, while implementation is firm-by-firm and case-by-case,
policies cannot be disaggregated to the level of the individual or the single firm
(as in distribution), because individual decisions must be made by application of
a general rule and therefore become interrelated within the broader standards of
law. Decisions cumulate among all individuals affected by the law in roughly the
same way. Since the most stable lines of perceived common impact are the basic
sectors of the economy, regulatory decisions are cumulative largely along sectoral
lines; regulatory policies are usually disaggregable only down to the sector level.

Redistributive policies are like regulatory policies in the sense that relations
among broad categories of private individuals are involved and, hence, individual
decisions must be interrelated. But on all other counts there are great differences
in the nature of impact. The categories of impact are much broader, approaching
social classes. They are, crudely speaking, haves and have-nots, bigness and
smallness, bourgeoisie and proletariat. The aim involved is not use of property
but property itself, not equal treatment but equal possession, not behavior but
being. The fact that our income tax is in reality only mildly redistributive does
not alter the fact of the aims and the stakes involved in income tax policies. The
same goes for our various "welfare state" programs, which are redistributive only
for those who entered retirement or unemployment rolls without having contributed at all. The nature of a redistributive issue is not determined by the outcome of a battle over how redistributive a policy is going to be. Expectations
about what it *can* be, what it threatens to be, are determinative.

ARENAS OF POWER

Once one posits the general tendency of these areas of policy or governmental
activity to develop characteristic political structures, a number of hypotheses
become compelling. And when the various hypotheses are accumulated, the
general contours of each of the three arenas begin quickly to resemble, respectively, the three "general" theories of political process. The arena that develops
around distributive policies is best characterized in the terms of E. E.
Schattschneider's findings on the politics of tariff legislation in the nineteen-
twenties. The regulatory arena corresponds to the pluralist school, and the
school's general notions are found to be limited pretty much to this one arena.
The redistributive arena most closely approximates, with some adaptation, an
elitist view of the political process.

(1) The distributive arena can be identified in considerable detail from
Schattschneider's case-study alone.[1] What he and his pluralist successors did not
see was that the traditional structure of tariff politics is also in largest part the

structure of politics of all those diverse policies identified earlier as distributive. The arena is "pluralistic" only in the sense that a large number of small, intensely organized interests are operating. In fact, there is even greater multiplicity of participants here than the pressure-group model can account for, because essentially it is a politics of every man for himself. The single person and the single firm are the major activists.

Although a generation removed, Schattschneider's conclusions about the politics of the Smoot-Hawley Tariff are almost one-for-one applicable to rivers and harbors and land development policies, tax exemptions, defense procurement, area redevelopment, and government "services." Since there is no real basis for discriminating between those who should and those who should not be protected [indulged], says Schattschneider, Congress seeks political support by "giving a limited protection [indulgence] to all interests strong enough to furnish formidable resistance." Decisionmakers become "responsive to considerations of equality, consistency, impartiality, uniformity, precedent, and moderation, however formal and insubstantial these may be." Furthermore, a "policy that is so hospitable and catholic . . . disorganizes the opposition."

When a billion-dollar issue can be disaggregated into many millions of nickel-dime items and each item can be dealt with without regard to the others, multiplication of interests and of access is inevitable, and so is reduction of conflict. All of this has the greatest bearing on the relations among participants and, therefore, the "power structure." Indeed, coalitions must be built to pass legislation and "make policy," but what of the nature and basis of the coalitions? In the distributive arena, political relationships approximate what Schattschneider called "mutual noninterference"—"a mutuality under which it is proper for each to seek duties [indulgences] for himself but improper and unfair to oppose duties [indulgences] sought by others." In the area of rivers and harbors, references are made to "pork barrel" and "log-rolling," but these colloquialisms have not been taken sufficiently seriously. A log-rolling coalition is not one forged of conflict, compromise, and tangential interest but, on the contrary, one composed of members who have absolutely nothing in common; and this is possible because the "pork barrel" is a container for unrelated items. This is the typical form of relationship in the distributive arena.

The structure of these log-rolling relationships lead typically, though not always, to Congress; and the structure is relatively stable because all who have access of any sort usually support whoever are the leaders. And there tend to be "elites" of a peculiar sort in the Congressional committees whose jurisdictions include the subject-matter in question. Until recently, for instance, on tariff matters the House Ways and Means Committee was virtually the government. Much the same can be said for Public Works on rivers and harbors. It is a broker leadership, but "policy" is best understood as cooptation rather than conflict and compromise.

Distributive issues individualize conflict and provide the basis for highly stable coalitions that are virtually irrelevant to the larger policy outcomes; thousands of obscure decisions are merely accumulated into a "policy" of protection or of natural-resources development or of defense subcontracting. Congress did not "give up" the tariff; as the tariff became a matter of regulation (see below), committee elites lost their power to contain the participants because obscure decisions became interrelated, therefore less obscure, and more controversy became built in and unavoidable.

(2) The regulatory arena could hardly be better identified than in the thousands of pages written for the whole polity by the pluralists. But, unfortunately, some translation is necessary to accommodate pluralism to its more limited universe. The regulatory arena appears to be composed of a multiplicity of groups organized around tangential relations or David Truman's "shared attitudes." Within this narrower context of regulatory decisions, one can even go so far as to accept the most extreme pluralist statement that policy tends to be a residue of the interplay of group conflict. This statement can be severely criticized only by use of examples drawn from non-regulatory decisions.

As I argued before, there is no way for regulatory policies to be disaggregated into very large numbers of unrelated items. Because individual regulatory decisions involve direct confrontations of indulged and deprived, the typical political coalition is born of conflict and compromise among tangential interests that usually involve a total sector of the economy. Thus, while the typical basis for coalition in distributive politics is uncommon interests (log-rolling), an entirely different basis is typical in regulatory politics.

Owing to the unrelatedness of issues in distributive politics, the activities of single participants need not be related but rather can be specialized as the situation warrants it. But the relatedness of regulatory issues, at least up to the sector level of the trade association, leads to the containment of all these within the association. When all the stakes are contained in one organization, constituents have no alternative but to fight against each other to shape the policies of that organization or actually to abandon it.

What this suggests is that the typical power structure in regulatory politics is far less stable than that in the distributive arena. Since coalitions form around shared interests, the coalitions will shift as the interests change or as conflicts of interest emerge. With such group-based and shifting patterns of conflict built into every regulatory issue, it is in most cases impossible for a Congressional committee, an administrative agency, a peak association governing board, or a social elite to contain all the participants long enough to establish a stable power elite. Policy outcomes seem inevitably to be the residue remaining after all the reductions of demands by all participants have been made in order to extend support to majority size. But a majority-sized coalition of shared interests on one issue could not possibly be entirely appropriate for some other issue. In regulatory decision-making, relationships among group leadership elements and between them on any or more points of governmental access are too unstable to form a single policy-making elite. As a consequence, decision-making tends to pass from administrative agencies and Congressional committees to Congress, the place where uncertainties in the policy process have always been settled. Congress as an institution is the last resort for breakdowns in bargaining over policy, just as in the case of parties the primary is a last resort for breakdowns in bargaining over nominations. No one leadership group can contain the conflict by an almost infinite subdivision and distribution of the stakes. In the regulatory political process, Congress and the "balance of power" seem to play the classic role attributed to them by the pluralists.

Beginning with reciprocity in the 1930's, the tariff began to lose its capacity for infinite disaggregation because it slowly underwent redefinition, moving away from its purely domestic significance towards that of an instrument of international politics. In brief, the tariff, especially following World War II and our assumption of peacetime international leadership, became a means of regulating the domestic economy for international purposes. The significant feature here is not the international but the regulatory part of the redefinition. As the process of redefinition took place, a number of significant shifts in power relations took place as well, because it was no longer possible to deal with each dutiable item in isolation. Everything in Bauer, Pool, and Dexter points toward the expansion of relationships to the level of the sector. The political problem of the South was the concentration of textile industry there. Coal, oil, and rails came closer and closer to coalition. The final shift came with the 1962 Trade Expansion Act, which enabled the President for the first time to deal with broad categories (to the sector) rather than individual commodities.

Certain elements of distributive politics remain, for two obvious reasons. First, there are always efforts on the part of political leaders to disaggregate policies because this is the best way to spread the patronage and to avoid conflict. (Political actors, like economic actors, probably view open competition as a necessary evil or a last resort to be avoided at almost any cost.) Second, until 1962, the basic tariff law and schedules were still contained in the Smoot-Hawley Act. This act was amended by Reciprocal Trade but only to the extent of allowing negotiated reductions rather than reductions based on comparative costs. Until 1962, tariff politics continued to be based on commodity-by-commodity transactions, and thus until then tariff coalitions could be based upon individual firms (or even branches of large and diversified firms) and log-rolling, unrelated interests. The escape clause and peril point were maintained in the 1950's so that transactions could be made on individual items even within reciprocity. And the coalitions of strange bedfellows continued: "Offered the proper coalition, they both [New England textiles and Eastern railroads] might well have been persuaded that their interest was in the opposite direction."

But despite the persistence of certain distributive features, the true nature of tariff in the 1960's emerges as regulatory policy with a developing regulatory arena. Already we can see some changes in Congress even more clearly than the few already observed in the group structure. Out of a committee (House Ways and Means) elite, we can see the emergence of Congress in a pluralist setting. Even as early as 1954–1955, the compromises eventually ratified by Congress were worked out, not in committee through direct cooptation of interest, but in the Randall Commission, a collection of the major interests in conflict. Those issues that could not be thrashed out through the "group process" also could not be trashed out in committee but had to pass on to Congress and the floor. After 1954 the battle centered on major categories of goods (even to the extent of a textile management-union entente) and the battle took place more or less openly on the floor. The weakening of the Ways and Means Committee as the tariff elite is seen in the fact that in 1955 Chairman Jere Cooper was unable to push a closed rule through. The Rules Committee, "in line with tradition," granted a closed rule but the House voted it down 207–178. Bauer, Pool, and Dexter saw this as a victory for protectionism, but it is also evidence of the emerging regulatory arena—arising from the difficulty of containing conflict and policy within the governing committee. The last effort to keep the tariff as a traditional instrument of distributive politics—a motion by Daniel Reed to recommit, with instructions to write in a provision that Tariff Commission rulings under the escape clause be final except where the President finds the national security to be involved—was voted down 206–199. After that, right up to 1962, it was clear that tariff decisions would not be made piecemeal. Tariff became a regulatory policy in 1962; all that remains of distributive politics now are quotas and subsidies for producers of specific commodities injured by general tariff reductions.

(3) Compared particularly with the regulatory area, very few case-studies of redistributive decisions have ever been published. This in itself is a significant datum—which C. Wright Mills attributed to the middle-level character of the issues that have gotten attention. But, whatever the reasons, it reduces the opportunities for elaborating upon and testing the scheme. Most of the propositions to follow are illustrated by a single case, the "welfare state" battle of the 1930's. But this case is a complex of many decisions that became one of the most important acts of policy ever achieved in the United States. A brief review of the facts of the case will be helpful. Other cases will be referred to in less detail from time to time.

As the 1934 mid-term election approached, pressures for a federal social security system began to mount. The Townsend Plan and the Lundeen Bill had become nationally prominent and were gathering widespread support. Both schemes were severely redistributive, giving all citizens access to government-based insurance as a matter of right. In response, the President created in June of 1934 a Committee on Economic Security (CES) composed of top cabinet members with Secretary of Labor Perkins as chairman. In turn, they set up an Advisory Council and a Technical Board, which held hearings, conducted massive studies, and emerged on January 17, 1935, with a bill. The insiders around the CES were representatives of large industries, business associations, unions, and the most interested government bureaucracies. And the detailed legislative histories reveal that virtually all of the debate was contained within the CES and its committees until a mature bill emerged. Since not all of the major issues had been settled in the CES's bill, its members turned to Congress with far from a common front. But the role of Congress was still not what would have been expected. Except for a short fight over committee jurisdiction (won by the more conservative Finance and Ways and Means committees) the legislative process was extraordinarily quiet, despite the import of the issues. Hearings in both Houses brought forth very few witnesses, and these were primarily CES members supporting the bill, and Treasury Department officials, led by Morgenthau, opposing it with "constructive criticism."

The Congressional battle was quiet because the real struggle was taking place elsewhere, essentially between the Hopkins-Perkins bureaucracies and the Treasury. The changes made in the CES bill had all been proposed by Morgenthau (the most important one being the principle of contribution, which took away the redistributive sting). And the final victory for Treasury and mild redistribution came with the removal of administrative responsibility from both Labor and Hopkins's Federal Emergency Relief Administration. Throughout all of this some public expressions of opinion were to be heard from the peak associations, but their efforts were mainly expended in the quieter proceedings in the bureaucracies. The Congress's role seems largely to have been one of ratifying agreements that arose out of the bureaucracies and the class agents represented there. Revisions attributable to Congress concerned such matters as exceptions in coverage, which are part of the distributive game that Congress plays at every opportunity. The *principle* of the Act was set in an interplay involving (quietly) top executives and business and labor leaders.

With only slight changes in the left-right positions of the participants, the same pattern has been observed in income tax decisions. Professor Stanley S. Surrey notes: "The question, 'Who speaks for tax equity and tax fairness?,' is answered today largely in terms of only the Treasury Department." "Thus, in tax bouts . . . it is the Treasury versus percentage legislation, the Treasury versus capital gains, the Treasury versus this constituent, the Treasury versus that private group. . . . As a consequence, the congressman . . . [sees] a dispute . . . only as a contest between a private group and a government department." Congress, says Surrey, "occupies the role of mediator between the tax views of the executive and the demands of the pressure groups." And when the tax issues "are at a major political level, as are tax rates or personal exemptions, then pressure groups, labor organizations, the Chamber of Commerce, the National Association of Manufacturers, and the others, become concerned." The "average congressman does not basically believe in the present income tax in the upper-brackets," but rather than touch the principle he deals in "special hardship" and "penalizing" and waits for decisions on principle to come from abroad. Amidst the 1954–1955 tax controversies, for example, Ways and Means members decided to allow each member one bill to be favorably reported if the bill met with unanimous agreement.

Issues that involve redistribution cut closer than any others along class lines and activate interests in what are roughly class terms. If there is ever any cohesion within the peak associations, it occurs on redistributive issues, and their rhetoric suggests that they occupy themselves most of the time with these. In a ten-year period just before and after, but not including, the war years, the Manufacturers' Association of Connecticut, for example, expressed itself overwhelmingly more often on redistributive than on any other types of issues. Table 1 summarizes the pattern, showing that expressions on generalized issues involving basic relations between bourgeoisie and proletariat outnumbered expressions on regulation of business practices by 870 to 418, despite the larger number of issues in the latter category. This pattern goes contrary to the one observed by Bauer, Pool, and Dexter in tariff politics, where they discovered, much to their surprise, that self-interest did not activate both "sides" equally. Rather, they found, the concreteness and specificity of protectionist interests activated them much more often and intensely than did the general, ideological position of the liberal-traders. This was true in tariff, as they saw, because there the "structure of the communications system

TABLE 1. PUBLISHED EXPRESSIONS OF MANUFACTURERS' ASSOCIATION
OF CONNECTICUT ON SELECTED ISSUES

	Number of References in Ten-Year Period (1934–40, 1946–48)		Percent of Favorable References
1. Unspecified regulation	378		7.7
2. Labor relations, general	297		0.0
3. Wages and hours	195		0.5
Total expressions, redistribution		870	
4. Trade practices	119		13.8
5. Robinson-Patman	103		18.4
6. Antitrust	72		26.4
7. Basing points	55		20.0
8. Fair-Trade (Miller-Tydings)	69		45.5
Total expressions, regulation		418	

Source: Lane, *The Regulation of Businessmen* (New Haven, 1953), 38ff. The figures are his; their arrangement is mine.

favored the propagation of particular demands." But there is also a structure of communications favoring generalized and ideological demands; this structure consists of the peak associations, and it is highly effective when the issues are generalizable. This is the case consistently for redistributive issues, almost never for distributive issues, and only seldom for regulatory issues.

As the pluralists would argue, there will be a vast array of organized interests for any item on the policy agenda. But the relations among the interests and between them and government vary, and the nature of and conditions for this variation are what our political analyses should be concerned with. Let us say, in brief, that on Monday night the big associations meet in agreement and considerable cohesion on "the problem of government," the income tax, the Welfare State. On Tuesday, facing regulatory issues, the big associations break up into their constituent trade and other specialized groups, each prepared to deal with special problems in its own special ways, usually along subject-matter lines. On Wednesday night still another fission takes place as the pork barrel and the other forms of subsidy and policy patronage come under consideration. The parent groups and "catalytic groups" still exist, but by Wednesday night they have little identity. As Bauer, Pool, and Dexter would say, they have preserved their unanimity through overlapping memberships. They gain identity to the extent that they can define the issues in redistributive terms. And when interests in issues are more salient in sectoral or geographic or individual terms, the common or generalized factor will be lost in abstractness and diffuseness. This is what happened to the liberal trade groups in the tariff battles of the 1950's, when "the protectionist position was more firmly grounded in direct business considerations and . . . the liberal-trade position fitted better with the ideology of the times . . ."

Where the peak associations, led by elements of Mr. Mill's power elite, have reality, their resources and access are bound to affect power relations. Owing to their stability and the impasse (or equilibrium) in relations among broad classes of the entire society, the political structure of the redistributive arena seems to be highly stabilized, virtually institutionalized. Its stability, unlike that of the distributive arena, derives from shared interests. But in contrast to the regulatory arena, these shared interests are sufficiently stable and clear and consistent to provide the foundation for ideologies. Table 2 summarizes the hypothesized differences in political relationships drawn above.

Many of the other distinctive characteristics of this arena are related to, perhaps follow from, the special role of the peak associations. The cohesion of peak associations means that the special differences among related but competing groups are likely to be settled long before the policies reach the governmental agenda. In many respects the upperclass directors perform the functions in the redistributive arena that are performed by Congressional committees in the distributive arena and by committees and Congress in the regulatory arena. But the differences are crucial. In distributive policies there are as many "sides" as there are tariff items, bridges and dams to be built, parcels of public land to be given away or leased, and so on. And there are probably as many elites as there are Congressional committees and subcommittees which have jurisdiction over distributive policies. In redistribution, there will never be more than two sides and the sides are clear, stable, and consistent. Negotiation is possible, but only for the purpose of strengthening or softening the impact of redistribution. And there is probably one elite for each side. The elites do not correspond directly to bourgeoisie and proletariat; they are better understood under Wallace Sayre's designation of "money-providing" and "service-demanding" groups. Nonetheless, the basis for coalition is broad, and it centers around those individuals most respected and best known for worth and wealth. If the top leaders did not know each other and develop common perspectives as a result of common schooling, as Mills would argue, these commonalities could easily develop later in life because the kinds of stakes involved in redistributive issues are always the same. So institutionalized does the conflict become that governmental bureaucracies themselves begin to reflect them, as do national party leaders and Administrations. Finally, just as the nature of redistributive policies influences politics towards the centralization and stabilization of conflict, so does it further influence the removal of decision-making from Congress. A decentralized and bargaining Congress can cumulate but it cannot balance, and redistributive policies require complex balancing on a very large scale. What William H. Riker has said of budget-making applies here: ". . . legislative governments cannot endure a budget. Its finances must be totted up by party leaders in the legislature itself. In a complex fiscal system, however, haphazard legislature judgments cannot bring revenue into even rough alignment with supply. So budgeting is introduced—which transfers financial control to the budget maker. . . ." Congress can provide exceptions to principles and it can implement those principles with elaborate standards of implementation as a condition for the concessions that money-providers will make. But the makers of principles of redistribution seem to be the holders of the "command posts."

None of this suggests a power elite such as Mills would have had us believe existed, but it does suggest a type of stable and continual conflict that can only be

TABLE 2. ARENAS AND POLITICAL RELATIONSHIPS: A DIAGRAMMATIC SURVEY

Arena	Primary Political Unit	Relation among Units	Power Structure	Stability of Structure	Primary Decisional Locus	Implementation
Distribution	Individual firm, corporation	Log-rolling, mutual noninterference, uncommon interests	Non-conflictual elite with support groups	Stable	Congressional committee and/or agency**	Agency centralized to primary functional unit ("bureau")
Regulation*	Group	"The coalition," shared subject-matter interest, bargaining	Pluralistic, multi-centered, "theory of balance"	Unstable	Congress, in classic role	Agency decentralized from center by "delegation," mixed control
Redistribution	Association	The "peak association," class, ideology	Conflictual elite, i.e., elite and counterelite	Stable	Executive and peak associations	Agency centralized toward top ("above bureau"), elaborate standards

* Given the multiplicity of organized interests in the regulatory arena, there are obviously many cases of successful log-rolling coalitions that resemble the coalitions prevailing in distributive politics. In this respect, the difference between the regulatory and the distributive arenas is thus one of degree. The *predominant* form of coalition in regulatory politics is deemed to be that of common or tangential interest. Although the difference is only one of degree, it is significant because this prevailing type of coalition makes the regulatory arena so much more unstable, unpredictable, and non-elitist ("balance of power"). When we turn to the redistributive arena, however, we find differences of principle in every sense of the word.

** Distributive politics tends to stabilize around an institutional unit. In most cases, it is the Congressional committee (or subcommittee). But in others, particularly in the Department of Agriculture, the focus is the agency or the agency *and* the committee. In the cities, this is the arena where machine domination continues, if machines were in control in the first place.

understood in class terms. The foundation upon which the social-stratification and power-elite school rested, especially when dealing with national power, was so conceptually weak and empirically unsupported that its critics were led to err in the opposite direction by denying the direct relevance of social and institutional positions and the probability of stable decision-making elites. But the relevance of that approach becomes stronger as the scope of its application is reduced and as the standards for identifying the scope are clarified. But this is equally true of the pluralist school and of those approaches based on a "politics of this-or-that policy."

NOTE

1. E. E. Schattschneider, *Politics, Pressures, and the Tariff* (Hamden, Conn.: Shoe String, 1935).